Restaurants from 101 Colorado Small Towns

Sequel to the
Colorado Small Town Restaurant Guide

Benjamin James Bennis

Benjamin James Bennis

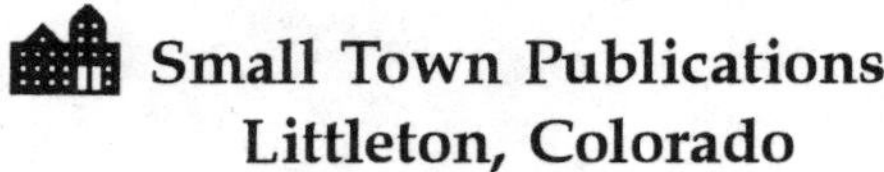

Small Town Publications
Littleton, Colorado

Front cover: Tivoli Deer in Kittredge

Back cover: Black Forest Inn in Black Hawk

Cover design and copy editing assistance by Dianne Borneman

Maps and photos by Benjamin James Bennis

Published by Small Town Publications
PO Box 621275
Littleton, CO 80162

Printed in the United States of America

To obtain additional copies, write directly to:

Small Town Publications
PO Box 621275
Littleton, CO 80162
(303)978-0316

ISBN 0-9629799-1-0

Dedicated to those who believe in the magic of their dreams.

John and Kathy,

Enjoy discovering Colorado's small-town restaurants. Merry Christmas and Good Eating!

B

TABLE OF CONTENTS

* Includes the towns of Norwood and Nucla.

PREFACE

As soon as I completed ***The Colorado Small Town Restaurant Guide*** in 1991 I knew I wanted to write a sequel. While this first attempt to produce a state-wide restaurant guide devoted exclusively to small towns (under 25,000 population) did cover all parts of Colorado, it lacked some key, popular places, most notably Summit County and several resort towns. If you picked up a copy of my first book, consider it an appetizer for this (***Restaurants from 101 Colorado Small Towns***), the main course. In addition to 190 restaurants from the first book, you now have 175 additional restaurants to choose from. I returned to some of the towns from the first book, like Crested Butte and Georgetown, and increased the number of selections. In addition, there are 52 entirely new towns spread across the state from Wray and Holly in the East to Pagosa Springs and Montrose out West. Most notably, perhaps, are the additions of places like Black Hawk, Breckenridge, Copper Mountain, Dillon, El Rancho, Frisco, Golden, Grand Lake, Idaho Springs, Keystone, Kittredge, Louisville, Morrison, Silver Plume, Silverthorne, Steamboat Springs, Vail and Winter Park.

This restaurant guide, like its predecessor, is intended to assist Colorado travelers in deciding where to dine. Here in one volume are 365 restaurants to choose from with reviews, comments and opinions on food, service, decor and atmosphere to make your decision easier. In addition, vital information such as prices, times of operation, address, telephone number and policies are provided. There are also maps of each town to assist you in finding the restaurant of your choice. I still keep running across hidden treasures out there. With the aid of this book, you will too.

ACKNOWLEDGEMENTS

Several professional associates, friends and acquaintances are owed my gratitude. Among them are Dianne Borneman, of Shadow Canyon Graphics, for responding to my numerous questions on hyphen and comma usage; Alan Stark, Executive Director of the Rocky Mountain Book Publishers Association, for his humor, kind words of encouragement, and referrals; Bob Kissel for his continued computer technical support; Piet and Carolyn Kallemeyn, of Pages, for their assistance in salvaging my first book out of their Macintosh system; Kathy Cooper and Deb Milano for their editorial help; and Steve Phillips of American Source Books for his advice. A special thanks goes out to my hiking and cross-country skiing friends without whose patience and cooperation, several restaurants would not have made it into this book. This group includes Deb Milano, Dee Raisl, Sandy Hendrickson, Brooke Heckman, and Jim Channel. I would also like to thank the many people who stopped by the State Fair and my many book signings to offer their comments and restaurant recommendations, many of which I followed up on in this guide.

INTRODUCTION

Like its predecessor, ***Restaurants from 101 Colorado Small Towns*** is intended as a guide for any overland traveler through Colorado. Whether you are from Colorado or out-of-state, here for business or pleasure, with 365 restaurants to choose from in 101 towns, this book will be a useful, and hopefully entertaining, asset to your glove compartment. Only towns with populations under 25,000 qualify (in my book) as a small town. While it would be impossible to include every incorporated village from the state, this guide can assist travelers on the eastern plains, the front range, the mountain areas and the western slope. It is intended for use by a wide spectrum of people, which is why you will find hum-drum hamlets, reverberating resorts, and everything in-between. Business and out-of-state travelers may need to find a place to eat in a small town like Holly or Walsh. Skiers, hikers and out door enthusiasts will want to use this guide in Clear Creek, Summit and Grand Counties. Denverites, who want to take a short drive for a meal, will appreciate the selections offered in Jefferson, Boulder, Douglas, and Weld Counties. So no matter where you are from or where you are going, if you plan to travel on the ground in Colorado, and love to eat, this book is for you.

How To Use This Guide

In this restaurant guide you will find a few hidden treasures, some excellent to outstanding discoveries, several good restaurants, and an occasional inferior one. It was my intention to bring the best and the worst to the reader. In selecting restaurants to visit, I attempted to 1) include every type of restaurant a town had to offer; and 2) dine at the better restaurants. During the course of my research, only 13 restaurants were excluded because they went out of business over the past year (10 from the original book). Each restaurant was confirmed, by telephone, to be in business in March, 1992, one month before printing. 11 restaurants were excluded to bring the total to the desired 365. Therefore, this guide contains 365 out of 376 potential restaurants, or 97% of the places that I visited. With only a small percentage of restaurants deliberately excluded, you will see the best, the worst and everything in-between in what Colorado cuisine has to offer.

The layout of this book is by town, alphabetically, and the restaurants within each town are also listed alphabetically. Simply look up the town you are driving through (or plan to drive through) and see if there is a restaurant of interest. If nothing looks appealing, try the next town on your trip.

As an introduction to each town, I included certain historical and pertinent information such as the derivation of the town's name or a place of interest that you may want to visit. I thought these additional insights might enhance your trip through beautiful Colorado. A town map follows with each restaurant identified by a circled number. The circled numbers refer to the "Restaurants and Ratings" chart which follows, listing the restaurants reviewed and their ratings by food, service, decor, atmosphere, and overall. With this information, a quick comparison of restaurants can be made on all factors. For example, if you are looking for the restaurant with the best food and quality service, you can find it quickly with this chart. Following this listing, is a brief summary of the better restaurants: the ones that I would recommend for a certain meal or, in some cases, because of some particular item of decor. Also included in this summary are the restaurants' policies regarding the acceptance of major credit cards, nonsmoking sections, and alcohol. Occasionally, you will see the restaurant summary precede the "Restaurants and Ratings" chart in order to position the entire chart on one page and to economize on space.

After this introductory information are the restaurants themselves and my reviews. You will notice that I used two styles of review. All restaurants with ratings of three ★'s or better were given a complete review on all factors (food service, decor and atmosphere). Restaurants below three ★'s were only given a short paragraph review on all factors. This was necessary to keep the size of the book down to around 500 pages. Otherwise, this guide would have ballooned to over 700 pages (much too fat for your glove box!). By the way, do not disregard a restaurant simply because it fails to have three stars overall. There are several good ★★½ restaurants in this book, some with ★★★ or better rated food, and many that I recommend.

The first two lines of each review give the restaurant's name, overall rating, street address, and phone number. The next section of information indicates what meals they serve and the price ranges of these meals. You are then provided with the days and hours of operation. In some cases, this information is divided into months and seasons. Next, the type of restaurant, for example Mexican or Continental, and additional policy information, such as automatic gratuities for large groups, are given. Occasionally, you will see a few special comments if the restaurant is exceptional or is an item of historical interest. Following all this is my review: what I found noteworthy or of particular interest.

The Ratings

Each restaurant is given an overall rating and rated individually on the basis of food, service, decor and atmosphere. The ratings are from one to five stars as follows:

★★★★★	Outstanding
★★★★	Excellent
★★★	Good
★★	Fair
★	Poor

Half-stars are also used. For example, a mere ½ is considered very poor, ★★½ is average, ★★★½ is very good.

During the course of the past year I have been asked on a few occasions how I rate each restaurant, "what do I look for?". In response to this inquiry, a few words are worth mentioning here. For food, I look for quality, freshness of ingredients, creativity in combining elements (like the apple-horseradish at the Glenn Eyrie in Montrose), originality in preparation, and, to a lesser extent, quantity. Price is not considered in rating food. In rating service, efficiency, courteousness, friendliness, helpfulness and attention are all important. A smile helps, too. In the category of decor, I take note of color combinations, artworks and wall decorations, cleanliness, table and seating arrangements, creativity in designs and patterns, and overall appeal. In judging atmosphere, music, noise level, scenic views (if any), the "air" created by management and clientele, the degree of sophistication or casualness, and to a certain extent, the clientele itself, all play a factor in the rating. The overall rating is a combination of all these elements. If I had to weigh the importance of each element, they would be in the order presented with food being most important, followed by service, then decor and atmosphere.

Prices of Meals

Each restaurant review indicates which meals are served (breakfast, lunch, dinner, and/or Sunday brunch) and the price range for each meal:

$	For meals under $5.00
$$	For meals between $5.00 and $10.00
$$$	For meals between $10.00 and $15.00
$$$$	For meals between $15.00 and $20.00
$$$$+	Over $20.00

The price range is for entrees only. Extra should be expected for drinks, appetizers, dessert, tax and tip. Also, the price range is intended as a guide and not as an absolute. For example, a common price range for breakfast is $ (under $5). The vast majority of breakfast meals will be under $5, but you should not be taken aback if you find the steak and eggs are $6.50. Another common exception is restaurants that serve lobster or crab legs, which are generally either at market price or at least priced higher than other meals.

Special Notes on Breakfasts, Mexican Food, Sandwiches, and Seating:

Because so many restaurants offer the same items on their menu when it comes to breakfasts, Mexican food, and to a certain extent, sandwiches, to eliminate repetition, I have made a list of these items below. Wherever breakfast, Mexican food, or sandwiches are mentioned, you may expect the vast majority, if not all, of the following "basic fare" items to be on their menu.

Breakfast	**Mexican food**	**Sandwiches**
eggs	tacos	grilled cheese
bacon	tostados	ham & cheese
sausage	burritos	BLT
ham	enchiladas	
steak	chili rellenos	
omelets	sopapillas	
French toast	rice	
pancakes	beans	
biscuits & gravy	chips & salsa	
hot & cold cereals	quesadillas	
hash browns	guacamole	
tea & coffee	nachos	
milk & juices		

Despite the above list, specific mention may be made of special items, such as blueberry pancakes or stuffed sopapillas.

Under the decor section, you will frequently see comments like "there are seven tables for 28 people." This means there is enough seating for a total of 28 people. It does not means <u>each</u> table can seat 28 people.

Disclaimers

Occasionally I will quote the price of a certain item. I should point out that these prices were in effect when I visited the restaurant. They may have changed since. Hence, these prices should be used as a guide only, not an absolute, and under no circumstances should they be presented to restaurant management as a guaranteed price.

Rating restaurants is a subjective endeavor and no matter how objective one may try to be, this business is still opinions and perspectives. I have dined at all of the restaurants at least once, some more than once, and some with fellow diners. Without exception, I have approached each restaurant without prejudice or preconceived notions and have attempted to be consistent and fair in all respects. I have no reason to rate any restaurant unfairly one way or the other. I am not a paid consultant or advisor for any restaurant. Many food critics differ on their opinions of the same restaurant and your opinion may differ as well. Please keep in mind that I am reporting what I encountered at the time(s) that I dined at each restaurant. Knowing that, it should also be remembered that restaurants, like everything else, do change over time. To minimize the effects of inevitable change, a confirmation of all restaurants in this book was performed within 30 days before going to print. As a result of this confirmation process, 13 restaurants had to be left out of this book because they were no longer in business. Still, this is a small percentage (about 3%) of the 389 restaurants I actually visited.

Comments and Additional Copies

Comments about The Guide or restaurants are most welcome. Comments and/or requests for additional copies of this book may be addressed to:

Small Town Publications
P.O. Box 621275
Littleton, CO 80162
(303)978-0316
Please see order form at back of book.

COLORADO MAPS

The four maps below and on the following pages are to be used as a quick reference guide. They include only the 101 small towns found in this book and the highways on which they are located. Each of the four maps represents a different quadrant of the state: northeast, southeast, northwest, and southwest. Interstate 25 divides the state from north to south. Interstate 70 divides the state from east to west.

NORTHEAST COLORADO
(North of I-70, East of I-25)

SOUTHEAST COLORADO
(South of I-70, East of I-25)

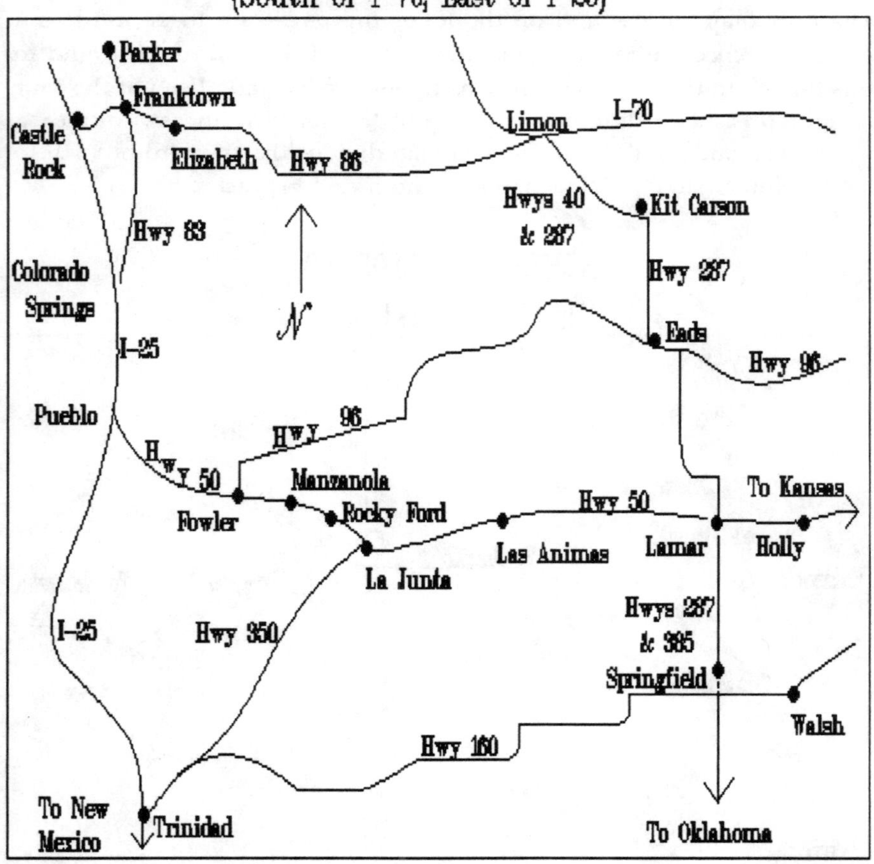

NORTHWEST COLORADO

(North of I-70, West of I-25)

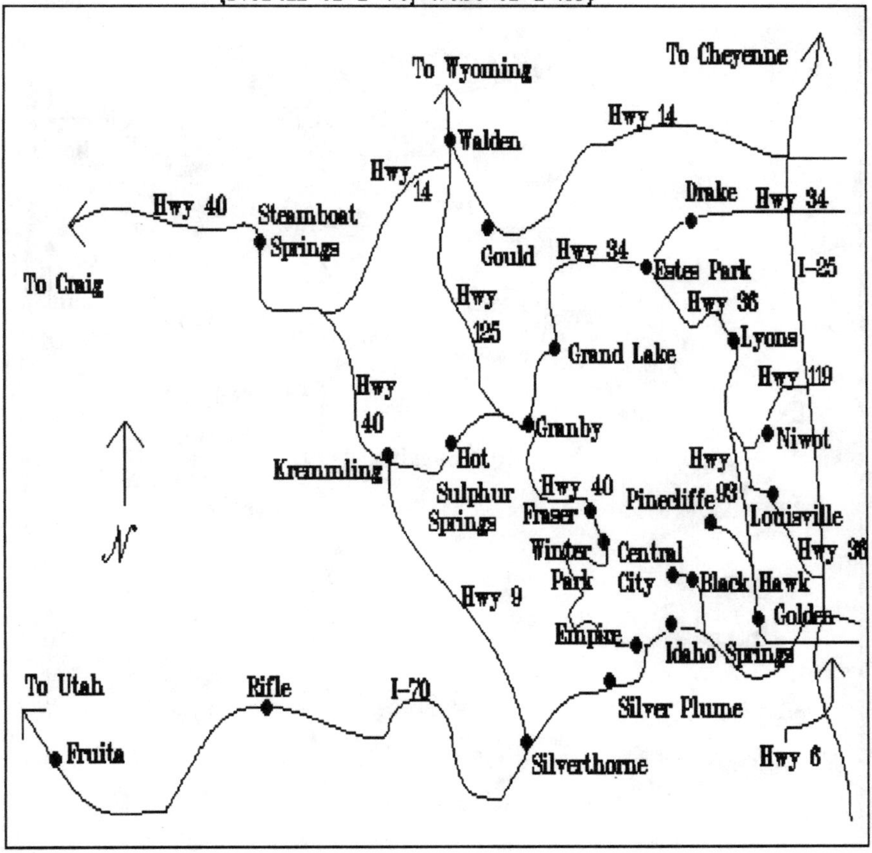

To Wyoming
To Cheyenne
Hwy 14
Walden
Hwy 14
Hwy 40
Steamboat Springs
To Craig
Gould
Drake
Hwy 34
Hwy 34
Estes Park
I-25
Hwy 125
Hwy 36
Lyons
Grand Lake
Hwy 119
Hwy 40
Granby
Niwot
Kremmling
Hot Sulphur Springs
Hwy 93
Hwy 40
Pinecliffe
Louisville
Fraser
Hwy 36
Winter Park
Central City
Black Hawk
N
Hwy 9
Golden
Empire
Idaho Springs
To Utah
Rifle
I-70
Silver Plume
Fruita
Silverthorne
Hwy 6

SOUTHWEST COLORADO
(South of I-70, West of I-25)

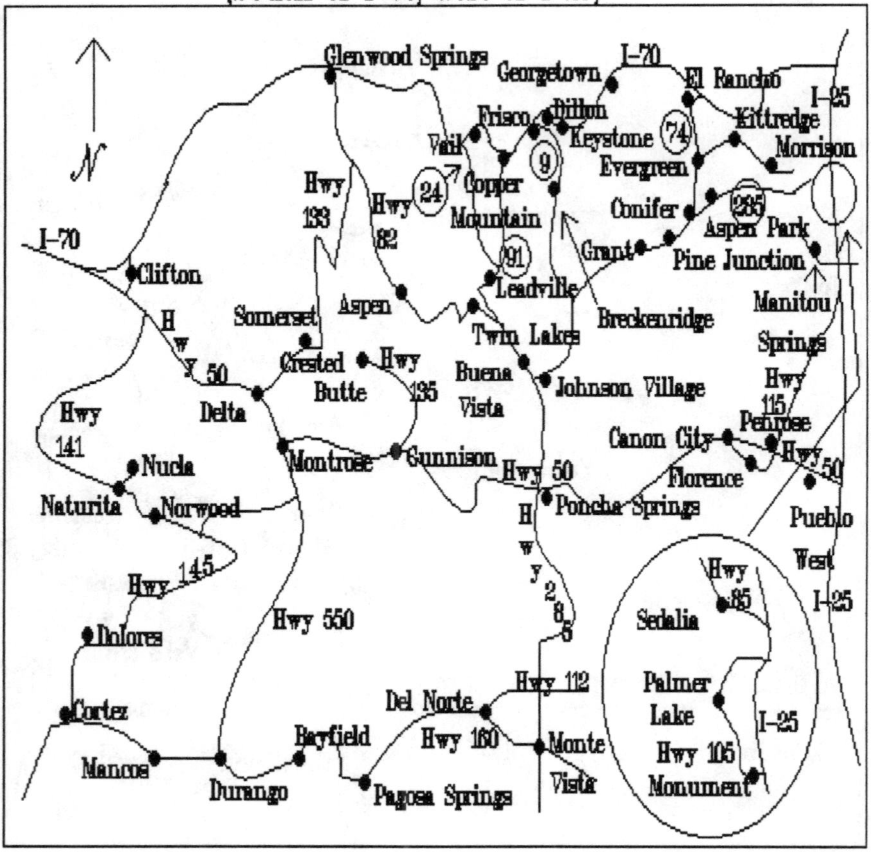

Note: Highways 9, 24, 74, 91 and 285, on the map above, are identified with circled numbers.

ASPEN

Originally named Ute City by H.B. Gillespie in 1879 for the local Ute Indians, Aspen's name was changed by B. Clark Wheeler for the abundant quantity of trees by that name in the vicinity. Another Wheeler, Jerome B. (no relation to the first), built the Wheeler Opera House, the Hotel Jerome (reviewed below), and the Wheeler-Stallard House. Over the last eleven decades Aspen has gone through several incarnations. It was first known for its booming silver mines but, following the establishment of the gold standard in 1893, Aspen reverted to a sleepy cow town. Today, Aspen is a prosperous, world-renowned ski resort.

Aspen has two off-seasons: one from the end of ski season in mid-April to Memorial Day and the other from Labor Day to the start of ski season in late October. Expect a decrease in services during these times.

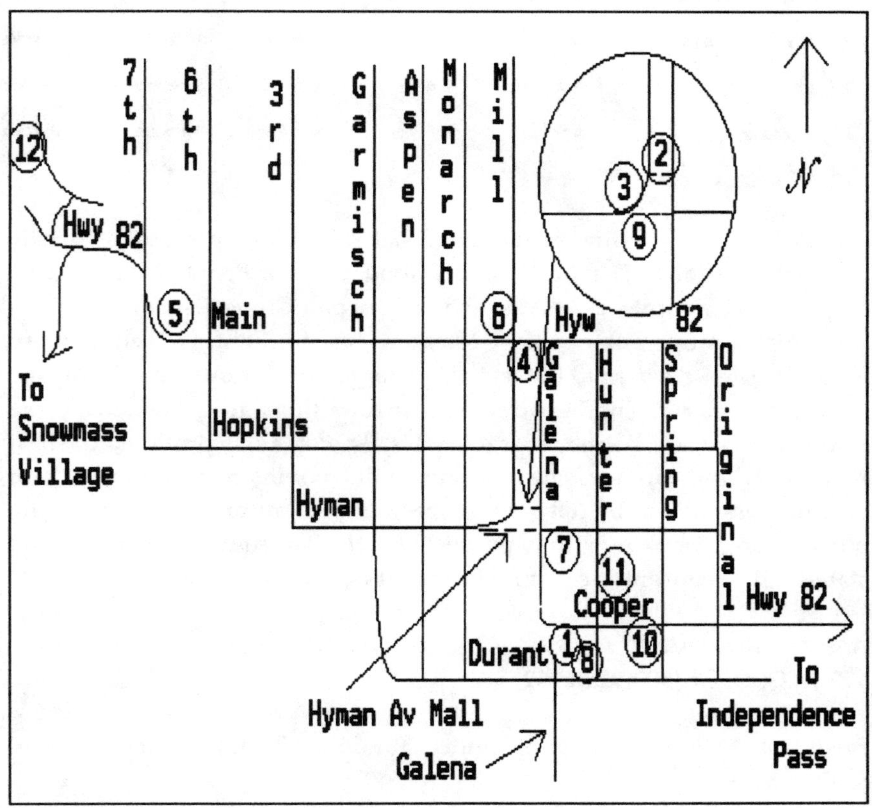

ASPEN

Restaurants and Ratings:	Food	Service	Decor	Atm	Overall
1. Aspen Grove	★★★★	★★★	★★★★½	★★★★	★★★★
2. Aspen Mine	★★★½	★★½	★★★½	★★★	★★★
3. Bentley's	★★★★★	★★★★½	★★★★½	★★★★½	★★★★½
4. Cantina	★★★★	★★½	★★★½	★★★	★★★½
5. Hickory House	★★★	★	★½	½	★½
6. Jacob's	★★★★	★★★½	★★★★½	★★★½	★★★★
7. Little Annie's	★★★	★★½	★★★	★★★½	★★★
8. Mama Maria's	★★½	★★	★★	★★	★★
9. NY Pizzeria	★★★	★★	★★½	★★	★★½
10. Poppycock's	★★★★½	★★½	★★½	★★★★	★★★½
11. Thai Kitchen	★★½	★★½	★★½	★★½	★★½
12. Woody Creek	★★	★	★	½	★

Aspen has so many fine restaurants, that it is difficult to make specific recommendations. The best quality food was at Bentley's. For great crêpes, go to Poppycock's. After that, it's Aspen Grove Cafe or Jacob's in the Hotel Jerome. For excellent Mexican, try the Cantina. The Hickory House serves great ribs, but get them to go. If you are into decor, the selection is easier. The best physical surroundings are provided by the Aspen Grove Cafe, Bentley's, and Jacob's. Bentley's also provided the best service and atmosphere. The following will be of interest to smokers and nonsmokers alike: by city ordinance, all restaurants in Aspen are nonsmoking. Smoking is only permitted at the bar. Also, unless otherwise stated, all restaurants accept major credit cards and serve alcohol.

Aspen Grove Cafe ★★★★
525 E. Cooper (303)925-6162

Breakfast $, lunch $$, and dinner $$$-$$$$. 7 days, 7AM-3PM and 5:30PM-8:30PM

Type: Continental. 15% gratuity may be added for parties of six or more. Children's portions available (under 12 years). Reservations accepted.

Food: ★★★★ Fresh and well prepared by Chef John Sisson. I ordered veal saltimbocca, but the waitress brought me the chef's special, salmon with noodles, instead (see service). For a mistaken order, it was quite good: tender and flavorful chunks of pink salmon on a bed of soft egg noodles. Judging from the menu, you would be safe ordering anything. They have an extensive breakfast menu featuring porridge, lox and bagels, cappuccino, espresso, smoothies (egg and yogurt blended with various fruits), Mexican specialties, eggs Benedict, eggs sardoux and l'eggs Benedict (with crab legs). Lunch includes a couple of linguine dishes, soup, chili, several salad selections and cold and grilled sandwiches. Dinner entrees feature pasta, seafood, poultry and meats. The selection includes linguine marinara, spinach ravioli, chicken & shrimp pasta, blackened red snapper, seafood Wellington, broiled salmon, soft shell crab, hazelnut chicken, Cajun duck, pistachio schnitzel, beef Stroganoff, veal saltimbocca, steak au poivre and a nightly chef's special. Also available are after-dinner specialties like Baileys and coffee, and desserts featuring pies, cakes, creams and chocolate delights.

Service: ★★★ As I stated above, I ordered the veal saltimbocca. The waitress, who had been working since early that morning, mistakenly switched my order with that of the restaurant manager's. Being new in town and not accustomed to Aspen ways, I figured the folks here cut their veal in small pieces and the cook exchanged noodles for the rice. After a few bites, I realized the error, but I also realized I was really enjoying the dish. I said nothing. The manager, on the other hand, had a different reaction. He made an uncomplimentary remark to the waitress and sent my veal back to the kitchen. Despite the error, the waitress was quite cheerful and pleasant with a good sense of humor and very apologetic.

Decor: ★★★★1/2 This restaurant can seat 50 people in one long narrow dining room with 13 tables and a small bar. Seating is in wicker chairs at tables covered with pink cloths. There are several fashionable works of art for sale. Lighting comes from several sources: subtle studio ceiling lights, stair-shaped sconces with light coming out of the top and bottom, and black shade ceiling lamps on long chains. Fans and a black iron sculpture in crystal with a wooden frame hang from the ceiling. Two wine racks are in plain view: one behind the cashier's station and the other extending from the wall in the rear. Everything seems to fit together very nicely. A professional decorating job.

Atmosphere: ★★★★ Soft jazz plays in the background. The restaurant has a quiet, subdued atmosphere.

ASPEN MINE COMPANY ★★★
HYMAN AVE. MALL (303)925-7766

Brunch/Lunch $$, dinner $$-$$$. 7 days 11AM-10PM. No dinner in the off-seasons.
Type: Burgers. 15% gratuity added to parties of six or more. No separate checks.

Food: ★★★1/2 I had a very good charbroiled burger made with fresh ingredients. The brunch/lunch menu features omelets, eggs Benedict, eggs sardoux (with artichoke hearts and spinach), the "eggs mine company" (with artichoke hearts and crab meat), huevos rancheros, the miners express (fresh fruit, yogurt and granola), Buffalo wings, nachos supreme, homemade French onion soup, salads, croissants (turkey & avocado, Reuben, and vegetarian), sandwiches (French dip, Philly steak, club, teriyaki chicken, roast beef, and turkey), and burgers. The dinner menu has the same appetizers, soups, salads, sandwiches and burgers as the lunch menu, plus the following entrees: baby-back pork ribs, half-roasted chicken, combination ribs and barbecue chicken, prime rib, NY strip, lasagna, rainbow trout, and boneless breaded chicken breast.

Service: ★★1/2 The bartender is friendly. I ate here for lunch, shortly before noon, and the place was almost empty. Then again, this was the off-season.

Decor: ★★★1/2 This restaurant can seat 106 people in two rooms. The large front dining room has five booths, 13 tables, three elevated tables that extend from the wall and are accompanied by high stools, and a small bar. A small back room has four tables. There is a red-brick wall on the right, raw unfinished wood on the left, and a full front window with hanging plants. Colorful mosaic lamps hang on ceiling chains. Seating is on green-cushioned benches and chairs with rib-backs. Very cheerful and well lit.

Atmosphere: ★★★ Comfortable.

BENTLEY'S AT THE WHEELER ★★★★1/2
328 E. HYMAN AVE. (303)920-2240

Lunch $$, dinner $$$-$$$$. 7 days 11AM-3PM and 5:30AM-10PM. Closed for lunch on SAT-SUN during the off-seasons.
Type: American/Continental

Food: ★★★★★ They have a limited but outstanding selection of steak, seafood, chicken and pork. I recommend the grilled paprika chicken breast for a flavorful and light dinner. Wine suggestions for each meal are on the menu. Burgers made from chicken, barbecue pork, fried cod, grilled ahi, and 'old fashioned' hamburger are served at lunch and late at night along with side orders of potato skins, chicken, zucchini, and home fries. A few items are on both the lunch and dinner menus: snow crab legs, smoked whitefish and seafood cakes for appetizers; German beefsteak (with Burgundy sauce), grilled halibut (with Newburg sauce) and the salad plate for entrees. Other lunch selections include grilled chicken salad, steak sandwich, corned beef and cabbage, and seafood cakes. Dinner-only entrees are pork loin roasted in shallots, chargrilled prime rib eye, NY strip, and steak churrasco (marinated in olive oil, parsley and garlic). Also on the dinner menu are a nightly aperitif, a soup selection, several wine selections by the glass (mostly from California), espresso, cappuccino, iced coffee and an evening creation from the pastry chef.

Service: ★★★★1/2 I came here for dinner, but was handed the burger menu (another limitation of the off-season). When I got up to leave, explaining that I was not in the mood for a burger, the waitress asked what I wanted and said she would see if the cook would do a special order. To my surprise and delight, he prepared the paprika chicken for me.

Decor: ★★★★1/2 This is an elegant looking restaurant. The tables are emerald green marble in a wood border with matching green-cushioned chairs. The gold chandeliers have 12 globe-shaped lamps. There are ten tables in the dining area and ten chairs at the bar for a total seating capacity of about 48. There are two televisions at the bar. Large wood-framed windows are decorated with white Christmas lights; potted plants add color to the sills. Pictures of turn-of-the-century scenes of tycoons, "fat cats," horse auctions, horseback riding and a man in a regal military uniform adorn the walls. A wood rail with gold coat hangers and a gold footrest separates the bar from the restaurant.

Atmosphere: ★★★★1/2 A fine clientele is attracted here. Relaxing jazz plays in the background.

THE CANTINA ★★★1/2
CORNER OF MAIN ST. AND MILL ST. (303)925-3663

Lunch & dinner $$-$$$. 7 days 11AM-10:30PM.
Type: Mexican.

Food: ★★★★ I was impressed by the high quality and freshness of their flour tortillas and chips. The tortillas are fluffy and light. The chips are crisp and light. They are among the best in the state. The Mexican fare includes guacamole, flautas, chili con quesco fundido, quesadillas, super nachos, hongos con chorizo (sautéed mushrooms, green onions and Mexican sausage), camarones (shrimp) sautéed or barbecued, pescado (fish) sautéed, chimichangas, fajitas (chicken or beef), pollo marinated or broiled, and salads. Also available are NY strip, burgers, desserts and a children's menu.

Service: ★★1/2 Satisfactory, but understaffed.

Decor: ★★★1/2 There is a lot of seating area both indoors and out. The patio is on the Main St. side and has 13 black iron tables for 52 people. The inside has two dining rooms plus a bar area with additional tables. The room straight back from the entrance has two booths and ten tables. The room to the right of the entrance has 20 tables. The bar area seats eight at the bar and has 18 tables. Total seating capacity is 180 indoors and 230 overall! The wicker, low-back, cushioned chairs are comfortable. The tables are finished wood. There is very little wall space as windows surround three sides of the building. A few works of Southwest art hang on the little wall space there is. There are wood beams on the white plaster ceiling with both in-set ceiling lights and studio lights. Plants, mostly philodendrons, divide the two dining rooms.

Atmosphere: ★★★ Mexican music plays softly in the background.

HICKORY HOUSE ★1/2
730 W. MAIN ST. (303)925-2313

Breakfast/lunch $, dinner $$. 7 days 6AM-10PM.
Type: Barbecue. $.25 charge to in-house prices for take-out.

Food: ★★★ *Service:* ★ *Decor:* ★1/2 *Atmosphere:* 1/2

They have very good baby-back ribs, but I recommend this place for take out only. The evening that I was here about half the tables on the right side of the restaurant were piled high with dirty dishes and the bar was filled with loud mouth louts who laughed hysterically at their own jokes, which were not particularly funny. Check your take out order before you leave. My server forgot the roll and barbecue sauce for the ribs.

ASPEN

JACOB'S ★★★★
330 E. MAIN ST. (303)925-5518

Breakfast/lunch $$, dinner $$$-$$$$. MON-FRI 11:30AM-10PM. SAT-SUN 5:30AM-10:30PM.
Type: American.

Food: ★★★★ There was a lot of garlic aftertaste in the meatloaf with horseradish potatoes. Otherwise, it was expertly prepared. The breakfast menu contains everything from continental to specialties like potato and wild mushroom cake; a fritata with asparagus, Monterey jack, mushrooms and tomato; smoked salmon, poppy seed waffle, pancakes with bran and raspberry, and vanilla French toast. Additional breakfast items include croissants, banana bread, bagels, English muffins, a selection of international teas, espresso, and cappuccino. Lunch offers daily specials like chicken quesadilla, barbecued pork sandwich, southern-style meatloaf, roast loin of pork, and Cajun catfish. Soup or salad and dessert are included with the specials. The regular lunch menu includes a half dozen appetizers such as smoked salmon, zucchini and tomato tarts, and shrimp & date skewers. Corn and shrimp chowder are available every day along with a soup du jour. There are several inventive salad entrees: grilled ahi tuna; grilled chicken breast; warm spinach; grilled prawn, papaya, and avocado; and a seasonal fruit plate. Equally imaginative are the sandwiches and hot entrees: avocado and tomato; grilled chicken with mozzarella and sweet peppers; grilled hickory cured ham and aged Herkimer; penne pasta with tomato, basil, and asiago cheese; and bamboo-steamed salmon and stir-fried vegetables. You can also order a burger, pizza of the day, or the vegetable platter. Dinner also offers daily specials: roast loin of pork, spinach fettuccine, roast beef, grilled chicken breast, and grilled baby coho salmon. Most of the lunch appetizers and soup appear on the dinner menu, as well as five of the lunch entrees. The other entrees include roast chicken on herb polenta, grilled strip sirloin, and grilled trout.

Service: ★★★1/2 Most accommodating.

Decor: ★★★★1/2 This place, in the Hotel Jerome, has a lot of seating area: a main dining room with 15 tables; two side dining rooms, one with 15 tables and half booth/tables, the other with eight tables; plus a lounge. Total seating is for about 160 people. This is a Victorian-style restaurant in a nineteenth century hotel. It has huge mahogany doors, high ceilings, a big silver chandelier, ceiling fans, potted plants, white tablecloths and curtains, wood chairs, and old photos of the hotel and the town. Each table is provided with crayons and paper for the children. Very elegant, even with the crayons.

Atmosphere: ★★★1/2 Sophisticated.

LITTLE ANNIE'S ★★★
517 E. HYMAN AVE. (303)925-1098

Lunch/dinner $$-$$$. 7 Days, 11:30AM-11:30PM.
Type: Burgers

Food: ★★★ The potato pancakes are thick and heavy, but the burgers and fries are great. They have all food items on one menu. However, dinner platters are only served after 5:00PM This is primarily a burgers, sandwich and salad place. The following items are served any time: burgers, sandwiches (Reuben, barbecue beef, grilled bratwurst, grilled teriyaki chicken breast, grilled tuna, or turkey), chili, homemade soup, a vegetarian plate, beef stew, salads (Greek, chef, and spinach), potato pancakes, pizza, and western wings. The dinner platters include barbecue pork ribs and chicken, marinated grilled chicken breast, rainbow trout, halibut, chicken fried steak or NY strip. Homemade desserts are baked daily.

Service: ★★1/2 This is a busy place for lunch. Service is a little slow.

Decor: ★★★ There are four tables across the front of the building facing the street. Behind this is one long, narrow dining room with 17 tables, plus a bar that seats nine people. Total capacity is about 95 people. Five-lamp wagon-wheels on chains hang from the ceiling. Several western items adorn the walls, including bridles, saddles, horns, and pictures of cattle rustling. The inside structure consists of wood walls and wood-beamed ceilings. Chairs are the wood-ribbed, low-back kind and the tables are covered with red-and-white-checkered tablecloths.

Atmosphere: ★★★1/2 A favorite local hangout.

MAMA MARIA'S ★★
520 E. DURANT (303)925-4300

Lunch/dinner $-$$$$. 7 days 11:30AM-2:30PM and 4:30PM-9:30PM.
Type: Italian. Carry-out and limited delivery available. Credit cards are not accepted.

Food: ★★1/2 *Service:* ★★ *Decor:* ★★ *Atmosphere:* ★★

The pizza is fair, but not the best in town. The salad choices are antipasto and Greek. The sub selection is Italian, ham & cheese, meatball, vegetarian, and turkey & cheese. Also available are calzones and garlic bread. Order and pick up from the counter. There are 15 tables for 60 people in a divided rectangular room with upper and lower levels. Prints of sports figures (bicyclists, skiers, tennis and soccer players) in glass and metal frames hang on the wall. Casual atmosphere.

NEW YORK PIZZERIA ★★1/2
409 E. HYMAN (303)920-3088

Lunch/dinner $-$$$$. 7 days, 12PM-2AM (depending on business).
Type: Italian. Delivery and carry-out available. Credit cards are not accepted.

Food: ★★★ *Service:* ★★ *Decor:* ★★1/2 *Atmosphere:* ★★

This restaurant features Italian specialties, pizza, sandwiches and salads. I recommend the pizza or Philly steak sandwich. Pizza can be ordered New-York-style or deep-dish Sicilian-style. The specialties include calzones, strombolies and manicotti. Other sandwiches include a chicken breast Parmesan and an Italian meatball or sausage submarine with green pepper. Antipasto, green salad, garlic bread, beer and wine are also available. This is another order-at-the-counter place. This restaurant is a one small upstairs room with an interesting view of the mall below. There are nine tables for 28, plus a small bar for four, making the total seating capacity only 32. The decor includes posters of New York and a wall mural of New York with Batman and King Kong. Rather humorous, I thought. Rock music plays medium loud.

POPPYCOCK'S CAFE ★★★1/2
609 E. COOPER AVE. (303)925-1245

Breakfast $-$$, lunch $$. MON-SAT 7AM-3PM. SUN 7AM-2PM.
Type: Continental.

***Food:* ★★★★1/2** I highly recommend the creamed spinach and cheese crêpe for lunch. The crêpe is thin, light, and nicely browned. Breakfast offers fresh-squeezed juices; cappuccino; espresso; mineral water blends; smoothies (fruits, juices and ice whipped in a blender); health drinks; fresh fruit; French toast made with thick sliced cinnamon bread and a choice of toppings including bananas and Grand Marnier; a variety of pancakes including macadamia nut oatmeal and blueberry granola; eggs Benedict; avocado eggs; spinach eggs; and a variety of crêpes made with eggs, cheese, vegetables, or fruits. Lunch also offers several exceptional selections: creamed spinach and cheese soup; chili; sandwiches, such as Italian chicken, grilled turkey and Cheddar, crispy mustard chicken breast, and a vegetarian; spinach salad with warm curried fruit; warmed Stilton on French bread; and linguine with either pesto, a tarragon wild mushrooms and pistachio sauce, or steamed fresh vegetables. A small children's menu and daily prepared desserts are also available. This little cafe was a pleasant surprise. Give it a try.

Service: ★★1/2 Satisfactory, but nothing special.

Decor: ★★1/2 A single long narrow room with 12 tables and a counter provides enough seating for 45 people. Modern art watercolors are for sale with "price on request" from the local artists. White tablecloths cover small round glass tables. The seating is on green, natural wood, rib-back chairs with grey cushions that are not very comfortable. Pink walls are on the left. Grey walls are on the right and back. Fans and white shade lamps on four- to six-foot cords hang from a high ceiling. The front door is about ten feet high and made of glass. The room did not have my favorite colors or artworks.

Atmosphere: ★★★★ Mexican guitar in the background. Quiet. Friendly.

THAI KITCHEN ★★1/2
308 S. HUNTER ST. (303)925-5518

Lunch/dinner $$. 7 days, 11:30AM-10:30PM.
Type: Oriental (Thai). Checks are not accepted. Gratuity added for parties of five or more.

Food: ★★1/2 *Service:* ★★1/2 *Decor:* ★★1/2 *Atmosphere:* ★★1/2

Their food is tasty and spicy, but precooked and waiting for a hungry customer. Service is fast, perhaps too fast. It was almost like a fast food restaurant. This is a small single-room restaurant with ten tables and seating for only 34. The clientele consisted of couples, small families and groups. Both locals and tourists appeared to be attracted here. For myself, I found everything rather average.

WOODY CREEK TAVERN ★
2 WOODY CREEK PLAZA (303)923-4585

Lunch/dinner $-$$. 7 days 11:30AM-10PM.
Type: Tavern. Credit cards are not accepted.

Food: ★★ *Service:* ★ *Decor:* ★ *Atmosphere: 1/2*

This place was smoke bombed on April 29, 1989, by a juvenile in his 50s who does not deserve to be mentioned by name. As you walk in the front door, on your left you will see a letter from this perpetrator promising not to smoke bomb the place again. I differed with my two local friends about the food here. I thought their buffalo sausage was not as good as Polish or Italian, but my friends liked the chicken fried steak and burgers and gave high marks to the onion rings. I found the service to be a little less than friendly. Outside, a statue of a pig sits on a gabled entrance. Inside, are a buffalo's head, a blue marlin, and a wide assortment of pictures: underwater photos of trumpet fish, lobe coral, and a squirrel fish; a photo of a state patrolman; and pictures of bikers. The walls look crowded. The restaurant consists of one small room with nine tables for 32 and a small bar for six. As for atmosphere, I am not much into juvenile behavior and smoke bombs.

ASPEN PARK

If you have done any traveling on Highway 285 southwest of Denver you have probably noticed the funny shaped building on the north side of the highway that resembles a hot dog covered with mustard and relish. This is Coney Island and the little town of Aspen Park.

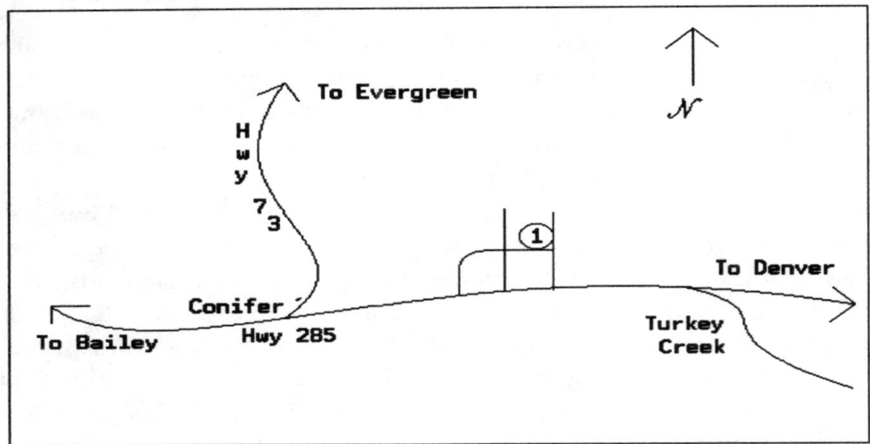

1. CONEY ISLAND ★★½
   25877 CONIFER ROAD (303)838-4210

Breakfast/lunch/dinner $ (All items under $2.50). 7 days, 9AM-9PM. Type: Burgers (and hot dogs). They do not accept major credit cards, do not offer a nonsmoking section, and do not serve alcohol.

Food: ★★★ *Service:* ★★ *Decor:* ★★½ *Atmosphere:* ★★★

While it may not look like much, Coney Island is worth checking out. I have eaten here twice and tried their hot dogs, Polish sausage, fries and onion rings. The dogs and sausage are excellent, the fries and rings, good. Coney Island was voted "Best Hot Dog - 1991" by Westword (a small Denver weekly newspaper). The hot dogs are very "meaty" and come in regular, jumbo, and foot-long sizes with your choice of sauerkraut, cheese, dill pickle, catsup, mustard, relish and onions. They also have corn dogs, taters, homemade burritos, and breakfast muffins with sausage or ham, egg and cheese. You can also get a soft ice cream cone, sundae, shake, float, or soda. Orders and pick ups are made at the counter. There is no table service. They forgot the sauerkraut on my hot dog and I had to return for it. Seating is limited to four formica tables inside for 12 and five formica tables outside for 20. The decor consists of a bulletin board with local announcements, one end-wall devoted to business cards, and Coney Island T-shirts and sweatshirts ($16) hanging on display behind the counter. The view out the window faces the eastern hills. I liked the uniqueness of the building, the country setting, the quality of the beef, and the "hot dog stand" atmosphere. Put this on your list of "drop-ins" for return trips to Denver, especially during the summer.

Coney Island - Aspen Park

BAYFIELD

Bayfield was originally called Los Pinos, Spanish for The Pines, and was later renamed for William A. Bay, a pioneer from Missouri who settled here with his family in 1890.

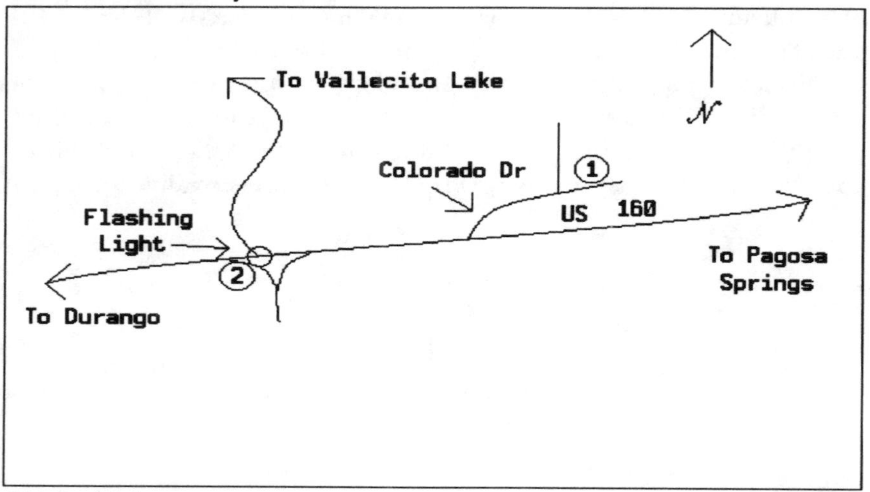

Restaurants and Ratings:	Food	Service	Decor	Atm	Overall
1. CHOICE BURGERS	★★★★	★★★½	★★	★★	★★★
2. THE HOMESTEAD	★★★	★★½	★★½	★★½	★★½

Choice Burgers serves one of the best charbroiled burgers in the state with great onion rings. The Homestead provides a filling half pound burger and some good country cooking. Neither restaurant accepts credit cards, has a nonsmoking section, or serves alcohol.

CHOICE BURGERS ★★★
581 COLORADO DR. (303)884-9339

Lunch/dinner $. MON-FRI 11AM-8PM. SAT-SUN 11AM-9PM.
Type: Burger

Food: ★★★★ Quite possibly the BEST charbroiled burgers in the state and terrific onion rings. A condiment bar to fix the burger your own way.

Also, fish, chicken, hot dogs, sandwiches (steak, roast beef, and pastrami), cheese sticks, fries, soft drinks, soft ice cream, shakes, malts and floats. Fish and fries are just average quality.

Service: ★★★½ Jovial and with a smile.

Decor: ★★ Eleven blue-top tables seat 44 people on black-cushioned chairs. Pictures of dogs and ducks adorn blue wallpaper and blue painted walls. There are six, four-lamp ceiling fans and curtains with blue trim on top. There is a lot of blue. A game room in the back has a pool table and video games.

Atmosphere: ★★ A basic burger place without a nonsmoking area.

THE HOMESTEAD ★★½
695 BUCK HIGHWAY(HIGHWAY 160 AND COUNTY ROAD 521) (303)884-9055

Breakfast $, lunch/dinner $-$$. MON-THU 6AM-8PM (9PM from APR-NOV). FRI-SAT 6AM-9PM. SUN 7AM-8PM (9PM from APR-NOV).
Type: Country.

Food: ★★★ *Service:* ★★½ *Decor:* ★★½ *Atmosphere:* ★★½

I ordered a half-pound cheeseburger with fries which was quite filling with lettuce, tomato, pickle, onion and mustard. The curly fries were thin and average. If you want quantity in a burger, come here. The service was satisfactory, with a sense of humor, and easy going. The restaurant is in two sections divided by a counter and can seat 62. The varnished pine walls are sparsely decorated with an old advertisement for Winchester rifles and cartridges, a photo of the corner where the restaurant is located, and a comical photo of a woman who just shot dead a man's horse. The caption reads: "He's yours lady, just let me get my saddle off your elk." A country music radio station plays through the restaurant. This seems to be a popular place with locals from a variety of ethnic backgrounds.

BLACK HAWK

As one of three Colorado towns to legalize gambling in October, 1991, the face and future of Black Hawk is sure to make a drastic change in 1992. Born in the gold mining days of the nineteenth century, that face may resemble the wild and raucous days of the 1860's. Along with Central City, Black Hawk produced over a half million dollars in gold and other metals during those great mining days. Rich in history, as well as precious metals, Black Hawk has several distinctions including the establishment of the first smelter in Colorado in 1868, the first telephone in Colorado, and the Gilpin House where President Grant slept. Also worth seeing while you are in town is the Lace House built in Gothic style in 1863.

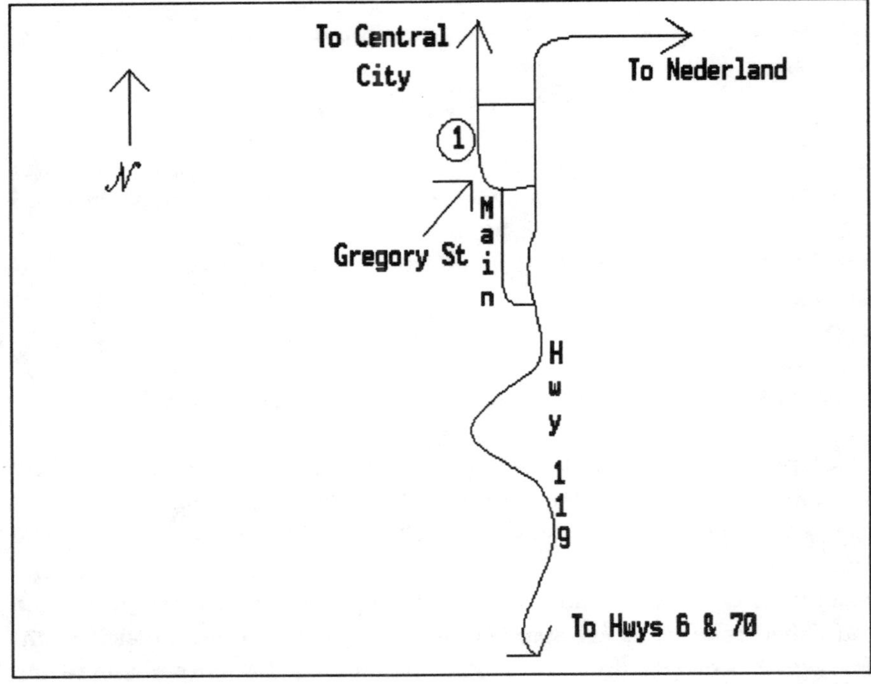

1. BLACK FOREST INN ★★★★
260 GREGORY (303)279-2333 (DENVER) OR (303)582-9971 (BLACK HAWK)

Lunch $$, dinner $$$-$$$$. MON-SAT 11:30AM-9:30PM. SUN 11:30AM-8PM.

Type: American/Continental. Established in 1958, ninety-nine years after John Gregory discovered gold in "The Richest Square Mile on Earth", the Black Forest Inn features the finest in German and American food in a family dining atmosphere. Owner Bill Lorenz, who may seat you to your table, is friendly and proud of his third generation restaurant. He aims to please both the gambling crowd next door and family diners as well, but has no intention of catering to the "dirty, foul-mouthed or drunk." Reservations are recommended. There is no designated nonsmoking area, but management tries to honor individual desires. If a room starts out nonsmoking, it stays nonsmoking. They try to take care of people. Credit cards are not accepted, but alcohol is served.

Food: ★★★★ The dinner salad (lettuce, tomato, cucumber and parsley) was served in a sweet vinegar & oil dressing. My sauerbraten (pork roast) was well done and smothered in a rich, thick brown sauce. The potato pancakes, one of my personal favorites, were crisp and dark brown on the outside, moist on the inside. The red cabbage had a pleasing tart taste. The meal also came with homemade applesauce. I actually preferred my dinner companion's filet of stroganoff better than my own meal: very tender medium rare tenderloin tips on a bed of homemade noodles with mixed steamed vegetables. The luncheon menu features continental entrees such as Hungarian goulash, a Wiener schnitzel sandwich and a French patty shell filled with diced veal in white wine sauce and mushrooms. More traditional American dishes like pork chop, NY sirloin, halibut, hamburger, avocado seafood salad and cold sandwiches are also available. Dinner appetizers feature a Russian egg (caviar with German potato salad and mayonnaise), tartar steak on rye toast, vichyssoise and German ox tail soups. Additional dinner entrees include chicken baked in burgundy with Champignon mushrooms, schnitzel holstein (veal steak with one egg, caviar, lox, and anchovies) and seafood selections (French fried jumbo gulf shrimp, rocky mountain rainbow trout, and Australian rock lobster tail). Various specials are offered on certain evenings, like elk, prime rib, Canadian geese and mallard duck.

Service: ★★★1/2 Amiable, efficient, prompt and professional.

Decor: ★★★★ The dining area can seat about 160 including 40 in the rathskeller downstairs, 45 in the main-floor dining room, about 20 in a small, side dining room one flight up, and 55 in the upstairs dining room. There is also a lounge between the restaurant and Auto's Casino next door. Auto's was named after Auto Blake, an early pioneer. Also available is a 200-seat banquet room with crystal chandeliers, named Gregory Hall after the miner who discovered gold here in 1859. Lots of room for a lot of gamblers, as well as family members. Brass candelabras with white candle-shaped lights hang from the vaulted ceiling which features hand-painted, Shakespearean-style figures. Pink and white carnations and candles in red glass tubes decorate the red-and-white-checkered tablecloths. Brass and cognac-colored glass lights adorn the wood-paneled walls. Watercolors of romantic country cottages and gala evenings in beer halls hang here as well. A six-point elk rack looks over the upstairs exit leading to the banquet room and a four-point mule deer rack hangs on the wall next to the main entrance to the restaurant. The style and grace of this carefully planned restaurant will enhance your dining experience.

Atmosphere: ★★★★1/2 The atmosphere in here picks up where the decor leaves off. There is a feeling of "old world Germany" in here. Perhaps it is the accordion player who tells jokes and socializes well with the customers. Afterwards, taped instrumental music was played. Situated well at the base of a large hill surrounded by fir trees, this fine German/American restaurant looks like it came right out of the Alps.

The Village at Breckenridge

BRECKENRIDGE

Named after former U.S. Vice President, John Cabell Breckinridge, the spelling was changed because of Breckinridge's sympathy for the Confederacy during the Civil War. The town's citizen's were fervent Unionists who petitioned Congress to change the name of the town. Hence, the spelling change to disassociate Breckenridge from the vice president. On July 23, 1887, the largest single gold nugget ever found in Colorado was discovered by miner Tom Groves at nearby Farncomb Hill. It weighed in at 13 pounds, 7 ounces! Today, Breckenridge can boast that they have over 350 buildings on the National Register of Historic places.

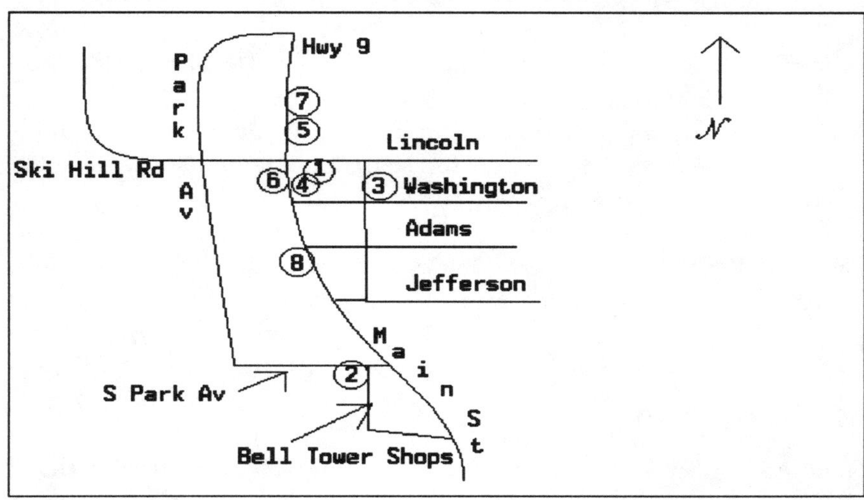

Restaurants and Ratings:	Food	Service	Decor	Atm	Overall
1. Briar Rose	★★★★	★★★★½	★★★★	★★★★	★★★★
2. Fa-Heatas	★★★	★★½	★★	★★	★★½
3. Fatty's	★★★½	★★★½	★★	★★★	★★★
4. The Prospector	★★½	★★★½	★★★	★★★½	★★★
5. The Red Orchid	★★★½	★★★½	★★★½	★★★	★★★½
6. St. Bernard Inn	★★★★½	★★★★	★★★★½	★★★★★	★★★★½
7. Steak & Rib	★★★½	★★★½	★★★★	★★★	★★★½
8. Whale's Tail	★★½	★★½	★★★	★★½	★★½

BRECKENRIDGE

Breckenridge has many very fine restaurants. Two of the "crème de la crème's" would be the Briar Rose and St. Bernard. The Red Orchid serves excellent Chinese food and the Steak & Rib is a good choice for either of those. Visit Fatty's for a good Italian lunch or Fa-Heatas for a light fajita. All of the restaurants accept major credit cards and serve alcohol. Only Fa-Heatas, Fatty's and The Prospector do not offer nonsmoking sections.

BRIAR ROSE ★★★★
109 E LINCOLN ST (303)453-2569

Dinner $$$$. Thanksgiving to Mid-April: 7 days 5PM-10PM. Mid-April to Thanksgiving: MON-SAT 6PM-10PM. Closed SUN.
Type: Steak (and seafood). 15% gratuity added to parties of five or more. No separate checks. $5 charge for shared dinner plate. The entire restaurant is nonsmoking.

The Briar Rose was built in the 1960's to resemble the Briar Rose Mine, a boarding house frequented by miners in the late 1890's for food and shelter. The boarding house was abandoned and later burned to the ground. This remake of the original serves fine meals in a traditional setting.

Food: ★★★★ My salad with honey/mustard dressing was sweet with not much mustard taste. I ordered the Canadian walleye: one of my favorites since I first had it on a Minnesota Outward Bound canoe trip in 1971. (Somehow, I remember it being a lot tastier on the back waters of Dryden, Ontario.) This, however, was a very good meal, served with baked potato and peas, but lacked the flavor that comes with fresh fish. Their trout is flown in daily from Denver, but all other fish are frozen. You can start your meal with an appetizer of New Zealand cockles, crab stuffed mushroom caps, escargot or a shrimp cocktail. The dinner entrees feature prime rib, veal, steak, seafood, and wild game when available. A few of the selections include veal Oscar, filet mignon, beef tips, Rocky Mountain trout amandine or marnier, shrimp Venetian (sauteed with mushrooms, green peppers and onions in a seasoned butter and wine sauce), Alaskan king crab legs, lobster tail, chicken Marsala, elk, moose, buffalo, caribou and quail. There is a "Little Miner's Menu" for the children. The choices for dessert include French cream cheese cake, ice cream, sherbet, and bread pudding with lemon sauce. International coffees with your favorite liqueur are also available.

Service: ★★★★½ Very friendly and efficient. My waitress made all of her customers feel at ease. A class act dressed in a white blouse with brocade tie of golds and reds on a black background and a long black skirt.

Decor: ★★★★ This single-room, L-shaped restaurant contains 15 tables with white cloths and napkins for 54 diners. The dining room is elegant looking with gold wallpaper, bronze framed sketches and paintings, and bronze five-lamp chandeliers with frosted tulip-shaped glass shades. Peach curtains with a flower pattern are drawn back with gold chords from the square pattern windows. A tall, ten-foot by six-foot mirror stands in the middle of the far wall. To enter the dining room you walk under an arched doorway next to a stain glass window. This place has some nice touches, like the black border plates. The lounge and bar to the back of the building have nine tables for about 24 and 10 barstools. There is a television in one corner of the bar, two large nude murals, a half-dozen deer heads with antlers, and a classy 110 year-old back bar with four frosted globe-shape lights and a large mirror. It was taken from the old opera house on Main St. Seating is on chairs with red cushions, rib-backs and armrests set at tables with white cloths. A wine rack at the end of the bar takes up the entire wall.

Atmosphere: ★★★★ Relaxed, yet refined. "Strangers in the Night", "Spanish Eyes" and other instrumental arrangements play 'oh so softly' in the background. A sophisticated and professional clientele, but definitely not stuffy or snooty. You should feel comfortable here, even if you come dressed in corduroys and flannels.

Fa-Heata Bar & Grill ★★½
605 S Park Av (303) 453-0801

Lunch/dinner $ ($$ if you are hungry). DEC-MAR: 7 days, 11AM-12AM. JUN-SEP: 7 days, 11AM-11PM. OCT-NOV and APR-MAY: MON-THU 11AM-10PM, FRI-SAT 11AM-11PM, SUN 11AM-9PM.
Type: Mexican.

***Food:* ★★★ *Service:* ★★½ *Decor:* ★★ *Atmosphere:* ★★**

This is a tiny one-room restaurant that uses part of its dining area to stock beer cases. I had a gyro fajita that was shy on quantity, but high on quality. Service was satisfactory and the place seems to attract a lunch crowd dressed in both Levi's and suits.

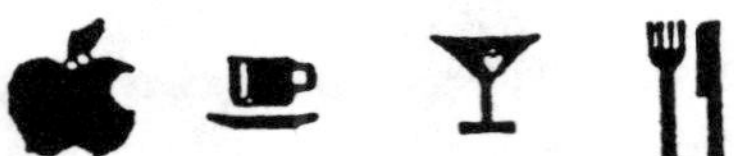

Fatty's ★★★
106 S Ridge (303)453-9802

Lunch/dinner $$. 7 days 11AM-10PM.
Type: Italian. 15% gratuity for parties of five or more. No separate checks.

***Food:* ★★★½** Their homemade meatball soup had a lot of little spicy meatballs, carrots, onion, celery, and mushrooms in a beef broth. A great homemade soup. My entree was the calabrian pasta roll: Italian sausage and ham rolled in a pasta roll with marinara sauce. The three pasta rolls came with two pepperoncini and a serving of sautéed, spicy zucchini and mushrooms. This was an above average lunch that was not over filling. The pasta was firm, not stiff or al dente either. The marinara sauce had a nice tangy, slightly bitter taste. Their 25 item salad bar features pasta and potato salads, cole slaw, cottage cheese, eggs, kidney beans and pepperoncini. Garlic bread, onion rings and potato skins are included with the appetizers. The sandwich selections include burgers, Italian sausage or beef, meatball, Reuben and veggie. They have a limited selection of homemade dinners that include lasagne, spaghetti and NY strip steak. Pizza is available in 10-, 12-, and 16-inch sizes on white, whole wheat or Sicilian pan style. Some of the regular specials include spaghetti and ravioli, stuffed manicotti, stuffed eggplant, chicken tetrazini, hot turkey and Swiss, and a ham, turkey & Swiss club.

Service: ★★★½ A very friendly young female transplant from West Virginia with a terrific laugh and sense of humor.

Decor: ★★ The main dining room, straight back from the entrance, with 11 tables for 52 diners, is divided from the bar/lounge by a wood wall with window level openings. The room is sparsely decorated with posters in black metal frames of "Bach, Beethoven and Breckenridge" (that has a nice ring to it), the "Second Annual Breckenridge Country and Bluegrass Festival in 1989" and black diamond ski trail signs of "Joker" and "Outer Horseshoe Bowl". The wall separating the dining room from the entrance has green and yellow stained-glass windows. White curtains with a flowered-pattern are used on the windows facing the garden level. Frosted, globe-shaped lights hang on brass chains from the arched wood-beam ceiling and posts. A cranberry carpet runs throughout the dining room and lounge. Seating is on red-cushioned chairs. The lounge has five tables for 14, and eight barstools. There are three televisions, a "Go Bears" banner (the owner is from Chicago) and a collage of rugby photos (the restaurant sponsored a rugby team at one time). Between the entrance and lounge are two video games and a pinball machine.

Atmosphere: ★★★ The sounds from the bar do not filter into the restaurant as much as they do in other bar/restaurants. I was here on a chilly afternoon after one of the first snowfalls of the fall season. Cold tourists stumbled in looking for food, hot chocolate and warmth. A very comfortable atmosphere.

The Prospector ★★★
130 S Main St (303) 453-6858

BRECKENRIDGE

Breakfast $, lunch $-$$, dinner $$-$$$. May-Oct: 7 days 7AM-9PM. NOV-APR: 7 DAYS 7AM-10PM.
Type: Country. Take-out available. To compensate for no nonsmoking section, they discourage smokers by not providing any ashtrays.

The Prospector Restaurant, built in 1893 as a private residence and converted into a restaurant in the mid-1900's, is registered as a Colorado State Historical Building.

***Food:* ★★1/2** Their homemade soup, potato cheddar with ham, was thick and had a rich cheddar flavor. It was spiced with paprika, parsley, a little red pepper and garlic, and had big chunks of potato and several smaller pieces of ham. I ordered the house special: calamari. It was more tender and not as chewy as most calamari. It was served on a bed of rice which I thought "tasted strange". The steamed vegetables were crisp, but a little overdone, and spiced with tarragon. I stayed long enough to have dessert: caramel pecan cheese cake with whipped topping on a chocolate graham cracker crust. It was creamy and smooth. Try some.

The breakfast menu has several omelet selections. House specialties include Prospector potatoes with bell peppers, mushrooms and onions covered with melted cheese; a scrambled egg, cheddar and bean burrito smothered with salsa; and huevos rancheros. The lunch offerings include more omelets, burgers, sandwiches (turkey/avocado, barbecue beef, and French dip), homemade soup, red or green chili, salads, and chicken fried steak. Dinner features several steak, fish and chicken entrees, along with barbecued pork chops and fettucini Alfredo. They have a children's menu.

Service: ★★★1/2 Friendly and helpful. My waitress explained the history behind some of the blown-up photographs and talked freely about Sylvia, the ghost that purportedly haunts the establishment. I stayed after dinner and discussed Sylvia with my waitress and two patrons. It was a week before Halloween and there was a full moon out. The setting was right for ghost stories.

Decor: ★★★ This is a small, single-room restaurant with 13 booths made out of wood that is scratched and carved extensively. Total seating capacity is only 43. It is a modest, unpretentious dining room with a small 13-inch television in the rear. All of the walls are decorated with blown-up old photographs of prospectors and miners, the Cashier Mine, a train making its way through snow on Boreaus Pass, logging, a woman with a big smile and a ski in each hand, and a 1928 photo of the old Tiger dredge (half sunk by its workers). The barn wood walls are completely unfinished with knots, cracks and carvings. A very natural look. Lighting is provided by bright studio lights (don't look up).

Atmosphere: ★★★½ The restaurant is rumored to be haunted by a ghost named "Sylvia". Sylvia did not show up the evening that I was there. Too bad, that would have been worth five stars for atmosphere. No one seemed to know what her last name was or where she was buried or whether she was even buried at all. The story goes that Sylvia was a young woman of 16 or 17, in love, when she was killed by a fire either in the same building where the Prospector is now located, or in a building across the street. If ghosts are supposed to be troubled spirits who have not been able to accept their own death, then Sylvia would seem a likely candidate. Robbed of her life before it started, and apparently cheated out of a happy life at that, it is understandable that she would have difficulty making the transition to the next life. However, her death happened almost a century ago and that is long time, at least by our world's standards. Come on Sylvia! Get on with your afterlife! Or at least rest in peace.

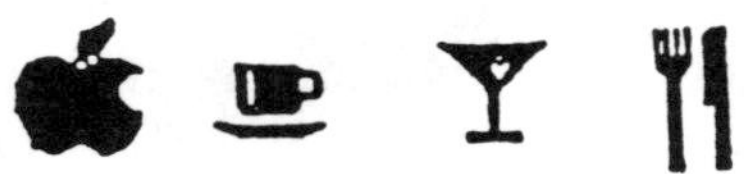

RED ORCHID ★★★½
206 N MAIN STREET (303)453-1881

Lunch $$, dinner $$-$$$. 7 days 11:30AM-10PM.
Type: Oriental (Mandarin & Szechuan). 15% gratuity added for parties of five or more. Take-out and delivery available.

BRECKENRIDGE

Food: ★★★½ I ordered Peking shrimp (sesame shrimp with water chestnuts and scallions). Although I found the egg drop soup to be a little weak and watered down, I did think the entree, fried rice and egg roll, was far better than what is served in most typical Chinese restaurants. The breading on the shrimp was not too heavy, the fried rice had pieces of egg and pork mixed in, and the egg roll was browned to a delicate perfection. Both the ingredients and their preparation seemed superior to most Chinese restaurants that I have encountered. Some of their house specialties include a seafood combination, Hunan duck, chicken and scallops in a delicate cream sauce with vegetables, steamed salmon, and jumbo shrimp in Szechuan chili sauce with chicken. For an appetizer you can order a pu-pu platter — a combination of other appetizers like crab rangoon, barbecue ribs, and silver wrapped chicken. Soups, like shrimp with sizzling rice and seafood, are available, along with the more traditional selections. Poultry, pork, beef, lamb, seafood, vegetables, fried rice and chow mein entrees may be ordered. Eleven lunch specials are on their daily menu.

Service: ★★★½ My American waiter was efficient and fast. My soup was served a couple of minutes after I ordered and my entree a couple of minutes after I finished the soup.

Decor: ★★★½ There are few decorations in this restaurant with orchid walls and ceiling, but the few are very attractive. There are frosted orchid patterns in the glass panels dividing the two dining areas; fiberglass crystalline arrangements on the posts along this dividing wall; and an indented pattern of white glass squares on the ceiling featuring red, pink, blue and purple orchids. There is plenty of natural light coming from windows on the right side, including a bay window area big enough to hold three tables. Altogether there are 18 tables in the nonsmoking section and nine tables in the smoking section for a total of 106 diners. Studio lights and rib-glass wall light fixtures enhance the natural light. Around the corner to the left of the entrance is a bar/lounge with ten tables for 30 and 8 black cushioned, silver, metal-framed barstools. The lounge faces Main Street and has windows on three sides. The entire restaurant and lounge has a very clean, new look.

Atmosphere: ★★★ There were only a few tables occupied on the afternoon that I was there. They seemed to be all tourists, except for a table of four who lingered long after the meal was over discussing some private business. There was no music for the lunch hour.

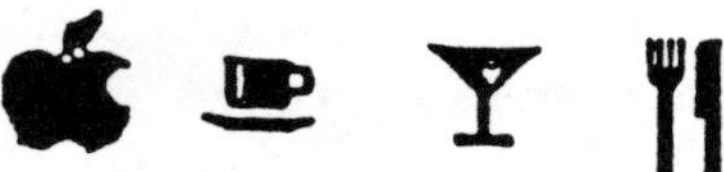

ST. BERNARD INN ★★★★1/2
103 SOUTH MAIN STREET (303)453-2572

Dinner $$$-$$$$. Mid-NOV to APR: TUE-SUN 5PM-10PM. Closed MON. Closed MAY. JUN-SEP: 7 days, 5:30PM-9:30PM. OCT to Mid-NOV: FRI-SAT 5:30PM-9:30PM. Closed SUN-THU.
Type: Italian (Northern). 15% gratuity added for parties of five or more. No separate checks. The entire restaurant is nonsmoking.

Named for the famous alpine pass between Italy and France, the St. Bernard Inn specializes in the cuisine of northern Italy: the egg pastas of Bologna, the beef dishes of Piemonte and Tuscany, the seafood of Venice, the veal dishes of Florence, Milan and Parma, the game dishes of Milan, and the lamb of Emilia Romagna. Built in 1880, the St. Bernard was originally a mercantile for miners. In 1899, the building became a grocery store and in 1908 it turned into a pharmacy and continued as such through the 1930's. In the 1940's the building returned to a grocery store. The St. Bernard Inn Restaurant began serving in 1971. This was my favorite restaurant in Breckenridge.

Food: ★★★★½ Three interesting homemade dressings are offered for your salad: honey-mustard vinegarette, toasted sesame and creamy garlic. I chose the first with grated Parmesan cheese on the side. My lasagna was made with all the right ingredients: mozzarella and ricotta cheeses, tomatoes and meat; and baked to an overflowing "gooey" perfection. Served with a side of spinach squash topped with marinara sauce and two small Italian bread loafs, this was truly a wonderful Italian meal. Other pasta dishes include fettuccine verdi (spinach pasta) Alfredo (plain, with mushrooms, or with mushrooms and Italian sausage), and sautéed eggplant Parmigiana. The antipasto dishes feature Italian toast, pasta and stuffed mushrooms. For those wanting something other than just pasta, there are seafood and meat dishes on the menu: shrimp sautéed with leeks, garlic and mushrooms served over pasta with a white wine and cream sauce; grilled salmon, basted with garlic, pine nut and tarragon, and served over pasta; beef tenderloins; baby lamb chops; veal chops; veal scallopini; veal steaks; and breaded or grilled chicken breasts. There is a children's menu. The dessert menu features Italian ices with amaretto, white chocolate, or chocolate; and Italian, hazelnut liqueur-flavored pudding with toasted coconut topping and amaretto.

Service: ★★★★ An efficient, professional sounding waiter: quite good...quite good.

Decor: ★★★★½ This is a single-room restaurant with eight booths — five on the left, three on the right — and five tables in the middle. In addition, there are two tables on a small balcony in the rear. Total seating capacity is 74. This is an olde-world-looking restaurant, almost something out of a Charles Dickens' tale, with its gold, symmetrical frieze ceiling, gold & red paisley wall paper, and a wood railing, 8 to 11 feet off the ground. The railing serves no particular purpose, but it sure looks stylish. The alcove in the rear has two old portraits — one of an older woman, the other a younger woman; a painting of an adobe chapel with a monk standing in front; and a painting of an old wood farm house, perhaps something out of "The Legend of Sleepy Hollow". Well-placed brass lanterns with candle-shaped bulbs, combined with kerosene lamps, provide the ideal amount of light for a romantic evening without eye strain. There is a bar/lounge in the rear of the building with four tables for 14, two couches, and nine barstools. A brass coat rack along the left wall of the dining area leads to the back bar and a collage of party photos, photographs of rafting, and a picture history of the St. Bernard.

Atmosphere: ★★★★★ This place does have a romantic atmosphere and would be my first recommendation in Summit County to bring your spouse or date. I was here on a snowy night and thoroughly enjoyed watching the falling snow through the trellis front window as I sat in the alcove and listened to the "1812 Overture".

Steak and Rib ★★★½
208 N Main Street (303)453-0063

Dinner $$$-$$$$. Mid-NOV to Mid-APR: 7 days, 5PM-10PM. Mid-APR to Mid-Nov: SUN-THU 5PM-9:30PM. FRI-SAT 5PM-10PM.
Type: Steak. 15% gratuity added for parties of five or more.

Built in the 1880's as one of the original cabins of Breckenridge, this building was also used as Breckenridge's first ski shop and owned by local celebrity Trygve Berge, 1956 downhill gold medalist.

Food: ★★★½ The salad bar included potato salad, cottage cheese, and green beans that were not completely thawed. I ordered the West Indian baby-back ribs, a recipe from St. Martin in the Virgin Islands. They are slow cooked in their own smoker and served with their tasty and tangy homemade barbecue sauce. Dinner was a healthy serving of 10 baby-back ribs with a pile of curly fries. (Baked potato and rice are also available). Warm rolls and butter come with the meal. These ribs are worth checking out. To start your meal you can choose an appetizer like steamed New Zealand green lip mussels, spicy orange shrimp or crab stuffed mushrooms. Other barbecue entrees include roast suckling pork, Martinique barbecued chicken and old-fashioned smoked sausage. On the list of house specialties are veal Oscar, roast duckling with cherry wine sauce and a daily fresh fish selection. Steaks, including roast prime rib, and seafood, such as shrimp scampi, crab filet and trout macadamia, complete the entrees.

Service: ★★★½ Friendly, enthusiastic and possessing a good sense of humor. The type of service that makes you feel right at home.

Decor: ★★★★ The main dining area is upstairs with two rooms that seat 30 each in a combination of booths and tables. This is the nonsmoking area that includes the 15-item salad bar. Downstairs is a small smoking section with four booths for 16. The back dining room upstairs is a new addition (about 10 years old), but it has the same split- log walls that are used throughout the restaurant. Blue and white curtains frame the small wood windows. Behind the top of the stairs is a wine rack. Four small wine shelves also hang on the wall next to the stairs. The front dining room upstairs has an old photo taken on March 17, in the early part of the century, of horses hauling a considerable number of logs. The upstairs is dimly lit by kerosene table lamps and stained-glass lights hanging on brass ceiling chains. The ceiling itself is arched and the doorway between the two dining rooms is decorated with ski tips. The bar/lounge area, just past the smoking section downstairs, is decorated with photos of the West Indies, scuba diving and rafting.

Atmosphere: ★★★ A quiet rock music station plays in the background. A table of three, the only other diners, were engaged in a lively discussion. The people here seem very honest, down to earth and open.

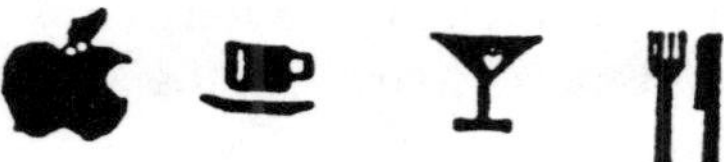

WHALE'S TAIL ★★½
323 S MAIN STREET (303)453-2221

Lunch $$, dinner $$$-$$$$ (a few $$$$+). 7 days 11:30AM-3PM (2:30PM DEC-APR) and 5:30PM-10PM (9PM OCT-NOV). Happy hour 3PM-6PM. Closed last two weeks of APR.
Type: Seafood. 15% gratuity added to parties of six or more. One check per table. Children's portions available on request for certain items. Smoking in bar area only.

Food: ★★½ *Service:* ★★½ *Decor:* ★★★ *Atmosphere:* ★★½

The bar and lounge has some authentic seafaring decor — like the cannon and compass at the entrance, a ship's steering wheel over the fireplace, fishing spears and knives, a life saver and a fish net dividing the bar and lounge. The dining room around the right from the entrance had some interesting photos of orcas, dolphins, and whales' tails. The dining area, however, seats 52 and is actually smaller in area than the bar/lounge which seats 48. A rock music station played some heavy rock tunes. My clam chowder soup, not homemade, only had a few pieces of clam. The tuna sandwich, with pickle and celery, was satisfactory.

BRIGHTON

Brighton was preceded by the Hughes stage station in the 1860's, the Hughes railroad station in the 1870's, and later Hughes Junction, all named after Bela M. Hughes, Civil War General, stagecoach company official and railroad company president. The town was named after Brighton, Massachusetts, hometown of Mrs D. F. Carmichael, who, with Daniel Carmichael, filed the plat for Brighton in 1881. The Kuner Canning Factory was built in 1889 and the Great Western Sugar factory followed in 1917.

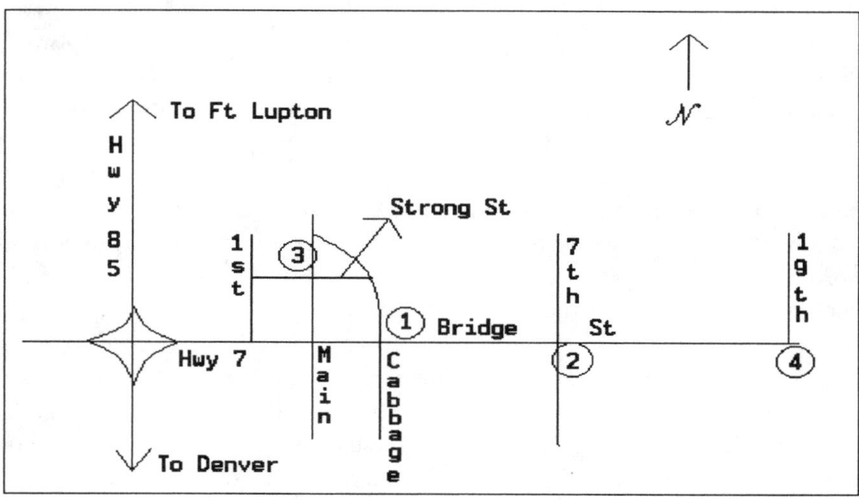

Restaurants and Ratings:	Food	Service	Decor	Atm	Overall
1. BRIGHTON DEPOT	★★★½	★★★	★★★	★★½	★★★
2. SING ON	★★½	★★	★★	★★	★★
3. SOUPS ON	★★	★½	★	★★	★½
4. SUNDOWN INN	★★★	★★½	★★½	★★½	★★½

The Brighton Depot, built in 1907 as the New Union Pacific Depot, serves some very good Mexican food. All of the restaurants except Soups On accept major credit cards. Only the Brighton Depot and the Sundown Inn offer nonsmoking sections. Only the Brighton Depot and Sing On serve alcohol.

BRIGHTON

BRIGHTON DEPOT ★★★
269 BRIDGE STREET (303)659-7787

Sunday Brunch $$, lunch, dinner $$ (a few $$$). MON-FRI 11AM-2PM and 5PM-9PM. SAT 5PM-9PM. SUN 10AM-2PM.
Type: Mexican (and American). A 15% gratuity is added to parties of six or more. Reservations are accepted.

Food: ★★★½ I ordered a combination chili relleno and beef & bean burrito. Both entrees came smothered in spicy green chili, lettuce, tomato and melted Montery jack and cheddar cheeses. The chili relleno was not overwhelming in size, but quite good with melted cheddar inside. I particularly liked the flour tortilla: light and chewy. The meal came with Spanish style refried rice in tomato sauce with onions that had some extra "pizazz". The refried beans were wholesome and good. Lunch also came with two light and not overly sweet sopapillas and honey. The only drawback to the meal was that they served me an all beef burrito, instead of the one I ordered.

The rest of the lunch menu has quite a bit to offer: prime rib or turkey, bacon & cheese croissants; flame-grilled beef or chicken burgers; sandwiches, like Monte Cristo and Italian sausage; seafood and steak selections; calves liver, barbecued chicken, roast turkey breast, soup, stuffed potatoes, and salads. There is more to the Mexican menu as well: Indian blue corn enchiladas, tamales, chorizo omelets, homemade chili, and beef or chicken fajitas. Homemade pies, cheesecakes and fruit cobblers are baked daily. Sopapilla sundaes, ice cream and fried ice cream complete the dessert menu. Wings, rings (onion and calamari), nachos and peel & eat shrimp lead off the dinner menu. The rest of the menu includes steaks, seafood, prime rib (including Cajun style), chicken fried steak, teriyaki chicken, pork chops, Mexican specialties, Southwest selections made with green or red chili, soup, salad, sandwiches, a children's menu and the same dessert choices from lunch. The Sunday brunch buffet includes the soup of the day, coffee & tea, champagne, three entree choices (a quiche, roast beef roulade, and chicken legs stuffed with apple & almond), roast beef & gravy, pancakes, biscuits & cream gravy, salads, fruit, sausage, bacon, and desserts (chocolate mousse cups, homemade turnovers and chocolate covered strawberries).

Service: ★★★ Attentive and prompt. My meal was served timely and my request for menus fulfilled. My server came back often with information, food, and drink.

Decor: ★★★ A short foot bridge separates the side entrance of the restaurant from the parking lot on the west side. The nonsmoking section is in the front of the restaurant. It is divided into two sections by an unfinished wood wall with stenciled windows showing a cattleman, a trapper, and a cowboy. The walls of the inner section are decorated with an array of framed photos under glass showing steam engine trains, calendars from the 50's and 60's with train pictures, and train time tables. A pair of ice tongs hang on one wall designed to imitate a barn door. The rest of the room is fashioned with white-laced curtains, a single ceiling fan, a wreath, and a shelf over the dividing wall with a milk bucket, an old typewriter and kerosene lamps. There is seating for 40 in eight booths and three tables. The outer section, facing the street, is a sun room with windows on three sides, several hanging plants, and six booths and one table for 20. The smoking section in the rear has seven tables for 30. One interesting item of decor is an old newspaper dated April 19, 1918 with articles on the First World War. Downstairs, there is a lounge with 23 small square tables for 50 to 60 people and nine barstools. A blue cushioned bench extends around three sides. There is a fish tank behind the bar and Mexican pictures of an adobe and a señorita with a basket of chilies. Food is served in the lounge.

Atmosphere: ★★½ There were only a few other diners when I was there: a small family at one table and a single woman at another. The place is popular with locals who come in every week. Light rock music could be overheard coming out of the kitchen.

SING ON ★★
702 E BRIDGE STREET (303)659-6513

Lunch $, dinner $$. MON-THU 11AM-9PM. FRI 11AM-10PM. SAT 4PM-10PM. SUN 12PM-9PM.
Type: Oriental (Chinese). Take-out available.

Food: ★★½ *Service:* ★★ *Decor:* ★★ *Atmosphere:* ★★

I had their "all you can eat" lunch buffet: a rice dish, a noodle dish, vegetables (broccoli, mushrooms, and water chestnuts) breaded meats (with too much breading), spring rolls, hot & sour soup (which had a peculiar taste), egg drop soup, and salad. I found the food to be of only fair quality. With a buffet, there is not much service. My server did return to fill my water glass once during the meal and once as I was getting up to leave. There are two dining rooms for 40 people each with limited decor, but attractive off-white wallpaper with a flowered-pattern. A quiet rock station plays in the background. A combination of local working men, housewives and children were dining here.

SOUPS ON ★1/2
115 N MAIN (303)659-7881

Breakfast/lunch $. MON-FRI 6AM-2PM. SAT 7AM-2PM. Closed SUN.
Type: Cafe

Food: ★★ *Service:* ★1/2 *Decor:* ★ *Atmosphere:* ★★

My breakfast burrito was smothered with luke warm green chili containing just a few small pieces of pork, which left me asking the question of the 1980's: "Where's the Beef?" The inside had egg and undercooked hash browns. The coffee was only fair. The present management had taken over this restaurant just one week before I visited, so they were still very disorganized. A slow waitress kept forgetting orders and getting them mixed up. A fellow who came in 10 minutes after I arrived got his meal ahead of mine. This is a very tiny, single-room restaurant with eight tables for 22. Country music played in the kitchen. A quiet place for locals.

SUNDOWN INN ★★1/2
1830 E BRIDGE ST (303)659-8244

Breakfast/lunch $, dinner $$. SUN-THU 6AM-8:30PM. FRI-SAT 6AM-9PM. Type: Family.

***Food:* ★★★ *Service:* ★★½ *Decor:* ★★½ *Atmosphere:* ★★½**

I enjoyed their breakfast burrito with hash browns and scrambled eggs stuffed in a flour tortilla and topped with green chili and melted cheddar. The chili with pork and bacon tasted just fine. I just did not like its glazed look. Their coffee, however, was weak. Service was very fast. They were ready to take my order before I had a chance to look at the menu. I think they are used to locals coming in and knowing what they are going to order before they sit down. Square cut log dividers, cross ceiling beams, hanging philodendrons, cactus, and a lot of windows decorate this three section restaurant with a counter.

BRUSH

Formerly known as Beaver Creek among cattlemen, Brush was a shipping point on the old Texas-Montana cattle trail. The town was later named for a pioneer cattleman, Jared L. Brush. Today, cattle is still big business with cattle auctions held in the same building as the restaurant listed below.

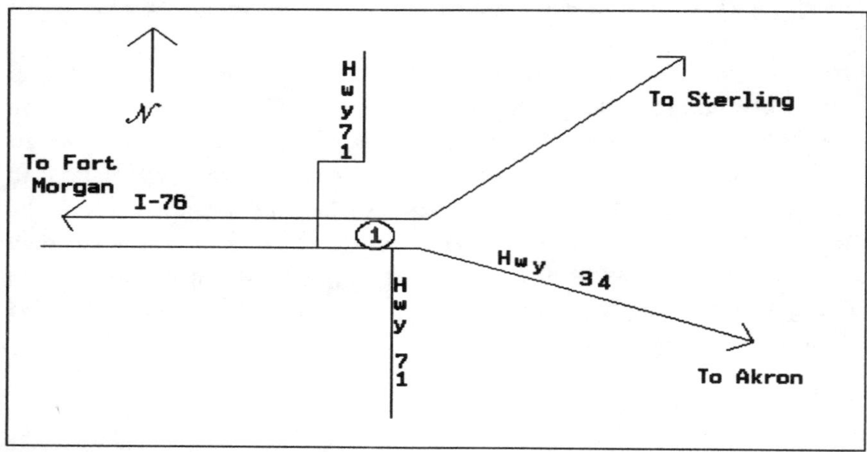

1. **DROVER'S RESTAURANT ★★★**
   28601 U.S. HWY. 34 (EAST END OF TOWN) (303)842-4218

Breakfast/lunch/dinner $. MON-SAT 6AM-8PM. Closed SUN.
Type: Country.

Food: ★★★½ Good and very, very cheap. The breakfast menu has the usual, plus cinnamon toast. Lunch is primarily burgers (chili, cheese, bacon, or taco) and sandwiches (French dip, barbecued beef, steak, patty melt, egg or tuna salad, hot beef, fried egg, cold beef and cheese, or cold ham). Inexpensive meals can be had for chicken fried steak, hamburger steak, deep-fried shrimp, roast round beef, and haddock. Hot or iced tea and lemonade go for a mere 15 cents and coffee is only 40 cents. There are great homemade pies in addition to ice cream, donuts, sundaes and ice cream bars. Soup, a diet plate, chef salad and chili are also available. Daily lunch specials are offered, such as corned beef and cabbage (which I can recommend), beef Stroganoff and Reuben sandwiches.

Service: ★★★ Fast before the lunch rush, but a little slow when it came time for our check.

Decor: ★★½ There is enough seating for 75 people at 17 tables and a counter. This is one large rectangular room with three windows, blue curtains, wood-paneled walls on three sides and concrete blocks on the fourth, acoustic tile ceilings with fluorescent in-set lights, three photos of local town folk by a local photographer, an aerial view of the sale barn area, and short-cushioned chairs. The chairs provide a minimum amount of comfort. This is a plain and simple place.

Atmosphere: ★★½ Suits and sport coats are out. Jeans, caps, cowboy hats and sport shirts are in. The flies are a little distracting. Cattle auctions are held in the same building, which is also part of a motel and a western store. The smell inside the restaurant is better than the smell outside. It gets a little crowded at lunch time.

BUENA VISTA

Buena Vista, Spanish for "beautiful view," lives up to its name. Fourteen "fourteeners" (14,000-foot peaks), known as the Collegiate Peaks, are located in the Buena Vista region. The town lies in Chaffee County where the residents changed the county seat in 1880 by stealing the courthouse records from Granite and transferring them to Buena Vista. From the adage "what goes around, comes around," the records were stolen from Buena Vista in 1928 and moved to Salida, the present-day county seat.

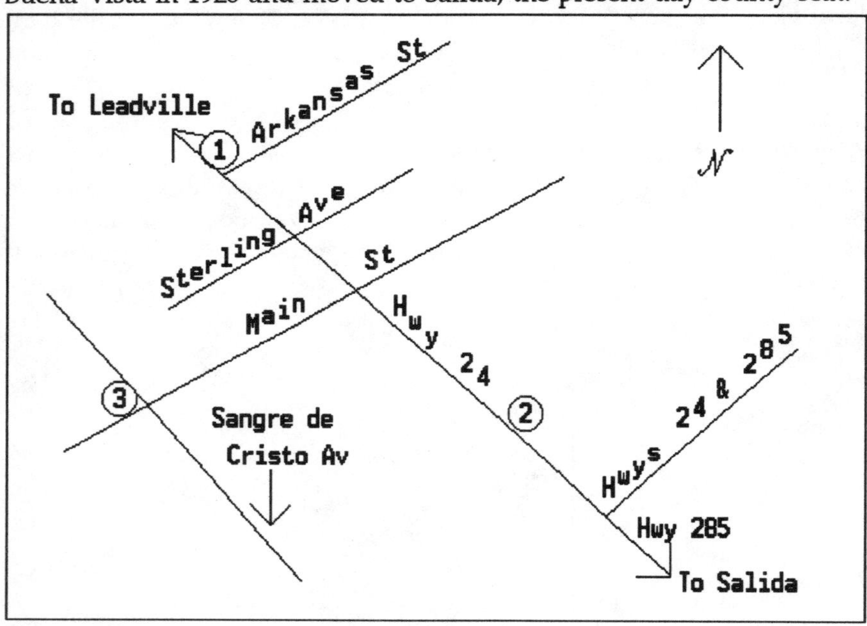

Restaurants and Ratings:	Food	Service	Decor	Atm	Overall
1. Casa Del Sol	★★★★½	★★½	★★★★½	★★★★½	★★★★
2. Delaney's Depot	★★★	★★★	★★★½	★★★	★★★
3. Talk of the Town	★★★★	★★½	★★★★	★★½	★★★½

For excellent authentic and different Mexican food, go to Casa Del Sol. For great sandwiches try Talk of the Town. For mouth watering homemade biscuits and good breakfasts, visit Delaney's Depot. Only Delaney's Depot does not accept major credit cards. Only Talk of the Town does not have a nonsmoking section and does serve alcohol.

CASA DEL SOL ★★★★
303 U.S. HWY. 24 (719)395-8810

Lunch $$, dinner $$-$$$. Winter: FRI-SAT & MON 11:30AM-3PM and 4:30PM-9PM. SUN 11:30AM-9PM. Closed TUE-THU. Summer: MON-SAT 11:30AM-3PM and 4:30PM-9PM. SUN 11:30AM-9PM.
Type: Mexican. Reservations advised.

***Food:* ★★★★1/2** I ordered the Pechuga Suiza, a recipe from Southern Mexico. It is a light, toasted, flour tortilla with chicken breast, Monterey jack cheese, mild green chilies onion, and sour cream. Chicken, cheese and onion is a delightful combination. I was impressed by the freshness of the ingredients and strongly recommend it. This restaurant's motto is "a little bit of Mexico in the Rockies." For thirty years the owners have traveled throughout Mexico sampling cuisine and bringing back traditional Mexican dishes. Other Mexican specialties that you may not find in a typical Mexican restaurant include a baked chili relleno, crab enchiladas with chile conqueso, chicken enchiladas with almonds, stuffed olives with sour cream or a homemade sauce, and carne cesada (broiled sirloin smothered in green chili). Combination dishes are available, along with more traditional items, including chimichangas. American dishes include chicken or cheese sandwiches, sirloin steak, and broiled shrimp. There are some creative desserts, like Mexican candy, rum, butternut cake and chicken mollé (chicken with chocolate, for the adventuresome), and the more common hot fudge sundae, ice cream, and a nonalcoholic pina colada.

***Service:* ★★1/2** I sat on the back patio. Service was a little slow, but acceptable.

***Decor:* ★★★★1/2** There are three small rooms with four to five tables each that can seat 40. A back patio seats twenty, plus a small building off the patio with two tables seats six. Kachina dolls and lanterns hang from the vaulted, log-beam ceiling in the main dining room. Red chili ristras hang in the patio. The small building in the rear is very interesting with a firewood stove, candles in buckets and kachina dolls. It seems very romantic.

BUENA VISTA

Atmosphere: ★★★★1/2 Mexican guitar music and a warm summer breeze in a cozy outdoor setting made for a most pleasant dining experience.

DELANEY'S DEPOT ★★★
605 U.S. HWY. 24 S. (719)395-8854

Breakfast/lunch $, dinner $$-$$$. Winter: SUN 7:30AM-7:30PM. MON 7:30AM-2:30PM. TUE-SAT 7:30AM-8PM. Summer: 7 days 6:30AM-9PM. Type: Country. Local checks only accepted.

Food: ★★★ I had eggs over easy with Italian sausage and homemade biscuits. This was an above average breakfast. The eggs were turned and retrieved at just the right moment. I had the waitress bring me some tabasco sauce, but the Italian sausage patty did not need any. The biscuits were exceptional: light, fluffy, rich in flavor, and they broke in half easily. Other breakfast items include pancakes with fruit (hot diced apples, strawberry nectar, or blueberry sauce), ground round, smoked minced ham, pigs in a blanket, and a mini breakfast for children. The lunch menu specializes in homemade soup, salad, fresh hot bread, and a daily entree, like mini shrimp. It also features burgers, hot dogs, tacos, barbecue spare ribs, onion rings, hot sandwiches (grilled Polish sausage, Reuben, barbecue beef, ham, corned beef, or chicken breast), and cold sandwiches (club, deli deluxe, chicken or tuna salad, roast beef, or ham). Dinner offers spaghetti, meat lasagna, prime rib, five steak selections, five chicken choices, rainbow trout amandine, fantail shrimp, barbecue beef ribs, pork chops, roast beef, and liver & onions. Homemade pies and ice cream are available for dessert. An "all-you-can-eat" buffet is offered on SUN from 11:30AM-7:30PM.

Service: ★★★ Just fine. The waitress was a pleasant young girl.

Decor: ★★★1/2 There is seating for 116 people in three front sections and a single back room. The center and right sections have 15 tables with red or blue tablecloths for 58 smokers. The section to the left has 10 tables for 34 nonsmokers. The back room has six tables for 24 people and looks out onto railroad tracks just a few yards away. Wood rail dividers with white and blue curtains, pulled back, separate the front sections. Very attractive beige curtains with blue steam engines cover the windows. All of the pictures depict trains, railroad tracks, or rail track bridges. There is a stone fireplace along the back wall in the center section. The real attraction in this restaurant, though, is the two toy trains on two sets of track that circle the entire room on a shelf just one to two feet from the ceiling. Behind the tracks is a mural showing everything from a skyline to steamboats to scenes from Monument Valley. In the back of the right section, over the salad bar, there is a mountain display that the trains pass through and around. The entire setup is quite imaginative.

Atmosphere: ★★★ This is a favorite stopping point for tourists and locals. The place is quiet with no music. There is a great view of the Collegiate Peaks out the front window.

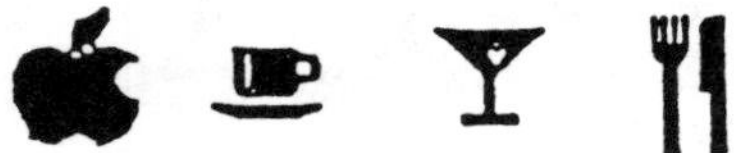

TALK OF THE TOWN ★★★1/2
1004 W. MAIN (719)395-8860

Breakfast/lunch $, dinner $$. Winter: FRI-SAT 7AM-2PM and 5PM-9PM. SUN 7AM-2PM and 5PM-8PM. Closed MON-THU. Summer: TUE-SAT 7AM-2PM and 5PM-9PM. SUN 7AM-2PM and 5PM-8PM. Closed MON.
Type: Barbecue. Established in 1989. $1 extra plate charge. Look for the Vista Court sign. The restaurant is the small brown building with the "Cafe" sign on the overhang.

Food: ★★★★ I ordered the (mild) Italian sausage with mushrooms, onions, and green peppers. It is an excellent sandwich with fresh vegetables and tasty meat. It comes with spicy fries which were quite good also. Other lunch sandwiches, which also look good, are beef brisket, ham, teriyaki chicken breast, vegetarian, and Wisconsin Bratwurst (charbroiled and simmered in beer & onions, but only offered in the summer). Additional lunch items include burgers, a limited Mexican selection, and a children's menu. Breakfast offers huevos rancheros, corned beef hash, grits, and herb & spice teas. The dinner menu features a half-dozen appetizers including chili con queso, sautéed mushrooms, and chicken; and the following entrees: mesquite-smoked baby-back ribs or chicken, beef brisket; charbroiled ham, chicken, or steaks; fried shrimp or catfish, halibut, chicken fajitas, and quesado (Mexican stir fry). There is a children's menu and for dessert there are peach schnapps ice cream, chocolate cake, home-baked apple pie, and a weekly house special.

Service: ★★1/2 Satisfactory. The owner was waiting tables.

Decor: ★★★★ This is a small one-room restaurant with nine tables for 34 people and sharp decor. It has fresh pine walls, eggshell wallpaper, and an artfully decorated wall shelf about eight feet above the floor. On the shelf you will find an assortment of old business paraphernalia: an old-fashion telephone, ticker tape machine, an old coffee grinder, a clock, vases, pitchers, plates, and dried grain. The wall decor includes a trombone, a horn, a small whip, a crooked cane and needlepoint art works. The slanted ceiling comes down to the Venetian blinds and windows. Attractive gold light fixtures with flower-shaped shades hang from the walls and ceiling. Kerosene lanterns add a nice touch to the tables.

Atmosphere: ★★1/2 It was quiet when I arrived with only two other tables occupied, but it was quite busy when I left. It was Good Friday and a religious radio station could be heard from the kitchen. I found this very strange. Without trying to be sacrilegious, I do not think a recount of the crucifixion enhances anyone's appetite. Another annoyance was a crying infant.

Burlington

Originally named Lowell in 1886, the name was changed in the following year to Burlington by the settlers that came from Burlington, Kansas. A couple of local attractions you should visit if you have the time are "Old Town", a turn-of-the-century museum and town with everything from the local saloon to a huge two-story red barn; and the carousal, a real carnival carousal from earlier in the century. Old Town is open year-round for tours, but is only active with live shows during the summer months. The carousal only operates in the summer.

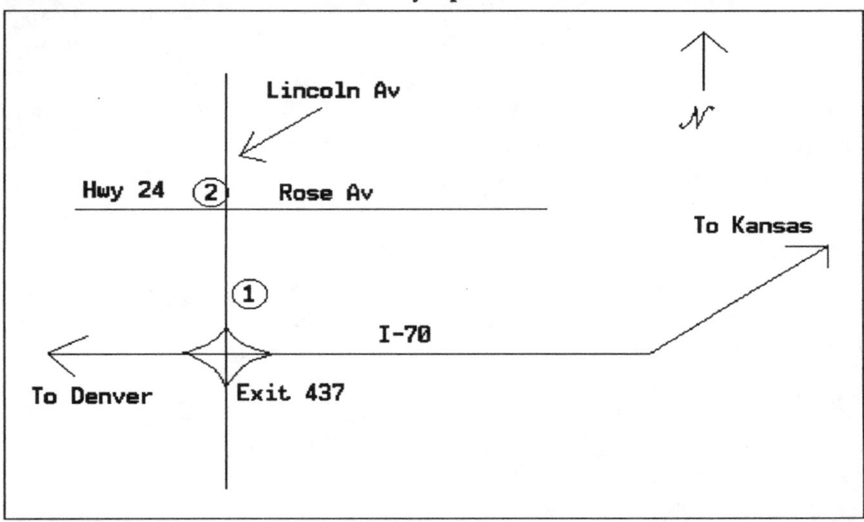

Restaurants and ratings:	Food	Service	Decor	Atm	Overall
1. Econo Lodge	★★½	★★★	★★½	★★½	★★½
2. Western Motor Inn	★★★	★★★	★★	★★★	★★★

The Western Motor Inn serves some very good broasted chicken. Both restaurants are part of motels. Both accept major credit cards, but do not have nonsmoking sections. Only the Western Motor Inn serves alcohol. Strangely enough, the downtown area, 14th St. north of Rose Avenue, does not have any restaurants.

Econo Lodge ★★1/2
450 S. Lincoln (719)346-5555

BURLINGTON

Breakfast $, lunch/dinner $-$$$. 7 days 6AM-9PM.
Type: Family.

Food: ★★1/2 *Service:* ★★★ *Decor:* ★★1/2 *Atmosphere:* ★★1/2

My four golden fried jumbo shrimp were satisfactory, as was the rest of the meal, but not great. Service was quick and with a smile. Eight booths, four along the back wall and four along the right wall, plus 11 tables, can seat 78 people. A trellis pattern is used on the front walls and in the booths. The booths are open with no dividers or wall separations. All tables have a two-quart red barrel-style water pitcher. The left wall has a large mural of a mountain cabin in fall with a stepped waterfall. The mural is surrounded by a diagonal cut wood panel. The place was quiet with a sparse crowd for dinner.

WESTERN MOTOR INN ★★★
123 LINCOLN (719)346-8115

Breakfast $, lunch/dinner $$-$$$. MON-SAT 6AM-9PM. SUN 6AM-2:30PM
Type: Country.

Food: ★★★ The broasted chicken is their specialty and requires a twenty-minute wait. It is crispy on the outside and slightly underdone on the inside, served with a good baked potato, but frozen vegetables. Their breakfast menu has corned beef hash, blueberry pancakes, homemade cinnamon rolls, and a western sandwich. The lunch/dinner menu has sandwiches (fish, pork, hot beef, and Reuben), steaks, jumbo fried gulf shrimp, halibut, grilled chicken breast, trout amandine, Rocky Mountain oysters, roast beef, onion rings, a chef salad, a soup and salad bar, a children's menu, daily chef specials, pies, and ice cream. They have a burger bar set up on Saturdays and a buffet on Sundays.

Service ★★★ Accommodating, helpful, willing to converse.

Decor: ★★ This is a big restaurant with total seating for 210 people. On the right side is an L-shaped dining area around the kitchen with 15 booths for 60 people. On the left side is a second dining area with five booths and eight tables for 58 people. Behind this is a bar, lounge and pool table for 40 more people. Upstairs to the left is a final dining area with 11 tables for 52 people. The walls downstairs are decorated with several paintings of cowboys, cattle, horses and Indians, and a piece of polished driftwood. The ceiling is a wood panel vault. The room to the left has windows to the front and left, a fireplace in the rear, and saddle-shaped mirrors on the brick wall over the fireplace. The upstairs has the same fireplace, brick wall and saddle-shaped mirror decor.

Atmosphere: ★★★ A quiet clientele.

CAÑON CITY

A former favorite meeting place of the Ute Indians, Cañon City derived its name from the Royal Gorge, the "Grand Canyon of the Arkansas River" eight miles to the west and sight of the world's largest suspension bridge. Zebulon Pike camped here in 1806. The Colorado State Prison is located in Cañon City.

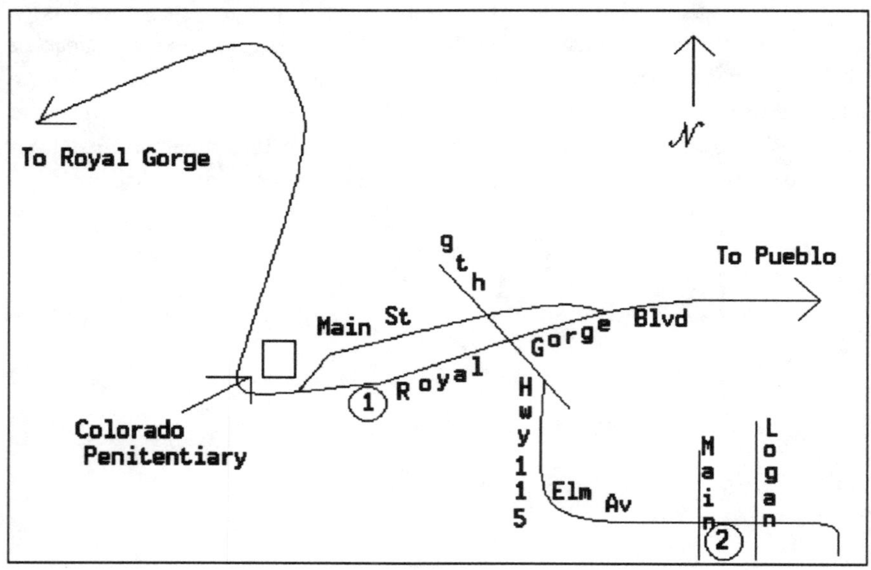

Restaurants and Ratings:	Food	Service	Decor	Atm	Overall
1. Le Petite Chablis	★★★★½	★★★★½	★★★½	★★★½	★★★★
2. Merlino's Belvedere	★★★★	★★★	★★★★	★★★½	★★★½

Le Petit Chablis is a rare classy restaurant in these parts with superb French cuisine, along with country and Cajun. Merlino's is a combination steak and Italian restaurant decorated with water fountains and paintings of Venice. Both come highly recommended, accept major credit cards, have nonsmoking sections, and serve alcohol.

Le Petit Chablis ★★★★
512 Royal Gorge Blvd (719)269-3333

Lunch $$, dinner $$$. TUE-FRI 11:30AM-1:30PM. TUE-THU 6PM-9PM (5:30PM NOV-MAR). FRI-SAT 6PM-10PM (5:30PM NOV-MAR). SUN 4PM-8PM (APR-OCT only). Closed MON.
Type: Continental (French). Make reservations.
French chef Daniel Petit and his southern wife Leigh have put together a rather unique restaurant featuring French, country and Cajun cuisine.

***Food:* ★★★★1/2** This restaurant specializes in little extra touches. The petit French rolls are served in a small clay crock with a lid. Rippled butter comes on a side dish. I ordered the "Carre d'agnesee Provencale": New Zealand rack of lamb. Chef Daniel gladly substituted a fresh garden mint sauce with garlic, shallots, herbs, parsley seasoning in a brown stock base with white wine, in place of the tomato, garlic, herb sauce that was on the menu. The chef uses fresh vegetables and prepares seasonal dishes depending on which crop has just ripened. My meal included four lean, medium rare slices of lamb. The sauce was delicious. Accompanying the lamb were mixed seasoned vegetable and baked potatoes in the shape of mushrooms. I had room for dessert, having skipped over the appetizer, soup and salad selections, so I ordered the bananas Foster. It was a delightful hot and cold combination: vanilla ice cream with sauteed bananas in a warm, brown sugar, butter, rum and banana liqueur sauce. If this scrumptious dessert has a drawback, it is a minor one: when the sugar and butter cools over the ice cream, it forms a formidable caramel that will stick to your gums and teeth. I personally did not mind one bit.

For appetizers, escargot, pâtés, and fromages are standards, but you may also see oysters Rockefeller or artichokes provencale (baked with a tomato, garlic and herb sauce). French onion soup, a soup du jour, and a varying third selection, like seafood gumbo, are on the menu. For entrees you may expect some regular selections like filet mignon, pork, veal, lamb and seafood prepared with a variety of delicious sauces, like Bernaisse, Roquefort, fruit, Dijon, apple brandy & cream mushroom, or mint in a brown sauce with parsley. The seafood dishes vary each evening and may include red snapper, salmon, scallops, swordfish or catfish. This is one place where you might want to save some room for dessert. Try one of these: gateau au fromage (cheesecake, like peach with fresh peaches baked inside), chocolate mousse, cigne a la crème (a swan cream puff swimming in a lake of strawberries, peaches or other fruit), crêpe a la praline (a crêpe filled with butter and pecan ice cream with hot pecan sauce), or crème caramel (vanilla flavor custard). Order some espresso or café au lait to go with your dessert.

Service: ★★★★1/2 Your server will explain the items on the blackboard menu and even substitute a sauce on your entry, if it is available. The chef uses a variety of 30 sauces which differ nightly, so if you like a particular entry, but would prefer a different sauce, consult with your server.

Decor: ★★★1/2 This restaurant is in an old house having four dining rooms downstairs with 13 tables for 45 people. The upstairs dining area has 13 tables for another 35 diners. To the right of the entrance is an old-fashioned wood champagne cooler and a wine cooler. There are white-laced curtains in every window and hardwood floors throughout. Tasteful figure studies, a Paris street scene, and horse drawn sleighs in the countryside decorate the upstairs. The upstairs front room has three tables with windows facing Highway 50. The room is not insulated and, thus, is closed in winter.

Atmosphere: ★★★1/2 It was raucous and rollicking on the August evening I was here. The folks from nearby Royal Gorge Bridge were celebrating the end of the season and they were having a real "blow-out", which lasted at least an hour and a half past closing. I may not have been here on a typical evening. "Clare du Lune" and other classical favorites played softly in the background.

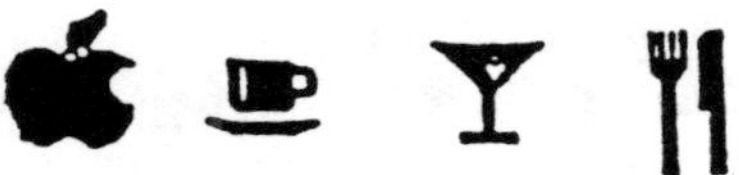

MERLINO'S BELVEDERE ★★★1/2
1330 ELM AVE (719)275-5558

Lunch/dinner $$-$$$$ (a few $$$$+). Summer: MON-THU 5PM-10PM, FRI 5PM-11PM, SAT 4:30PM-11PM, SUN 12PM-9PM. Winter: MON-THU 5PM-9:30PM, FRI 5PM-11PM, SAT 4:30PM-11PM, SUN 12PM-8PM.

Type: Steak (and Italian). Reservations are required for 12 or more. Belvedere's is a third generation restaurant run by the Merlino family. It was started in 1946 by Joe and Tony Merlino, sons of Ubaldo Merlino, a tough coal miner who later became "the cider and juice man" producing Colorado's largest supply of fruit beverages and the second largest supply of apple cider. The family tradition of original recipes has passed down to Tony's son, Michael, who, with his wife Cathie and their children Adam and Michelle, took over sole operation of the restaurant. Today, Mike oversees every operation of the restaurant and does some of the cooking.

Food: ★★★★ To get you started, a dish of blue cheese is served with a small loaf of Italian bread. The salad, which I found to be quite good with a few sprinkles of the blue cheese, is delivered in a bowl with a serving spoon and fork. My sirloin was a delicious combination of charcoal black on top and juicy pink inside with some flavorful seasonings. Their steaks are aged and cut in their own butcher shop. My dinner came with a medium sized baked potato, but no vegetables. I would highly recommend their steaks, and based on their long history and reputation, I think their homemade pasta would be an excellent choice also.

This place is primarily noted for its steaks and pasta, although they also serve seafood, chicken, pork and hamburgers. Other entrees from their steak dinner selection include prime rib, rib eye, filet mignon, lamb chops and prime calves liver. The Italian dinners include ravioli, manicotti, cavatelli, spaghetti, fettuccini, veal Parmigiana, homemade sausage and lasagna. The seafood entrees feature deep fried shrimp, red coho salmon, lobster tail, Colorado rainbow trout and frog legs. Homemade soups, chili and sandwiches are available for the lighter appetite. The dessert offerings include mud or grasshopper pie, chocolate suicide cake, spumoni, and white chocolate raspberry cheese cake.

Service: ★★★ My waitress was forgetful (She forgot I ordered "just butter" on my baked potato and served it with "just sour cream". She forgot the menu that I requested and she had to confirm how I ordered my steak.), but she was actually very friendly and accommodating. In her defense, she was quite busy. If she carried a note pad, I did not see it. The water boy kept busy and apologized when my glass got too empty. A nice kid. The bus boys did an effective job of cleaning the entire seating area between customers.

Decor: ★★★★ Straight back from the entrance is the main dining room with six booths for 25 and a bar for eight. Portraits of three Merlinos hang in one corner. To the right of the entrance is the Grotta Sotterranea lounge which seats 60 in black, glossy, cushioned chairs with adjustable backs. The chairs are set at small round tables and it looks like a comfortable place to come for a drink before or after dinner. The Grotta is underground, below the parking lot. There is a small bar with four stools and a field stone wall along the far right side. Lighting is provided by black-iron, frosted-glass wall lights. Gold-framed portraits of beautiful women in a black background also decorate the wall space.

To the right of the entrance is the two tier Mediterranean Room. Three large booths and two small tables overlook the lower tier, four feet below, which has two booths plus tables for about 64 people. The upper tier only has two paintings on its wood-paneled walls — one of the canals of Venice, the other a still-life of fruit and jars. The lower tier is much more decorative with a small water fountain inset in the middle of the back wall and arched shaped tapestries of sailing ships, doves and rocky islands at sea: very Mediterranean looking indeed.

To the far left of the entrance is the Roman Room with wall mirrors, a large mural of Roman scenes, and seating for 55 in gold-cushioned chairs on the lower level. Above this level is a divided dining area with nine booths for about 40 people. Total seating in all dining areas is about 280. In addition, there is a large banquet room upstairs which seats 200.

Atmosphere: ★★★*1/2* I was here on a Wednesday night in August, but I had to remind myself that it was not a Friday or Saturday. It was very busy with families casually dressed: a lot of shorts, t-shirts, and cool casual clothes. They play some instrumental music which can barely be heard above all the voices. Despite the crowd, I had no problem getting seated. They have a lot of room and try to be very accommodating.

CASTLE ROCK

Castle Rock, named for the large rock formation at the top of the hill, was elected county seat in 1874 and incorporated in 1881. The town is settled among thousands of acres of rolling hills, scrub oak and ponderosa pine. Each year, around the Holiday Season, a yule star is lit on top of the large rock marking the town. In the summer, Castle Rock is home to a PGA golf tournament - the International at Castlepines. In March of 1978, the county courthouse was destroyed by a distraught lover who tried to free her imprisoned boyfriend by setting the courthouse on fire. The new courthouse now stands in its place.

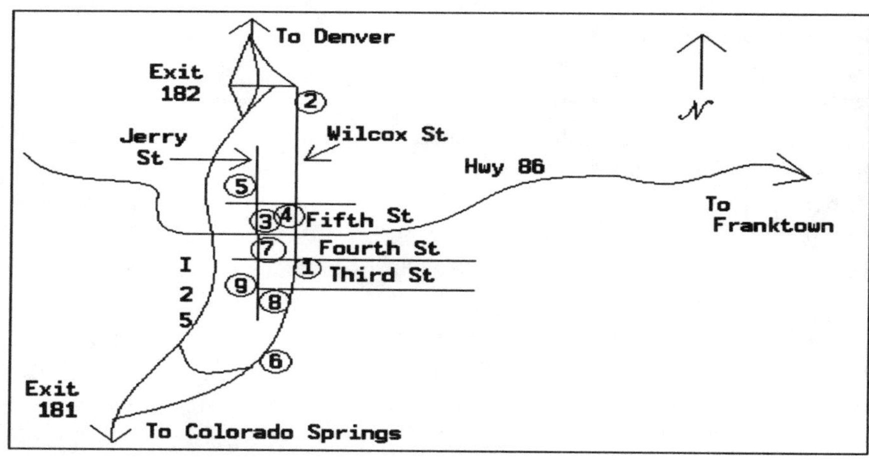

Restaurants and Ratings:	Food	Service	Decor	Atm	Overall
1. B & B Cafe	★★	★★	★★★	★½	★★
2. China Dragon	★★	★★½	★★	★★	★★
3. Cliff O'Deli's	★★★	★★½	★½	★★½	★★½
4. Golden Dobbin	★★★★½	★★★★★	★★★★½	★★★★	★★★★½
5. Khaki's	★★★½	★★★½	★★★	★★	★★★
6. Nicolo's	★★★★	★★★	★★★	★★★	★★★½
7. Pablo's	★★½	★★★	★★	★★½	★★½
8. Pegasus	★★★★	★★★	★★½	★★½	★★★
9. Stone Church	★★★½	★★★½	★★★★	★★½	★★★½

CASTLE ROCK

My favorite place in Castle Rock was The Golden Dobbin, located in a charming old, white, wood house run by two delightful and pleasant ladies. The Stone Church offers the setting of a Franciscan Church for its meals. Pegasus has some delicious Greek food and Nicolo's has some worthy Italian selections. For the best burger and sandwiches in town visit Khaki's. Only the B & B Cafe and Cliff O'Deli's will not take your major credit card or serve alcohol. The only restaurants that offer nonsmoking sections are the China Dragon, Pegasus and the Stone Church.

B & B CAFE ★★
322 WILCOX (303)688-9983

Breakfast $, lunch $-$$. MON-FRI 6:30AM-5PM. SAT 6:30AM-4PM. Closed SUN.
Type: Cafe.

Food: ★★ *Service:* ★★ *Decor:* ★★★ *Atmosphere:* ★½

There is a lot of history to be found in this restaurant, like the bullet hole left in the tin ceiling when the Town Marshall was killed in 1946, or the marble bar made in Italy, or the photos and news clippings of the county courthouse that burned in March, 1978. Despite the decor, I found their food to be slightly greasy and salty, the service a bit slow, and the restaurant itself crowded, noisy and smoky.

CHINA DRAGON ★★
820 WILCOX (303)688-2300

Lunch $, dinner $$. MON-THU 11AM-9:30PM. FRI 11AM-10PM. SAT 5PM-10PM. SUN 5PM-9PM.
Type: Oriental (Szechuan & Mandarin). Carry-out available.

Food: ★★ *Service:* ★★½ *Decor:* ★★ *Atmosphere:* ★★

Nothing special here. I ordered the seafood combination spicy: it was anything but. The decor is sparse, the service satisfactory, the atmosphere bland.

CLIFF O'DELI'S ★★½
205 FIFTH ST (303)688-3470

Breakfast/lunch $. MON-FRI 8AM-6PM. SAT 9AM-4PM. Closed SUN. Type: Deli. Free delivery available.

Food: ★★★ *Service:* ★★½ *Decor:* ★½ *Atmosphere:* ★★½

I found their roast beef sub to be quite good and filling, but too heavy on the onions. The man behind the deli counter is a nice guy and the atmosphere is relaxed with easy listening music playing. This is a one room deli with nine wood tables with wooden folding chairs. The walls are extensively covered with sports pennants.

THE GOLDEN DOBBIN ★★★★½
519 WILCOX (303)688-3786

Lunch $$. TUE-SAT: 2 sittings at 11:45AM and 1:15PM. MON 11:30AM-2PM. Closed SUN.

Type: American/Continental. Reservations required TUE-SAT. No reservation required on MON when they offer a blue plate special.

This combination tea room and gift shop was built in 1905 and originally owned by the town lamplighter. The previous owner played an organ that could be heard in town during the evening. It has been a tea room since 1965. They try to accommodate both smokers and nonsmokers, but they only have two small rooms.

CASTLE ROCK

Food: ★★★★½ This is a specialty restaurant that serves only one complete meal twice a day (except on Monday). The afternoon that I was there, lunch featured Caesar's salad, lemon caper chicken, scallion rice, ratatouille and bread pudding for dessert. The same entree is served TUE-THU each week. On FRI and SAT, homemade soup, bread and dessert is on the menu. The Caesar's salad came with a wonderful lemon and extra virgin olive oil dressing and Parmesan cheese. This is a buffet style lunch served from the gift shop room. The chicken was thick & meaty and had a delicate white sauce with lemon and capers. The rice was steamed with peas and scallions. The ratatouille was a delicious combination of eggplant, tomatoes and green peppers. The bread and lemon pudding was very weak, like milk toast, but oh, what flavor! Some of the other soups you may see here are Brazilian red bean and smoked cheddar potato. Other salad dressings include sesame herb, raspberry vinegarette and cilantro lime. The lunch entree could be canneloni crêpes, chicken étouffée, curry meatloaf with chutney, apricot champagne chicken, Stroganoff meatballs or beef Bourguignonne. For Sunday brunch, you may find brisola (a spicy turkey patty), round steak, sour cream cheese potatoes, mixed vegetables with basil butter and strawberry short cake. The menu varies weekly, so you have to call ahead to see what's on the menu for the day you plan to dine here.

Service: ★★★★★ The owner/host/server and chef are two cheerful and dignified ladies who do a superb job of preparing food and serving their customers. The waitress will assist you to the entree while you help yourself to the rest of the meal. During your meal, she will return with rolls, rice and vegetables for a second helping. After the meal, the chef will come by with the days dessert selections.

Decor: ★★★★½ Located in an old white house with black awning, shutters and doors, the restaurant inside is artfully decorated. Wreaths, paintings of pastoral scenes, and assorted knick-knacks give this tiny restaurant a comfortable, homey look. For seating, there are only two small rooms with seven tables for 19 people. There is outdoor seating in the summertime: four tables under umbrellas on the patio for 16 and a gazebo with two tables for eight. Also, in the summer, some people will just sit out on the lawn or on one of the two circular benches around two trees. Separating the two dining rooms is the gift shop. Human and animal figurines, fresh scents, traditional rose potpourri, candle holders, vases, egg coddlers and dinner bells are just a few of the items for sale. The original wood floor combined with the fresh, clean, white and tan wallpaper provide a charming mix of the old and new. Seating is on small, round-cushioned chairs at tables with white tablecloths: comfortable in a dainty kind of way; not a good stop for truck drivers.

Atmosphere: ★★★★ A classical radio station plays very quietly in the background. This restaurant appears to be popular with women — especially older women. This is not a place to bring a large group, unless you plan to sit outside.

KHAKI'S ★★★
600 JERRY STREET (303)688-5257

Lunch/dinner $$. MON-THU 11AM-9:30PM. FRI-SAT 11AM-10:30PM. SUN 11AM-9PM.
Type: Burgers. 15% gratuity for parties of eight or more. No separate checks. To go orders available.

Visible from Interstate 25, Khaki's is an off-the-road restaurant that is worth finding if you are in the mood for a good burger or sandwich in a comfortable, sporty atmosphere.

Food: ★★★½ Their Mexican bean soup with cayenne pepper and pieces of pork is exceptional. The roast beef sandwiches, filled high with lean beef, lettuce & tomato, are very good. Probably their best item on the menu, though, is their burger. Thick, meaty, charbroiled and very tasty: it is a super burger and comes with curly fries. For appetizers, you can choose from super nachos, quesadillas, potato skins, onion rings, or jalapeno Buffalo wings. New York style pizza comes in three sizes, but a limited selection of seven toppings. There are several salads to choose from, including spinach, avocado-artichoke, and taco. Soup and green chili are also on the menu. The list of specials includes veal cutlet

Parmesan, linguini with baby clams, T-bone and rib eye steaks, chicken tettrazini or teriyaki, shrimp primavera, and roast prime rib. There a few good Mexican selections like fajitas, chili rellenos, Mexican London broil, and smothered burritos. Other sandwich selections include hot pastrami & Swiss, steak with onions & cheese, French dip, and Monte Cristo. There is a children's menu and, for dessert, cheesecake, homemade pies, and Southern style pound cake with ice cream and strawberries.

Service: ★★★½ A very friendly waitress with a good sense of humor. Very helpful and willing to find answers to my questions, but slow with the check.

Decor: ★★★ There are ten booths and eleven tables for 86 in the dining room with a 30-foot, vaulted ceiling made of blue wood. Square, maroon platforms with ceiling fans and lights, hang about 12 feet from the ground disguising the true height of the room. Windows along the front face the parking lot while windows on the opposite side face the patio. Black and white photos decorate the other two walls, including a picture of the old county courthouse before it burned down in 1978 and a picture of the old train station with the enormous town rock in the background. Photos of snow-capped buttes and glaciers decorate the tan wall paper with maroon trim. Blue and maroon are the primary colors here with blue tablecloths and blue-clothed bench seats. Opposite the dining room is the bar/lounge with a large, square brick wall in the middle. Both square and round tables can seat 60. There are eight barstools, a juke box in one corner, and a collage of photos taken at a pajama party. The patio out back is in two sections with a trellis over the inner section. Orange plastic seats attached to wood tables are used on the inner section. Circular glass-tables with umbrellas and lounge chairs are used on the outer section. There is room for about 80 people outside. Total seating is 234.

Atmosphere: ★★ No nonsmoking section hurts, even with fans. There are quite a few smokers. This is a yuppie crowd. The name, Khaki's, was derived in 1985 when khaki pants were popular among yuppie's.

NICOLO'S ★★★½
190 S WILCOX (AT THE SOUTH END OF THE SAFEWAY SHOPPING CENTER)
(303)688-9800

Lunch/dinner $-$$ ($$$ for large or family size pizza). MON-SAT: 11:30AM-9:30PM. SUN: 11:30AM-8:30PM.
Type. Italian. Nicolo's is one of the more popular restaurants in town because of their pizza. They were voted "Best Pizza in Denver" by a June 1989 Denver Magazine readers poll.

Food: ★★★★ I heard of Nicolo's reputation for great pizza, so I thought I would try one of their pasta dishes. I was not disappointed with their lasagna: a flavorful marinara sauce, al dente lasagna noodles, and a good mix of cheeses. Their pizza comes in four sizes with a choice of eight toppings and is available in pan style or regular. The other pasta choices include spaghetti in red sauce, linguini in white clam sauce, and fettucini Alfredo. Calzones, sandwiches (Italian sausage, meatball or sub), and salads (pasta and tossed) are also available. For dessert, plain or amaretto cheesecake are on the menu. Their selection is limited, but their quality is noteworthy.

Service: ★★★ Just fine. They are pleasant, helpful and prompt.

Decor: ★★★ This is a single, long narrow restaurant with a bench along the full length of the right wall and small, wooden chairs opposite. There are two booths and three small, mauve tables on the left. Total seating is 40. The walls are decorated with posters of Toscana, Marsala, pasta, a paint brush coming out of a can dripping red, white and green paint (the colors of the Italian flag), and a cute, small child in a pot with the caption "There's a little Italian in everything we do". Accompanying the posters are pictures of Chicago harbor on Lake Michigan and a baseball stadium.

Atmosphere: ★★★ I was here about 2PM, after the lunch crowd had left, so I did not get to sample much atmosphere. It was quiet and the staff was mostly cleaning up. The setting seemed pleasant enough.

CASTLE ROCK

PABLO'S ★★½
201 4TH ST (303)660-8511

Lunch/dinner $. MON-SAT 11am-9pm. SUN 4pm-9pm.
Type: Mexican. Carry-out available.

Food: ★★½ *Service:* ★★★ *Decor:* ★★ *Atmosphere:* ★★½

I dined here with several co-workers so I obtained opinions on a variety of meals. Their chips are light and very crispy and their salsa is fairly mild and filled with tomatoes. Both are good, but here's where the meal ends. Their enchiladas are watery, their tostados tasteless, and their tacos greasy. Their burritos use fresh, but contain plain ground beef. I ordered their chili relleno which came wrapped in their own egg batter. I did not care for it. I prefer the traditional flour tortilla. This tasted more like huevos rancheros. Their chili sauce is good, but their rice and beans are bland. This is a one-room restaurant in two sections for 66 diners. The decor is a hodge-podge of Mexican, t-shirts, beer signs and wood parrots perched on rings hanging from the ceiling.

PEGASUS ★★★
207 WILCOX STREET (303)688-6746

Breakfast $, lunch/dinner $-$$. MON-THU 6:30AM-9PM. FRI 6:30AM-10PM. SAT 7AM-10PM. SUN 7AM-9PM.
Type: Mexican (Greek and American).

Food: ★★★★ I ordered the Grecian platter: a Greek salad with lettuce, tomato, cucumber, bell peppers, Greek olives, pepperoncini (they call them Greek peppers, but I think they are strictly Italian), onions, feta cheese (one of my favorites), and Greek salad dressing with plenty of oregano. The entree featured a generous portion of grilled, marinated pork, a blend of lamb and beef ground together, two pita breads to make your own souvlaki (pork) and gyro (lamb & beef), and a side of sour cream with cucumber. Greek food has always been "so-so" with me, but

I found this delicious! The Greek platter will also make two meals for an average appetite.

Breakfast includes cinnamon rolls, souvlaki, hickory smoked ham, eggs benedict, huevos rancheros, and breakfast burritos. The highlight of the appetizer list is the dolmades, or marinated rice wrapped in grape leaves & served with lemon wedges. You can create your own salad by choosing four items and dressing to go with your lettuce. They offer the following sandwiches: cheesesteak, grilled chicken breast, souvlakis, gyros, and club. The entrees feature steak (Mexican, rib eye, top sirloin or chicken fried), chicken (Mexican, or smothered), halibut, and the basic Mexican fare.

Service: ★★★ Satisfactory. Helpful in answering my questions. The owner, John T. Delay, is a young, friendly, energetic and jovial fellow.

Decor: ★★½ There is a small bar as you enter with seven director's chairs and a television in the corner. The dining room is divided into three sections. The first section has five tables for 22. The end balcony section has two booths and five tables for 28. The third seating area is parallel to the first and separated by a white plaster wall with four-inch thick crystal-glass bricks and potted plants. It seats 34 at four booths and four tables. The decor is rather sparse and includes pictures of cattlemen, cattle, horses, and mountain scenery. Combined with this is a Mexican artwork and tapestry. There are in-set ceiling lights and several potted plants dispersed throughout. Seating is on brown-cushioned chairs in silver aluminum frames or on turquoise- and grey-cushioned bench seats.

Atmosphere: ★★½ These are mostly local folks who know each other. This is a pleasant place. It was a little chilly the evening that I was there. A few tornados had touched down in Castle Rock that afternoon. Live music is played on FRI and SAT beginning at 9PM.

STONE CHURCH ★★★½
210 THIRD STREET (303)688-9000

CASTLE ROCK

Lunch \$-\$\$, dinner \$\$-\$\$\$ with a few \$\$\$\$ and \$\$\$\$+. MON-FRI: 11AM-10PM. SAT: 4PM-10PM. Closed SUN.
Type: Steak (and seafood). Reservations accepted. 15% gratuity for groups of six or more.

The historic Stone Church Restaurant is in what once was the St. Francis of Assisi Church built by the Franciscan Friars in 1888. They used rhyolite stone from a quarry south of Castle Rock. The stained glass windows were added in the early 1920's. In 1966, the congregation built a larger church east of town and left the original church vacant. In 1975, a group of local businessmen purchased the property and remodeled the structure. The original choir loft was expanded and the confessional is now an intimate table for two.

Food: ★★★½ Their cauliflower and cheese soup came with celery, only a few small pieces of cauliflower, and was only fair. The entree lunch special was better: a charbroiled teriyaki chicken that was moist and tender with just enough flavor and mixed vegetables that were crisp, not over cooked. It was served with pineapple, lettuce, tomato and honey dew mellon. Their BLT is also good and comes with fresh, crispy potato chips. Lunch features sandwiches like baked ham on toast, Polish sausage and barbecue beef tips; burgers; appetizers like Rocky Mountain oysters; salads; and dinners like steak, broiled Icelandic cod, and honey dipped chicken. The dinner menu will start you off with onion rings, zucchini sticks or shrimp cocktail. The entrees include prime rib; several steak and seafood selections like filet mignon wrapped in bacon, Australian lobster tail and Alaskan salmon steak; combination steak and seafood dinners; three chicken choices including teriyaki and barbecue; and ham steak. There is a combination child's/senior's menu for those under 12 or over 60. You can finish your meal with cheese cake, mudd or pecan pie, a sundae or sherbet.

Service: ★★★½ Very good. Cooperative and helpful, yet unobtrusive.

Decor: ★★★★ The nonsmoking section is an addition to the original church on the west side. It has an uneven floor, a slanted wood-beam ceiling (to go with the uneven floor) with two skylights and hanging plants. There is seating for 52 at 13 finished wood tables with rust-colored, cushioned wood chairs. Oil paintings on the wood panel wall opposite what used to be the stone exterior of the church include scenes of a horse drawn carriage crossing the prairie, "dudes" playing poker, cowboys and horses on the plain, and a cowboy doing tricks on a horse. The smoking section is a small room with four tables for 10 with a stained-glass window and a painting of a small girl. Across from the smoking room is the alcove that used to be the confessional in the old church. The lounge downstairs is visible from upstairs and has seating for 36. It occupies the main part of the church, decorated in a combination of stained-glass, wood, red brick and plaster. A semi-circular stairway decorated with old pictures of the church, Castle Rock, and the surrounding area, leads to the upstairs dining area. There is seating on three sides with an open space in the middle looking down onto the lounge. 12 tables can seat 42. Square, black, metal and clear-glass electric light fixtures hang from the vaulted wood ceiling. The main feature of the room is a single, circular, stained-glass window with a yellow and blue border. Oil lamps are at each table throughout the restaurant. In front of the church is a small patio with five tables with umbrellas for 20 diners.

Atmosphere: ★★½ Country music plays a little louder than it should and contradicts what otherwise might be a peaceful and serene church setting.

CENTRAL CITY

As one of three towns in Colorado where gambling is legal, Central City began as a trading center for miners. The town was named by Rocky Mountain News publisher, William N. Byers, for its centralized location among the gold camps. Central City became known as "the richest square mile on earth". The first legal execution under the Colorado territorial government occurred here in January 1864. In the early 1930's, the Opera House was reopened to stars like Lillian Gish, Ruth Gordon, and Mae West. The Teller House next door is home to the famous "Face on the Barroom Floor".

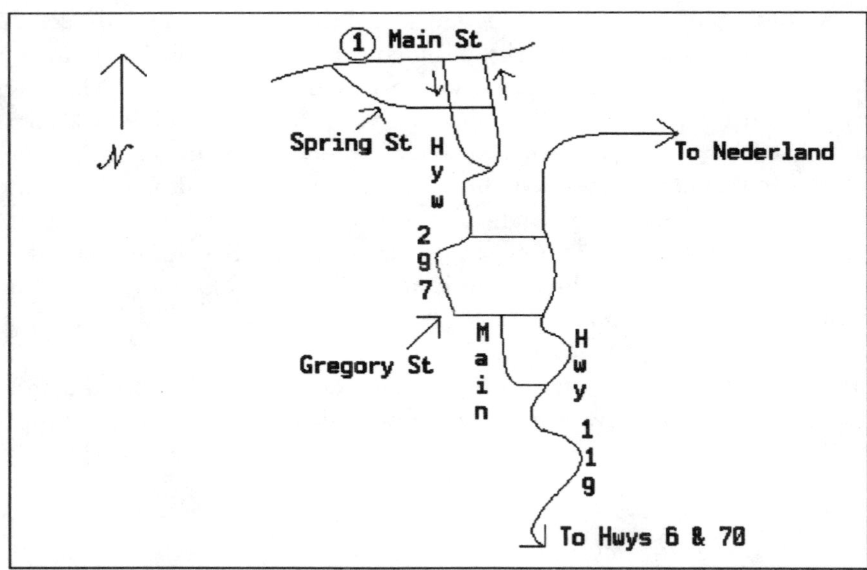

1. **Gilded Garter Saloon ★½**
   129 Main Street (303)582-5915

Breakfast $, lunch/dinner $-$$. SUN-THU 7AM-11PM. FRI-SAT 24 hours. They accept major credit cards, do not have a nonsmoking section and definitely serve alcohol.
Type: Tavern.

Food: ★★ *Service:* ★ *Decor:* ★ *Atmosphere:* ★½

This is a dark saloon with grey window shades blocking 90% of the sunlight. A live country music band plays at a reasonable noise level in the back. There is a lot of smoke, black leather vests, hats, and coats, and a preponderance of flies in this country atmosphere. I had a very flat, over cooked, unimpressive buffalo burger (the folks from Buffalo would not be proud!) served with thin, frozen style fries and a pickle. The "all you can eat," mild sauce, barbecue beef ribs that my service rep from Gilliland Printing ordered were a better choice, served with real pinto beans, fries and toast. Our server provided us with no silver - or plastic - ware, forgot the cheese on my cheeseburger (it wouldn't have helped, anyway), and never returned to pick up payment on the check. My rep had to track him down.

Main Street - Central City

CLIFTON

Clifton was named after the nearby Denver & Rio Grande Railroad tracks and station that took the name for the book cliffs in the area.

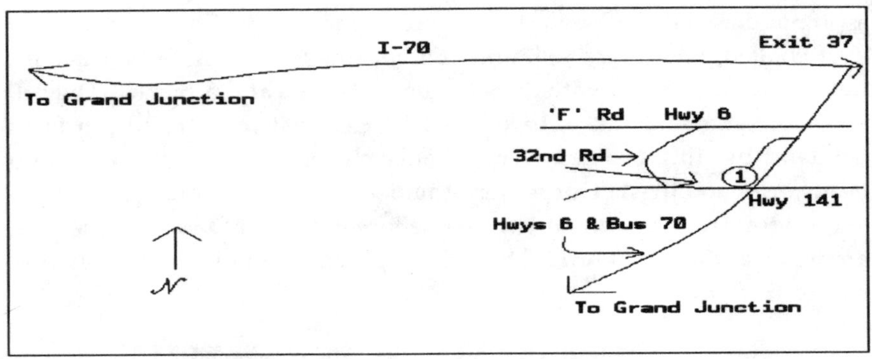

1. Brown's Pointe ★★½
3210 I-70 Business Loop (303)434-1505

Breakfast/lunch $, dinner $$-$$$. MAR-NOV: MON-SAT 6AM-9PM, SUN 6AM-8PM. DEC-FEB: 6AM-10PM, SUN 6AM-8PM. They accept major credit cards, have a small nonsmoking section, and serve alcohol. Type: Family.

***Food:* ★★★ *Service:* ★½ *Decor:* ★★½ *Atmosphere:* ★★**

This is a V-shaped restaurant with a large smoking section for 124 and a nonsmoking section for 17, to give you some idea of where their priorities lie. The decor is nice enough, with large murals and framed posters of lakes, pine trees and snow-capped peaks. Windows along both sides of the "V" allow plenty of natural light. I had an interesting, but bland breakfast of hash browns with ground beef and one egg in a cream sauce served with toast. It could have used some salsa, chili, jalapeños or seasoning. Service was cool to the point of being ignored. My meal was served in a hurry, but my waitress never returned to refill my coffee. I did notice her refilling coffee at other tables, though. The hostess finally brought me a second cup. I don't think they took kindly to my suit and tie. This is a place for locals, not tourists or strangers.

CONIFER

Originally known as Hutchison, for early settler George Hutchison and later as Junction City, the town's name was changed to Conifer in 1900 for the abundance of that tree in the area.

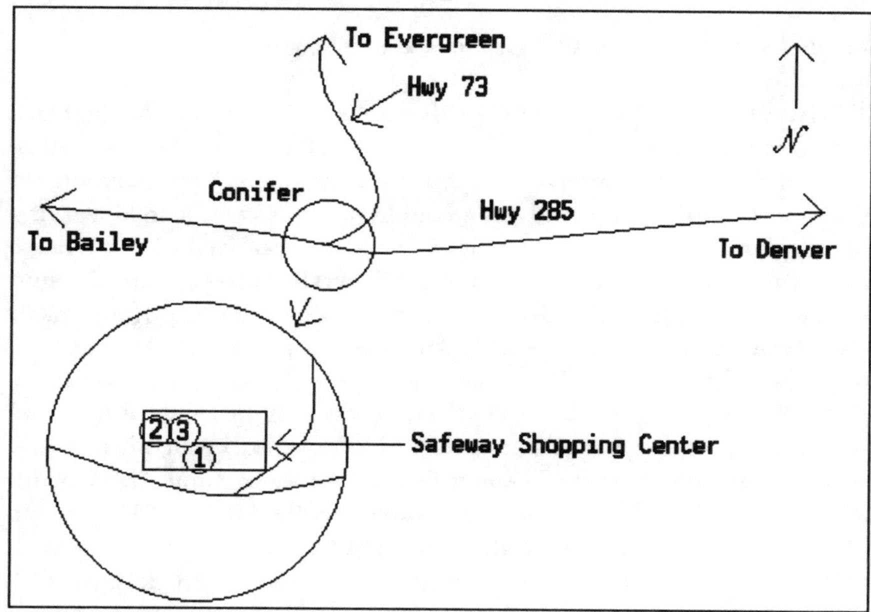

Restaurant and Ratings:	Food	Service	Decor	Atm	Overall
1. ITALIAN TOUCH	★★½	★★½	★★★	★★	★★½
2. LA CANTINA II	★★★½	★★	★★★½	★★★	★★★
3. New China Dragon	★★★	★★★	★★½	★★★	★★★

La Cantina II serves some good fajitas and other Mexican specialties. The New China Dragon offers some good, spicy chicken, pork and shrimp dishes. All three restaurants accept major credit cards and have nonsmoking sections. Only the New China Dragon does not serve alcohol. However, they have applied for a liquor license, so they may be serving alcohol by the time you visit.

ITALIAN TOUCH ★★½
10875 US HWY 285(AT HWY 73, CONIFER SHOPPING CENTER)(303)838-7870

CONIFER

Lunch $, dinner $$. SUN-THU 11:30AM-8:30PM. FRI-SAT 11:30AM-9:30PM. Type: Italian. 15% gratuity added to tables of 8 or more. All menu items available for take-out.

Food: ★★½ *Service:* ★★½ *Decor:* ★★★ *Atmosphere:* ★★

The twenty item salad bar with six dressings included mozzarella, black olives, macaroni & potato salads, Jello and cottage cheese. The lettuce was a little wilted. I ordered the ravioli and eggplant Parmigiana dinner (one meal) thinking I would get a couple of ravioli and a small serving of eggplant. Wrong! I was served six moderate sized ricotta cheese ravioli in a bland tomato sauce and a full serving of eggplant. I found the eggplant on the dry side. The ravioli, with a little help from grated Parmesan and red peppers, was better. These are good sized portions of average Italian food. They also have pizza, calzones, sandwiches, linguini, manicotti, and lasagna. Service was very quick until the meal was served, then I became invisible. Norman Rockwell posters and covers from the Saturday Evening Post adorn the natural wood walls. An attractive stone wall in the back separates the kitchen. There is an abundance of lighting from ceiling fan lights, single hanging lights with colorful mosaic shades, and fluorescent tubes. Moderate rock music was playing, rather loud, until the Lion's Club arrived. They complained and the management turned it off.

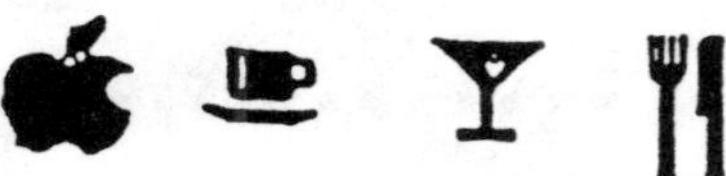

LA CANTINA II ★★★
10903 U.S. HWY 285 (AT HWY 73 IN THE CONIFER SHOPPING CENTER)
(303) 838-6138 IN CONIFER, (303)674-0424 IN DENVER

Breakfast $, lunch/dinner $-$$$. 7 days 7AM-11PM.
Type: Mexican.

Food: ★★★½ My dinner companion ordered a cheese enchilada which he found spicy and to his liking, I had the chicken fajitas. They serve a dish with warm (not hot) chicken, green peppers, onion, cold lettuce and tomato; a second dish with guacamole, American cheese, sour cream, and more tomatoes; a cup of green chili; and three flour tortillas (not nearly enough for the quantity of ingredients in front of you). It was quite good, but cold since most items were cold and the heated items were only luke-warm. The breakfast menu includes fluffy hot buttermilk pancakes and waffles, cinnamon rolls, turnovers, eggs Benedict, a breakfast burrito and huevos con chorizo. The lunch/dinner menu features sandwiches like French dip and chicken fried steak, weekday specials like a smothered beef & bean burrito, buffalo specials (steaks, ribs & burgers), a complete Mexican menu including chicken filets, fajitas and Mexican sirloin steak. There is a limited "Gringos" menu with burgers, steaks, chicken, fish and shrimp. Sopapillas, ice cream, cinnamon rolls and homemade pies are on the dessert menu.

Service: ★★ The owner, who got my card from the waitress, greeted me with "what's the deal here?" I think he thought I was here to sell him some advertising. Actually, he turned out to be an "alright Joe". The waitress was somewhat less sparkling, though.

Decor: ★★★½ There is a bar/lounge to left as you enter with seven tables for 24 people and 12 barstools. To the right of the hostess station is a small dining room for 20 with beige wallpaper featuring a turquoise & maroon, flower & leaf pattern. The decor consists of hanging and potted plants and a yellow kachina doll. The main dining room, farther back, seats 66 at ten tables, seven booths and three combination bench seats opposite brown-cushioned chairs. This room has two crooked-hanging pictures of a niño playing a guitar and a niña carrying a basket in a black velvet background. Gold-plated and wood chandeliers in clear-glass, globe-shaped fixtures hang from the acoustic ceiling. A short 18-inch trellis with a gold banister on top separates the main and small dining rooms. The booths are made of pinewood with gold banisters on top of the backs. A turquoise and maroon, speckled egg shell wallpaper covers the top two-third of the rear wall, pinewood covers the bottom one-third. A continuous row of windows extends along the right wall facing the highway. Attractive pictures of cattails in a lake hang on the tan and beige, tree pattern, wallpaper on the left side.

Atmosphere: ★★★½ Soft rock music played in the background. It was a quiet atmosphere on the Saturday afternoon that I visited in early summer. There were a lot of tourists, stopping on their way down Highway 85.

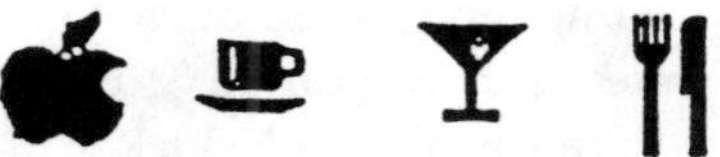

NEW CHINA DRAGON ★★★
10875 US HWY 285(AT HWY 73, CONIFER SHOPPING CENTER)(303)838-7870

Lunch $, dinner $$. 7 days 11AM-9:30PM.
Type: Oriental (Chinese).

Food: ★★★ I tried their hot & sour soup and three meats (chicken, pork & shrimp) with hot pepper sauce. The soup was the spicier of the two, but I liked the sauce used in the entree. Plenty of "meats" with green peppers, carrots, peanuts and water chestnuts in this one. The rice was fluffy (nonsticky). The menu is typical Chinese with the usual appetizers, like the pu pu platter and scallion pancakes (which I was tempted to order), soups, three family dinners for two or more, a few chef specials like roast duck, an array of 92 dinner entrees with chicken, pork, beef, shrimp and vegetables, and 43 quick lunch combinations, most under $5. 12 are classified as hot & spicy.

Service: ★★★ Pleasant, thoughtful and quick.

Decor: ★★½ This is a long, single-room restaurant with nine brown-cushioned booths along the left wall, four along the right wall, and four tables in-between. Total seating for 74. There are the familiar gold ceiling light fixtures with red tassels and pictures of Chinese life, wild life and nature. Most of the wall space is barren with only three pictures of Chinese women (fan ladies) in the front of the restaurant and two nature pictures in the rear. They recently expanded and may not have had time for their decor to catch up.

Atmosphere: ★★★ Easy listening and light rock music. A lot of tourists in the summertime, mostly all locals the rest of the year.

COPPER MOUNTAIN

Copper Mountain is often referred to a "the skier's mountain" and was recently voted No. 1 trail and slope design by "Snow Country Magazine". The resort is undergoing a $40 million dollar expansion, including a second high-speed quadruple chairlift, and offers ski lessons, snowboarding, and cross-country skiing. In the summer, there is Copper Creek Golf Club, the highest golf course in the U.S. at 9,700 feet.

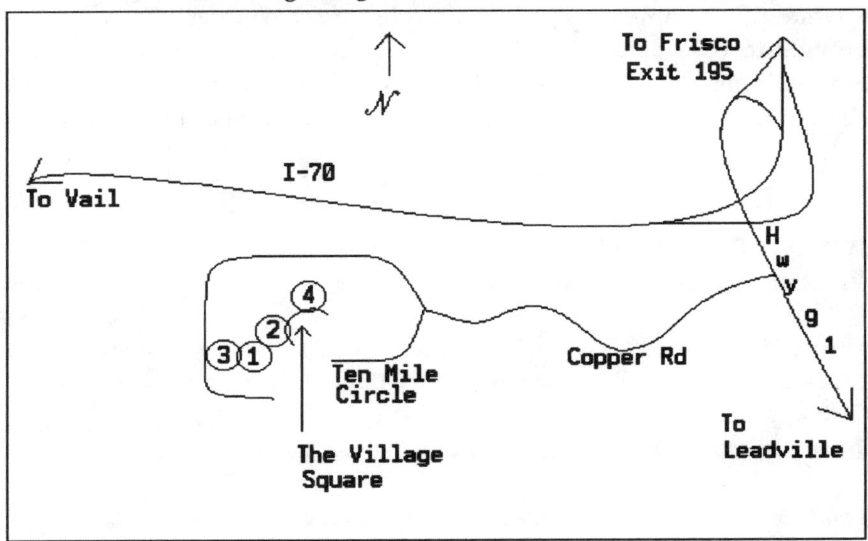

Restaurant and Ratings:	Food	Service	Decor	Atm	Overall
1. Copper Deli	★★½	★★	★★	★½	★★
2. Imperial Palace	★★	★★½	★★★	★½	★★½
3. Pesce Fresco	★★★★	★★	★★★★	★★★½	★★★½
4. That Soup Place	★★½	★★½	★★½	★★	★★½

I would recommend Pesce Fresco for their sandwiches and That Soup Place for a good bowl of chili. Only the Imperial Palace and Pesce Fresco accept major credit cards and serve alcohol. Only the Imperial Palace does not offer a nonsmoking section. The others are all nonsmoking.

Copper Deli ★★
Mountain Plaza Building (303)968-6168

Breakfast/lunch $. 7 days 8AM-5PM.
Type: Deli.

Food: ★★½ *Service:* ★★ *Decor:* ★★ *Atmosphere:* ★½

I had an average quality barbecued beef sandwich with tomato sauce on a white roll. Nothing special. You order at the counter. Food will be brought to your table. This is a sandwich, ice cream and pastry place. Seating is limited to 7 hardwood tables for 25 people seated on cushioned chairs with low wicker backs. I found this to be a quiet lunch spot.

IMPERIAL PALACE ★★½
VILLAGE SQUARE (303)968-6688

Lunch $$, dinner $$-$$$$. NOV-APR: 7 days 11AM-10PM. JUN & SEP: TUE-SUN 11AM-9:30PM. Closed MON. JUL-AUG: 7 days 11AM-9:30PM. Closed MAY & OCT.
Type: Oriental (Chinese). Take-out available.

Food: ★★ *Service:* ★★½ *Decor:* ★★★ *Atmosphere:* ★½

Their hot & sour soup could have been hotter in both temperature and spice. The twice cooked pork was heavy on the soy sauce and grease. The decor was interesting with posters of famous stars like Elvis Presley and Humphrey Bogart, photos of antique cars, and a full length mirror in the middle section of the restaurant. The service was quick and curt, but efficient. The atmosphere had too many boisterous local workers.

PESCE FRESCO ★★★½
MOUNTAIN PLAZA (303)968-2882 x6505

Breakfast $-$$, lunch $$, dinner $$$-$$$$. 7 days 7AM-10PM (Breakfast 7AM-11AM, lunch 11AM-2PM, afternoon menu 2PM-5PM, dinner 5PM-10PM).

Type: Seafood (and pasta). Smoking is only permitted in the lounge.

Food: ★★★★ Their menu changes monthly. That's right, monthly! So management did not want me to print anything in particular. They do serve sandwiches for lunch and I ordered an excellent turkey & gouda on wheat with honey-mustard sauce. Actually, you start with a BLT, pile it high with turkey, add the cheese and sauce, and you have this scrumptious sandwich. It comes with a big pile of tasty, spicy fries and fruit garnish. The dinner menu offers a variety of fresh fish and pasta dishes. The selection of pasta and sauces are changed on a regular basis. They have, in the words of the manager, a very creative chef.

Service: ★★ Somewhat cool. I was the only customer. Perhaps they wanted a quiet afternoon.

Decor: ★★★★ There is a bar/lounge to the left of the entrance with seven barstools and seven tables for 17. There is a bar extension from one wall and bars along two sides facing the windows. A fish tank separates the lounge and dining room. The patio in front has six wood bench tables with warped seats and tables, plus seven glass-topped tables with metal-framed lounge chairs. Total seating outside is 76. There are two dining rooms to the right of the entrance. The first has three booths and 12 hardwood tables for 56 diners. Seating is on wood-framed chairs with armrests and green-clothed, cushioned seats and backs. The restaurant has a clean, fresh, modern look. The center of the dining room ceiling has a wood-framed structure with a shiny, copper-cratered pattern bordered by diagonal mirrors that allow viewing of fellow diners without staring (if that is what you are into). Impressionistic paintings following a theme of marshes and plains decorate the walls. The second dining room, farther back, has eight tables for 20. It is a completely enclosed room — except for the single entrance at one corner — with no windows.

Atmosphere: ★★★½ Pleasant, quietly playing jazz, and an excellent view of the ski slopes and lifts, makes this an ideally aesthetic spot to dine. I was here on a Saturday afternoon in the off-season. A piano is put into use TUE-SAT evenings during the winter.

COPPER MOUNTAIN

THAT SOUP PLACE ★★½
VILLAGE SQUARE (303)968-2629

Breakfast/lunch $. Mid-NOV to Mid-APR: SUN-THU 8AM-4:30PM. FRI-SAT 8AM-8PM. Mid-APR to SEP: 7 days 8AM-3PM. OCT to Mid-NOV: 8AM-2PM.
Type: Cafe.

***Food:* ★★½ *Service:* ★★½ *Decor:* ★★½ *Atmosphere:* ★★**

They have good chili with beef, beans, celery and tomatoes. Their turkey pitas however, are only fair quality. Everything, including the water for my hot tea, is microwaved. You order at the counter and the food is served at your table. The decor is limited and lacks imagination. No music and there is a partially blocked view of the ski slope.

Mountain Plaza - Copper Mountain

CORTEZ

The town was named after Hernando Cortez (1485-1547, sixteenth century Spanish explorer and conqueror of Mexico) despite the fact that the man never stepped foot in this area. Located in the heart of the Montelores Valley where the San Juan Mountains meet the Arizona desert, the town is centrally situated for excursions to Mesa Verde National Park, Hovenweep National Monument, the Four Corners, and Monument Valley. During the 1950s the town boomed as a result of the area's oil, gas and uranium activity.

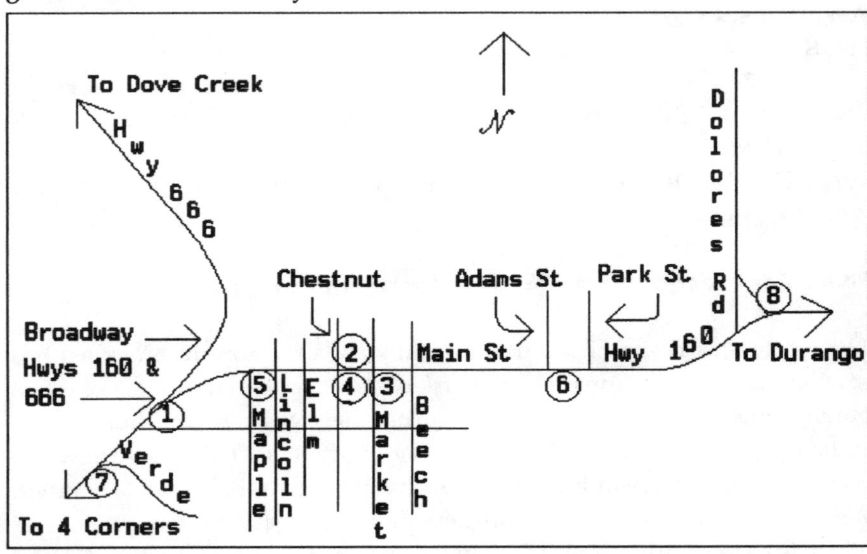

Restaurants and Ratings:	Food	Service	Decor	Atm	Overall
1. Appletree	★★★	★★★½	★½	★★	★★½
2. El Grande Cafe	★½	★★½	★★	★½	★★
3. Francisca's	★★★★	★★½	★★★½	★★★½	★★★½
4. Homesteaders	★★★½	★★½	★★★★	★★★★	★★★½
5. Nero's	★★★	★★★	★★★½	★★½	★★★
6. Pony Express	★★★	★½	★★½	★★½	★★½
7. Stromsted's	★★★★½	★★★★	★★★★½	★★★★	★★★★½
8. Warsaw Inn	★★½	★	★★	★	★½

CORTEZ

The best restaurant in town, on all counts, is Stromsted's. For very good barbecue pork ribs and original and natural decor, visit Homesteaders. If you like Mexican food you can not go wrong with Francesca's. Only the El Grande Cafe does not accept major credit cards. The Appletree, Pony Express and Stromsted's are the only restaurants that offer nonsmoking sections. Only the Appletree and El Grande Cafe do not serve alcohol.

APPLETREE ★★½
666 S. BROADWAY (303)565-3773

Breakfast $, lunch/dinner $-$$. MON-SAT 5:30AM-10PM. SUN 5:30AM-9PM.
Type: Family. 10% senior citizen discount, except for buffets. $1 per meal to go charge.

***Food:* ★★★ *Service:* ★★★½ *Decor:* ★½ *Atmosphere:* ★★**

The food is good and cheap in this family style restaurant. Breakfast has several hearty selections: chicken fried steak, pork chops, a breakfast burrito, huevos rancheros, waffles, corned beef & hash, and homemade cinnamon rolls. Service is fast and very courteous. This restaurant can accommodate 116 people at eighteen booths, ten tables and a counter. Windows on all sides preclude any paintings or wall hangings. The windows are divided by brick columns painted white. Like the decor, I did not find much in the way of atmosphere here either.

EL GRANDE CAFE ★★
28 E. MAIN (303)565-9996

Breakfast/lunch/dinner $. MON-SAT 6:30AM-5PM. Closed SUN.
Type: Country.

***Food:* ★½ *Service:* ★★½ *Decor:* ★★ *Atmosphere:* ★½**

I had breakfast here. Everything was fair, but the hash browns were under cooked. There was only one waitress in the morning, but she did just fine. Eleven booths, four tables, plus a counter provide seating for 60 diners. A three-foot-high mirror runs the full length of the right side of this long single-room restaurant with the counter on the left side. The decor theme here is cowboys and Indians: pictures of cowboys and Indians on horses, cowboys around the camp fire, Indians on a buffalo hunt, and figures of cows and bulls on a mantel behind the counter. There are jukebox selections in each of the large booths. Typical "good ol' boys" yuck it up here. Watch out for the smokers.

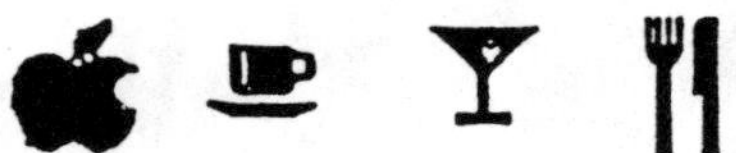

FRANCISCA'S ★★★½
125 E. MAIN (303)565-4093

Lunch/dinner $-$$. MON-SAT 11AM-10PM. Closed Sundays.
Type: Mexican.

Food: ★★★★ Especially good Mexican food goes by special Mexican names here, like the "Spicy Matador". It is actually a smothered burrito. I liked their salsa: thick, but not too thick with just the right amount of tomato and onion flavor. One of the best. In addition to the spicy matador, which I strongly recommend, there are 16 other dinner entrees: everything from stacked enchiladas to a gordita (stuffed sopapilla) to huevos rancheros. If none of these satisfy you, there are three "charbroiled especiales": pollo asada, a super grande burger or an 8-oz. sirloin. For dessert, order a Cherry or apple empanada with ice cream.

Service ★★½ Not bad until the food is served, then you become virtually invisible. Overall, average, at best.

Decor: ★★★½ This restaurant has 17 tables, three in white wicker gazebos. Total seating is for 68 people in white wicker chairs with green or orange cushions that are actually very comfortable. The tables are set with white tablecloths and either baby blue place mats or white placemats with prints of strawberries and cherries. The gazebos are decorated with several hanging plants. Orange crepe paper is used as a covering for the small basement-style windows. The white plaster walls are decorated with a couple of sombreros, a picture of a matador fighting a bull and a picture of children dressed in Mexican costumes. White globe lights hang about six inches from the white plaster ceiling. The entire restaurant is well lit. Decor is simple and inexpensive, as is the building. However, I have a strong fondness for gazebos.

Atmosphere: ★★★½ Quiet, country music plays in the background. A very casual, comfortable atmosphere.

HOMESTEADERS ★★★½
45 E. MAIN (303)565-6253

Breakfast/lunch $, dinner $$. MON-SAT 7AM-9PM. Closed SUN & HOL. Type: Country. 10% senior citizen discount.

Food: ★★★½ They have very good barbecue spare ribs. These are the larger pork ribs, not the baby-back kind. The sauce is very good also. Breakfast features waffles and huevos rancheros. Fresh baked breads, pies and cakes are available to take home, but 24-hour notice is required for full pies and cakes. Lunch offers a large choice of burgers, salads and sandwiches (club, Reuben, roast beef & cheese, chicken breast, tuna bagel, corned beef, turkey, French dip, and steak). A smaller selection of omelets is also available in case you missed breakfast. Additional items include deep fried zucchini, mushrooms or onion rings, chili con carne, soup, and a pot of beans. They also advertise that if there is something you would like that is not on the menu, they will try to meet your request: an offer you do not see in many restaurants. The dinner selection is varied: burgers, salads, barbecue spare ribs and chicken, steaks, seafood (catfish, trout, halibut and shrimp), Mexican food, and a few "old fashion favorites" like roast beef, fried chicken, chicken fried steak, and liver and onions. A children's menu is included.

Service ★★½ Mostly adequate.

Decor: ★★★★ The inside of Homesteaders resembles a barn with wood beamed ceilings, diagonal beams, crossbeams, and ceiling posts between each booth. There are five booths on each side separated by ten tables. In addition, there is a small room up front with one table for five: ideal for a small family or private party. Total seating capacity is 84. There is a potato sack resting on one of the diagonal beams high overhead. Small low-back wood chairs around the tables do not look comfortable. Everyone was sitting in the booths. Old license plates are nailed on the crossbeams over the entrances to each booth. Lamps hang from two-foot poles extending from the ceiling beams. There is the same style lamp in each booth. This place is well lit. Yet, if you look around, one gets a kind of eerie feeling. The reason, I think, is that if you look up, you cannot really see the ceiling. It is high and the bright lights blind your view. I felt like I was on the set for a "Twilight Zone" episode. Photographs in glass and metal frames hang on the wall space in the booths: pictures of the Southwest taken in summer and winter, Indians on horseback, the Telluride Valley & ski area, The Stratter Hotel in Durango circa 1920, Cortez from the restaurant looking north circa 1895. These are some very interesting and nostalgic pictures. In front of the small room for five at the entrance to the restaurant stands a waterwheel. This restaurant has the most natural and historical decor of any restaurant in Cortez.

Atmosphere: ★★★★ Goes along with the decor.

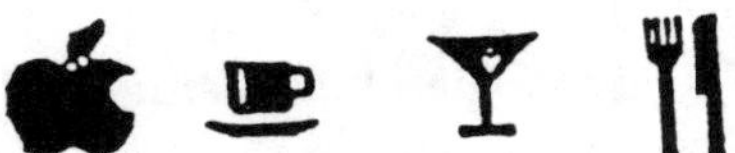

NERO'S ★★★
303 W. MAIN (303) 565-7366

Dinner $$. Winter: MON-SAT 4:30PM-9PM. Closed SUN. Summer: 7 days 4:30PM-10PM.
Type: Italian. Entrees may be ordered without soup or salad at a reduced price. No separate checks. Entrees may be split between two children at no extra charge.

Food: ★★★ The lasagna had a sour and bitter taste. I prefer a touch of sugar in my marinara sauce. Despite the peculiar taste, I would have to recommend it. The entry comes with a good-sized bowl of soup. It also comes with a cold corn relish which I did not like. I thought the Chianti was particularly weak and lacked that Chianti taste. The menu caters more to the food of northern Italy, with no mention of spaghetti or ravioli. There are several worthy Italian selections beginning with a wide choice of linguini dishes in tomato, meat or clam sauces; fettuccine Alfredo with mushrooms and zucchini; fettuccine with sausage and peppers; calzones; three chicken breast dishes: Parmesan, with fettuccine, or Florentine; three veal dishes: Parmesan, Marsala or lemon; three shrimp dishes: Parmesan, with butter and garlic, or with sirloin; a 10 oz. sirloin, and a catch-of-the-day. A lighter menu features soup and salad, a charbroiled burger, and sandwiches (grilled chicken breast, veal Parmesan, steak, meatball and sausage). They have a children's menu. Preludes to dinner include antipasto, shrimp cocktail, artichoke (in season), stuffed mushrooms, and deep-fried breaded zucchini or mushrooms.

Service ★★★ The food is a little slow coming, but the waitresses are friendly and eager to please.

Decor: **★★★½** There are tables for only 38, if you include the small booth across from the bar and the tiny table for two just off the entrance before the main dining room. The bar has stools for an additional five patrons. This is a small restaurant that is not capable of handling its own popularity. It could do well to expand its premises, if that is possible. In the summer, they have an outdoor patio, which, according to the waitress, seats an additional 25 to 30 people. The chairs have low-back, black-cushioned seats. The tables have turquoise blue tops with a finished wood border. Candles are at every table. The walls are filled with pictures from the ten-foot ceiling to tabletop level. A trio of pictures depicts the Sleeping Ute Mountain. There are some modern works of American Indians, a shepherd with his sheep, and a hunter in winter. A fish tank also graced the premises. The far wall had a mirror with white lights around its perimeter. There are two stained-glass decorations hanging from gold chains. A few of the wall hangings imitate hieroglyphics of animals. Finally, there is a black railing and potted plants on the window sills and room dividers.

Atmosphere: ★★½ Popular, crowded and noisy. Make reservations!

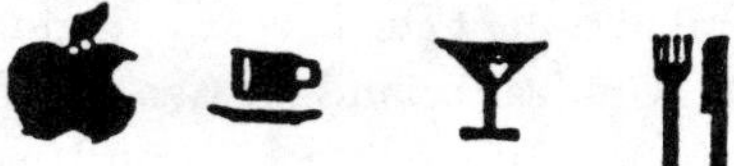

PONY EXPRESS ★★½
1603 E. MAIN (303) 565-3475

Breakfast/lunch $, dinner $$. 7 days 5:45AM-9PM.
Type: Family. This restaurant is in the Turquoise Best Western.

***Food:* ★★★ *Service:* ★½ *Decor:* ★★½ *Atmosphere:* ★★½**

I had a good light breakfast here. The breakfast menu includes waffles, eggs Benedict, egg burritos, cinnamon toast, sweet rolls, English muffins and donuts. The lunch menu offers salads, a soup/salad bar, chili, sandwiches, burgers, and fried chicken. The dinner menu is combination American/Mexican. The waitress was just fine, but the hostess definitely had "a creature of the arachnid variety stuck in her behind." There are two dining rooms, but the front dining room is used exclusively unless there is an overflow. It has 18 tables for 72 people. There are windows along the front and side. Virtually everything is in turquoise: seats, pattern wallpaper, and ceiling beams. The wall space displays pictures of the desert Southwest and Mesa Verde. The back room has eight tables with similar decor. This restaurant does not have the rustic, historic feel that some of the other restaurants in the area have.

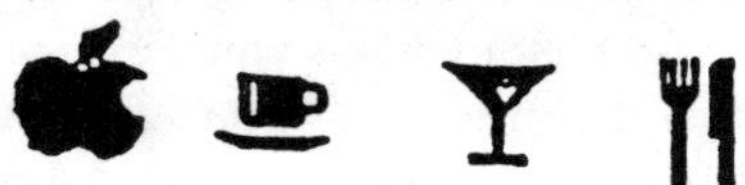

STROMSTED'S ★★★★½
1020 S. BROADWAY (303)565-1257

Dinner $$$-$$$$. 7 days 5:30PM-10PM.
Type: Steak.

Food: ★★★★½ Expertly prepared, flavorful and different. The artichokes on chicken Marsala was a deliciously different combination. For appetizers, you have artichokes, deep-fried zucchini or mushrooms, potato skins, shrimp cocktail, sautéed mushrooms, and nachos. The dinner menu has several excellent steak, seafood and fowl selections. The choice of steaks includes Chateaubriand for two, an 18-oz. tenderloin, filet mignon, and two steak specialties: Steak Stromsted, a bacon-wrapped center-cut filet stuffed with Alaskan king crab and topped with Bernaise sauce; and steak ranchero, a NY strip with cheddar cheese and green chilies. The chicken selections are deliciously different: chicken teriyaki with soy sauce and brown sugar, chicken Marsala with artichokes and mushrooms, and chicken ranchero with cheddar cheese and green chilies, same as the steak ranchero. There are several varieties of shrimp: scampi; Hawaiian style with pineapple, teriyaki and ginger; and deep fried. Other seafood items include Alaskan rock lobster, king crab, and daily fish specials, such as catfish and salmon. A vegetarian plate is included on the menu. Ice cream and dessert specials are available.

Service ★★★★ Efficient, friendly and fast.

Decor: ★★★★½ The smoking section has seating for 24 with a combination of booths, tables and a private alcove for two or three. The nonsmoking section seats 30. The restaurant offers great views of the Sleeping Ute Mountain and Mesa Verde. Seating is at finished-wood tables in low-back chairs and brown and white-cushioned benches. Windows are covered by horizontal shutters. Very attractive and colorful stained-glass lamp shades on gold chains hang from the ceiling. There are several hanging and potted plants and a picture of a charging bull. The inside provides interesting architecture and the outside is well landscaped. The restaurant is right on the highway, but you would never know it looking out on the yucca plants, brick walls, pinon pines, spruce and juniper trees just outside the restaurant. This is a romantic setting if you are with someone; poorly lit if you are alone. In addition there is a lounge downstairs with five small booths, six tables and a bar for 50 people.

Atmosphere: ★★★★ A place that combines good taste with casualness.

Warsaw Inn ★½
Highways 160 & 145 (303)565-8585

Breakfast/lunch $, dinner $$. 7 days 7AM-9:30PM.
Type: Steak.

***Food:* ★★½ *Service:* ★ *Decor:* ★★ *Atmosphere:* ★**

Don't be fooled by the name. The only thing continental about this restaurant is the Polish sausage & sauerkraut and the stuffed cabbage on the dinner menu. Otherwise it is primarily a steak place with a few Mexican dishes for dinner. This is not an authentic Polish restaurant as the name suggests. I ordered their potato pancakes for breakfast and they were, quite honestly, very good, not to mention plentiful (three large pancakes). However, they practically had time to grow and harvest the potatoes between the time I ordered and the time I was served. Service was slow and inefficient. My potato pancake order took just under a half-hour, and then, the waitress forgot the apple sauce (another four minute wait). There were two other tables occupied while I was there. Ten booths, two large round tables, three small round tables, and nine small square tables provide seating for 78 people. Windows cover the south and west sides. The heads and horns from four stags hang high on the crossbeam on the north side. The patio is open in the summer. Rock music plays for a few locals.

CRESTED BUTTE

The town derives its name from a nearby mountain whose top resembles the crest of a rooster's head. Since the 1860's, Crested Butte has been blessed with gold and silver mining, followed by coal mining, and now benefits from the ski industry with Mt. Crested Butte Ski Resort next door.

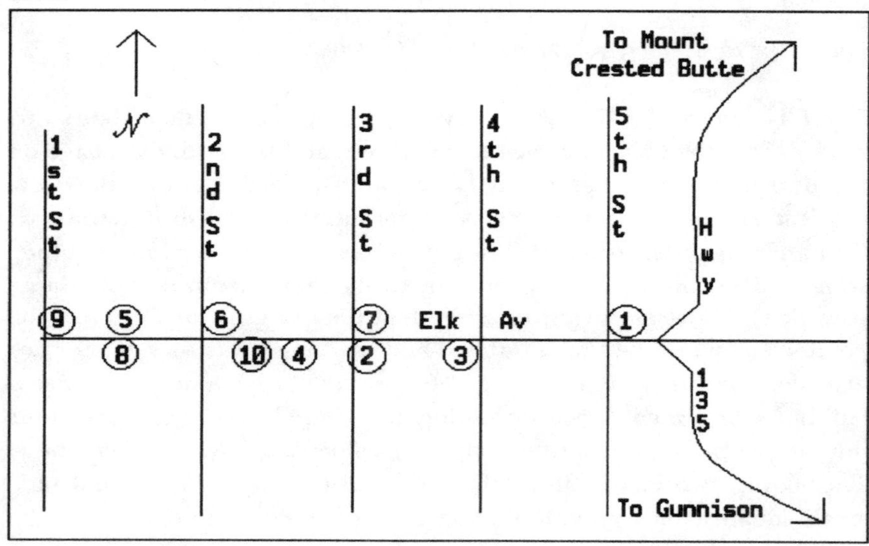

Restaurants and Ratings:	Food	Service	Decor	Atm	Overall
1. Angello's	★★★	★★★	★★	★★½	★★½
2. Bakery Cafe	★★½	★★	★★	★	★★
3. Donita's	★★★	★★½	★★½	★★½	★★½
4. Idle Spur	★★★½	★★★	★★½	★★	★★★
5. Karolina's	★★½	★★	★★½	★	★★
6. Le Bosquet	★★★★★	★★★★½	★★★★½	★★★★★	★★★★★
7. Paradise Cafe	★★★½	★★	★★★	★½	★★½
8. Powerhouse	★★★★	★★★★½	★★★½	★★★★	★★★★
9. Timberline	★★★★½	★★★★	★★★★	★★★★½	★★★★½
10. Wooden Nickel	★★★½	★★★	★★★	★★★	★★★

Last year I only had the opportunity to visit Le Bosquet and I thought it was one of the best restaurants in the book. This year I visited 10 restaurants in Crested Butte and Le Bosquet is still my favorite. My other top recommendations are the Timberline where I enjoyed a superb pasta dish and the Powerhouse, an 1891 establishment serving a wide variety of excellent Mexican food. The Paradise Cafe is the only restaurant that does not accept major credit cards and only the Bakery Cafe and Paradise Cafe do not serve alcohol. Half the restaurants have nonsmoking sections and half do not, so see each individual restaurant for that information.

ANGELLO'S ★★½
501 ELK AVENUE (303)349-5351

Lunch $$, dinner $$-$$$. JUN to Mid-APR: 7 days 11AM-9PM. Mid-APR to MAY: 7 days 5PM-9PM.
Type: Italian. 15% gratuity added to parties of six or more and to ski card holders. $1 charge for substitutions or extra plate. No separate checks. Smoking only permitted in bar.

Food: ★★★ *Service:* ★★★ *Decor:* ★★ *Atmosphere:* ★★½

My white clam sauce fettuccini had a very rich sauce with capers and lemon and was very filling. This was served with a salad that included pepperoncini and oregano, and a warm loaf of Italian bread. A good Italian meal. I had two waitresses attend my table. One was in training. The trainer handled everything in a pleasant and professional manner (a good role model for the waitress to be). The restaurant is divided into a main dining room to the right, two smaller dining rooms and a small bar/lounge area. The walls are decorated with snow shoes, Indian arrows, pastel watercolors, and a poster of Bill Johnson, gold medalist in the men's downhill at the 1984 Olympics. Country music plays in the background. There were only a couple of locals drinking at the bar.

BAKERY CAFE ★★
302 ELK AVENUE (303)349-7280

Breakfast/lunch/dinner $-$$. Mid-JUN to Mid-APR: 7 days 7:30AM-9PM. Mid-APR to Mid-JUN: 7 days 7:30AM-5:30PM.
Type: Cafe. Carry-out, take-out and mail-order available. No nonsmoking area.

Food: ★★½ *Service:* ★★ *Decor:* ★★ *Atmosphere:* ★

I stopped here for breakfast and had their microwaved spinach and feta cheese crêpe. It was actually fairly good with a cup of their African coffee. They serve bakery specialties, cakes, pies, sandwiches, soups, snacks and croissants. No table service. This is deli style where you order and pick up at the counter. The seating is rather uncomfortable on small round red-cushioned chairs. There are four seating areas for about 90 people. Framed glass posters and still lifes are the major items of decor. As for atmosphere, it was too early in the morning (for me anyway) to be listening to rock music. Quite a few local workers stopped in for a quick cup of coffee and a muffin before popping off to work.

DONITA'S ★★½
330 ELK AVENUE (303)349-6674

Dinner $$-$$$. Winter: 7 days 5PM-9:30PM. Summer: 7 days 5:30PM-9:30PM.
Type: Mexican. 15% gratuity added to parties of six or more. No separate checks. No reservations. No cigars or pipes. Nonsmoking area is provided.

Food: ★★★ *Service:* ★★½ *Decor:* ★★½ *Atmosphere:* ★★½

Their chips are excellent: light, crispy & flaky; and their salsa has a lot of tomato, onion and green chili. The spinach enchilada prepared with onions and spices tasted more like collard greens to me (which was fine. I like collard greens). I ordered green (hot) chili on my chili relleno but only my plate was hot. The rice and beans were standard, the entrees good, not excellent. The portions are large. No room for dessert here.

I ate at the bar because the dining room was a 25 to 30 minute wait. The barmaid was friendly and had a pretty smile, but my meal took about 25 to 30 minutes (perhaps they were looking for the spinach!). Hub caps are lined along the top part of the wall in the lounge extending into the dining room. A 50's style chrome bumper with "bullets" hangs over the bar. A rock fireplace separates the lounge from the dining area. The wood panel walls have an ample array of artwork, Mexican figures and figurines, plants and Mexican rugs. This is a popular place with mostly "yuppie" types and is fairly noisy.

IDLE SPUR ★★★
226 ELK AVENUE (303)349-5026

Lunch/dinner $$-$$$. 7 days 5PM-10PM (Happy Hour 3PM-5PM, Late Night Menu 10PM-12AM).
Type: Barbecue (also steaks, burgers and a brewery). No nonsmoking section.

Food: ★★★½ The menu's are on chalk boards which they bring to your table. No hand held or written menus. A fellow at the table next to mine seemed to thoroughly enjoy his baby-back ribs. I ordered the Garcia burger with green chili & cheese, lettuce, tomato and onion. It was charbroiled medium rare with a pink center (just the way I like it) and served on grilled toast. The green chili was mild and the steak fries lightly salted. Quite good. Their appetizers include chips & salsa, chicken wings, gazpacho soup, shrimp cocktail, and Cajun style popcorn shrimp. They offer top sirloin and barbecue beef or pork sandwiches. The list of entrees features roast chicken, barbecue ribs, and charbroiled steaks. Their brewery produces beer, dark-light beer, amber ale, red ale, pale ale, and an oatmeal stout made from chocolate, black flour & oat malts. Gary Garcia is the owner and cook.

Service: ★★★ A friendly young waitress was eager to provide answers and information. The waitresses are dressed in cowgirl outfits: black hats, white shirts and short blue denim skirts.

Decor: ★★½ There is seating for 185 in two dining areas, right front and left rear, separated by an 18-stool bar and the kitchen. Seating is on log wood-framed chairs with red-cushioned seats. Fork-shaped log supports run the length of the restaurant. There is a rock fireplace with a stuffed lion on the large log mantel, a stuffed bear head on the front wall, and a whole stuffed bear in the rear room pinning a trout. Next to the fireplace is a character painting of cowboys playing poker. Around the corner from the entrance is a six-point deer. Potted crocus, jade and cactus are set by the front window. Peach plaster covers the ceiling and top two thirds of the walls, wood logs the lower one third.

Atmosphere: ★★ Noisy! Very popular with young and old, but more so with the young. This was probably the busiest place I visited in Crested Butte during the off season. They just opened in February 1991 and plan to use the back room for live bands, hoping to snag some big names after they perform in Denver.

KAROLINA'S ★★
127 ELK AVENUE (303)349-6756

Lunch $-$$, dinner $$-$$$. SUN-THU 11:30AM-11PM. FRI-SAT 11:30AM-12AM.
Type: Country. No separate checks. Take-out available. Nonsmoking section provided.

Food: ★★½ *Service:* ★★ *Decor:* ★★½ *Atmosphere:* ★

They have excellent Reuben sandwiches full of very lean and fresh corned beef on large slices of dark rye. The curly Q fries were stale, though. The daily special, chicken fried steak, was a healthy portion with a big serving of real mashed potatoes that still had some chunks of potato in them (some folks like that, some don't). The steak itself had flavor, but was not very tender. Soups, sandwiches, fish, chops, steaks and kilbasi are also on the menu. Service was slow and inattentive. However, the owner did provide me with a copy of "Menu Magazine" featuring menus of most of the Crested Butte restaurants. This is a two-room restaurant with seating for 48 and old photos of the blacksmith shop that used to occupy this spot. Pulleys, axle shafts, a circular saw, axes, blacksmith tools, and a black iron stove provide some of the decor. Rock music, played too loudly, can be heard from the kitchen. Blue jeans, shorts, and flannel shirts seem to be the style.

LE BOSQUET ★★★★★
ELK AVE. & 2ND ST. (303)349-5808

Lunch $$, dinner $$$-$$$$. Winter: 7 days 5:30PM-10PM. Summer: 7 days 6PM-9PM. MON-FRI 11:30AM-2PM. Closed Mid-APR to Mother's Day and two weeks in NOV.
Type: Continental (French). No nonsmoking section.

Food: ★★★★★ I have eaten here on two occasions and both times the food was fantastic. On my first visit I had their salmon pastry with fresh asparagus for Sunday brunch (they, unfortunately, do not have Sunday brunch anymore). The salmon was flown in fresh from the West Coast, the asparagus was fresh, the pastry shell, light and fluffy. This was topped with hollandaise sauce made the "old fashion way" (without a blender). For my second (dinner) visit I had their toasted sesame seed vinaigrette dressing on a fresh and light salad of greens, carrots and tomato slices. The roast leg of lamb was two healthy slices with chives in a brown gravy, accompanied by French style scalloped potatoes and yams. The entree came with soup or salad, bread, beverage and sorbet or chocolate mousse. The strawberry sorbet was cool, light, refreshing and slightly frosted. It got better as it melted. The lunch menu features French onion soup plus a soup du jour, salads (Caesar's, gourmet mixed organic greens, chevre made with fresh goat cheese & basil, and grain & pasta salads offering items like Indian spiced rice and gingered millet), sandwiches (Reuben, mesquite smoked turkey, and Cajun chicken), and sweet & sour chicken stew. The soups and salads are also served at dinner along with some tempting appetizers: potato pancakes served with lox, caviar, sour cream & chives; escargots de Bourgogne; smoked duck sausage; and asparagus spears in a puff pastry with Parmesan hollandaise. For a lighter, less expensive meal, you can choose a typical country French one-dish dinner served with homemade French bread: Colorado lamb shank, bouillabaisse, or angel hair pasta with asparagus & tomatoes or with chicken. For the heartier appetite, there is chicken Oskar, large gulf shrimp, elk medallions in a cabernet sauce, and grilled duck breast. To finish your meal you can choose from chocolate mousse, fresh fruit in a meringue shell or chocolate cream Napoleon (a layered pastry and chocolate custard); and to accompany your dessert, a cup of café Frangelico, blueberry tea, or Italian coffee with sambucca and rum.

Service: ★★★★½ According to my waiter, their entire restaurant staff has been together for 12 years (which sounds incredible considering the turn over in the business, not to mention the staffs of most restaurants). Service is friendly, affable, courteous, with a sense of humor, relaxed yet efficient, and, as always, professional.

Decor: ★★★★½ This is a small single room restaurant with 14 tables for 48 and a deck with 11 white metal mesh tables and 28 chairs. The tables inside have pink cloths on top of brown cloths and decorative pink and white frosted oil lamps. Additional lighting is provided by five-lamp chandeliers with cute, small brown shades. Windows with white laced curtains take up most of the front and left sides leaving room for only a few well-placed photos and pictures of the Eiffel Tower. A large mural on one wall depicts a forest of aspens. There are some great photos of French peasants: standing next to two cows, sitting around drinking wine, carrying bread and meat, an old woman holding a ladle, and a man with his dog. There are also photos of Paris, a boy carrying a loaf of bread that is longer than he is, frosted crab apples, and a line of ferries crossing a river (the Seine?).

Atmosphere: ★★★★★ Despite the absence of a nonsmoking section, they do have an ionizer (smoke eater) on the ceiling. Smoking was not a problem the evening that I was there since no one in the restaurant smoked. This is an ideal place for young couples and most of the tables were occupied by pairs. Very relaxing slow jazz and big band tunes, like

"What's New?", play in the background. A very quiet, romantic clientele. Definitely my kind of place.

PARADISE CAFE ★★½
3RD & ELK (IN THE COMPANY STORE) (303)349-6233

Breakfast/lunch $. 7 days 7AM-3PM.
Type: Deli. $.35 charge for to go orders. No nonsmoking section.

Food: ★★★½ *Service:* ★★ *Decor:* ★★★ *Atmosphere:* ★½

I ordered a Maui pancake made with buckwheat batter, blueberries, bananas, seeds and nuts. This nine-inch pancake was full of delicious ingredients and tasted wonderful. The sausage was quite good also. If you come here for lunch there is a variety of steak sandwiches, burgers, sandwiches, deli sandwiches, and salads. The waitress and cook had a "tiff", apparently over someone who was at an all night party and did not show up for work. This is a small one-room restaurant that can seat 30. For decor there is a world map, tuna & blue marlin, and photos of Maui, skiing, and a pink cadillac between snow and a swimming pool. The decor is as varied, and a bit more bizarre, than the food. For atmosphere, I had noisy adults making sounds like children and a crying (screaming) baby. Ouch on the ears!

POWERHOUSE ★★★★
130 ELK AVENUE (303)349-5494

Dinner $$-$$$. 7 days 5:30PM-10PM. Closed APR.
Type: Mexican. 15% gratuity added for parties of six or more. No separate checks. $2 minimum charge per person. Nonsmoking section provided.

CRESTED BUTTE

The Powerhouse has an interesting history dating back to 1891. It served as Crested Butte's sole source of power generation until 1943 when power became available from the nationwide grid system. Abandoned, the original front of the building was removed in 1971 due to deterioration. Today, the main dining area remains in its original state and the new front is a close replica of the original. The bar was custom made at the request of two South Dakota businessmen, Cotton & Andrews, and their initials, "C & A" are still on the center of the bar.

Food: ★★★★ Their chips are light and crispy; their salsa, spicy with tomatoes and cilantro. The side salad came with a tasty mustard-vinaigrette dressing. The fried rice was very flavorful with onion, tomato, carrot, green pepper and celery. The entree was a delicious, thick slice of striped marlin, similar in texture to swordfish, with cilantro, lime and tequila butter. It is served along side a large potato slice that is deep fried, baked, then deep fried again in cumin butter right before being served, creating an interesting and different covering. The menu is large and includes all the basic Mexican dishes in addition to a daily selection of fresh fish, steaks, shrimp (mesquite-roasted, beer-battered fried, or with garlic & butter), chicken, quail (mesquite-roasted), and sizzling or mesquite fajitas. A flan, amaretto cheesecake, and ice cream are featured on the dessert menu. There is a children's menu.

Service: ★★★★½ The waitresses and bartender were very hospitable and enjoyed discussing the proud history and decor of this restaurant.

Decor: ★★★½ The entrance way is loaded with framed photos of good times from the past. Everyone seems to be enjoying themselves in these pictures. This looks like it would be a fun place when it gets busy. There is a large smoking dining room that seats 84 and a smaller nonsmoking section in the rear that seats 32. The decor in here is the structure of the building. It is unique: wood-framed walls inside a ripple pattern sheet metal exterior and a very high arched ceiling with cross beams, diagonal beams, posts, pipes, and slow moving fans. The bar is from Lead, South Dakota and behind the bar are three large arch-shaped mirrors. The rear room has two model sailing ships hanging over red doors that are no longer in use. Between them is a comical photo of a boy sucking a goat's udder with the caption "no adultered milk for this Mexican boy". Perhaps the best item of decor lies outside where Coal Creek passes directly below and is visible from tables and booths along the far wall and from the rear room which has windows on two sides. A sailing ship over the entrance to the kitchen was painstakingly made out of toothpicks by a local artist.

Atmosphere: ★★★★ Very pleasant, easy listening Mexican songs. According to one waitress, they attract a good combination of locals and tourists. For a restaurant with an atmosphere of a truly different flavor, you should visit here.

TIMBERLINE ★★★★½
21 ELK AVENUE (303)349-9831

Sunday brunch $$, dinner $$$$. Mid-JUN to Mid-APR: 7 days 6PM-10PM. SUN 8:30AM-1PM. Mid-APR to Mid-JUN: WED-SAT, 6PM-10PM. SUN 8:30AM-1PM. Closed MON-TUE.
Type: Continental (French). Reservations requested. Nonsmoking section provided.

Food: ★★★★½ I thought their salad with mozzarella cheese and homemade Italian vinaigrette dressing was very good. The entree, pesto fusilli with both fresh and sun dried tomatoes was excellent: rainbow pasta noodles with onions and grated Parmesan cheese, nicely seasoned with basil and Italian seasonings. It comes with garlic bread and is not overfilling. I definitely recommend this dish if you like Italian food. For dessert, I tried their lemon kiwi tartette: a delightful combination of very fresh kiwi and lemon filling in a light, fluffy pastry shell, or as the waitress said, "the best thing next to lemon meringue pie" (she must have known that was my favorite!). Their menu changes regularly, but may include many of the items listed here. Appetizers may include a duckling pâté, jumbo scallops and artichoke hearts, roasted garlic crêpes, mussels, or smoked trout. Soups and salads, not included with entrees, feature asparagus soup, a daily fish soup, and warmed spinach or lobster salad. For entrees, you may see offered blackened lamb with cassis sauce, boneless roast quail filled with chicken mousseline, sautéed duck breast with ginger cherry sauce, a fresh market whitefish, or medallions of venison with green peppercorns. For dessert, look for chocolate hazelnut puff pastry, white chocolate-blackberry moussecake, crème caramel with sliced apples and maple syrup, and ice cream. For Sunday brunch expect to find chicken apple sausage, quail salad, egg or crab Benedict, and prosciutto & melon.

Service: ★★★★ A most pleasant, helpful and courteous waitress who called me by my first name (I like that).

Decor: ★★★★ This is a small restaurant in a wood-framed house with four tables downstairs for 10 and seating for an additional 18 upstairs. Pink curtains with a flower pattern match the pink tablecloths and compliment the grey wood floors and plaster walls. The framed, matted posters downstairs show fall leaves and garlic cloves; the ones upstairs feature wine, Georges Duboeuf, and the Monterey wine festival. There are two wine racks: one under the stairwell; the other under the server's station. Red French wines seem to be their specialty. The stairwell is decorated with a sketch of "Robin's Shed's" in Crested Butte and a picture of an "old timer" holding a huge puff ball mushroom - bigger than his own head! At the top of the stairs is a column with red bricks housing some wine glasses. The upstairs is actually an attic with steeply slanted walls and a single front window. Seating is on wicker-seat, wood-framed chairs.

Atmosphere: ★★★★½ Very pleasant, relaxing and charming soft mellow piano and acoustic jazz. The clientele is top notch. I really enjoyed this place! This is a very comfortable atmosphere. Feel free to wear a suit & tie or come dressed casual.

WOODEN NICKEL ★★★
222 ELK AVENUE (303)349-6350

Dinner \$-\$\$\$\$. OCT to Mid-APR: 7 days 5PM-10PM. Memorial Day to SEP: 7 days 5:30PM-10:30PM. Closed Mid-APR to Memorial Day. Type: Steak. Reservations not accepted. No nonsmoking section.

Established in 1929, an interesting historical item about this place is that is burned down on Saturday night, August 24, 1985. The fire started about 8:30PM in the kitchen when the wall behind the stove overheated. The flames quickly spread along the roof. The bartender, who was present for the fire, told me the story. In the hallway between the front and rear rooms is a collage of pictures taken after the fire, while they were rebuilding the restaurant.

Food: ★★★½ I ordered the barbecue pork ribs, all two pounds of them! They came with average curly Q fries. The ribs were excellent, though. They broke off the bone completely and easily with a fork and had very little fat. I was less enthusiastic about their barbecue sauce. If you are more interested in meat than sauce, you must try them. The menu is featured on a chalkboard. No hand held menus here. The selection, though limited, includes some delectable offerings: shrimp bowl, steamed clams, Alaskan snow or king crab, prime rib, sandwiches (chicken, steak, chicken fried steak, and tuna steak), soup du jour, beer batter onion rings, house salad, jalepeño cheese potato skins, rib eye, NY strip, daily fresh seafood selection, half-pound burgers, baby-back ribs, and live Maine lobster.

Service: ★★★ An easy going friendly bartender, known by most who entered here. He fit right into the place. Of course, he had been working here for at least six years when I visited.

Decor: ★★★ This is a two-room restaurant and bar/lounge. The bar/lounge to the right has ten green-cushioned stools. A green-cushioned bench seat extends along the front, left, and back walls with round, brown-cushioned chairs opposite the tables. Enough seating for 45. The left wall is divided by a fireplace with a large model sailing ship above the mantel. Wood-framed, glass-covered beer ads, an ad for Dr McGillicuddy's mentholmint schnapps liquor, and Wooden Nickel t-shirts decorate the green velvet walls above the polished walnut panels. The same wood paneling is used for the ceiling. Polished two-by-fours are used on the floors. Brass chandeliers with yellow- frosted lights hang on four-foot brass chords. A deer head is mounted on the back wall. Behind the bar is an attractive trio of mirrors in a classical entablature with columns at both ends. The dining room in the rear is similar to the bar/lounge in front with a mounted deer's head, windows with no curtains, beer signs and green velvet walls. It seats 60.

Atmosphere: ★★★ A variety of rock music, from mild to hard, plays through ceiling speakers. A variety of young and old local folks are attracted here, but I did not see any children.

Totem pole carved by George Sibley, Professor at Western States College, in 1974 for the First Crested Butte Arts Festival. Gothic Peak is in the background.

DACONO

Dacono was one of three coal mining towns known as the "tri-cities," the other two being neighboring Frederick and Firestone. The town was named by coal miner C.L. Baum, who took the first two letters of his wife's name, DAisy, and combined them with the first two letters of the names of two of her friends, COra and NOna.

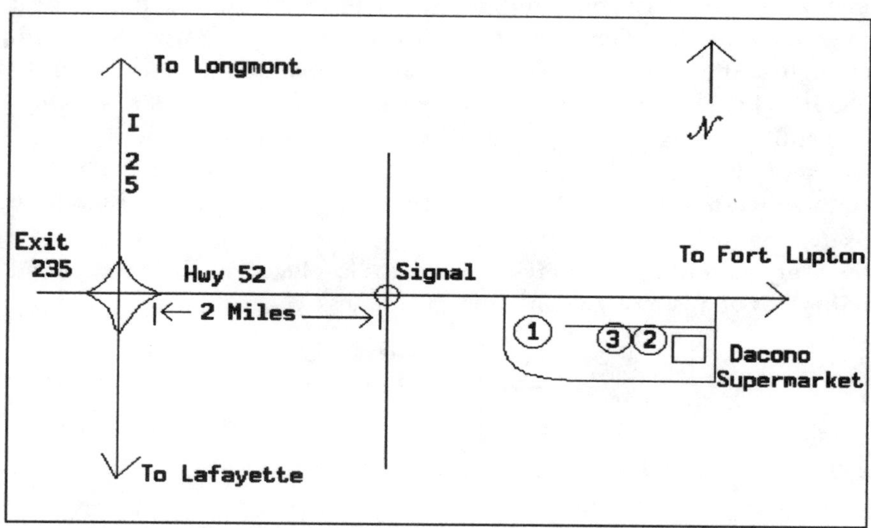

Restaurants and Ratings	Food	Service	Decor	Atm	Overall
1. BUCKO BOB'S	★★★	★★	★½	★½	★★
2. GABRIEL'S	★★	★★	★★	★½	★★
3. LAWANA'S	★★★½	★★★½	★★½	★★½	★★★

Lawana's serves good soup and sandwiches and delicious "dump cake". Only Bucko Bob's accepts major credit cards and offers a nonsmoking section. Only Lawana's does not serve alcohol.

BUCKO BOB'S (FORMERLY THE OXBOW) ★★
SOUTH SIDE OF HIGHWAY 52, WEST OF LAWANA'S (303)833-3369

Dinner $-$$. TUE-THU 4PM-9PM (10PM MAR-OCT). FRI-SAT 4PM-10PM (11PM MAR-OCT). Closed SUN-MON.

DACONO

Type: Steak.

Food: ★★★ *Service:* ★★ *Decor:* ★½ *Atmosphere:* ★½

I had an above average, but not great, cheeseburger. The locals claimed their steaks are very good, and, if you are in the mood, you might want to give them a try. Service was a bit slow. This is one large room with enough seating for over 200 people and a good-sized dance floor — about 25 by 50 feet. The dance floor is surrounded by a log fence, giving the entire setting the appearance of a horse corral. The walls are decorated with harnesses, horse shoes, collars, and other articles with a country western flavor. A wall painting of a covered wagon pulled by oxen hangs behind the bandstand. The restaurant was empty when I was there at 5PM on a Friday afternoon. A radio played in the background with a lot of ads and golden-oldie rock tunes.

GABRIEL'S ★★
909 CARBONDALE DR. (303)833-2633

Breakfast $, lunch/dinner $-$$. MON-THU 6AM-2PM & 5PM-9PM. FRI 6PM-9PM. SAT 7AM-9PM. SUN 8AM-9PM.
Type: Mexican.

Food: ★★ *Service:* ★★ *Decor:* ★★ *Atmosphere:* ★½

The chips were stale. The chili relleno and taco only fair. Service was also only fair. This is a one-room restaurant and bar with an adjacent lounge and dance floor. A fireplace is in the middle of the dining room. There are six booths along the left side separating the dining room from the lounge. The wall dividing the two rooms contains empty window frames. It appears there were glass windows here at one time. There are tables for about 40 and the bar has four red-cushioned barstools. There are a couple of murals in the back showing an Indian pueblo in the desert. There is Indian pottery on the fireplace mantels. Along the front are two booths and a table, making the total seating capacity 78. This place has an unfinished look about it. Rock music — some light, most moderately loud — was playing here.

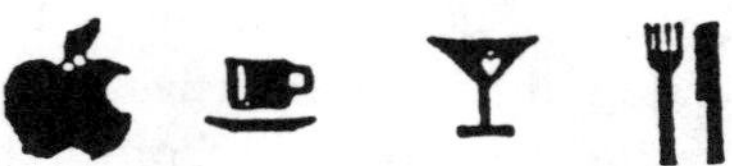

LAWANA'S ★★★
CARBON VALLEY SHOPPING CENTER (303)833-3773

Lunch/dinner \$-\$\$. MON-THU 11AM-8PM. FRI-SAT 11AM-9PM. Closed SUN.
Type: Diner.

Food: ★★★½ The broccoli cream soup and barbecue pork sandwich were surprisingly good. I say surprisingly because to look at this place one would think it is just a sandwich shop hangout for the local teens. If you do nothing else while passing through Dacono, you should stop here for a piece of their "dump cake" which has pineapples, cherries and pecans — a delicious mixture. On the menu are sub sandwiches (roast beef, pastrami, turkey, salami, ham, and Italian sausage) on white, wheat or rye in 4-, 6-, 12-, 18-, and 24-inch sizes; cannolis; daily specials, like Polish sausage, meatloaf, barbecue on a bun, tortellini, and tuna salad; deep-dish pizza in 6-, 12-, and 16-inch sizes; homemade cheesecake, banana pudding cups and spiced cider.

Service: ★★★½ Fast, friendly and very accommodating. For a small diner, they were uncommonly courteous. For example, they asked if I wanted to finish my soup before starting on the barbecue.

Decor: ★★½ This restaurant is a single-room with eight tables and brown vinyl benches for 32 people. Small decorative clocks, which are for sale, adorn the plain white walls. They also have pictures of ponds, butterflies, and flowers, along with some hanging plants.

Atmosphere: ★★½ A combination of local flavor: old-timers, professionals and workers in T-shirts. This is the kind of place that you would easily pass by if you were just passing through, but take my word for it, give it a try.

DEL NORTE

Del Norte derives its name from the Rio Grande del Norte, Spanish for "great river of the north." The Rio Grande River flows through the northern sections of town. The local economy is built around farming, ranching, beef cattle, and lumbering. Of particular interest is the fact that Del Norte only averages 8¼ inches of annual precipitation. Crops depend on mountain snowmelt and irrigation.

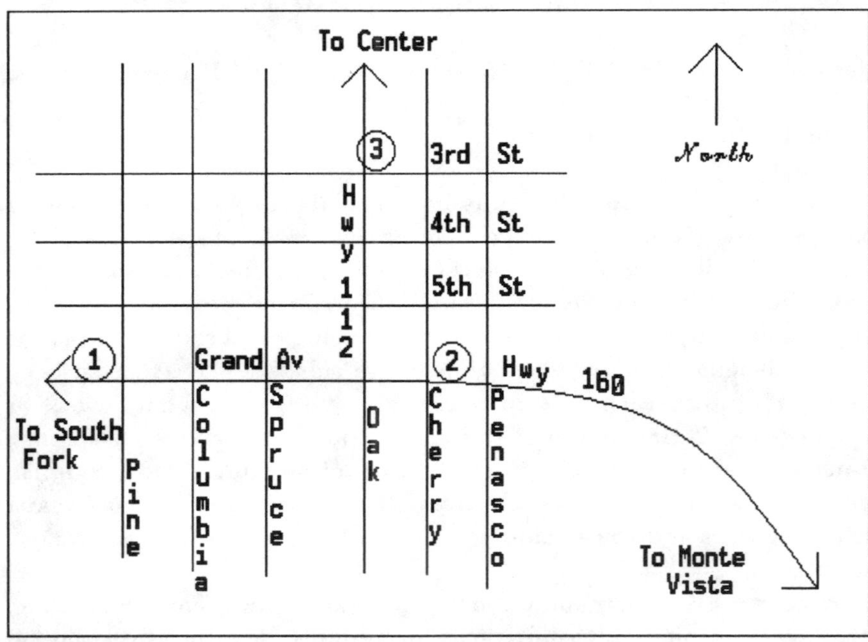

Restaurants and Ratings:	Food	Service	Decor	Atm	Overall
1. ARNOLD'S	★★	★	★★★	★★½	★★
2. DEL NORTE CAFE	★★★½	★★½	★★	★★	★★½
3. TIN CUP CAFE	★★★½	★★★	★★	★★½	★★★

For great ribs and burgers visit the Tin Cup. For a good bowl of homemade soup with a croissant sandwich, stop by the Del Norte Cafe. The Tin Cup is the only restaurant that does not accept credit cards and Arnold's is the only restaurant that has a nonsmoking section and serves alcohol.

ARNOLD'S STONE QUARRY ★★
540 GRAND AVE. (719)657-3492

Breakfast/lunch $, dinner $-$$ (some $$$). MON-FRI 11AM-8PM (9PM JUN-AUG). SAT-SUN 8AM-8PM (9PM JUN-AUG).
Type: Mexican. This restaurant was in a building that was built in 1914, but by the time you read this, the restaurant will have moved one block to the west on the same side of Hwy. 160, or Grand Ave. The address shown above is the new address. 580 Grand Av was their old address, which I describe below.

Food: ★★ *Service:* ★ *Decor:* ★★★ *Atmosphere:* ★★½

I had a beef enchilada and beef tostada. They were of fair quality and not very spicy. One member of our group ordered breakfast. The bacon, which I sampled, was crisp and nongreasy. I had ordered a chicken enchilada, but was served the beef enchilada, instead. The waitress said they may not have had any chicken, she was not sure, but she did not check with me before serving the substitute beef. Lunch took about 35 minutes from ordering to being served when the restaurant was not very busy. Service is very slow. There was also a mix-up when it came time to pay the bill. This is a single rectangular room with 21 tables for 76 people and a small bar in the rear. A quarry between Del Norte and Monte Vista provided the stone for this building. This restaurant looks like an antique, which is why I was sorry to hear they were moving. They have an old photo of the original stones being quarried for the restaurant that I visited. The clientele is mostly local townsfolk, including one interesting chap with a cowboy hat, mustache and little cigar sitting in the back. He reminded me of an outlaw. I thought he added color to the place, but one of my fellow diners had to get some fresh air because he thought the cigar smoke was so bad. We were sitting in the nonsmoking section, by the way.

DEL NORTE CAFE ★★½
1050 GRANDE AVE. (719)657-3581

DEL NORTE

Breakfast/lunch $. Thanksgiving to Memorial Day: MON-FRI 7AM-2PM. Closed SAT-SUN. Memorial Day to Thanksgiving: 7 days 6AM-3PM (Open at 4:30AM during hunting season — OCT to Mid-NOV).
Type: Country.

Food: ★★★½ *Service:* ★★½ *Decor:* ★★ *Atmosphere:* ★★

I ordered the lunch special: ham and cheese with a mild green chili in a toasted croissant. It was excellent: lean ham, Cheddar melted just right, and a fresh warm green chili. I also tried their soup: creamy chicken with wild rice. It was also very good with barley and carrots. This is good food at reasonable prices. The waitress was very pleasant and friendly. Owner, Jim Szatkowski, was eager to talk about his plans for future development of the restaurant. This is a tiny cafe with three booths and three tables for 22 people in the front. The back room brings total seating to 50 people. White-laced curtains border the windows. There is little wallspace for decorations: a wreath, a few prints of duck decoys, cattails and vases, a mountain-and-meadows scene, and a needlepoint of a duck with eggs. A rock 'n' roll radio station can be heard in the background. The clientele is mostly middle-aged and elderly.

TIN CUP CAFE ★★★
216 OAK ST. (719)657-3973

Lunch $, dinner $$. MON-FRI 11AM-7:30PM. Closed SAT-SUN.
Type: Burgers. $.25 charge per box for carry-out.

Food: ★★★½ I had their lunch special: barbecue ribs with potato salad, baked beans and tea or coffee, for only $5. I was served two meaty beef-ribs that were very tender and had very little fat. My only complaint was that they were a little too well-done. The barbecue sauce was good also. Most of the meals at the other tables, and the tables were all filled, were for burgers. One individual in our group of five had a burger, which was thick and well done, but also very good. Lunch offers sandwiches, hot meals like fish & chips or shrimp, the common Mexican fare, chili, salads, and cornbread or biscuits. The dinner entrees include pork chops, chicken, hamburger steak, liver & onions, and chicken fried steak. Pies, ice cream, and homemade sweet rolls can be ordered for dessert.

Service: ★★★ They only had one waitress, but she managed to get the job done without delays.

Decor: ★★ This is a small, one-room, square cafe with three booths and nine tables for 43 people. The decor is simple. It includes tan and brown horizontal shades, two ceiling fans, four triple-light ceiling lamp fixtures, and humorous animal posters of cats, dogs, and an orangutan. A sign on one of the booths reads "local gossip, this booth only."

Atmosphere: ★★½ This place had a variety of locals: a group of four housewives, a couple of families, local police, and one man in a cowboy hat. This is the most popular place I visited in Del Norte.

Arch over natural water well constructed in 1914 in Del Norte.

DELTA

Originally named Uncompahgre after the nearby river, mountain range and plateau, the town was later renamed for its location on the delta at the mouth of the Uncompahgre River. The Ute Indians named the river "Anacopogri" or Uncompahgre meaning Red Lake because there is a red-water spring near the source of the river. The first white man to visit the delta area was Don Juan Rivera in 1761. Today, Delta is a town of about 4,000 people.

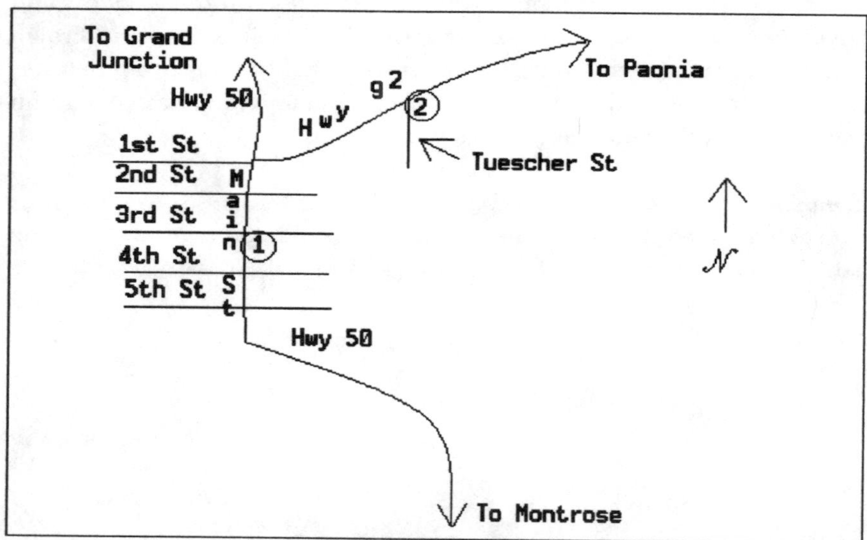

Restaurants and Ratings:	Food	Service	Decor	Atm	Overall
1. Davito's	★★★★	★★★½	★★½	★★★	★★★½
2. Fireside	★★★½	★½	★★★½	★★★½	★★★

Davito's has some excellent Italian food prepared with a wonderful tomato sauce. The Fireside is Delta's premier, elegant restaurant with some very good steak and seafood selections. Both restaurants accept major credit cards and serve alcohol. Only Davito's offers a nonsmoking section.

Davito's ★★★½
520 Main (303)874-8277

Lunch/dinner $-$$. TUE-THU: 11AM-9PM. FRI-SAT: 11AM-10PM. Closed SUN-MON.
Type: Italian. Family owned and operated.

Food: ★★★★ A fresh salad with mozzarella, pepperoni, croutons, lettuce, tomato and honey Dijon dressing preceded the dinner entree. The honey Dijon had just the right amount of both for a delicious sweet and spicy taste. They also serve a poppyseed dressing. My entree, baked ravioli with ricotta cheese, melted mozzarella on top, meatball and a sweet, spicy tomato sauce, was excellent. Other pasta items on the menu include spaghetti, rigatoni, tortellini, ravioli, and fettucini or tortellini Alfredo. Homemade ingredients are used in the preparation of sausage, meatball, deluxe and veggie canolis. Pizza in 12-, 14- and 16- inch sizes with 15 ingredients to choose from can be ordered on a regular or deep dish crust. Appetizers (chips & hot sauce, a veggie tray, and garlic pizza strips), sandwiches (Italian sausage, meatball or sub, turkey, and tuna subs), pizza burgers, salads, burritos, homemade green chili and desserts (fruit pizza with apple, cherry or peach, spumoni, and cinnamon crisps), complete the menu.

Service: ★★★½ Friendly, smiling and jovial. Quick to respond to my inquiries.

Decor: ★★½ This long narrow restaurant has two dining rooms: five booths and three tables for 28 in the front and four booths and three tables for 30 in the rear. The rear dining room is sparsely decorated with still-life prints of potted roses, fruits and vegetables, a painting of a country cabin, and two framed portraits. The front dining room has a most peculiar print showing a pumpkin, a water pump & pitcher, a moonshine bucket, a vase with daisies, an apple, an American Indian doll, an American flag, a duck, an ear of corn, a letter, a jar of strawberry jam and a bible. My assumption is that this is supposed to signify Thanksgiving. Another print by the same artist is a little less complicated and depicts just apples, a water pitcher, jar and bucket. Seating is on rust chairs and bench seats in the rear dining room and brown bench seats in the front dining room. All lighting comes from single-bulb ceiling lights. The front window has red & white curtain trim at the top and bottom.

DELTA

Atmosphere: ★★★ Easy, rock music plays in the background. A few locals and a family of seven were here for late dinner. This is a comfortable dining establishment.

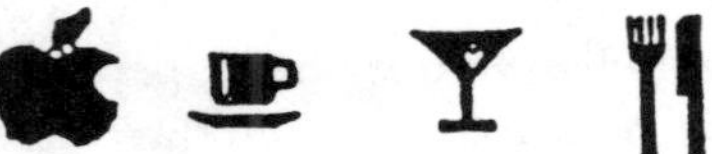

FIRESIDE ★★★
820 HIGHWAY 92 (303)874-4413

Sunday brunch $-$$, lunch $, dinner $-$$. 7 days: 4PM-10PM. SUN-FRI: 11AM-2PM.
Type: Steak. 10% cash senior (over 65) discount. American Heart Association approved meals.

This steak restaurant is owned and operated by the daughter of the owner the First National Fireside Restaurant in Rifle. She is also the niece of the owner of The Fireside in Glenwood Springs. All three restaurants are featured in this book.

Food: ★★★½ Their beef and bean soup is very thick with celery, carrots and seasoning. The 21 item salad bar with six salad dressings features mushrooms, mozzarella cheese, radishes, pepperoncini, cottage cheese, macaroni, potato & bean, and marshmallow & fruit cocktail salads, applesauce, and baked apples & raisins. My entree was the Alaskan pollack, a light, white mild fish in a mayonnaise and wine sauce, topped with seasoned bread crumbs and served with a baked potato. The entire meal was very good. The Sunday brunch offers eggs, a western Benedict, omelets, roast beef hash, huevos rancheros, hot roast beef, turkey & dressing, shrimp, chicken, steak, liver & onions, sandwiches (Monte Cristo, Reuben, and French dip), burgers, quiche and the salad bar. The lunch/dinner menu is the same here as the one at the First National Fireside Restaurant in Rifle. It offers light meals for lunch like spinach or chef salad, and beef or chicken lean meals. Other lunch items include soup, salad, onion rings, burgers, sandwiches (chicken, patty melt, club, pork cutlet, and Reuben), and specialties such as chicken fried steak, teriyaki chicken, Bratwurst hoagie, rib eye steak and clam strips. Dinner features German, Cajun, seafood, steaks, barbecue and chicken. The entrees include smoked chicken, pork or beef ribs, red snapper, jumbo shrimp, Cajun catfish, swordfish, chicken Marsala, and Wiener schnitzel. Both lunch and dinner offer a children's menu.

Service: ★½ Very slow. Several minutes lapsed before I was handed a menu and a glass or water. Several more minutes before the waitress returned to take my order. By now I had been here 15 minutes. It took another 35 minutes to get my entry after placing the order.

Decor: ★★★½ This is a rare tri-level restaurant. The middle level at the entrance has 13 tables for 45. The lower level is the bar/lounge area with seven tables for 24 and eight barstools. The upper level has 12 tables for 43. The entire restaurant has a look of elegance with high-back, red-velvet chairs and antique wood chairs with decorative red, flower-patterned backs. Pedestal-shaped lamp shades and ceiling fans hang from the natural-wood vaulted ceiling. Heads of deer, a buffalo, and a rare moose hang on the front wall over the entrance and a walnut cabinet. White curtains cover the windows to the left and railings separate the lounge below and the dining room above. At the end of the top level is an alcove with a banquet table. A large banquet room in the rear can hold 130 for a sit-down dinner.

Atmosphere: ★★★½ This was like a tale of two restaurants. The main dining areas on the second and third tiers had a couple of large families with very quiet, well behaved children and a two middle-aged couples. The lounge below had a younger crowd that was clearly enjoying itself and exhibiting boisterous laughter on a continual basis. Meanwhile, soft guitar music could barely be heard above the voices and laughs from below. It was an interesting mix. I did not find the behavior of the people in the lounge objectionable. It is hard to argue with someone having a good time and they were not the least bit obnoxious.

DILLON

Dillon was named after gold digger Tom Dillon who, after becoming lost and ending up in Golden, described a wide valley where three rivers met. Later explorers upon finding this area named it in his honor. (Sometimes getting lost has its advantages!). This town has moved three times since its original townsite in 1881: in 1882 when the railroads came to town, in 1883 when the town was moved between the three rivers, and in 1961 to make room for Dillon Lake. The original townsite lies under water on the south end of the lake and many of the original buildings are still visible.

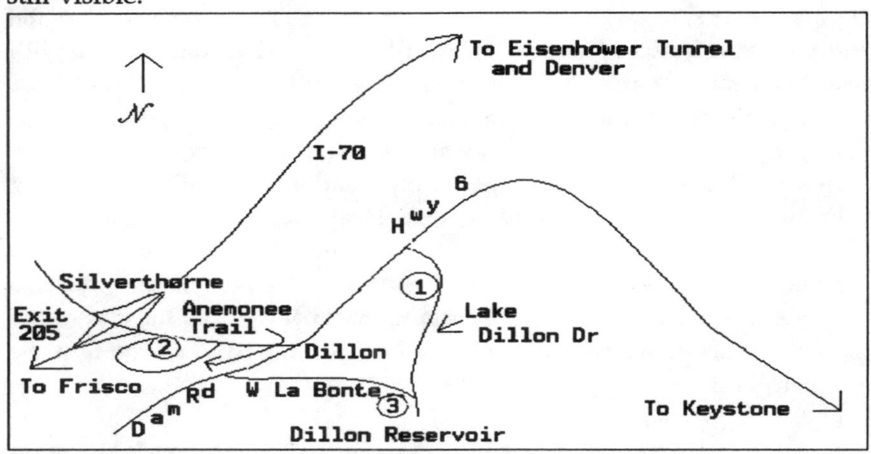

Restaurants and Ratings:	Food	Service	Decor	Atm	Overall
1. AL LAGO	★★★★½	★★★★½	★★★★	★★★★½	★★★★½
2. ANTONIA'S	★★★	★★½	★★★½	★★★	★★★
3. ARAPAHOE CAFE	★★★½	★★★	★★★	★★★½	★★★½

Al Lago serves delicious veal and pasta dishes in a warm and friendly atmosphere. Antonia's also serves some good Italian meals and salads. The Arapahoe Cafe serves good home-cooked meals, like beef Stroganoff, in large portions. All three restaurants accept major credit cards, have nonsmoking sections, and serve alcohol.

AL LAGO ★★★★½
240 LAKE DILLON DRIVE (303)468-6111

Dinner $$$-$$$$. TUE-SUN: 5PM-10PM. Closed MON. Closed NOV&MAY. Type: Italian (Northern). 15% gratuity added for parties of six or more. $5 surcharge added for any person not eating or splitting an entree. No checks. Owned and operated by the Ottoborgo family. Reservations not accepted.

Food: **★★★★½** All pasta and veal dishes are served with a warm, round loaf of Italian bread, soup and salad. The soup was homemade chicken tarragon with rice and it was excellent. The homemade Italian dressing, made with virgin olive oil, vinegar, mustard, herbs, and Parmesan cheese was quite good also. My entree was vitello alla fontina: sauteed veal with seasoned spinach & fontina cheese in a brown sauce with white wine & garlic. It is served with a side of fusilli: corkscrew pasta noodles in a homemade Bolognese sauce (a tomato sauce with spices). This was a superb combination. Thin medallions of prime veal and pasta with outstanding sauces. Many restaurants that I have dined at recently use thick slices of veal steak. I think this is fine for beef or pork, but veal, in my opinion should be served in thin medallions. Fortunately for me, Chef Ivano agrees. The dinner menu offers hot appetizers (eggplant Parmigiana, stuffed baked clams, garlic bread, and sautéed shrimp) and pasta, veal, chicken and seafood entrees. The pasta entrees are fettuccine all'Alfredo, linguini with clams and linguini with garlic, salami, fresh tomatoes and black olives. (Don't expect to find spaghetti, ravioli or lasagna here. They are southern Italian dishes.) There are three sautéed veal scallops entrees: with capers, mushrooms or artichoke hearts; and sautéed veal and shrimp topped with prosciutto. The three breast of chicken entrees, named after the three Ottoborgo daughters (Diana, Elisabetta and Loredana) are prepared with strawberry sauce; shrimp and cream sauce; and with onions, mushrooms and tomatoes. The seafood entrees are sautéed shrimp, sautéed sea scallops served over fettucini noodles, and sautéed trout with shrimp and mushrooms. Children can choose any item from the full menu and receive half-size portions for one-half the price. Off the menu desserts include crème caramel custard, chocolate mousse, strawberry short cake, blueberry & strawberry cheese torts, cognac log roll (yellow cake topped with butter cream cognac, rolled and topped with Ghiradelli chocolate, sprinkles and zabaglione sauce made from eggs, cream and Marsala wine), and tirra ma su (meaning "lift me up"): layered yellow cake soaked with espresso Angelico and mascarpone cheese mixed with chocolate & vanilla pudding, whipped cream and nuts. Have some coffee, espresso, cappuccino or hot chocolate with your dessert.

Service: ★★★★½ It would be difficult to find a warmer and friendlier family run operation in Colorado. I stayed long after my meal was over discussing food and restaurants with Chef Ivano and my server, Diana (Dee-an-a), while sampling a couple of their homemade wines (not for sale).

Decor: ★★★★ This is a two dining room restaurant. The smaller room has seven tables with mauve cloths for 22 diners. Frosted-glass and brass chandeliers and kerosene lamps light up this room which has windows on three sides and rose-patterned wall paper on the fourth. Climbing philodendrons and giant red geraniums decorate the window sills and divider separating the two dining rooms. The main dining room has 14 tables for 50. Both dining rooms face their own private game farm — complete with peahens, peacocks and deer. Diners can pet the animals through the fence. A double-sided fireplace separates the main dining room from the bar/lounge. The bar/lounge has two tables for eight, five barstools, a couch, love seat, cushioned chair, and a cabinet with plates and water pitchers. Past the lounge is a stairway leading to the rest rooms. At the bottom of this stairway are photographs of Venice in wood frames.

Atmosphere: ★★★★½ An appropriate and pleasing tape of Italian songs and lyrics greatly enhanced the mood in this empty restaurant during the off season. The Ottoborgo family owned the Berthoud Inn before it burned down on July 7, 1987. They opened Al Lago 51 weeks later on July 1, 1988 and have spent considerable time and effort expanding the restaurant and building the red-brick wall that surrounds the parking lot. They have made quite a comeback from their earlier misfortune.

ANTONIA'S ★★★
817 U.S. HIGHWAY 6 (303)468-5055

Dinner $$-$$$$. Easter-Thanksgiving: 7 days 6PM-10PM. Thanksgiving-Easter: 7 days 5PM-10PM.
Type: Italian. No half orders on pizza. This Italian restaurant that began in 1983 is entirely nonsmoking.

Food: **★★★** My dinner salad included shredded Parmesan and Italian olives with a basil vinegarette dressing. I ordered cavatelli: small pasta shells in a marinara sauce made with tomatoes and mild bell peppers, topped with a combination of melted imported Romano and mozzarella cheeses. It was served with two French rolls. I also had a side of meatballs with mushrooms in a brown sauce with Marsala wine. This was a good meal but not exceptional. I particularly liked the salad, especially the Italian olives. Besides pasta, the menu features veal, chicken, shrimp, beef and pizza. Appetizers include marinated artichokes, stuffed mushrooms, tortillini, fettucini, garlic bread and three meatball selections. The other pasta dishes feature linguini, fettucini, lasagna, spaghetti and tortelloni in a variety of marinara, cream and Alfredo sauces. There are five sautéed medallions of veal dishes to choose from; a half a dozen boneless breast of chicken entrees including cacciatore, Florentine, and Parmesan; shrimp scampi, formaggio (prawns rolled in imported cheeses), and di Medici (with garlic, tomatoes and artichoke hearts); and three charbroiled beef choices. Pizza comes in two sizes with a healthy selection of 15 toppings including capers, prosciutto, shrimp and filet of beef. A different selection of homemade desserts are offered every evening.

Service: **★★½** Friendly and helpful, although new.

Decor: **★★★½** The dining room is upstairs with 18 tables for 66 diners seated in sturdy and stylish oak rib-backed chairs with engraved leaf patterns. Several potted plants in window sills and hanging plants from a vaulted wood-beamed ceiling decorate the room. The south side of the restaurant faces the parking lot, night club next door, and the mountains. However, you can not see the mountains at night because of the bright parking lot lights. Lighting inside is provided by in-set ceiling lights, tables candles, and a chandelier with antlers hanging from a three-foot chain. A cabinet filled with wine glasses, red-clothed napkins and plates stands in the corner next to the kitchen. On the far left wall is an Indian rug with the imprint of the Taj Mahal. There are several framed and matted photos of Italy hanging on the white stucco walls: many of Venice, one taken from a cliff looking down on several boats in the Mediterranean, and one of a restaurant and alley. There is a deck off the east side of the dining room which is no longer used for dinner. However, diners can view the sunset in the northwest from here in the summer. Downstairs is the bar/lounge with nine wood tables for 22 and 8 barstools. A map of Italy and a photo of wine bottles decorate the white plaster walls. Several oil on fabric paintings, created by one of the waitresses, hang at the entrance. They depict a council of Indian chiefs and abstract patterns. Adjacent to these paintings is a cartoon poster of some of the establishments in Summit County.

Atmosphere: ★★★ New age guitar and piano selections create a comfortable environment. This is a popular place with couples.

ARAPAHOE CAFE ★★★½
626 LAKE DILLON DRIVE (303)468-0873

Breakfast $-$$, lunch $$, dinner $$$-$$$$. MON-FRI: 7AM-2PM and 5PM-9:30PM. SAT-SUN: 7AM-2:30PM and 5PM-9:30PM.
Type: Country. The entire restaurant is nonsmoking

Built in the early 1940's by Faye and Lenore Bryant, the Arapahoe Cafe had to be moved in 1960 to make way for Lake Dillon reservoir. The move was successful but left its mark on the building: some of the floors are uneven and the pine panel walls meet somewhere more or less than 90 degrees. This, however, only adds to the historic charm of the restaurant.

Food: ★★★½ I ordered the lunch special: beef Stroganoff with green peas and a fresh hot biscuit. This was a big meal. About half-a-pound of pasta noodles with more than two dozen pieces of beef. The sauce was a brown gravy rather than a cream sauce. This was good home cooking!

The breakfast menu has some choices which might interest you, like red meat trout, a no yolk mushroom and cheese omelet, or yogurt & granola. There are also eggs Benedict, Belgian or strawberry waffles, sautéed vegetables with egg and cheese, their own version of huevos rancheros, cinnamon vanilla battered French toast, blueberry or banana pancakes, and several omelets to choose from. The lunch menu is sure to please both the carnivore and vegetarian with burgers, sandwiches, salads and cafe classics. You can order a guacamole, bacon and cheddar burger or one made with soy meal. The sandwich selections include club, chicken teriyaki, turkey breast, and two for the vegetarian. There are three salads to choose from including spinach & bacon or oriental chicken with greens. The cafe classics feature chicken fried steak, their own quesadilla, a veggie filled tortilla, liver & onions and linguini marinara. The dinner menu centers around chicken, steak, fish and a nightly pasta specialty. Roast duck, sautéed scallops in Alfreda sauce, steak au poivre, rainbow trout and chicken Marsala are a few of the entrees. The linens and candles are brought out for dinner. These are all four-course meals with soup, salad, entree and dessert.

Service: ★★★ Satisfactory. I had an informative and friendly chat with the proprietor after lunch.

Decor: ★★★ The dining room to the right of the entrance hosts nine tables with cranberry-red linens for 30 diners. Blue drawn-back curtains frame the windows that look out onto a row of flowers and a hummingbird feeder. There are fresh flowers at every table. Old newspaper clippings on Dillon, an Ansel Adams poster and a wreath are among the decor on the wood walls. There are a lot of windows and very little wall space. Lighting is provided by a combination of brass, clear-glass lanterns hanging from chains, studio lights, and frosted ceiling lights. The dining room to the left of the entrance has five tables along the windows for 14 diners. Old photos of people on ski lifts, the Arapahoe Basin shelter, the

Dillon Hotel, and the Arapahoe Cafe & Motel, circa 1956, decorate the wall opposite the windows. Downstairs is the "Pub Down Under" which features its own menu of burgers, sandwiches, steak, trout, soup, salad, appetizers and a veggie grill. There are four booths and one table for 20 plus eight square barstools with plaid-cushioned seats. Decor consists of a stone wall with a black-iron, wood-burning fireplace, a television, a foos ball machine, a pool table, and old photos of W.C. Fields and Jackie Gleason, as "Minnesota Fats" shooting pool.

Atmosphere: ★★★½ Classical music plays in the background. This is a popular lunch spot for local business people.

Lake Dillon and the town of Dillon

DOLORES

Dolores was named after the river on which it is located. The Dolores River was given the name "Rio de Nuestra Senora de las Dolores," or "river of our lady of sorrow," by Father Escalente in 1776. Dolores was one of the last sections of the state to be settled by the white man. In 1877 William, Richard, and George May settled on the Dolores River. From that beginning, Dolores developed over the years as a shipping point for cattle and sheep. Ranching, farming, and lumber have been the town's major sources of survival and prosperity. Of particular interest today is the Anasazi Heritage Center, which opened in August, 1988, just two miles west of Dolores.

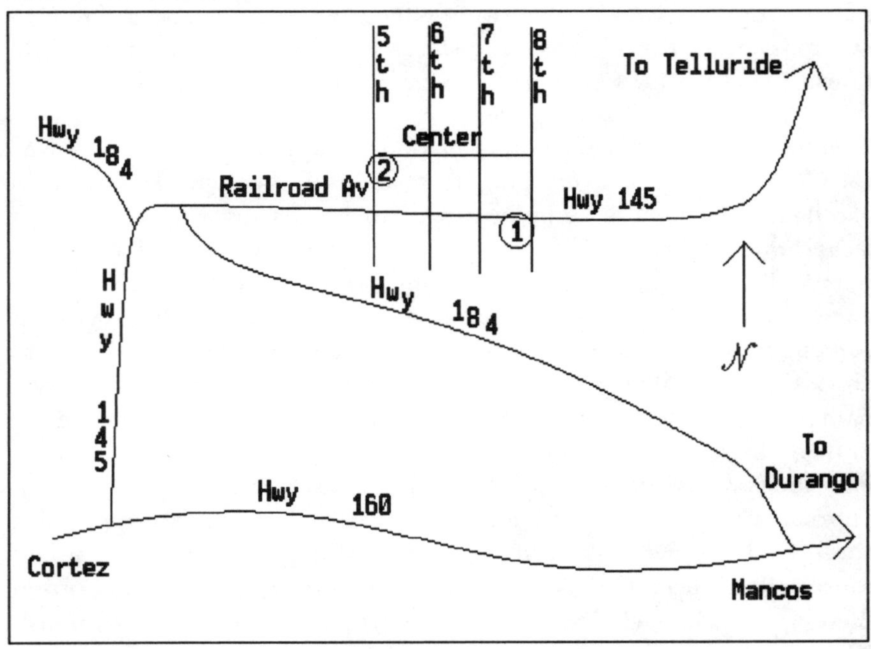

Restaurants and Ratings:	Food	Service	Decor	Atm	Overall
1. OLD GERMANY	★★★★★	★★★★★	★★★★★	★★★★½	★★★★★
2. RIO GRANDE	★★★★½	★★★★	★★★★	★★★½	★★★★

Dolores has two very fine restaurants and if you are in the vicinity you owe it to yourself to try at least one of them. Old Germany offers outstanding German food prepared by a Bavarian trained chef. The Rio Grande Southern has excellent country food with many homemade items. Both restaurants accept major credit cards and serve alcohol, but only Old Germany has a nonsmoking section.

OLD GERMANY RESTAURANT ★★★★★
HWY. 145 & 8TH ST. (303)882-7549

Dinner $-$$$. TUE-SAT 4PM-9PM. Closed SUN & MON.
Type: German. This is truly an outstanding restaurant that I am sure many people pass on the highway without giving a second thought to stopping. From the outside, the restaurant looks like an ordinary white house. Don't let that fool you. There are many pleasant surprises inside.

Food: ★★★★★ In this authentic Bavarian Restaurant where the chef was certified in Bavaria, everything is made from scratch. The soup is excellent. The potato dumplings are superb, as are the sauces. My jaegerbraten (pork roast in mushroom sauce) with red cabbage was outstanding. It doesn't get any better! To start with, escargot and zucchini, or onion rings are on the appetizer menu. If you want something light, there are several American and German sandwiches to choose from: schnitzel with ham & cheese, German-style meatloaf on rye, hamburger, Reuben, or patty melt with grilled onions. The following list of menu items comes with the soup & salad bar: Bratwurst, Knackwurst, kasseler (smoked pork chop), grilled pork loin, grilled tenderloin with paprika sauce, and Hawaii toast (covered with ham, pineapple and cheese). The dinner entrees include rump steak pilze (with mushroom sauce), rump steak "Old Germany" (with fried onions), pork loin Cordon Bleu, Jaegerschnitzel, Paprikaschnitzel (with bell peppers & onions), Wiener schnitzel, Hungarian chicken (with bell peppers & onions in paprika sauce), cod, sauerbraten (marinated roast beef), pork roast, pork tenderloin with Béarnaise sauce, and trout. Side orders of German potato salad, German fried potatoes, spatzle, and sauerkraut can also be ordered and, in some cases, are included with the meal. They have a children's menu. For dessert try some apple strudel, Bavarian cream pie, Eiskaffee (vanilla ice cream on coffee with whipped cream), or Fruechtebecher (mixed ice cream and fruits with whipped cream).

Service: ★★★★★ Fast, cordial, and ready and willing to talk about the restaurant, the food and their philosophy. One of the owners gave me a personal tour.

Decor: ★★★★★ This is an old refurbished house with nicely varnished door frames. There are four dining rooms with total seating for about 75, in addition to a lounge downstairs and seating outside in the summer. The room on the right has five tables for 23 people. The middle room has five tables for 19 people. The room on the left has two tables for 10 people. The rear room, which is only used if they are busy or for private parties, has six tables for about 20 people. I sat in the room on the right where two philodendron vines wrap around two walls. A mantel also extends around the room supporting pewter and blue ceramic plates, wine bottles, shot glasses, candle holders, a mug and a cup. Very attractive baby blue curtains hang in front of the windows. In one corner is a wood china cabinet with two glass panels divided by a shelf and four drawers. The cabinet contains beer steins and mugs , a punch bowl, a tea kettle and candle holders. On top, there are brass tea kettles. The center room has the soup and 11-item salad bar, a five-lamp chandelier hanging from three-foot chains, and a page out of the February 3, 1918, edition of the Denver Post with the following headlines: "Hun Strikers, Kiev Victory," "America must recognize Reds," and "Americans must Smash Detachment/Huns Attack." The room on the left has coasters from Germany on the mantel. Toward the rear of the restaurant are deer horns over the entrances to the rest rooms and the cashier's station. The rear dining room with its pink curtains and trellis-pattern white walls holds the biggest surprise. Hanging on the wall in an air-tight glass enclosure is the emblem of the twelfth century village of Wipfelt in northern Bavaria. This priceless 800-year-old flag was once carried into battle. The flag was discovered in 1974 by the current proprietors who were remodeling an old house in Bavaria built in the early 1200s. When a portion of the roof was ripped out, this 800-year-old emblem fell to the ground. It had been hidden in the roof, covered with boards. The lounge downstairs has eight tables and six bar stools for an additional 50 people, a television, beige and white stripped curtains, and a couple of beer advertisements. Two white tables with metal chairs on the porch and four picnic tables on the lawn are used in the summer.

Atmosphere: ★★★★½ German polkas play quietly in the background. This is a warm and friendly place. An outstanding find.

RIO GRANDE SOUTHERN HOTEL AND RESTAURANT ★★★★
CENTRAL & 5TH (303)882-7527

Breakfast/lunch $, dinner $$. WED-MON 7AM-9PM. Closed TUE.
Type: Country. Dinner entrees half-priced for children 10 and under.

Food: ★★★★½ This restaurant offers homemade soup, breads, cakes and pies. They have excellent food. The breakfast menu has Canadian bacon, an egg sandwich, fruit pancakes, waffles, and French crêpes. Lunch offers a soup & salad bar, sandwiches (roast beef, club, turkey breast, and French dip), burgers, chef's salad, and a diet plate. Dinner entrees include T-bone steak, roast beef, country fried steak, ground steak with either mushrooms and gravy or onions and green chilies, barbecue ribs, fried chicken, liver & onions, cod, a dieter's plate, and the soup & salad bar. A children's menu is available as well as daily offerings on dessert.

Service: ★★★★ Fast and amiable.

Decor: ★★★★ The building housing the hotel is old (built in 1931), but the restaurant is new, having just opened in June 1989. This is a small one-room restaurant with seven booths plus a single table in a small alcove. Total seating for 34 people. There are several interesting old photos taken between the 1890s and 1930s, including one of a group of men standing in front of the "Dolores Akin Mercantile Co. General Merchandise Store." Accompanying the old photos are paintings of adobe brick buildings in Southwest settings. The tables and benches have the new look of finished wood. Old silver and bronze teapots sit on the mantels.

Atmosphere: ★★★½ These are pleasant surroundings. Honky-tonk and easy listening music plays quietly from a portable cassette player.

DRAKE

The town was named after State Senator William A. Drake, who represented the district from 1903 to 1907. Locally, the town is referred to as "The Forks" because it is situated at the junction of the North Fork and main stream of the Big Thompson River.

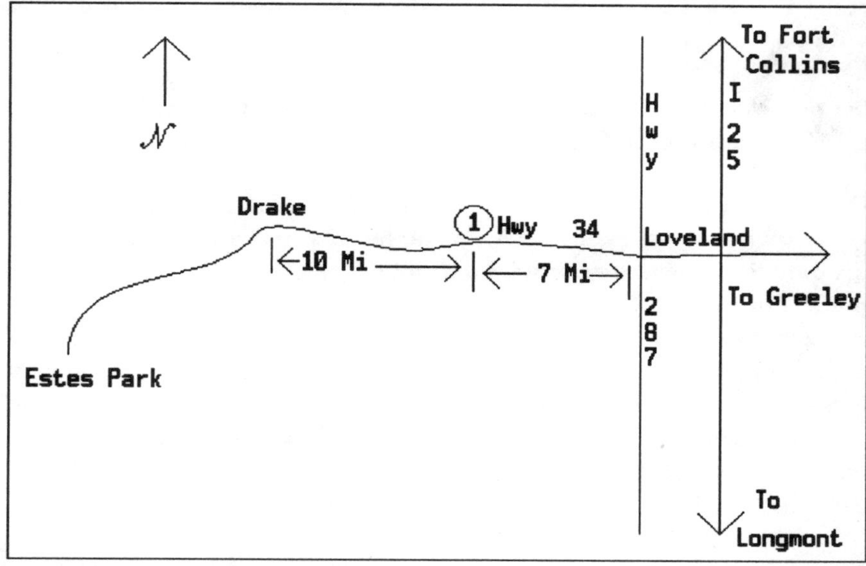

1. Bohemian Cottage ★★★★★
8039 West U.S. Hwy. 34 (303)667-3718

Dinner $$$. TUE-SUN 5pm-10pm. Closed MON.
Type: German. Major credit cards are accepted, alcohol is served, but they do not have a nonsmoking section. Reservations recommended.

This restaurant, owners Henry and Lucy Lampert, my first book, and I were featured on "Friday Feast" with Kristen McClousky on KCNC-TV, Channel 4 on August 2, 1991. We all enjoyed a meal of jaegerschnitzel for the cameras.

Food: ★★★★½ There are many wonderful Czechoslovakian and German dishes on the menu, like sauerbraten "Prague Style" with herbs, vegetables, and sour cream gravy. It came with spongy Bohemian dumplings, sliced like bread, and was delicious! Dinner is served with homemade soup and bread. Other beef dishes include Stroganoff and Hungarian goulash. The rest of the menu features veal (Cordon Bleu and Wiener schnitzel), pork (Holland schnitzel: breaded ground pork with ham, bacon, & Swiss; roasted pork, and jager schnitzel), chicken (Vienna style: a breaded breast with fried potatoes and lemon; sweet & sour, and with paprika), and specials like duck or buffalo.

Service: ★★★★½ Henry & Lucy Lampert, your hosts, will provide a genuine central European experience.

Decor: ★★★★★ This is such a quaint little one-room restaurant that you really owe it to yourself to come to dinner if you are in the area. There are only ten tables, covered with red cloths, for 42 people, so reservations might not be a bad idea. Bear skins and deer antlers adorn the wood-paneled walls and ceiling beams. The rear wall has an array of paraphernalia from plates and mugs to post cards and a flag. One wall is an entire mural depicting a waterfall, waterwheel and cabin in a fall mountain setting. Tiny baskets with artificial daisies and tulips are set in the window sills. It all blends together much better than I am able to describe.

Atmosphere: ★★★★★ German "Ooom-pah-pah" music play in the background. The country setting of the restaurant adds to the authentic European flavor found inside. However, due to the size, there is no nonsmoking section.

DURANGO

The town was named by former Territorial Governor A.C. Hunt upon his return from Durango, Mexico. The name Durango itself is derived from the town Urango (meaning "water town") in the Basque Province of northern Spain. The "D" was added by the Spanish. Once a predominant coal mining community and commercial center, Durango is known today for its Victorian architecture and the Durango to Silverton narrow gauge railroad. The railroad offers daily round trips, from May to October, through the scenic San Juan Mountains. The train depot, the Palace Grill (reviewed below), located in what used to be the Palace Hotel, and the Strater Hotel are three of the best examples of early architecture that still remain today.

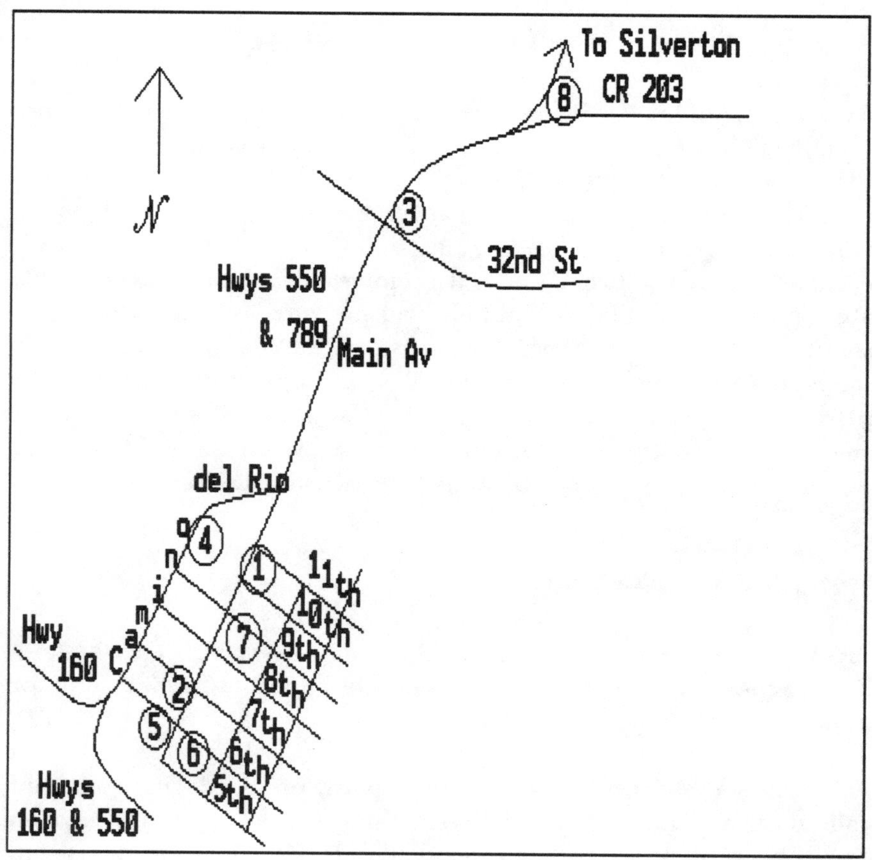

DURANGO

Restaurants and Ratings:	Food	Service	Decor	Atm	Overall
1. CARVER'S	★★★★	★★½	★★★	★★★★	★★★½
2. FRANCISCO'S	★★★★½	★★★★½	★★★★★	★★★★½	★★★★½
3. MAY PALACE	★★★★	★★★½	★★★★	★★½	★★★½
4. OSCAR'S	★★	★★★	★★	★	★★
5. PALACE GRILL	★★★★★	★★★★½	★★★★★	★★★★★	★★★★★
6. PRONTO'S	★★½	★★★	★	★★★	★★½
7. RED SNAPPER	★★★★½	★★★★★	★★★★½	★★★★	★★★★½
8. SWEENEY'S	★★★★	★★★★	★★★★½	★★★	★★★★

Durango sports many fine and excellent restaurants. Some of the ones described here are among the best in town. With several restaurants in the four-to-five-star category, I found it imperative to select the very best, or my personal favorite, as a five-star restaurant. The Palace Grill, along with its Quiet Lady Tavern, offers outstanding food, professional service, enchanting and historical decor, and a comfortable, relaxed and enjoyable atmosphere. You will not want to leave here. For excellent seafood, you should visit the Red Snapper. Francisco's, in their large restaurant, has the best Mexican food. If you are looking for excellent beef and ribs, the place to go is Sweeney's Grubsteak. Only Oscar's does not accept major credit cards nor serve alcohol. Except for the May Palace, Oscar's and Sweeney's Grubsteak, all restaurants have nonsmoking sections.

CARVERS ★★★½
1022 MAIN AVE. (303)259-2545

Breakfast/lunch $, dinner $$. MON-SAT 6:30AM-10PM. SUN 6:30AM-2PM. Type: American/Continental. 15% gratuity added to parties of six or more.

Food: ★★★★ My eggs Florentine were expertly prepared. This restaurant calls itself a "bakery, cafe & brewery" and it is all three. Opened on December 31, 1988, Carvers' brewery and pub offers their own house tap beers: a pilsner, stout and ale. They also make their own bread. Beer and bread: the "staffs of life" they call it. Other breakfast items are eggs Benedict; potatoes with green peppers, mushrooms, onions and Cheddar cheese, or Mexican style with green chili; huevos rancheros, and a breakfast burrito. The lunch menu has a couple of special items: chicken stew and ratatouille, as well as subs, soup, salads, hot sandwiches (tuna & Cheddar, turkey & Provolone, a vegetarian Reuben, or chicken), and cold sandwiches (club, tuna or chicken salad, and a garden with cream cheese). For dessert, you can order homemade fruit pies, custard pies or cakes to go with a cup of espresso, cappuccino or mochaccino. Start your dinner off with an appetizer of Buffalo chicken wings, nachos made with blue corn chips, or Hungarian mushrooms in a sour cream dill sauce with paprika. From here, you have a choice of salads (garden, chef, vegetarian or chicken), the soup of the day, a hot sandwich, chicken stew, a pot pie, ratatouille, or chili. There is a limited, but excellent, selection of entree specialties: basted snapper, sirloin strips, barley glazed almond chicken, and chicken Florentine.

Service: ★★½ Fast on the food, but slow on the coffee.

Decor: ★★★ Modern art by a local artist adorns the white plaster-finished walls. Studio ceiling lights hang from the stucco ceiling. The ceiling is rather interesting with a wood frame covering the left and rear sections, and ceiling beams in the middle section.

Atmosphere: ★★★★ It seems like an arty/intellectual crowd comes in here.

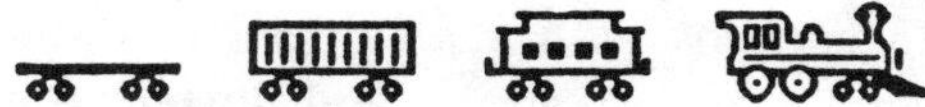

FRANCISCO'S ★★★★½
619 MAIN AVE. (303)247-4098

Breakfast $, lunch $-$$, dinner $$-$$$. MON-SAT 11AM-10PM, SUN 8AM-10PM.
Type: Mexican.

DURANGO

Food: ★★★★½ Superb. I have eaten here for breakfast and dinner. Whether it's bacon & eggs or your favorite Mexican dish, this restaurant is an excellent choice any time of day. Breakfast (only served on Sundays until 1:30PM) specializes in huevos rancheros, a breakfast burrito, and homemade Danish pastry. Lunch offers sandwiches like breast of chicken in green chili, turkey and avocado; burgers, a marinated pork burrito, chicken fried steak, salads (guacamole, chef, crab Louis, tossed, and a tostada), some interesting Mexican items: a chicken tamale, sour cream enchilada, guacamole tostada, and an enchilada made with Indian blue corn tortillas. Dinner appetizers include beer steamed shrimp, shrimp cocktail, and blue corn quesadillas. There are several beef, chicken and seafood entrees to choose from: filet mignon, top sirloin, chicken Oscar, chicken with white wine sauce, Rocky Mountain trout, salmon, Cajun-style snapper, shrimp scampi, lobster tail, and Alaskan king crab legs. There is a lot of good food to choose from.

Service: ★★★★½ Very accommodating.

Decor: ★★★★★ The size of the restaurant accompanies the size of their menu: an 8,000-square-foot area that can seat up to 250 people. Established in 1968, this is probably the most popular restaurant in Durango. Their 250-seat capacity is put to good use. The restaurant is divided into many sections by pink adobe walls. The left front section has five booths and four tables. The right front section has 10 tables, five booths and a bar with 10 seats. The ceiling has log beams that pass through a plaster wall and a wood divider that hangs three feet from the ceiling. Below that is open space and the pink adobe walls. There are white water fountains, several potted and hanging plants, arched entrances between sections with stained glass overhead, spiral wood columns, and several wreaths, mirrors and flower arrangements on the walls and shelves. The south wall is made of stone and decorated with pictures of nature scenes. There are a few small Mexican rugs. Seating is at booths, and tables with a bench seat on one side and chairs on the other. The booths are very comfortable with high-back brown cushions with gold buttons. The tables are finely finished wood with decorative splashes of color in green & blue resembling daisies. A lot of work went into designing the interior.

Atmosphere: ★★★★½ Easy listening, romantic, soft Spanish music in the background. Very comfortable dining.

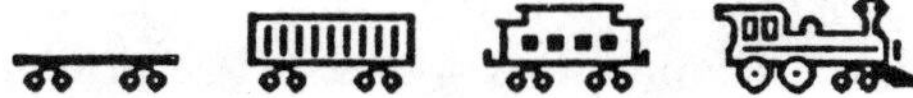

MAY PALACE ★★★½
3206 MAIN AVE. (303)259-4836

Lunch/dinner $$-$$$. MON-FRI 11AM-9:30PM. SAT & SUN 5PM-9:30PM. Type: Oriental (Mandarin & Szechuan) They do try to separate smokers from nonsmokers.

Food: ★★★★ Their house specialty duck is one of the most tender and tastiest I have ever had. It comes with bean sprouts, water chestnuts and celery, but it is mostly duck. Ask for the chili hot sauce served on the side. It had the effect of a delayed anesthetic. When I first tried it, I had no reaction, but by the time I could count to ten, the back of my throat was numb. This is a must for people who like to feel their food as well as taste it. This Mandarin and Szechuan Chinese restaurant features some hot and spicy dishes. However, the "spiciness can be altered to your taste." The lunch/dinner menu has several choices of appetizers, soup, fried rice, chow mein, poultry, pork, beef, lamb, seafood, vegetables, specialty dinners and desserts. Appetizers include egg rolls, fried prawns, won ton, rumaki (liver & water chestnuts wrapped in bacon), and paper-wrapped chicken. For soup, there is egg flower; shrimp with rice; chicken, black mushroom & abalone; and crab meat & corn. There are 14 poultry dishes including chicken in plum sauce and chicken with black mushrooms & snow peas; seven pork selections, such as twice cooked, shredded and moo-shu; eleven beef choices including pepper steak in oyster sauce and flaming Chinese steak; three lamb meals: Mongolian, Hunan, and kung pao; fifteen seafood selections, such as Peking shrimp and Mandarin-style crispy fish; seven vegetable dishes including Szechuan-style eggplant and Chinese cabbage; and a dozen specialty dinners including volcano shrimp and pineapple duck. The desserts are chilled lychee fruit and sugar-spun bananas or apples.

Service: ★★★½ Friendly.

Decor: ★★★★ This restaurant has front, rear, and downstairs sections. The front has 12 tables plus some booths for about 60 people. The rear has ten tables for 38 people. Downstairs is the bar area and dart board with five stools and ten tables for 25 people. Food is served downstairs sometimes, depending on the bartender. Total seating is for about 123. Most of the chairs are the low-back cushioned type. There are studio lights between the wood-framed windows with no curtains or shades. The walls are 2 by 6 diagonal wood panels and overhead is a trellis with very real looking (but artificial) grapes and grape vines. Several hanging plants and just a few Chinese decorations add flavor without overdoing it. I was impressed by the grape vine trellis. While you're here, check out the piece of art work downstairs behind the pipe-stove. It is made entirely from nails and bronze.

Atmosphere: ★★½ There's nothing Chinese about the host, wine stewardess or waitress. The busboy looked Chinese, but sounded like he was from California. This does seem to be a Chinese family affair, however, as I overheard what appeared to be a mother and daughter conversing in Chinese as they left the restaurant.

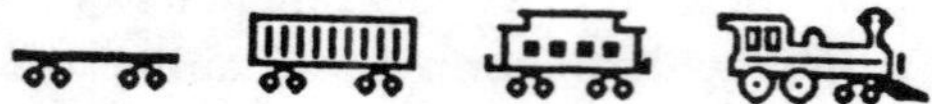

OSCAR'S ★★
18 TOWN PLAZA (303)247-0526

Breakfast/lunch $. MON-SAT 7AM-5PM. SUN 8AM-1PM.
Type: Country.

Food: ★★ *Service:* ★★★ *Decor:* ★★ *Atmosphere:* ★

I ate a standard breakfast here. The potato pancakes (one of my favorites) were fair. I was here in March when the waitress was talking about what a "yummy" summer it was going to be in Durango. I'm sure she did her part to make it just that. This place is a single long room with ten tables and a counter. Total seating is for 52. The walls are part wood panel, with pictures of the Colorado mountains and cowboys, and part decorative beige wallpaper with a pattern of roosters, weather vanes and water pitchers. Bring your cowboy hat or feel like a tourist.

THE PALACE GRILL AND QUIET LADY TAVERN ★★★★★
NEXT TO THE TRAIN DEPOT (303)247-2018

Lunch $$, dinner/Sunday brunch $$$$. Mid-May to late Sept: MON-FRI 11:30AM-2PM. All year: 7 days 5:30PM-10PM and SUN 10AM-2PM. Type: American/Continental.

Food: ★★★★★ Their French onion soup is outstanding, as is their honey duck. Actually, it would be difficult to go wrong with anything on their menu. It all sounds good to me. There are several delectable hot and cold appetizers on the dinner menu: chopped chicken liver pâté, jumbo shrimp cocktail, oysters on the half shell, gazpacho, sautéed mushrooms, grilled shell shrimp, escargot, skewered oysters in bacon, the baked French onion soup, crab Rangoon (with cream cheese in a won ton skin), pasta primavera, and onion rings. The salad selections include a julienne, Caesar's, chicken curry and spinach, just spinach, and the Maurice (turkey, avocado, bacon and bleu cheese). There are several excellent and interesting entrees primarily in the steaks, poultry and seafood categories: sirloin, beef tenderloin, rib eye, hickory smoked baby-back ribs, brandy pepper steak, beef tenderloin goulash, the honey duck, mesquite grilled chicken breast, chicken & shrimp with artichokes, chicken dumplings, Colorado trout, shrimp ajo (in garlic butter), beer batter shrimp, lobster tail, shrimp & sea scallops, a catch of the day (like snapper or ahi), fettuccine primavera, and stir-fried vegetables. The desserts are equally tempting: sour cream apple, grasshopper, or Turkish coffee pies; cheesecake, chocolate torte cake, crème brulee (with brandy), sherbet, ice cream, and fudge brownies. The lunch menu in summer offers fried clams, fettuccine primavera, barbecued ribs, sandwiches (steak, Mexican club, turkey croissant, mesquite-grilled barbecued pork tenderloin and a burger) and either a soup and sandwich or soup and salad combination.

Service: ★★★★½ Excellent. The management is eager to discuss the history of the restaurant and former hotel.

Decor: ★★★★★ There's indoor and outdoor dining. Outside there's a patio with five tables for 16 people. Inside there's the Palace Grill: one room with a fireplace and nine tables for 28 people. Elegant, decorative stained-glass lamps hang by a chain over each table. White curtains hang over the windows with potted plants on the window sills. Pewter plates sit on high wall shelves. The walls are adorned with turn-of-the-century photographs of Durango and the surrounding area; this is a marvelous collection circa 1897 and earlier: scenes of horse-drawn carriages, pipe stoves, mule trains, and the Durango-Silverton Railroad. There are some later twentieth century photographs showing a group of firemen, and some individual photographs, like the one of Black Bart in the Little Lady Tavern. It's on the wall on your left as you enter from the doorway next to the host's station. Behind the host's station is a picture of the old Palace Hotel. Just beyond the host's station is a wine rack in what used to be one of the windows of the Palace Hotel. The swinging door entrance from the Tavern to the rest rooms and telephones used to be the arched entrance to the Hotel. Have the host point these items out to you. You will be able to see how the restaurant is part of the original hotel, while the Tavern, built in 1977, is an addition to the front of the Hotel. By the way, the Rocky Mountain Chocolate Factory, around the corner from the restaurant, is in one corner of the former Palace Hotel. Take a look at the whole building from across the street to get a good overall view. The Quiet Lady Tavern, adjacent to the Palace Grill, has nine small round tables for 26 people and 6 high barstools. There's also darts and a small library with couches. An ideal place for a before- or after-dinner drink.

Atmosphere: ★★★★★ Very quiet rock music in the background that you hardly notice (the way rock music should be played). With elegant decor, soft music, remarkable old photographs, a good clientele, and history. This restaurant may have the best atmosphere of any in Colorado.

PRONTO'S ★★½
160 E 6TH ST. (303)247-1510

Dinner $-$$. 7 days 4:30PM-10PM.
Type: Italian.

Food: ★★½ *Service:* ★★★ *Decor:* ★ *Atmosphere:* ★★★

My spaghetti was just a little under cooked and the sauce could have used more oregano and basil. The menu is almost exclusively Italian. The waiter had a good sense of humor. I asked for a large glass of ice water and he brought me a 24-oz. goblet, the largest glass in the house. The restaurant is in two sections: an upper front level by the windows has four tables for 14 people; the lower level has ten tables for 38 people. There are also six seats at the ice cream counter making a total seating capacity of 58. The decor is gimmicky, if not downright laughable. I'll describe it and let you be the judge. On the positive side, the entire restaurant is decorated in the colors of the Italian flag: green, red and white: a high green ceiling, white plaster walls, and red-cushioned seat covers and buffet tablecloth. On the negative side, the chairs have low metal backs and are not very comfortable. Now comes the humorous side. There are two glass & metal frame posters: one advertising salami, the other Ferraris. Another wall hanging advertises the 15th Annual Durango Bicycle Classic. A green motor scooter (not a poster of one, but an actual scooter) hangs on one wall. A large Italian flag hangs over the buffet table and twelve smaller Italian flags rotate about a pole hanging horizontally over the ice cream counter. I can't help laughing just thinking about it. A place for young and old. A good family restaurant.

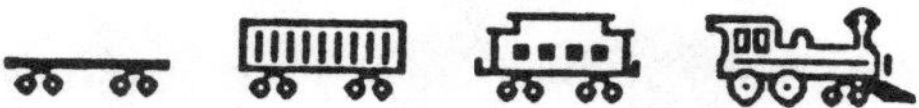

THE RED SNAPPER ★★★★½
144 E. 9TH ST. (303)259-3417

Dinner $$$-$$$$ (some $$$$+). 7 days 5PM-10PM
Type: Seafood.

DURANGO

Food: ★★★★½ My red snapper was very moist and easy to break apart with a fork. Their seafood is flown in twice weekly so it is fairly fresh. Oyster hour is from 5PM to 6PM. Other appetizers include shrimp cocktail, oysters Rockefeller or Parmesan, artichoke, escargot in mushrooms, and Cajun shrimp skewer with sausage and vegetables. There are several excellent seafood entrees including several varieties of red snapper (Cajun, Parmesan; with spicy mushrooms, peppers and onions; or with Monterey jack cheese), scallops baked with Dijon mustard and white wine, shrimp (scampi, Cajun or teriyaki), lobster, king crab, Hawaiian ahi, swordfish, halibut, Atlantic salmon, and trout amandine. Clam chowder, a salad bar, Hawaiian chicken, prime rib, filet mignon and top sirloin are also available. For dessert, you can try peach pie, cheesecake, mint Alaska pie, or "Death by Chocolate" (chocolate crumb pie crust, chocolate ice cream, chocolate fudge, nuts and whipped cream).

Service: ★★★★★ Top rate.

Decor: ★★★★½ There are three sections to this restaurant: the left section has eight combination bench & chairs for 32 people; the center section has eight tables for 30 people; and the right section has five booths and six tables for 42. Total seating capacity is 204. The high-back, wood-rib chairs are very comfortable. The tables are finished wood. There are artificial flowers and a candle at each table. Several colorful and appropriate posters in glass & metal frames of whales, angelfish and triggerfish adorn the walls. Plants are on the counters separating the three sections. A single lamp hangs over each booth. The ceiling is a low acoustic tile and the walls are a combination wood panel and cloth fabric. A very nice place.

Atmosphere: ★★★★ Soft jazz plays in the background. This was a very quiet place except for one loud customer who could be heard clear across the right section. He was actually very funny, speaking in a low guttural voice. He made one comment, not too surprisingly, about his mother being a "very vocal person."

SWEENEY'S GRUBSTEAK ★★★★
1644 COUNTY RD. 203 (303)247-5236

Dinner $$$-$$$$. SUN-THU 5PM-10:30PM. FRI-SAT 5PM-11:30PM.
Type: Steak. Management tries to separate the smokers from the nonsmokers. They are working on providing a nonsmoking section.

Food: ★★★★ Kow-bi, their spicy, tangy teriyaki sauce, is quite good. It comes with the beef brochette and Choi's ribs. (Choi is their former cook). The menu is primarily seafood, steak and poultry. The seafood choices include orange roughy, rainbow trout, mahi-mahi, halibut, flounder, shrimp, Alaskan king crab, broiled Australian lobster, trout stuffed with crab meat, and a catch of the day (sea bass the day I was here). The red meat selections are beef brochette with green peppers, onions & tomato sauce; top sirloin, plain or teriyaki style; Choi's ribs; filet mignon; prime rib; beef short ribs; and NY steak. There are some good white meat selections, like chicken breast teriyaki, Cornish game hen, chicken Cordon Bleu, roast duckling, and lamb chops. If none of the above suits you, you could try their sweet and sour frog legs.

Service: ★★★★ Friendly and easy going. A nice group to talk to.

Decor: ★★★★½ The restaurant was opened on St. Patrick's Day, 1973, and has some fine looking wood used in the decor. Check out the arched ceilings in the "greenhouse" (a lounge with lots of plants) next to the bar upstairs. The restaurant is downstairs and contains some stained-glass, antique light fixtures, Navajo rugs, plants, prints and paintings, cedar wood tables and chairs, a fireplace, stone walls, and a slanted wood ceiling with skylights. I counted about 22 tables downstairs for about 90 people. Management says they can hold 150 people in all with additional seating in the lounge, the "greenhouse," a deck outside and the foyer with fireplace. The bar/lounge upstairs has darts and backgammon tables. The bartender says it gets really busy on special weekends in the summer.

Atmosphere: ★★★ Unusual. Everything from strict Mormons to intellectuals to drunks.

EADS

Eads was named after James B. Eads, the engineer who built the Eads Bridge across the Mississippi River in St. Louis. Eads was originally named Dayton, and was located about three miles south of the route of the Missouri Pacific Railroad. When the railroad was completed, the townspeople decided that if the railroad was not going to come to them, they were going to the railroad. They literally picked up their buildings, moved three miles north, and renamed the town Eads.

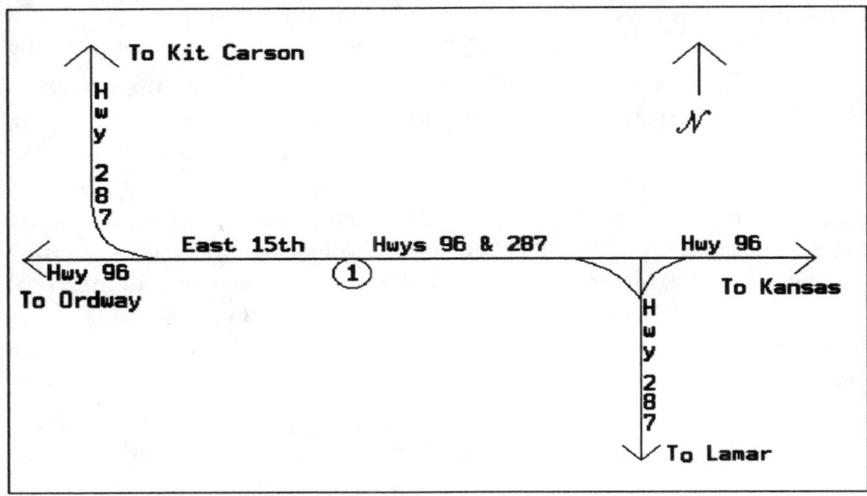

1. COUNTRY KITCHEN RESTAURANT ★★
505 E 15TH (HWY 287-NEXT TO THE MANOR HOUSE MOTEL)
(719)438-9902.

Breakfast/lunch \$, dinner \$\$. 7 days 5:30AM-10PM.
Type: Country. Credit cards are not accepted. They do not have a nonsmoking section and do not serve alcohol.

Food: ★★★½ *Service:* ★★ *Decor:* ★½ *Atmosphere:* ★

The Country Kitchen serves good home-cooked meals, like ham, potatoes and vegetables, and terrific homemade pies. Lunch specials are on the menu FRI, SAT, and SUN. Service is fair. This is a one-room restaurant with eight booths, seven tables, and a counter for a total of 65 people. Baby knits and bibs hang on the wooden wall. Not much atmosphere.

Elizabeth

Elizabeth was named by Governor John Evans in honor of his sister-in-law, Elizabeth Gray Kimbark Hubbard. The Denver & New Orleans Railroad (later the Denver, Texas & Gulf Railroad) reached the site of Elizabeth in 1881. The railroad was promoted and principally owned by Evans. The town was incorporated in 1890.

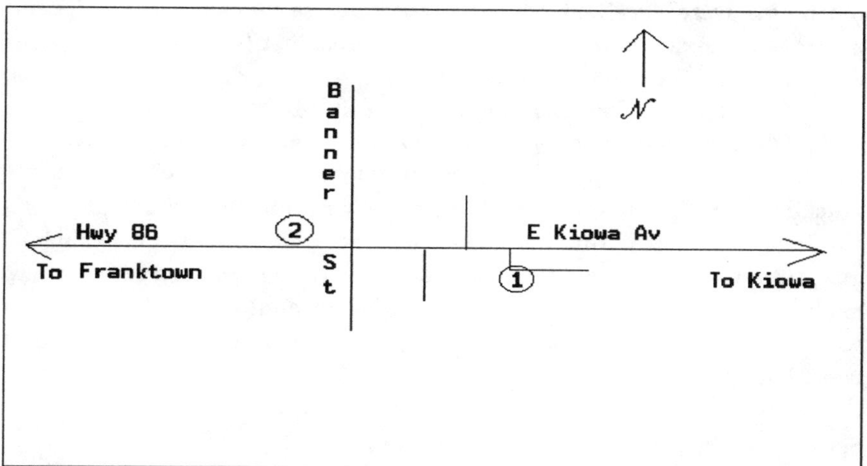

Restaurants and Ratings:	Food	Service	Decor	Atm	Overall
1. BOTANA JUNCTION	★★★½	★★½	★★½	★★★	★★★
2. MONA'S	★★	★★½	★★	★★½	★★½

Botana Junction serves some excellent charbroiled beef fajitas. Both restaurants accept major credit cards and serve alcohol, but do not have nonsmoking sections.

BOTANA JUNCTION ★★★
742 HIGHWAY (303)646-3163

Breakfast $, lunch/dinner $$. MON-THU: 11AM-9PM. FRI: 11AM-10PM. SAT: 6AM-10PM. SUN: 6AM-8PM.
Type: Mexican.

ELIZABETH

Food: ★★★½ The salsa with chips is all tomatoes and very little spice. However, I was surprised by the quality of their beef fajitas: a generous portion of lean, charbroiled beef chunks in two big, thick flour tortillas with lettuce, tomato, guacamole and pico de gallo (a spicy relish) on the side. The tortillas were large enough to hold this platter full. The beans were an unrecognizable mush and the rice fried. They were not bad, but the fajitas were excellent. Breakfast is only served on weekends and includes a Mexican omelet, a Texas style breakfast (two scrambled eggs with chorizo & potatoes, beans and tortilla), huevos rancheros, pancakes, Texas French toast, breakfast burritos, Bloody Mary's and hot cider. The lunch/dinner menu serves basic Mexican food plus fajitas (steak or chicken), chicken burritos, tamales, chimichangas, T-bone steak, carne guisada (beef tips in spicy Mexican gravy with tortillas) chili rellenos, a combination plate, quesadillas, chili, burgers, appetizers (nachos, guacamole dip, taco salad, chicken taco salad, and panchos, which are nachos with homemade beans & carne picada), and desserts like sopapillas, cheese cake with fruit topping, key lime or pecan pie and chocolate tortes.

Service: ★★½ Friendly and satisfactory.

Decor: ★★½ The front dining room has eight booths around the perimeter accompanied by six tables for 60 people. Wreaths made with dried leaves, flowers, chilies and pine cones, a few Mexican artworks, and a collage of magazine and newspaper clippings showing people, places and food decorate the white plaster walls. Electric fans hang from the ceiling which has in-set lights. The front window is used to advertise breakfast specials, by the number, in white chalk. Brown curtains with white polka dots trim the tops of the windows, front and right. The rear dining room, which was not in use the evening that I was there, has seven tables and three booths for 38 and very little decor —
a few Mexican-style decorations, but mostly empty wall space.

Atmosphere: ★★★ "Goldy, oldy" rock tunes ("I got you babe" by Sonny & Cher) play overhead. Local couples, young & old, families, children, teenagers: every age group seemed to be represented here. This was a quiet clientele in pleasant surroundings.

MONA'S ★★½
273 E KIOWA AV (303)646-4900

Dinner $-$$. TUE-THU: 4PM-9PM. FRI-SAT: 4PM-10PM. SUN: 4PM-8PM. Closed MON.
Type: Italian. Carry-out available.

Food: ★★ *Service:* ★★½ *Decor:* ★★ *Atmosphere:* ★★½

The dinner salad came with a tart tasting creamy Italian dressing. The manicotti noodles were stiff and crisp with far too little sauce, most of which was baked onto the dish. Service was sporadic: frantic in the beginning, absent towards the end. This is a small, three-dining-room restaurant in an old house with seating for 45. There is very little decor: a few tiny mirrors, beer signs, knick-knacks, and only two noteworthy artworks. The rooms are so dimly lit I could hardly see what I was eating. This does seem to be a family place, though.

El Rancho Restaurant

EL RANCHO

El Rancho (meaning "the ranch" in Spanish), the restaurant, was established in 1948 by Ray Zipprich.. The town was established later in 1953. The El Rancho Restaurant has its own post office and visitor center.

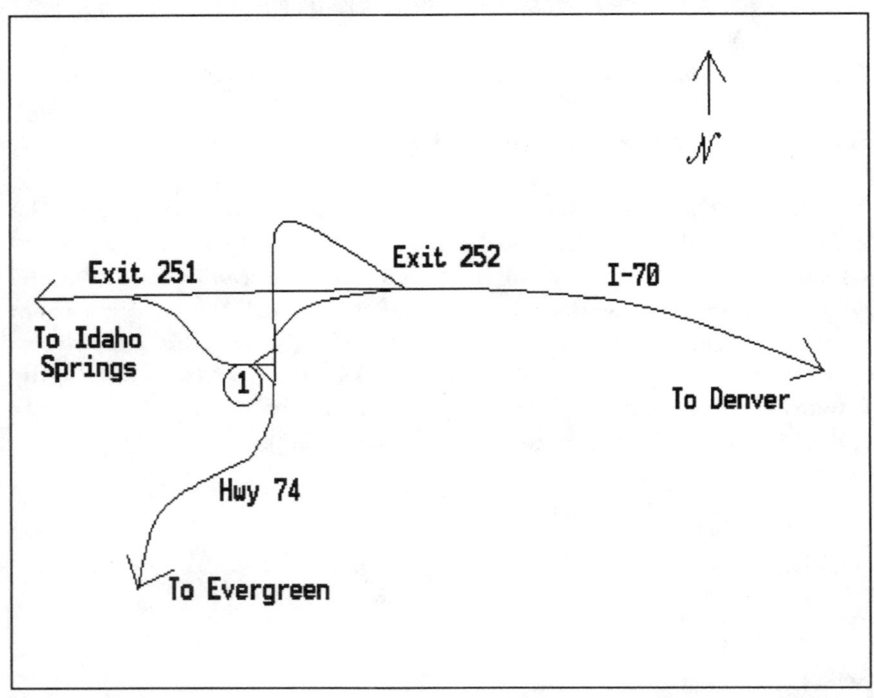

1. EL RANCHO ★★★½
   I-70 EXIT 252W, EXIT 251E (303)526-0661

Sunday buffet $$, breakfast/lunch $-$$, dinner $$$. SEP-APR: MON-FRI 8AM-9PM. SAT 8AM-10PM. SUN 8AM-8PM. MAY-AUG: MON-THU 8AM-9PM. FRI-SAT 8AM-10PM. SUN 8AM-9PM.

Type: Country. 15% service charge added to parties of seven or more. Seniors (62 and over) can receive smaller portions and special pricing on specially marked menu items. $5.95 extra plate charge. Reservations accepted. Wheel chair access. Major credit cards accepted, nonsmoking section provided, pipe or cigar smoking is prohibited, and alcohol is served. Dinner served 365 days a year.

Food: ★★★½ The waitress brought a relish tray while I was deciding what to order. On it were sweet gherkin pickles; black olives; carrot, celery and turnip sticks; cauliflower; broccoli; and their red onion ranch house dressing, which I particularly found to my liking. The small dinner salad with poppyseed dressing had fresh, crisp, and chilled lettuce, tomato slice, cucumber slice, carrot slivers, cabbage and croutons. Dinner was served with soft and sweet homemade rolls. My dinner entree, pork chops, were medium rare, as ordered, tender, juicy, and with a flavorful broiled taste. The baked potato seemed to have more potato taste, like it was fresh from the garden. The meal was complimented by slices of grannie apples and red grapes. Dessert, which was included with the price of the meal, was chiffon pie: creamy, thick, and rich, but the crust was hard and not flaky.

The Sunday buffet offers a variety of waffles, vegetables and homemade pastries. Breakfast items include corned beef hash, eggs Benedict, buttermilk pancakes, Belgian waffles, chicken fried steak, huevos rancheros, broiled boneless trout, and homemade cinnamon rolls.
Lunch features sandwiches (turkey on grilled sourdough, grilled chicken, and cheese & tomato), burgers, including one made with buffalo, French onion soup, western chili, salads (cobb, chicken walnut and taco), and entrees (chicken fried steak, fettuccini primavera marinara, Monterey chicken, fresh trout, and prime rib). Dinner appetizers include stuffed mushrooms, shrimp cocktail, crab claw scampi, onion rings, and smoked buffalo. Entrees feature fried chicken, chicken breast with apple raisin stuffing, orange roughy, salmon steak, jumbo fried shrimp, shrimp scampi, lobster tail, roast prime rib of beef, filet mignon, T-bone, and buffalo steak. Desserts, included with the meal, are chocolate or lemon chiffon pie, or a sundae with your choice of topping. Additional desserts include a double delicious brownie, carrot cake, fruit pies and ice cream.

Service: ★★★ Pleasant, cordial and helpful.

Decor: ★★★½ The El Rancho was built in 1948 and is currently owned by Skip and Mary Roush. There is one large dining area to the right for about 125 people and an adjacent dining area along the front of the building with nine tables for 27 in three sections. There is a smaller dining area in the rear for about 40. Polished wood log beams and posts are used throughout as dividers. There are windows along the front, rear and right sides with potted plants in the sills . Tri-lamp, brass, frosted glass lights on wagon wheels hang from the acoustic ceiling. There is a wood burning stone double fireplace separating the main dining area from the one in the rear. On the main dining area side are a pair of long horns over the mantel and elk racks on either side of the fireplace. With all the windows, there is little room for decor. However, in the back corner of the main dining area is a bookshelf with 600 antique cookbooks from the U.S. and Canada, a pair of cowboy chaps circa 1905-1915 from Kiowa, and a blown up photo of El Rancho Restaurant taken in 1964. Straight back from the entrance is the bar and lounge with five bar stools, a buffalo head, and a lounge area in the shape of a horseshoe with a gas fireplace in the middle. They call the lounge "The Forge". To the left of the entrance is the Trading Post Gift Shop where you can purchase chimes, mandalas and an assortment of other items. Downstairs you will find the banquet room which can serve up to 150 people; the Sweet Shoppe, General Store, and American southwest room & museum, which are opened every day in the summer but only on weekends in the winter; and a patio with a bar that seats about 50 in the summertime. There are three more fireplaces downstairs, making the total five, including two double fireplaces. The walls are decorated with many Indian rugs and antiques, including a rifle, a saddle and branding irons circa 1880.

Atmosphere: ★★★★ Instrumental music plays faintly in the background; at times, it is barely audible over the voices of the diners. Couples, older folks, families and larger groups were all here. With its close proximity to Denver and easy access from I-70, this has become a favorite of the Denver dining crowd. There are terrific views of the mountains with a lot of windows on the south, west and north sides.

EMPIRE

Empire was named after New York, the "Empire" state, and the original home of the men who founded the town.

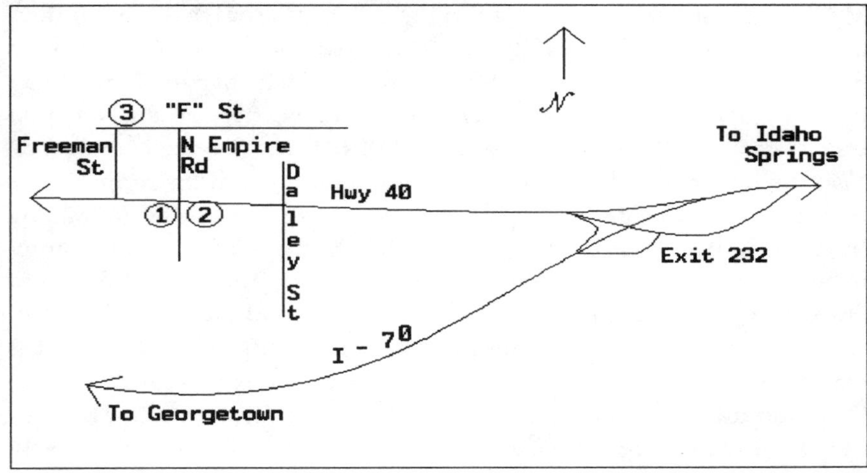

Restaurant and Ratings:	Food	Service	Decor	Atm	Overall
1. Hard Rock Cafe	★★★	★★	★★½	★★★	★★½
2. Jenny's	★★★½	★★★½	★★★	★★	★★★
3. The Peck House	★★★★★	★★★★★	★★★★½	★★★★★	★★★★★

The Peck House serves a marvelous brunch with very attentive service in a serene setting providing great mountain views. Jenny's delivers some good hearty breakfasts for those heading up to the mountains and has some interesting paraphernalia hanging around. The Hard Rock Cafe also dishes out big portions and has a gift shop. All three restaurants accept major credit cards. Only Jenny's offers a nonsmoking section, and only the Hard Rock Cafe does not serve alcohol.

Hard Rock Cafe ★★½
W. side of Hwy. 40 (303)569-2061

Breakfast/Lunch $, dinner $$. THU-TUE 7AM-8PM. Closed WED.
Type: Country.

EMPIRE

Food: ★★★ *Service:* ★★ *Decor:* ★★½ *Atmosphere:* ★★★

My biscuits and gravy were plentiful with lots of sausage. Many of their menu items advertise "lots of" and "extra," so you can expect generous portions. The quality is there also. Dinners, which change nightly, may include a smothered burrito, beef stew, barbecue ribs, or chicken fried steak. Pasta and pizza are offered on FRI & SAT. Service is adequate. Visit the gift shop before you leave. It is interesting and the proprietor is friendly. This is a small one-room restaurant with five booths, four along the right wall and one on the left, two tables in the middle, and a counter in the back. Total seating is for only 36 people. There is artificial red brick in the front and rear. The side walls are wood panel on the lower half and a decorative wallpaper print of swamps, ducks, and elk on the upper half. Painted buckskins on circular racks showing scenes from the Colorado mountains and Monument Valley hang on the wall. They call themselves "the original hard rock cafe," so-named for the "hard rock" mining in the area. The cafe was started in 1932 in a building which is now over 100 years old. It proudly distinguishes itself from the nationally owned corporation which started in the late 1950s when hard rock music was in its heyday. There is a lot of local flavor here.

JENNY'S ★★★
WEST SIDE OF HWY 40 AT NORTH EMPIRE RD (303)569-2570

Breakfast $, lunch/dinner $-$$. MON-FRI 11:30AM-9:30PM. SAT-SUN 8AM-9:30PM.
Type: Country. $1 extra plate charge. $.25 charge for requesting separate checks after order is placed. 15% gratuity for parties of six or more.

Food: ★★★½ If you are really hungry, order their ham and pancakes: a generous 8-10 ounce portion of ham with four huge pancakes. Their breakfast sandwiches and eggs are also quite good. The home fries are real fried potatoes and rate A+. There are daily soup, sandwich, quiche and dessert specials for lunch. The menu includes half-pound burgers, 100% pure beef franks with hot saucy German potato salad, and a meatless enchilada. For those under 12 and "old folkses" there are a few special items. The dinner entrees include top sirloin, jumbo gulf shrimp, fried chicken, scallops, quiche and burritos. Jenny's serves homemade pies, cakes, sundaes, ice cream and other concoctions for dessert.

Service: ★★★½ Fast, friendly and efficient.

Decor: ★★★ This is a two room restaurant with 12 tables for 40 people. From top to bottom, the list of paraphernalia includes two black iron chandeliers, each with four lantern style electric lamps; old white pots & pans; posters advertising "pear's soup", a $3 shoe by W. L. Douglas, and a $100 Phaeton horse-drawn carriage; a shelf with tea kettles, funnels and cans for olive oil, potato chips, and crackers; a mug rack, rug beater, record albums; and a glass cabinet with jars, bottles, pitchers and plates. Even the half and half has a tiny milk bucket container. Quaint and cute.

Atmosphere: ★★ A quiet clientele. People were stopping here on their way up the mountains. However, it was too early in the morning (for me, anyway) to be listening to the rock music they played in the kitchen.

THE PECK HOUSE ★★★★★
"F" STREET AT FREEMAN STREET (EAST OF HWY 40) (303)569-9870

Brunch/lunch $$, dinner $$$$. Year around: SUN 10AM-2PM and 4PM-9PM. MON-THU 4PM-9PM. FRI-SAT 4PM-10PM. JUN-SEP: MON-SAT 11AM-4PM.
Type: Country. The Peck House, built in 1862, is the oldest hotel in Colorado still in operation. It served to accommodate visiting mining executives, was a stage coach stop for stages heading over Berthoud Pass, and was headquarters for miners, prospectors, and sportsmen during Colorado's territorial days. The names of William Tecumseh Sherman and Phineas T. Barnum are on the original hotel guest register.

EMPIRE

Food: ★★★★★ I stopped here for Sunday brunch, which included complimentary champagne, coffee or tea, a fruit cup of fresh strawberries and raspberries, and a plate of homemade breakfast breads (raisin and nut) and coffee cakes. For my entree, I chose the holiday omelet, which on this particular Sunday was a wonderful combination of prosciutto, cream cheese and asparagus. I do not remember ever having a better omelet. It was incredible and was served with fried potatoes. Other Sunday brunch entrees that you may find on the menu are: quail, smoked trout, or steak with eggs; a pâté platter, and alder-smoked salmon. The lunch menu features sandwiches (roast filet mignon, steak and cheese, and BLT with turkey) and entrees (broiled NY steak, barbecued chicken, smoked trout, and a Monte Cristo). The list of dinner entrees sounds delicious: beef tenderloin or NY strip au Poivre (sautéed with peppercorns), steak Béarnaise, sautéed veal medallions, rainbow trout stuffed and baked, shrimp Sarah (broiled and covered with chutney-curry sauce), raspberry duck, brace of quail (roasted), medallions of venison, and Mrs. Peck's beef and oyster pie. Desserts include hot fudge cake, apple strudel, tortes, and raspberry Romanoff (raspberries and cream covered with French vanilla ice cream, Kirschwasser and B&B).

Service: ★★★★★ Superb! Always there to warm the coffee, fill the water and see to your every need. They take great care of their customers.

Decor: ★★★★½ The main dining room, to the left of the entrance, has 13 red-clothed tables and 40 comfortable hardwood rib-backed chairs with armrests. A small room with a piano and five tables for an additional 10 diners lies between the entrance and main dining room. Red velvet curtains and red-clothed napkins compliment the red-brick fireplace. A pair of deer racks adorn both ends of the mantel. A few small windows offer terrific views of the mountains and pines. A pick, a hay saw, a branding iron, and frosted, globe-shaped, brass lamps hang from the white plaster walls. The decor includes prints of Pikes Peak, Colorado City and Empire City; a portrait of Gracie Peck; and old photos of Big Chief Mill and Empire during its gold mining days.

Atmosphere: ★★★★★ Pleasant classical music and great mountain views in a serene setting. A perfect place for Sunday brunch. What a delight!

ESTES PARK

Formerly known as Estes Park Village, the town was named after its first permanent settlers, Joel Estes and his family, who came to this beautiful mountain-enclosed meadow in 1859 and later built a cabin on Fish Creek. Today, Estes Park is the entrance to Rocky Mountain National Park.

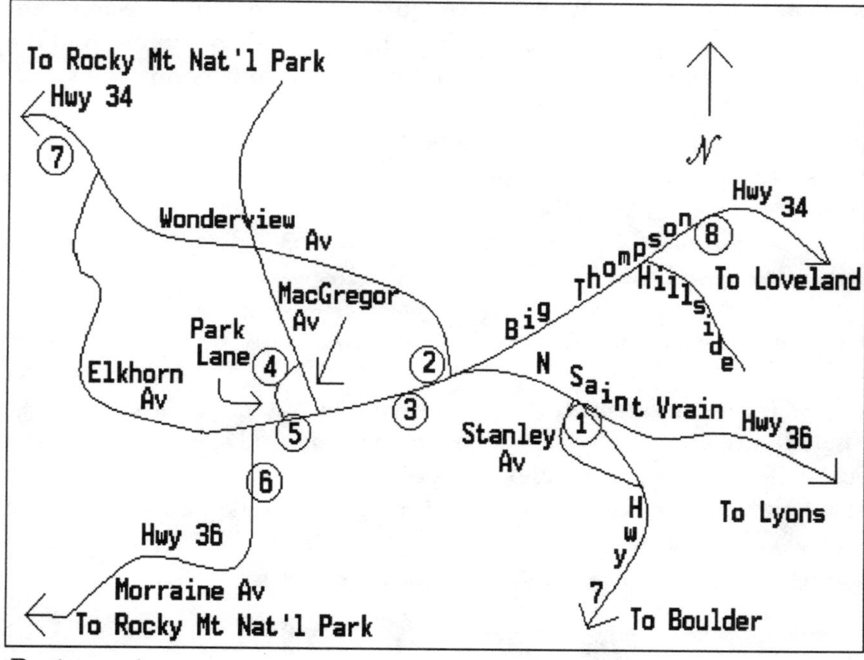

Restaurants and Ratings:	Food	Service	Decor	Atm	Overall
1. ASPENS	★★	★★½	★★★	★★★	★★½
2. ELKHORN JUNCTION	★★	★★	★★	★★	★★
3. ED'S CANTINA	★★★	★★½	★★½	★★	★★½
4. GAZEBO	★★★★½	★★★★	★★★★½	★★★★½	★★★★½
5. LA CASA	★★★★	★★★	★★★½	★★½	★★★½
6. MOLLY B	★★½	★★★½	★★★½	★★½	★★★
7. NICKY'S	★★★★	★★★	★★★★	★★★★½	★★★★
8. ROTH'S	★★★★	★★★	★★½	★★½	★★★

ESTES PARK

I found the food, ambience, scenery, even the service, to be superior at the Gazebo. For a good burger, sandwich or oysters, go to Nicky's. For great Cajun or Mexican food, the place to be is La Casa. Unless otherwise stated, all restaurants in Estes Park accept major credit cards and have nonsmoking sections. The only restaurant that does not accept credit cards nor serve alcohol is the Elkhorn Junction. It, Ed's Cantina, and the Molly B do not have nonsmoking sections; all the others do.

ASPENS (IN THE HOLIDAY INN) ★★½
101 S. ST. VRAIN AVE. (303)586-2332

Breakfast $, lunch $-$$, dinner $$-$$$. 7 Days 7:30AM-9:00PM.
Type: Family. The entire dining room is nonsmoking.

***Food:* ★★ *Service:* ★★½ *Decor:* ★★★ *Atmosphere:* ★★★**

I thought their barbecued ribs were only fair. Service was satisfactory. This is a one-room restaurant with two large plants behind a wall in the center. Total seating is for about 80 people, mostly in booths. The chairs and benches have peach cushions with a pastel ripple pattern. Sketches and watercolors decorate the walls. The room is well lit with in-set ceiling lights. This is a quiet, family-style restaurant.

ELKHORN JUNCTION ★★
401 E. ELKHORN (303)586-8472

Lunch/dinner $. MAY-SEP: 7 days 10:30AM-9PM. OCT-APR: 7 days 11AM-8PM.
Type: Diner.

***Food:* ★★ *Service:* ★★ *Decor:* ★★ *Atmosphere:* ★★**

This is a typical small-town diner. The single menu includes burgers, fries, onion rings, soup and salad, hot dogs, patty melts, barbecued beef, chicken strips, chicken or turkey & Swiss sandwiches, shakes, malts, floats, sundaes and cones. Place order and pick up at counter. Total seating is for 28 people at booths and tables. This is a small place with a hanging light fixture with antlers and pictures of trains and rail yards. More suitable for children and adolescents.

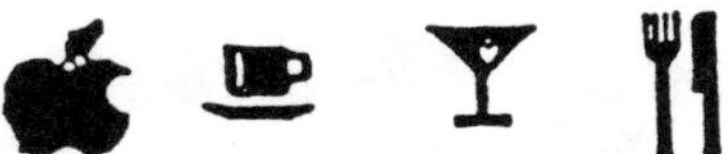

ED'S CANTINA ★★½
362 E. ELKHORN AVE. (303)586-2919

Breakfast/lunch/dinner $. Seven days 7AM-9PM (8PM on SUN-THU in winter).
Type: Mexican. Take-out available. They have installed a couple of "smoke eaters" in the ceiling.

***Food:* ★★★ *Service:* ★★½ *Decor:* ★★½ *Atmosphere:* ★★**

Their taco salad is not half bad. Breakfast has a few specialties like Belgian waffles, huevos rancheros and breakfast burritos. The lunch/dinner menu features nachos, guacamole salad, Buffalo wings, and homemade vegetable soup for starters; taco and seafood salads; burgers, a marinated chicken sandwich, chicken or steak fajitas, Mexican combination platters, and specialties like a stuffed burrito or taco burger. Mexican dishes also come a la carte. There is a children's menu and, for dessert, fried apple pie or turtle cheesecake. Service is satisfactory. This is a sports bar restaurant with country flavor: pennants, posters and pictures of football, baseball and basketball occupy most of the wall space with a large-screen television in the corner. There are two rooms with total seating for about 100 people. The atmosphere fits the decor.

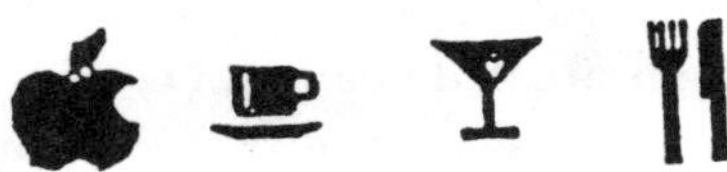

GAZEBO ★★★★½
225 PARK LANE (ACROSS FROM CITY HALL) (303)586-9564
Sunday brunch/lunch $$, dinner $$-$$$. SUN 11:30AM-4PM. MON-SAT 11:30AM-4PM and 5PM-9PM.

Type: American/Continental. The entire restaurant is nonsmoking. 20% senior (over 60) discount off total dinner guest check. No personal checks without check guarantee card. Special diet or menu requests prepared for $1.50 service charge.

Food: ★★★★½ This was my favorite place in Estes. The Sunday brunch comes with Champagne, fruit and muffin. The entree selections include eggs Benedict or Florentine, a Monte Cristo, quiche du jour, Belgian waffles and California chicken. An appetizer menu is offered anytime: chicken fingers, ground steak wrapped in bacon, baked French onion soup, sauteed mushrooms and shrimp cocktail. For lunch, there's a wide variety of salads, pastas (fettuccini Alfredo, primavera or carbonara), burgers, sandwiches (turkey melt, roast beef & Cheddar, French dip, Reuben, club, vegetarian, or broiled chicken), entrees (jumbo shrimp, NY strip, clams, and baked halibut), and, their specialty, spuntini: a hollowed-out homemade bread filled with chili, beef stew, seafood or chicken. The dinner menu is a combination of fowl, seafood, beef and veal: fried chicken, chicken Dijon or Parmesan, stuffed fillet of sole, baked halibut, shrimp scampi, Rocky Mountain trout, king crab legs, filet mignon, prime rib, steak Diane, steak au poivre (with black peppercorn sauce), liver & onions, veal Parmesan and Wiener schnitzel. For a lighter meal, there's fruit with assorted cheeses, and stir-fried vegetables or chicken. The house specialty is Khyber chicken or beef.

Service: ★★★★ Friendly and willing to talk about the restaurant, their meals and history.

Decor: ★★★★½ The Gazebo moved from 205 Virginia Dr in March, 1992, right before this book went to press. Their former location had indoor seating for about 50 people with a balcony for about 80, plus additional seating upstairs. They were situated in an "out of the way" place accessed by walking up brick steps, past a waterfall, to a third level from the street. Perhaps that is why they decided on the move: to get more visibility.

Atmosphere: ★★★★½ Their former location was very comfortable and quiet and catered to a professional clientele. Their new location should be just as pleasant.

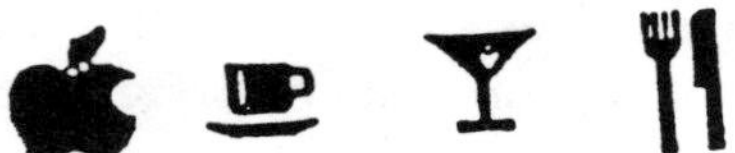

LA CASA ★★★½
222 E. ELKHORN (303)586-2807

Lunch/dinner $$. SUN-THU 11AM-9PM. FRI-SAT 11AM-10PM. (Closing times are one hour later between MAY and SEP.
Type: Mexican. $1 for special requests. 15% gratuity for groups of eight or more. Out of town checks accepted with guarantee card and adequate identification.

Food: ★★★★ I recommend the blackened prime rib, Cajun-style. It is sure to open your sinuses and please your palate. It is served with paprika potatoes, carrots, beans, kiwi, and a whole shrimp that will watch every bite you take. I recommend turning the shrimp to one side and leaving it alone. You might lose your appetite if you try cracking it open.

This restaurant's several-page lunch/dinner menu begins with appetizers: popcorn shrimp, guacamole dip, chili con queso, gator legs (chicken wings), super nachos and a 35-item salad bar. The lunch selections include blackened redfish, seafood gumbo (which I also recommend. It's served in an edible Parisian bread bowl), shrimp scampi, chicken breast, burgers, sandwiches (Cajun chicken breast, turkey & Swiss croissant, blackened prime rib, and French dip), and Mexican a la carte (soft tacos, enchiladas, and chili rellenos). The Mexican listing is available all day and includes an Estorito (named after Estes Park, it is a flour tortilla with beef, chicken, turkey or vegetarian frijoles), chimichanga, beef or chicken fajita, and soft taco. The international dinner menu, served after 4PM, has Cajun, Mexican, Italian, Indian and American choices: steak with bell pepper, tomato & onion; blackened or grilled trout, chicken breast, blackened or regular prime rib, blackened redfish, lime chicken, seafood fettuccini, blackened shrimp, shrimp scampi, and chicken Marsala. Domestic, imported (Mexican, Canadian, Dutch) and nonalcoholic beer, wine and Margaritas are available. Finally, the dessert menu has some interesting items, such as cherry or apple turnovers, hot pecan goo (poured over vanilla ice cream), pecan pie, cakes, mousse, and ice cream. Before you leave the restaurant, pick up a bottle of Chef Lee's gourmet voodoo sauce for marinating: only three calories per ounce.

Service: ★★★ Friendly.

Decor: ★★★½ This restaurant has two rooms and a bar. The front room will seat about 40 people. The window shelves have figurines of conquistadors carrying fish nets or bottles. Southwest Indian tapestries adorn the wall. Lamps and artificial flower baskets hang from the ceiling. On one wall, there is a model of an old Spanish sailing ship.

Atmosphere: ★★½ They feature live guitar music, but the clientele is loud and annoying.

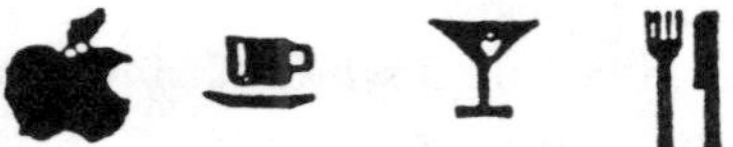

MOLLY B ★★★
200 MORAINE AVE. (303)586-2766

Breakfast/lunch $, dinner $$. APR-OCT: 7 days 6AM-9PM. NOV-MAR: 7 days 6:30AM-3PM.
Type: Country. 15% gratuity added for groups of six or more.

Food: ★★½ I had an average bacon & eggs breakfast here. However, there are some more interesting, and probably better, selections if you have enough appetite: a tortilla stuffed with scrambled eggs, potatoes and cheese; scrambled eggs, Mexican style, on a flour tortilla; quiche; crêpes Benedict; steak; and an egg & muffin. The lunch/dinner menu has appetizers: a fried vegetables & cheese plate, nachos grande, potato skins, or chilled shrimp; sandwiches: Reuben, turkey Reuben, and a gyro; burgers; light selections: quesadillas, snow crab (a half-pound), a 12-inch stuffed tortilla or quiche du jour; and vegetarian selections: a crêpe, pasta primavera, a 12-inch tortilla stuffed with vegetables, or lasagna. The dinner entrees, served after 5PM, are snow crab (a full-pound), mahi

mahi, and NY strip. There are fresh fish selections daily and prime rib on Thursday and Saturdays.

Service: ★★★½ Professional.

Decor: ★★★½ This restaurant has two small rooms with four booths in the front room for 16 people and total seating for about 35. The building is colonial style with wood tables, wood beams on a stucco ceiling, wood panel walls on the lower half, and wallpaper on the upper half. The kitchen is in view. There are stained-glass window dividers, and hanging lamps and plants. Specials are listed on the blackboard over the entrance to the back room.

Atmosphere: ★★½ Local clientele.

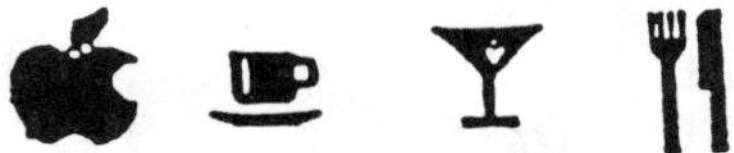

NICKY'S ★★★★
1350 FALLRIVER RD. (303)586-5376

Breakfast/lunch $-$$, dinner $$-$$$. 7 days 7AM-10PM.
Type: Steak. Menu designates "good for you" items approved by the American Heart Association.

Food: ★★★★ They have two big menus for breakfast and lunch/dinner. The breakfast menu has fruits & juices, breads & pastries, Canadian bacon, trout, Belgian waffles, and eggs Benedict. The lunch/dinner menu has a combination of seafood, steak, chops, Greek and Italian food. For appetizers there is an oyster bar which also serves a seafood cocktail, crab and shrimp. There are light sandwiches such as corned beef, roast beef or pork; deluxe sandwiches including several burger selections, Italian sausage, fish, and an open-face Reuben; and hot sandwiches with roast beef, pork, turkey, or meat loaf. The Greek & Italian specials are souvlaki, Greek salad, spaghetti, and gyros. Seafood dinners include Rocky Mountain trout, perch, jumbo fried shrimp, red snapper, and walleyed pike. The list of steaks and chops include filet mignon, T-bone, center-cut pork chops, and lamb chops. They also have a choice of crêpes: crab meat; spinach; or mushroom, ham & cheese. Cold specialties feature a baked ham or turkey plate and a stuffed tomato. Specialty dinners include grilled ham steak, breaded veal cutlet, fried calves liver, southern fried chicken, chicken fried steak, and honey-dipped fried chicken. There is a large selection of desserts such as sundaes, homemade cheesecake, fruit and cream pies, German layer cake, rice pudding, shakes, and malts.

Service: ★★★ Most adequate.

Decor: ★★★★ This restaurant can seat 140 people in two large rooms with a wood-beam ceiling. Decor consists of a front window loaded with plants, a brick column, American Indian rugs, a small salad bar and pewter cups & plates.

Atmosphere: ★★★★½ Relaxed.

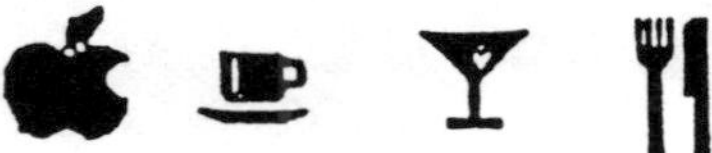

ROTH'S ★★★
HWY. 34 EAST (303)586-6194

Breakfast $, lunch $-$$, dinner $$. OCT-APR: 7 days 7:30AM-2PM and 4:30PM-8PM. MAY-SEP: 6:30AM-2PM and 4:30PM-9:30PM.
Type: Family.

Food: ★★★★ They have great barbecued ribs that I would recommend to any ribs lover. This is good, home-cooked food at reasonable prices.

Service: ★★★ Friendly and homey.

Decor: ★★½ This is a large restaurant that can seat over 100 people with windows all around and not much in the way of decor.

Atmosphere: ★★½ A pleasant and peaceful atmosphere in a country setting aimed at families.

EVANS

Evans was named after John Evans, the second Colorado Territorial Governor, serving during the Civil War from 1862 to 1865, and former president of the Denver Pacific Railroad. Of historical interest is the fact that John Evans founded Northwestern University in Evanston, Ill., which was also named for him. He also was a founder of the University of Denver.

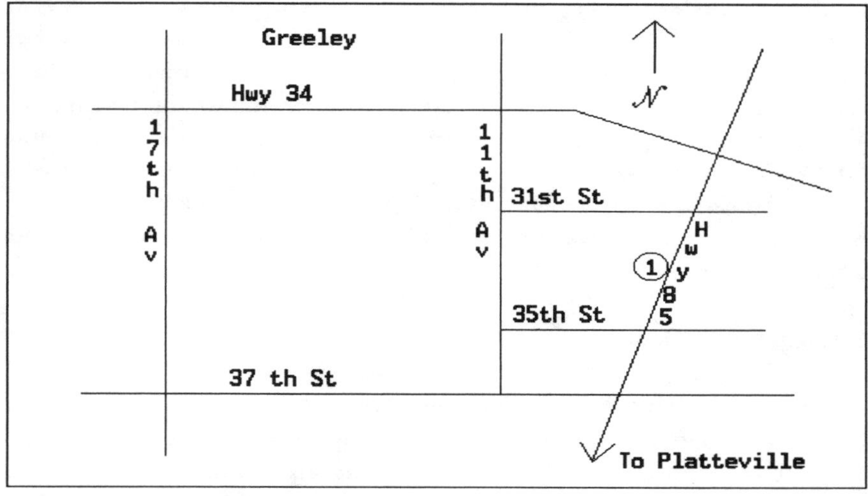

1. PORTOFINO'S ★★★
   3301 U.S. HWY. 85 (WEST SIDE, IN THE HERITAGE MOTEL) (303)339-5900

Breakfast $, dinner $$-$$$. MON-FRI 6AM-9:30AM. SAT-SUN 6AM-11AM. MON-THU 6PM-8:30PM. FRI-SAT 6PM-9PM.
Type: Italian. Major credit cards are accepted. They do not provide a nonsmoking section and alcohol is served.

Food: ★★ All dinner entrees are served with breadsticks and marinara sauce. As it turned out, this was the best part of the meal. The marinara sauce was just the sort of thing that I would indulge in if I were doing some homecooking. The dinner itself was less appealing. The noodles were stiff and rubbery. The ingredients — spinach, Italian sausage, and tomatoes — were not of the "garden fresh" variety. The dinner menu features Italian food, steaks and seafood. The list of appetizers includes shrimp cocktail, stuffed mushrooms, calamari, Buffalo wings, mozzarella marinara, and antipasto. There is a soup of the day along with minestrone and onion. The choices of salad are Caesar's, Portofino's (with sliced meats, cheeses & egg), and a house dinner salad. The Italian specialties include a stuffed baked chicken breast, breaded chicken breast in a marinara sauce, sautéed veal with mushrooms & onions, veal scallopini in white wine, pasta (lasagna, canneloni, fettuccine Alfredo or pesto); spaghetti marinara, in a meat sauce, or with meatballs; and pizza. There are three steaks to choose from: filet mignon, T-bone, and a chopped sirloin in Italian seasonings. The seafood selections are shrimp scampi, linguine vengole (with clams), seafood marinara (shrimp & scallops with fettuccine), and the catch of the day. A children's menu offers chicken nuggets, hamburger, lasagna, spaghetti and a cheese melt. An Italian sausage sandwich and an Italian sub are available if you are not hungry enough for a full meal. Homemade desserts, domestic and imported beer, and a wine list are also available.

Service: ★★★ Good.

Decor: ★★★½ This is a one-room restaurant with nine booths and eight tables for 74 people. There is a fireplace in the middle of the room, plants hanging from the ceiling between the booths, and windows on opposite sides: one side faces the highway, the other faces the bar/lounge. The tables are decorated in green and white; the cushioned seats are orange and rust. The paintings in the booths are of islands in the misty clouds. They reminded me of the fjords of Milford Sound in New Zealand.

Atmosphere: ★★★ Quiet and comfortable.

Special Note: Despite the three-star rating, this place did little justice to the Italian seaport it is named after. I traveled by car from Genoa to Portofino, about a one-and-a-half hour drive the way Italians drive in the mountains, when I was just 14 years old. It was an unforgettable night: a dozen 18 and 19 year old Italians and me in three Fiats racing from Genoa to Portofino just to stop for coffee, listen to some music, and race back to Genoa. It was a fun night I just had to mention!

EVERGREEN

Formerly called The Post, after Amos F. Post, the son-in-law of Thomas Bergen who first settled nearby Bergen Park, the name was changed to Evergreen by D.P. Wilmot in honor of the huge evergreen trees in the area. Ute Indians used to camp along nearby Soda Creek. Evergreen has had a varied history of trappers, traders, gold miners, ranchers and lumberjacks.

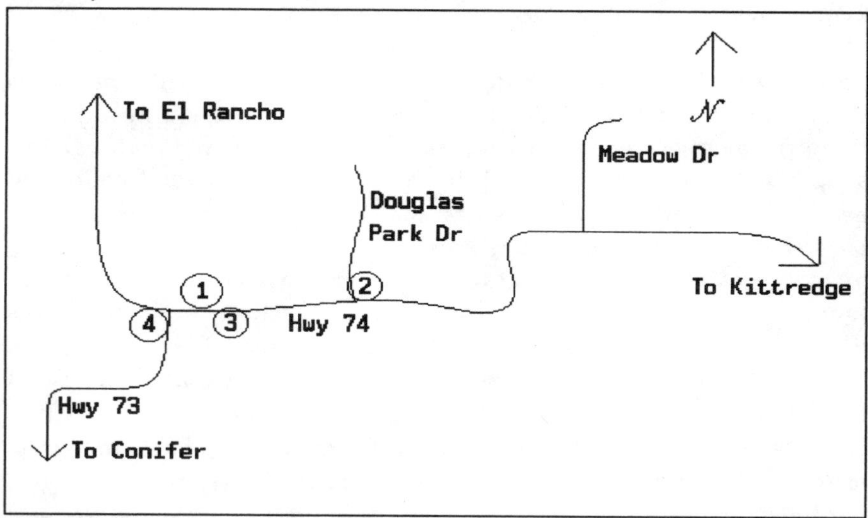

Restaurants and Ratings:	Food	Service	Decor	Atm	Overall
1. JONATHAN WOLF'S	★★★	★★★	★★★	★★★½	★★★
2. LITTLE BEAR	★★★½	★	★	★	★½
3. LIZBETH'S	★★★★	★★★½	★★★★	★★★	★★★½
4. RIVER SAGE	★★★★½	★★★★	★★★½	★★★★½	★★★★

The River Sage, which borrows a little on history and legend, serves delicious homemade soups, breads, sauces and desserts on a most appealing location on Bear Creek. Lizbeth's, also on Bear Creek, is modern and elegant and offers excellent crêpes and other continental cuisine. Jonathan Wolf's prepares a combination of American and Continental dishes under the pictorial auspices of their favorite wild animal.

EVERGREEN

JONATHAN WOLF'S ★★★
28215 HWY 74 (303)674-3173

Sunday brunch $$, breakfast/lunch $-$$, dinner $$-$$$$. MON-TUE 11AM-2:30PM and 5PM-9PM. WED-FRI 7:30AM-2:30PM and 5PM-9PM. SAT 8:30AM-2:30PM and 5PM-9:30PM. SUN 8:30AM-2:30PM and 5PM-8:30PM. Type: American/Continental.

Food: ★★★ I ordered half a dozen clams on the half shell. They were chilled and delicious. (They always are.) I could make a meal just of these. Dinner was served with warm rolls and apple & nut muffins. The soup was a beef burgundy with fresh mushroom slices and chunks of beef in a thick parsley flavored broth. Excellent! The entree, bayou blackened chicken, came in a rich cream sauce with a touch of tabasco, mixed vegetables and baked potato. The chicken was moist and tender, topped with tiny bay shrimp. The Sunday brunch menu features eggs with several tempting selections: asparagus, veal medallions, and Cajun blackened catfish. At noon, croissants, salads, burgers and a smothered burrito are added to the fare. The breakfast menu offers Belgian waffles, French toast with melted cheese and blueberry sauce, and a combination of bay shrimp, mushrooms and cream cheese scrambled with two eggs. For lunch, you can choose from specials like chicken picata and linguini Napoli. Lighter dinner fares feature vegetable strudel and pork chops, while the entree list includes elk medallions Diane, Wiener schnitzel, and veal coachella. There are several homemade pasta selections to choose from as well: chicken Tuscany, spinach fettuccine and chicken Florentine. A children's section is a part of each menu.

Service: ★★★ Satisfactory. Quick on the water refills and plate take-aways. I thought the bus girl did a great job.

Decor: ★★★ The nonsmoking section is the first dining room to the left with 13 hardwood tables that seat 46. Pictures of wolves and a dried-flower arrangement decorate the stucco walls. Below the stucco is white painted wood with dark green trim and borders. The door and window frames are in the same dark green. Dim lighting is provided by brass, six-light chandeliers; brass, two-light wall fixtures; and kerosene lamps.

The smoking section has a mountain goat's head hanging over the entrance, 10 tables for 34, and flower prints and wicker cages with flower arrangements for decoration. On top of the wall separating the two dining sections is a coral tank, sans fish. The bar/lounge to the right of the entrance hosts two tables and three booths for 18 and seven barstools. Sailing ship wallpaper, photos of parties and rafting, and more wolf pictures in the booths adorn the casual surroundings.

Atmosphere: ★★★½ A mix of easy listening, jazz, instrumental and country music plays comfortably overhead. It looked like some regulars were visiting the evening that I was there.

LITTLE BEAR ★½
MAIN STREET (303)674-9991

Lunch/Dinner $. 7 days 11AM-11:30PM.
Type: tavern.

***Food:* ★★★½ *Service:* ★ *Decor:* ★ *Atmosphere:* ★**

Their Bratwurst is very tender and tasty. Their onion rings, which are quite good, are big and come in a generous serving as well. I saw a lot of people ordering pizza and it also looked good. The crust appeared to be thick and fluffy with lots of mozzarella cheese on top. Order and pick up at the counter. The service is slow. I waited 20-25 minutes for my Bratwurst and onion rings at a time when they were not particularly busy. This is a bar/restaurant. The bar has 15 stools on three sides. The left dining area is more subdued and has seven tables, rather tightly spaced, for 32 people. The right side has about 16 small triangular tables for about 40 people, plus a row of tables along the wall for 20 more. There is also an upstairs loft with a double row of wood benches overlooking the stage where the band plays. There's room for another 50+ up there. The downstairs has a low ceiling and is poorly lit. There are dozens of license plates and road signs, photos of parties from "days gone by," carved graffiti in the woodwork, and a row of skis. There was one road sign in particular that I liked. It was a yellow diamond-shaped warning sign with a picture of a kangaroo and the words "kangaroos next 18 miles" — evidently brought back from Australia. The men's room was one of the dirtiest in Colorado. Their sign on the men's room door read "caution, wet floor" and they meant it. Beware! When I arrived, about 7:30PM, hard rock music was playing — Steppenwolf stuff. However, the band which came on later was better. They played "new age" and "blues." There is a small dance floor.

LIZBETH'S ★★★½
28186 HWY 74 (303)670-0710

Sunday brunch $$-$$$, lunch $$, dinner $$-$$$$. TUE-SAT 11AM-2:30PM and 5PM-9PM. SUN 10AM-3PM. Closed MON.
Type: Continental. The entire restaurant is nonsmoking.

Food: ★★★★ The leaf lettuce salad with sesame seed vinaigrette dressing was simple, fresh, and quite good. The entree, vegetable gateau of crêpes, was delectable: an open-face crêpe with flaky crust and a layered offering of creamed broccoli, mushrooms and carrots in a fresh basil sauce with a sprig of fresh basil (so intoxicating it should be illegal!); served with red potatoes cut into swirls with a carrot peeler. My dinner was complimented with some excellent fresh French roast coffee. The Sunday brunch entrees include brioche beef Burgundy, scallops St. Jacque, and peaches and cream French toast. The lunch menu starts off with gravlax, baked brie, and roasted peppers with chevre (goat cheese) as appetizers; French onion au gratin soup; and salads. Featured on the list of entrees are pasta primavera, grilled filet of salmon or tuna, Wiener schnitzel, bouché bourguignonne, and chevre or oriental chicken supreme. The dinner appetizers offer smoked salmon with caviar caper cream and grilled & chilled shrimp. For dinner entrees, select either rouleau of salmon, chicken supreme Dijonnaise, cornish hen, sauteed medallions of veal, or strudel of beef bourguignonne. To finish your meal, souffle au Grand Marnier and a pecan Chantilly roll are on the dessert menu.

Service: ★★★½ A little slow getting seated, but my meal was served quickly. The waitress was a very pleasant young lady.

Decor: ★★★★ The bar at the entrance has seven tan leather stools. Beyond is the dining area with seating for 64 at tables with white cloths and booths with emerald green cushions. The decor in here is modern, with in-set ceiling lights over the bar, white columns & arches, and sconces. Simple, yet elegant, describes the prints of fruit, flowers, ships in a harbor, and a mother cow with her calf. The tables are set with kerosene lamps, solid white and black plates, white napkins, and fresh columbines. Seating is on comfortable tan cloth-cushioned chairs in bronze metal frames. A series of glass doors extends along the back and far right wall. There is a gas fireplace in the back corner with no mantel, but an adjacent statute of Don Quixote (an appropriate place for him, I thought). A patio out back extends along two sides of the building and seats 30 at 15 tables directly above Bear Creek, with ducks floating by.

Atmosphere: ★★★ Vivaldi's Four Seasons played pleasantly in the background, three outspoken middle-aged women gossiped in the foreground about houses and other peoples' children, and a quieter group of five older adults and one child spoke quietly amongst themselves. A bit on the high-class side. An obvious attraction for yuppies.

RIVER SAGE ★★★★
4651 HWY 73 (303)674-2914

Weekend brunch $$, breakfast $-$$, lunch $$, dinner $$-$$$. MON-THU 7AM-8:30PM (9PM in summer). FRI 7AM-9PM. SAT 7:30AM-9:30PM. SUN 7:30AM-8:30PM (9PM in summer).
Type: Seafood. Personal checks with I.D. welcome. Reservations recommended on weekends and holidays. Smoking only on the deck.

While some restaurants have histories, this restaurant has a dream. There is a legend of an old wise man who lived long ago on the banks of Bear

Creek. He lived a reverent, harmonious life, respected the wisdom and balance of nature, and appreciated the gift of life. His life reflected the tranquility and gentle energy of the water by which he lived, and he became known as the River Sage. The dream behind this restaurant is to pass on some of the wisdom and inspiration of the Old River Sage by providing nourishment for both body and spirit.

Food: ★★★★½ The corn chowder bisque came in a crock bowl, was thick, creamy, and lightly seasoned, and was served with corn bread. It was very good. The entree was a mesquite-grilled, yellow-fin tuna in a dill butter sauce. It was mild, tender and cooked medium rare. While I liked the lightly grilled taste, I would have liked more mesquite flavor. It was still a delicious dish, served with baked potato and fresh vegetables. All their soups, breads, sauces and desserts are homemade. The weekend brunch specials feature eggs Benedict or Florentine, a seafood scramble, and a fresh trout and eggs platter. Their regular breakfast menu is most innovative, offering turkey sausage, scrambled tofu, and an assortment of whole-grain buttermilk pancakes. You can make your own omelets with your choice of 20 additions, including soy cheese, roast chicken, and jicama. Their lunch menu is no less innovative, or extensive. Their sandwiches, served closed or "bubbly" style (open-faced with broiled cheeses), include spinach & mushrooms, curried tuna, and turkey with roasted cashews and raisins. They have specialties like spinach or seafood lasagna, spanikopita (a Greek filo pastry with feta & ricotta cheeses), tandoor chicken, and a southwestern tempeh sauté. If you like mesquite grill, you can have Rocky Mountain trout, chicken, or organic beef prepared that way. Four wok selections, homemade soups, and salads are also available. The dinner offerings include fresh seafood (a Caribbean sauté, Cajun sea scallops, seafood lasagna, or blackened red snapper), mesquite-grilled fresh fish (swordfish, marlin, shark, tuna, coho salmon, or trout), and chicken specialties (Tahitian, blackened Cajun, Indonesian, tandoor, grilled barbecue or Baja style). If you have room for dessert, you can choose from a flan, mocha custard pie, baklava, white raspberry chocolate swirl cheesecake, tofu blueberry cheesecake, or carrot cake.

Service: ★★★★ Very friendly, helpful, pleasant, courteous and relaxed.

Decor: ★★★½ The restaurant sits right on Bear Creek with a walkway along the river and a foot bridge connecting Highway 74. Dining inside is in two small areas that seat a total of 43. A deck used in the summer can seat an additional 32. From inside the restaurant you can look out onto Bear Creek or inside to the mall. The decor consists of studio lights, brass wall lanterns, Indian art works in colored pencil, pen & ink prints, a black cast-iron wood-burning stove, wood carvings of faces, amethyst logs, hanging wood logs, and a lithograph of a bald eagle.

Atmosphere: ★★★★½ The restaurant has a romantic tone with its unique setting on the river. They play new age music. My waitress stated that the deck was extremely enjoyable in the summer. I'll bet she's right.

River Sage Restaurant - Evergreen

FLORENCE

Ute Indians lived in the area around Florence in the fifteenth century, and later, French and Spanish trappers and explorers passed this way. The town was formerly known as Frazerville after "Uncle Joe Frazer who developed the coal mines in nearby Coal Creek. Florence, named after the youngest daughter of Senator James A. McCandless, was founded in 1872. Oil was discovered here in 1862 making the Oil Creed oil field the second oldest in the U.S. McCandless was the first to refine oil in Florence.

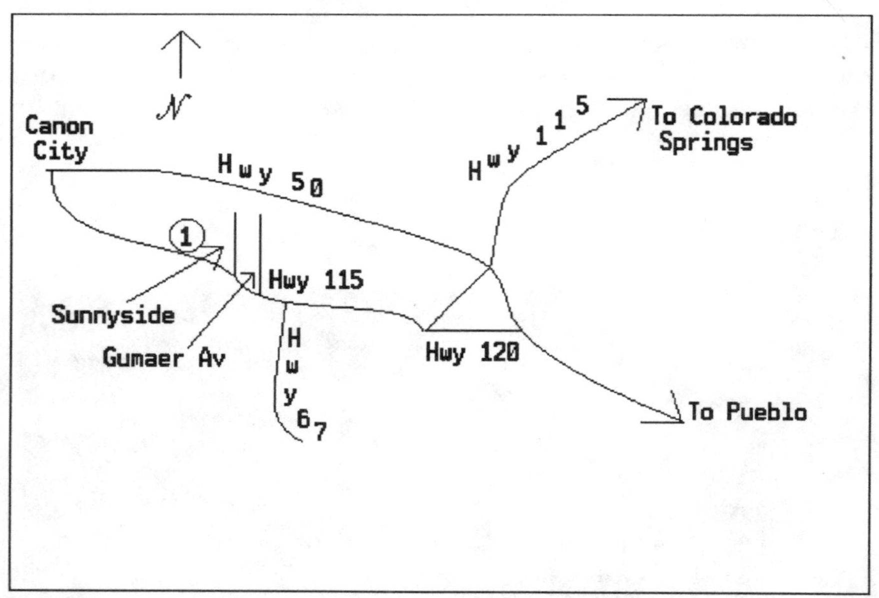

1. MORELLI'S ★★
   727 EAST MAIN STREET (719)784-3798

Lunch $, dinner $$-$$$. WED-SAT: 11AM-2PM and 4:30PM-9PM. SUN: 11AM-8PM. Closed MON-TUE.
Type: Italian (and steaks).

Food: ★★★ *Service:* ★ *Decor:* ★★★ *Atmosphere:* ★★

I arrived here on a week night at 8:40PM. The sign outside said "Open" but the door was locked. When I knocked, a little girl on the other side asked "who is it?!" "A customer" I responded. (Who did she think it was, the Big Bad Wolf?). The little girl said "we close at nine". I said "It's only twenty to nine". She opened the door and let me in. Actually, I was surprised they served me. The place was empty and they told me they had only taken in $12 that evening. They blamed the slow night on the State Fair in nearby Pueblo. The little girl who answered the door also waited on me. She failed to bring my soup and salad and did not refill my water. Upon serving me four cold pieces of Italian bread, she asked if I wanted butter and when I responded with "yes" she wanted to know "how many?" (butter patties). My personal feeling is that 10 year olds should not be waiting tables, especially when they should be getting ready for bed. As for my meal, I ordered the taconels. (No, they aren't Italian style tacos!). They are wide pasta noodles with tomato sauce, served with a meatball & sausage. There was plenty of zesty sauce, but the noodles were a little stiff. The restaurant is in an old building decorated with a large square red-brick fireplace leading up to a vaulted ceiling, more Mexican decor than Italian, and sandstone paintings. They serve meals on three floor levels and a deck that looks out over the entrance.

FORT LUPTON

Fort Lupton was originally a trading post called Fort Lancaster by Lieutenant Lancaster P. Lupton, a member of Colonel Henry Dodge's 1935 expedition to the Rocky Mountains. The post was abandoned in the 1840s but was later used as a mail station between Missouri and Denver.

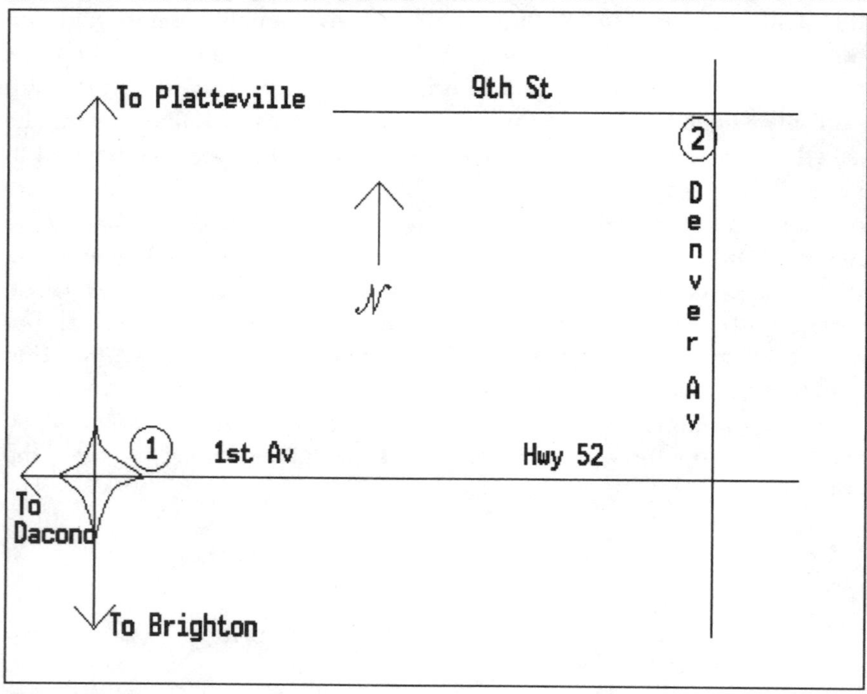

Restaurants and Ratings:	Food	Service	Decor	Atm	Overall
1. BRANDING IRON	★★★½	★★★	★★★½	★★★	★★★
2. HOUSE OF SMOKE	★★★★	★★	★★	★★	★★½

For great venison sausage, hickory-smoked pork ribs, elk, buffalo, and pheasant, visit the House of Smoke. For very good soup and sandwiches go to the Branding Iron. Both restaurants accept major credit cards, but only the Branding Iron has a nonsmoking section and serves alcohol.

BRANDING IRON ★★★
11 1ST ST. (303)857-6770

Breakfast $, lunch/dinner $-$$$. SUN-THU 6AM-10PM. FRI-SAT 6-11PM. Type: Family.

Food: ★★★½ My toasted ham & Swiss had plenty of lean ham. The beef barley soup had a lot of both: beef and barley. Their breakfast menu offers a host of good items: banana pancakes, pigs in a blanket, Belgian malted and strawberry waffles, grits, homemade cinnamon rolls, a selection of skillet meals, and a children's menu. The lunch/dinner menu primarily features steaks, seafood and chicken. Appetizers include chili fries, deep-fried vegetables and chicken tenders. There is homemade western chili, green chili, a soup du jour and salads. For a light meal there's a shrimp basket, fish & chips, ground round steak, chicken breast tenders, and a soup & salad bar. The sandwich selections include corn dogs, turkey & Swiss, tuna melt, and roast beef. Burgers, sides of vegetables or corn bread, and a children's menu are also available. The list of house specialty meals includes a Lancaster cheese steak sandwich (similar to the one from Philadelphia which is just outside of Lancaster), a turkey pastrami Reuben, barbecue beef with homemade barbecue sauce, and a beef dip (similar to the one the French make). The dinner entrees feature sirloin & shrimp, rib eye, chicken breast (which comes either barbecued, chargrilled, in teriyaki sauce or sesame style), chicken fried steak, honey-dipped fried chicken, pork chops, roast beef, catfish, and NY strip. For dessert, there are homemade pies, cinnamon ice cream, cheesecakes, dessert waffles, sundaes and pudding.

Service: ★★★ Friendly and with a smile. The food is served fast.

Decor: ★★★½ This is a red-brick building with brown shingles on the northeast corner of Highways 85 and 52. The nonsmoking section to the right has five booths and five tables with benches on one side and rib-backed, wood chairs on the other. This section seats 36. The smoking section to the left has 10 booths, one table, and more tables with bench seats opposite chairs. This section seats 65. There is a counter in-between for 15. There is also a banquet room in the rear. The decor is Western-style, with pictures of horseback riders, cattle, and an old timer — all done in bright colors: a lot of greens, blues, yellows and oranges. The tainted-glass hanging lamps are also colorful exhibiting blue, tan, white, green and red. The ceiling is painted a rust color, the horizontal shades are brown, and the booths are tan vinyl with clothed backs. This is a colorful, bright and cheerful place.

Atmosphere: ★★★ A well-dressed clientele mixed with soft country music.

HOUSE OF SMOKE ★★½
825 DENVER AVE (303)857-2750

Lunch/Dinner $. MON-SAT 9AM-6PM. Closed SUN.
Type: Steak.

Food: ★★★★ *Service:* ★★ *Decor:* ★★ *Atmosphere:* ★★

I ordered the venison sausage. It seemed like a cross between cotto and hard salami, only better. The homemade broccoli soup was quite good also. Sandwiches are served with chips and a large dill pickle slice, which had a strong taste. This restaurant has some great tasting meats and cheeses not found in most restaurants: hickory-smoked turkey breast, country beef or ham; various sausages (buffalo, venison, Norwegian, or spicy hot beef); cheeses (hot pepper, onion, American camel, Swiss and Cheddar), bacon, Bratwurst, buffalo Bratwurst, buffalo roast, and German sausage. sauerkraut. They have salads, sauerkraut and submarine sandwiches. You can also purchase many of these fine items at the counter and take them home. Some additional items which you can buy by the pound are salmon, elk sausage, venison or buffalo ribs, ham hocks, duck, pheasant and Cornish game hen. This place is for anyone who is not a vegetarian. Order at the counter. This combination deli-restaurant is in a brown building with brown shingles. There are two dining rooms divided by the meat counter. The walls are made of unfinished wood and have pictures in unfinished wood frames showing prepared roasts and fish. The room to the left has posters of Canada and Austria, stuffed elk and buffalo heads, ceramic fish and pheasant decorations. A country-western music station plays in the kitchen.

FORT MORGAN

This former military post went by the names of Camp Tyler and Fort Wardwell before being named after Colonel Christopher A. Morgan in 1866. The town became an agricultural center about 40 years later when the North Western Sugar Company built a factory north of town.

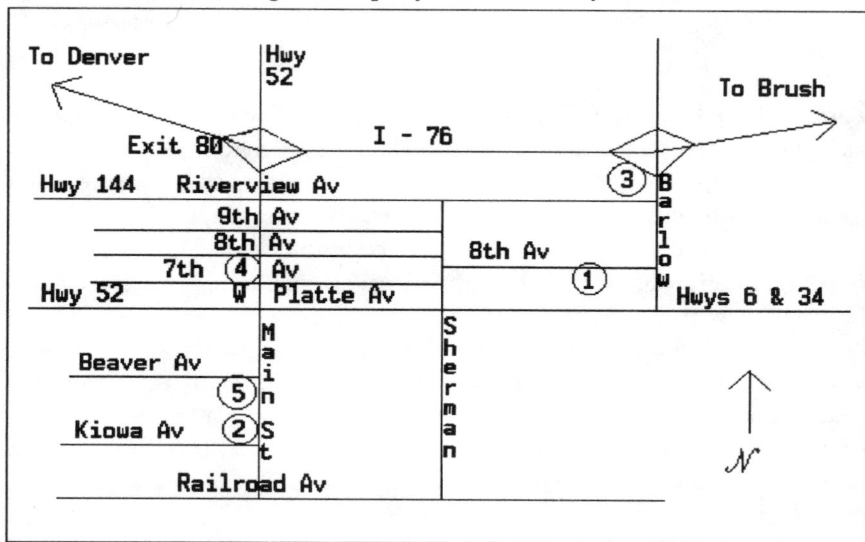

Restaurants and Ratings:	Food	Service	Decor	Atm	Overall
1. COUNTRY STEAK OUT	★★★★½	★★★★	★★★★½	★★★½	★★★★
2. HOME PLATE	★★	★★½	★★	★½	★★
3. MOMA'S KITCHEN	★★½	★★½	★★½	★★★	★★½
4. PARK TERRACE	★★★½	★★★	★★★	★★½	★★★
5. SHANGHAI TERRACE	★★½	★★½	★★½	★★½	★★½

For thick, juicy steaks, as well as a great homemade soup and salad bar, visit the Country Steak Out. If you are looking for good home-cooked food that includes German sausage with breakfast or a good sandwich for lunch, then you should stop by the Park Terrace. Home Plate and Moma's Kitchen are the only restaurants that do not accept major credit cards nor serve alcohol. Shanghai Terrace is the only restaurant that offers a nonsmoking section.

FORT MORGAN

COUNTRY STEAK OUT ★★★★
19592 E. 8 AVE. (303)867-7887

Lunch $, dinner $$-$$$. TUE-SAT 11AM-9PM. SUN 11AM-2PM. Closed MON.
Type: Steak.

Food: ★★★★½ I had lunch here twice and this is by far the best place to eat in Fort Morgan. They have excellent homemade soup, like beef barley and cream of potato, daily luncheon specials, and a salad bar that includes Jello with fruit and chocolate mousse. As their name implies, steak is their specialty and comes highly recommended. The lunch menu is a combination of steaks, chicken, burgers, croissants, sandwiches and Mexican. Feature items include a steak sandwich, chopped sirloin, honey-dipped chicken, chicken fried steak, hot beef sandwich, spaghetti, patty melt, a low-calorie special with broiled fish, taco salad, and the Marco Polo (ham & turkey croissant). Derby pie, NY cheesecake, ice cream sundaes, and sherbet are on the dessert menu. The dinner menu is primarily steaks and seafood: rib eye, sirloin, filet mignon, NY strip, prime rib, lobster, crab legs, shrimp, salmon, halibut, and trout. Also on the menu are Italian chicken and Rocky Mountain oysters, The appetizers are all deep-fried: vegetables, cheese or shrimp.

Service: ★★★★ Top notch.

Decor: ★★★★½ There are two sections on either side of the entrance with total seating for about 150. On the right side, the first section seats 38, 12 in booths and 26 in tables. The second section seats 40, all at tables. On the left side, the upper section seats between 32 and 40 in eight circular booths. The lower section seats 40, all at tables. The left side has pink tablecloths and comfortable brown-cushioned chairs with wooden arms. The right side has pictures of ranching and farming. Ropes, cattle prongs, and branding irons hang on the walls. There is an old mural of the Colorado Mountains that is literally bubbling with age. The ceiling is vaulted with wood beams. The walls are wood panel. Fans and lights on wagon wheels hang from the ceiling. There are a lot of windows on the right side, but none on the left.

Atmosphere: ★★★½ A very busy and noisy place at lunch time, but a friendly crowd. Management claims their ceiling is high enough and they have enough air circulation to compensate for smokers. They are probably right.

HOME PLATE (FORMERLY DELRICH'S) ★★
207 MAIN (303)867-4416

Breakfast/lunch/dinner $. MON-SAT 6AM-8PM. Closed SUN.
Type: Country.

Food: ★★ *Service:* ★★½ *Decor:* ★★ *Atmosphere:* ★½

A limited basic food selection, but very inexpensive. The breakfast menu has a breakfast burrito. The lunch menu includes sandwiches, burgers, soup, salad, the basic Mexican fare, and entrees: Salisbury steak, pork chops, ground round steak, chicken fried steak, and ham. Dinner offers more American and Mexican choices. Service is average. There are two rooms. The front room can seat 35 people at seven booths, a small table, and a counter with five stools. The back room seats 26 at seven tables. The ceiling is low with no hangings. There are two decorative mirrors and some wicker decorations in the front. The back room has a clock and American Indian rugs hanging on the walls.

MOMA'S KITCHEN ★★½
I-76 & BARLOW ROAD (303)867-6569

Breakfast/lunch $ dinner $$. 7 days 24 hours.
Type: Country.

Food: ★★½ *Service:* ★★½ *Decor:* ★★½ *Atmosphere:* ★★★

Their breakfasts are average. They include corned beef hash, daily breakfast specials for $2 and the usual breakfast fare. The lunch menu has sandwiches, burgers, hot dogs, and onion rings. The dinner menu offers a variety with steaks, chicken, chicken fried steak, shrimp, pork chops, liver & onions, a low-calorie burger patty, soup, salad, and chili. There's also a children's menu and pie and ice cream on the dessert menu. Moma does the cooking while the "kids" (all in their 50s) wait on tables. A large one-room restaurant with seven tables and six booths for a total of 52 people. Practically everything is light blue in this restaurant: the ceiling, beams, curtains, tablecloths, cushioned bench seats, glasses, ceiling fans and lamp shades. While I was there, a trucker pulled up in a semi with a light blue cab. As luck would have it, I just happened to be wearing my light blue sports coat. I guess I fit right in. This, like most other restaurants in Fort Morgan, is a "good ol' boys" hangout. Still, it had better atmosphere than most.

PARK TERRACE ★★★
725 MAIN (303)867-8205

Breakfast/lunch $, dinner $$. 7 days 5:30AM-9PM.
Type: Country.

Food: ★★★½ "Good home cooked food," like the sign says inside. Breakfast offers cinnamon rolls, breakfast burritos, Belgian waffles, German sausage, and chicken fried steak with country gravy. The lunch menu has sandwiches, spaghetti, soup, salad, and a limited Mexican fare. The dinner menu is strictly steaks, seafood, and fried chicken. For dessert, there are homemade pies, ice cream and sundaes.

Service: ★★★ Quite good.

Decor: ★★★ There is enough seating for 45 at seven counter stools, plus tables. Ceiling fans, globe light fixtures and plants hang from a steep vaulted wood-beam ceiling. Eggshell wallpaper with prints of tiny apples decorate the walls. Above the counter is a high wall extending to the peak of the vaulted ceiling decorated with pots, pans, pictures, a broom, a rolling pin, wicker baskets and other culinary paraphernalia.

Atmosphere: ★★½ Country music.

SHANGHAI TERRACE ★★½
209 MAIN (303)867-4842

Lunch $, dinner $$. MON-THU 11AM-9PM. FRI-SAT 11AM-9:30PM. Closed SUN.
Type: Oriental (Chinese).

Food: ★★½ *Service:* ★★½ *Decor:* ★★½ *Atmosphere:* ★★½

I had the curry shrimp for lunch. It had a fair portion of large shrimp, about six. Unlike most Chinese restaurants, their lunch dishes will not stuff you, just fill you. There are several lunch specials under $4. Service is satisfactory. This restaurant has one long narrow room with 13 booths for 52 people and three tables for 20. Chinese zodiac place mats are set on red tablecloths. Red curtains hang in the windows. The walls are wood panel with paper butterflies, gold Chinese letters and symbols, and painted dragons on black framed glass with red & green tassels. For good measure, there are rotating chandeliers, a large mural, and orange, pumpkin-shaped ceiling lamps hanging from the acoustic ceiling. It is fairly dark in here.

FOWLER

Previously called South Side, Oxford Siding and Sibley, Fowler was named in 1887 by Professor O.S. Fowler, a phrenologist — or one who studies the configurations of a person's skull to determine mental faculties and character traits.

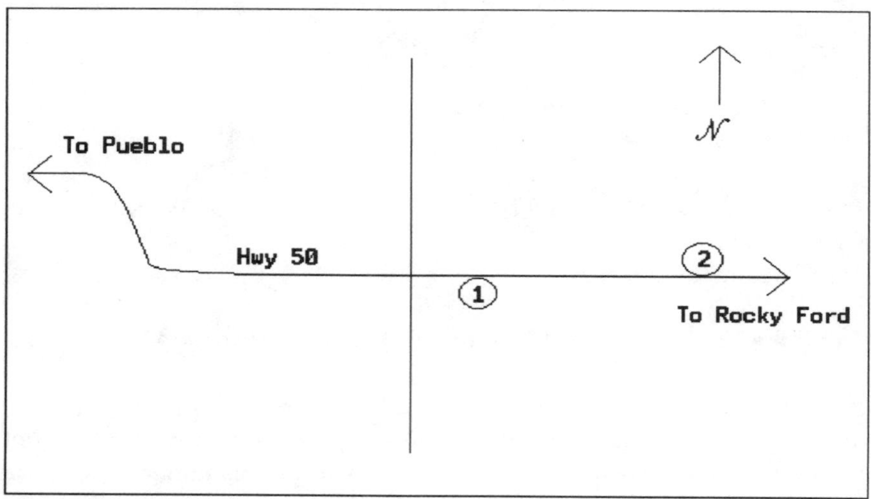

Restaurants and Ratings:	Food	Service	Decor	Atm	Overall
1. Mother's Kitchen	★★½	★★★	★★	★★	★★½
2. Stockman's	★★★	★★★★	★★½	★★★½	★★★½

If you want a steak or burger, go to the Stockman's. For a good hot lunch, visit Mother's Kitchen. Only Mother's Kitchen accepts major credit cards. Neither restaurant has a nonsmoking section or serves alcohol.

Mother's Kitchen: ★★½
120 E. Cranston Ave. (719)263-4441

Breakfast/lunch$, dinner$-$$. MON-SAT 7AM-2PM and 5PM-8PM. SUN 9AM-2PM
Type: Country.

Food: ★★½ *Service:* ★★★ *Decor:* ★★ *Atmosphere:* ★★

Their lunches are plentiful. I had barbecue beef, mashed potatoes, mixed vegetables, cole slaw, Texas toast and soup, all for only $4. Lunch is a combination of sandwiches, Mexican food and burgers. Dinner offers charbroiled steaks, roast beef sirloin, liver & onions, fried chicken, grilled ham, halibut, deep-fried shrimp, and a fish fillet. For a lighter meal, there are salads and fish or chicken low-calorie plates. The dessert menu has fresh-baked pies, sundaes, gelatin, malts and shakes. Service is good. There are nine booths for 36 people and tables for 24. The decor consists of artificial flowers and plants, small mirrors in the booths, acoustic tile ceiling, and wood paneling. A quiet place, but then this is a quiet town.

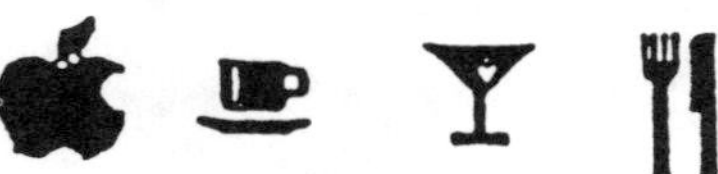

STOCKMAN'S RESTAURANT ★★★½
3377 HWY. 50 (719)263-9994

Breakfast/lunch $, dinner $-$$. 7 days 6AM-8PM (9PM APR-OCT).
Type: Steak.

Food: ★★★ This is primarily a steak place, so, of course, I had the lasagna lunch special. It had a good sauce, but they used cottage cheese instead of ricotta. Breakfast includes pork chops and cinnamon rolls. The lunch menu has burgers, sandwiches, soup, French fries, baked or mashed potatoes, onion rings, and the vegetable of the day. The dinner steaks include T-bone, rib, chicken fried or sirloin. Also on the menu at reasonable prices are chicken, cod, breaded shrimp, liver & onions, and salads. Pastries, cream & fruit pies and ice cream make the dessert menu.

Service: ★★★★ The waitress is very talkative and friendly.

Decor: ★★½ There are three sparsely decorated rooms with enough total seating for 90 people. This is the only place in town big enough for banquets, and the local chamber of commerce meets here. There's water damage to the ceiling right at the entrance.

Atmosphere: ★★★½ Old-time locals and tourists passing through visit here. The place has a nice, rustic, woody feeling.

FRANKTOWN

Franktown was formerly known as California Ranch, once called Russelville for Green Russell who discovered gold in the area, and later called Frankstown after James Frank Gardner, a pioneer who owned the site on Cherry Creek. The 's' was later deleted by postal authorities. Franktown was a stop on the stage line from Denver to Colorado City and became the county seat in 1861, a distinction it lost in 1875 to Castle Rock which was serviced by the railroad.

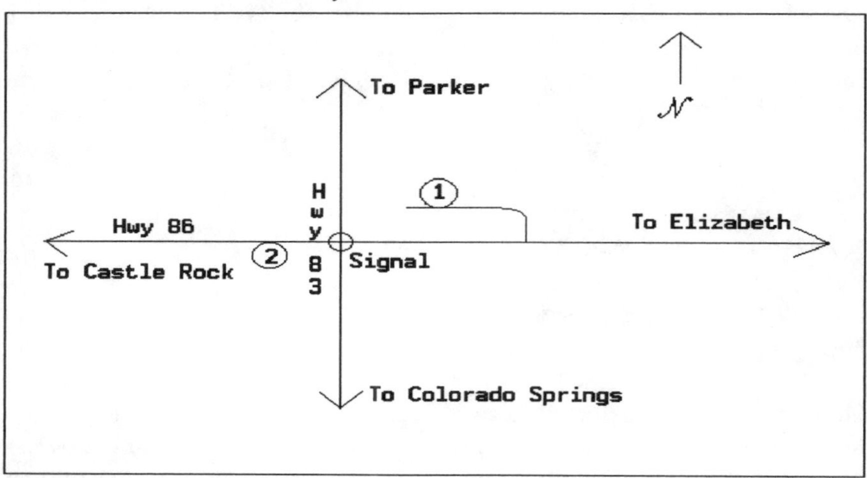

Restaurants and Ratings:	Food	Service	Decor	Atm	Overall
1. COURTYARD	★★★½	★★★	★★★½	★★★	★★★½
2. ESTHER'S	★★½	★★	★½	★★	★★

The Courtyard serves lean and tender steaks in a family atmosphere. Only the Courtyard accepts major credit cards, has a nonsmoking section, and serves alcohol.

COURTYARD ★★★½
7517 E STATE HIGHWAY 86 (303)688-7562

Lunch $$, dinner $$ (a few $$$). TUE-SAT: 11AM-9PM. SUN: 11AM-7PM. Closed MON.
Type: Steak.

Food: ★★★½ I ordered the charbroiled London Broil, medium-rare. It was surprisingly good for one of the smaller small towns, cooked just the way I like it: charbroiled on the outside, pink inside, tender & lean, with very little grizzle or fat. It came with warm, sweet tasting rolls, a dinner salad with croutons, a modest size baked potato and corn off the cob. If you stop here for lunch, you have your choice of sandwiches (club, Philly cheese, French dip, Italian sausage or meatball, prime rib, charbroiled chicken), burgers, a few Mexican dishes, pizza (a medium or thick crust with homemade sauce and nine topping choices), French onion soup, chili and salads. Dinner features appetizers like nachos and Buffalo style chicken wings. The entrees include chicken fried steak or chicken, charbroiled chicken breast, steaks, prime rib on FRI and SAT after 5PM, liver & onions with bacon, pork chops, barbecue beef ribs, spaghetti, and seafood (deep-fried shrimp, shrimp scampi and fried white fish).

Service: ★★★ Attentive without being obtrusive.

Decor: ★★★½ The front dining room has 13 tables and nine booths for 91. White-laced curtains hang across the top of the windows which occupy three sides of the room. Between the windows is attractive flower-patterned wallpaper on a brown background. Wreaths and short wall shelves holding cast-iron pans, plants and bottles decorate the wood-paneled back walls. There are a few well-placed pictures: one showing a little girl "herding" some geese, another featuring a carriage in front of a barn. Leading into the rear dining room is a dresser & mirror to the right and a small divider to the left. It can seat about 30 and has a red-brick wall along the back with a piano in front. Lighting is provided by in-set ceiling lights and brass, clear-glass wall fixtures. There is a patio that can seat 24 on white, metal lounge chairs set at six white circular tables with umbrellas. This is a nicely decorated restaurant. Somebody put some thought and care into the look.

Atmosphere: ★★★ A country western radio station plays quietly overhead. The clientele was also very quiet. I found the atmosphere to be unpretentious and friendly.

FRANKTOWN

ESTHER'S ★★
7272 EAST HIGHWAY 86 (303)688-6387

Breakfast $, lunch/dinner $-$$. MON-SAT 10AM-9PM. Closed SUN. Type: Mexican.

Food: ★★½ *Service:* ★★ *Decor:* ★½ *Atmosphere:* ★★

The large combination of bean burrito, chili relleno and cheese enchilada was average, except for the rice with peas in tomato sauce which was dry and the green chili in the relleno that I needed a knife to cut. They offer the typical Mexican fare and serve sodas in the can from the cooler. The stucco white walls and brown frame windows are dirty and peeling. The menu is posted in four places throughout the restaurant. They have two dining rooms. The service was average. However, the waitress was sitting and "fooling" with a friend who spilled pop on the floor. This seems to be a local visiting hole that few tourists stop at.

Byers Peak - Fraser

FRASER

Formerly known as Easton, for George Easton who laid out the townsite, the town was later called Frazier, for Reuben Frazier, an early settler. The postal service later adopted the simpler spelling. Today, Fraser attracts both Nordic and downhill skiers to the area. Fraser experimental forest is a favorite holiday spot for those interested in chopping down their own Christmas trees for a small park fee.

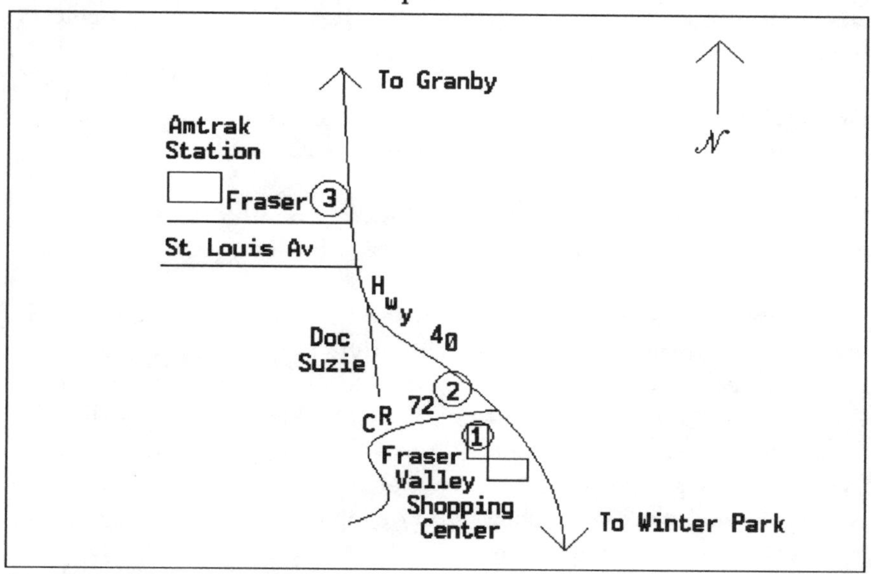

Restaurants and Ratings:	Food	Service	Decor	Atm	Overall
1. AMAZENBURGERS	★★★★	★★★	★★	★★★	★★★
2. BYERS PEAK	★½	★½	★★★½	★★★★	★★½
3. CROOKED CREEK SALOON	★★★	★★½	★★½	★★	★★½

Amazenburgers is the place to go for great charbroiled burgers and big onion rings. The Crooked Creek Saloon serves good sandwiches and fries. All three restaurants accept major credit cards and serve alcohol, but none of them offers a nonsmoking section.

AMAZENBURGERS ★★★
FRAZIER VALLEY SHOPPING CENTER (303)726-9555

FRASER

Lunch/Dinner $. 7 days 11AM-9PM.
Type: Burgers. Delivery available.

Food: ★★★★ They have terrific charbroiled burgers (some of the best in the state) and big, fluffy, flavorful onion rings. The burger was just a tad overcooked. They also have a great French mint ice cream with big chunks of chocolate chips. They also serve hot dogs, marinated chicken breast or steak sandwiches, chicken or beef fajitas, French fries, salads, and ice cream (cones, cups, floats, shakes, malts and sundaes). There is also a children's menu. Beer, wine, wine coolers and soft drinks are available. Thursday night is all-you-can-eat-fajita night.

Service: ★★★ Order at the counter. The owner/counterman told me about the games that can be played in the maze (see decor).

Decor: ★★ This place has just what it says in its name. There really is a walk-through maze here, not to mention video games and a nine-hole miniature golf course. The restaurant is located on the second tier of shops just to the right of Safeway on the west side of Highway 40. Look for the signs "Maze," "Golf," and "Burgers." Seating is in two sections. In the front along a solid row of windows are four bright red formica tables with green mid-back wood chairs for 17 people. In the back are six tables for 41. Next to the order counter is a big cartoon maze with the word "Colorado" written across it. In the rear are prints of mazes in gold frames. The walk-through maze can be played a couple of different ways. You can go through the maze and find the four letters M-A-Z-E. Or, you can play a laser game with teams equipped with "laser" guns. It sounded kind of fun, even for adults.

Atmosphere: ★★★ There is a great view of the mountains out the rear window. This was offset by the sounds of video games. I was here at an off-hour (3:30PM-4:00PM) when the place was empty. The owner informed me, however, that they get quite busy in the evening, especially on Thursdays. The logical assumption is that the place is packed with kids playing the maze, videos, and golf.

Byers Peak ★★½
5 Grand County Road 72 (303)726-8256

Dinner $$$ (a few $$$$). Mid-NOV to Mid-APR: 7 days 5PM-9:30PM. JUN-SEP: 7 days 5PM-9:30PM. MON-FRI 11:30AM-2PM. Closed OCT to Mid-NOV and Mid-APR to May.
Type: American/Continental. 15% gratuity for parties of 8 or more. Children's plates for kids 10 and under. No split dinners. The restaurant is in the old Gaskill house, built in 1885.

***Food:* ★½ *Service:* ★½ *Decor:* ★★★½ *Atmosphere:* ★★★★**

The food and service, as you can tell from the ratings, were a real disappointment. The potato soup had pieces of onion, but no potato. It was creamy, thick and fresh. The 12-item salad bar was modest but good. I recommend the spicy French with white-pepper dressing. The entree, lamb curry, had exactly four bite-size pieces of lamb buried in a cup of sliced onions and curry sauce. It would have been more appropriately named onion curry. They need to switch the quantities of lamb and onions. The small stuffed potato was mixed with cheese, (more) onions and chives. The beans tasted like they had been frozen. Service was either humorous or flippant, depending on your view. I was their first customer, and when I asked the waitress if she minded if I walked around and took a look at the place, she replied, "I don't care. I'm not the owner. I just work here. Someone else will tell you if they mind." She forgot the mint jelly with the lamb, and when she brought the check, she stated (somewhat sarcastically, I thought), "Thank you. It was simply a pleasure waiting on you." Also, they cannot handle gratuities on credit cards. You have to leave your tip in cash. Now for what I did like about the restaurant. There are two dining rooms for about 60 people and a small bar. Both dining rooms are decorated with blue-clothed napkins, white tablecloths under glass and white-laced curtains. The front dining room has a single red-brick column, paintings of mountains, trees and lakes in winter and spring, and several decorative plates, many in blue ceramic. The dining room to the left has several wreaths, two stained-glass tulips in an octagonal wood frame, a pair of antlers, and a series of mountain scenes. They play classical music and have some terrific views to the south and west. You may want to just pull into their parking lot, take a good look around, take a few pictures, and leave.

CROOKED CREEK SALOON ★★½
401 ZEREX (303)726-9250

Breakfast $, lunch/dinner $$. MON-FRI 11AM-10PM. SAT-SUN 7AM-10PM. Type: Tavern. 15% service charge added for parties of six or more. 15¢ per order carry-out charge. No separate checks.

I spent an impromptu evening here the day after New Year's Day in 1988 when the train to Denver was four hours late. It proved to be an enjoyable wait. My review is based on a more recent visit in 1991.

***Food:* ★★★ *Service:* ★★½ *Decor:* ★★½ *Atmosphere:* ★★**

My Philly beef sandwich was filled with a lot of beef, but they serve the onions on the side instead of sautéeing them. The fries are flat, round, real potato slices. Both were good. The lunch/dinner menu features Colorado beef, chicken, seafood, Mexican, burgers, and a dessert du jour. Service is adequate and seating is open. To reach the two dining rooms, you have to pass through the bar/lounge, where there is a big-screen television, stage, small dance floor, pool table, darts, and seating for 18. The two dining rooms can seat about 90 and are decorated with old photos of the local logging industry and turn-of-the-century Fraser, a piano, a pipe stove, a foos ball machine, several Frank Howell posters of American Indians, and a red velvet sleigh. Glass doors and door-size glass windows let in plenty of light. Rock music, moderate to heavy, plays in the bar area. Their slogan, posted at the entrance, reads "eat until it hurts, drink until it feels better!" Sounds like a profound statement.

FREDERICK

Originally called McKissick, the town was later named for Frederick A. Clark, owner of the townsite. The founders of the town were three women: Mary M. Clark, Maud Clark Reynolds, and Mary Clark Steele. Along with Firestone and Dacono, it is one of the "tri-cities."

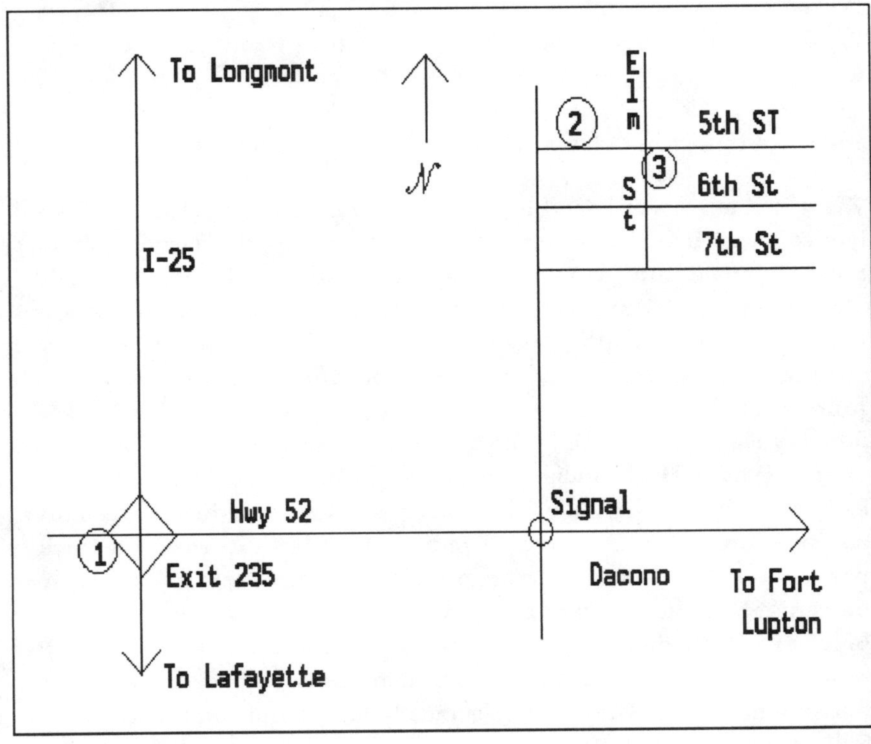

Restaurants and Ratings:	Food	Service	Decor	Atm	Overall
1. COFFEE URN	★★½	★★★	★★	★★½	★★½
2. MUGG-N-PYE	★★★	★★	★	★	★★
3. NINA'S	★★★★	★★★★	★★½	★★½	★★★½

For surprisingly excellent Mexican food, see Nina's. For a good-sized, home-cooked meal at a reasonable price, and close to the highway, stop at The Coffee Urn. None of the restaurants has a nonsmoking section or serves alcohol, and only The Coffee Urn accepts major credit cards.

FREDERICK

THE COFFEE URN ★★½
I-25 & HWY. 52 (303)833-4361

Breakfast/lunch $, dinner $$. SUN-THU 5:30AM-9PM. FRI-SAT 11AM-10PM.
Type: Country. This restaurant, which used to be in the town of Erie, was annexed into Frederick.

***Food:* ★★½ *Service:* ★★★ *Decor:* ★★ *Atmosphere:* ★★½**

You get a lot of food for the price. My four-ounce chicken fried steak looked more like six or seven ounces. It came with mashed potatoes, broccoli, bread, and soup. The big meals start with breakfast, which offers burgers, huevos rancheros, eggs Benedict, buttermilk pancakes, and Belgian waffles. The lunch menu features burgers, sandwiches, Mexican and side orders. Dinner is served anytime after 11AM and includes the soup & salad bar, a stuffed tomato, salads, steaks, country fried chicken, breaded shrimp, cod fillet, grilled ham steak, and beef pot roast. Cream or fruit pies, waffle sundaes, ice cream and root beer floats are on the dessert menu. Service is quick, friendly and concerned. This restaurant has two rooms for 85 people. The first room has pictures of a truck, a parade, a hot air balloon, a weather vane and a mechanic's bench with an oil can. Shade lamps hang on gold chains over the tables & booths. A blue brick wall divides the two rooms. On the shelf between the two rooms are a couple of pieces of Western art: a horse lying on its side and a man with a calf. The clientele is mostly farm hands and field workers. Suits & ties look out of place here.

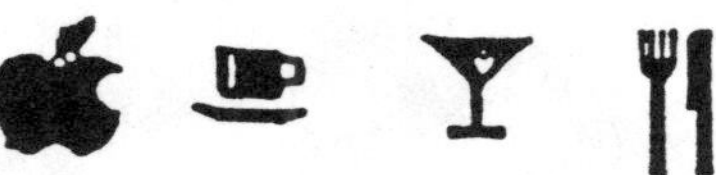

MUGG-N-PYE: ★★
141 5TH ST. (303)833-2270

Dinner $-$$. 7 days 4PM-8PM.
Type: Italian. Take-out and delivery available.

***Food:* ★★★ *Service:* ★★ *Decor:* ★ *Atmosphere:* ★**

Pizza is the primary menu item, but they also have canolis, sandwiches spaghetti & meatballs, and garlic bread. Order at the counter. This restaurant has wood panel walls with a low acoustic tile ceiling, a fireplace with trophies, some sports banners and video games. There are 12 tables for 48 people. The place is dark. Go with the take-out or delivery if you go with this place at all.

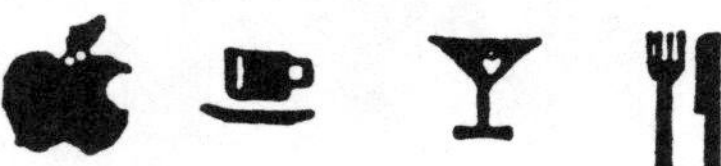

NINA'S ★★★½
5TH & ELM (303)833-3937

Lunch $, dinner $-$$. MON-SAT 11AM-9PM. Closed SUN.
Type: Mexican.

Food: ★★★★ I had a smothered burrito for lunch. The tortilla was light. There was plenty of beef and beans and just the right amount of spices. This was one of the best smothered burritos in northeast Colorado. Excellent! Their daily lunch specials include tamales, flautas, stuffed and plain sopapillas, Mexican burgers, nachos, green chili, and guacamole dip. The dinner menu has smothered tamales, huevos rancheros, Mexican steak, chicken, pizza, burgers and hot dogs.

Service: ★★★★ Lunch specials are prepared ahead. I was waited on and served within five minutes of walking into the place.

Decor: ★★½ This is a small, long, narrow, one-room restaurant with a high ceiling, 10 booths and three tables for 42 people. There is a small strip of yellow flower wallpaper around the room about a foot below the ceiling. My only guess is that it is there to cover some crack or damage to the wall. Wall decorations include a single mantel with three potted plants; Mexican pictures, mostly of bull fights; a large rug depicting a festival; a few black Mexican hats; one picture of a bald eagle and another of two black cats.

Atmosphere: ★★½ A pesky fly joined me for lunch, but the waitress and clientele were friendly.

FRISCO

A Swedish emigrant, Henry A. Recen, built the town's first log cabin in 1871, and four years later the townsite was named "Frisco City" by an old Indian scout named Henry Learned. In its early days, Frisco was known for its dancehalls and saloons. Today, it is the center of Summit County, with easy access to several surrounding ski areas.

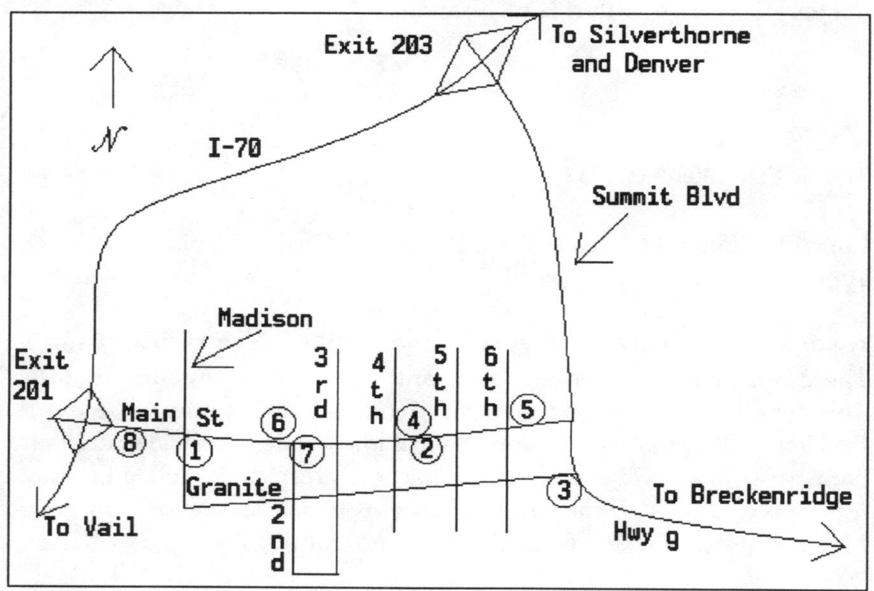

Restaurants and Ratings:	Food	Service	Decor	Atm	Overall
1. Blue Spruce Inn	★★★★★	★★★★	★★★★	★★★★½	★★★★½
2. Butterhorn Bakery	★★★	★★★	★½	★★	★★½
3. Frisco's	★★½	★★	★★★	★½	★★½
4. Ge-Jo's	★★	★★½	★★	★★	★★
5. Golden Annie's	★★★★	★★★½	★★★½	★★★	★★★½
6. Log Cabin Cafe	★★★½	★★½	★★½	★★½	★★★
7. Moose Jaw	★★	★½	★½	★	★½
8. Trail Head	★★★★½	★★★½	★★★★	★★★★	★★★★

The Blue Spruce Inn is my favorite restaurant in Frisco. It offers delicious soup and seafood & meat entrees in a well-decorated historic log cabin. The Trail Head, a popular locale, serves some excellent wild game, smoked and broasted selections. Golden Annie's prepares very good mesquite charbroiled fish and meats in a Southwest-style setting. All of the restaurants listed accept major credit cards. Only Frisco's, Ge-Jo's, and the Moose Jaw do not provide nonsmoking sections, and only the Butterhorn Bakery does not serve alcohol.

BLUE SPRUCE INN ★★★★½
20 WEST MAIN (303)668-5900

Dinner $$$-$$$$ ($$$$+ for a few seafood entrees). 7 days 5PM-10PM. Type: Continental. The entire restaurant is nonsmoking. A 15% gratuity is added to parties of 6 or more, and separate checks are not prepared.

Food: ★★★★★ This 50-year-old restaurant (formerly a lodge) specializes in slow-roasted prime rib and seafood. The soup for the evening when I dined there was cream of broccoli with smoked jalapeño cheese. It was delicious! I ordered the seafood special: salmon with shrimp, spinach and Parmesan cheese, topped with lemon beurre (butter) blanc. It was wonderful! This was one of the most tender and freshest-tasting salmon that I have had the pleasure of trying in Colorado. Their seafood is flown into Denver three times a week. The entrees feature fowl, meats and seafood. They offer milk-fed veal and aged, unfrozen beef shipped from Wichita, KS. Roast duckling, chicken Marsala, chicken in a lemon wine sauce, and chicken with coarse mustard are the fowl selections. Tenderloin filet bearnaise, steak Diane, lamb chops coated with pesto, and veal rolled with mushrooms, asparagus tips, artichoke hearts and Aloutte cheese top the choices of meat. Rocky Mountain trout, shrimp scampi, Alaskan king crab legs, and Australian broiled lobster tail are featured under seafood. A children's menu offers grilled chicken, shrimp scampi and prime rib. Homemade mud pies, chocolate eclairs and a daily special are on the dessert menu.

Service: ★★★★ Very efficient and relaxed. They make you feel comfortable and welcome.

Decor: ★★★★ There is a small, divided dining room downstairs with a bar/lounge and second dining room upstairs. The downstairs dining room can seat 50 people at 16 tables. A stuffed deer head with antlers and a pair of old broken snowshoes hang over the small red-brick fireplace along the back wall. The natural-wood log walls are decorated with an array of posters from Sterling, Cabernet Cellars and Kenwood vineyards, and with pictures of pheasants, ducks, a lonesome cowboy crossing a snowfield, and three Indians pondering the depths below from a high precipice. Effuse lighting reaches out from brass, yellow-tinted glass, hexagonal wall and ceiling fixtures and from kerosene table lamps. A wood beam traverses the length of the dining room with wood post supports. Philodendrons and spider plants hang in front of the windows and alongside the wood posts. The bar/lounge at the top of the stairs has two small tables with five chairs and eight bar stools. Overhead is an old-fashioned wood sled. To one side is an artist's rendition of "The Rockies, the high plains and the intermountain west." The dining room beyond the bar is in the attic of the building. There is one booth in a corner with a mini-arch and a large brass light fixture hanging from a cross beam. A wood bench extends along one wall. There is seating for 36. A black kettle for wood burning stoves hangs from three-foot chains. Posters celebrating everything from Rocky Mountain National Park's 75th Anniversary to the Georgetown Loop Railroad decorate the log walls.

Atmosphere: ★★★★½ This is a good place to unwind. Soft jazz plays in the background. There are good views of the blue spruces outside.

BUTTERHORN BAKERY AND DELI ★★½
408 MAIN ST (303)668-3997

Breakfast $, lunch $-$$. Thanksgiving-SEP: TUE-SAT 7AM-6PM, SUN 8AM-4PM, Closed MON. OCT-Thanksgiving: WED-SAT 7AM-5PM, SUN 8AM-4PM, Closed MON-TUE.
Type: Deli. The entire restaurant is nonsmoking.

Food: ★★★ *Service:* ★★★ *Decor:* ★½ *Atm:* ★★

This four-year-old restaurant is owned by a husband and wife team. Always willing to try anything once (well, almost anything), I decided to give their strawberry omelet a try: a plain egg omelet topped with fresh strawberries and whipped cream. It was different and good, but I think I still prefer strawberries on a waffle or pancake. The service is pleasant, helpful and cheerful. This is a popular place, and you may have to wait at peak hours on weekends, during the ski season, or in the summer. This is a very small, single-room restaurant with two window booths and seven tables for only 28 diners. This is a no-frills place with plants hanging in front of the windows without any curtains or drapes, a couple of breakfast posters decorating the wood panel walls, and fluorescent ceiling lights.

FRISCO'S BAR & GRILL ★★½
720 GRANITE (303)668-5051

Lunch $$, dinner $$$. 7 days 11:30AM-10PM.
Type: Burgers. Take-out available.

Food: ★★½ *Service:* ★★ *Decor:* ★★★ *Atmosphere:* ★½

My blue-cheese burger that I ordered medium rare was served well done. It came with a sharp-tasting red onion. However, my onion rings did not have a strong onion flavor. Overall, this was only an average meal. Service was friendly but somewhat less than efficient. My waitress noticed the slice of tomato missing from my burger when she served it, then she forgot to return with one. She compensated by bringing a piece of French silk pie. The pie was about three inches high with chocolate pudding on a flaky crust swamped with whipped cream and slices of chocolate. There is a bar at the entrance with pool tables, four televisions and a video game. Dining is in secluded booths, but this place is anything but romantic. The entire restaurant has a bar-type atmosphere. Six tables with umbrellas and 24 lawn chairs are set on the deck.

GE-JO'S ★★
409 MAIN STREET (303)668-3308

Lunch/dinner $$-$$$. Mid-NOV to Mid-APR: 7 days 11:30AM-10PM. Mid-APR to Mid-NOV: 7 days 4PM-10PM.
Type: Italian. Delivery and take-out available. No personal or separate checks. 15% gratuity added to parties of six or more. $1 plate charge for second plate.

***Food:* ★★ *Service:* ★★½ *Decor:* ★★ *Atmosphere:* ★★**

The manicotti is made with cottage cheese instead of ricotta cheese, and the tomato sauce had no seasoning. This was a very weak Italian meal. The service was satisfactory, but nothing special. The dining area to the right of the entrance is decorated with pictures of pasta, skis & poles, chateaus & cottages, and fig trees. The bar/lounge to the left has a pinball machine, pool table, large-screen television and three fish tanks. The music and television from the lounge give the dining room a barlike atmosphere. A deck is open in the summer.

GOLDEN ANNIE'S ★★★½
603 MAIN ST (303)668-0345

Lunch $, dinner $$$-$$$$. 7 days 11:30AM-3PM and 4:30PM-10PM. (appetizers served between 3PM and 5PM).
Type: Mexican (Southwest, seafood, and barbecue). 15% gratuity added for parties of six or more. No separate checks.

Golden Annie's was named after a claim within the Masontown Mine, located in Mountain Royal overlooking Frisco. The legend goes that the mine was destroyed by an avalanche on New Year's Eve, 1912. This restaurant has a definite Southwest appearance and flavor, closely resembling the restaurants in Santa Fe or Taos, New Mexico. Smoking is permitted only in the bar and lounge.

Food: ★★★★ The chicken Mexicali soup was made with barley, tomatoes, and just a little green chili to spice it up. My entree, mesquite char-broiled salmon filet, was very tender, juicy and flavorful. It was served with hot butter on the side and brocciflower - a hybrid that has the color of broccoli and the texture of cauliflower. This was the first time I had tried this unique vegetable, and I was favorably impressed. Bean & cheese or chicken nachos, smoked trout and a rib sampler are a few of the more interesting-sounding appetizers. The lunch menu offers slow-smoked barbecue ribs, sausage, pork, and beef, grilled chicken or fried catfish sandwiches, Texas chili, soup, salad, fajitas, and mesquite burgers. Mesquite-grilled fish and meats are featured on the dinner menu and include Pacific snapper, swordfish, salmon, shrimp, NY strip, rib eye, T-bone, and filet mignon. Their seafood is flown in three times a week. The salmon comes from the Northwest. The same slow-smoked barbecue items and fajitas from lunch are offered at dinner also. Both menus have turtle cheese cake, mud pie and a daily special for dessert.

Service: ★★★½ Satisfactory in the dining room, warm and friendly at the bar. I also had an opportunity to talk to chef Paul and his brother. Paul trained at the New York Culinary Institute.

Decor: ★★★½ The restaurant's most distinctive feature is its deep skylights with artificial plants hanging from a wood fixture in the ceiling indenture. There are large Mexican rugs, a gallery poster, pictures of a buffalo lost in a fog or sandstorm, a window with wooden shutters, and an old photo of Mexicans standing around a cannon during the 1911 insurrection. The dining room has five booths with green-cushioned seats and 13 tables for 41 hardwood, rib-backed chairs with armrests. Total seating in the dining room is 61. Artificial cactus and kerosene lamps decorate the hardwood polished tables. The bar/lounge area in the front has a stone fireplace with artificial cactus in vases and bowls on the mantel. There is seating on a clothed-cushioned, log-framed couch and a chair with a Southwestern-pattern cover. Decor includes some old, old photos of a cowboy, the rebel General Costilla, and General Francisco Villa. Lighting is provided by in-set ceiling lights and kerosene lamps.

Atmosphere: ★★★ Bring your flashlight for the dining room. Attempting to read the menu is this dimly lit restaurant is a real eye strain. It is brighter in the smoking lounge area than in the nonsmoking dining room. The very friendly and relaxed bar will make you feel welcome. Say hello to Mookie, the barkeep.

LOG CABIN CAFE ★★★
121 OLD MAIN STREET (303)668-3947

Breakfast/lunch $, dinner $$. SUN: 7AM-2PM. MON: 6AM-2PM. TUE-FRI: 6AM-9PM. SAT: 7AM-9PM.
Type: Cafe. Separate checks only if you tell the server before ordering. 15% gratuity charge for parties of six or more. 20¢ container charge on orders to go.

Food: ★★★½ This is very good, plain country cooking: nothing more or less. I was here for Sunday breakfast with my usual hiking buddies. We gave thumbs-up on their eggs, sausage patties, short stack, and biscuits & gravy with sausage gravy. The huevos rancheros, smothered with lettuce, tomatoes, sour cream and pork green chili, was a plentiful serving and quite good also. The locals raved about their large sausage patty. I thought it was good, but I would probably order links or bacon next time. Grits, a favorite of mine, were good, as usual, with a little sugar on top. The lunch menu offers burgers, sandwiches, soup, salad, Mexican, chicken fried steak, and hot dogs. The dinner specialties include char-broiled beef or buffalo burgers, grilled beef liver & onions, a half broiled chicken, fried chicken, Rocky Mountain trout, rib eye steak, and pork chops. There is a children's menu and nightly specials. Homemade cobblers and ice cream are on the dessert menu.

Service: ★★½ The same waitress that I had at the Frisco Bar & Grill works here also, except she was a little more awake on Sunday morning than she was on Thursday night. Expect about a half hour wait for your meal on a busy Sunday morning. All 16 tables were filled when I was here.

Decor: ★★½ This is a two-room cafe with five formica booths and three tables in each room for a total of 60 diners. Lighting is provided by fluorescent ceiling lights behind a plastic panel in a narrow rectangular wood structure. Paintings of the Colorado Rockies, cowboys, buffalos, and a poster of the Arapahoe Basin decorate the white plaster walls.

Atmosphere: ★★½ This is a very popular breakfast place that attracts both locals and tourists. They do not take reservations. It is on a first come, first serve basis. There were about half a dozen people waiting to get in when we left.

MOOSE JAW ★½
208 MAIN ST (303)668-3931

Lunch/dinner $. 7 days 12PM-12AM.
Type: Tavern. 15% service charge added to parties of five or more. No separate checks.

The home of the Moose Jaw was originally built in the old town of Dillon in the late 1950's and was used as a bunkhouse for the Dillon Dam construction workers. In 1961, it was split in half, moved and reconstructed in Frisco, where it became the first supermarket in town. It was later used as a furniture store, donut shop, and various cafes, before it became the Moose Jaw in 1973.

Food: ★★ *Service:* ★½ *Decor:* ★½ *Atmosphere:* ★

Everyone that I talked to in Frisco told me that the Moose Jaw had the best burger in town. Maybe I hit them on an off night, but my burger was definitely dry. The fries were big slices of potato and I would recommend them. Some of my hiking friends ordered the fish and chips. They also liked the chips (fries) but would not recommend the fish. They are not too quick to return to your table, so try to do all of your ordering when you get the waiter the first time. There are a lot of moose pictures, stuffed animals, baseball & volleyball trophies and team photos. The square, wood barstools with no finish show a lot of wear. There is a big-screen television to the left, a pool table and games in the rear, and an old wooden ice chest on the right side. Long hair, flannel shirts, working people, cowboy hats and caps describe the clientele.

TRAIL HEAD ★★★★
450 WEST MAIN STREET (303)668-5757

Lunch $-$$, dinner $$$-$$$$. JUN-SEP: MON-SAT 11AM-4PM and 5PM-10PM. SUN 10AM-2PM. Mid-NOV to Mid-APR: 7 days 5PM-1PM and SUN 10AM-2PM. OCT to Mid-NOV and Mid-APR to MAY: WED-MON 5PM-9PM. FRI-SAT 11AM-4PM. SUN 10AM-2PM. Closed TUE.
Type: Country. 15% gratuity added to parties of six or more. No separate checks.
Located at the base of Mt. Royal next to the site of the old Colorado Southern Railroad station, the Trail Head today is at the head of a bicycle trail.

***Food:* ★★★★½** I ordered the wild game sausage (elk and buffalo) served open face on French bread and topped with Monterey jack cheese and their own rich & spicy barbecue sauce. I found the sausage to be top quality. It came with "tater logs" - about 10 steak fries. A tasty, very good lunch. Wild game sausage nuggets, Rocky Mountain oysters, artichoke hearts, potato skins, and smoked Rocky Mountain trout are on the lunch and dinner appetizer menus. Salads, burgers made from buffalo and turkey, sandwiches (broiled or broasted chicken, turkey, and deep-fried fish), Rocky Mountain trout, and wild game cider stew are the lunch entrees. Wild game, smoked meats, chicken and fish are featured on the dinner menu. Entrees like flame-broiled T-bone or elk, in a red wine currant sauce, quail, venison, lamb chops with a cranberry wine sauce, roasted turkey or trout with cornbread stuffing, smoked baby back ribs, broasted fried chicken, pan-fried walleye pike, and spinach salad are available. There is also a children's menu and, for dessert, homemade mud pie, old-fashioned peach cobbler and cinnamon apple crisp.

Service: ★★★½ Very cooperative and pleasant.

Decor: ★★★★ The bar/lounge area is straight back from the host station. It has five tables for 20, 13 barstools, a couple of framed harnesses in one corner and a television in another. Beyond the lounge, separated by a two-sided stone fireplace, is the nonsmoking dining room with 11 wood tables. Seating is on 38 wood, rib-backed chairs with maroon-cushioned seats and armrests. White-laced curtains with white horizontal shades cover the windows. Kitchen utensils and pots & pans decorate one barn-wood wall. The back wall has four watercolors of mountain scenes and cabins in winter. The wall to the left has more paintings of a bear, a moose and a mountain goat, and photos of a mine and some men standing by a railroad track with mountains in the background. Lighting is provided by square, brass, clear-glass wall fixtures. The second dining room is to the left of the host station. This is a small room with five tables for 18, bookshelves built into the barn-wood walls, beer signs, and a scrub board for decor. With a few more books, this room could have a cozy, library feel to it. There is an outdoor patio used in the summertime with eight Plexiglass tables and 34 lawn chairs overlooking the creek below.

Atmosphere: ★★★★ A combination of old rock and country music plays in the background. There is a nice view of the creek from the patio. This was a rather quiet place for lunch in the off season. However, one of my friends who frequents the mountains informed me that it was quite lively in here on a winter Sunday.

FRUITA

Named by William E. Pabor in 1883 in recognition of the fruits grown on the western slope. Today, Fruita hosts the second busiest Welcome Center in Colorado.

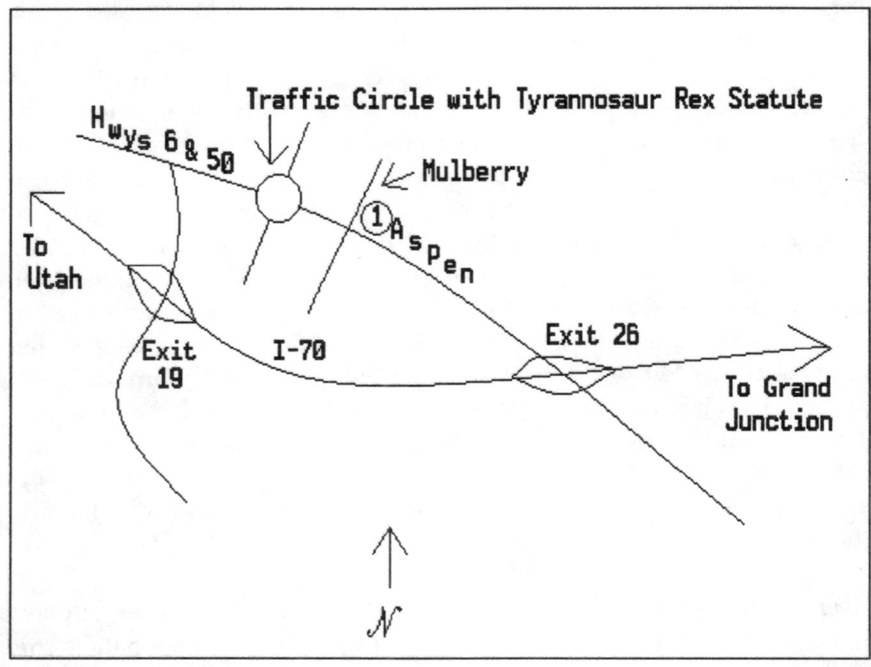

1. Dinosaur Pizza ★★★
201 E Aspen @ Mulberry (303)858-1117

Lunch/dinner $-$$. TUE-THU 3PM-9PM. FRI-SAT 11AM-10PM. SUN 11AM-9PM. Closed MON.
Type: Italian. Delivery available. Senior citizen discounts.
Credit cards are not accepted. There is no nonsmoking section and they do not serve alcohol. However, smokers are asked to sit in the back.

Food: ★★★ I ordered their barbecued ribs with cole slaw, beans and garlic bread. Ribs were not on the menu when I was there, but the waitress informed me that they were going to be added. Everything is homemade. The ribs are broasted, just like their chicken, and this helps keep the moisture and tenderness in the meat. They were meaty, too, with very little fat or bone. The cole slaw was sweeter than most. Chef Warren uses some honey in his recipe. The garlic bread only had a hint of garlic with no aftertaste. The beans...were beans. I would recommend this meal, and restaurant, if you are in the area. Pizza comes in individual, 7-, 12-, and 14-inch sizes, made thick or thin, with a choice of 12 toppings. They also advertise that "if you do not see it, ask for it". Their breakfast pizza is a combination of eggs, blended and baked, with cheese, vegetables, and choice of meat. The dinner entrees feature lasagna, spaghetti, ravioli, chicken Parmesan and Louisiana catfish. Lighter meals include homemade soup, salad, chili, and sandwiches (Philly cheese steak, Italian meatball or sausage, steak fajita, and burgers). Sundaes, floats, cheese cake, shakes, and ice cream made with real fruit are on the desert menu.

Service: ★★★ Charming. A very likeable couple run this friendly restaurant: Warren and Sherri Harrison. Warren has a very interesting past and will gladly tell you about any decoration in the restaurant. The Harrisons have been at their current location since 1987.

Decor: ★★★½ The largest philodendron I have ever seen crawls along the front window, halfway down the left wall and the full length of the right wall. There is a very interesting mix of decor in here: framed posters identifying dinosaurs; photos of Owner/cook Warren Harrison after he harpooned a shark off Nova Scotia during his deep sea fisherman days; a photo of a Mayan relic; large stained-glass ceiling lamp shades on gold chains; an upright piano; a letter from Chief Seattle to President Franklin Pierce dated 1855 entitled "Where is the Eagle gone?"; a black iron stove; a mobile of silver sailing ships and paintings of sailing ships; a rifle with a 330 year old musket; a lock that dates back to 1810 (used by the British on the Khyber Pass in their 1839 invasion of Afghanistan); and a fish tank that the giant philodendron has found (remember him?). This place not only has a different name, it is different!

Atmosphere: ★★★ This restaurant is built around a local clientele base, perhaps because there are two other restaurants closer to the highway (but it is worth the trip!). Some light music plays in the background.

GEORGETOWN

Georgetown was named after George Griffith, who, with his brother David, discovered gold here in 1859. Despite the discovery of gold, silver mining became the true source of wealth in the 1870s and 1880s. Georgetown, which became known as the "Silver Queen of the Rockies," and nearby Silver Plume, 2.1 miles away and 638 feet higher, became centers of Colorado's mining boom. To overcome the 6 percent grade between the two towns, Union Pacific engineer Robert Blickensderfer designed a circuitous route covering 4.47 miles, but with only a 3.5 percent grade. Today this stretch of railroad track is known as the Georgetown Loop and is open to the public. With the establishment of the gold standard in 1893, the value of silver plummeted and Georgetown dwindled. In 1966, the Georgetown/Silver Plume Mining Area was declared a National Historic Landmark District.

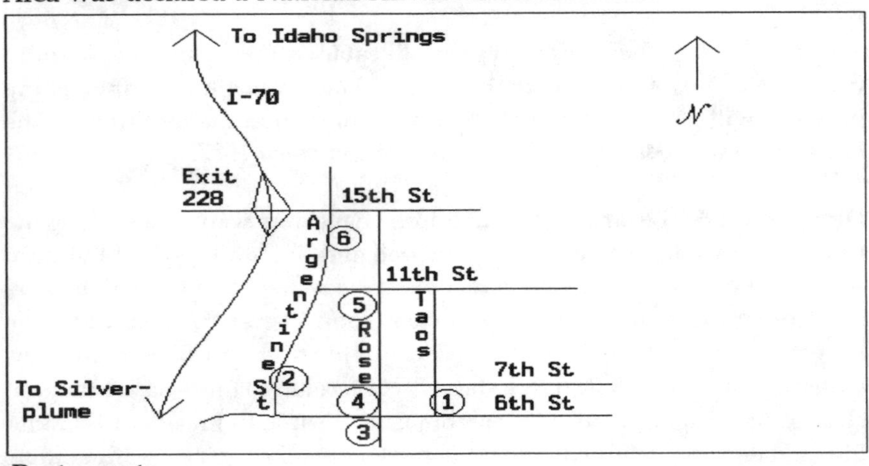

Restaurants and Ratings:	Food	Service	Decor	Atm	Overall
1. THE HAPPY COOKER	★★★★	★★½	★★★★	★★★★	★★★½
2. THE PLACE	★★★	★★½	★★★½	★★★½	★★★
3. THE PRETZEL	★★★	★★	★★★	★★	★★½
4. THE RAM	★★★	★★½	★★	★½	★★½
5. THE RENAISSANCE	★★★½	★★★	★★★½	★★★½	★★★½
6. THE SWISS INN	★★★½	★★★	★★★	★★★	★★★

The Happy Cooker offers delicious light crêpes and hearty European waffles. The Renaissance serves very good four-course northern Italian meals. The Swiss Inn dishes up spicy Italian sausage & potatoes. The Pretzel is the only restaurant that does not accept major credit cards or serve alcohol. Only The Renaissance and The Place have nonsmoking sections.

THE HAPPY COOKER ★★★½
412 SIXTH STREET (303)569-3166

Breakfast/lunch$$, dinner$$$. MON-THU 8AM-4PM. FRI-SAT 8AM-9PM. SUN 8AM-8PM.
Type: American/Continental. 15% service charge may be added for parties of six or more. No personal checks. No pipe or cigar smoking.

Food: ★★★★ For breakfast, you can order ham & cheddar, chicken à la king, or chipped beef & artichokes over a European waffle or crêpe. If you want a light breakfast, order the crêpe. If you are looking for a "He-Man" breakfast, order the waffle. I had the chipped beef & artichokes over crêpe served with peaches. The crêpes were light, the sauces divine, and the peaches, though canned, tasted fresh. My cross-country ski buddies enjoyed fluffy scrambled eggs and crisp bacon. Waffles also come with your choice of shrimp in sherry wine sauce, vanilla ice cream & hot fudge, or fruit. Cinnamon rolls and children's portions are also available. The lunch menu offers a barbecue beef sandwich, a chicken salad croissant, baked vegetarian lasagna, homemade soup or chili, and a dinner salad. Baked brie and smoked trout are offered as dinner appetizers. The dinner entrees feature chicken pasta, a pasta du jour, chicken Marsala, steak Diane, veal lemon pepper, a daily fresh seafood special, and shrimp or vegetable en croutes (in puffed pastries). Cheesecake, hot apple pie, pecan pie and sundaes are on the dessert menu. Specialty drinks like Tuaca hot apple pie can be ordered.

Service: ★★½ Service was not overly attentive but certainly satisfactory.

Decor: ★★★★ This restaurant, converted from an old house, is filled to overflowing with pastel paintings of nasturtiums, flowers, gardens, and

Taos, NM. Seating is on rattan chairs at tables with mauve cloths and maroon paper placemats. Fresh poinsettias were set at every table. (We were here Christmas week). This is a very neat and clean restaurant with white-laced curtains, a blue painted ceiling, and brass chandeliers with frosted tulip-shaped light shades. Even the rest rooms are clean. The three dining rooms can seat 72 people at 21 tables.

Atmosphere: ★★★★ They play classical music for your listening pleasure. I ran into some folks here who drove all the way from Aurora just to have breakfast: a nice testimonial for a classy restaurant!

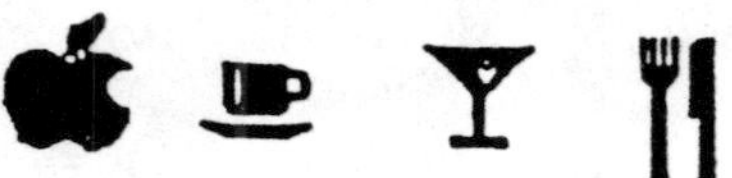

THE PLACE ★★★
SEVENTH & BROWNELL (303)569-2552

Breakfast/lunch$, dinner$$-$$$. MON-FRI 11AM-8PM. SAT-SUN 8AM-8PM. Type: Country. 15% gratuity added for parties of six or more.

Food: ★★★ Our eggs over easy were uneven. I had one egg overcooked. My snowshoe buddy had his eggs watery. The potatoes were real, but bland. The bacon and pancakes were good choices. The coffee was average. The limited breakfast menu offers a homemade bread bowl filled with scrambled eggs, topped with ham and hollandaise sauce, and served with fresh fruit; oatmeal; and hot cider. The lunch menu features burgers, sandwiches, a low-cal plate, chef's salad, soup, and a vegetarian croissant or omelet. For dinner you can order a broiled steak topped with mushrooms sautéed in garlic butter, a vegetarian plate, chicken kabob, cod, and jumbo shrimp. The list of desserts includes warm apple crisp with French vanilla ice cream, apple or strawberry rhubarb pie, walnut cream layer cake, cheesecake, chocolate cake, and sundaes.

Service: ★★½ Slow taking our orders and delivering our food, but frequent returns to refill our coffee. The potatoes were not served warm.

Decor: ★★★½ This is a two-room restaurant with 10 tables for 40 in the first room and five tables for 22 in the nonsmoking second room. The attractive yellow-print wallpaper that matches the yellow window and door frames is decorated with a copper pan, a 100th anniversary poster of the Georgetown Loop railroad (1884-1984), and several colored-pencil drawings of country scenes. White-laced curtains hang in the windows of the first room facing the outside and separating the second room. Shelves over the entrance display an array of alarm clocks, ceramic horses, cups, scales and a coffee pot. Attractive hexagonal-shaped brass light fixtures with drawings of sleds and mountain cabins hang from the ceiling. There is a very nice brass-framed mirror on one wall. Wood columns are used at the entrance to the server station. The second room has windows on three sides with hanging plants and ceiling fans.

Atmosphere: ★★★1/2 They play 40's tunes in here (Spike Jones). The clientele is quiet and older.

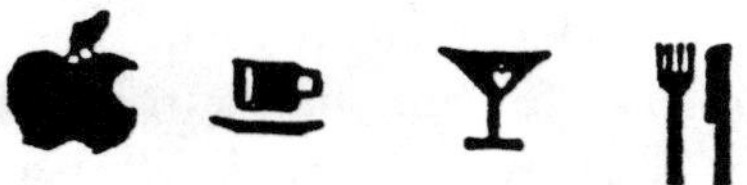

THE PRETZEL KAFFEE HAUS ★★½
511 ROSE STREET (ACROSS FROM STRAUSS PARK) (303)569-3404

Breakfast/lunch $. MON-FRI 7AM-3PM. SAT-SUN 7AM-5PM.
Type: Cafe.

Food: ★★★ *Service:* ★★ *Decor:* ★★★ *Atmosphere:* ★★

The French toast was a little well done, but otherwise, the hash browns with onions, pancakes, bacon, toast and coffee were all good. My eggs, ordered over easy, were a little watery, so you may want to order them over medium if you normally order them over easy. The meats were especially good: the Polish sausage and a whole Bratwurst sliced in half. The lunch offerings include soup, chili, sandwiches and burgers. The service was fair. This is a small, single-room restaurant with eight hardwood tables for 34 and nine short red-cushioned stools at a counter. Emblems from German and Austrian towns and provinces (Hamburg, München, Tirol and others) adorn the white wallpaper, along with old photos of Georgetown and prints of ducks and sailing ships. There is ample lighting from the fluorescent ceiling lights. The door and window frames and doors themselves are painted red. Heavy rock music was playing in the kitchen. The few other occupants appeared to be all locals. The smokers seemed to gravitate to the table in the middle of the room.

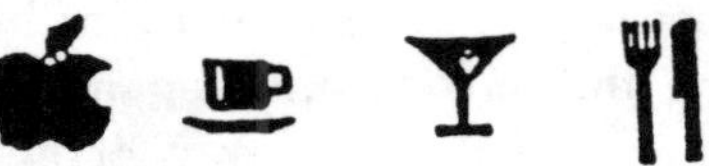

THE RAM ★★½
606 6TH ST. (303)569-3263

Lunch/Dinner $$. WED-MON 11AM-9:30PM; Closed TUE.
Type: Tavern.

Food: ★★★ *Service:* ★★½ *Decor:* ★★ *Atmosphere:* ★½

The Ram has good sandwiches and burgers. The entrees include an omelet croissant or quiche du jour, hamburger, steak sandwich, hot corned beef with Swiss & sauerkraut, hot Philly beef, a pita vegetarian sandwich, a diet plate, and seafood pasta salad. For appetizers, there's zucchini legumes, cheese & fruit, and con queso & chips. You can order French onion soup or salad (spinach, tossed, or Mediterranean). Dinner specials include veal Parmesan, stuffed trout, seafood linguini, and chicken teriyaki. Service was satisfactory. The downstairs has 12 tables for 50 people, plus a bar for 12. The upstairs balcony has about 12 tables for another 50. The decor consists of hardwood walnut chairs, tables, balcony rails, and stools; old-time photos of the town; a ram's head with horns; and framed beer posters. This place has a bar atmosphere.

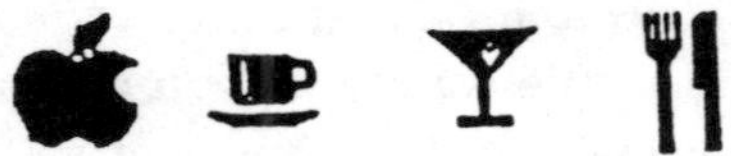

THE RENAISSANCE ★★★½
1025 ROSE STREET (303)569-3336

Lunch $$, dinner $$$$ (a few $$$). JAN to Memorial Day: WED-THU 4PM-10PM. FRI-SUN 11:30AM-10PM. Closed MON-TUE. Memorial Day to DEC: TUE-SUN 11:30AM-10PM. Closed MON.
Type: Italian (northern). Reservations recommended. They can arrange for transportation to and from the restaurant. Limo service is available.

Food: ★★★½ Warm, fresh garlic bread is served with an appetizer of chicken in a cream sauce with Perno, a French liqueur. This is followed by a spicy tomato bisque with onions, basil and chili pepper: a delight to the senses. The Caesar's salad was rich and fresh. The lasagna entree had a lot of beef and vegetables but lacked the sauce and cheeses that would have been used if this were a Sicilian-style restaurant. The Parmesan table cheese was stale and tasteless. Both lunch and dinner menus offer escargot, clams casino and scampi for appetizers and a seafood du jour, veal, chicken (Vesuvio or Romana), wild game (in season), and linguini (marinara, garlic & herbs, or clam sauce) for entrees.

Service: ★★★ One extremely busy waiter handled the whole restaurant. While I think he did an admirable job, it would have been more relaxing if he had some help. He had to run around "like a terror" and it was somewhat disconcerting just watching him.

Decor: ★★★½ There are 17 tables in four different dining sections for 54 people. The two tables in the front can be used for nonsmokers. Chianti bottles are everywhere: in stands, between the wood beams and vaulted ceiling, and hanging from the wall and ceiling. Seating is on comfortable hardwood, rib-backed chairs with armrests set at tables with red cloths. A wood trellis separates the last section, where there is a small bar. The decor consists of a combination of posters from Italy with photos of urban and country settings. A glass case in the middle of the dining area displays brass pigs, a hippo, a duck, and an eagle sitting on a globe.

Atmosphere: ★★★½ Pleasant classical music. Incredibly dark. Lighting is uneven, with some areas having no light except for kerosene lamps. A five-globe light fixture hangs in the center of the dining area just outside the kitchen. There are a few other multi-colored lanterns and light fixtures hanging from the ceiling, but they are few and far between. I was surprised how busy they were on a Sunday night. It really filled up.

GEORGETOWN

SWISS INN ★★★
1414 ARGENTINE ST (303)569-2931

Breakfast $, lunch $-$$, dinner $$-$$$. THU-TUE 7AM-9PM. Closed WED. Type: American/Continental. 15% gratuity on parties of six or more. No separate checks or substitutions.

Food: **★★★½** Breakfast was very much to my liking: a large serving of Italian sausage, potatoes and green peppers with two eggs and toast. Spicy and good. My cross-country ski buddies enjoyed thick slices of French toast and crispy bacon. Coffee was average. We also sampled their escargot à la Bourguignonne on another visit: petit and tender snails in garlic butter. Their French onion soup with large croutons is also quite good, and they have excellent hot butter rum. The breakfast menu offers Bratwurst, Knackwurst, and espresso. Lunch entrees include lasagna, fish, chopped steak, a diet plate, sandwiches and omelets. Soups, salads, pasta, veal, fish, beef and chicken are on the dinner menu.

Service: **★★★** Efficient, cordial and good.

Decor: **★★★** Empty wine bottles are lined up on shelves hanging from walls decorated with cranberry and white-striped wallpaper. There are several pictures of nature and mountain scenes featuring a bobcat, foxes and geese, combined with pictures of Indians, a sailing ship and puppies. White-laced curtains hang in the only window on the back wall. Kerosene table lamps and brass, two-bulb, wall light fixtures are the only additional sources of light. A wood-burning fireplace occupies one corner. Polished square-cut wood beams run across the low flat ceiling. There are 18 tables for 60 diners. The bar/lounge has eight stools and four tables with two wood benches for eight more. It is decorated with numerous glass-enclosed beer signs and flags of the Swiss states.

Atmosphere: **★★★** This is a quiet, comfortable place with light rock music.

GLENWOOD SPRINGS

Previously called Defiance, Glenwood Springs was first called Glenwood Hot Springs for the mineral springs in the vicinity, and for Glenwood, Iowa. The Ute Indians were the first people to use the mineral hot springs. Later visitors included Doc Holiday, Kit Carson, Buffalo Bill Cody, President Theodore Roosevelt, and Tom Mix. Today, Glenwood Springs is home of the world's largest hot springs pool.

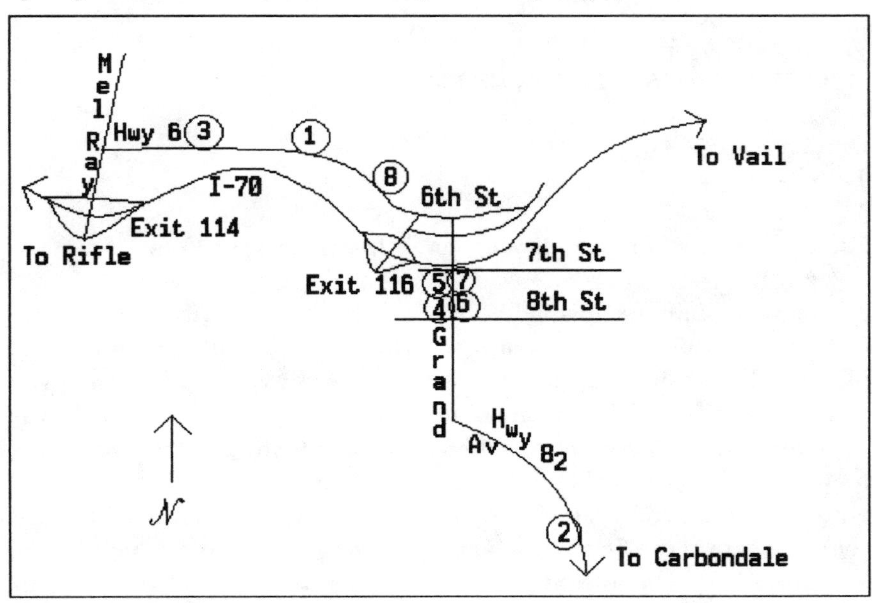

Restaurants and Ratings:	Food	Service	Decor	Atm	Overall
1. The Bayou	★★★	★★	★★	★★½	★★½
2. Buffalo Valley	★★★	★★★	★★★	★★½	★★★
3. The Fireside	★★★★★	★★★½	★★★★½	★★★★★	★★★★½
4. Florindo's	★★★★	★★★	★★★½	★★★★	★★★½
5. Ital Undergrnd	★★★	★★½	★★★½	★★★	★★★
6. The Loft	★★★★	★★★★½	★★★★	★★★½	★★★★
7. Riviera	★★★	★★★½	★★★	★★★★	★★★½
8. Rosi's	★★★★½	★★★★	★★★★	★★★★	★★★★

GLENWOOD SPRINGS

For great soup and steaks, visit The Fireside. Rosi's Bavarian Inn features homemade preserves and pastries and delicious Vienna Bratwurst and quiche. The Loft offers well prepared, plentiful servings of American/ Continental cuisine with a pleasant second story view. All restaurants accept major credit cards and serve alcohol. Only the Buffalo Valley Inn does not have a nonsmoking section.

THE BAYOU ★★½
52103 U.S. HWY. 6 & 24 (303)945-1047

Dinner: $$-$$$. 7 days 4PM-10PM.
Type: Seafood.

***Food:* ★★★ *Service:* ★★ *Decor:* ★★ *Atmosphere:* ★★½**

As the name implies, this is hot, spicy, Cajun food. I visited here with friends on two separate occasions. The shrimp, Buffalo wings, and blackened red fish were all good. Service was not very professional. The waitress was eating ice cream sandwiches while serving, but she was reliable. The patio in front has almost as much seating as the two dining rooms inside this log cabin restaurant. The patio, which is partly covered with umbrellas, can seat 44 people in fairly comfortable, metal-framed chairs. There is the figure of a large green frog on the roof which can be seen from I-70. The interstate noise is a major distraction. However, this is offset by a great view of the mountains and Glenwood Canyon. They pipe in Mo-town music, jazz and rock. This is considered a "funky" place and a good choice by the younger crowd. A mixed review from me.

BUFFALO VALLEY INN ★★★
3637 STATE HWY. 82 (1½ MI. S. OF GLENWOOD SPRINGS) (303)945-5297

Dinner: $$-$$$. 7 days 5PM-10PM.
Type: Steak.

Food: ★★★ I recommend the prime rib. This is a steak, seafood and barbecue restaurant. For appetizers, you have chicken livers, a rib sampler, and Rocky Mountain oysters. Your choice of steaks includes teriyaki beef kabob, porterhouse, buffalo, and hamburger. The seafood selections are Rocky Mountain rainbow trout, swordfish, deep-fried shrimp, and lobster. They barbecue the following items: chicken, spareribs, smoked beef and baby-back ribs. For a lighter dinner they have sandwiches of barbecue beef, sirloin steak, and pork; soup and salads, and chicken teriyaki. There is a children's menu. Desserts include pecan pies, cheesecake and ice cream.

Service: ★★★ Friendlier than most.

Decor: ★★★ There are three large rooms, two in front on either side of the entrance, and one main dining room. The main dining room has 25 tables for 116 people. The two dining rooms in the front have ten tables for 36 people. Also, there is a double-row bar with 18 seats. Total seating capacity is 170. This is a large restaurant with a rock fireplace that extends up to the wood log vaulted ceiling. There are several oil paintings of cowboys at work and play: cooking, hanging their laundry, playing cards, building a dam, and mending fences. Buffalo and deer heads hang from the walls, log beams and rock fireplace. Wagon-wheel chandeliers hang from the ceiling. They use red-and-white checkered tablecloths and red curtains. Wooden walls with windows, a dried eucalyptus plant and silk flowers in atriums separate the main dining room from the two front rooms. A black iron sculpture made by Benedictine monks greets you as you enter the main dining room. It is a figure of a mule train going over a hill.

Atmosphere: ★★½ Western and rustic.

THE FIRESIDE ★★★★½
51701 U.S. HWY. 6 (303)945-6613

Lunch: $-$$. Dinner $$-$$$. MON-FRI 11AM-2PM. MON-SAT 4PM-10PM. SUN 10AM-10PM.
Type: Steak. 15% gratuity for parties of eight or more. 10% senior citizen (over 65) discount, with identification, cash only.

Food: ★★★★★ The Russian cabbage soup with big chunks of pork was excellent. My T-bone was charbroiled to perfection. With baked potato, it made for a very filling meal. There was no need for a side vegetable and I was glad there was none. The salad bar had several side salads to choose from: a couple with macaroni, one with peas, another potato. The lunch menu offers a wide selection of burgers, sandwiches, light meals and mostly seafood dishes. The appetizers include fried mozzarella, shrimp or mushrooms, and onion rings. The choice of sandwiches are French dip, beef & cheddar, chicken, Philadelphia roast beef, and Reuben. The light meals are salads, vegetable primavera, pita bread, stuffed potato, and fettuccine Alfredo. The dinner menu features smoked oysters, potato skins, clams, escargot and shrimp cocktail as appetizers. Slow roasted, juicy prime rib is available in three sizes. Chicken is offered in a variety of ways: southern fried, marinated in teriyaki sauce, and Cordon Bleu. From the sea come clam strips, fried-shrimp, trout, shrimp scampi, king crab legs and lobster tails. There's a good selection of steaks to choose from: teriyaki sirloin, filet mignon, rib eye, NY strip, and T-bone. Dinner specialties include pit-smoked barbecue beef or pork ribs, Wiener or jaeger schnitzel, and kassler rippchen. For a lighter dinner you can choose from a burger, the soup & salad bar, steak kabobs with spinach salad, chicken fried steak, liver & onions, or London broil. Desserts include homemade German apple or cherry cheese strudel, double chocolate cake, pies, cheesecakes, and ice cream.

Service: ★★★½ Unpredictable. I waited about five minutes to get seated, then had a good-humored waiter who was quick with my requests to light the candle and bring a menu that I could take home. However, he was slow with the bread and the meal. Still, I found the service, overall, to be well above average.

Decor: ★★★★½ This restaurant consists of two divided rooms. The front room with its two sections has eight booths and three tables for 34 people. The rear room has six booths along the back wall behind 13 tables, plus an additional five tables in a section to the left, for a total of 104 people. Total seating capacity is 138. The front room hosts a fireplace, a variety of tablecloths in different flower patterns under glass, green wallpaper with a pyramid-shaped pattern, and a low ceiling with hanging plastic plants and a fan with lights. Pictures of flowers and mountain pines in winter adorn the walls, and there is a candle at every table. A circular fireplace stands in the middle of the rear room. A wood beam extends the length of the ceiling and there is a single wall lamp in each booth. The pictures, which are for sale, show an Indian woman weaving a rug and scenes of trees and mountains — some in winter. The far left wall has beer and wine pictures in glass frames. There is also a small lounge with six stools and a couch. The outside of the building has a log cabin appearance with flaming torches lighting the way.

Atmosphere: ★★★★★ This is a pleasant dining experience. I felt very comfortable here. Light instrumental music in the background, barely noticeable if you are not listening, adds to the "at-ease" ambience.

FLORINDO'S ★★★½
721 GRAND AVE. (303)945-1245

Lunch $$, Dinner $$-$$$. MON-FRI 11:30AM-3PM & 5PM-10:30PM. SAT 5PM-10:30PM. Closed SUN.
Type: Italian. $3.95 extra plate charge for sharing at lunch, $4.95 at dinner. All items available for take-out. The restaurant is all nonsmoking.

Food: ★★★★ I liked the tomatoes and spices on the veal Siciliana (scallopine) which I highly recommend. The lunch menu starts off with appetizers: shrimp cocktail, fried mozzarella marinara, and hot or cold antipasto. There are three very good soups to choose from: minestrone, pasta e faggioli (white kidney beans sauteed with prosciutto), and stracciatelle all romana, made with homemade chicken broth. A tossed or Caesar's salad is available. Lunch specialties include baked lasagna Florentine, cannelloni, manicotti, ravioli, fettuccine Alfredo, chicken

Parmigiana, veal Siciliana, and egg plant Parmigiana or rollatini (with ricotta, tomato & mozzarella). For a lighter meal have a hot sub. There is also a children's menu and, for dessert, Italian cheesecake, cannoli, and cassata ice cream. There are several tempting appetizers on the dinner menu: mozzarella marinara, two antipasto dishes, clams oreganato or posillipo (steamed, Neapolitan style), fried calamari, and shrimp cocktail. Insalata fantasia (a green lettuce salad with creamy garlic dressing) and a fish salad made with shrimp, snapper and squid are available. Additional pasta dishes include gnocchi a la marinara (potato dumplings), fettuccine primavera (with sauteed vegetables), spaghetti, and baked ziti a la Siciliana. There are five veal scallopini dishes; veal Parmigiana; five chicken dishes; shrimp scampi, marinara or fradiavolo (over linguini); red snapper; a seafood combination of clams, mussels, shrimp, calamari, and snapper, in either a red sauce or scampi sauce, served over linguini; and NY steak. For the vegetarian there is eggplant Parmigiana or rollatini and side dishes of vegetables. You can compliment your meal with espresso or cappuccino.

Service: ★★★ Quite pleasant.

Decor: ★★★½ This restaurant has two, long narrow rooms. The room to the left has five tables for 22 people. The room to the right has three booths and eight tables for 40 people. Total seating for 62. Still-life paintings of pears, plants, a flower pot, and a patio hang on the mauve plaster walls with red trim at the corners and entrance. The tables have glass over green tablecloths. The chairs are comfortable and sturdy — made of wood with mauve-cushioned seats. I found this place had good color coordination and was not overly done. The lighting is from in-set ceiling lights and sconces.

Atmosphere: ★★★★ Quiet and sophisticated.

ITALIAN UNDERGROUND ★★★
715 GRAND AVE. (303)945-6422

Dinner $$. Daily 5PM-10PM.
Type: Italian.

Food: ★★★ I found their pizza to be above average, but not great. They have some interesting appetizers, like cocktail meatballs, pizza clambakes, and cannoli. Entrees, all Italian, include spaghetti prepared a variety of ways (with meat sauce, meatballs, Italian sausage, or butter), pizza, linguini & clam sauce, cannoli, spinach lasagna, chicken Cacciatore, and a combination plate of spaghetti, sausage, meatballs, cannoli, and lasagna. They have a full bar, including mineral water, and ice cream is available for dessert.

Service: ★★½ A little slow.

Decor: ★★★½ As implied in the name, the restaurant is downstairs in a single room with two sections. The lower first section has eight tables for 33 people. The higher second section has six tables for 24 people, plus a bar for three or four more. Total seating for 60. Old wood skis and poles made of hickory adorn the sandstone walls which go well with the brick floors. There are old pictures of the hot springs, and the St. James Hotel of the 1800s which is no longer around. Candles are at all the tables, which have red-and-white checkered tablecloths. Track globe lights hang from the low stucco ceiling.

Atmosphere: ★★★ A family restaurant. However, in retrospect, I recall this place as being dark.

THE LOFT ★★★★
720 GRAND AVE. (303)945-6808

Lunch $$, Dinner $$-$$$, Sunday brunch $$. MON-SAT 11:30AM-2PM and 5PM-10PM. SUN 10AM-2PM and 5PM-10PM.
Type: American/Continental. Senior citizens and children's dinner portions ½ price plus $1.50.

Food: ★★★★ My chicken teriyaki was well prepared and a lot of food for lunch. It was topped with fresh pineapple and served with a large salad, rice and asparagus. An excellent meal. For a lunch appetizer you can choose from New England clam chowder, shrimp cocktail, or a hot or cold artichoke. Follow this with a burger or sandwich (steak, chicken breast, Monte Cristo, Reuben, club, or vegetarian). There is also a big selection of salads: Caesar's, chicken and snowpea, pasta, and steak & spinach. Lunch specialties include fettuccine, spaghetti with Swiss cheese, ground sirloin, honey-dipped chicken, omelets, Swiss veal Bratwurst, and a chicken burrito. The dinner appetizers include baked brie, chicken livers, and fettuccine Alfredo. The light dinner menu includes salads, a charburger, and cold roast beef or grilled chicken sandwich. The rest of the menu is divided into beef, pasta, seafood, poultry and house specialties. Steaks include filet mignon, NY pepper, and top sirloin. The pasta entrees are fettuccine Alfredo, straw & hay (white and spinach noodles in cream), and linguini with shrimp. From the sea comes pan-fried trout, broiled Alaskan salmon, grilled white Mexican shrimp, and baked Australian lobster tail. From the farm house comes grilled teriyaki chicken breast, chicken moutard (sautéed with brandy cream and mustard) and wiener backhendel (chicken, prepared with the chef's special sauce). The house specialties complete this varied menu which must require a skilled staff of chefs. They include Hungarian paprika filet goulash, calves liver, lemon veal, veal in a wine, cream and mushroom sauce, Wiener schnitzel and a chicken breast stuffed with prosciutto and Swiss. There are several good choices for dessert to finish your meal: mud or apple pie, ice cream, chocolate sundae or mousse, caramel custard, and cheesecake with strawberries.

Sunday brunch offers specialty drinks like Bloody Marys and Champagne. The egg entrees include eggs Benedict, Florentine and Neptune (with spinach & crabmeat); omelets, French toast, and a fritatta or open-face omelet. Many of the sandwich and salad selections from lunch are also on the brunch menu as are the following specialties: fettuccine, chicken burrito, and honey-dipped chicken.

Service: ★★★★½ Very, very good. One of the best in town.

Decor: ★★★★ There are three dining rooms to this restaurant. The nicest is the non-smoking room which overlooks Grand Ave. and has 13 tables with bench seats on one side and chairs on the other, plus five tables, for a total of 46 people. The center dining room has nine of the bench/chair combinations and three tables for 34 people. The room to the right has five tables and a bar which overlooks the indoor shops and seats 27 people. Total seating capacity is 107. Four light ceiling fans hang from the stucco ceiling. The rear wall is brick. The front has long vertical windows with shades, divided by cut logs. On one wall is a lighted mosaic of mountains and stream. Plastic flowers are set on glass-covered, red tablecloths. There is a modern art sculpture of sea gulls. The chairs have short, ribbed backs and are made of wood.

Atmosphere: ★★★½ A busy, popular place, but friendly.

RIVIERA SUPPER CLUB ★★★½
702 GRAND AVE. (303)945-7692

Dinner $$-$$$$. TUE-SUN 5PM-10PM Closed MON.
Type: Steak. Carry-out available.

Food: ★★★ Prime rib is their specialty. It's very good, but not great. All dinners come with baked potato and the all-you-can-eat soup, salad and baked beans bar. There were a few good items here, like hard-boiled eggs and fried apple crisp. The soup was also very good, but the beans were only fair. You can start your dinner with an appetizer of mushrooms with escargot and crabmeat, a crab cocktail, mushroom cheese, deep-fried mushrooms, or Rocky Mountain oysters. Prime rib, in three cut sizes, leads off their entrees. It also comes in combination with lobster and shrimp, as does the steak. The steak choices are NY strip, rib eye, teriyaki, chopped sirloin, and a steak or prime rib sandwich. Barbecue beef or pork ribs and chicken in a special Southern-style sauce are available. There are a couple of veal entrees: Francaise (lightly breaded, sauteed, with mushrooms) and in lemon juice with mushrooms. Rocky Mountain oysters can be ordered as an entree, as well. Broiled or teriyaki chicken is available. A good selection of seafood completes the entree selections: shrimp scampi; stuffed baked shrimp or flounder with a crabmeat dressing; deep-fried shrimp, trout, oysters or scallops; baked trout amandine or scallops; and Australian twin lobster tails. There is a children's menu and the dessert list includes parfaits with a variety of liqueurs, chocolate mint, or wine; sundaes; and cheesecake.

Service: ★★★½ Very good.

Decor: ★★★ This is a one-room restaurant with 17 tables for 70 people. The restaurant is located on a corner with one side higher than the other. The result is the windows, which have short white curtains for trim at the top, are at different levels. The windows along the front are at thigh level while the windows on the side are above the head. This makes for a rather strange appearance. The ceiling is brown and flat with no lights. Lighting is provided by candles at tables with beige tablecloths and by wall lights that shine over paintings of a mountain lake in winter, an Indian chief, a scene from Monument Valley, and a trapper at night viewing the desert. The chairs have short wood panels and yellow cushions.

Atmosphere: ★★★★ This is a quiet place with soft music playing in the background. It caters to an older crowd and is very pleasant.

ROSI'S BAVARIAN INN ★★★★
141 W. 6 (303)945-8412

Breakfast/Lunch $. MON-FRI 7AM-1PM. SAT-SUN 7AM-2PM.
Type: German. Lunch is only served on weekends. No separate checks. Pastries available to go. Reservations are not accepted.

Food: ★★★★½ They prepared a special order for me that was not on the menu: Vienna bratwurst on a French roll with German potato salad. This is fresh authentic German food. Homemade preserves and pastries, which I understand are very good and very popular, can be found on the breakfast menu along with the usual breakfast fare, as well as Bavarian or strawberry waffles, and a continental breakfast with a German hard roll. Champagne and mimosa (champagne & orange juice) are also available. The weekend lunch menu offers quiche, soup, chili, sandwiches (steak, Reuben, assorted European lunch meats, patty melt, grilled turkey or cheese, and French dip), salads (spinach, fruit, tuna, chef, small green, German potato, sauerkraut, and cottage cheese), burgers, and Bavarian sausages (veal or pork Bratwurst and Vienna). Wine and imported bottled beer are also available.

Service: ★★★★ Very friendly and willing to accommodate special orders.

Decor: ★★★★ This is a small single-room restaurant that bends at a 150-degree angle in the middle. There are 13 tables for 46 people — not enough for the crowd from Denver. Breakfast, according to the owners, is a 45-minute wait sometimes just to get seated. This speaks well for the quality of the restaurant. However, you might try to arrive at an off-hour between breakfast and lunch, if there is one. I was here on a Friday morning in spring, about 11AM, and there were tables available. Your best bet is to visit during the week.

The windows have blue curtains with white frilly borders. The wood panel walls are adorned with pictures of Heineken and Beck beer in wood frames with glass, photographs taken in Germany of "Rothenburg Ob Der Tauber" and Bavaria, a colorful rug depicting horses hauling logs from a mountain mill, and antique-looking plates showing German castles and a wolf in winter. The tables have blue-and-white checkered tablecloths under glass and fresh flowers. The low plaster ceiling with beams has white, three-bulb, light fixtures.

Atmosphere: ★★★★ The atmosphere gives the impression of a Bavarian inn and complements the decor.

GOLDEN

Originally called Golden City, the town was named after Thomas L. Golden. He and fellow settlers James Saunders and George W. Jackson established a temporary camp near the mouth of Clear Creek Canyon in 1858. The following year, the Boston Trading Company sent a wagon train led by General George West to partake in the gold discovery. From 1862 to 1867, before Colorado acquired statehood, Golden City was the capital of Colorado Territory. The building used for the Colorado territorial capitol is still located on the corner of Washington and 12th. Once a railroad center associated with the metal-production industries, Golden today is a tourist center, home to Coors Brewery, established in 1872 by Adolph Coors Sr., Colorado School of Mines, founded in 1874, and county seat of Jefferson County.

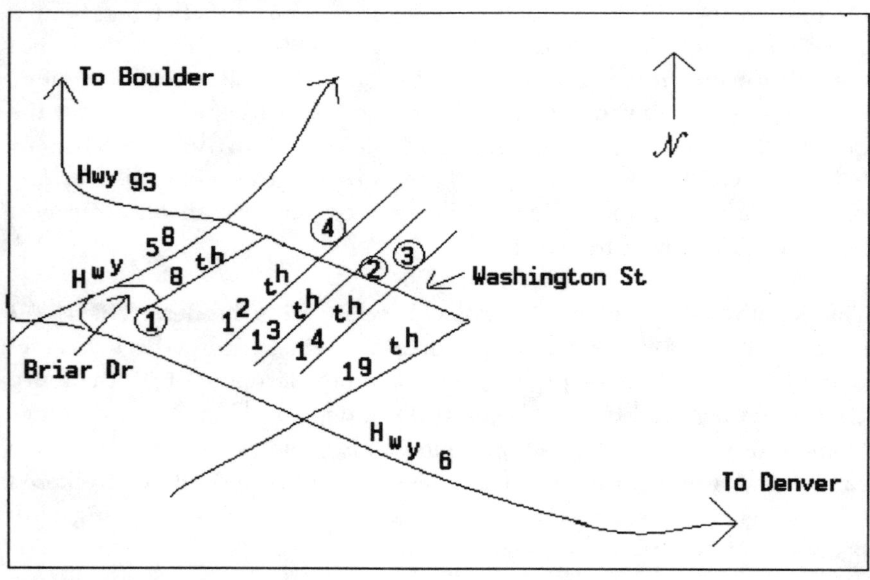

Restaurants and Ratings:	Food	Service	Decor	Atm	Overall
1. Briarwood Inn	★★★★½	★★★★	★★★★½	★★★½	★★★★
2. Golden Eagle	★★★	★★	★★½	★★½	★★½
3. Guido's	★★★½	★★★	★★★½	★★★★	★★★½
4. Kenrow's	★★★½	★★½	★★★	★★★	★★★

The Briarwood Inn offers a variety of classic dishes from around the world in a country mansion atmosphere. Guido's serves some well-prepared Italian dishes in an old house purported to be haunted. Kenrow's is a good breakfast stop and is very popular. All four restaurants accept major credit cards and serve alcohol, only the Golden Eagle does not offer a nonsmoking section.

BRIARWOOD INN ★★★★
1630 8TH STREET (303)279-3121

Lunch $$, brunch $$$, dinner $$$$+ (mostly $25-$30). MON-SAT 11AM-2:30PM and 5:30PM-10PM. SUN 10:30AM-2:30PM and 5PM-9PM.
Type: American/Continental.

Food: ★★★★½ An array of long crackers awaits you when you are seated: whole wheat, garlic, sesame and poppy seed and Norwegian flat bread. I ordered the crêpes Rheims: a wonderful combination of chicken, mushrooms and onions in just the right proportions in a feather-light crêpe with cream sauce and topped with melted cheddar. This was a delicious and flavorful entree, served with a sorbet on the side. Other lunch entrees include homemade pastas like angel hair with fresh basil & Italian pear tomatoes, scampi au cognac, cioppino (a fish stew), chicken Rochambeau prepared with Danish ham and Swiss cheese, several salad selections (a Hawaiian chicken platter, avocado shrimp, and Long Island duck), and a few traditional fares (prime rib sandwich, Monte Cristo, and a smothered burrito). You can finish your meal with hot or iced cappucino or espresso along with homemade ice cream, cheesecake, or a torte. The desserts vary but may include sabyon (a filo pastry filled with homemade lemon ice cream, Grand Marnier, and fresh fruit) or white chocolate lasagna (homemade peanut butter ice cream topped with chocolate and caramel). Full-course dinners include an appetizer tray filled with gulf shrimp boiled in beer, liver pâté, and chilled ratatouille; spinach or vinaigrette salad, vegetable du jour, fresh fruits, toasted coconut bananas and nut-filled brownies. As for the entrees, they feature beef (tournedos "excelsior" made with eggplant, filet Wellington, and pepper steak au cognac), several veal dishes (picatta, a l' Oskar, and Martinque), lamb, duck a l'amaretto, roast pheasant, and a variety of seafood selections (Dover sole, salmon hollandaise, Rocky Mountain rainbow trout, broiled swordfish, and lobster thermidore).

The single ($14.95) price Sunday brunch offers a glass of champagne, seasonal fruits, freshly baked pastries, and a choice of nine entrees including eggs Benedict, prime Benedict, omelets, seafood crepes, Monte Cristo, roast prime rib of beef, eggs Briarwood with avocados and sliced tomatoes in place of the ham, eggs Columbia made with Norwegian king salmon and crêpes Rheims.

Service: ★★★★ Friendly, very helpful, and with a smile.

Decor: ★★★★½ A red-brick walk and foot bridge lead up to this restaurant at the end of a dead-end street. Inside is an elegant, eclectic European arrangement of white tablecloths, red-clothed napkins, white-laced curtains with brown drapes and ties, white stencil window dividers, a high wood-beamed vaulted ceiling, antique hutches & mirrors, turn-of-the-century Edwardian cabinets from Belgium, tan and gold wallpaper in a flowered-pattern, and chandeliers hanging on brass ceiling chains. The pictures in the booths have pastoral scenes of pheasants, cows, cottages and gypsies. The east dining room, which features a dresser and mirror between two glass-enclosed wood wine cabinets, seats 120. The west dining room, with its stone fireplace and shiny copper heat duct in the middle, seats 125. In the middle is the library, with books on a high wall shelf extending around the room, and a lounge.

Atmosphere: ★★★½ I was here in December, so instrumental Christmas carols were playing. There is a high-fashion, upper-class atmosphere about this place and it was occupied primarily by elderly ladies for lunch.

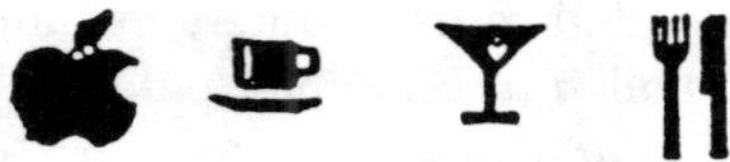

Golden Eagle ★★½
1305 Washington (303)279-5257

Lunch $-$$, dinner $$-$$$. MON-SAT 11AM-9PM. Closed SUN.

Type: Tavern.

Food: ★★★ *Service:* ★★ *Decor:* ★★½ *Atmosphere:* ★★½

A friend and I happened upon this place on a Monday night in mid-winter. We had their two-for-one sirloin steak special. It came with cream of cauliflower soup, which was creamy but had only a few tiny pieces of cauliflower. The steak was a thin, lean, tender, six-to-seven ounce piece with no seasoning. The baked potato was a little undercooked. We also tried their nachos: a half order filled a nine-inch plate high with American and Monterey jack cheeses, scallions, burger, beans, tomatoes, and jalapeños. Guacamole and sour cream were served on the side. They were good, not great. Service was friendly but forgetful and inefficient. Our waitress forgot to give our nacho order to the cook and served our steaks first. We had the nachos for dessert. There are practically no windows in here except for four-inch-square glass blocks in the front of the restaurant. Western art decorates this restaurant/lounge/bar/pool hall. The lounge can seat 48 at six booths and six tables. The main dining room farther to the right seats 58 at 11 tables. There is a pool table at the end of the main dining room which was in use the entire time my friend and I were there. About a half-dozen televisions provide additional entertainment. This place is strong on country-western clothes, styles and nonstop music (which got to be a little too much and too loud after a while). You will find a quiet, peaceful crowd of country-western folks here.

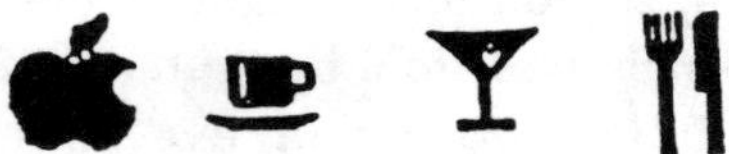

GUIDO'S ★★★½
714 14TH STREET (303)278-8226

Lunch $$, dinner $$-$$$. Mon-Fri 11AM-2:30PM and 4:30PM-10PM. SAT 4:30PM-10PM. Closed SUN.
Type: Italian. 15% gratuity added to checks for parties of six or more.

Food: ★★★½ Their dinner salad had fresh, crisp, cold vegetables including sliced mushrooms and black olives. Entrees are served with fresh soft dinner rolls made with pizza dough and Italian spices (oregano, basil, & hot pepper). The lasagna seemed to have just the right amount of noodles, sauce, tomatoes, ricotta and mozzarella cheeses, beef in the form of tiny, spicy meatballs, and spices. For dessert, try some of their fruity and nutty spumoni with walnuts and candied fruit. The rest of the dinner menu starts out with a cold antipasto plate, garlic bread, and stuffed mushrooms or artichoke hearts for appetizers; Caesar's, Italian chef or dinner salads; entree specials (chicken or veal Parmigiana, steak pizzaiola, veal saltimbocca, seafood fettucine, and a seafood spinach fettucini in their own Agli Ioli sauce); pastas (baked rigattoni, penne with sausage, pasta agli ioli, spaghetti and fettucini Alfredo); regular and deep-dish 14-inch pan pizza made with homemade crust and thirteen topping choices, including anchovies, broccoli and artichoke hearts; sausage rolls; calzones; and spaghetti for the kids. The lunch menu offers a seven-inch individual pizza in addition to the large one, calzones, sausage rolls, the same salads and pastas and chicken Parmigiana. In addition, there are several sandwiches to choose from: meatball, sausage & peppers, Philly steak, turkey, ham & cheese or turkey clubs; and ham & Provolone, alone or with salami, cappicola, or both. All food is prepared fresh using imported cheeses and Italian coldcuts.

Service: ★★★ Friendly, informative and with a good laugh.

Decor: ★★★½ This restaurant is located in an old two-story house built in 1908 and recognized by the historic preservation board of Golden. There is a small seating section to the right of the entrance with four tables for eight and a small, two-stool bar to the left. Straight back and to the right is one small dining room with five mauve-clothed tables for 18. It is decorated with an in-set wall cabinet made of wood with a mirror back; cupboard doors; and shelves containing red glass & white ceramic candle holders, salt & pepper shakers, and preserve serving jars. Across the hall to the left is another small dining room with five tables for 20. This room leads to a patio with five round tables, a bar and several benches. About 40 people can fit here. Both dining rooms have gas fireplaces set in old wood frames. White-laced curtains hang in the wood-framed windows. Lighting is provided by a ceiling fan structure with a trio of lights in frosted, flower-shaped shades. Seating is on wobbly, fragile, small wood-framed chairs; not uncomfortable, just fragile. Neither dining room has any pictures. The lack of paintings may be a plus for this old house. It somehow maintains its simplicity and holds onto its age better. I think artworks would distract from the antique qualities of the building itself. I liked the setting for what it was. There are also two dining rooms upstairs for banquets and private parties.

Atmosphere: ★★★★ Easy listening music in stereo plays from two corner speakers. I found this place to have a comfortable setting that will make you "feel at home." Like The Prospector in Breckenridge, this old house restaurant is purported to be haunted according to co-owner Angie Larson. The ghost in this case is a Mrs. Delaney, and either she or her two children died in this building. Neither Mrs. Delaney nor her two children, to my knowledge, were present the evening that I was there. Then again, maybe I was just too busy eating and taking notes to notice.

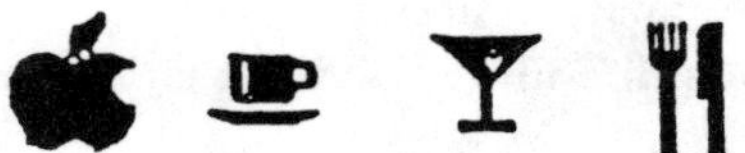

KENROW'S ★★★
718 12TH STREET (303)279-5164

Breakfast $, lunch/dinner $-$$$. 7 days 6AM-10PM.
Type: Family (featuring Mexican, American and Italian).

Food: ★★★½ All seven of our breakfasts were very good with oversized portions. For something different, try their Reuben omelet made with corned beef, sauerkraut and Swiss. It comes with hash browns and either toast or two big biscuits & gravy, which are a meal by themselves. The pancakes, bacon, eggs and sausage were all quite good. The avocado omelet is made with guacamole rather than fresh slices of avocado. The hash browns were undercooked and the coffee was only fair. Other breakfast selections include pork chops, chicken fried steak, huevos rancheros, a hard egg sandwich, pigs in a blanket, ground-beef patty, and diced ham & eggs. The lunch/dinner menu begins with Buffalo wings, peel & eat shrimp, and a barbecue rib basket for appetizers. This is followed by a soup du jour, homemade chili, salads (taco, dinner or antipasto), hot dogs and burgers. They have cold deli sandwiches (turkey, roast beef, chicken or tuna salad on your choice of breads), hot sandwiches (Philly steak, Reuben, French dip, meatball and/or sausage, Parmesan, and vegetarian), pasta (spaghetti, lasagna, and eggplant or Italian cutlet Parmigiana), calzones, and traditional and Sicilian-style pan pizza in 12- or 16-inch sizes with a dozen toppings to choose from, including jalapeños and pineapple. The dinner entrees feature seafood (shrimp Provencal or scampi, Cajun catfish, and salmon steak); chicken (Cordon Bleu, Cajun, fried, or Parmigiana); chicken or beef chimichangas and fajitas; barbecue baby-back ribs, beef ribs and country ribs; prime rib; pork chops; and steaks. For dessert, you have your choice between fruit or cream pies, cheesecake, brownies, cake, and ice cream sundaes.

Service: ★★½ Understaffed. The waitresses were hustling at "warp 6" and we still had to wait. Coffee was not served until several minutes after we had placed our breakfast orders. Our waitress was quite pleasant, helpful and hustled about to try to please everyone. She maintained a cheerful smile under difficult circumstances.

Decor: ★★★ There is a small dining room at the entrance with four tables for 16. In my opinion, this created an awkward situation. The folks that were eating in this room had to deal with several guests waiting nearby to be seated. If it were me, I would have refused to sit in this room. The main (smoking) dining room, to the right of the entrance, has sixteen tables and a red-brick wall at the far end with a large mural depicting a street scene. The dining room to the far right is nonsmoking and has seven tables, a red-brick wall, several pictures of cowboys, and a Western display of rusty latches and chains. The other end room to the left of the entrance is also nonsmoking with seven tables, wicker baskets and trays, a still-life of vases and flowers, white-laced curtains, and a life-size statue of a bearded man with a black hat and suspenders holding a mug in his hand. Total seating for about 140 people.

Atmosphere: ★★★ This is a busy, busy place on Sunday mornings. A lot of regulars must come in here because our hostess asked us if we wanted menus thinking we already knew what they had to offer. A little later, some regulars did come in and ordered the special without looking at the menu.

GOULD

Preceded by a community called Penfold, Gould was named after Edward B. Gould, who settled here in 1898. Today, the town of Gould is nonexistent and the site is privately owned. Gould is a small one-restaurant town (or should I say "one-restaurant private site"?) but its one restaurant is one of the best in the North Park area.

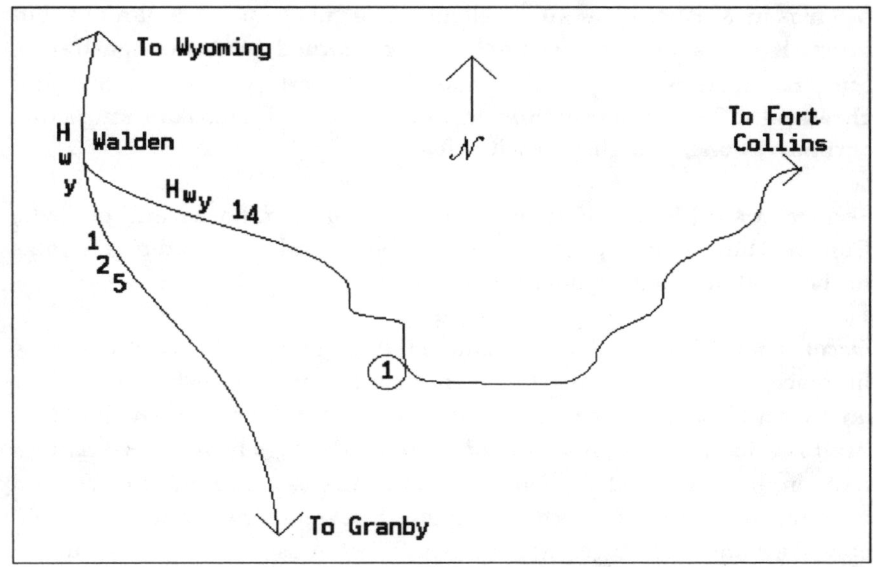

1. COOKHOUSE ★★★½
HWY 14, SOUTH SIDE (303)723-8339

Lunch $, Dinner $$-$$$. WED-MON 11AM-10PM (9PM in winter). Closed TUE, except during hunting season (Mid OCT-Mid NOV).
Type: Steak. They accept major credit cards with a $15 minimum charge, do not have a nonsmoking section, and serve alcohol.

Food: ★★★★ They have excellent homemade soup: cream of potato (made with fresh cream) and vegetable beef the evening I was there. The salad bar has 18 items including two pasta salads, pineapple, mandarin oranges, chives and creamed peas. The ribs are tender and juicy; however, they use store-bought bottled barbecue sauce. The broasted chicken was done to perfection: tender and moist on the inside and crispy on the outside. It is one of the best broasted chicken in Colorado. Their steaks are also super. I was with a group of nine so I managed to get some reactions to several items on the menu. Although no one ordered a seafood dish, the five types of meals that were ordered (filet mignon, NY strip, barbecue spare ribs, honey-dipped chicken and a combination of chicken & ribs) were all excellent. The lunch menu is limited, but good. It offers hot sandwiches (roast or corned beef, and pastrami), burgers, burritos, soup, salad and, for dessert, pie, ice cream and cheesecake. The dinner entrees include lobster tail, Alaskan king crab, shrimp, T-bone, and shrimp with ribs.

Service: ★★★ I had a short chat with the cook, Tim Lucas, and his wife, Connie. They are nice people and well known and respected by the folks in the local area that frequent this place.

Decor: ★★★★ This is a single rectangular dining room with a circular stone fireplace in the middle and tables for about 56 people. Adjacent is a bar area with 12 barstools and three tables for 12 more people. The building itself is a log cabin with a vaulted ceiling. The logs have a very natural look on the inside and, combined with the fireplace, provide a warm and cozy feeling. On the far right wall hangs a seven point elk next to an old cow skull and eight black iron skillets. There are several prints — under glass and in wood frames — of mountain lakes, elk, ranches, rams, a log cabin by a mountain stream, a cowboy wearing a white scarf riding a horse-drawn carriage, and a summer sunset. To your right, as you first enter the dining room (which must be accessed through the bar), is an old photo, circa 1900 I would guess, of some gentlemen dressed in suits. Some baseball trophies in the far right corner and two posters, one of Monaco and the other of Theatre Magazine with a flapper girl on the cover, add a different touch to the otherwise western decor.

Atmosphere: ★★★ The television from the bar could be overheard in the dining room. However, later, they played soft country music.

GRANBY

Named for Granby Hillyer, a Denver attorney, the town is located near the confluence of the Colorado and Fraser Rivers and is known as "the dude ranch of Colorado". Six famous guest ranches are all within a half hour drive of Granby. Nearby Granby Reservoir is the second largest reservoir in Colorado.

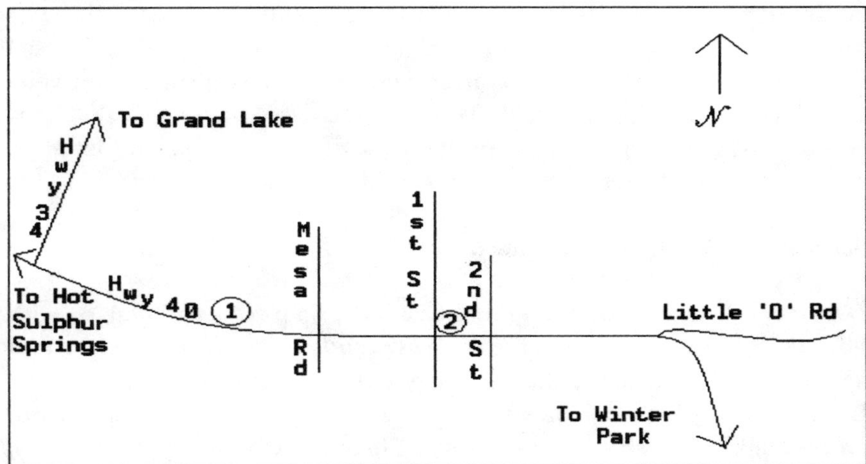

Restaurants and Ratings:	Food	Service	Decor	Atm	Overall
1. El Monte	★★★½	★★½	★★★	★★½	★★★
2. Longbranch	★	★	★★½	★★	★½

The El Monte Motor Inn is a family-style restaurant that serves a very good Monte Cristo in a puff shell. Both restaurants accept major credit cards and serve alcohol, but neither offers a nonsmoking section.

El Monte ★★★
519 West Agate Av (303)887-3348

Breakfast/lunch $, dinner $$-$$$. 7 days 6AM-9PM.
Type: Family. 15% discount offered to all senior citizens.

Food: ★★★½ I ordered the Monte Cristo which came in a puff shell rather than grilled. Having been used to the grilled variety, I found that

I liked the puff shell Monte better. It was filled with ham, turkey, American and Swiss cheeses and topped lightly with powdered sugar. If you like Monte Cristo sandwiches, you should try this one. It came with two pickle slices and thin French fries, á la McDonald's style. Breakfast offers chicken fried steak, huevos rancheros, a breakfast burrito, an English muffin sandwich, pigs in a blanket, and cinnamon rolls. The lunch fare includes soup du jour, salads, red or green chili; appetizers like hot wings, onion rings and deep fried mushrooms; burgers, sandwiches, and Mexican food. Dinner is a choice between steaks, fried chicken, grilled chicken breast, pork chops, trout amandine and breaded shrimp. There is a children's menu for all three meals.

Service: ★★½ Quiet and satisfactory.

Decor: ★★★ The main dining room can hold 56 people at 15 tables with white plastic covers. Seating is on hardwood chairs with rib-backs and armrests. The same polished aspen wood carvings found at the Longbranch — horses, hands at prayer, a moose, a bear, a howling wolf, an owl, and a cross — are here also. Three photos of rock formations, rivers and blue sky hang on one wall. White transparent-laced curtains hang in the front windows. Philodendrons and wagon wheels with lights in frosted shades hang on brass chains from the vaulted ceiling. An adjoining banquet room to the rear seats an additional 50 to 55 people and is used for any overflow. Two stained-glass windows in the shapes of mountains using purple, blue, orange, and brown separate the main dining and banquet rooms.

Atmosphere: ★★½ Austere and quiet with no music. More tourists than most places in town because of the motel, but still many locals.

LONGBRANCH ★½
185 E AGATE AVENUE (303)887-2209

Lunch $, dinner $$-$$$. MON-SAT 11AM-9:30PM. SUN 5PM-9PM.

Type: Continental (German) and American. Children's menu. Take-out available.

Food: ★ *Service:* ★ *Decor:* ★★½ *Atmosphere:* ★★

I had an overcooked chicken fried steak (beef chuck, I would say) in a brown glazed gravy with packaged mashed potatoes, no vegetables or salad, and a roll. Service was infrequent and unprofessional. The waitress "bopped around" like a pinball, leaving customers waiting at a table in the middle of taking an order to seat another party standing at the door. She never returned to my table after I was served and told a couple of guys waiting at the door that they could seat themselves at a table that had not been cleared yet. This is a single-room restaurant with an adjacent bar/lounge. A gas fireplace — set in front of a real red-brick fireplace — brass lanterns, wood carvings, and paintings are the major items of decor. There is very little natural lighting because of an overhang outside. Consequently, all the dining room lights are kept on in the middle of the day when it is bright and sunny outside. This is a very busy and noisy place at lunch time, popular with the locals.

Grand Lake and the town of Grand Lake

GRAND LAKE

Grand Lake is situated on the north shore of the largest natural body of water in Colorado, after which the town got its name, and on the headwaters of the mighty Colorado River. It was founded as a mining settlement at first, but today it is a popular summer resort, serving as the west entrance to Rocky Mountain National Park.

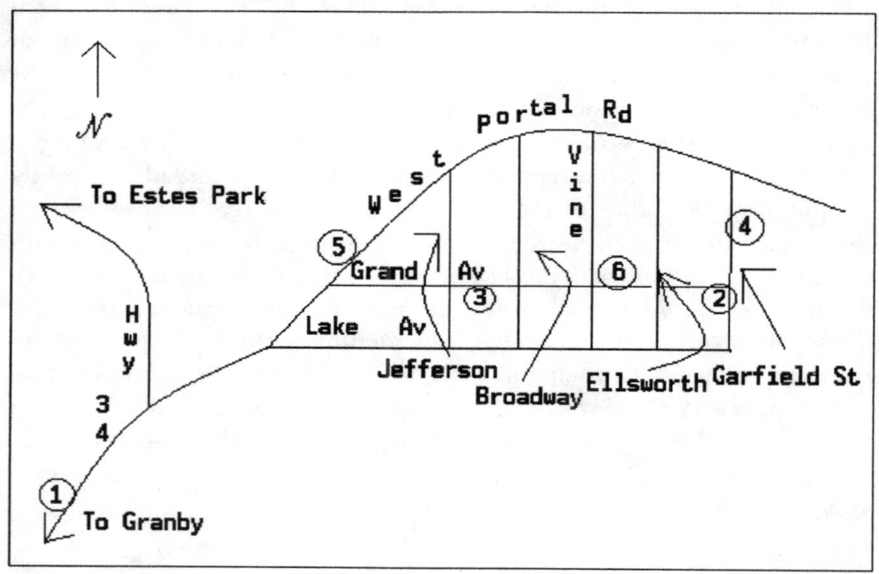

Restaurants and Ratings:	Food	Service	Decor	Atm	Overall
1. Caroline's Cuisine	★★★★½	★★★★★	★★★★★	★★★★½	★★★★★
2. Maxine's	★★½	★½	★★	★	★★
3. Mountain Inn	★★★½	★★½	★★★	★★★	★★★
4. Rapids	★★★★	★★★★½	★★★★	★★★★★	★★★★½
5. Red Fox	★★★★	★★★½	★★★★½	★★★★	★★★★
6. Terrace Inn	★★★	★★½	★★½	★★	★★½

I dined at three excellent to outstanding restaurants in Grand Lake. My favorite was a restaurant that had just opened its doors the weekend before: Caroline's Cuisine. Chef Caroline prepares delicious continental food that is served by an enthusiastic waiter in a comfortable setting with great views of the hills. Rapids was a close second, featuring Italian, beef, fish and veal specialties with haunting nighttime views of the rock-filled Tonahutu (or Colorado) River. The Red Fox was also excellent — with its offerings of seafood and beef — in a setting high atop the town, lake, and surrounding hills. All restaurants accept major credit cards and serve alcohol, but only Caroline's Cuisine offers a nonsmoking section.

CAROLINE'S CUISINE ★★★★★
9921 U.S. HIGHWAY 34 (303)627-9404

Breakfast $, lunch $-$$, dinner $$$. TUE-SUN: 5PM-9PM. SUN: 10AM-2PM. Closed MON.
Type: Continental. In business since October 1991. Reservations recommended.

Food: ★★★★½ Dinner is preceded by a warm French roll served with garlic and chive cream cheese: a good start! A Caesar's salad follows with Romaine lettuce and croutons. I ordered Caroline's roasted one-half chicken: chicken grandmere (or Grandma's chicken) with gratin dauphinoise (potatoes au gratin) and vegetables (green beans and tomatoes topped with almonds). The chicken was moist on the inside and crispy on the outside and was served with sautéed mushrooms, bacon, and pearl onions. This is a hearty meal, so plan on some leftovers. The breakfast menu includes eggs Benedict, huevos rancheros, waffles with walnut butter, buttermilk pancakes and fresh-baked muffins. Lunch features nachos, shrimp cocktail, and Buffalo chicken wings for appetizers; corn chowder and French onion soups; and taco salad. Also on the lunch menu are burgers, sandwiches (Reuben, vegetarian and steak with onions), and entrees like chicken pot pie, fish & chips, burritos, fettucini Alfredo, and tabouleh salad. The dessert selections include tirra ma su, baked Alaska, chocolate cake, apple pie, ice cream, and crème caramel. Dinner entrees feature baked trout, fettucini with jumbo garlic shrimp, filet mignon, lamb chops, veal, and rigatoni.

Service: ★★★★★ I had a very thorough and enthusiastic young waiter. Jean-Claude, the other host besides Caroline, is a French chef, raised in

Italy, who has worked from coast to coast in the U.S. before opening this restaurant. He is most interesting and pleasant. His restaurant was off to a good start and had many things going for it. I think Caroline and Jean-Claude will have a big success on their hands.

Decor: ★★★★★ The main dining room is in two adjoining sections facing south with 16 tables for 68. A blue swordfish hangs on the far right wall. Windows with horizontal shades and maroon velvet curtains extend the full length of the south wall. A shelf sets over the windows occupied by books, plates, a Grand Marnier bottle and canisters. There is a small wood cabinet and mirror with coffee cups and glasses along the far left wall beneath two wine racks. Off the dining room is a small patio with two tables for eight. Between the entrance and dining room is a bar with six stools and three lounge areas. The one nearest the entrance has two small round tables with five high chairs and two red velvet couches next to a fish tank. The lounge to the right of the bar has a piano and two green couches. The lounge to the left of the bar has two tables for eight, a red velvet couch, and a wood-burning stove in front of a stone wall. The louvre upstairs features a circular walkway with five small tables for 10: ideal for couples. The tables are on the circular path with green velvet love seats set into the mauve walls. All seats look outward and down onto the bar, lounge and dining room below. The ceiling is hexagonal in shape with a fan and tinted glass.

Atmosphere: ★★★★½ There is a great view of the hills from the dining room. Combined with Italian music, a piano, a lounge area that will make you wish for a wait before dinner, and a rather unusual louvre, plan on spending an enjoyable evening here.

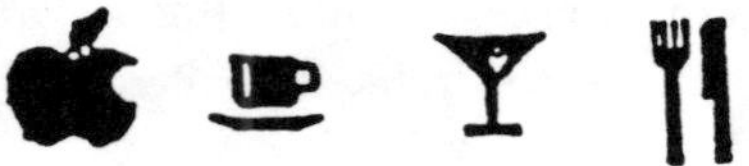

MAXINE'S ★★
928 GRAND AV (303)627-8897

Breakfast $, lunch/dinner$-$$. NOV-APR: 7 days 8AM-8PM. MAY-SEP: 7 days 7AM-9PM. OCT: MON-WED 8AM-2PM, THU-SUN 8AM-8PM. Type: Country.

Food: ★★½ *Service:* ★½ *Decor:* ★★ *Atmosphere:* ★

They were out of Philly steak sandwiches, so I ordered the green chili made with pork, large tomato pieces, beans and onions. It packed a fairly good kick. The flour tortillas, though, were part soft, part crisp, from being overcooked. Service was slow, with only one waitress covering both dining rooms. Wagon wheel light fixtures hang from the stucco ceiling . Posters and pictures of the surrounding area hang from the stucco walls. Irritating rock music is played in the kitchen to accompany the irritating smoke drifting over from the next table.

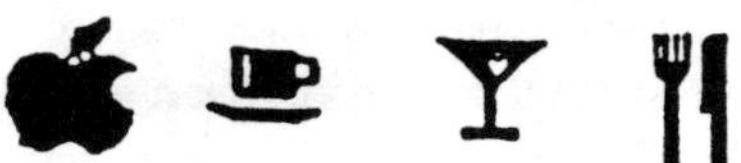

MOUNTAIN INN ★★★
612 GRAND AV (303)627-3385

Lunch $$, dinner $$$. 7 days 11AM-9PM. Closed three weeks in NOV. Type: Family. 15% gratuity added to parties of six or more. $3.95 plate charge for adults sharing; $2.00 if children under 12 share.

Food: ★★★½ I ordered the beef and bean burrito for lunch. It filled a 9x12 inch platter and was my only meal of the day. It was 95% beef (actually, I would have preferred something closer to 50% beef and 50% bean) and smothered with an ample amount of cheese and green chili sauce. Onion and green and red peppers added a nice spicy touch to the meal. I came here with an appetite, having not yet eaten that day, and left with a box of leftovers for dinner. Make sure you come here hungry. Their lunch menu offers sandwiches (chicken breast, fish, hot roast beef and burgers), vegetarian or beef stew, chicken pot pie, soup, and salad. Sautéed mushrooms, vegetable tempura and Rocky Mountain oysters can be ordered as appetizers. The dinner entrees include prime rib, fried shrimp, salmon, trout almandine, pot roast, chicken fried steak, country-fried or oven-baked chicken, barbecued beef ribs; and charbroiled pork chops, NY strip, beef kabob and rib eye prepared with Colorado beef. Also on the menu is an item referred to as "Fixings": soup, salad, vegetable, potato, biscuits and ice cream. Sounds like a good meal for a vegetarian. There is a children's menu.

Service: ★★½ Understaffed with one young waitress handling late lunch (1PM-2PM). She forgot my water and was late returning, but was friendly and tried hard.

Decor: ★★★ True to its name, the inside of this restaurant resembles a mountain inn with log wood walls, posts, and ceiling beams. The vertical wall logs are joined by solid concrete. Four-sided, clear-glass, brass lanterns, a shovel, posters of Grand Lake's Centennial (1981), Rocky Mountain National Park, Italy, and North Denver are some of the items of decor hanging on the wall. There is a main dining room in two sections with the rear section partly divided by the log walls. Seating is on hardwood chairs set at tables with maroon and white plastic covers. The front section has 14 tables for 60. The rear has seven tables for 28. There is a second dining room to the far left of the entrance with hardwood tables without covers and hardwood chairs that seats about 30. It is used for meetings as well as for diners when they are very busy. "Doc Lee's Saloon" is to the right of the main dining room and has four tables for 12, seven barstools, beer signs, and old photos of Doc Lee.

Atmosphere: ★★★ This is much more of a family restaurant than it appears on the outside. It is a quiet place with easy listening music in the background.

RAPIDS ★★★★½
209 RAPIDS LANE (303)627-3707

Dinner $$$-$$$$. Memorial Day to OCT: 7 days 5PM-9:30PM. NOV to Memorial Day: WED-SUN 5PM-9:30PM. Closed MON-TUE.
Type: Italian (and steak). Patrons requested to refrain from smoking pipes or cigars. A 15% gratuity is added for tables of six or more. There is a $1.00 per ticket charge for separate checks and a $3.00 per plate charge for sharing.

Food: ★★★★ My dinner started with an hors d'oeuvre tray of broiled shell on shrimp with cocktail sauce, prime rib pâté, blue cheese pâté, and crackling bread (you could hear everyone in the dining room making crackling sounds as they bit into these crisp crackers). A Caesar's salad of Romaine lettuce, tomato sauce and croutons followed. Dinner was preceded by a delicious and intriguing apricot sorbet. My entree was succulent prime rib, medium rare, new potatoes, sweet carrots, and fresh but firm asparagus spears in a white wine-and-cheese sauce. An excellent meal with all the trimmings. The dinner menu features several pasta and beef selections plus a few fish, veal and chicken entrees. Fettuccine Alfredo, linguini with white clam sauce, olive oil, shrimp, garlic, or marinara sauce, lasagna, manicotti, and eggplant with marinara sauce are the Italian entrees. Prime rib, T-bone and NY pepper steak are the beef choices. Trout with almonds or capers, a fish of the evening; veal picatta, Marsala or with capers; and Sicilian chicken or chicken with capers are the other selections. A children's menu for 10 years old and under includes pasta, hamburger, chicken and salad. The wine list has several domestic and imported reds, whites and sparkling selections, including Dom Perignon. A special dessert of the evening can finish your dining experience — or inquire about one of their famous ice cream drinks.

Service: ★★★★½ Friendly, cordial, efficient and professional. They know when to come to your table and when to stay away: a sign of a well-trained, proficient staff.

Decor: ★★★★ The main dining room is straight back from the entrance overlooking the Tonahutu River. It has 14 tables for 50 diners. Exterior lights provide haunting views of the rock-filled river below. Artificial garland drapes the tops of the windows and brass, frosted-glass lanterns hang on the wood log beams separating the long row of windows that face the river. A gas, black metal fireplace sets to one side of the room. Hanging plants and stained-glass pictures of ducks, a pheasant and a carnival horse separate the open dining room from the lounge and lobby. The log beam ceiling slants down toward the river. Seating is on comfortable brown, tan & beige striped chairs in wood frames with armrests. The tables are covered with mauve cloths. The lounge to the left of the main dining room has six barstools, four tables for eight, and a television. A second dining room in the back with eight tables for 32 is decorated with paintings by a local artist showing ducks in flight. There are more glass-framed posters of carousel animals. My waitress, Kathrina, the owner's daughter, explained that their family used to own a restaurant in Estes Park called The Carousel, and these pictures keep those memories alive. They are building a terrace on the river which they plan to have open in the summer of 1992. They may also be open for lunch at that time.

Atmosphere: ★★★★★ Kathrina also told me that this restaurant was built on Indian holy ground and that it used to be a brothel at one time. It was also used as a gambling house until the late 1940's. There is a lot of history and character in these walls. A combination of relaxing jazz, soft rock and easy listening music plays throughout the restaurant. The clientele is soft spoken and sophisticated. This is a very pleasant dining experience.

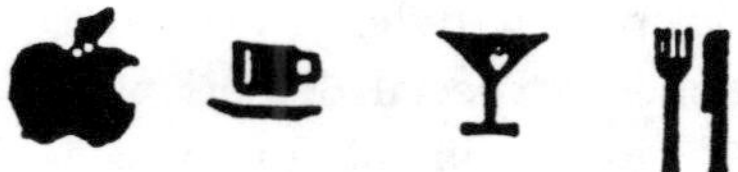

THE RED FOX ★★★★
414 WEST PORTAL ROAD (303)627-3418

Dinner $$$-$$$$. OCT-DEC: FRI-SUN 5PM-10PM. Closed JAN-MAY. JUN-SEP: 7 days 5PM-10PM. SAT 11AM-2PM. SUN 10AM-2PM. (Note: SAT lunch and SUN brunch are new starting in 1992.)
Type: Seafood (steak and continental).
The Red Fox was established in 1975 and named in honor of the fox families playing on the nearby rocks.

Food: ★★★★ I opted for the salad with the sweet and spicy French dressing instead of the mushroom soup. It was made with bib lettuce, cucumber, carrot slivers, onion slice and croutons: a better variety than most of the other salads in town. This was followed by a rainbow sorbet of raspberry, lime and orange. For my entree I chose frog legs! This was the first time in twenty years I had the tailless amphibian's legs and only the second time ever. Six large frog legs were served on a bed of lettuce with a baked potato and sautéed mixed vegetables on the side. The first time that I had frog legs they were from a frog that I had caught and killed to use for fish bait. I was on my three-day solo on a four-week Outward Bound course in Minnesota. I caught three fish, the largest being about six inches. All I had for cooking was a tin cup, so the frog legs were thrown into the boiled fish stew and tasted more like fish. They were just a little bit different the second time around. Actually, as you probably know from experience (or have heard), frog legs taste a lot like chicken — except when I eat chicken I do not get visions of frogs leaping from one lily pad to the next. I guess when you eat something for the first or second time you think more about what it is you are actually eating. The frog legs, by the way, were from Bangladesh (couldn't those people eat them?), and they were very tender with a light breading. Warm garlic butter was served on the side.

To start your meal you have several appetizers to choose from, including seafood egg rolls, escargots, and brie cheese. Seafood, steaks, house specialties, and a light appetite menu are featured for dinner. You can order rainbow trout almandine, northwestern salmon, blackened red fish, shrimp scampi, or lobster. Grilled and seasoned Colorado beef is offered from the broiler: filet mignon, steak oscar, or double lamb chops. The house specialties include fettucini Alfredo, cajun pork chops, steak Diane, and Chateaubriand bouquetiere for two. If you are looking for something lighter, you might order baked French onion au gratin, lemon pepper chicken or seafood salad, or a filet. A children's menu is available. The gourmet burger bar in the lounge has Buffalo wings, soups, salads, burgers, fish, chicken, and a steak sandwich.

Service: ★★★½ A friendly, jovial and talkative young waitress. Very pleasant and efficient.

Decor: ★★★★½ This is not an ideal place for the handicapped. You have to walk up 69 steps to reach the entrance to the bar and lounge, then go up 13 more steps to reach the dining room. Both the lounge and dining room are in a rather unusual octagonal-shaped building with a domed ceiling that has eight wood beams stretching outward from the center down to the walls and a square pole in the middle of the room. Eight maroon cloth tables ring the perimeter of the dining room for 24 people. Four tables for 14 fill the center. Total seating is 38. White-laced, drawn-back curtains with maroon trim, top and bottom, decorate the windows. Pink table napkins compliment the maroon look. Vases with plastic flowers are set on the window sill. Brass wall lamps hang on the narrow wall spaces separating the six windows. A stuffed red fox sets on a wood carving in front of a wood railing looking over the stairway. The wall along the stairway has a Persian rug and a black iron candle fixture with ten blue candles. The other wall not occupied by windows has a stone fireplace with a brass, leaf-pattern, circular plate hanging over the hearth. The burger bar downstairs has nine wood-framed tables, a few small round ones along the back wall, a few square ones in the middle, plus four barstools. There is an organ around to the left of the entrance. Total seating is 35.

Atmosphere: ★★★★ Tapes of Henry Mancini play theater favorites like "Mame" and "If I Were a Rich Man", plus popular tunes like "Help" and "Michelle." The view of the town and lake below is "Grand" indeed. This is an interestingly different place.

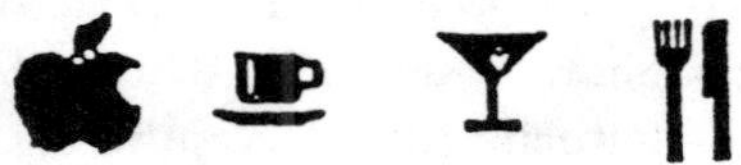

TERRACE INN ★★½
813 GRAND AV (303)627-3079

Breakfast $, Lunch $$, dinner $$$. MON-FRI 11AM-8PM. SAT-SUN 8AM-9PM. Closed Mid-OCT to Thanksgiving and two weeks in April.
Type: Country.

***Food:* ★★★ *Service:* ★★½ *Decor:* ★★½ *Atmosphere:* ★★**

This inn and restaurant dates back to 1908. They serve some good hot and cold sandwiches for lunch. Their Italian sausage in tomato sauce is fairly spicy and good tasting. There are a few Mexican items to choose from as well as pasta and prime rib for dinner. Service is a little on the slow side, but satisfactory. They have a patio outside for 12 and a small rectangular room inside for 36. The decor is a combination of blues, violets and white. This seemed like a quiet place for local business people to gather over lunch and discuss the affairs of the day.

GRANT

Grant is thought to be named after President Ulysses S. Grant and was once known as Grantville.

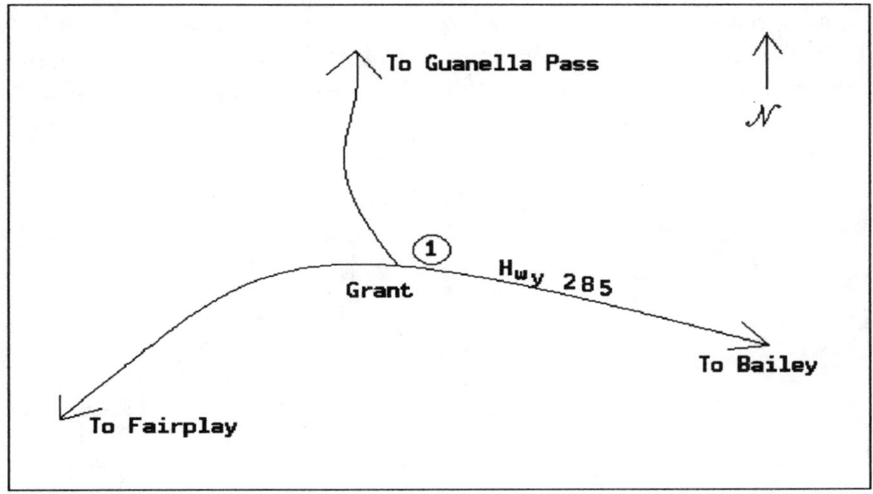

1. PLATTE RIVER INN ★★½
49491 HWY 85 (AND GUANELLA PASS ROAD) (303)838-4975

Breakfast/lunch $, dinner $-$$. 7 days 10AM-9PM.
Type: Country (tavern). Major credit cards are accepted, alcohol is served, but there is no nonsmoking section.

Food: ★★½ Service: ★★ Decor: ★★★ Atmosphere: ★★½

I have eaten here twice and have tried their burgers and pizza. The pizza is thin crust with bland tomato paste. This is an average pizza. The burger was equally average. Service was not very attentive, but fair. There is a bar as you enter with the dining room to your right that seats 36. The plastic table covers are colorful and homey looking with pictures of fruit, bread baskets, bowls, ladles, towels, jars and kettles. There are stuffed deer, foxes, and skunks on the walls and mantel above the stone fireplace. Comical-looking stuffed squirrels are dressed up like people and placed in tiny chairs. A big-screen television plays MTV tunes. A family of five "having a ball" and a couple deep in a quiet and private conversation provided an interesting contrast in clientele.

GUNNISON

Gunnison was named for Captain John W. Gunnison who led a surveying team through the area in search of a railroad route to the west. He and most of his company were killed by Ute Indians in Utah in the fall of 1853. Today, the Pioneer Museum on Hwy. 50 displays many of the artifacts and buildings representing Gunnison's heritage, including a narrow gauge engine, boxcar, and caboose.

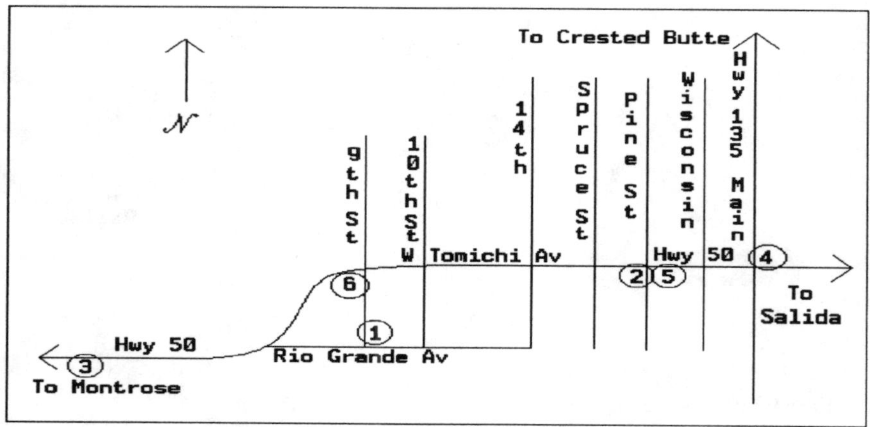

Restaurants and Ratings:	Food	Service	Decor	Atm	Overall
1. Cactus Jack's	★★½	★★½	★★½	★★	★★½
2. Cattleman Inn	★★★★	★★★	★★★½	★★★½	★★★½
3. Dos Rios	★★★½	★★★	★★★★	★★★	★★★½
4. Epicurean	★★★★★	★★★★★	★★★★½	★★★★	★★★★½
5. Mario's	★★½	★★	★★	★	★★
6. Sundae Shoppe	★★½	★★★	★★★½	★★½	★★★

The Epicurean has delectable quiche and wonderful soup made with homemade kibasa sausage. Go to the Cattlemen Inn for barbecue and steaks or Dos Rios for steaks and homemade bread fresh out of the oven. Cactus Jack's, Cattleman Inn and Dos Rios are the only restaurants that accept major credit cards. Only Cactus Jack's and the Epicurean have nonsmoking sections and only the Sundae Shoppe does not serve alcohol.

CACTUS JACK'S ★★½
9TH & RIO GRANDE (303)641-2044

Lunch/Dinner $$. TUE-SAT 11:30AM-2PM and 5PM-10PM. Closed SUN-MON.
Type: Mexican. Take-out available.

***Food:* ★★½ *Service:* ★★½ *Decor:* ★★½ *Atmosphere:* ★★**

I ordered their Guadalajara: a chili relleno stuffed with mushrooms and jack cheese, rolled in batter and deep-fried. It was heavy on the batter with few mushrooms, but the relleno and cheese mixed well. The menu offers Mexican combination plates and a la carte items. Also available are taco salads, huevos rancheros, Mexican pizza, burgers, onion rings, nachos, sopapillas, and ponsanitas (a fluffy pastry with cinnamon and vanilla ice cream, topped with homemade wine). Service is adequate. This is a big, single-room, open restaurant in two sections with no windows. The first section has six booths and seats 30 people. The second section has tables and one booth for 60. There is a pipe-stove, chili ristras hanging from huge log beams, Mexican rugs and hats, antlers, and a large mural of a snowy mountain. There is also a bar area with six stools, four tables, a booth, a pool table and a television. A young crowd, that was noisy at times, was hanging out here.

THE CATTLEMEN INN ★★★½
301 W. TOMICHI AVE. (303)641-1061

Breakfast/Lunch $, Dinner $$-$$$$. 7 days 6:30AM-11PM.
Type: Steak. Take-out available.

***Food:* ★★★★** I had a light dinner of barbecue tips on a kaiser roll. The tips were excellent. The lunch menu offers burgers, fish & chips, sandwiches, a super burrito, liver & onions, soup, and salad. The dinner appetizers include a shrimp bowl, breaded zucchini and onion rings. The house specialties are liver & onions, burrito supreme, chicken fried steak and fish & chips. Main courses include steaks (sirloin, prime rib, filet mignon, Delmonico, rib eye, NY strip, club, and shish kabob), chicken (Cordon Bleu, barbecue or teriyaki), seafood (shrimp, lobster tail, crab legs, trout), barbecue beef ribs, burgers, sandwiches (prime rib, steak, French dip, and club), soup, and salad. There is also a children's menu and cheesecake or ice cream for dessert.

Service: ★★★ Good.

Decor: ★★★½ This restaurant has an upstairs and downstairs. The upstairs has two rooms with circular and square tables. The first room has ten tables and six booths for 64 people. The rear room can be used for banquets and holds 30 people. The downstairs is one long, narrow-room with a salad bar on the right and a service bar on the left. It has a combination of 11 tables, 15 booths and a bar for total seating of 122. The walls are brick, rock, wood, or painted red. There is very little in the way of wall decorations. The front wall has horseshoes and saddles. There is a illuminated picture of Hawaii and a big-screen television in the rear. The booths have pictures of prairies, home on the range and horses.

Atmosphere: ★★★½ This seems to be one of the more popular places for the well-to-do in town.

DOS RIOS ★★★½

1½ MILES WEST OF GUNNISON ON HWY. 50, SOUTH SIDE (303)641-1000

Breakfast $$, lunch $-$$, Dinner $$-$$$. Winter: MON-SAT 7AM-9PM. SUN 7AM-2PM. Summer: MON-SAT 6AM-10PM. SUN 6AM-8PM.
Type: Steak.

Food: ★★★½ Their homemade bread had that right-out-of-the-oven taste. The cream of mushroom soup was creamy with fresh mushrooms. The medium-rare sirloin came with fresh mushrooms also and was prepared just the way I like it. Both the lunch and dinner menus are quite extensive. The lunch menu features soups, appetizers, light lunches, salads, hot and cold sandwiches, burgers and specialty dishes. Among the soups and appetizers: French onion, sautéed mushrooms, Rocky Mountain oysters, and Mexican chicken wings. The salad choices include chicken curry, taco, and spinach. The light lunches feature a fresh fruit plate or lime chicken. For a hot sandwich there's sliced beef, Reuben made with corned beef, and French dip. The cold sandwiches are chicken curry salad and Italian hero. The specialty lunches include grilled NY steak, sautéed chicken breast, and burritos. The dinner menu offers beef (filet mignon, top sirloin, chicken fried, or prime rib), sautéed chicken breast in either cilantro or curry sauce, a stuffed pork chop, Danish baby-back ribs, seafood (trout amandine, shrimp scampi, or deep-fried shrimp) and Mexican food. Sunday brunch includes baron of beef, chicken livers, chicken enchiladas, fruit pastries, champagne and mimosa.

Service: ★★★ The service was quite good. My waitress was very courteous and friendly despite her case of laryngitis.

Decor: ★★★★ This is a large one-room restaurant with an elevated section (two steps up) to the far right with seven tables for 20 people. The main dining area has 15 tables for 54 people. They also have room in the rear for banquets and club meetings. There are some fine paintings in here — mostly of pastoral scenes: fall colors, ponds, children playing, a farm house, a summer cottage, a girl feeding rabbits, a forest stream in summer, wild flowers, an old sailor with children; and some still lifes of vases, flowers and Indian pottery. Adding to the elegant decor are handsome gold chandeliers with white candle-shaped lights. The two entrances to the elevated section are bordered by these same candle-shaped bulbs in smoked-glass containers on a gold tubular base with gold-ornament tops. The tables are attractively decorated with mauve placemats, turquoise napkins, water goblets, and a small ceramic vase with artificial wild flowers. Two mantels on opposite sides of the room display two gold candle holders with mauve candles, a gold basket and vase, and two wicker baskets with artificial flowers.

Atmosphere: ★★★ This is a quiet place with country music and news playing in the background.

GUNNISON

EPICUREAN RESTAURANT ★★★★½
108 N. MAIN (303)641-2964

Breakfast/Lunch $-$$. MON-SAT 7AM-5PM. SUN 7AM-2PM.
Type: Continental. The entire restaurant is nonsmoking.

Food: ★★★★★ I had a superb lunch special. I chose the cabbage soup over the cinnamon apple soup. It was so good I had to have a second bowl. It was wonderful: filled with homemade kibasa sausage, onions, potatoes, and dill seeds. Equally terrific was the spinach and feta cheese quiche in a fluffy pastry made with all fresh ingredients. It was served with homemade cranberry bread which was soft and delicate. The breakfast menu features an interesting Danish dish that I have not seen before: Ebelskiver. It is two-inch ball-shaped Danish pancakes filled with fresh apples. Seven of these make one dish alone or it comes with eggs and ham, bacon or kibasa. They also have wild rice pancakes, souffles, omelets, eggs Florentine, eggs Benedict, eggs Don Quixote (with Mexican sauce), spinach crêpes, stuffed croissants, fruit cups, bagels and cream cheese, French toast, and mocha. The lunch menu has a daily quiche special and soup du jour, a chicken salad croissant, crabmeat or garden salads, a vegetarian sandwich, Reuben (made with ham), roast beef, hamburger, carrot soup, and a fruit cup served with ham slices and yogurt. Espresso, cappucino and fresh specialty desserts are available.

Service: ★★★★★ The owner/chef/waitress has been in the business twenty years and knows her food.

Decor: ★★★★½ This is a small single-room restaurant with ten tables for 42 people. The furniture is of high quality: wood-framed, high-backed chairs with brown cushions and finished wood tables. Finely polished logs on the right and left walls with a single wood beam extending the length of the ceiling give the appearance of a log cabin. Candle-shaped lights in wide-rimmed glasses and brass holders decorate the walls which only have two paintings: a young woman with a little girl by a stream and horses on a street on a rainy day in Denmark. Two wreaths, one simply made with branches, the other decorated with acorns, also adorn the walls. Fresh daisies were on a few of the tables. Each of the two front windows, divided by the entrance, has a glass mosaic: one of a mallard duck, the other of a hawk, both in flight. A cabinet with shelves containing glasses and bottles sits along the rear wall.

Atmosphere: ★★★★ The only annoying factor to this fine restaurant that I highly recommend is the noisy heater hanging from the ceiling in the rear of the room. The clientele is top quality. The innkeeper of the Nordic Inn in Crested Butte was dining here when I had lunch.

MARIO'S ★★
213 W TOMICHI AVE. (303)641-1374

Lunch/Dinner $-$$$. 7 days 11AM-11PM.
Type: Italian. Take-out available.

Food: ★★½ *Service:* ★★ *Decor:* ★★ *Atmosphere:* ★

I found their pizza to be of average quality and ingredients. The Italian food specialties include a stuffed pizza, spaghetti, calzones, veal Parmesan, and ravioli. The sandwich choices are Italian sausage or meatballs, ham, hamburgers, a Monte Cristo, chicken breast, and a patty melt. Tossed or pasta salads, chili, fries and soup are also available. A Mexican-style pizza, with jalapeño peppers, is on the menu. Service is slow. This is a single-room restaurant with 16 booths and six tables that can accommodate 120 people. The booths are completely enclosed on three sides and lit with candles. There are dimly lit ceiling lights, hanging plants, and pictures of the Old West. This might be considered a good romantic spot to bring a date with the closed-in booths and poor lighting. Otherwise, you might feel as I did, that I was in a cave.

SUNDAE SHOPPE ★★★
901 W. TOMICHI (303)641-5051

GUNNISON

Breakfast $, Lunch/Dinner $-$$. 7 days 7AM-8PM (9PM in summer). Closed one week at Christmas.
Type: Country. Checks accepted with proper I.D.

Food: ★★½ The burgers are fried and the soup is canned, but they make a good corned beef and Swiss on rye. The breakfast menu offers homemade sweet rolls and hot spiced cider. The lunch/dinner menu has a host of burgers and sandwiches, including barbecue beef, beef & Cheddar, club, fish, patty melt, grilled chicken breast, and a chili burger. The entree selections include rib eye steak, chicken fried steak, pork chops, clam strips, shrimp, steak fingers, ham, and fried vegetables. Chili, soup, and salads (dinner, taco or chef) are also available. A short Mexican menu offers burritos, tacos, and chimichangas. There is a children's menu, and for dessert, homemade baked pies, hot apple delight, banana splits, hot fudge parfaits, sundaes, shakes, malts, frosties, and floats.

Service: ★★★ Friendly and fast.

Decor: ★★★½ There is a single table in the front for ten people. The main dining area has 17 booths and two tables for 66 people. The rear and left rear walls have an array of picture clocks on polished wood, carved in oblong, square, and rectangular shapes with a variety of pictures: from John Wayne to Jesus Christ to everything in-between: cats, ducks, unicorns, a poem to mother, a husky dog, a mountain lion, a tiger, an owl, a mountain cabin, deer, and Elvis Presley. They also have wood-framed colored prints of waterfalls, deer, elk and an owl. All items are for sale. The right rear wall has brown wallpaper with prints of trees, shrubs and hills. The rear wall is made of carved wood resembling picture frames. The front and right front walls have windows with orange verticals matching the orange-cushioned bench seats. The picture clocks and prints are quite attractive and I liked their choice of print wallpaper.

Atmosphere: ★★½ A popular local hangout. It was very busy for lunch. Only one or two booths were open at any time.

HOLLY

Named after pioneer cattleman Hiram S. Holly, whose SS ranch extended from Granada, 11 miles to the west, to Kansas, just three miles to the east. The Holly Sugar Company was built here in 1905. The lowest point in Colorado (3,350 feet above sea level) is located near Holly.

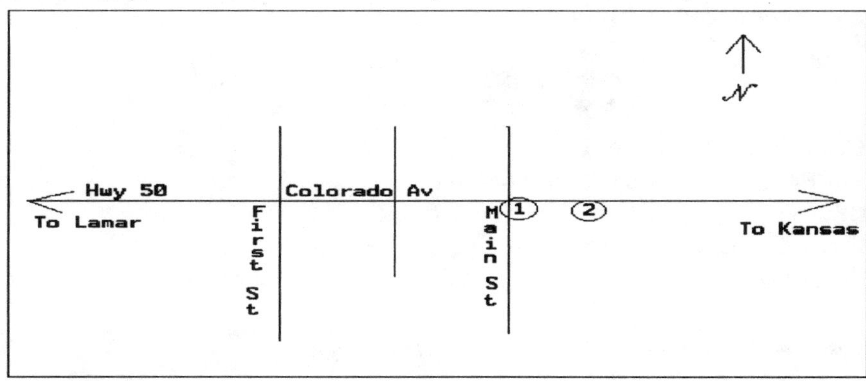

Restaurants and Ratings:	Food	Service	Decor	Atm	Overall
1. BILLY JOHN	★★½	★★½	★★	★½	★★
2. COUNTRY PEDDLER	★½	★★	★	★	★½

Only the Country Peddler will accept major credit cards. Only the Billy John Restaurant offers nonsmoking. Neither restaurant serves alcohol.

BILLY JOHN RESTAURANT ★★
SE CORNER OF HWY 50 (COLORADO AV) & MAIN ST (719)537-6090

Breakfast/Lunch/dinner $$. MON-SAT 6AM-8PM. SUN 6AM-2PM. Type: Country.

Food: ★★½ *Service:* ★★½ *Decor:* ★★ *Atmosphere:* ★½

They have good homemade soup and fair sandwiches. The lunch/dinner menu includes salad, chili, burgers, onion rings, French fries, hot dogs, fish, and hot meals like barbecue beef, roast beef, or chicken fried steak, with mashed potatoes and vegetables. Service was no problem. They have a coffee shop which holds about 50 people and a dining room for about 150. The all glass window front has red-and-white-checkered curtains covering the bottom half. Seating is on red- or brown-cushioned chairs at brown formica tables. The high ceiling has two single-lamp fans. The rear wall has a brick pattern. There are two wall clocks, but no other decor and no plants. Lots of local gossip.

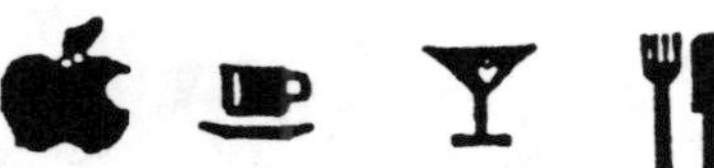

COUNTRY PEDDLER ★½
118 EAST COLORADO (719)537-6061

Pizza & sandwiches $-$$. 7 days 24 hours.
Type: Deli.

***Food:* ★½ *Service:* ★★ *Decor:* ★ *Atmosphere:* ★**

You can get pizza or a sandwich at this walk up counter. They have five booths for 20 people. There are no particular items of decor. This was a local hang out for young people.

Colorado River East of Hot Sulphur Springs

HOT SULPHUR SPRINGS

The town is named for the hot springs in the area and was once owned by William N. Byers, founder of the Denver Rocky Mountain News.

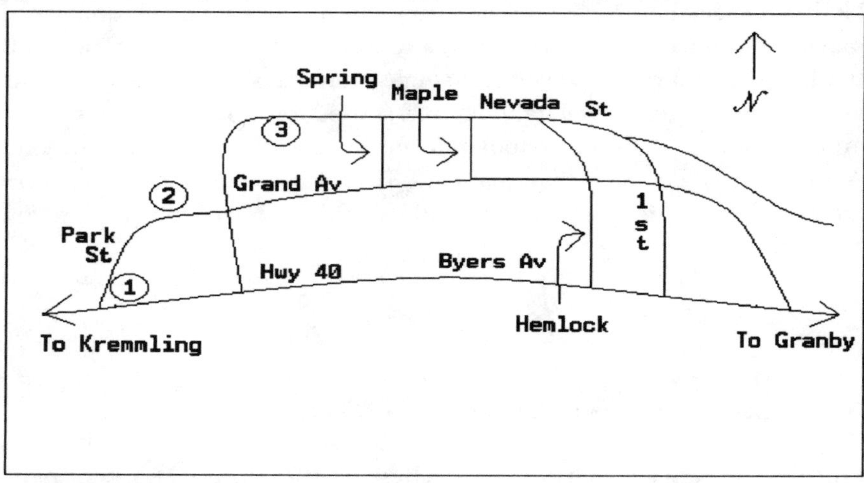

Restaurants and Ratings:	Food	Service	Decor	Atm	Overall
1. COUNTY SEAT CAFE	★★½	★★½	★★½	★★½	★★½
2. RIVERSIDE	★★★½	★★★½	★★★	★★★	★★★½
3. STAGE COACH STOP	★★★	★★	★★★½	★★★½	★★★

The Riverside offers some very good country-cooking with a view of the Colorado River running below. The Stage Coach Stop prepares homemade salsa, warm chips, and some good Mexican fare in a building dating back to 1875. None of the restaurants listed here accept credit cards or have a nonsmoking section. Only the County Seat Cafe does not serve alcohol.

COUNTY SEAT CAFE ★★½
517 BYERS (303)725-3309

Breakfast/lunch/dinner $. 7 days 6:30AM-9PM.
Type: Cafe.

Food: ★★½ *Service:* ★★½ *Decor:* ★★½ *Atmosphere:* ★★½

I ordered a quarter pound beef patty with blue cheese & bacon and onion rings. The rings were not greasy and the burger was satisfactory. Nothing special. The prices are very cheap, however: all under $6, including dinner items. Service was a little slow in bringing out the food, but friendly and helpful. This is a single-room restaurant with a vaulted ceiling, four wagon-wheel light fixtures, stuffed toy animals and windows on three sides. A lot of customers from the courthouse eat lunch here. Actually, they do more than just eat. They "jaw" with each other long after their meal is finished. A radio could be heard playing in the kitchen.

RIVERSIDE ★★★½
509 GRAND AVENUE (303)725-3589

Lunch $-$$, dinner $$. JUN-AUG: TUE-SUN 11AM-3PM and 5PM-8:30PM. Closed MON. SEP-MAY: THU-SUN 5PM-8:30PM. Closed MON-WED. Type: Country.

Food: ★★★½ Their clam chowder is a clear broth, rather than a cream sauce, with a lot of vegetables, but only a few small clams. Croutons are served on the side. The cornish hen was stuffed with pimentos, topped with stewed tomatoes, and served with green olives. The fried rice is prepared with onions, pickle relish, stewed tomatoes, and stuffed green olives. This is accompanied by a mixture of corn, green beans, red peppers and broccoli. The hen was well prepared. Host and replacement chef Abraham Renta took the time to serve it right. I liked the choice of enhancements, also. The dinner items were displayed on a small chalkboard brought to your table. The other entrees were chicken fried steak, Rocky Mountain rainbow trout, breaded pork chops, pepper steak, 16-oz. T-bone, and salmon steak. Sometimes the dinner selections include roast chicken, barbecue ribs, or roast pork. Homemade soup, sandwiches (Reuben, roast beef, German sausage, pastrami, fish, and meatball), sides of potato salad or French fries and burgers are usually on the lunch menu. Homemade pies, like deep-dish apple pie and rhubarb, are available for dessert.

Service: ★★★½ It was the cook's night off, so the owner handled it all — cooking and serving. He had a sense of humor and did a few extras, like serving the rye bread warm, and the butter at least a few degrees above –273 degrees Celsius (absolute zero) so it could be spread. It was not busy, so Abe joined me at my table. He has been in business about nine years and is a very down to earth guy. His philosophy is service with an upbeat attitude and a smile. We had a very pleasant chat.

Decor: ★★★ The dining room is at the end of the hotel with windows on three sides overlooking the Colorado River. There are 13 tables for 40 diners. A wood-burning black-iron stove stands directly back from the entrance. Brass, clear-glass lanterns hang on the wood-framed posts. Brass, frosted-glass electric lamps are set on some of the tables with white linen cloths and napkins. Seating is on hardwood, rib-backed chairs with armrests. Glass, wood-framed prints of geraniums, anemones and other flowers decorate what little wall space there is.

Atmosphere: ★★★ Soft jazz plays in the background. A couple of elderly ladies and an elderly gentleman occupied two other tables on this off-season evening.

STAGECOACH STOP ★★★
NEVADA ST & ASPEN ST (303)725-3910

Dinner $$. MON-SAT 6PM-9PM. Closed SUN.
Type: Mexican. Reservations recommended in the summer and on FRI and SAT the rest of the year. Built by Captain Dean, a former confederate soldier. President Teddy Roosevelt slept here.

Food: ★★★ Warm chips are served with homemade salsa made with tomato pieces, onion slices and green chili in a clear, watery, moderately hot soup. I ordered the Stagecoach Mexican turnover: a crunchy and soft fried flour tortilla (crunchy on the edges, soft in the middle) stuffed with ground beef, cheese & onions, smothered in green chili, and topped with jalapeño slices, cheese, lettuce, tomato, sour cream, and a large black olive. It was very good, but I was less excited about the bean paste and rice topped with American cheese and green chili. The Mexican menu has taco salads, huevos rancheros, chimichangas, and fajitas. There are two American dishes: T-bone steak and fried chicken. For dessert, you can choose deep-fried or regular ice cream and honey sopapillas.

Service: ★★ Take your time finishing your chips and salsa. Your entree will take a while. I came in about 7:15, ordered at 7:25, and was served at 8:08, almost 40 minutes later. The service is pleasant enough. They have just one cook: owner Jean Crouch. Jean's daughter-in-law, a pleasant, cheerful woman with a good laugh, took me for a tour of the upstairs bedrooms, and chatted with me about the hotel, the locals and the local cuisine.

Decor: ★★★½ This is a single-room restaurant, located at the end of the hotel, with 10 tables for 38 diners. Three old wood-framed windows and a brown wood door with windows facing the street, add to the historic ambiance of the room. The wallpaper, in shades of black and white, shows caricatures of women, poems, and advertisements for "Lundborg's Perfumes". There are two large paintings, one on the far wall of a sailing ship at sea, the other on the right wall of two grisly bears. The painting of the grisly bears and one of a six-point elk hanging in the foyer were created by Jean's son. Seating is on wood-framed chairs, with either rust cushions, or rib-backs and white seats. Brass, frosted-glass lanterns hang by a trio of chains from the ceiling. At the opposite end of the hotel is a bar/lounge with six stools, two tables for eight, a pool table, two ceiling fans, a black pipe-stove, a juke box, and a deer head with antlers.

Atmosphere: ★★★½ This is an active, popular place on Fridays and Saturdays where you will find families and couples both young and old. It was quite noisy on the Saturday evening that I was there: a lot of talking and laughing. If you are in the mood for good food and a good time, consider stopping here. A combination of Mexican and country music plays in the background. You will notice the lights flicker every now and then from their self-generator.

IDAHO SPRINGS

Formerly known as Sacramento City, Idaho City, Idaho and Idahoe, the final name for the town may have been derived from an Indian word meaning "gem of the mountains", or it may have come from the word "Idahi", the Kiowa-Apache name for the Comanches. In either case, the town is the outgrowth of the camp of George A. Jackson who discovered gold in the area on January 7, 1859. Idaho Springs is another Colorado town with a rich history of mining. The Argo Gold Mine, which was used to retrieve gold, silver, copper, lead and other valuable metals between 1913 and 1943, has been restored and is now open for tours. A locomotive stands in the center of town on a section of the original narrow gauge track that connected Idaho Springs with two other mining towns, Golden and Georgetown.

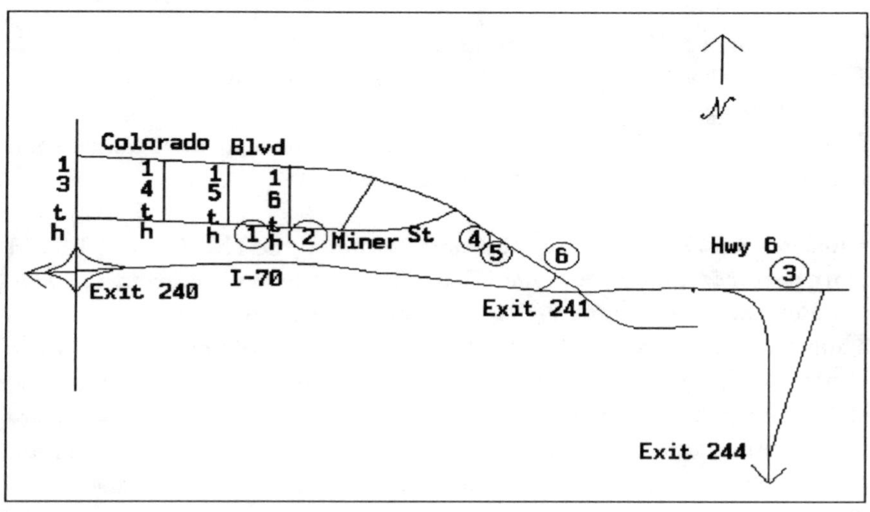

Restaurants and Ratings:	Food	Service	Decor	Atm	Overall
1. Beau Jo's	★★★★½	★★★½	★★★★	★★★½	★★★★
2. Buffalo Bar	★★★★	★★★	★★★½	★★★½	★★★½
3. Kermits	★★½	★★	★	★	★½
4. King's Derby	★★	★★	★★½	★★	★★
5. Marion's	★★★	★★★	★★★	★★½	★★★
6. 6 & 40	★★	★★★	★★	★★★	★★½

IDAHO SPRINGS

Beau Jo's has long had a reputation for one of the best pizzas in the state, and deservedly so, both in terms of variety of ingredients and quality. They also have some unique decor, thanks to the help of many of their patrons. The Buffalo Bar is the place to go for lean Buffalo burgers, homemade onion rings, or a big crock of French onion soup. Marion's would be my choice for best breakfast stop in town. Only Kermits does not accept major credit cards. Only Beau Jo's, the Buffalo Bar and Marion's offer nonsmoking sections. Only King's Derby does not serve alcohol.

BEAU JO'S ★★★★
1517 MINER STREET (303)567-4376 IN DENVER, CALL (303)573-6924.

Lunch/dinner $-$$ (per person for pizza). Mid-OCT to Mid-APR: SUN-THU, 11AM-9:30PM. FRI-SAT, 11AM-10PM. Mid-APR to Mid-OCT: 7 days 11AM-10PM.
Type: Italian (pizza). This well known pizzeria has consistently been voted BEST Pizza in the Denver Metro area.

Food: **★★★★½** A friend of mine and I sampled the Thai Pie and a build your own Mountain Pie. The Thai Pie is made with curried chicken, mushrooms, green peppers, onions, tomatoes, and sweet & sour sauce on a standard thick crust. My friend ordered the Mountain Pie with butter white bread, thin crust, Beau Jo's pizza sauce, mozzarella and provolone cheeses, pepperoni, Canadian bacon, spinach and pineapple. They were both scrumptious! The butter on the white bread makes for a lighter, more flavorful crust and there is no arguing about the freshness and quality of the ingredients. We also split an order of genuine Buffalo wings made with Frank's hot sauce and butter: quite good ... and hot! Beau Jo's offers a wild variety of ingredients for their primarily pizza menu, which states: "We offer more creative, more varied combinations of pizza than anybody we know." Their pizzas come in five sizes (6-,8-10-,13-, and 16-inches), four different types of dough made with Colorado honey (white, butter white, whole wheat and sesame wheat), four types of thickness (extra thin, thin, thick or standard, and extra thick), five selective sauces (Beau Jo's pizza sauce, barbecue, sweet & sour, taco, and white wine sauce), seven choices of cheese (mozzarella, provolone, cheddar, Montery jack, Swiss, fontina-provolone, and no-cholesterol), and a whopping 27 meat, seafood and vegetable items, including curry chicken, shrimp, chicken, sweet peas, zucchini, tofu, spinach, artichoke hearts, and alfalfa sprouts. The menu also features some pizzas with interesting sounding names, like the Conestoga made with Canadian bacon, zucchini, artichoke hearts and tomatoes; shrimp Zapigh (named after Pete Zapigh, the mythical French fur trapper given credit for Beau Jo's recipe) containing shrimp, mushrooms, and scallions in a white wine sauce; and Jose gold which has chicken or hamburger, green peppers, onions, taco chips and taco sauce. Beau Jo's also serves baked stuffed mushrooms, garlic bread, a limited selection of sandwiches, and a soup and salad bar. Of particular interest, to those of you who like a challenge and pride themselves on their gastronomical abilities, is Beau Jo's Challenge: any two people capable of eating Beau Jo's Grand Sicilian in one hour get the pie for free, $100 and two free Beau Jo T-shirts. The pie is 12 to 14 pounds, made with a super thick 16" crust piled high with green peppers, onions, mushrooms, pepperoni, and sausage or hamburger! Our waitress said she only knew of one pair capable of accomplishing this feat in the last few years.

Service: ★★★½ Very informative about Beau Jo's past, present and future. If you order your pizza with extra thick crust allow 30 minutes.

Decor: ★★★★ This five dining-room restaurant can seat up to 300 people! Its most distinctive items of decor are the hundreds of patron designed napkins on the old barn wood and log walls. People who have come here to enjoy Beau Jo's outstanding pizza have left their mark with drawings, caricatures, and witty phrases on the restaurant's napkins. Management has immortalized these by tacking them onto their walls. In addition to this unique, personal concept in decoration, this restaurant features old photos of the Copper Home Ensemble - 1890, The Blazing Arrow Band, the Mercantile Co. in 1938, miners, Idaho Springs and trains. White-laced curtains hang in the front window. The wall to the far left is made of red brick with frosted wall lamps. Overhead there are exposed pipes. Seating is on solid-wood, rib-backed chairs at hardwood tables. The wall ledges have three-dimensional artworks of horse-drawn conestoga wagons. There is a small bar in the balcony. A bar/lounge, decorated with an old-fashioned safe and an elevator shaft, is planned for the back of the restaurant, along with a back patio that is scheduled to open in the summer of 1992. It will seat 75 outside and 25 inside.

Atmosphere: ★★★½ Soft rock music plays through the large wall speakers. I was here on a quiet mid-week day before ski season. During the ski season, especially on weekends, this place is packed between 4PM and 8PM when the skiers are returning from the mountains. Expect a 45 minute to one hour wait for your meal during these peak times.

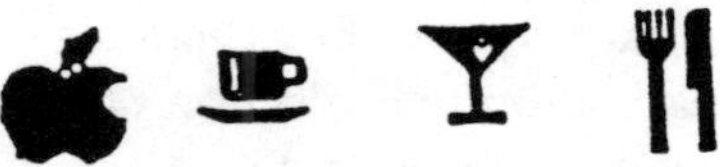

BUFFALO BAR ★★★½

1617 MINER STREET (303)567-2729. IN DENVER: (303)595-9018. USA TOLL FREE: 1-800-477-2227.

Breakfast/lunch $-$$, dinner $$. MON-FRI 11AM-10PM. SAT-SUN 8AM-10PM.
Type: Burgers (Mexican, Italian and steaks). A 15% gratuity is added to parties of six or more.

This restaurant has been family owned and operated for the past decade by Art, Darlene, and Jory Rosean. It has a rich and incredible history. The Buffalo Bar is a combination of six different buildings. The main building, built in 1881, was the home of the Golden Rule Mercantile Store. It was remodeled in 1906 and opened as John Rohner's Bar and Billiard Hall. The restaurant's antique bar originated in Chicago in the early 1860's, was transported to the Cosmopolitan Hotel in Telluride by wagon train, and moved to the Windsor Hotel in Denver before it finally found its current home in Idaho Springs. Celebrities from many fields have visited here including the Kennedys, Clint Eastwood, Karl Mecklenberg of the Denver Broncos, and a 2,280 pound Budweiser Clydesdale (no wonder their floors creak!). Numerous commercials and parts of six motion pictures have been filmed here as well.

Food: ★★★★ My hiking group stopped here on a fall Sunday afternoon after being in the mountains and enjoyed their lean Buffalo burgers, cole slaw made with raisins; big, crispy and juicy homemade onion rings; and a big crock of their flavorful and chewy French onion soup. Everything is made from scratch and they use only fresh ingredients. You won't go wrong ordering anything on their menu. They offer a large and varied selection that features Mexican, Italian, steaks, buffalo burgers and pizza. Their breakfast menu features eggs Benedict, trout & eggs, a breakfast burrito, huevos rancheros, cinnamon rolls & Danish. Both the lunch and dinner menus offer appetizers (potato skins, vegetable or mushroom tempura, chili con queso fondue, and super deluxe nachos), homemade soups, red or green chili, and taco or spinach salads. The lunch menu features sandwiches (Italian sausage or meatball, Reuben, Philly steak, club and barbecue beef); burgers (patty melt, guacamole, chili cheese, pizza and barbecue); Vienna all beef hot dogs; a few Mexican specials like smothered burrito, chimichanga, and chili rellenos; and specials made with buffalo meat: burgers, Philly sandwiches, black bean chili, and fajitas. The dinner menu includes homemade spaghetti, chicken Parmesan, Rocky Mountain trout, chicken fajitas, top sirloin, and a children's menu. Pizza is available in 12- and 16-inch sizes with a choice of 10 ingredients. Four different lunch specials, like meatloaf and a Monte Cristo, and four dinner specials, are offered every day.

Service: ★★★ Very helpful and friendly. They provided me with a six-page guide to their restaurant. If you are interested in learning more about their history, decor and food, ask them for a copy.

Decor: ★★★½ Seating is offered for 210 people in five different dining areas. From the Miner Street entrance there is the Pub to your left: a small dining area for 20 with a full bar. Straight back is the main dining room with an elevated dining section in the back; two black, wood-burning stoves; a full bar; a thorough display of advertising signs on the red-brick walls; and seating for about 100. To the right of the main dining room is a smaller room with a red-brick fireplace; a double oxen yoke, three foot flask and potted plants on the mantel; and photos of Navajo medicine men and a Sioux family with the sheriff circa 1870. This room seats 24. Further to the right is a dining room for 20 decorated with paintings of wolves howling at the moon and a full-length shelf with cups and various brass and ceramic ornaments. The fifth dining room is directly behind the room with the red-brick fireplace. It hosts a wood pile for a black, wood-burning stove; a couple of elk heads with antlers; skylights; several old advertising signs; a 1911 player piano; and a 1900's peep show. Forty-six people can sit in here at 11 tables. You will also find a 1948 Rockola jukebox with original recordings, a collection of old tin signs, a framed newspaper of the day Lincoln was assassinated, and World War I & II posters. The pressed-tin ceiling is original as is the 110-year-old wood floor that creaks.

Atmosphere: ★★★½ This is a popular place in the summer (JUL-AUG) and in the middle of the ski season (JAN-FEB). A sports bar with a casual atmosphere, this is a place to have a good time. Occasionally noisy, but always friendly.

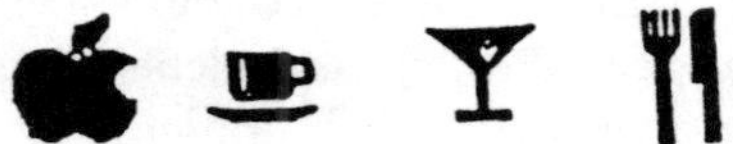

KERMITS ★½
I-70 & HWY 6 (EXIT 244 OFF I-70) (303)567-4113

Lunch/dinner $. 7 days, 12PM-10PM.
Type: Tavern.

***Food:* ★★½ *Service:* ★★ *Decor:* ★ *Atmosphere:* ★**

They serve good homemade chili with beef and beans, but their burgers are only fair, at best. Their limited menu also features hot wings, Mexican, and sandwiches. Service is fair: quiet and quick. Beer signs and old photos of gun slingers decorate this restaurant with 10 tables, seating for 40, two televisions, pinball, video game, darts, juke box and pool table. Rock music played quietly from the juke box. Bikers (motorcyclists) were using this place for a stop-over on a Sunday afternoon.

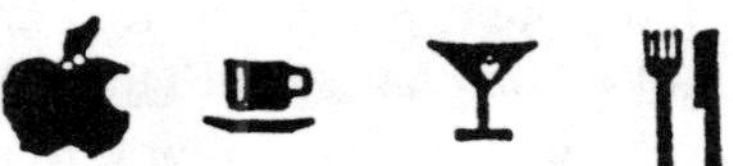

KING'S DERBY ★★
2801 COLORADO BLVD (303)567-2185

Breakfast/lunch $, dinner $$. 7 days 5AM-12AM.
Type: Country. Senior discounts and take-out available.

Food: ★★ *Service:* ★★ *Decor:* ★★½ *Atmosphere:* ★★

My hiking group stopped here for breakfast where we experienced lean crisp bacon, slightly underdone hash browns, flour tasting waffles, satisfactory French toast and pancakes, and dish-pan coffee. Service was not fast: twenty minutes between ordering and being served. This is a single rectangular-room restaurant with brown carpet, brown formica tables and brown wood-paneled walls. Paintings of pastoral scenes with mountains in the background decorate the walls. There is a juke box at the entrance. No music unless someone pays the jukebox. Then, it is 50's tunes. There was a quiet local crowd here on Sunday morning.

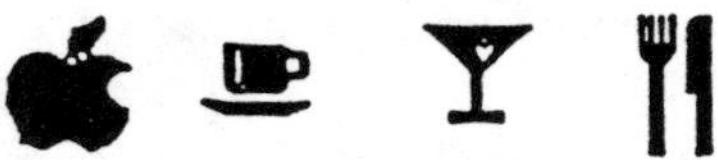

MARION'S (OF THE ROCKIES) ★★★
2805 COLORADO BLVD (303)567-2925

Breakfast/lunch $, dinner $$. WED-MON 6AM-9PM. TUE 6AM-2PM.
Type: Family.

Food: ★★★ This was another breakfast stop for my hiking group. I ordered the country burrito. It was quite a concoction: a flour tortilla filled with two eggs, American & cheddar cheeses, and hash browns; then topped with sausage gravy and more cheese. Personally, I found it to be too "cheesy", but if you are a cheese lover, you might really like it. My hiking friends both gave thumbs up to the eggs Benedict special with hash browns. Breakfast features a croissant sandwich, corned beef hash, Polish sausage, blueberry hot cakes, and a Belgium waffle with peaches. The lunch menu offers burgers, sandwiches (French dip, Reuben, and charbroiled chicken breast), spaghetti, and a beef & bean burrito. Dinner features steaks, fish (salmon, tuna, rainbow trout, and fried shrimp), roast turkey breast, meat loaf, fried or mesquite-smoked chicken, and hickory-smoked beef brisket or pork spare ribs. Soup, salads and chili are also available. There is a children's menu and, for dessert, fruit pies, cheesecake, sundaes, and carrot or chocolate suicide cake.

Service: ★★★ Pleasant and satisfactory, but you may have to wait at the cash register to pay your bill.

Decor: ★★★ This is a two-room restaurant. The divided smoking room, to the right, has nine tables and seven booths for 72 diners. Oil paintings of cabins in winter, snow-capped mountain peaks, adobe structures, a pair of Indian women, and a pastoral scene decorate the back pinewood polished wall. Pictures of a water wheel and mine hang on the green plaster front wall. The nonsmoking dining room to the left has seven tables for 28, three wood cabinets, several hanging plants, windows along the front that extend into sky lights, baskets filled with straw and flowers, and Easter bonnets hanging from the walls.

Atmosphere: ★★½ A quiet place for locals and skiers on their way to the slopes.

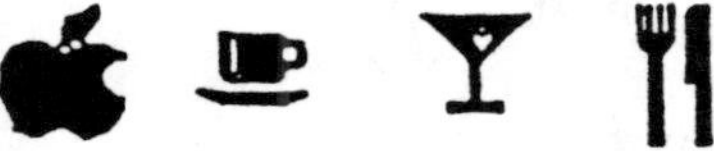

6 & 40 RESTAURANT ★★½
2910 COLORADO BLVD (303)567-4891

Breakfast $, lunch/dinner $-$$. THU-TUE 7AM-7:30PM. Closed WED.

***Food:* ★★ *Service:* ★★★ *Decor:* ★★ *Atmosphere:* ★★★**

My eggs were under cooked. Otherwise, everything else was satisfactory. They serve burgers, salad, chili, soup, sandwiches, steaks, seafood, fried chicken, meatloaf, and homemade pies. Service is provided by a jovial lady. They have a single dining room with 13 tables and a small bar for 54 people in total. In addition, there is a small banquet room for private parties. The dining room is decorated with plastic, flower-patterned tablecloths; blonde-wood cabinets with figures of horses and elephants; and a black-iron rail divider separating the restaurant from the bar. The bar is open, but only when the bartender shows up. It is very informal.

JOHNSON VILLAGE

This town started as a cafe and service station by John Johnson. As others started buying property in the area, the settlement began to be called Johnson Village. The town was established in 1947 and has appeared on the state highway map since 1976.

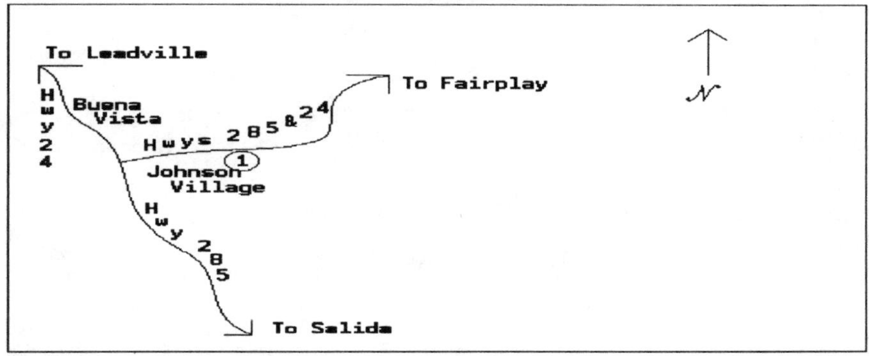

1. **BURGER TIME ★★½**
   12974 HWY 24 & 285 (303) 395-4858

Lunch/dinner $. Labor Day to Mid-MAY: THU-MON 10:30AM-9PM. Closed TUE-WED. Mid-MAY to Labor Day: 7 days 10AM-9PM.
Type: Burgers. No credit cards, no nonsmoking section, and no alcohol.

Food: ★★★½ *Service:* ★★ *Decor:* ★½ *Atmosphere:* ★★

I have eaten here three or four times over the past few years. Every time, except for the last, I ordered one of their excellent burgers. The last time I ordered a chicken sandwich just to try something different. It was quite good, crispy on the outside, moist and tender on the inside, but I think I'll stick with their burgers. Their sides of French fries, onion rings and fried mushrooms are all good. The fried mushrooms, about a dozen, are completely nongreasy, deep-fried, golden-brown, and tender & juicy on the inside. They do a good job of preparing their food. Try one of their burgers with an order of fried mushrooms. You order and pick up at the counter. This is a small single-room burger stand with 10 tables for 30 people, windows on three sides with good views of the Collegiate Peaks, no pictures, no posters, five potted plants, and a U.S. map at the far end. It is quiet (no music) and most customers come in for take-out.

KEENESBURG

First known as Keene, for an area rancher who built the Keene Improvement Company which developed the town, the name was changed to Keenesburg in 1907 to avoid postal confusion with Keene, Nebraska.

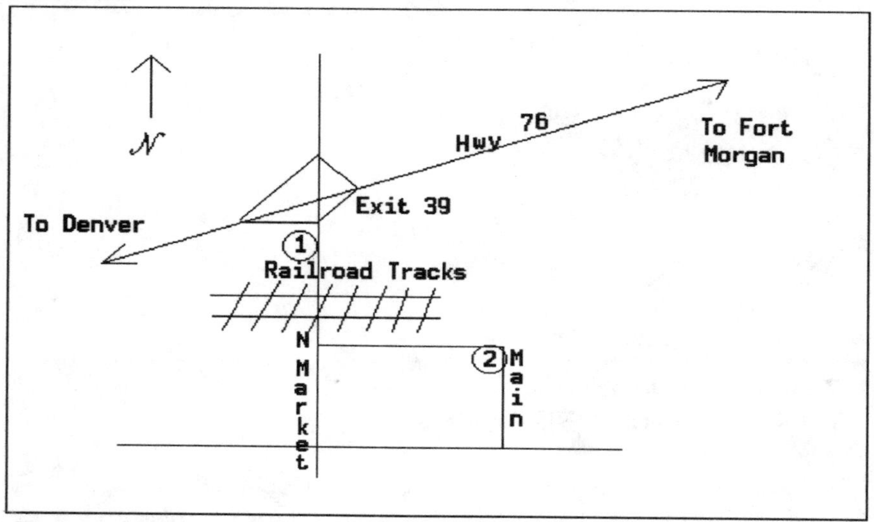

Restaurants and Ratings:	Food	Service	Decor	Atm	Overall
1. Charlie D's	★★★	★★★	★★★½	★★★	★★★
2. Korner Kitchen	★★	★★★	★★	★★½	★★½

Charlie D's serves up some good soup and sandwiches for lunch. Neither restaurant has a nonsmoking section and only Charlie D's accepts major credit cards and serves alcohol.

Charlie D's ★★★
245 N. Market (303)732-4846

Breakfast/lunch $, Dinner $$-$$. THU-TUE 6AM-9PM. WED 6AM-2PM. Type: Country. 10% senior citizen discount. Personal checks accepted with check guarantee card.

Food: ★★★ Their clam chowder was good and thick with a lot of clams. They also have good sandwiches. The breakfast menu has hamburger, huevos rancheros, Belgium waffles, pigs in a blanket, buttermilk biscuits & sausage gravy, and homemade cinnamon rolls. Lunch items include burgers, sandwiches (steak, Italian sausage or meatball subs, French dip, club, ground round, Reuben or hot roast beef), Mexican food, homemade chili, soup, and salads. You can start off dinner with Rocky Mountain oysters, barbecued chicken wings, potato skins, or deep-fried breaded mushrooms. The dinner entrees are a mixture of steaks (sirloin, sirloin tips, filet mignon, T-bone, NY strip, or chicken fried), seafood (beer-battered jumbo shrimp, breaded catfish, Alaskan king crab legs, or lobster tail), Italian food (veal Parmesan and homemade spaghetti), lite meals (a smaller sirloin, cod, burger, or shrimp dinner), chicken (teriyaki or fried), liver & onions, Wiener schnitzel and Rocky Mountain oysters. The dessert menu includes ice cream cones, shakes, sundaes or floats, home baked pies, cheesecake, banana splits and a brownie delight.

Service: ★★★ Ask for Terri.

Decor: ★★★½ This two-room restaurant is more elegant than you would expect for a town of this size. The front room has seven booths, four tables and a counter for about 60 people. The rear room has nine booths and 11 tables for about 80 people. There is also a bar area with 12 stools and tables for 28. The front room has red booths, horizontal shades, a stucco ceiling, and a chain lamp over every booth. The rear room has turquoise booths, wood chairs at wood trim tables, cream walls and print wallpaper, several wood-framed mirrors, pictures of an Indian pueblo and Indians by a mountain stream in winter, and ceiling lights with tulip-shaped shades.

Atmosphere: ★★★ The clientele is mostly elderly and retired. A calm setting.

KORNER KITCHEN CAFE ★★½
15 S. MAIN (303)732-9990

KEENESBURG

Breakfast $, lunch $-$$. MON-TUE & THU-SAT 5:30AM-3PM. WED 5:30AM-8PM. SUN 5:30AM-12PM.
Type: Country. 25¢ extra per item on carry-outs.

***Food:* ★★ *Service:* ★★★ *Decor:* ★★ *Atmosphere:* ★★½**

Their beef noodle soup had no beef, but the broth and narrow noodles were good. Their sandwiches and burgers are fair. The lunch menu offers daily specials, salads, soup, burgers, sandwiches, and dinners (schnitzel, ham or chicken fried steak, roast beef, and deep-fried shrimp or chicken). Pies and ice cream are available for dessert. Service is fast, friendly and with a smile. Beverly, the owner, is jovial. This is a small one-room white building that seats 34 at eight tables and a counter. There are wood-paneled walls on three sides. The right wall and ceiling are made of formica, as are the tables. The decor consists of cute pictures of small children, video games, horizontal shades on the front windows, and brown and rust curtain tops on the small side windows. It is all basic and clean. This is a place for local gossip. The noise level is low.

Dick's Hickory Dock - Kittredge

KEYSTONE

Keystone's mineral and precious metal history dates back as far as 1810 when mountain trappers discovered gold and silver in the rivers, but kept it secret for 40 years. The first reported discovery of silver in Colorado occurred in 1863 in nearby Saints John, ten miles up the Montezuma Canyon from Keystone Village. The famous Comstock Lode was uncovered there in 1865. Old Keystone was used as a railhead for the silver mines in Montezuma Canyon. The Ski Tip Lodge served as a stagecoach stop before becoming Colorado's first ski lodge. If you want to learn more about the history of Keystone, the Activities Center hosts an historical presentation of the area every Sunday night, with complimentary wine and cheese.

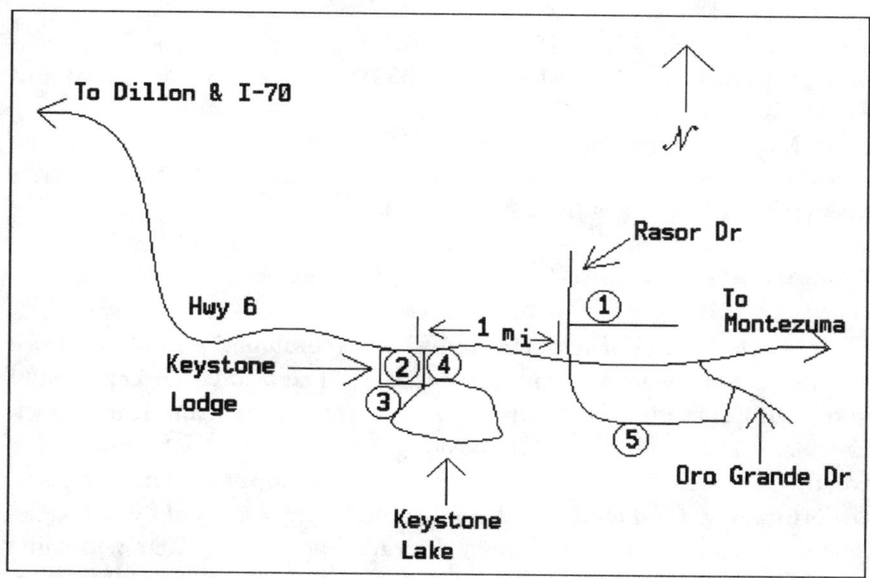

Restaurants and Ratings:	Food	Service	Decor	Atm	Overall
1. Bandito's Cantina	★★★½	★½	★	★	★★
2. Bighorn Steakhouse	★★★★	★★★½	★★★½	★★★	★★★½
3. Commodore	★★★½	★★½	★★★	★★★½	★★★
4. Edgewater Cafe	★★★	★★★	★★★	★★★½	★★★
5. Razzberrys	★★★★½	★★★½	★★★★½	★★★★	★★★★

KEYSTONE

Razzberrys was my favorite restaurant in Keystone, both for the quality of their American cuisine and their relaxed, unpretentious atmosphere. The Bighorn Steakhouse serves some top quality meats. The Commodore does a superb buffet on Fridays and I found a good sandwich lunch stop at the Edgewater Cafe. A 4.7% surcharge, in addition to state and local taxes, is added to your bill in Keystone. All restaurants accept major credit cards and serve alcohol. Only the Bighorn Steakhouse does not offer a nonsmoking section.

BANDITO'S CANTINA ★★
MOUNTAIN VIEW PLAZA, HWY 6 (303)468-0404

Lunch/dinner $$. Mid-NOV to Mid-APR: SUN-THU 11AM-10PM. FRI-SAT 11:30AM-11PM. Mid-APR to Mid-NOV: 7 days 11:30AM-2:30PM and 4:30PM-10PM.
Type: Mexican. On Sundays from June 1 to October 31, beer & Bratwurst is served-up on the patio with Austrian folk music. On MON-SAT, a disk jockey plays tunes from 9PM to 1:30AM.

***Food:* ★★★½ *Service:* ★½ *Decor:* ★ *Atmosphere:* ★**

Their beef taco/chili relleno/cheese enchilada combination, with fried rice and real pinto beans, was very good indeed. The taco was exceptionally good with shredded beef, whole lettuce leaves, and American & jack cheeses. The chili relleno had enough chili & cheese to make it a worthwhile selection also. The rice was topped with cheeses. Unfortunately, good food was the only noteworthy aspect of this Mexican Restaurant. The barkeep/waiter, the only server for lunch with nine people at four tables, was not very helpful, conscientious, prompt or alert. He did not check on my meal or refill my water and seemed "out of it" on this particular day. The restaurant itself has a closed in feeling with only a few narrow windows on the front side which are partially obstructed by the disk jockey's booth, outside posters, plants and a big screen television. An overhang outside obstructs light even more in this almost claustrophobic setting. Rock music BANGS through some powerful speakers.

Bighorn Steakhouse ★★★½
Keystone Resort, U.S. Hwy 6 (303)468-2316

Dinner: $$$$. DEC-APR: SUN-THU 5PM-10PM. FRI-SAT 5PM-10:30PM. MAY-NOV: SUN-THU 5:30PM-9:30PM. FRI-SAT 5:30PM-10PM.
Type: Steak.

Food: **★★★★** Dinners are served with a small loaf of warm wheat bread and the soup & salad bar. The soup of the day was a thick and spicy sirloin steak with mushrooms, white pepper, pimentos and onions. The 30-item salad bar includes gherkins, pepperoncini, pasta & potato salads, black & green olives, fruit salad and hot bacon dressing. My entree was the herb marinated top sirloin topped with "onion hair" and served with a brown demiglaze sauce and baked potato on the side. The "onion hair" is very fine, thin strands of onion rings. The sirloin was very tender and lean with no fat or gristle and I found it did not need the demiglaze sauce, although it was quite good also. This was a top quality piece of meat. Appetizers include escargot, French onion soup, and shrimp cocktail. Dry-aged steaks, prime rib, crab stuffed shrimp, Rocky Mountain rainbow trout, smoked chicken, and a game meat of the day are the major entree items. Vegetables, like steamed asparagus bernaise sauce, can be ordered a la carte. There is a children's menu. For dessert, you can end your meal with mud pie, Grand Marnier cheesecake, rhubarb strawberry cobbler, or warm gingerbread with hard brandy sauce.

Service: **★★★½** Very well spoken and observant. The waitress spotted that the burner had gone out on the hot bacon dressing and immediately offered to heat some in the kitchen and bring it out to me.

Decor: **★★★½** This high-class looking restaurant is located at the bottom of the stairs from the Keystone Resort Lobby. It has 15 semi-circular booths with brown vinyl seats and tan corduroy backs that seat about 50. The polished wood-paneled walls are sparsely decorated with paintings of mountains, valleys, lakes, open fields and snow. Dried sunflowers and cattails in shiny brass pots and basins are set in the center section and in the corners. The lighting scheme is sophisticated with lights set in a hidden louvre about a foot from the ceiling. The light actually reflects off the ceiling before reaching the diner. Additional lighting is provided by brass lamps with frosted shades hanging on the walls behind the booths.

Atmosphere: ★★★ Soft jazz plays quietly in the background. People speak in whispers so as not to be overheard. It was a little too high-brow and stuffed-shirt for my style. I felt a little uneasy in here.

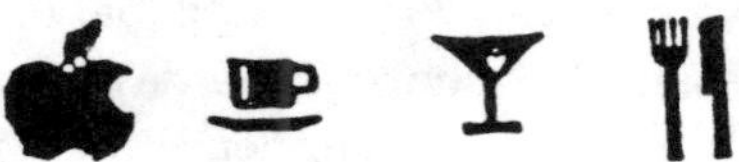

COMMODORE ★★★
KEYSTONE RESORT AND PEDESTRIAN VILLAGE, U.S. HWY 6 (303)468-4295

Dinner: $$$$-$$$$+. DEC-APR and JUN-SEP: 7 days 5:30PM-9:30PM. MAY, OCT & NOV: FRI-SAT 5:30PM-9:30PM. Closed SUN-THU.
Type: Seafood (and steak). A number of entrees are marked with a heart figure indicating they are low in cholesterol, sugar and fat.

Food: ★★★½ I dined here on a Friday night (the only night they serve a seafood buffet and nothing else) having had nothing to eat all day. After a cup of New England Clam Chowder, a roll, a trip to the salad bar, 20 peel-away shrimp, 10 oysters on the half-shell, a dish of pasta, an entree of grilled hickory glaze salmon over pasta with almonds, another entree of pork chops and honey glazed beef with apple horseradish sauce, a piece of raspberry chocolate cake and a chocolate covered strawberry, I was full. The oysters from the Florida keys and the shrimp from Thailand were the best. I could have just eaten my way through all the oysters, but then I could not have told you about the rest of the buffet. The salad bar featured pasta, artichoke hearts, and basil vinaigrette and honey-mustard dressings. The tri-color pasta in pesto sauce was very rich — too rich. The pasta bar also offers fettucini and two other sauces: Alfredo and white wine olive oil. The pork chop with rosemary was dry, but I think that is one of the drawbacks of having a buffet. Food dries out from staying under those burners. The grilled hickory glazed salmon, though, had a flavorful barbecue taste. The other entrees were Southern-fried catfish with avocado and black bean salsa, sautéed chicken breast with wild mushrooms, honey-glazed beef, broiled

Rocky Mountain trout, and vegetable florettes with roasted potatoes. Fruit cobbler and assorted cakes were also on the dessert buffet. If you arrive here on an evening other than Friday, you can still order an appetizer of shucked oysters on ice, smoked trout cakes, bay shellfish, or tiger prawns. The soup and salad bar is still available. The seafood selections include sautéed bay shrimp & scallops, grilled ginger tuna, mahi mahi, sea scallops, blue river trout, steamed ruby red trout, and Maine lobster. If you are in the mood for beef you can order filet mignon with bearnaise sauce, a NY steak, or a combination beef tenderloin and hickory-glazed salmon. Rosemary grilled chicken completes the choice of entrees. There is a children's menu.

Service: ★★½ Very good at the beginning. It was a buffet, so service was limited. I had just come from working out and my waitress could not keep up with my demands for ice water. Towards the end, a large party and several smaller ones arrived and I became lost in the maze.

Decor: ★★★ Located on Keystone Lake, when you enter this restaurant you are greeted by seafaring decor: fish nets and cages, sailing flags, a lobster tank, a fish tank, pictures of The American Schooner and The British Queen sailing ships, three propellers mounted on a wall, boiler gauges, a Navy binnacle, and three life savers. Straight back is the bar with a thick, tan, vinyl-cushioned rail and nine barstools. The lounge to the left has a stone fireplace at one end and looks out onto the gazebo and Keystone Lake. It has nine tables for about 30. In the summertime they can serve food to about 50 diners in the gazebo. In front of the bar, next to the hostess stand, is a small seating area with two couches, a globe on a coffee table and 15 more propellers, some damaged. The dining room, back and to the right of the hostess stand, is decorated with thick ropes wound around square posts, sailing flags over the salad bar, and several low hanging plants, mostly philodendrums and spider plants, that I found myself bumping into more than once. Lighting is provided by ceiling lights in mosaic shades hanging on short chains, studio lights, and kerosene table lamps.

Atmosphere: ★★★½ This restaurant hosted a mixture of couples, singles, families, and friends. The clientele is casual here, but still somewhat formal in comparison to most restaurants in Summit County. I was here in October, an off-season, which the management here told me they refer to as "shoulder season". They did not know, however, how this name came about.

EDGEWATER CAFE ★★★
KEYSTONE RESORT, U.S. HWY 6 (303)468-2316

Breakfast/lunch $$, dinner $$$. Mid-APR to Thanksgiving: 7 days 6:30AM-3PM. Thanksgiving to Mid-APR: 7 days 6:30AM-9PM.
Type: Cafe.

Food: ★★★ I ordered their Philly steak sandwich for lunch: tender & tasty grilled buffalo beef strips, lightly sautéed green peppers, slightly more sautéed onions, and melted cheese on a roll. Fruit salad, a mix of different melons, was served on the side. The breakfast menu offers some deliciously different meals: items like huevos Montezuma (similar to huevos rancheros, only with scrambled eggs), French toast stuffed with strawberries and cream cheese, French toast made with custard raisin nut bread, blueberry and buttermilk flapjacks, and strawberry filled cantaloupe. Eight different salads are featured for lunch including bay shrimp & vegetables, ginger fruit, and smoked chicken with black beans. Shrimp gazpacho and French onion are the soups. Other sandwich selections include seafood croissant, burger, smoked Colorado beef dip, and hot corned beef. Before dinner you can order calamari, pizza, steamed mussels, or a calzone. Minestrone soup is served at dinnertime. The entrees include veal picatta, herb marinated beef, chicken breast with green peppercorn sauce, grilled tuna, and a nightly pasta special. There is a children's menu and the choices for dessert include Heath bar cheesecake, black & white brownie sundae, ice cream or sherbet. Non-dairy creamer, margarine, and a variety of other low salt, low cholesterol, low sugar, and low fat items are available.

Service: ★★★ Friendly, concerned, helpful and with a smile. Just fine.

Decor: ★★★ Located on Keystone Lake, this restaurant has windows all around for great views of the mountains, lake, and neighboring shops. The dining room is divided in two by a concrete wall with open window spaces filled with wood-framed, mosaic glass showing a green-leaf pattern. The lake front side has 15 tables for 59 diners. The inside lane has eight tables for 29 with lighting provided by lamps under white shades hanging from an arched brass wall structure. A few of the tables are in secluded alcoves. The entrance is decorated with potted plants, red bricks, and baskets with plastic vegetables. To the left of the entrance is a bar/lounge with eight tables for 32 and eight barstools. Except for several hanging plants and an awning with a "splashy pattern", the decor in here is primarily exterior (the view outside).

Atmosphere: ★★★½ A business-type crowd that discusses skiing a lot is attracted here. Light jazz plays in the background. A lot of natural light and good views make for a pleasant atmosphere.

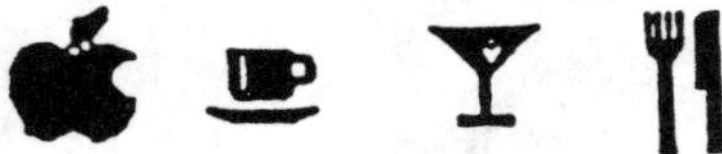

RAZZBERRYS ★★★★
23044 U.S. HWY 6 (303)468-1334

Breakfast $, lunch $$, dinner $$$-$$$$. Mid-NOV to Mid-APR: 7 days 7AM-10:30AM and 11AM-10PM. Mid-APR to MAY and OCT to Mid-NOV: MON-FRI 7AM-10AM and 5:30PM-10PM. FRI-SAT 7AM-10AM and 11AM-10PM. JUN-SEP: 7 days 11AM-10PM.
Type: American/Continental (mostly American). A 15% gratuity is added to parties of six or more.

Food: ★★★★½ The ten-item salad bar is included with all entrees and features prime rib salad (green & red peppers and carrots in a Stroganoff sauce). For my entree I ordered Colorado lamb T-bones with sour cherry chutney. The lamb was lightly seasoned, broiled and mixed wonderfully with the cherry chutney: a delicious combination. It came with two mushroom-shaped potatoes, long thin baby carrots, a couple of raspberries and garnish. The breakfast menu features fresh seasonal berries, natural yogurt, granola, and homemade fruit breads and muffins.

The lunch appetizers include potato skins, Cajun hot wings, and homemade onion rings. You can also choose between two salads: a hearty deli or smoked chicken and honeydew. If you are looking for something more substantial for lunch, a half-pound hamburger, grilled chicken or open-faced prime rib sandwiches, barbecue baby-back ribs and deluxe pizzas are also on the menu. The dinner appetizers are much more imaginative: wild mushroom ravioli, margarita cured salmon, and grilled Anaheim chilies. The list of entrees includes a variety of different meats, fish, pastas and vegetables: chargrilled NY sirloin or swordfish steak, sautéed rainbow trout, smothered duck breast, roasted prime rib of beef, smoked double pork chop, steeped salmon, grilled chicken breast, ragout of rabbit, and tomato fettucini. For dessert, try pound cake with raspberry sauce or a frozen alpine white chocolate and raspberry parfait.

Service: ★★★½ Friendly, efficient and very helpful. My waiter, Harry, was eager to provide answers to all my questions and enhanced the relaxed atmosphere.

Decor: ★★★★½ The nonsmoking section with salad bar has 11 tables with black cloths and 40 black wood cushioned chairs with armrests. The smoking section has six tables, no artwork, and room for 20 diners. The entire dining room is done is black, platinum and pink with in-set ceiling lights and turquoise napkins. The restaurant faces the patio and ski slope. Except for a tri-color (black, turquoise and pink) hanging on the wall separating the smoking and nonsmoking sections, the dining area is void of artwork. Not that there is much space for it. A mirrored wall behind the salad bar separates the nonsmoking section from the lounge. Philodendrons in platinum pots hang along the window row of tables. Lighting is provided by platinum wall sconces. The restaurant is very elegant, modern and different. The unique color combination does not require substantive art work and in this case I think "less is better". The bar/lounge can seat 42 at seven tables and 16 barstools. Adjacent to the lounge is a seating area in front of a fireplace with three couches and four lounge chairs.

Atmosphere: ★★★★ Classical and instrumental music. This is a popular place with couples. I imagine night skiing would be fun to watch.

KIT CARSON

Named after the famous pioneer scout and guide, the original town was on the banks of Sand Creek, three miles west of its present site. The Kansas-Pacific railroad reached Kit Carson in 1870 and three years later the Arkansas Valley railroad connected the town to Las Animas.

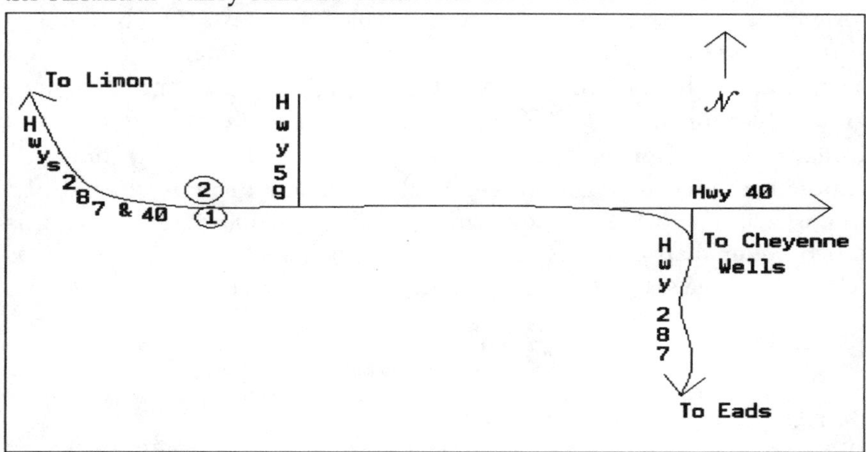

Restaurants and Ratings:	Food	Service	Decor	Atm	Overall
1. CHUCK WAGON	★★★	★★★	★	★★½	★★½
2. TRADING POST	★★★	★★	★★½	★	★★

Only the Trading Post accepts major credit cards and has a nonsmoking section. Neither restaurant serves alcohol.

CHUCK WAGON ★★½
WEST SIDE OF TOWN ON THE SOUTH SIDE OF HWYS 287&40 (719)962-3456

Breakfast $, lunch/dinner $-$$. Daily 5AM-10PM.
Type: Family.

Food: ★★★ *Service:* ★★★ *Decor:* ★ *Atmosphere:* ★★½

My Denver omelet had a lot of ham with green peppers, cheese & onions. There was no scrimping of food here. The coffee, however, was weak. The lunch/dinner menu features burgers, sandwiches, soups, salads, nachos, steaks, pork chops, fried chicken, seafood, ice cream and fruit pies. There is a children's menu for "12 and under and 55 and over" with smaller portions and prices. Service was satisfactory and friendly. This restaurant has two rooms with a counter in-between. The front room resembles a cafe, has six white formica tables, and seats 20. The counter seats six. Around the corner to the left of the counter is the second seating area which resembles a dining room. It has ten, formica, wood-grain tables for 31 people. The salad bar separates the two rooms. The walls, composed of white and brown panel boards in both rooms, are almost bare. There was only one wall ornament: a square clock in the dining room which keeps the wrong time. The lighting in here was much better than in the restaurant across the street. The clientele was much the same, except this restaurant had a few women.

(Kit Carson) Trading Post ★★
West side of town on the north side of Hwys 287&40 (719)962-3355

Breakfast/lunch $, dinner $$. 7 days 5:30AM-10PM.
Type: Country.

***Food:* ★★★ *Service:* ★★ *Decor:* ★★½ *Atmosphere:* ★**

This is a good place for burgers and chili. Breakfast, which is served anytime, includes Cinnamon rolls and blueberry muffins. The lunch menu features burgers, soup, chili, salads, and sandwiches. There are daily specials, homemade pies, ice cream and cheesecake. The dinner entrees include steaks, rainbow trout, shrimp, halibut, scallops, chicken and pork chops. Service is fair. This is a two-room restaurant. However, the room to the right was not in use. The room to the left has five booths, nine tables and a counter for a total of 58 people. A plastic imitation red-brick divider separates the dining area from the waitress pick-up station. Chained ceiling lamps hang from the wood-beamed ceiling that has a polished look. Old photographs of the local area hang in the booths which are divided by a trellis design. This is a dark place. Expect a lot of local cowboys, ranchers and farmers.

KITTREDGE

Established in 1920 when the Kittredge Town Co, owned by Charles M. Kittredge, purchased 300 acres of the Luther ranch. A year later postal officials named the settlement after the Kittredge family which had lived in the area since 1860.

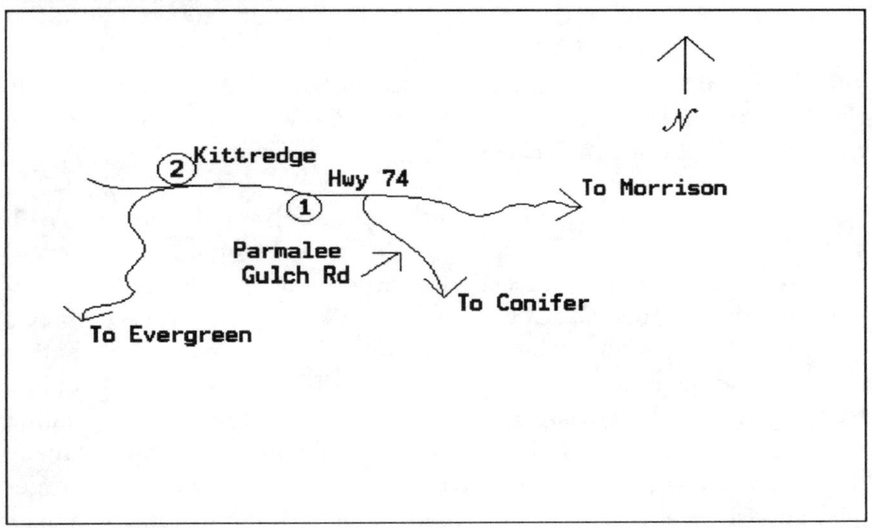

Restaurants and Ratings:	Food	Service	Decor	Atm	Overall
1. Dick's Hickory Dock	★★★★	★★★	★★★	★★★½	★★★½
2. Tivoli Deer	★★★★★	★★★★★	★★★★½	★★★★★	★★★★★

If I had to pick my favorite restaurant, the best restaurant in small town Colorado, the Tivoli Deer would be it. They serve exquisitely delicious brunches and dinners, have outstanding servers who can tell you anything and everything you want to know about any meal, its ingredients, or how it is prepared, and offer this in a most congenial and warm country atmosphere. The Tivoli Deer is "Tops" in my book! Somewhat overshadowed, but still an excellent choice for barbecue is Dick's Hickory Dock. You simply can not go wrong with either of these restaurants. Both restaurants accept major credit cards, have nonsmoking sections, and serve alcohol.

KITTREDGE

DICK'S HICKORY DOCK ★★★½
26220 HIGHWAY 74 (303)674-9612

Lunch/dinner $$. MAR-SEP: SUN-THU 11:30AM-9PM. FRI-SAT 11:30AM-10PM. Closed MON. OCT-DEC & FEB: TUE-THU 5PM-9PM. FRI-SUN 11:30AM-9PM. Closed MON. Closed JAN.
Type: Barbecue. 15% gratuity for parties of eight or more. No separate checks. $1.50 extra plate charge. Personal checks with check guarantee card only. No out-of-state checks.

Food: ★★★★ The homemade turkey & lentil soup was fair to good with several small cut pieces of turkey in a thin broth. I would have preferred a thicker base. I ordered the combination two-rib special: one pork and one large (about nine inches) beef rib in their homemade barbecue sauce, served with a gigantic baked potato topped with sour cream, butter, cheddar cheese, chives and bacon bits; ranch style beans with onion, bacon, garlic and brown sugar; and homemade corn bread. A very filling enterprise. Great ribs and 'fixins'! They do their own smoking and make their own desserts as well. For something lighter, you can try a burger or sandwich (French dip or club), smoked red snapper or catfish, quiche, salad (country or taco), or a diet special. Also on the menu are sandwiches or platters of hickory smoked sliced beef, ham, or turkey; spicy hot Polish sausage; and sliced roast pork. NY, filet mignon, and rib eye steaks complete the list of entrees. The weekend specials are a half barbecued chicken on Friday night and hickory-smoked pork spare ribs on Saturday and Sunday nights. There is a children's menu and the list of desserts includes cheese cake, chocolate sundae and ice cream.

Service: ★★★ Accommodating. The waitress will set you up with a big bib that says "I ♥ ribs", just in case.

Decor: ★★★ This is a very rustic-looking building, inside and out, with a big patio on Bear Creek. A board walk leads up to the entrance that has a long brown-wood overhang. The nonsmoking section to the left has nine hardwood tables for 32 with windows on three sides and natural-looking, but finished, wood walls. There are a few stained-glass artworks, an elk photo, a nature picture and dried flowers for decor. The smoking section to the right has five tables for 18 with pictures of sea gulls over a sandy deserted beach and ducks. The patio has 13 picnic tables with umbrellas.

Atmosphere: ★★★½ I was here in winter, but I imagine it would be very pleasant to be on the patio in summer and listen to the sounds of the creek roll by. This is another superb country/mountain restaurant.

TIVOLI DEER ★★★★★
26300 HILLTOP DRIVE (303)670-0941

Sunday brunch $$$, lunch $$, dinner $$$$+ ($32 for any four course dinner). MON and WED-SAT 11AM-3PM and 5:30PM-9:30PM. SUN 10AM-2PM and 5:30PM-9:30PM. Closed TUE.
Type: Continental (Danish). The Tivoli Deer was started in 1982 by Mogens Sorensen, a native of Denmark, and Lynn Sorensen, a native of Colorado. The name came from "Tivoli Gardens", a famous amusement park in Denmark, combined with a recognizable symbol of the Colorado mountains, a peaceful deer.

Food: ★★★★★ I have had Sunday brunch here eight or nine times since the Tivoli Deer opened for business on June 17, 1982. I have tried most of the brunch entrees at least once and they are all wonderful. Brunch includes a glass of champagne or soft drink, coffee or tea, Danish pastry, and fresh orange juice or fruit. Special cocktails, like mimosa, Bloody Mary, fresh fruit daquiri, and a Danish Mary with Aquavit, along with specialty coffee drinks are available. A dozen delicious entrees are on the menu for your choosing. Most come with fresh vegetables and pommes gratin dauphinoise (similar to scalloped potatoes with a crusty cheese & bread topping). On my last brunch visit I ordered the Pojarski: a homemade chicken sausage that has a kind of fish texture. It was served on a buttered croissant with poached eggs, green & red peppers, and Hollandaise sauce. The fresh vegetable was an interesting hollowed out zucchini slice stuffed with mushroom pâté. Other brunch entrees that I have equally enjoyed and would all highly recommend include the

Stroganoff crêpe (tenderloin tips sautéed medium-rare in bordelaise, onion and mushroom sauce, then folded in a homemade crêpe), the garden brioche (filled with sautéed spinach, poached egg and Hollandaise), the French (two chicken and ham croquettes served with poached eggs on a croissant with Hollandaise), the Nordic chicken (breast stuffed with deviled crabmeat in a light paprika shrimp sauce), the smoke house (fresh smoked trout with scrambled eggs and chives), and the cheese blintzes (with three types of cheese, blueberries and raisins, served with blueberry yogurt sauce). The other brunch entrees feature filet mignon, Danish waffle, Danish open face omelet, a combination seafood tart, and salmon with cream cheese and bagel.

I have never been here for lunch, but the menu offers gravad lax (marinated salmon served with mustard dill dressing) as an appetizer; baked onion soup and a soup du jour; duck, herring or chicken curry salad, and the Tivoli salad with romaine lettuce, greens, spinach and the house dressing. For sandwiches they have Swedish meatballs, steak and hamburger. The lunch specialties feature breast of chicken Frangelico, Aeggekage (an open face omelet with Danish ham, tomato, scallions and Jarlsberg cheese), beef sauté Stroganoff, sirloin steak, seafood spaghetti, moules marinee (green lip mussels in olive oil and white wine), braised lamb shank, Wiener schnitzel, and beuf lindstrom (broiled Swedish style chopped sirloin).

My sole dinner experience here was a delightful one on the patio under a warm summer sky. I strongly recommend you make dinner reservations here and plan to spend two to three hours to fully enjoy this marvelous dining treat. Take your time, relax and feast! Your four course meal begins with your choice of appetizer or soup. The choices are: imported herring in three different marinades, escargot en papillote (baked in parchment paper), smoked game sausage cumberland (encased in boned rabbit, chilled and sliced), the gravad lax, duck salad, baked onion soup, smoked pheasant in a consommé of veal and beef, seafood cocktail, or Danish (veal and pork) liver terrine. My dinner companion and I ordered the herring trianon and the seafood cocktail. We enjoyed dipping the herring in each of the marinades (the tomato sherry, vinaigrette & horseradish, and the curry & mayonnaise) and delighted in the Norwegian bayshrimp and scallops in Louis dressing made with mayonnaise, tabasco, and sweet onion & pickle. The second course is the Tivoli salad. The ten dinner entree selections feature everything from spaghetti to lamb. There's the Nordic chicken, tornedos marsala (filet mignon), squire coho salmon (stuffed with shrimp and scallops), breast of duck Danoise (oven roasted, stuffed with apples and prunes, served crisp and tender), emincé of veal Zurichoise (sautéed veal in a white wine sauce served on Swiss rosti potato), sweetbreads with crayfish tails en cocotte (bits of sweetbreads and crayfish tail meat enclosed in a crock with a puff pastry), roast saddle of lamb, beuf sauté Stroganoff (made from beef tenderloin, served on fresh linguini), seafood spaghetti, and a daily special, usually fresh fish. We ordered the duck and the veal. The duck is basted a day in advance in its own juices and it was moist on the inside and crispy on the outside. Served along side potatoes with brown sugar glaze and red cabbage, it was simply outstanding! The veal and mushrooms in sour cream and chardonnay was no less outstanding. It is served on a rosty (roo'sty), similar to a potato pancake with onion, herbs and spices. It also is prepared a day in advance. If you made it this far in the meal you simply can not stop until you have had one of their mouth watering, absolutely incredible desserts. We had the floderand (flu-der-and): chocolate mousse with whipped cream layered between, on top of a bed of blueberries, topped with strawberries; and the coupe Denmark in meringue shell: hot ghirardelli chocolate on homemade vanilla ice cream with roasted almonds on top of a baked meringue shell. For me, the baked meringue shell does it. For some, it is the ghirardelli chocolate. Actually, the combination of all ingredients makes this a positively irresistible dessert. I dare you - no matter how full you are - to take just one bite and stop! We complimented the ending of this wonderful dining experience with Colorado coffee — made with kahlua, Grand Marnier, courvoisier, and amaretto; topped with whipped cream; and served with a sugar crystal stick.

Service: ★★★★★ It would be difficult to find better trained, more informed servers in small town Colorado. Each server goes through a three month training program and is well versed on the ingredients and preparation of every item on the menu. It is like having the chef at your table. They can answer every question you might have about food or drink and do not mind if you ask then to repeat something. They will flood you with information. The service itself has always been pleasant, cheerful, intelligent, professional, and with a light hearted rather than business like attitude. They are simply the BEST!

Decor: ★★★★½ The patio is a delightful place to dine in the summertime. There always seems to be a cool breeze and the surrounding pines and firs are wonderful. Thirty-two people can be seated at eight white-metal tables with green and white "Carlsbad Beer" umbrellas. There is a wall mural of two deer in a field with aspen trees in the background. Tiny white Christmas lights provide additional lighting to the table candles. Inside, the dining room to the right has 17 tables for 60 diners. The entire restaurant is decorated in blue and white — the colors of Denmark. There are white-laced tablecloths and blue and white wallpaper. They have some interesting, rather unusual blueprints on how to make various dishes. These are in gold frames with dark blue matted backgrounds. They resemble the blueprints for a building project with specifications for materials and equipment, an isometric cut of the finished product, and the ingredients — except they are for gourmet dishes and cocktails, like Grand Marnier souffle, boiled crab, a dry martini, a Bloody Mary, a whiskey sour, a margarita, and stuffed lobster. A framed poster of the Tivoli Gardens in Copenhagen also adorns the oak-stained walls and there are some colorful plates on the top section of one wall. The bar/lounge area to the right has 11 tables for 42 with a small dining section off to the side with two tables for 14. About 15 potted and hanging plants occupy the front window area. Lighting is provided by white, globe ceiling lights with wicker shades. There is a wine rack along the rear wall and tapestries from France showing wine drinkers in a garden. A diamond-shaped, stained-glass fixture in a wood frame, with a picture of grapes in the middle, hangs in the back of the room also. Two deer heads are mounted on the wall.

Atmosphere: ★★★★★ Since this is my favorite restaurant, I obviously love the atmosphere. Always comfortable and relaxed. They play classical music. The setting is perfect. It is a charming country/continental experience you soon won't forget and well worth the short drive from Denver.

KREMMLING

Kremmling was established by Rudolph Kremmling in 1874. He had a retail business in Dillon and started a subsidiary on the Dr. Harris Ranch on the north side of the Muddy River in Grand County. Kremmling later moved his store to the south side of the river and the new site soon became know as Kremmling.

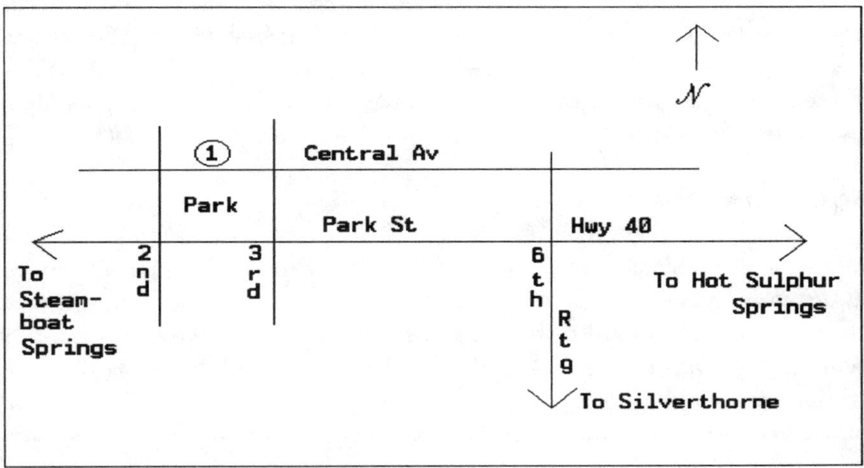

1. THE WAGON ★★★
   207 CENTRAL AVENUE (303)724-9219

Breakfast/lunch $, dinner $$-$$$. 7 days 7AM-10PM (9PM OCT-MAY). Type: Country. 10% added for orders to go. They accept major credit cards and serve alcohol, but do not have a nonsmoking section.

Food: ★★★½ I have stopped here for breakfast and lunch while passing though town. This is a "good ol' country restaurant" where you can get a hearty hot sandwich or a filling omelet loaded with your favorite ingredients. Whatever you order, it is sure to satisfy your appetite without putting a dent in your pocketbook. Some of the locals have their own favorite dishes not shown on the menu. The Sunday morning that I was there, a fellow at the next table told the waitress he wanted "hash browns topped with an egg, over easy, salsa and cheese". The waitress had a little trouble taking the order, but when she finally got it the fellow said "It's a Tom's Special. Don't forget it!" Audacious! Later, the waitress told me that other regular local customers also have their own personal special meals. For example, there is a Jodi Hill omelet made with ham, cheese, tomato, green pepper, salsa and onions. So if you don't see something you want on the menu, try dictating it to the waitress, then giving it your own name. The lunch menu offers soup; salad; chili; appetizers; sandwiches, like corned beef or Bratwurst with sauerkraut and Swiss; burgers; and a few Mexican specialties. The dinner entrees feature steaks, chicken, fish, shrimp, and roast beef. Prime rib is served on Fridays, Saturdays and Sundays. There is a children's/senior's menu and, for dessert, home-baked pies, ice cream and sherbet.

Service: ★★½ Satisfactory.

Decor: ★★★ This is a single-room restaurant with 11 tables for 40 people A brown vinyl bench seat stretches across the back wall and accompanies three of the tables. All of the pictures have a country-western flavor: a woman milking a cow with a little girl looking on, a small cow poke trying on a cowboy hat, a cowboy taking a fall at a rodeo, a sunset (or sunrise) over a lake, and several ducks in flight over a marsh.

Atmosphere: ★★★ This is a country restaurant with a lot of country folks. It is very popular with the locals. Rather quiet with no music.

Colorado River East of Kremmling

LA JUNTA

The town was formerly named Otero, after Miguel Otero, who established the town in 1875. The name was changed to La Junta, the Spanish word for "junction," in 1878 when the town became a junction for the Santa Fe Railroad lines to Pueblo and Trinidad. Two items of local interest are the Koshare Indian Museum and Bent's Old Fort. The museum is patterned after the Indian ceremonial kivas of the Southwest and home of the famous Koshare Indian dancers. Several years ago the curator of the museum, a fellow named "Buck", who has since passed away, treated me to a tour of his private collection. Bent's Old Fort is a reconstruction of the original fort as it was in 1845. It was a major trading outpost on the Old Santa Fe Trail.

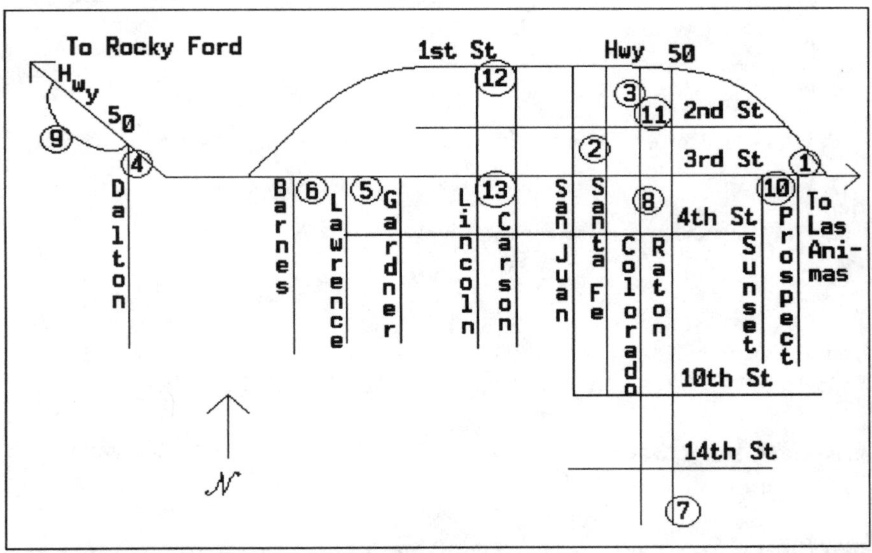

La Junta has three excellent restaurants. Chiaramonte's is surprisingly elegant looking, the Hickory House has great barbecue and El Cid's is by far the best Mexican restaurant in this part of the state. For a feeling of history, dine at the Kit Carson, an old hotel with very high ceilings. Only four restaurants, The Copper Kitchen, Cristina's, El Camino, and New China offer nonsmoking sections. Five restaurants do not serve alcohol: Copper Kitchen, Cristina's, El Azteca, El Patio, and Rosita's. Five restaurants do not accept major credit cards: Copper Kitchen, Cristina's, El Azteca, El Patio, and Rosita's.

LA JUNTA

Restaurants and Ratings:	Food	Service	Decor	Atm	Overall
1. CAPRI	★★★	★★½	★★★½	★★★	★★★
2. CHIARAMONTE'S	★★★★	★★½	★★★★½	★★★★½	★★★★
3. COPPER KITCHEN	★★★	★★★	★★	★★	★★★
4. CRISTINA'S	★½	★★½	★½	★★	★★½
5. EL AZTECA	★★★	★★½	★★★	★★★½	★★★
6. EL CAMINO INN	★★★	★½	★★★½	★★½	★★★
7. EL CID	★★★★★	★★★★½	★★★½	★★★★½	★★★★½
8. EL PATIO	★★½	★★★	★★	★★½	★★½
9. FELISA'S	★★★	★★★	★★★	★½	★★½
10. HICKORY HOUSE	★★★★½	★★★½	★★★★	★★★½	★★★★
11. KIT CARSON	★★★½	★★★½	★★★½	★★★	★★★½
12. NEW CHINA	★★	★★½	★½	★★	★★
13. ROSITA'S	★½	★★½	★★	★★	★★

CAPRI ★★★
1325 E. 3RD ST. (IN THE QUALITY INN) (719)384-2571

Breakfast/lunch $, Dinner $$. MON-SAT 5AM-10PM; SUN 5PM-9PM.
Type: Family.

Food: ★★★ I tried this place for breakfast and was generally well-pleased with their country breakfast (eggs, biscuits & gravy, and sausage). They also offer Belgium waffles and a continental breakfast. The lunch/dinner menu offers the following lunch items: burgers, soup, salads, and sandwiches (patty melt, deli, Reuben, hot or barbecued beef, and French dip). Dinner appetizers include shrimp cocktail, sautéed or tempura mushrooms, and escargot. The dinner entrees are primarily steaks, seafood, or white meat. The choice of steaks includes T-bone, filet, beef kabob, chicken fried, and roast beef. From the sea comes lobster tail, trout, snow crab, frog legs, shrimp, tempura, and salmon. The barnyard selections are rock Cornish game hen, chicken strips, lamb or pork chops, and ham steak. They have a children's menu. There are several good choices for dessert: homemade pies & cakes, sundaes, crème de menthe & vanilla parfaits, and Swiss Delight with cherry chocolate liqueur.

Service: ★★½ Adequate.

Decor: ★★★½ This restaurant is in the Capri Motel. It has two rooms and a counter. The front room has three booths and four tables for 30 people. The rear room seats about 40, mostly at tables. The two rooms are divided by grey wood columns that imitate the Tuscan order of classical architecture. Plants sit atop the cornice. Paintings of the local area adorn the walls and are for sale.

Atmosphere: ★★★ Quiet and somewhat dignified.

CHIARAMONTE'S ★★★★
208 SANTA FE AVE. (719)384-8909

Lunch $, dinner $$$. MON-FRI 11AM-2PM. MON-SAT 5PM-9PM. Closed SUN.
Type: Steak. I dined here on three or four occasions over the last few years. It has been and still is one of my favorite restaurants in Colorado. It has a charm and elegance that is uncommon for this part of Colorado. At the same time, I found the atmosphere to be relaxing and easy going.

Food: ★★★★ Their sandwiches, burgers, steaks, homemade soups, and salads are all excellent. The choice of salads includes cottage cheese with fruit or ground sirloin, chef's, and taco. The sandwich board includes croissants with either ham, turkey, or beef; roast beef & Swiss; ham, turkey & Swiss; club sirloin; ground sirloin & cheese; beef & Cheddar; and French dip. Sourdough rolls and French bread are used for most of the sandwiches. The offer a limited Mexican selection. You can start your dinner off with an appetizer of breaded mushrooms, clam strips, nachos, or onion rings. The list of steaks includes filet mignon, rib eye, and club sirloin. The seafood menu has salmon, scallops, shrimp tempura, trout amandine, king crab legs, and lobster tail. If you're not very hungry, there are lighter meals to choose from: chef salad, burrito supreme, French dip, ground sirloin & cheese, club steak sandwich, and burgers. Finally, there are a few dinner specialties: beefsteak Neptune (a combination of crabmeat, petite filet and asparagus); marinated pepper steak; chicken Divan; and, on Friday and Saturday only, prime rib and the lighter prime rib sandwich. A children's menu is available.

Service: ★★½ Generally, the service here has been quite good. However, on my last visit it was somewhat inefficient. There were mixed up orders, forgotten requests, and unclean lettuce. So overall, I will have to give them an average rating.

Decor: ★★★★½ This is a large restaurant with four dining rooms and a bar area that can seat about 150 people. The first of the two front rooms has nine tables and five booths and can seat 60 people. The second front room has seven tables for 22 people. The first of the two back rooms can seat about 40 people. The second back room can seat about 20. The decor in the first front room consists of comfortable brown-cushioned chairs with armrests, pink tablecloths, red-brick and dark-wood walls, a low ceiling, and hardwood walnut doors. The second front room has a large mirror on one wall and imaginative wood artworks on two other walls resembling the sun and Saturn with its rings and moons. In-set ceiling lights provide good lighting in here. The first room provides a darker, more romantic, look. This is definitely the most elegant restaurant in Southeast Colorado.

Atmosphere: ★★★★½ This place is a jewel in the grasslands.

COPPER KITCHEN ★★★
116 COLORADO AVE. (719)384-7216

Breakfast/lunch/dinner $. MON-SAT 6AM-2PM; SUN 7AM-12PM.
Type: Country.

Food: ★★★ This is good food at very cheap prices. Their biscuits & gravy are plentiful. Other breakfast items include pork chops, huevos rancheros, pigs in a blanket, blueberry hot cakes, raisin bread French toast, sweet rolls, and melons (in season). The lunch/dinner menu has burgers, sandwiches (patty melt, Reuben, club, Italian sausage, French dip, fried cod; cold ham, turkey or beef; and hot beef, hamburger or turkey with mashed potatoes & gravy), a few Mexican items (a giant burrito, taco salad, taco plate, and homemade red or green chili), soup, salads (ham or turkey chef, and a stuffed tomato), and dinners (roast beef, fried cod or chicken, chicken fried steak, liver & onions, pork chops, ground round, and baked ham). There is also a children's menu and pies & ice cream available for dessert.

Service: ★★★ Simple, plain and good.

Decor: ★★ The wall shelves are decorated with teapots and spice canisters. The walls themselves have several paintings for sale by a local artist. One painting is of a Koshare Indian.

Atmosphere: ★★ The clientele is primarily local ranchers and farmers.

CRISTINA'S ★★½
101 DALTON AVE. (719)384-7508

Lunch/dinner $. MON-SAT 11:00AM-2PM and 5PM-8:30PM. Closed SUN. Type: Mexican. Personal checks taken. The restaurant is all nonsmoking.

Food: ★½ *Service:* ★★½ *Decor:* ★½ *Atmosphere:* ★★

I ordered the combination plate which comes with cheese enchilada, chili relleno, beef taco, refried beans and vermicelli. It was quite soggy and the beef was burned. This was below average. The folks that run this place speak Spanish and seem friendly. This small one-room restaurant has only five brown formica tables for a total of 22 people. It is located in a small red stucco building. The cushioned chairs are red, the curtains are orange, the walls are white, and the trim around the doors and windows is brown. There is not much color coordination here. The decor consists of political posters, a painting of a Mexican hat on a post next to a saddle and other cowboy accouterments set on a blanket, two wood artworks of vegetables and bread, and a shelf in one corner with hanging plants. I noticed most people came in here for takeout. This could be due to the small size of the dining room.

EL AZTECA ★★★
710 W. 3RD (719)384-4215

Lunch/dinner $. TUE-SUN 11AM-2PM and 5PM-9PM. Closed MON.
Type: Mexican.

Food: **★★★** They serve "red hot" green chili with chips. The food here is good but not the best in town. They offer three different combination plates: the special comes with a taco, enchilada, chili relleno, beans and vermicelli; the original comes with a taco, enchilada, beans and vermicelli; and the small comes with just a taco, enchilada and tostada. You can also order a la carte.

Service: **★★½** Adequate.

Decor: **★★★** Seating is at dark wood chairs and tables. The walls are pine-wood panel on the lower half and white plaster on the upper half. Fans with lights and ceramic models of parakeets on rings hang from the wood-beam, stucco ceiling. The window coverings are a colorful multi-colored array of greens and blues with some red, orange and pink. The wall decor includes Indian rugs and Mexican paintings of conquistadors with a black background. They also have a fish tank, which adds a nice touch.

Atmosphere: **★★★½** The piped in Mexican "La Bamba" music is very pleasant and a good addition to the atmosphere.

El Camino ★★★
816 W. 3rd (719)384-2871

Lunch/dinner $. TUE-SAT 10AM-2PM and 3PM-10:30PM. Closed SUN-MON.
Type: Mexican.

Food: ★★★ Their Margaritas are made from a mix and are overpriced. The chalupas or stuffed sopapillas are very good, though. They offer the usual Mexican fare, plus fried ice cream and sopapillas for dessert.

Service: ★½ I was not impressed by the ten-year-old girl who served our food. She was quick to return a menu but never returned to see if we wanted to order anything additional.

Decor: ★★★½ There are two small rooms in this restaurant. The one in front only has two tables for six people. The room to the rear has eight tables for 30 people and a small bar for four. A shotgun and branding iron hang over the bar. Some of the decor is rather interesting: Mexican hats & guitars; Indian rugs & paintings; two wagon wheels; two old stoves; an old gasoline pump; old-fashioned telephones; and shelves decorated with colorful vases, jars, clocks, and water pitchers. There's one chandelier with candle-style bulbs hanging from the wood beam ceiling.

Atmosphere: ★★½ Not quite as interesting as the decor. The place was empty.

El Cid's ★★★★½
1617 Raton Ave. (719)384-9818

Dinner $. MON-SAT 5PM-8:45PM. Closed SUN.
Type: Mexican.

Food: ★★★★★ The all-Mexican menu here is hard to beat. This is by far the best Mexican restaurant in La Junta and one of the best in Colorado. I've eaten here on several occasions over the past few years. Everything on their menu is superb, including the Margaritas. This restaurant is by no means any secret so try to arrive by 6:15PM because it is very popular. You will be guaranteed excellent food at very reasonable prices. The dinner entrees include sanchos (white flour tortillas with beef, cheese, tomatoes, onions and red & green chili); chimichangas; con questas (corn tortillas with beef & beans, cheese, and onions); a combination plate which includes a chili relleno, taco, enchilada, vermicelli & beans; and a la carte items, including Mexican steak and sopapillas.

Service: ★★★★½ Consistently pleasant and efficient.

Decor: ★★★½ There are 16 tables that seat 60 people plus a bar for six. Two of the tables are in a small side room. Mexican rugs & hats, and small white lamps adorn the white walls. The tables have red plastic tablecloths and red place mats. There is a fireplace and the ceiling has wood beams.

Atmosphere: ★★★★½ It just feels Mexican to be here.

EL PATIO ★★½
315 COLORADO AVE. (719)384-6787

Lunch/dinner $. MON-TUE,THU, & FRI 11AM-7PM; WED & SAT 11AM-3PM; Closed SUN.
Type: Mexican.

Food: ★★½ *Service:* ★★★ *Decor:* ★★ *Atmosphere:* ★★½

I suggest their tamale and chili relleno. They have always been a couple of my favorites. The menu is basic Mexican except for the Biscoshitos, which are cookies made with anise and covered with cinnamon and sugar. Service is friendly. Seating is both indoors at four tables and outdoors in a side alley with five tables. Total seating capacity is only 26. Access to the outside seating is direct from the street through a black-iron gate. The walls are clay and concrete. The formica tables are flesh colored. The carpet is green and you can look up at the sky through a trellis. There is also a log decorated with artificial flowers. Rock music is played softly from a speaker hooked up to a tape player inside. A sign asks guests to limit their smoking.

FELISA'S ★★½
27948 FRONTAGE RD. (719)384-4814

Lunch/dinner $. MON-SAT 11AM-9PM. SUN 11AM-7PM.
Type: Mexican. 15¢ per plate charge for orders to go.

***Food:* ★★★ *Service:* ★★★ *Decor:* ★★★ *Atmosphere:* ★½**

I dined here for both lunch and dinner. The salsa has a touch extra chili pepper, which I like. The chips are crispy and spicy. The refried beans are original. For dinner I ordered one of their combination plates. The chili relleno was excellent. The taco, however, was noticeably absent any tomato or salsa. It just came with ground beef, lettuce and cheese. For lunch I recommend the pachanga, a deep-fried flour tortilla with ground beef, green pepper, green onion, and cheese. The service is good and friendly. The decor is a nice combination of mirrors, artwork, plants, lights and sculpture. Seating is on red-cushioned chairs at 16 brown formica tables in a single room that holds 62 people. Black iron plays a significant part in the decor with this material used for the entrance gate, bars on the front window, wall ornaments, and a sculpture of a matador and bull. Pink plaster walls have six octagonal-shaped mirrors, dolls of Spanish dancers, Mexican hats and blankets, a picture of an Indian brave, and ristras. Kachina dolls and artificial plants in wicker baskets hang from the low acoustic-tile ceiling. To top it off, there is a fountain with plants set on a bed of rocks in the middle of the room. The first time I visited here I took note that this was a family place. The second time I visited, the family was acting the way families sometimes do. There was a heated argument going on in the kitchen between employees or family members. A second argument ensued when a customer came in to pick up an order and there was a disagreement over prices and a cheese enchilada. Neither incident made a favorable impression about the staff or clientele.

HICKORY HOUSE ★★★★
1220 E. 3RD (719)384-9250

Lunch $, dinner $$. TUE-SUN 8AM-2PM Closed MON and holidays.
Type: Barbecue.

Food: ★★★★½ They have excellent country-style pork ribs. However, they do not serve baby-back ribs. The rib dinner comes with great Mexican beans, salad, baked potato or fries, ice cream and coffee. My only complaint is with the salad. It is a poor man's salad as they confuse lettuce with salad. The lunch menu includes barbecued beef or ham; burgers, including one with hickory sauce; chicken; shrimp; and sandwiches. Besides ribs, the dinner menu has soup, salads (chef, tossed, cole slaw, and cottage cheese with peaches), steaks (T-bone, NY cut, club, rib eye, chopped sirloin, and dinner), barbecued beef or ham, smoked pork chops, chicken, fried chicken gizzards & livers, French-fried shrimp or oysters, breaded cod, and Rocky Mountain oysters. Prime rib is served on Saturdays only. Ice cream, sherbet, sundaes, and pies are available for dessert.

Service: ★★★½ Very good.

Decor: ★★★★ There are two rooms. The front room has nine booths and seven tables for about 70 people. The back room has 20 tables, 15 of them along a wall bench, and seats 84 people. The front room has red print curtains, tri-lamp ceiling lights, a branding iron and branding marks on two wall murals, hanging plants, the skull and horns from a steer, wood-rail ceilings and walls, and window overhangs inside the building. The back room has red velvet curtains, a fireplace with a model train on the mantel, pictures of mountain and sea scenes, and maroon and white wallpaper. This is a very rustic restaurant.

Atmosphere: ★★★½ It does get busy in here. This is a popular place for both the locals and out-of-towners. I have dined here several times. On the last occasion, members of the visiting college basketball team were eating in the back room.

KIT CARSON ★★★½
CORNER OF COLORADO AVE. & 2ND ST. (719)384-4471

Breakfast/lunch $, dinner $-$$. MON-THU 6AM-8PM; FRI-SAT 6AM-8:30PM; SUN 6AM-2PM.
Type: Country.

Food: ★★★½ I have eaten here for breakfast and lunch on several occasions. They have a good light breakfast which includes cold cereal, a poached egg and English muffin. The lunch specials provide a good nourishing meal as well. Breakfast items include huevos rancheros, sweet rolls, and cinnamon rolls. Regular lunch items include salads (seafood, chef, and a fruit plate), roast beef with gravy, a low cal lunch featuring hamburger and cottage cheese, cod, and sandwiches (Reuben, French dip, steak, hot beef, club, and hamburger). They also have lunch specials: chicken & noodles, Swiss steak, a cold beef sandwich, and turkey salad sandwich. The Mexican lunch specials include a hot Mexican sandwich and salad bar. The dinner menu features shrimp on ice, deep-fried vegetables, liver pâté, and sautéed mushrooms for appetizers. The dinner entrees are steaks (pepper, rib eye, club, filet mignon, chicken fried, and hamburger), roast beef, pork chops, shrimp, a catch of the day, and breast of chicken. For dessert, you have your choice of ice cream, sherbet or a sundae.

Service: ★★★½ Consistently good.

Decor: ★★★½ This historic restaurant consists of two large high-ceiling rooms. The front room has 15 tables for 65 people. The back room has both tables and booths and seats about 85. The decor consists of red-flowered wallpaper, ceiling fans with lights, several paintings, and a large mural of Indians.

Atmosphere: ★★★ An established clientele comes here. It is a quiet place, old and well established.

NEW CHINA ★★
414 WEST 1ST ST. (719)384-8504

Lunch $, dinner $-$$. MON-FRI 11:30AM-2:30PM and 4PM-9PM. SAT 4PM-9PM. SUN 12PM-2PM and 4PM-8PM.
Type: Oriental (Chinese). Take-out and delivery available.

***Food:* ★★ *Service:* ★★½ *Decor:* ★½ *Atmosphere:* ★★**

They have a good hot & sour soup. The Szechuan chicken wings had a good, hot sauce, but too much breading. I guess it is difficult to bread that small an amount of meat. Like most Chinese restaurants, the menu is extensive. There are 28 lunch specials featuring chicken, pork, beef and shrimp. All four of these are served chow mein, chop suey, or kung pao. All but the beef are served sweet and sour. All but the pork come with broccoli. The additional chicken dishes are with almond, moo goo gai pan, and the Szechuan wings. The additional pork dishes are twice cooked, and shredded. The additional beef dishes are pepper, Mongolian, and chicken fried steak. The additional shrimp dish is in lobster sauce. Oh, and in case you're counting, the 28th lunch special is mixed vegetables. Their sign reads "we guarantee fast service no matter how long it takes." Actually, their service was not bad. They even have a couple of Chinese waitresses. This is a two-room restaurant. The front room has four large round tables and six booths for 46 people. The back room has four booths and five tables for 48 people. Artificial plants and red lanterns with red tassels and pictures of dragons and mountains hang from the low stucco ceiling. There are a few pictures of Chinese people in pastoral scenes. The windows are dirty and cracked. The carpet on the floor is rust color; the one on the wall is green. The restaurant is in an old pink and red building. It is comfortable but lacks an air of Chinese authenticity. Easy listening piped in music is played very low.

ROSITA'S CAFE ★★
408 WEST 3RD ST. (719) 384-9060

Breakfast $, Lunch $-$$. 7 days 8AM-8PM.
Type: Mexican. Personal checks accepted.

***Food:* ★½ *Service:* ★★½ *Decor:* ★★ *Atmosphere:* ★★**

I had the lunch special: cheese enchilada, beef tostada, rice and beans. The salsa was watery but hot. The chips unflavorful. The meal itself fair. No complaints on the service. This is a small one-room restaurant with three booths on the right, two booths on the left, and two tables between for a total of 32 people. The walls are wood panel on the lower half and white plaster on the upper half. The right side has three hangings that look more Japanese than Mexican. The largest shows a pagoda and bridge. The two smaller ones are almost identical pictures of mountains in the distance viewed between trees. They are very colorful in greens and browns, but they look out of place. Seating is on black benches and orange-cushioned chairs. I was here around Halloween so the colors were appropriate and complemented their Halloween decorations. There are two mirrors on the back wall, several hanging spider plants and philodendrons, and a gold wall decoration on the left depicting two swords with an emblem of a knight in the middle. This is a place where local workers come.

LAMAR

The town was named after former Secretary of the Interior, L.Q.C. Lamar, in 1886, the year of its establishment. Lamar is primarily an agricultural and cattle-raising community. It is the home of many Canadian geese during winter and is considered the Goose Hunting Capital of the world.

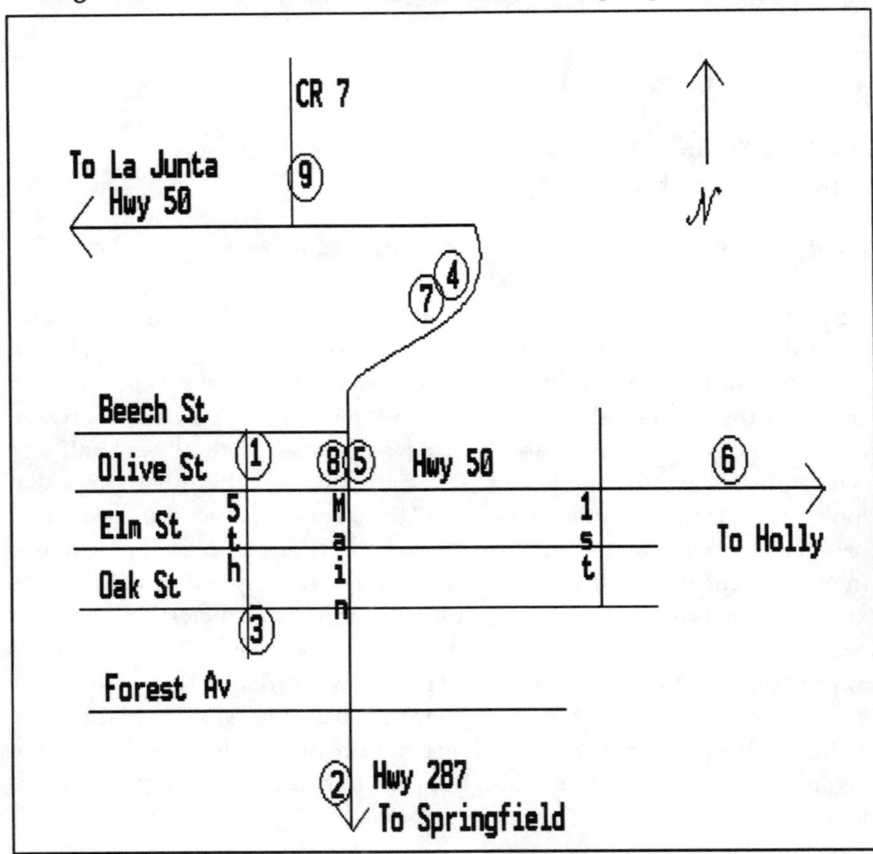

The Green Garden has the best Chinese food in southeast Colorado, and the Hickory House has those great baby-back ribs and sauce. For very good Mexican food featuring tantalizing tortillas, see Abitia's. All but three restaurants accept major credit cards: B.J.'s, Coffee Cup and Daylight Donut. The Cow Palace and Ranchers are the only restaurants that offer a nonsmoking section. Four restaurants do not serve alcohol: B.J.'s, Coffee Cup, Daylight Donut and Ranchers.

Restaurants and Ratings:	Food	Service	Decor	Atm	Overall
1. ABITIA'S	★★★★	★★★½	★★★½	★★★	★★★½
2. B.J.'S	★★	★★½	★	★	★½
3. COFFEE CUP	★	★	★	★	★
4. COW PALACE	★★½	★★½	★★★	★★	★★½
5. DAYLIGHT DONUT	★★	★★	★★	★★½	★★
6. GREEN GARDEN	★★★★½	★★★★½	★★★½	★★★½	★★★★
7. HICKORY HOUSE	★★★★★	★★★★	★★★½	★★★½	★★★★
8. THE MAIN	★★★½	★★★	★★★½	★★½	★★★
9. RANCHERS	★★★	★★½	★★½	★★½	★★½

ABITIA'S ★★★½
121 W. BEECH (719)336-9985

Lunch $, dinner $-$$. MON-SAT 11:30AM-2PM and 5PM-9PM. Closed SUN. Type: Mexican. Take-out available.

Food: ★★★★ The chimichanga comes in a light and crispy flour tortilla that is loaded with beef and cheese. I found it very filling. They have a daily all-you-can-eat lunch buffet for $4.75. Otherwise, you can order off the lunch/dinner menu which features a number of appetizers such as nachos especial, guacamole salad, and a stuffed quesadilla. The choice of salads includes tossed, taco, chicken, and chef. For your dinner entree you can choose between a combination plate, pork with green chili, chicken flautas, the chimichanga, sopapillas stuffed with rice and beans, chili rellenos, or beef fajitas. Additional entrees are huevos rancheros, huevos con chorizo (with Mexican sausage) and steak. All items can be ordered a la carte. An el chiquito or child's plate is also available. For dessert there are sopapillas, cinnamon sopapillas and chips, ice cream, and sherbet.

Service: ★★★½ Friendly and efficient.

Decor: ★★★½ This is a two-room restaurant with three booths and 14 tables in the front room for 82 people and enough tables in the rear room for about 65 people. However, the rear room is only used for parties, banquets and large crowds. This is a colorful place with striped woven curtains in various colors (tan, red, brown and blue), brown or orange chairs, and a brown, artistic-patterned wallpaper. Kachina dolls, fans, and lamps in black-iron square fixtures hang from the ceiling. Mexican hats and paintings of dancing señoritas hang from the walls. Potted plants are set in the window sills.

Atmosphere: ★★★ A popular place for local people and visitors. This is the place to go to for Mexican food in Lamar.

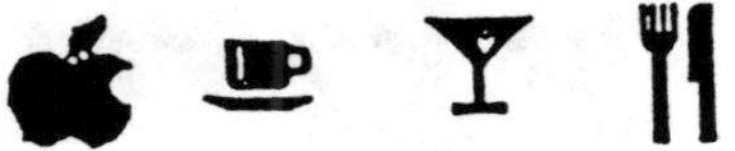

B.J.'S ★½
1510 S. MAIN (719)336-5386

Lunch/dinner $. 7 days 11AM-10PM.
Type: Diner.

Food: ★★ *Service:* ★★½ *Decor:* ★ *Atmosphere:* ★

They prepare a fair grilled burger. Nothing special. They also have foot-long, chili, and korn dogs; chef, shrimp, and tossed salads; sandwiches; dinners (chicken nuggets or strips, shrimp, and fish); Mexican food (deep-fried smothered green chili burritos); and desserts (slushes, shakes, malts, hard & soft ice cream, floats, and sundaes). Service is quick. There is one divided room with 20 booths for 80 people, plus drive-up parking for 20 cars. Food ads are on the windows, meal pictures on the walls and plants on the divider. This is a burger-and-shake place for teenagers.

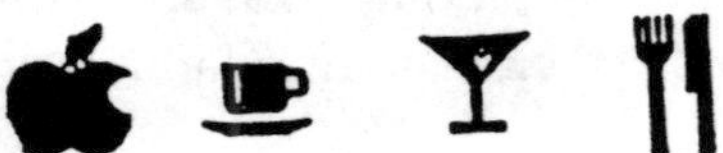

COFFEE CUP ★
401 SOUTH 5TH (719)336-5643

Lunch $. MON-FRI 10AM-5PM; Closed SAT-SUN.
Type: Diner.

Food: ★ *Service:* ★ *Decor:* ★ *Atmosphere:* ★

This is the home of the joker burger made with four patties and the Big G burger made with three patties. You can also order pizza, hot dogs, soft ice cream, shakes, sundaes, floats, and lemonade, but no French fries. This is strictly order-at-the-counter and takeout. No seating. This place caters to Junior High kids: a younger version of B.J.'s.

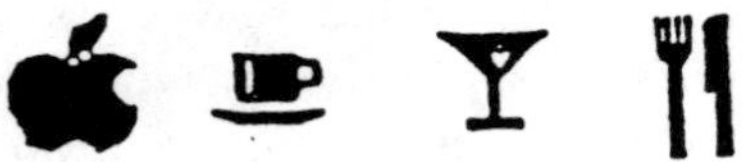

COW PALACE ★★½
1301 N. MAIN (719)336-7753

Breakfast $, lunch $$, dinner $$-$$$. 7 days 5AM-10PM.
Type: Steak. This restaurant is in the Best Western Cow Palace Inn.

Food: ★★½ *Service:* ★★½ *Decor:* ★★★ *Atmosphere:* ★★

I have eaten here several times for breakfast, lunch and dinner. Their salad bar impressed me the most. I found almost everything else, from bacon & eggs to steaks, to be average. Breakfast features Belgian waffles. The lunch menu includes salads, soup, sandwiches, burritos, and steaks. Dinner entrees are chicken breast, broiled halibut, lobster tail, and king crab legs. The soup & salad bar always has two good soup choices, a complete selection of greens, vegetables, side salads, Jellos, puddings and cakes. It is not a light meal. Service is generally average to good. This is a single two-tier room. The upper tier has four booths for 16 people. The lower tier has eight booths and eight tables for 58 people. There is a brick wall on one side, glass on the courtyard side, and a fireplace separating the bar/lounge. The mantel above the fireplace has the accouterments for a nineteenth century sheriff: knife, rifle, revolver, spurs, badge, and handcuffs. The salad bar is outside the restaurant in the courtyard (which is still inside the motel). A lot of "good ol' country boys" come in here along with folks staying at the motel.

DAYLIGHT DONUT ★★
100 BLOCK OF SOUTH MAIN, EAST SIDE (719)336-7911

Breakfast $. MON-SAT 6AM-5:30PM. Closed SUN.
Type: Diner.

Food: ★★ *Service:* ★★ *Decor:* ★★ *Atmosphere:* ★★½

This is basically a coffee and donut shop, but they did have one item I liked a lot: sausage rolls: a sausage link with cheese wrapped in a lightly toasted roll. The limited selection includes sweet rolls, cinnamon biscuits, cookies, fudge, and daily specials like honey wheat cake or peanut butter cake. You order and pick up at the counter and pour your own coffee. This is a small one-room restaurant with ten tables for 38 people. There's blue wallpaper on the lower half of the wall below the blue painted walls and pictures of rocking horses and trees. Fans and plants hang from the ceiling. Two wall mantels, plates, and old photographs provide additional decor. Actually, I thought this was a quiet and comfortable place to get a quick cup of coffee and a donut, or better yet, a sausage roll.

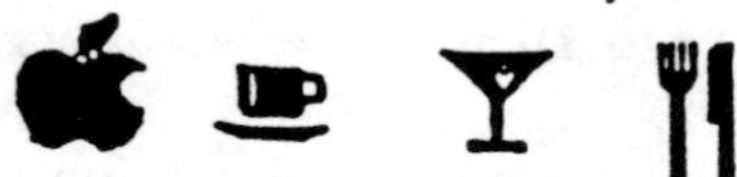

GREEN GARDEN ★★★★
601 E. OLIVE (719)336-3264

Lunch/dinner $-$$. MON-SAT 11AM-2:30PM, 4:30PM-9:30PM. Closed SUN.
Type: Oriental (Mandarin & Szechuan). Carry out available.

Food: ★★★★½ The pu-pu platter is outstanding as an appetizer or light meal. It has paper-wrapped chicken, fried prawn, wanton, rumaki, egg roll, and chow chow beef. It is sure to whet your appetite for more of their delicious food. The rumaki is one of my favorites: an intriguing combination of liver, water chestnuts and bacon. I ate here on three or four occasions and every meal was a delight, whether I had soup, appetizer, or an entree. Other appetizers include barbecue pork and ribs, and pan fried dumplings. The choices of soup are egg flower, wanton, hot & sour, shrimp with sizzling rice, and chicken with black mushrooms

& abalone. The poultry, pork, beef and shrimp entrees look something like this: all four are offered with fried rice, mixed vegetables or Mandarin-style chow mein. All but the beef come sweet-and-sour style. Chicken and shrimp come kung pao, Szechuan style. Chicken and beef come with mushrooms and snow peas, while barbecued pork and shrimp come with just snow peas. Chicken and beef come with garlic. There is Szechuan chicken, pork, beef, shrimp, scallops, or lobster, and Mandarin beef or fish. There is also crispy or Peking duck and whole fish. For dessert, try some fried banana or apple and chilled lychee fruit.

Service: ★★★★½ Most accommodating and friendly.

Decor: ★★★½ This is a small single-room restaurant with seven booths along adjacent sides and five tables in the middle for a total of 48 people. Separating the booths and tables are four-foot dividers with artificial plants on top. Needlepoint of Samurai warriors and colorful paintings of temples adorn the paint and wallpaper walls which, unfortunately, are an unattractive green. Ceiling studio lights plus attractive lamps with stained-glass Chinese paintings and tassels provide ample lighting.

Atmosphere: ★★★½ The place appears to be popular with a certain segment of the local populace and is very busy at lunchtime.

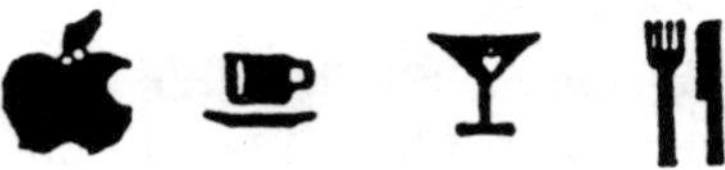

HICKORY HOUSE ★★★★
1115 N. MAIN (719)336-5018

Lunch/dinner $-$$. 7 days 5:30AM-9PM.
Type: Barbecue. Take-out available.

Food: ★★★★★ This restaurant is owned by the same people who own the Hickory House in La Junta. They serve some of the best baby-back ribs in the state with their own special barbecue sauce. Their lunch/dinner menu features barbecue beef, ham, or ribs; burgers, including a hickory burger; sandwiches; fried chicken, shrimp, or cod; chef salads; steaks; soup; a child's plate; chicken teriyaki; a diet plate; fried chicken gizzards

& livers; French-fried shrimp or oysters; and Rocky Mountain oysters. They also have daily specials including prime rib on the weekends.

Service: ★★★★ Consistently very good.

Decor: ★★★½ This restaurant has three dining rooms. The room to the left has six booths and two tables for 32 people. The room to the right has six booths and three tables for 36 people. The room to the far right has 15 tables for 60 people. There are windows along the front and left side with maroon and white curtains. The room to the right has a wall mural with branding iron markings.

Atmosphere: ★★★½ This place is not as rustic as the one in La Junta, but it is better lit.

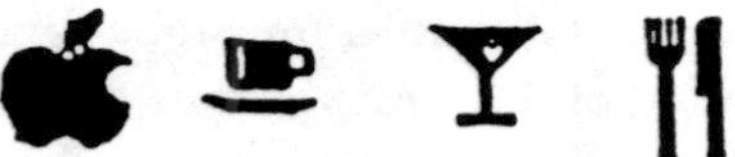

THE MAIN ★★★
114 S. MAIN (719)336-5736

Lunch/dinner $-$$. MON-SAT 6AM-9PM. SUN 6AM-2PM.
Type: Steak (and Mexican).

Food: ★★★½ This is a combination Mexican and steak place. I would recommend them for their steaks first. The selection includes sirloin, rib eye, chicken fried, and hamburger. Other dinner entrees are jumbo shrimp, cod, roast beef, and chicken strips. They also have a child's dinner and a weight watchers' dinner. The Mexican selection is basic. Ice cream, homemade pies, and chocolate sundaes are available for dessert. The breakfast menu offers blueberry muffins and huevos rancheros.

Service: ★★★ The service has been good the three times I have eaten here.

Decor: ★★★½ This is a two-room restaurant. The front room has nine booths, five tables, and a bar for 62 people and resembles a cafe. The back room has four booths, nine tables, and a bar for 64 people and resembles a dining room. The back room is nicely furnished with black-vinyl, high-back chairs and bench seats. This is complemented by a red carpet. There are no windows in the back and only a small window in the front room. In the back room, Mexican hats and big pictures of an old carriage, a wagon, and an abandoned cabin adorn the dark-red wallpaper with wood-paneled walls. Four-lamp, wagon-wheel chandeliers add a nice touch to this room that is without too much clutter.

Atmosphere: ★★½ The back room is dimly lit, which could make for a romantic dinner. Also, it is a quiet place.

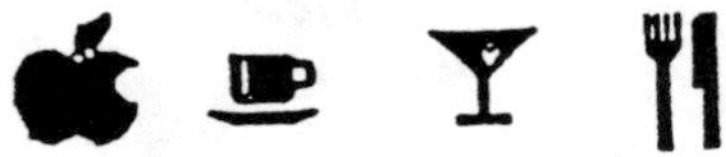

RANCHERS ★★½
33110 COUNTY RD. 7 (AT LAMAR TRUCK PLAZA) (719)336-3445

Breakfast/lunch $, dinner $$. 7 days 24 hours,
Type: Country.

Food: ★★★ *Service:* ★★½ *Decor:* ★★½ *Atmosphere:* ★★½

This place has good country-cooking with plentiful servings and low prices. I recommend their sausage gravy & biscuits. Other breakfast items include corned beef hash, huevos rancheros, Belgian waffles and grits. The lunch menu has an all-you-can-eat soup & salad bar; burgers, including a patty melt and one with chili; and hot sandwiches (beef, meatloaf, or turkey). The dinner selections offer a wide variety, like chicken fried steak, roast sirloin, broiled pork chops, meatloaf, spaghetti, fried chicken, chopped beef steak, cod, and top sirloin. For dessert there is strawberry shortcake, fresh baked pie, and ice cream. Service is satisfactory. This is a big restaurant with enough seating for half the truckers in Colorado. The front section has a bar and 21 booths for 95 people. The first back room has three tables and seven booths for 48 people. The second back room has tables and booths for 60 more. Seating is at brown-cushioned seats with hanging lamps over every booth. Matching decor is provided by the light brown and tan wallpaper, horizontal window shades, and ceiling beams with a railroad track design. This is a very well-lit and clean place. Expect a lot of truckers.

LAS ANIMAS

The town was named after the Las Animas River and was first established in 1869 about six miles to the east of its present location. In 1873, the Arkansas Valley Railway built a line from Kit Carson which connected to the Kansas Pacific Railroad six miles west of the original Las Animas. The town of West Las Animas was established at this junction and renamed Las Animas in 1886.

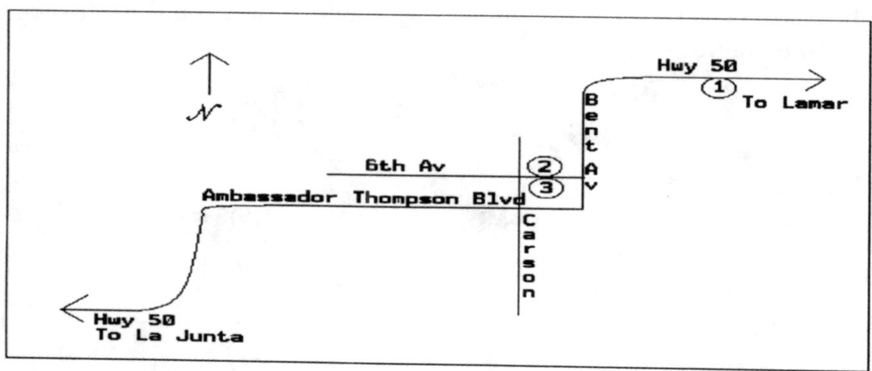

Restaurants and Ratings:	Food	Service	Decor	Atm	Overall
1. BENT'S FORT INN	★★★½	★★½	★★★½	★★★	★★★
2. CHADDERBOX	★★★	★★★	★★	★½	★★½
3. MEDINA'S	★★	★½	★★★	★	★★

For a good charbroiled steak, go to Bent's Fort Inn. For Mexican, visit the Chadderbox. Only Bent's Fort Inn accepts major credit cards and has a nonsmoking section. Only the Chadderbox does not serve alcohol.

BENT'S FORT INN ★★★
EAST END OF TOWN ON THE SOUTH SIDE OF HWY 50 IN THE BEST WESTERN MOTEL (719)456-0011

Breakfast/lunch $, Dinner $-$$. 7 days 6AM-8PM (9PM in summer).
Type: Steak. 15% gratuity added for service in The Bent Rim Saloon or outside of the dining room.

Food: ★★★½ I had the chopped sirloin wrapped in bacon with mushroom sauce. It had a nice charbroiled taste with a delectable sauce. It was excellent. However, I thought they overcooked my order. The soup and potato were just average. The breakfast menu features huevos rancheros, blueberry pancakes, Belgian waffles, oatmeal and cinnamon rolls. For lunch, the choices are chicken fried steak, country fried chicken, roast beef, hot sandwiches (burgers, Reuben, French dip, beef, or a Monte Cristo), cold sandwiches, soup, salads and desserts (homemade pie, ice cream, sherbet, and sundaes). This is primarily a steak house with charbroiled rib eye, top or chopped sirloin, filet mignon, chicken fried steak, beef kabob, and sautéed sirloin tips. The rest of the menu includes country fried chicken, rainbow trout, deep-fried shrimp, and lo-cal meals of grilled halibut or chicken breast.

Service: ★★½ Satisfactory.

Decor: ★★★½ This restaurant is a single room in two sections divided by a pair of steps. The first section has five booths and eight tables for 52 people. The second section has four booths and seven tables for 44 people. Wagon-wheel chandeliers on black-iron chains hang from the vaulted, wood-beamed ceiling with matching wall lanterns. Adorning the white stucco walls are colored sketches (a blacksmith and an open space with a mountain range in the background); a painting of a mother and child in front of an Indian pueblo; and octagonal- and diamond-shaped knit artworks in orange and yellow. Plants hang from rope-style macrame holders in the area separating the two sections. In the second section there are pictures of deer and a bull.

Atmosphere: ★★★ The clientele consists mostly of elderly and professional.

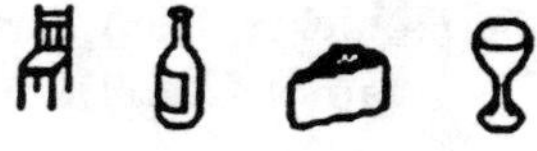

CHADDERBOX ★★½
324 W. 6TH (719)456-1734

Lunch/dinner $. 7 days 11AM-8PM (9PM in summer).
Type: Mexican.

LAS ANIMAS

Food: ★★★ *Service:* ★★★ *Decor:* ★★ *Atmosphere:* ★½

I liked the Mexican food here, which included tamales, fajitas, and smothered crispittas. The American menu includes burgers, sandwiches (Polish sausage, pepper steak, pork tenderloin, and chicken), a full submarine menu, breaded mushrooms, and the following dinners: fish & chips, shrimp and chicken fingers. For dessert, there are shakes, sundaes, and floats. Service is quite good. This is a long, single, narrow-room restaurant with six tables and three booths for only 36 people. The tables in the front did not have comfortable chairs. Old poster advertisements of soap, Coca Cola, and Grapenuts hang on one wall. One of the posters, by Maud Humphrey, depicts "wash day." Green curtains with white trim cover the windows. Most of the clientele were dressed slovenly.

MEDINA'S ★★
333 W. 6TH (719)456-9973

Lunch/dinner $. MON-FRI 11AM-2PM and 5PM-8PM. Closed SAT-SUN.
Type: Mexican.

Food: ★★ *Service:* ★½ *Decor:* ★★★ *Atmosphere:* ★

I had a chili relleno, beef & bean burrito, and guacamole taco served with spicy hot salsa on the side. The food was dry and the hot salsa only made it hot, not less dry. The Mexican fare can be ordered individually or in combination plates. The American side of the menu has burgers, sandwiches, salads, soup, and dinners (shrimp, fried chicken, ham, hamburger steak, pork chop, chicken fried steak, and diet plates). The first order of chips & salsa was not free. The front seating area has six booths and two tables for 36 people. Up a short ramp into the rear seating area are four tables for 18 people, plus a single table for four off to the left behind a trellis with hanging plants. Mirrors with flowered-patterns and pictures of Indian pueblos hang on the wood-paneled walls. I liked the turquoise seats and benches. It made the room feel more authentically Mexican. A Mexican radio station played mostly talk.

LEADVILLE

Silver was first struck in 1876 and the town began with many names: Agassiz, Boughtown, Carbonate, Cloud City, Harrison and Slabtown. Controversy raged when it came time for legal adoption of a name. One faction wanted Harrison for the Harrison Reduction Works, while another supported storekeeper, Horace Tabor, who favored the name Leadville. The name was chosen for the large amount of argentiferous lead ores in the area. Leadville is an historical treasure chest. The Matchless Mine Cabin and adjacent mining area are now open for tours, as are the Healy House and Dexter Cabin, restored to nineteenth-century decor, and The Old Tabor Home, where Horace and his first wife, Augusta, lived before they moved to Denver in 1880. Two other attractions are Leadville's Heritage Museum and Gallery, which tells the town's story in miniature, and the new National Mining Hall of Fame and Museum, which has exhibits dealing with the mining heritage here and throughout the nation.

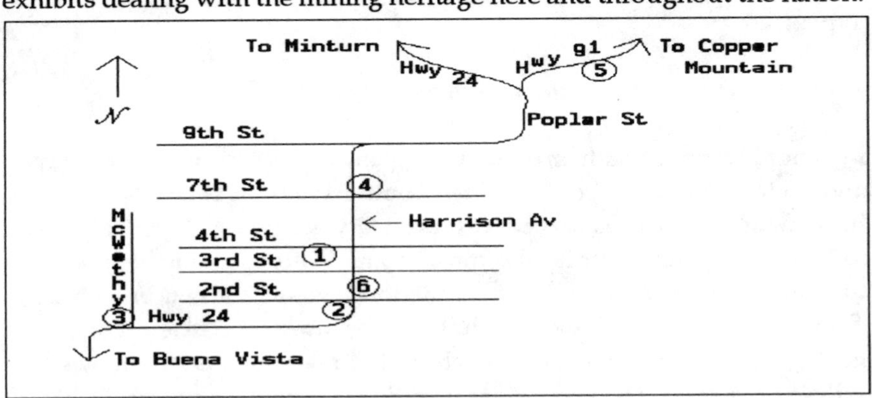

Restaurants and Ratings:	Food	Service	Decor	Atm	Overall
1. GARDEN CAFE	★	★	★½	½	★
2. HIGH COUNTRY	★★★	★★★½	★★½	★★½	★★★
3. LA CANTINA	★★★	★★★½	★★★	★★½	★★★
4. PINE CONES	★★	★★	★½	★★½	★★
5. PROSPECTOR	★★★★	★★★★	★★★★	★★★★½	★★★★
6. WILD BILL'S	★★½	★★	★★★	★½	★★½

LEADVILLE

By far the best restaurant in the Leadville area is the Prospector, three miles north of town. I recommend their steak, chicken and onion rings. If you like wallpaper with very old advertisements, visit Wild Bill's, but be prepared for tight seating. La Cantina, the Prospector and Wild Bill's are the only restaurants that accept major credit cards. High Country, Pine Cones and Wild Bill's are the only restaurants that have nonsmoking sections. All the restaurants, except Pine Cones and Wild Bill's, serve alcohol.

GARDEN CAFE ★
115 W. 4TH (719)486-9917

Breakfast/lunch/dinner $?? (see below). 7 days 7:00AM-2:00PM (2:30PM in summer). WED-SUN 5:30PM-9:00PM (9:30PM in summer).
Type: Cafe.

***Food:* ★ *Service:* ★ *Decor:* ★½ *Atmosphere:* ½**

My soup, when it finally arrived, was lukewarm with no body, no flavor, and no texture. A bowl of hot water would have been better. None of the burgers or sandwiches served at our table were warm. My Philly steak sandwich was dry despite the mushrooms, onions, green peppers and tomatoes. The best food item was the long, golden-brown French fries. They had not had a chance to chill yet because the grease retained the heat. I requested breakfast, lunch and dinner menus when we first ordered our food. The waiter forgot, and, as I became more familiar with the place, I did not bother to remind him. Service was slow ... very slow. There was only one waiter and two cooks during the lunch hour when all the tables were taken. In all fairness to the waiter, he was trying his best. He just had an impossible task handling seven tables and three booths by himself. This is a small two-room restaurant with four tables in the front and three booths, three tables in the back for a total of 24 people. There are two park benches behind the building which could seat an additional 24 people. The narrow booths have green-cushioned benches and green tabletops. There are only a few pictures, showing Arches National Park, mountain scenes, and a columbine flower, all hanging crooked on the white plaster walls. The windows have orange trim and white curtains with orange flowers. The roof is slanted with skylights. This is a hangout for nail-biting, long-hair, grubby people who put their feet up on chairs. With regards to smoke, if you just returned from the Middle East, bring your gas mask.

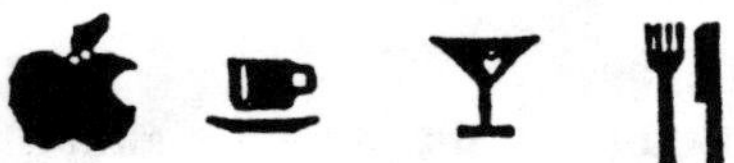

HIGH COUNTRY ★★★
115 HARRISON AVE. (719)486-3992

Lunch/dinner $-$$. SUN-THU 11AM-9PM. FRI-SAT 11AM-10PM.
Type: Country.

Food: **★★★** Their open-faced hot beef sandwich is good. Other sandwich choices include turkey, steak with cheese & jalapeño, pepper steak, barbecue roast beef, and cod. Burgers, soup, salad, breaded mushrooms, onion rings, applesauce, potato salad, cole slaw, garlic bread, French fries, and a children's menu are also available. The list of dinners includes hamburger steak, hot beef or turkey, shrimp basket, chicken fried steak, trout, prime rib, and pizza in 8-, 12-, 13- or 15-inch sizes.

Service: **★★★½** Very accommodating and prompt with the check.

Decor: **★★½** This two-room restaurant has a divided front room with seven booths and 14 small tables for 62 people. The back room is smaller with nine tables for 26 people. The low-back, brown-wood chairs are comfortable and match the brown booth benches, walls, window frames, and vaulted wood-beamed ceiling. Red brick covers the lower section of wall. A beige pattern curtain covers the small windows in the front room. There are two identical pictures of a ram in a mountain scene, plus pictures of a mountain lion, elk, and small pictures of miners. The back room is decorated by framed windows on three sides. However, they only face a picket fence and parking lot. The ceiling is slanted with skylights and several hanging plants and brass lamps.

Atmosphere: **★★½** This place appeared to be more popular with local people than with tourists.

LA CANTINA ★★★
1942 U.S. HWY. 24 (719)486-9927

Lunch/dinner $-$$. 7 days 11AM-10PM.
Type: Mexican.

Food: ★★★ Their stuffed sopapilla is very big and filling, but the flavor and quality is just average. This is strictly a Mexican restaurant offering the usual fare.

Service: ★★★½ The service is very good. I arrived here shortly before closing, but they took my order and did not rush me to finish.

Decor: ★★★ This is a two-room restaurant. The main dining room is to the left and has four booths and seven tables for 44 people. The room to the right has a bar with six stools, a pool table, a large dance floor and is usually used for private parties with bands. This room has two tables, four booths on the left and three more in the back for 40 people. Large Spanish arches separate the two rooms. Spanish rugs and oval mirrors adorn the walls, which are made of white plaster or unfinished wood. The ceiling is stucco, and there are wood ceiling beams and posts. I liked the Spanish arches.

Atmosphere: ★★½ According to my server, they can get very busy during prime dinner hours.

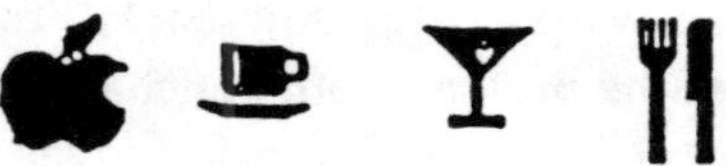

PINE CONES ICE CREAM PARLOR & DELI ★★
700 HARRISON IN THE DELAWARE HOTEL MALL (719)486-3700

Lunch/dinner $. 7 days 11AM-9PM.
Type: Deli. The entire restaurant is nonsmoking.

Food: ★★ *Service:* ★★ *Decor:* ★½ *Atmosphere:* ★★½

This is primarily an ice cream parlor and the ice cream is not homemade. In addition to sugar, plain and waffle cones, they offer shakes, floats, malts, and sundaes. Selections from the deli include soup, a salad and potato bar, sandwiches and popcorn. Service is satisfactory. You order and pick up at a counter. Seating is at six tables with small cushioned chairs having wire backs that are very uncomfortable. The counter has six stools. Total seating is for 30 people. A circular stairway in the middle of the room is interesting, but makes the place feel a little cramped. Located in the Delaware Hotel, which is of some historic significance.

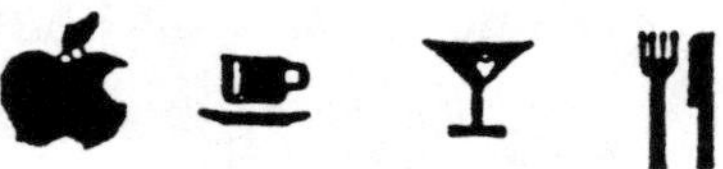

PROSPECTOR ★★★★
THREE MILES NORTH OF LEADVILLE ON THE EAST SIDE OF HWY. 91
(719)486-2117

Dinner $$-$$$. TUE-SUN 5PM-9PM (10PM in summer). Closed MON. Type: Steak. 15% gratuity for parties of six or more. No separate checks on parties of five or more.

Food: ★★★★ They have superb onion rings. They are big, have a great batter, and break off easily. I highly recommend them. Dinner comes with homemade soup, salad and bean bar, bread and potato. I recommend their steaks or chicken. Besides the onion rings, you have your choice of shrimp cocktail, Rocky Mountain oysters, or tempura mushrooms as an appetizer. The dinner entrees feature steak with wild rice and mushrooms, chicken Kiev, Alaskan king crab, shrimp tempura, walleye, baked Icelandic filet, Rocky Mountain trout, scallops, or lobster. If you are not too hungry you can order a steak sandwich, fish & chips, or the soup, salad and bean bar alone. On Fridays, they offer a seafood bar. Prime rib is served on SAT only. The dessert menu includes cheesecake with berries, chocolate mousse, and hot fudge sundae.

Service: ★★★★ Excellent.

Decor: ★★★★ This decorative restaurant has two rooms. The front room has 18 tables for 72 people and the back room has nine tables for 28 people. The windows along the front face west and look out onto red and yellow hummingbird feeders, a wood sculpture of a miner, and blue spruce and fir trees decorated with white Christmas lights year-round. Inside, to the left of the entrance, is a display of ore samplings in a long, rectangular, glass-covered display case. There are several appealing pictures of mallard ducks, a mountain lion, a mountain sunset, a map of Leadville, gophers, and one of the 1895 Leadville Ice Palace. Hexagonal, black-metal light fixtures with yellow-tinted glass hang on two-foot chains from a low acoustic tile ceiling. There are several philodendrons, ferns, and flowering plants on the window sills and hanging.

Atmosphere: ★★★★½ A higher class of clientele comes here. Big-band music plays softly in the background. A very nice setting.

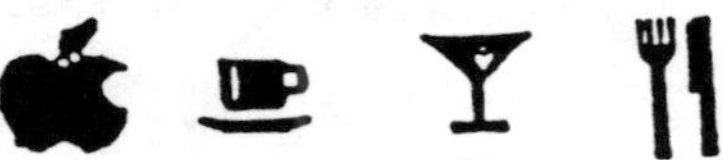

WILD BILL'S ★★½
200 HARRISON (719)486-0533

Lunch/dinner $. 7 days 11AM-10PM.
Type: Burgers. Delivery available during lunch.

***Food:* ★★½ *Service:* ★★ *Decor:* ★★★ *Atmosphere:* ★½**

Their charbroiled hamburgers are not half-bad, the curly-Q fries, with cayenne pepper, are quite good, and the chicken is also good. Their large single-page menu features appetizers, burgers, fried chicken nuggets, sandwiches, Mexican meals, a shrimp dinner, a children's menu and desserts (fried pies and ice cream). You order and pick up at the counter. This is a single-room restaurant with six booths and three tables for 38 people. The back and side walls have black and white nineteenth century soap and hair restoration advertisements. Items like "Mousson's cocoa butter soap," and "Edward's 'Harlene' for the hair: world renowned hair producer and restorer/remedy for baldness." I liked the advertisement wallpaper. There are several hanging plants from the low, flat ceiling that has two skylights and two fans. These are tight quarters. The tables and booths are right up against each other. Local townsfolk frequent here.

LIMON

Formerly known as Limon's Camp, then Limon's Junction, the town was named after John Limon, a construction foreman on the Rock Island Railroad, built through the area in 1888. Limon lies on the route of the historic Smokey Hill Trail and the old Butterfield Stage route. Today, agriculture, tourism and retail trade are the town's major industries.

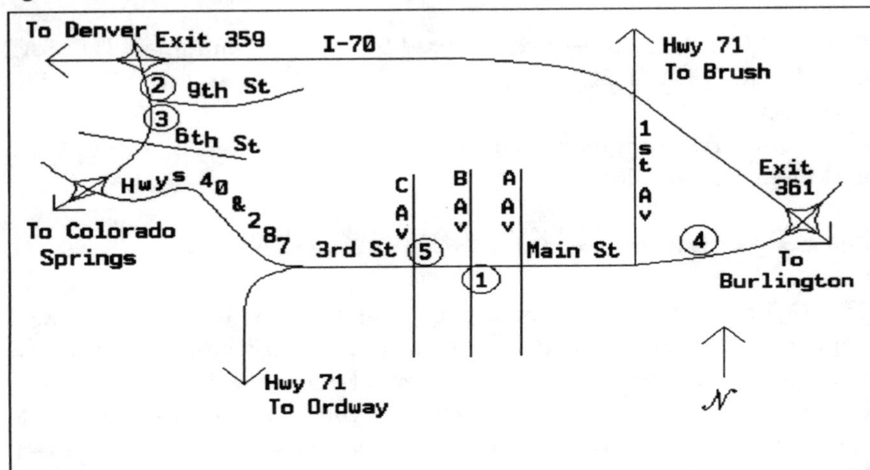

Restaurants and Ratings:	Food	Service	Decor	Atm	Overall
1. Bo-Mar	★★★	★★	★★★	★★	★★½
2. Country Fare	★★½	★★★	★★½	★★	★★½
3. Fireside Junction	★★★	★★★★	★★★★	★★★	★★★½
4. Flying J	★★½	★★★½	★★	★★★½	★★★
5. Southside	★★★	★★½	★★★½	★★★	★★★

I found Limon to be difficult to rate. Nothing stood out as exceptionally good or bad. Each restaurant had its strong and weak factors. The Bo-Mar had good food and original decor created by the owner. The Country Fare had good service. The Fireside was stronger on service and decor. The Flying J had excellent service which created a cheerful atmosphere. The Southside, Limon's newest restaurant, is clean, fresh and new. Overall, the best restaurant would have to be the Fireside.

LIMON

Only the Bo-Mar does not accept major credit cards. Only the Fireside Junction and Southside offer nonsmoking sections and serve alcohol.

BO-MAR ★★½
599 MAIN (719)775-2433

Breakfast/lunch $, dinner $-$$. Closed SUN-MON. Summer: TUE-SAT 6AM-2PM. TUE-FRI 5PM-8PM. Winter: TUE-SAT 6AM-2PM. WED-FRI 5PM-7:30PM.
Type: Country. Additional charges for carry-out containers, extra plates, and menu substitutions.

***Food:* ★★★ *Service:* ★★ *Decor:* ★★★ *Atmosphere:* ★★**

The Cajun white-bean soup is good and thick with tomatoes, green peppers, onions and big chunks of ham. The grilled cheese sandwich was average. Their entire menu is limited, but it does offer a few good items. Lunch offers burgers, including a chili burger; chili; a dinner salad; cole slaw; onion rings; sandwiches; hot open-faced sandwiches (beef, hamburger, or ham) with mashed potatoes and gravy; and pies for dessert. The dinner specialty is broasted chicken. Other entrees are fish, chicken fried steak and roast beef. Daily specials like lasagna are offered. Bo-Mar is short for Bob and Marlene, the owners. Bob does the cooking and is the artist of the portraits and cards on display. Marlene serves the customers. Bob and Marlene typify the local people. They are friendly. This restaurant is in an old brown building with an orange roof. It is a single-room, small restaurant with 12 white or brown formica tables for 44 people. Bob's portrait sketches in frames and cards decorate the whole restaurant. Some of the portraits are of local people Bob once knew. The curtains have an attractive pattern of early Airplanes: "Spirit of St. Louis," "Sopwith Camel" and the "Wright Brothers Aircraft" to mention a few. The rest of the restaurant is very plain with wood panel walls and a brown carpet. The clientele on the day I stopped by included local workers in plaid shirts and blue jeans, a young woman with two children, and some older folks. Located in the middle of town, they do not appear to attract many tourists.

COUNTRY FARE (RIP GRIFFIN'S) ★★½
I-70 & HWY. 24 (719)775-2811

Breakfast $, lunch $-$$, dinner $$. Seven days 24 hours.
Type: Family. All items available for take out.

This is a 24-hour, seven days a week truck stop where you can expect to find a lot of truckers, as well as tour busses with everyone from high school athletic teams to senior citizens. The food is average to good, but the service is very attentive. The front dining area looks like a truck stop, but the back looks more like a dining room. All-you-can-eat buffets are offered most hours on most days.

Food: ★★½ *Service:* ★★★ *Decor:* ★★½ *Atmosphere:* ★★

I had their all-you-can-eat Sunday breakfast buffet that featured apple or blueberry compote, Polish sausage and muffins. Some of the sausage was slightly crispy black, which I like. I have had leaner bacon, though. During the summer, May through October, buffets are served for breakfast, lunch and dinner every day from 5:30am to 9pm. During the winter months, the three buffets a day are offered THU-SUN. The lunch choices include charbroiled burgers, chicken breasts, catfish fillets, beef patties, red or green chili, Sloppy Joe's, Rocky Mountain oysters, a stuffed tomato with tuna salad, Mexican dishes, and sandwiches. Dinner features soups, salads and entrees (chicken fried chicken or steak, meatloaf, beef liver & onions, spaghetti with meat sauce, roast beef, pork chops, chopped beef steak, broasted chicken, stir-fry beef or chicken, smoked barbecue brisket, catfish, and an all-you-can-eat sirloin). For dessert there is ice cream, fruit and cream pies, homemade red velvet cake, hot fudge cake, donuts and cinnamon rolls. Despite the fact this was a help-yourself buffet, the waitress frequently returned to see if I wanted more coffee or water and to see how I was doing in general. She was very attentive. The restaurant area is to the left of the entrance with a gift shop to the right. The first dining room has sixteen counter seats in a semicircle around six booths, a pair of tables next to the salad wagon, and a section beyond the wagon/buffet with three booths and ten tables. Total seating in this area is 100. Decor consists of cowboy hats and paintings of cowboys, meadows, and trees. The second dining room to the rear has 11 tables for another 50 people and is much nicer with blue wallpaper and curtains, several mirrors, electric candle-light fixtures on the walls, and a piano at the far end. As a truck stop, expect a lot of truckers and tourist buses. This is a clean restaurant where it is doubtful you will go hungry.

FIRESIDE JUNCTION ★★★½
I-70 & U.S. HWY. 24 (719)775-2396

Breakfast $, lunch $$, dinner $$-$$$. 7 days 6AM-9PM (10PM MAY-OCT). Type: Family.

This is another restaurant with a big seating area like the Country Fare next door. This one is generally better in all areaus and probably the best overall restaurant in Limon. Expect to see fewer big groups as they appear to stop at the first restaurant off I-70 (Country Fare).

Food: **★★★** Their clam chowder had big pieces of clam and potato, but few spices. It was excellent, though. The combination sliced brisket and German sausage was a very filling eight ounces of meat. Their own barbecue sauce was good, but by far not my favorite in the state. The sausage was mild to moderately spicy. The beef was well cooked, but tender. The meal comes with baked beans, potato, and onion and dill pickle on the side. The beans, made with onion, pickle relish, Worcestershire sauce and brown sugar, were particularly good. The breakfast menu features huevos rancheros, assorted pastries, blueberry muffins and a children's menu. The lunch offerings include barbecue; soup and salad bar; chicken fried steak; fried chicken; liver & onions; another children's menu; and sandwiches, such as a Philly steak & cheese, hamburger, patty melt, and Reuben. For dinner, there are steaks, seafood (fried shrimp, catfish and halibut), a basic Mexican fare, and desserts (ice cream and fruit or cream pies).

Service: ★★★★ Service was fast, efficient, friendly and very, very pleasant. Their bus service was very fast, also, and I was there on a busy Friday night.

Decor: ★★★★ This restaurant can hold 186 people in one large dining room in two sections and a smaller second dining room. There are 18 booths with light rust/brown cushioned benches, plus tables with very comfortable wood-framed chairs. The section to the right of the entrance is for smoking. The rest of the restaurant is for nonsmokers. There is a fireplace to your left as you enter. The wallpaper in the rear of the smoking section has an attractive pattern of wheat. There is a nice blend of colors and decor in here with tan vertical curtains, a tan, brown and rust blend rug, and white walls decorated with knit wreaths and weather vanes. Pictures of deer and ducks adorn the nonsmoking front section. Indian artworks made of sandstone decorate the second dining room. Except for the fireplace, windows extend the full length of the front, the right side, half of the left side, and the left wall of the second dining room. Combined with the cognac glass-shaped chandeliers and in-set ceiling lights, they provide good lighting for this very clean and well-kept restaurant.

Atmosphere: ★★★ This is a very popular restaurant with both the locals and tourists. It is suitable for families, couples, young and old.

FLYING J ★★★
198 MAIN (719)775-2725

Breakfast/lunch $, dinner $$. 7 days 24 hours.
Type: Country.

This is the small truck stop on the east end of town. It is sparse on decor, but high on atmosphere and a good place for sandwiches.

Food: ★★½ Their gear jammer sandwich is quite good. It comes on a French roll with lots of thin slices of beef, melted Swiss, grilled onions, mushroom, bell peppers, cold lettuce and thick tomato slices. The vegetable no-beef soup, with tomatoes, celery, carrots, corn and peas, was only fair. However, their cup is bowl size, which means their bowl is giant size. Breakfast has a few interesting items, like their skillet specials that feature vegetables, scrambled eggs and hash browns. Other breakfast entrees include chicken fried or rib eye steak. The lunch menu features burgers made from beef, chicken or fish; and sandwiches, including hot roast beef, ground beef or chicken fried steak with country gravy. The dinner selections are primarily steaks and your basic Mexican foods. Fried chicken, pork chops, cod, ham, soup and chili are also available. Light meals and salads, including a taco salad, can be ordered if you are not too hungry. For dessert, there are cakes, pies, ice cream, sundaes, and hot fudge ice cream cake.

Service: ★★★½ My waitress, Sabine (Sa been' ah) was very pleasant and enhanced the cheerful atmosphere.

Decor: ★★ This is a single divided room with a counter. There are three tables and seven stools on one side for 19 people, and seven tables on the other for another 30. Windows above red brick extend along the front and half way down the left side. The remainder of the restaurant is covered with white textured wallpaper with specks of blue and rust. The decor is sparse with just a few pictures of ducks and flowers.

Atmosphere: ★★★½ I noticed a lot of interaction between the waitress, cook and local customers. There was a lot of joviality and "joking around." These folks sure seem to enjoy each other 's company. This is a very cheerful place.

SOUTHSIDE ★★★
NE CORNER OF MAIN & C AVE. (719)775-9593

Lunch/dinner $-$$ ($$$ for a large pizza). 7 days 10AM-9PM
Type: Tavern.

This is Limon's newest restaurant. Owners Pat and Bob Younger built this restaurant after their former restaurant was blown away by the June 6, 1990, tornados. It is a clean, fresh place with much of the decor from the old restaurant. This would be a good stop for beer and pizza.

Food: ★★★ They have a limited menu that specializes in pizza and features calzones, sub sandwiches (turkey, ham, roast beef or corn beef), regular sandwiches, tacos, nachos, burritos, a few appetizers (cheese sticks, chicken wings, and chips & salsa), and a chef or dinner salad. They have a salad bar set up on one side of a large pillar which may be used for happy hour or a Rocky Mountain oyster buffet in the future. Pat Younger hopes to expand the menu, too. I had the soft shell tacos which were good. They had a soft tortilla shell with all fresh ingredients.

Service: ★★½ Pleasant. Ask for the owners. They can tell you a little about the history of some of the decor.

Decor: ★★★½ This is a single-room restaurant and bar with 13 booths, nine tables, and 12 barstools for about 100 people. The restaurant is in a brand new, clean building. It looks and smells clean. There are two big gold-framed pictures of "The Duke" — John Wayne — on the east wall. The north section of the building has two pool tables, a snooker table and framed beer posters. The long south side of the building has natural-wood framed posters under glass of the Coors Brewery depicting women in turn-of-the-century attire. There is a large pillar in the middle of the room on the west end with decorative wood-framed mirrors in different shapes. On the west side of the pillar is the salad/buffet bar. Many of the decorations came from the old destroyed restaurant. I found the new walls and old decor mixed exceptionally well.

Atmosphere: ★★★ This place seems to be a hit with the local residents. It just seems to "click." The proprietors have plans for a deck, horseshoes and volleyball behind the building. For a restaurant/bar, the atmosphere was most comfortable. Classical, rock 'n roll or country music played from two large speakers on an antique cabinet and mirror behind the bar. There are four televisions in all.

LOUISVILLE

Named after Louis Nawatny who led the first coal boring expedition after C.C. Welch discovered coal in 1877. Nawatny also owned the land on which the original settlement was located and filed the town plat in 1878.

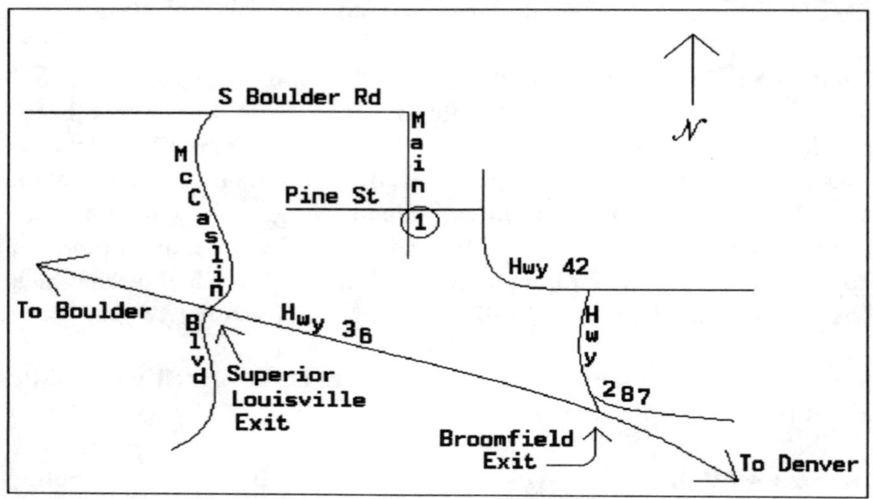

1. BLUE PARROT ★★★
640 MAIN STREET (303)666-0677

Breakfast/lunch $, dinner $$. MON-THU 8AM-9PM. FRI-SAT 8AM-10PM. SUN 8AM-8PM. (½ hour later every evening in the summer).
Type: Italian. No separate checks. Personal checks accepted with driver's license and guaranteed check card. Carry-out available. Deli next door. 35¢ per container except for breakfasts, sandwiches, and luncheon specials (unless you bring your own).
Louisville is known for its many Italian restaurants. The Blue Parrot, established in 1919, was the first and has a reputation as one of the best, if not the best. It was burned down in April 1988, rebuilt, and reopened less than a year later in February 1989.

Food: ★★★ The dinner salad was a combination of lettuce, cabbage and one small pepperoncini without any of the ingredients I like to see on an Italian salad, like black olives, tomatoes, mozzarella cheese, green peppers, oregano, basil, and Italian seasoning. It was fresh, however. Dinner was served with a cold loaf of Italian bread. For our entrees, my dinner companion and I ordered a couple of Italian specialties: a half-order of raviolis & spaghetti and lasagna. We also ordered sides of meatball and mild Italian sausage. The pasta and meats are all homemade. The half-order had three beef, chicken & cheese raviolis and a huge portion of wide noodle spaghetti with additional sauce on the side. The lasagna was prepared with beef, sausage and mozzarella. We both agreed the meals were good, not great. For breakfast, you can order a side of spaghetti, blueberry pancakes, a Danish, fried egg & sausage sandwich, or Italian sausage. There is also a children's menu for those under 12. The lunch menu offers sandwiches (Italian sausage or meatball), burgers, spaghetti, salads, and desserts (ice cream, spumoni, sherbet, and cheesecake). Other dinner entrees include gnocchi (potato noodles), chicken cacciatore, steaks, hamburger, chicken, and shrimp.

Service: ★★★½ The waitress was low keyed and earthy, simple yet efficient. Gary, one of the managers, was very hospitable, talkative and jovial. He came over to our table twice to discuss food, decor, family and history. A most interesting and pleasant fellow.

Decor: ★★★½ This restaurant is in two dining areas that can seat about 160. It is very well color coordinated with some nice touches. They use three different patterns of teal and mauve wallpaper (diamond, roses, and flowers & leaves) that compliment the blue carpet. Pella windows, two with matching stained-glass, are used along the front. Most of the decor is historical in nature: a March, 1984 letter from the Louisville Historical Commission designating the Blue Parrot as a Louisville landmark, a collage of 12 photos of the April 1988 fire, photos of the staff, and newspaper reviews & clippings. In-set ceiling lights and frosted sconces with brass fittings provide plenty of light. Unpretentious is the word that best describes the surroundings. A bar/lounge at the entrance has six booths and nine barstools. Along the far wall are family portraits, a letter of appreciation from the Governor of Wyoming, and a letter of sympathy from Colorado Governor Romer after the fire.

Atmosphere: ★★½ No music. The bar television could be overheard in the dining area. There was a triple birthday party (they sang Happy Birthday and served cake) at the next table. A family style atmosphere.

LYONS

The town was named after Mrs. Carrie Lyons, pioneer editor of the weekly Lyons News which had a brief existence in 1890-91. The Lyons family was also instrumental in quarrying superior sandstone, used in many buildings at the University of Colorado campus. Geographically, Lyons is the gateway to the Rocky Mountains on Hwy. 7 and to Estes Park and Rocky Mountain National Park on Hwy. 36.

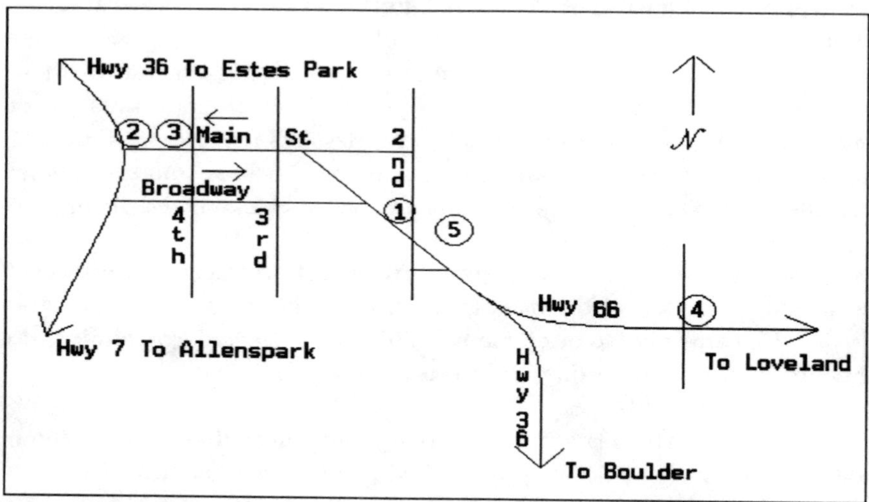

Restaurants and Ratings:	Food	Service	Decor	Atm	Overall
1. ANDREA'S	★★★★	★★★★½	★★★★	★★★★	★★★★
2. DON DAVID	★★★½	★★★	★★	★★★	★★★
3. GATEWAY CAFE	★★★	★★½	★½	★½	★★
4. OLD PRAGUE INN	★★★★★	★★★★	★★★★★	★★★★½	★★★★½
5. SUNRISE CAFE	★★½	★★★	★★	★★★	★★½

The Old Prague Inn, offers some of the best German/Czech cuisine in the state and Andrea's serves excellent German specialties. Both restaurants have classic country settings and together they overshadow Don David's good sauces, spices and Mexican food. Only the Sunrise Cafe does not accept major credit cards. Only Andrea's has a nonsmoking section. Only Andrea's and the Old Prague Inn serve alcohol.

ANDREA'S ★★★★
216 EAST MAIN STREET (303)823-5000

Breakfast $ (a few $$), lunch $-$$, dinner $$-$$$. THU-TUE 8AM-9PM. Closed WED.
Type: German. Take-out available. Minimum charge of 25¢ each for all substitutions. 50¢ charge for extra plates. No cigar or pipe smoking.

Food: ★★★★ The veal Bratwurst was tender, juicy and lightly grilled; the French toast was thick, toasted golden brown, and served with warm maple syrup; and the eggs were done just right. This was one of the better breakfasts I have had in Colorado. Some of their breakfast specialties are eggs Benedict, huevos rancheros "German style", croissant sandwiches, homemade potato pancakes (one of my personal favorites), German apple-pecan pancakes with melted brown butter, and a variety of coffees from Viennese to Irish. In addition to soup, salads, sandwiches, burgers, steaks, seafood, poultry and Mexican dishes, the lunch menu offers several tempting German specialties: vegetable cheese strudel, Bratwurst, kassler rippchen, Wiener or turkey schnitzel, and zwiebel rostbraten (ribeye with grilled onions & mushrooms). Dinner features appetizers (chicken tenders, Bratwurst, and potato pancakes) and entrees from the same luncheon food groups. Some of the selections are chicken breast Lauenstein (sautéed in olive oil), chicken Dijon, broasted chicken, pork roast with homemade potato pancakes and red cabbage, petite filet mignon, medallions Bordelaise, scampi, and Rocky Mountain trout almondine.

Service: ★★★★½ Top notch. They do the little things often missing from most restaurants, like bringing butter when you run out, always being there for more coffee & water, and knowing when to take away your plate at the right time. Very pleasant and professional.

Decor: ★★★★ The nonsmoking front dining room has nine tables for 30. Beige wallpaper with touches of blue match nicely against the blue curtains with tan four-leaf clovers. Windows along the front look out on geraniums and pansies. Philodendrons hang in the corners. A frosted, octagonal-shaped stencil window of ducks in a marsh divides two paintings on the rear wall and is bracketed by brass lanterns. Seating is on tan-cushioned wood chairs and benches. The back smoking section has stuffed deer, moose, buffalo, elk and long horn sheep, five booths and six tables for 42, and a bar for four. Stained-glass, wood-framed ornaments hang from the ceiling separating the two dining rooms.

Atmosphere: ★★★★ Pleasant and relaxed with classical music playing lightly in the background.

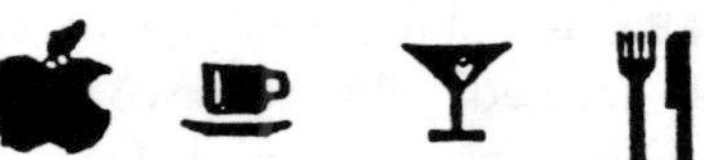

DON DAVID ★★★
450 MAIN (303)823-5014
Lunch/dinner$-$$. MON-SAT 12PM-10PM. SUN 12PM-8PM. Closed TUE. Type: Mexican.

Food: ★★★½ The smothered burrito is big and tasty. I especially liked the sauces and spices and the ingredients were fresh. Order a tortilla if your meal does not come with one. They are big, light and fluffy. They also offer burgers, nachos, flautas, quesadillas, bean dip, garden or avocado salad, huevos rancheros, guacamole dip and a child's combination plate. Items used in the combination specials are also available a la carte.

Service: ★★★ This place is a family affair. They are nice people.

Decor: ★★ This is a one-room restaurant with booths to the right and left, tables in the center, a single booth at the front window, and a small bar with six stools in the rear. Total seating capacity is 60 people. The building itself is made of red brick. The booths have very high black-vinyl bench seats in hardwood frames. The tables have low-back wood chairs. A black dresser with a large mirror set along the right wall is adorned with trophies, mugs, and stereo speakers. Framed beer signs and pictures of matadors and bulls are set on a wall rail. Additional decor on the white plaster walls is provided by two oval artworks — one depicting two cowboys crossing a stream; the other, a ship at sea. Masking the height of the high ceiling are diamond-shaped wood trellises. The red carpet and short white curtains provide some color.

Atmosphere: ★★★ They put their sound system to use after we had been there a while and played some entertaining Mexican music.

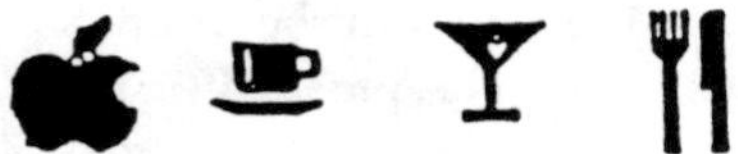

GATEWAY CAFE ★★
432 MAIN (303)823-5144

Breakfast/lunch $. WED-MON 7AM-2PM. Closed TUE.
Type: Cafe.

Food: ★★★ *Service:* ★★½ *Decor:* ★½ *Atmosphere:* ★½

This is one of your basic small-town cafes. However, I did find their pigs-in-a-blanket to be quite good. The pancakes were light and fluffy, my egg-over-easy was done just the way I like it, and the sausage links were good. Additional breakfast items include a pancake sandwich, grits, and muffins. Lunch features salads, hot & cold sandwiches, burgers, chili, and the following entrees: veal Parmesan, spaghetti, and chicken fried steak. They offer pastries for dessert: cinnamon rolls, pies, cakes, and cookies. Service is fast. This is a long, single-room restaurant with seven pinewood tables in the front for 28 people, a long gold bench seat along the right rear wall with four tables and eight chairs across for 16 people, and a counter with 12 black stools. The clientele consisted of six local townsfolk men and one townsfolk woman dressed in plaid shirts, blue jeans and caps, discussing local gossip. This is not a tourist spot.

OLD PRAGUE INN ★★★★½
7521 UTE HWY. (5 1/2 MILES EAST OF LYONS ON 66) (303)772-6374

Dinner $$-$$$. WED-MON 5PM-10PM. Closed TUE and major holidays.
Type: Continental (German/Czech). Reservations suggested.

Food: ★★★★★ My roast pork tenderloin was tender and succulent with plenty of spicy juice. It came with sauerkraut and dumplings. Each is so flavorful and fresh that they should be tried separately. The onion dumpling soup was delicious. The most difficult part of the meal was deciding what to choose. They offer a wide selection of wonderful dishes, superbly prepared with the best ingredients and spices. Their menu advertises: "Central European with a Czech accent. The execution rather than the composition of the menu makes the difference." I definitely found this to be the case here. For an appetizer, you can choose from a Russian egg (potato salad with egg, special sauce, ham, asparagus and tomato), herring salad, or escargots Bourguignonne. The beef entrees included sauerbraten Czech-style (with sweet & sour wine sauce), filet goulash "Haushofmeisterart" (beef tenderloin flamed in cognac), and Tournedos Henry IV (beef wrapped in bacon and topped with artichoke hearts). The veal entrees list has veal steak praka (sautéed and topped with ham, asparagus and Swiss), Rahmschnitzel (thinly sliced and topped with mushrooms), and Wiener schnitzel. The seafood choices are broiled lobster tail, Rocky Mountain rainbow trout, and fish gratin haus Habsburg (a poached fillet of sole topped with shrimp and wine sauce). The poultry and game selections include Czech-style roast duck, Cornish hen, chicken Kiev, and Medallions of Venison in port wine sauce. Many of the dinner entrees come with sauerkraut, potato or spatzel. A dessert tray specializes in strudel and other pastries.

Service: ★★★★ Formal, but definitely most courteous.

Decor: ★★★★★ This restaurant, resembling an inn, sets by itself in the countryside, It has four dining rooms with a total of 22 tables for 78 people. There is also a lounge with four tables and six barstools for 22. The main dining room has a fireplace. The natural wood-grain looking walls have several pictures of people dancing and celebrating in Prague and the Czechoslovakian countryside — showing centuries-old architecture, arched bridges, and country cottages. Large plates add color to the window ledges and wall racks. Potted plants decorate the room dividers. The chandeliers are large brass fixtures with flower-petal-designed lamps. The double door entrance and small, quaint, wood-framed windows make this a charming place indeed. The decor extends into the lounge where you can see a picture of the Orloj (or-loi) clock in Prague. The story behind this copper clock is that the man who built the clock, several centuries back, had his eyes burned out to prevent him from building another one like it. Red curtains and beer mugs on mantels add to the lounge decor.

Atmosphere: ★★★★½ Very pleasant classical music. I was here on a January mid-week evening when the only patrons were a young couple.

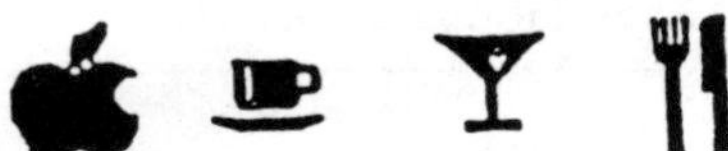

SUNRISE CAFE ★★½
138 MAIN (303)823-5419

Breakfast/lunch $, dinner $$. MON-SAT 6AM-2PM (3PM MAY-AUG). SUN 7AM-2PM (3PM MAY-AUG). Closed WED.
Type: Cafe. Delivery service available on all menu items.

Food: ★★½ *Service:* ★★★ *Decor:* ★★ *Atmosphere:* ★★★

Their Italian sausage sandwich was a substandard quality patty dressed up in green pepper, mozzarella, onions and spicy tomato sauce on a big hoagy bun. Too bad the main ingredient was inferior. Their pancakes are light, fluffy and huge — about 12 inches in diameter. The onion rings are satisfactory. The breakfast menu includes Italian sausage, corned beef hash, pork tenderloin, blueberry pancakes, and homemade pies. The lunch menu features pizza, subs, burgers, soup, chili, a low cal plate, salad, red or green chili burritos, kraut dogs, and sandwiches. The dinner entrees are liver & onions, roast beef, Rocky Mountain oysters, catfish, broasted chicken, and shrimp. There is also a children's menu. The cook/waiter has a friendly, smiling beard with a good sense of humor. This restaurant has an all-glass front with a great mountain view. Seating for about 40 people is on brown-cushioned, metal-framed chairs at 16 brown formica tables. The seating area runs into the kitchen with no real separation. A mandala and a circular cardboard picture of a mountain view are the few decorations on the white plaster walls. The clientele consists of locals with thick beards, cowboy hats, and caps.

MANCOS

The town was settled in the 1880s and named after the Mancos river, which, in Spanish, means "one handed," "faulty," or "crippled." Two of the early settlers, Richard Wetherill, son of a successful Quaker rancher, and his uncle, Charles Mason, discovered three of the larger ruins of Mesa Verde in December, 1888: the Cliff Palace, Spruce Tree House, and Square Tower House. Richard Wetherill and his five brothers later provided guide services for visitors to the ruins and began a large collection of artifacts. Ten thousand of these items later found their way into The Colorado Heritage House in Denver.

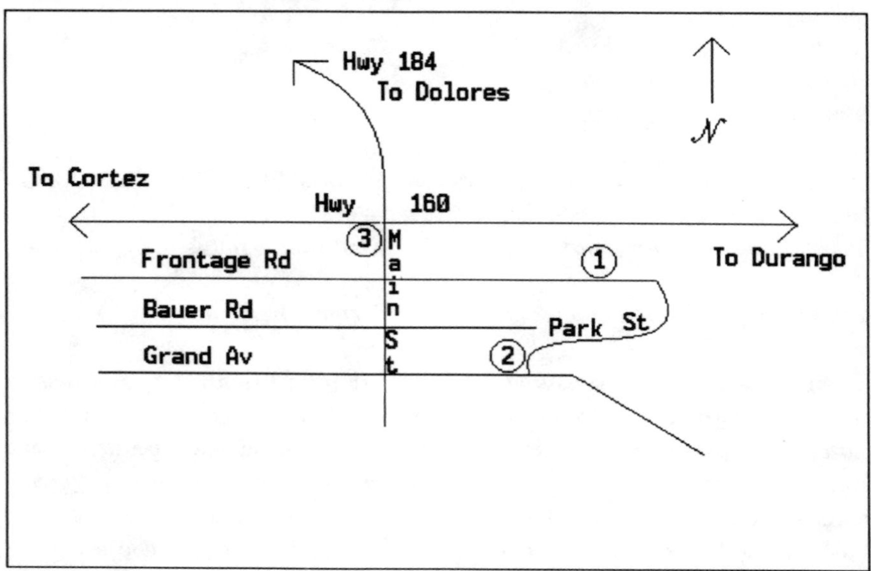

Restaurants and Ratings:	Food	Service	Decor	Atm	Overall
1. CANDY'S	★★★	★★½	★★	★★½	★★½
2. HAMBURGER HAVEN	★½	★★½	★	★	★½
3. MILLWOOD JUNCTION	★★★½	★★★	★★★½	★★★	★★★½

For dinner, the place to go is the Millwood Junction. For good, cheap food with large portions, go to Candy's. Only the Millwood Junction accepts major credit cards and serves alcohol. Only Candy's has a nonsmoking section.

CANDY'S COUNTRY CAFE ★★½
1602 FRONTAGE RD. (303)533-7941

Breakfast/lunch $, dinner $$. Winter: 7 days 7AM-8PM. Summer: 7 days 6AM-9PM.
Type: Cafe. Take-out available.

Food: ★★★ *Service:* ★★½ *Decor:* ★★ *Atmosphere:* ★★½

I had lunch here. The food is good, cheap and plentiful. Come here with a hungry appetite. The breakfast menu has a lot of local flavor: eggs are called "kackelberries," a pork chop is a "pig chop," ham goes by "pigbutt," "sowbelly" means bacon, "piglets" refers to sausage, pancakes are "chips," oatmeal is called a "rib sticker," toast is served as "shingles," and, my favorite, biscuits and gravy, is hailed as "wagon wheels & axle grease." Make sure you learn the slang before ordering or you may be surprised by what you get. The lunch offerings include burgers, sandwiches, chicken, fish, shrimp, a low-calorie plate, a few Mexican items, chili, and salad. This place turns into a steak house at dinner time. Other entrees include fried chicken, pork chops, halibut steak, ham, and breaded sole. Pies, ice cream and the house special, bread pudding with cream, are available for dessert. Service is fair to good. This is a small restaurant with nine tables and a counter with six stools. They have some interesting and attractive plates and paintings, a mirror inside a saddle, and a cow bell hanging on white concrete block walls. This is a very popular place with the locals at lunch time.

HAMBURGER HAVEN ★½
108 E. GRAND AVE. (303)533-7919

Lunch $. MON-FRI 10AM-8PM. SAT 10AM-5:00PM. Closed SUN.
Type: Burgers.

Food: ★½ *Service:* ★★½ *Decor:* ★ *Atmosphere:* ★

The food here was below average. The lunch menu has burgers, hot dogs, sandwiches, a few Mexican items, homemade cinnamon rolls, and ice cream desserts. Service was just fine. No complaints. This small one-room restaurant has a counter with six stools, six tables and two booths for 38 people total. Windows are on two sides. There are three pictures on the plaster walls depicting deer in winter and men relaxing.

MILLWOOD JUNCTION ★★★½
HWY. 160 & MAIN (303)533-7338

Dinner $$-$$$. 7 days 5:30AM-9:30PM (10:30PM FRI-SAT in the summer). Type: Steak.

Food: ★★★½ Big steaks and a large order of fries is the specialty here. Their shrimp is fairly good also. Some of their steak specialties include Chateaubriand (for two), steak Diane and steak au poivre (a NY strip rolled in peppercorns and sautéed with brandy cream sauce). Other dinner entrees include barbecue pork ribs, chicken breast, shrimp, fettuccine Alfredo, Alaskan king crab or lobster, blackened catfish, Rocky Mountain trout, and beer-battered catfish with pecan sauce. Burgers and sandwiches are available for a smaller dinner, as well as a small salad bar. For dessert, there is homemade ice cream and daily specials.

Service: ★★★ Nothing special, but good.

Decor: ★★★½ The dining room has 15 tables for 60 people separated by wood dividers. The dividers have openings that are filled with lanterns, bottles and, in one case, a wagon wheel. Prints of the Colorado mountains in fall and bighorn sheep adorn the walls. Adjacent to the dining room is a bar/lounge with six stools and 16 tables, providing enough room for 64 people. There are some old pictures in here, circa 1911, courtesy of the Colorado Historical Society.

Atmosphere: ★★★ Country music can be overheard from the bar area, but it is a fairly quiet place.

Manitou Springs

Famous for its bubbling natural mineral springs, this small town was originally called Villa La Font, or Fountain Village. It was renamed Manitou, the Algonquin Indian word meaning "Great Spirit", and became Manitou Springs in 1885. A few of the attractions which earned Manitou Springs a place on the National Historic District Register are Miramont Castle — a Victorian style spa built of stone by Father Jean Baptiste Francolon in 1896; the Manitou Cliff Dwellings Museum — an outdoor architectural museum established in 1904 with original stones from the Anasazi Indians; and the Manitou and Pike's Peak Railway — the world's highest cog railroad ascending to the top of 14,110 foot Pikes Peak.

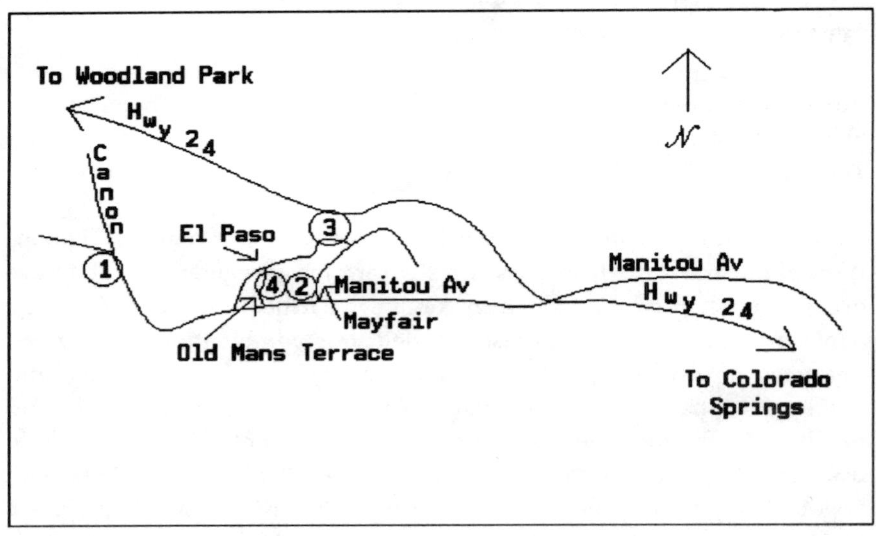

Restaurants and Ratings:	Food	Service	Decor	Atm	Overall
1. ADAM'S MOUNTAIN CAFE	★★★½	★★★★	★★★	★★★½	★★★½
2. BRIARHURST MANOR	★★★★	★★★	★★★★★	★★★★	★★★★
3. CRAFTWOOD INN	★★★	★★½	★★★½	★★★	★★★
4. HOUSE OF PRIME RIB	★★½	★★★½	★★½	★★½	★★½

MANITOU SPRINGS

Adam's Mountain Cafe has some deliciously different breakfast specialties. The 116 year old Briarhurst, a Tudor mansion set amongst spacious lawns and gardens, offers a variety of Continental and American cuisine prepared by renown Chef Sigi Krauss in an elegant Victorian setting. The Craftwood Inn is another English Country Tudor style restaurant built in 1912 specializing in the "hearty and robust cuisine that is truly Colorado". The House of Prime Rib serves good prime rib. All four restaurants have nonsmoking sections and serve alcohol. Only Adam's Mountain Cafe does not accept major credit cards.

ADAM'S MOUNTAIN CAFE ★★★½
733 MANITOU AVENUE (719)685-1430

Breakfast $, lunch/dinner $-$$. MON-SAT: 7:30AM-3PM and 5PM-9PM. SUN: 7:30AM-3PM.
Type: Cafe.

Food: **★★★½** This small, quaint cafe offers a variety of house specialties throughout the day. It is a good restaurant for a vegetarian. They use organic, fresh produce like fresh "organic" carrot juice. I ordered the Santa Fe potatoes for breakfast. A delicious combination of new red potatoes, homemade green chili, mild white cheddar, tomatoes, and scallions topped with two eggs. The ingredients were fresh and nutritious. Try this one for a different breakfast entree. You won't be disappointed. A second potato dish features scalloped potatoes with vegetables. The whole grain pancakes are homemade and their French toast is prepared with whole wheat sunflower bread. The house specialties include a breakfast burrito made with blue corn tortillas, two whole grain pancakes, and fresh fruit with either scalloped potatoes or scrambled eggs. There are several interesting omelets with scrumptious sounding ingredients to consider: one with avocado, sour cream and Parmesan; another with spinach and cream cheese. Soup, salad, sandwiches and new red potatoes are on the lunch menu. The soups of the day were turkey-vegetable and green chili potato stew. The sandwich selections include a grilled soy burger, three choices with roasted turkey, and two vegetarian options. Pasta, Mexican food and stir fries are the house specialty dinner entrees. Lasagna, eggplant Parmesan (recommended to me by a fellow diner), fettuccine Alfredo and pasta primavera or pesto are the Italian choices. Chicken, vegetarian & breakfast burritos, and nachos are on the Mexican menu. Stir fried vegetables, chicken or shrimp prepared in a Chinese wok are served with soup or salad. Cappucino and espresso are available. The dessert specials, on this particular day, were sour cream chocolate cheesecake, ginger cake with caramel pears, poppy seed cake and apple pie.

Service: ★★★★ They are quite friendly, helpful and accommodating. Everything is prepared to order using their own special recipes. They will try to accommodate any special dietary needs you may have. Their commitment to your dining experience is above and beyond the ordinary.

Decor: ★★★ This is a small, tight, single-room restaurant with 10 tables for 38. The eggshell wallpaper has a red and blue flowered-pattern. The walls are very well decorated with prints in pastel colors by a local artist: pictures of castles and cottages, pathways and pines, gardens and geese, sailing ships, lakes, tree houses and rivers. Lighting is provided by tulip-shaped wall fixtures and chandeliers hanging from a high acoustic ceiling. There are several hanging plants, mostly philodendrons. Seating is on wicker-seat, high-backed, wood-framed chairs at solid-wood tables. A Tuscan column made of wood stands in the back corner of the restaurant. Two cement figures of a farmer and his wife occupy the entrance. There are no shades or curtains in the front windows. A locked brown shutter door and a window with a laced curtain across the top separate the left side of the restaurant from the gift shop next door. A box display in the front window is decorated with seasonal items.

Atmosphere: ★★★½ Classical music plays pleasantly from the kitchen. This is a popular place with the locals and one of the best kept secrets from the traveling public. On MON-THU evenings they have live guitar music from 6:30PM until about 8:30PM.

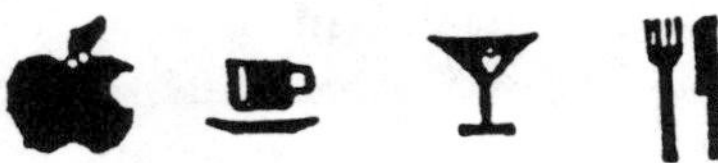

BRIARHURST MANOR ★★★★
404 MANITOU AVENUE (719)685-1864

Sunday brunch $$$, lunch $$, dinner $$$-$$$$+. SUN: 10AM-2PM and 5PM-8PM. MON-FRI: 11AM-2PM and 6PM-10PM. SAT: 6PM-10PM.
Type: Continental. Reservations are suggested and jackets are required for gentlemen at dinner. The entire restaurant is nonsmoking. However, Chef Sigi said they would set up a special room for smokers, if necessary. A 20% service charge is added for parties of 6 or more.

With the architecture and landscaping of a true English Country House, the Briarhurst Manor has many unique features. It is on the National Register of Historic Places, has its own organic gardens, and a Victorian gazebo. The Briarhurst was opened on May 30, 1975 by Chef Ziegfried Krauss. To reach this restaurant, go under the flesh-colored arches next to the Buffalo Bill Wax Museum at Manitou Avenue and Mayfair.

Food: ★★★★ With herbs, fruits and vegetables grown in their own organic gardens and meats and fish smoked on the premises, the Briarhurst is sure to start your mouth watering. I ordered the quail stuffed with sour cherries, served on a bed of goose liver pâté: a unique and delectable combination. It was served with lightly-glazed carrots, crisp green beans, and salty sliced potatoes and onions. The cauliflower soup with broccoli and paprika was deliciously different, also. The Sunday brunch buffet offers a lavish selection of appetizers, salads, hot dishes, carved meats, desserts, a glass of champagne or mimosa, and either an egg or fish entree of your choice. You can start off lunch at the Briarhurst in a couple of unique ways. Try their mixed chips (half French fry, half chip and all homemade) or half of an avocado stuffed with seafood. Alaskan seafood and smoked trout are a couple of the salad selections. Ham & Swiss or roast beef sandwiches are offered hot or cold. Cold smoked turkey or hot Rocky Mountain rainbow trout are also available on your choice of breads. They also have a weight watcher's meal and a children's menu. If pasta is to your liking, choose angel hair or fettucini with your choice of one of six sauces (pesto, Bolognese, Alfredo, marinara, seafood or New Zealand mussels). Iced coffee, espresso, cappuccino and desserts like crème caramel, chocolate mousse, fresh strawberries or raspberries, cheesecake, ice cream and cake complete the lunch menu. On Sunday evenings complete family dinners, American style, are offered. You have a choice of appetizer (Buffalo wings), soup

(New England clam chowder) or salad (cole slaw or dinner); a main course selection such as pork roast with apple rings, chicken sautéed with onions and bell peppers, or a sautéed rainbow trout. Desserts, like apple crisp baked with rum or rhubarb pie, and coffee, tea or milk, complete the meal. Chef Sigi has also prepared an "International Country Cuisine Series". Each month the culinary tastes of a different country are featured. It may be France in April, Germany in September or Russia in November. This is a full course meal, offered Mondays through Saturdays, and includes an appetizer, dessert and glass of wine.

Service: ★★★ I was not impressed, at first, by the quality of the service. After I was seated at my table the bus boy asked if I had a reservation. I told him rather frankly, "no, I did not have a reservation" and thought to myself why would the bus boy be concerned with whether I had a reservation. Besides, I was already seated. I later learned that he asked if I had a reservation so that he could check the reservation list to see if anyone would be joining me, but then he would have had to ask for my name as well. Besides, he could have just asked the maitre'd, or myself, if anyone would be joining me. After thoroughly reviewing the menu, I still did not have a server. I asked the busboy, who was just milling about, if he would bring my server over. When she finally arrived I asked what the plate du jour was, pronouncing plate with a long "a". She quickly "corrected" my pronunciation by stating "plate" with a short "a". Give me a break! The waitress did not return to ask how my meal was, but she did take me for an extended tour of this mansion after dinner. This was followed by a long talk and tour of the beer garden, band stand, gazebo and adjoining five acres with chef Ziegfried (Sigi) Krauss. Sigi would like to open a culinary school on the premises and start training future chefs personally. I found Sigi to be an extremely personable, friendly and interesting gentleman. If you get the opportunity, chat with him for a while.

Decor: ★★★★★ This is a rather elegant place (to say the least) with finely grained pink sandstone walls, a Gothic oak staircase, rich hardwoods, fine stonework (each stone in the building's exterior is 23 inches thick) and a fireplace in every dining room. Outside, the spacious lawns and gardens, deck, beer garden, gazebo and view of Pikes Peak enhance the charm found inside. When I visited here they had eight dining rooms on two levels with plans for another — the Palmer Room upstairs. I dined in Dr. Bell's Library, the second to last dining room on the first level. (Dr. William Bell, considered the founder of Manitou Springs, built the Briarhurst in 1876, and, along with the help of his good friend, General William J. Palmer, founded the Denver & Rio Grande Railroad). The room is filled with several volumes of encyclopedias on bookshelves and wall shelves close to the ceiling. There are seven tables that could seat 20, including a table for six situated in a small alcove, one step up from the main dining room. The back wall of the alcove is decorated with an array of differently-shaped mirrors, mostly in gold frames. The cranberry carpet and pink table clothes provide an attractive combination of colors.

Preceding Dr. Bell's Library are Cara's Room, which seats just 15, and the Drawing Room, with seating for 20, a white fireplace, and gold wallpaper decorated with blue plates. Closer to Dr. Bell's Library is the Captain's Table, a reclusive setting for four where Chef Sigi was gathered with friends. Adjacent to this is the Lounge with wood floors, pictures of officers on blue and maroon mats in gold frames, and seating for 12. Separating the Lounge from Dr. Bell's Library is a cherry wood fireplace with a mirror and two shelves above the mantel decorated with Van Briggle pottery. Beyond the Library is the end room of the first floor, known as the Garden Room. Stuffed pheasants, deer heads and a black chandelier decorate this room which can seat 12 at three tables. Windows on three sides face the beer garden outside that is used for Octoberfest.

There are three rooms upstairs (with the fourth in the making). The Oriel Room with bay windows overlooking the entrance seats 12 at four tables. The Master Bedroom (not used as that anymore) is larger and seats 20 at seven tables. The Sitting Room has an organ and seats 20 at six tables. Total seating inside, without the proposed Palmer Room, is about 130. Outside, you have a bandstand and dance floor across from the gazebo and movable white-trellis barriers. For Octoberfest, the last 10 days leading up to Labor Day, a huge tent is erected that can hold 2,500 people.

Atmosphere: ★★★★ Chopin plays pleasantly and profusely in the background. The background music and lighting are superb. The clientele, except for one loud, outspoken woman from California seated behind me, was quiet, subdued and sophisticated, but also on the "yuppie" side. The section of the restaurant where I was seated had a very open feeling, which is why I could so easily overhear the conversations at other tables. The Briarhurst also caters to special events like weddings, birthday parties, anniversaries, luncheons and the like.

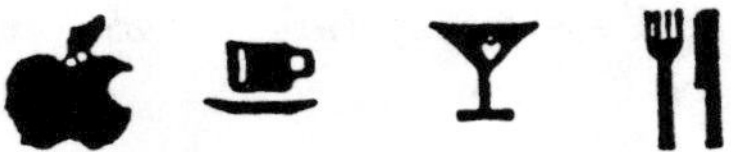

CRAFTWOOD INN ★★★
404 EL PASO BLVD (719)685-9000

Dinner $$$-$$$$. 7 days 5PM-10PM.
Type: Country.

This is another English Country Tudor style building, erected in 1912 by Roland Bautwell, with beamed ceilings, stained glass windows and a copper hooded fireplace. It was originally a coppersmith shop and became a restaurant in 1940. Extensively renovated in 1988 by new owners, chef, and hosts Cris Pulos and Rob Stephens, The Craftwood Inn offers the hearty, robust cuisine and flavors that are truly Colorado.

Food: ★★★ I had the roast duck with cranberry port sauce that sweetened and moistened this flavorful dish. It was served with wild rice and mixed vegetables. Duck is just one of the wild game entrees on the menu. Others include fried rabbit made with Dijon mustard and apples, juniper venison Bourguignonne with wild mushrooms, mixed game bird that includes stuffed quail, pheasant sausage and roast duck, and mixed wild grill with venison and elk. The list of dinner entrees also features grilled piñon trout with pine nuts, Colorado striploin steak, roast stuffed leg of lamb with spinach, king salmon, beef tenderloin and a vegetarian platter.

Before dinner you can have an appetizer like caramelized onion soup with duck consomme, duck and leek terrine with pine nuts and cognac, or escargot served under angel hair pasta. There are a few different and intriguing salads to choose from as well. For example, warm pheasant or smoked salmon. If you prefer, go with a more traditional spinach or Caesar's salad. Their wine list contains about 15 domestic and foreign whites, most by the glass as well as bottle, and about an equal number of reds. In the winter time they add a few special items to their menu like oysters au gratin, grilled mahi-mahi and Atlantic sea scallops.

Service: ★★½ A little on the slow side and not too enthusiastic. Anything above average would be over-rated.

Decor: ★★★½ This restaurant sits on a hill off the roadway. If you park down by the road there is a walkway that passes under two arches leading up to the restaurant. The alternative is to take the circular drive up to the restaurant and park by the restaurant, assuming you can find a space.

To enter the restaurant, you cross over a rock patio framed in a four-foot rock wall with flowers planted on top. A green and white striped awning stretches down from the restaurant over half the patio. Thirty-two people can be seated here at eight tables. Inside, there is a combination of booths and tables with mauve tablecloths. The seating is very comfortable with high-back, cushioned bench seats and sturdy wood chairs with rib-backs and cushioned seats. The walnut wood trim used around the doors and windows, as a wall divider and as ceiling beams offsets the pure white, rough edged plaster walls very nicely. The dining room has a few well-placed paintings of mallard ducks, hunters camping out, and a stone house in the mountains with an original looking horseless carriage parked in front. Fresh sunflowers and kerosene lamps are set at every table. There is a black-stone fireplace with a brass hood with the initials C.S, which stands for craftwood shops (the original function of this building). The two sections of the downstairs dining room seat 36. In addition, there is a small, separate dining room just for private parties that seats 16. Adjacent to the dining area is a bar/lounge with five barstools and two tables for 13. Upstairs there was a proposed dining room for about 50 people that did not have any decor yet, but had a terrific view of Pikes Peak.

Atmosphere: ★★★ The Craftwood Inn has attracted some noteworthy celebrities over the years, like Cary Grant, Bing Crosby, Lawrence Welk, and Liberace. The clientele seemed sophisticated. This is a most pleasant place to dine and with their new dining area opening upstairs, it could be an ideal setting for a meal.

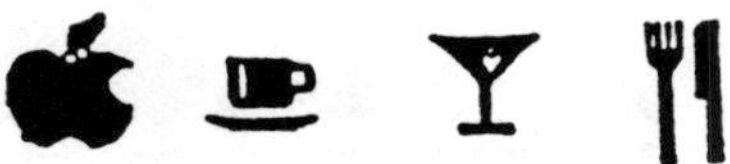

HOUSE OF PRIME RIB ★★½
10 OLD MANS TRAIL (719)685-1119

Dinner $$-$$$ (a few $$$). MAY-SEP: 7 days 4PM-10PM. OCT-APR: TUE-SAT: 4PM-10PM. Closed SUN-MON.
Type: Steak.

***Food:* ★★½ *Service* ★★★½ *Decor:* ★★½ *Atmosphere:* ★★½**

Established in 1902 as the Hiawatha Gardens, this was the most popular ballroom in Manitou Springs. Celebrities like Jimmy Dorsey, Benny Goodman and Rudolph Valentino came here to dance. Today, like the back of the menu states, you can come here to enjoy a quiet meal. Oh, how the times do change. A quiet meal is indeed what I had. Their potato soup was bland and without any potatoes. Their eight-item salad bar was lacking many common salad items. The prime rib was good, but not great. Perhaps the highlight of the meal was the homemade biscuits. Service was very attentive, showing an above average interest in the customer. The dining room is one large room with no dividers and NO WINDOWS. It is "decked out" as a 1930's style ballroom, but no artwork on the red and gold velvet walls. Golden piano tunes from the 30's and 40's are pleasantly played overhead. A restaurant without windows is atypical for Colorado, with all of our natural beauty, and I had a hard time accepting that. However, if you are into ballroom dancing and the big band era, you may just find yourself a good time here.

MANZANOLA

First settled in 1869 by two stockmen, Jaspar M. and James W. Beaty, and a grocer, William H. May, the town was first named Catlin after a nearby ditch. In 1895, the town was renamed Manzanola, Spanish for "red apples." The town is surrounded by apple orchards. If you pass through this area in the fall stop by one of their stands for some apple or strawberry cider.

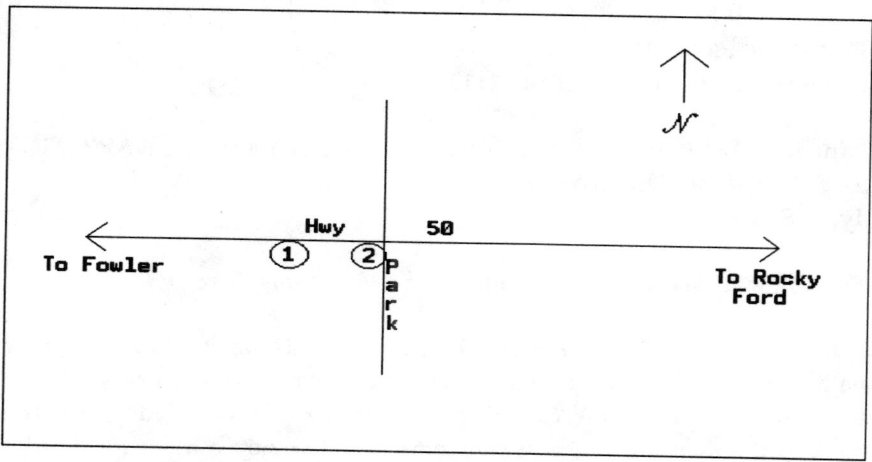

Restaurants and Ratings:	Food	Service	Decor	Atm	Overall
1. Patricio's Cafe	★★½	★★½	★★½	★★	★★½
2. Ranchers	★★	★★½	★★	★★	★★

Neither restaurant takes credit cards, offers a nonsmoking section, or serves alcohol.

Patricio's Cafe ★★½
115 W. 1 (719)462-5402

Lunch/dinner $. TUE-SAT 11:30AM-2:30PM and 5:00PM-8PM. Closed SUN-MON.
Type: Mexican.

Food: ★★½ *Service:* ★★½ *Decor:* ★★½ *Atmosphere:* ★★

They serve a healthy portion of chips and thick tomato salsa with a lot of red peppers. The salsa was similar to the one served at Delgado's in Sterling. My empanada was an ample portion served very (temperature) hot. The menu has the usual Mexican selections, plus hamburgers and hot dogs. Entrees include an empanada (beef, bean and cheese stuffed in a sopapilla), a smothered burrito, a concha (a taco salad shell with beans, rice, green chili, lettuce and cheese, but no beef), a taco salad, and daily specials. Service was fast. This is a small one-room restaurant with only eight tables for 30 people. The white concrete block walls are decorated with the appropriate Mexican decor: Mexican hats, Mexican rugs, and pictures of matadors, bulls, conquistadors and some small Mexican boys. This is a busy place that seems to be popular with the locals.

RANCHERS RESTAURANT ★★
101 S. PARK (719)462-5515

Breakfast, lunch and dinner $. MON-SAT 7AM-7PM. Closed SUN.
Type: Country.

Food: ★★ *Service:* ★★½ *Decor:* ★★ *Atmosphere:* ★★

I found their lunches to be of only fair quality. They serve a basic breakfast, lunch and dinner menu. Eggs & meats, hot cakes, French toast, and omelets for breakfast. Sandwiches, burgers, and common Mexican items for lunch. Steak, chicken, cod, liver & onions, and chicken fried steak for dinner. Salad, onion rings and chili are also available. Service is very considerate. This is another small one-room restaurant with four booths and seven tables for 44 people. Seating is on orange-cushioned chairs and benches. The curtains are beige. A craft work of a roadrunner and pictures of raccoons, tigers and buffalos decorate the walls. Most of the clientele are old-time locals.

MONTE VISTA

Formerly called Lariat and later Henry, Monte Vista, which means "mountain view" in Spanish, was named after the glorious mountains that surround it: Blanca Peak and the Sangre de Cristo Mountains to the east and the San Juan Mountains to the west. During my stay in this area, I visited the Monte Vista Wildlife Refuge at sundown with a co-worker, who also happens to be a falconer. We saw thousands of ducks and Canadian geese. It was an amazing sight on a chilly eve in early spring.

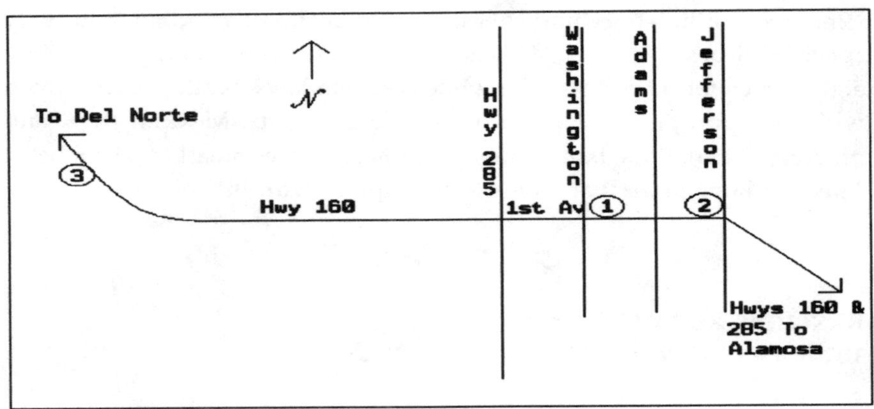

Restaurants and Ratings:	Food	Service	Decor	Atm	Overall
1. Hi Country Steakhouse	★★★	★★½	★★	★★½	★★½
2. Monte Villa Inn	★★★★½	★★★★½	★★★★★	★★★★★	★★★★★
3. Movie Manor	★★★½	★	★★★	★★★★	★★★

As the only five-star restaurant from Southeast Colorado, the Monte Ville Inn should not be missed. In addition to expertly prepared entrees and desserts, elegant oak and walnut antique decor, and efficient service, the dining room has an unusual, perhaps spiritual, atmosphere that I have only encountered on rare occasions. All three restaurants accept major credit cards. Only the Hi Country Steakhouse does not have a nonsmoking section or serve alcohol.

HI COUNTRY STEAKHOUSE ★★½
819 FIRST AVE (719)852-5866

Breakfast $, lunch/dinner $-$$. MON-SAT 6AM-8:30PM. SUN 8AM-2PM. Type: Steak.

***Food:* ★★★ *Service:* ★★½ *Decor:* ★★ *Atmosphere:* ★★½**

Their burgers are the best in the area: very meaty. However, their steaks are fatty and, what meat there is, no better than average quality. The fries are thin and unimpressive. Salads are average. The lunch/dinner menu has a varied selection of appetizers, burgers, sandwiches, salads, steaks, pork chops, seafood, chicken, choice dinners (roast beef, ham, and liver with onions or bacon), a children's menu and desserts (pies, ice cream and sundaes). The waitress is jovial. This is a long, single-room restaurant with a four-foot wood, undecorated divider down the middle. Six tables to the left, four tables to the right, and seven tables in the rear provide enough seating for 74 people. Wagon-wheel chandeliers with brass lanterns hang from a very high 18-foot ceiling. Brass lanterns and wood-framed paintings of cowboys and horses hang from the wood-paneled walls. This is a quiet place with no music. Only a few tables were occupied by local people.

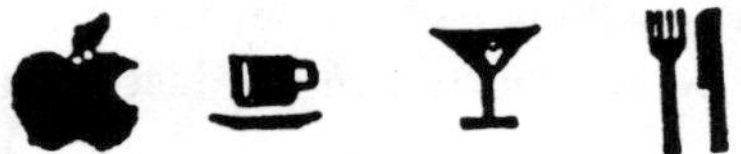

MONTE VILLA INN ★★★★★
925 FIRST AVE. (719)852-852-5166

Breakfast/lunch $, dinner $$-$$$. 7 days. Winter: Coffee Shop 6AM-5PM. Dining Room 5PM-9PM. Summer (mid-April to mid-September): Coffee Shop 6AM-6PM; Dining Room 6PM-10PM.
Type: Family.

***Food:* ★★★★½** I ordered the prawns, sautéed in butter and white wine: five jumbo shrimp served with lightly cooked vegetables (tomatoes, zucchini, yellow squash, broccoli and carrots). They are lightly flavored with parsley and served over rice. This made a delightful meal that was delicately flavored, but not heavy on the stomach. I even had room for burnt cream (a flan with whipped topping) for dessert. The custard had a smooth, consistent texture, a wonderful flavor, and was not over-filling. Try the burnt cream for a most flavorful and pleasant dessert. The breakfast menu offers huevos rancheros, fruit roll-ups (buttermilk pancakes filled with fruit and topped with whipped cream), breakfast croissants, the Monte special (scrambled eggs with ham, vegetables & cheese), and Swedish waffles (topped with fruit, whipped cream & nuts). Lunch features burgers, sandwiches, salads, soup, four fettuccine dishes, five lunch entrees (chicken strips, hamburger steak, shrimp, fish, and chicken fried steak), a children's menu, and desserts (homemade pies, cheesecake, burnt cream, ice cream, and Bailey's Irish Cream chocolate mousse). Dinner includes ten appetizers, such as sautéed mushrooms, sesame chicken, shrimp cocktail, and French onion soup; six steak entrees, French dip, liver & onions, roast beef, five chicken choices, nine seafood selections, like cod, trout, scallops, prawns, and shrimp, a limited Mexican fare, and the same pasta, salads, desserts and children's menu that is offered at lunch.

Service: ★★★★½ A quiet, but efficient and sophisticated, waitress. The most hospitable owner, Doris Hunt, took my dinner companion and me for a tour of some of the rooms at the Inn and her own personally made chapel- a place where travelers can go for quiet meditation or prayer. Doris has been to Medjugorje, Yugoslavia (where several miracles and sightings of the Virgin Mary have been reported in the last decade), four times since 1987.

Decor: ★★★★★ The minute I walked into this restaurant, which I entered from the lobby, I felt like I was stepping back into history. Few places have affected me this way (Taos Inn in Taos, N.Mex., is another). As I entered, I was greeted on my left by a balcony and a pair of aged wood benches with black-iron frames separated by a red-velvet couch. To my right was an elegant dining room behind a movable structure of wooden verticals set at an angle and only partly obstructing the view of the room. This room has nine tables for 48 people. It is elegant in its antique decor. There is an oak hutch, a walnut cabinet, a yellow-brick fireplace with an oak mantel and mirror, and one of two matching oak sideboards. The other is at the opposite end of the bar. The side boards date back to 1826 and were hand carved in Germany. The balcony seats 24 people at three booths and five tables. A third dining area straight back from the lobby entrance has nine tables for 38 people on a marble floor. Once a month they have a dance here. Total seating in the dining room is 110. The adjacent coffee shop seats 122.

Atmosphere: ★★★★★ I fell in love with the atmosphere here almost immediately. Perfect lighting is provided by antique brass chandeliers with candle-shaped lights: sufficiently well lit for easy reading yet subdued enough to be romantic. Bring your wife, bring your girl friend, bring your children, bring your grandmother. You will want to share this rare treasure.

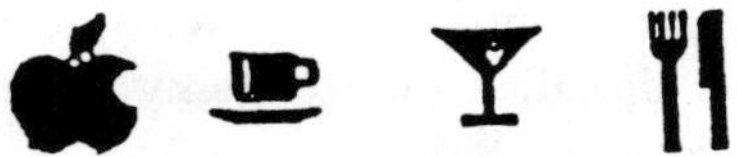

MOVIE MANOR ★★★
2830 U.S. HWY. 160 (½ MI. WEST OF MONTE VISTA) (719)852-3626

Breakfast/lunch $, dinner $$. 7 days 6:30AM-2PM and 5PM-9PM.
Type: Family. Sandwiches served in the lounge from 9pm-10pm.

Food: ★★★½ Dinner started with warm, fresh rolls and honey butter. The fish chowder, however, was barely warm and had no spices. My broiled mahi mahi was surprisingly good. It was tender, juicy, broke apart easily with a fork and had a delicious broiled seasoning. Remarkable for land-locked Colorado. The nightly special was a stuffed burrito despite the fact they only have one Mexican food item on their dinner menu. The house special is a "kibbie": an authentic Mediterranean dish consisting of ground beef steak with special spices and topped with gravy. It is served medium-well to well done. The kibbie is available for breakfast, lunch, or dinner. Breakfast items of special mention are the malted Belgian waffles with fruit topping and homemade sweet rolls. The lunch menu features burgers, including pizza, chili, and kibbie burgers; sandwiches, such as Italian sausage, hot beef, French dip, turkey, roast beef, Philly, and patty melt; a low-calorie plate; salads, like taco, chef or shrimp; bean burritos; and homemade soup. The descriptive dinner menu details four appetizers, including beer-battered mushrooms and shrimp cocktail; six steak selections, such as T-bone and filet mignon; eight seafood dishes, including jumbo shrimp, red snapper, Rocky Mountain trout, and stuffed flounder; chef's salad; honey-dipped chicken; and liver & onions.

Service: ★ VERY understaffed. They had one poor waitress to handle both dining rooms: an impossible task. It was a long wait between courses. The waitress had ten tables and 28 customers to satisfy. She did a hell of a job rushing around trying to please everyone. The hostess did not help out either. But then I guess that was not her job.

Decor: ★★★ This is actually a restaurant, lounge and coffee shop. The lounge, the Fireside Den, is to the right of the entrance with seven tables for 28 people. There is a stone fireplace on the right wall. The restaurant, to the left of the entrance, is called the Academy Award Dining Room and has both a nonsmoking and smoking section. As luck would have it, I was here the night they awarded the Oscars. Quite by accident, I dined here on a most appropriate evening. The nonsmoking section has 11 tables for 32 people and a fireplace. The smoking section has eight tables for 32 people and the view to the south. There was something wrong with this place that I could not put my finger on until after I had finished my meal. It was the coloring. The lime-green curtains and napkins against the tan tablecloths and flesh-colored walls create a very dull effect, which is too bad considering their extensive display of photographs of old movie stars. Further to the left of the dining room is the coffee shop, in three sections with 28 tables for a total of 108 people. The lounge, restaurant and coffee shop have an extensive selection of photos, mostly from Hollywood's Golden Age: Burt Lancaster, Rita Hayworth, Betty Davis, Spencer Tracy, Clark Gable, James Cagney, Frank Sinatra, Humphrey Bogart, John Wayne, Jimmy Stewart, Elvis Presley, Marilyn Monroe, and Spencer Tracy, to mention just a few.

Atmosphere: ★★★★ The atmosphere was the only noncontroversial aspect of this place. It had everything going for it: quiet instrumental music, subdued lighting from the in-set ceiling lights, and a great view of the mountains.

MONTROSE

Montrose, located in the Uncompahgre Valley, was settled by 2,000 Ute Indians in the early 1870's. In 1881 a military post named Fort Crawford was established under General McKenzie and, under the demands of white settlers, the Ute Indians were "escorted" into eastern Utah. Pioneers, ranchers and farmers followed in their place and incorporated the town of Pomona on September 16, 1881. The name was later changed to Montrose by Joseph Selig in honor of the character, the Duchess of Montrose, from the novel "Legend of Montrose" by Sir Walter Scott.

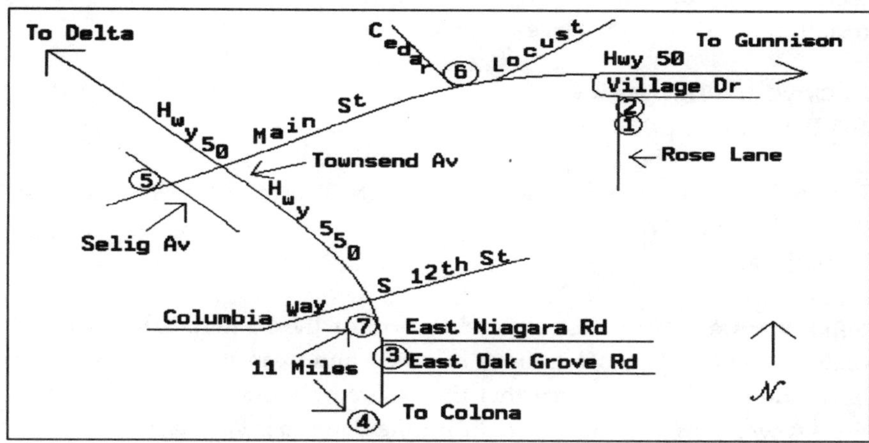

Restaurants and Ratings:	Food	Service	Decor	Atm	Overall
1. Backwoods Inn	★★★★½	★★★★	★★★★	★★★½	★★★★
2. El Sombrero	★★½	★★½	★★★	★★½	★★½
3. Glenn Eyrie	★★★★★	★★★★½	★★★★½	★★★★★	★★★★★
4. Jim's Texas Barbecue	★★★★	★★	★★★	★★½	★★★
5. Los Companero's	★★★	★½	★★½	★★	★★½
6. Red Barn	★★★½	★★★½	★★★½	★★★	★★★½
7. Starvin Arvin's	★★★	★★★	★★★½	★★★	★★★

MONTROSE

The Glenn Eyrie is by far the best restaurant in this area with superb soup, flavorful prime rib, apple horseradish and a garden view. The Backwoods Inn serves some incredible barbecue beef ribs and Jim's Texas Barbecue cooks up some excellent meats smoked slowly over smoldering oak wood. The Red Barn is a good choice for a bowl of soup and sandwich for lunch. All of the restaurants above accept major credit cards except Los Companero's. El Sombrero, Jim's Texas Barbecue and Los Companero's are the only restaurants that do not offer a nonsmoking section and Jim's Texas Barbecue and Starvin Arvin's are the only restaurants that do not serve alcohol.

BACKWOODS INN ★★★★
103 ROSE LANE (303)249-1961

Lunch $-$$, dinner $$-$$$. MON-FRI 11AM-2:30PM. MON-SAT 4:30PM-9PM. Closed SUN.
Type: Steak.

Food: ★★★★½ Dinners come with soup or the 20 item salad bar that features hard boil eggs, big, fresh radishes, and fresh strawberries. Their barbecue beef ribs, a special that they serve only once every one to two weeks, were terrific. The beef falls off the bone so if you drop your knife on the floor, don't bother the waiter for another one. You won't need it! Don't be shy about asking for some extra, warm barbecue sauce on the side. They are happy to accommodate. If you are fortunate enough to be here when they have these beef ribs, you MUST order them. They are some of the best I have had in the state. You might call ahead to see when they plan to serve them next and tell them you can not leave town until you have had some. (They are that good!). If you stop here for lunch, you can start with an appetizer of deep-fried zucchini, sautéed mushrooms, shrimp cocktail, or egg rolls; move on to soup or salad (crab, chef or shrimp); continue with a sandwich (burger, gyro, French Dip, barbecue or steak) or plate (marinated chicken breast, shrimp & clams, or hot roast beef); and finish it off with cheesecake or ice cream cake. The dinner menu offers steak, chicken and seafood entrees: prime rib, aged & seasoned NY strip, charbroiled chicken breast, chicken saltimbocca, chicken fried steak, burgers, deep-fried battered cod, shrimp scampi, and Australian lobster. Children's portions are available on some items.

Service: ★★★★ Quite good in a quiet way. They had no problem serving me ten minutes before closing, or serving a couple that came in a few minutes after closing, which is more than I can say for some restaurants. The waitress was very accommodating and unpretentious.

Decor: ★★★★ This small single-room restaurant is on two levels separated by a brass railing with red-velvet curtains and potted plants in wicker baskets. The top level is nonsmoking and has five completely divided booths for 20. Each booth is separated by a square frosted-glass window depicting a miner's pick and shovel. The varnished, dark-wood, back walls of the booths are decorated with still-life prints of vegetables. The lower level, for smokers, has orange and rust cloth bench seats that I found very comfortable and wood-framed, rib-backed, clothed-seat chairs. This area seats 36. There are photos of "Judge Roy Bean, Notary Public — Law West of the Pecos" and "Geronimo". (Hopefully, they did not steal it from the "Cheers" television series). The bar and saloon next door has ten barstools, 20 tables, a stage, and a good-sized dance floor. A disc jockey plays rock music WED-SAT starting at 9:30PM. The lounge is decorated throughout with wood-framed beer signs.

Atmosphere: ★★★½ Rock music could be heard from the kitchen, but I do not think it is intended for the enjoyment of the diners. The restaurant is dimly lit with attractive gold- and red-tinted glass shades in the nonsmoking section. The atmosphere is very casual and comfortable.

EL SOMBRERO ★★½
82 ROSE LANE (303)249-0217

Lunch/dinner $$. TUE-SAT 11AM-9PM. Closed MON. APR-OCT: SUN 11AM-3PM. NOV-MAR: Closed SUN.
Type: Mexican.

MONTROSE

Food: ★★½ *Service:* ★★½ *Decor:* ★★★ *Atmosphere:* ★★½

Their chili relleno and beef burrito in green (hot) chili had good ingredients, but was not very spicy. The beef in the burrito was greaseless, but also tasteless. This is a good Mexican restaurant if you like your Mexican food bland. Service was friendly. This is a very clean, square-shaped restaurant with windows on three sides and seating for 43. Rock music plays quietly. I was here for a late lunch, so there were only a couple of other tables occupied. I understand, though, that this is a fairly popular place with the locals.

GLENN EYRIE ★★★★★
2351 SOUTH TOWNSEND AV (303)249-9263

Sunday brunch/lunch $$, dinner $$$-$$$$. APR-DEC: TUE-FRI 11:30AM-2PM. TUE-THU 5:30PM-9:30PM. FRI-SAT 5:30PM-10PM. SUN 11AM-1:30PM and 5:30PM-9:30PM. JAN-MAR: TUE-FRI 11:30AM-2PM. TUE-SAT 5PM-8:30PM. Closed SUN-MON.
Type: Continental.

The Glenn Eyrie, or Eagles Nest in Gaelic, is located in a 50-year-old colonial house. The restaurant is owned and operated by Johannes "Hansl" and Barbara Schwathe from Austria and Switzerland. Hansl has 35 years experience in restaurants in Vienna, Toronto, Barbados, and elsewhere. Barbara has managed and worked in restaurants in Switzerland, Vail and Denver. Together they have combined their experience to provide an elegant, yet casual, experience in country dining.

Food: ★★★★★ Their red cabbage and duck soup was superb! It was thick, made with chives and carrots, and properly seasoned. The dinner roll is served with butter, apricot preserves and chokeberry jam. They grow their own apricots and chokeberries. I ordered the prime rib. (Served on FRI and SAT only). It comes with lightly cooked vegetables (yellow squash, zucchini, carrots, green peppers and onion), baked potato with sour cream, bacon bits or chives, and a popover. The prime rib was very flavorful, served with a unique apple-horseradish sauce. The fruity taste of the apple cut the sharp taste of the horseradish resulting in a well-balanced combination. If you have apricot preserves or chokeberry jam left over, try it on the popover or prime rib. The Sunday brunch offers your choice of eight entrees including smoked pork chop with herb scrambled eggs, spinach and shrimp quiche, black tiger shrimp baked with herb butter and brandy, and poached eggs on sautéed fish fillets with lime hollandaise sauce. The dinner menu features several salads to choose from — artichoke hearts, spinach, steak, crab Louie, shrimp Louie, or hot grilled chicken — with your choice of strawberry-vinaigrette, mustard-vinaigrette, ranch or blue cheese dressings. The list of entrees includes several steaks (filet mignon, Chateaubriand bouquetiere for two, beef tenderloin medallions, and steak Diane), seafood selections (black tiger shrimp, Idaho trout, west coast salmon, lobster ravioli, and broiled lobster tail), veal scalloppini, lamb or pork tenderloin, cheese tortellini, grilled turkey or chicken breast, and duck á la orange. They also have a children's menu, American and Viennese desserts, an in house bakery, and organically grown herbs, vegetables and edible flowers.

Service: ★★★★½ Relaxed, yet professional, the way excellent service should be.

Decor: ★★★★½ This is Montrose's most elegant and charming restaurant with three dining rooms and a garden for 115 people. I sat in the Garden Room: seven tables with white-laced cloths for 26 diners. Kerosene lamps with pewter plates and salt and pepper shakers are set at every table. There is a double-sided fireplace in the middle and two very distinctive Colorado murals — one of golden aspen in fall and the other a rugged mountain scene in winter. The wood-framed, green-clothed, cushioned chairs are very comfortable. Three sides of this room have windows. The long side opposite the fireplace looks out onto the garden with a trellis-arch entrance and eight glass-topped tables with 32 white aluminum-framed chairs. The Patio Room has seven tables for 25 and also has windows on three sides looking up to the Garden Room and out to the garden. The third room, the Antler Room, has three booths and four tables for a total of 32 diners and is decorated with small European deer antlers.

Atmosphere: ★★★★★ Very pleasant and relaxing classical music plays in the background. This is the place where locals bring their out-of-town guests and Coloradans bring their out-of-state guests. The outdoor patio, used for lunch and brunch only, looks like a delightful dining experience as well.

Jim's Texas Barbecue ★★★
Hwy 550, 11 miles south of Montrose in Colona (303)249-4809

Breakfast/lunch $, dinner $$. 7 days 7AM-9PM (8PM DEC-APR).
Type: Barbecue (Texas pit). Wheel chair access.

Food: ★★★★ I had the barbecued sliced beef: lean, tender, pink inside and with a most definite smoked flavor. It came with seasoned fries which were quite good also. Their special sauce is served warm on the side. All of their meats are smoked slowly over smoldering oak for up to 15 hours. Breakfast includes barbecued or smoked sausage; and cinnamon rolls served with vanilla, caramel, or caramel and peanut-butter topping. The lunch/dinner menu features barbecue sandwiches with your choice of sliced or chopped beef, Polish sausage, or ham; regular sandwiches like fish, steak, or tuna salad; hamburgers with bacon, mushrooms, jalapeños or green chilies; barbecue plates of sliced beef, ham, chicken, pork ribs, beef ribs, or Polish sausage served with bread, cole slaw, beans and your choice of potato; T-bone, rib and house charbroiled steaks; complete dinners: chicken fried steak, hamburger steak, butterfly shrimp or catfish; and a children's menu. Meats, cole slaw, beans and barbecue sauce are also for sale by the pound or pint. A senior's menu for those 60 and over offers lower prices on the barbecue plates and sandwiches. Pies and ice cream can be ordered for dessert.

Service: ★★ Helpful, but slow taking the order and bringing the check. The food was served promptly.

Decor: ★★★ This restaurant is in a two-story building with a pine vaulted ceiling and vertical and horizontal log beams. The downstairs has 10 tables for 40. The upstairs loft which looks down on the lower level has three long sections of tables side-by-side with enough seating for 48 on black-cushioned, metal-rimmed chairs. The downstairs is decorated with more caps than the population of Colona. There must be three or four hundred caps hanging on the walls. The proprietor told me there were only 48 people in Colona. This has turned into somewhat of a tradition here with people from all parts leaving their head wear behind when they leave. It's quite an interesting display. The entrance and far left wall are decorated with photos taken from an "old time emporium" where people dress up in turn-of-the-century garb to have their picture taken. The front and rear walls have heads and horns of deer and elk, a bear head and full bear skin. The front wall extends clear up to the top of the vaulted ceiling and has two rectangular windows providing superb views of the Uncompahgre Mountains.

Atmosphere: ★★½ They were very busy at 2PM when most restaurants are experiencing a slow down. This is a very popular place with people from Montrose to Ridgeway. Sit in the loft upstairs, if you can, to get a view of the mountains.

LOS COMPANEROS ★★½
147 MAIN (303)249-0902

Lunch/dinner $-$$. MON-FRI 11AM-8PM. Closed SAT-SUN.
Type: Mexican.

Food: ★★★ *Service:* ★½ *Decor:* ★★½ *Atmosphere:* ★★

I ordered the stuffed sopapilla which came with a thick green chili sauce. The sopapilla had a freshly baked soft texture and was stuffed with beef and beans, but not authentic pinto beans. I also ordered a red chili tamale with the same beans on top and lean chicken and beef inside. The waitress told me that their red sauce was the hot one, but I found the green chili sopapilla to be spicier than the red chili tamale, neither one of which will light any fire under your palate. My waitress did not return to check on my meal nor to refill my water glass. Considering there were only five other people in the restaurant at the time, I found the quality of service to be inattentive and disinterested. The restaurant is in an odd shaped building with walls meeting at odd angles and a 15 foot high stucco ceiling. There is one large dining room for 52 and a smaller one for 28. No music was played.

RED BARN ★★★½
1413 EAST MAIN (303)249-9202

SUN Brunch $$, lunch $-$$, dinner $$-$$$. MON-FRI 11AM-10:30PM. SAT 3PM-10:30PM. SUN 9AM-10:30PM.
Type: Country.

Food: **★★★½** I stopped here for soup and a sandwich on a very rainy summer day. The cream of mushroom soup (made with a rich, herb chicken base with garlic, white pepper, and parsley) had carrots, onions and celery and was very good. The beef and cheddar on a French bun with lean, nongreasy beef and horseradish on the side was even better. Sunday brunch lets you choose from omelets, eggs Benedict, eggs Arnold (with crab and artichoke), croissants, smoked pork chops, huevos rancheros, quiche and chicken fried steak. At 11AM, the following items are added to the brunch menu: chicken Santa Fe, tortellini with shrimp, and sirloin. Burgers and the 35-item salad bar with nine dressings — including red wine vinaigrette, poppyseed and Parmesan peppercorn — are also available. The lunch menu offers a variety of gourmet charbroiled burgers, including one topped with Canadian bacon, guacamole and cheddar; Monte Cristo and Reuben sandwiches; soup; chili; salads (shrimp or hot spinach); a quiche of the day; beef stew; and daily specials like Southwest meatloaf. For dessert you can order a fudge brownie delight, peanut butter and chocolate ice cream pie, a sundae, or fresh baked pie. Dinner features a number of light meals such as spaghetti, shrimp, fish & chips, or chicken fried steak. Filet mignon, top sirloin, steak & pasta, prime rib, baby-back ribs, jumbo shrimp, blackened chicken primavera, chicken or beef stir-fry, chicken Cordon Bleu, and

Australian lobster tail highlight the list of entrees. They also have daily specials like sirloin Bordeau and blackened fresh salmon. Desserts made fresh in their bakery include strawberry pie, hot fudge brownie and black forest cheesecake.

Service: ★★★½ Very friendly, helpful and with a sense of humor.

Decor: ★★★½ Mauve-cushioned bench seats and chairs accent this restaurant with artificial red-brick and natural-wood walls. The walls are decorated with prints of old western towns, horses, mule and cattle trains, covered and open wagons, travelers, mines, miners and country cabins. Lighting is provided by studio ceiling lights and brass lanterns. A stuffed bear stands next to the salad bar and a stuffed buck with head and horns is on a dining room wall. The lounge has carvings of branding marks cut into the natural wood. The dining room can seat 74 and the bar/lounge can seat 72.

Atmosphere: ★★★ Quiet, family-oriented, and friendly in the dining room; more sophistication and smoke in the lounge.

STARVIN ARVIN'S ★★★
1320 SOUTH TOWNSEND (303)249-7787

Breakfast/lunch $, dinner $$. 7 days 6AM-10PM.
Type: Family.

Food: ★★★ I ordered the lunch special Navajo taco with salad and a drink. The salad was very basic with lettuce, shredded American cheese and a couple of pieces of cabbage with your choice of one of four basic salad dressings. The taco salad, in an edible taco bowl, was made with real pinto beans; lean, nongreasy beef; and other good ingredients. Breakfast offers a few breakfast specialties, like strawberry or blueberry blintzes, a green supreme (hash browns topped with scrambled egg, green chili, sausage gravy and cheddar), a breakfast burrito, steak, ham, cinnamon rolls, and blueberry or California pancakes and waffles (the

California cakes and waffles are "loaded with nuts"). Lunch is charbroiled burger and sandwich time with patty melt, Reuben, French dip, steak, club, hot turkey or roast beef. Chili, French fries, salad and soup can accompany your meal. A light menu features chicken, fish, steamed cod, chef or seafood salad, and fruit with cottage cheese. Steaks, chicken and seafood (salmon, halibut, prawns and cod) highlight the dinner entrees. There is also a seniors menu (55 and older), a children's menu, appetizers (shrimp cocktail, sautéed mushrooms, and toasted cheese tortilla), and desserts (cheesecake with fruit, chocolate mousse, ice cream, pies and sundaes).

Service: ★★★ An amiable, cheerful waitress who nicknamed the shrimp (in the fish tank) "sebastian". She was most willing to help.

Decor: ★★★½ This restaurant has a divided nonsmoking section with 11 booths for 40 and a smoking section with 13 booths for 55. A large fish tank with angel fish, regal tangs, shrimp, coral and anemones separates the two nonsmoking sections. A second fish tank with a moray eel, a grouper, a sand shark and coral separates the nonsmoking and smoking sections. The second nonsmoking section has seven shelves of books stretching clear up to the ceiling. Quite appropriately, the first nonsmoking section has a painting of a scholarly, elderly gentleman on a ladder pulling books from the top shelf. Windows extend around the front and sides of the building leaving little room for decor. However, there is a print of a beautiful red horse (about as common as a unicorn!) and modern artworks of big cats and Monument Valley. Baskets in glass enclosures and another horse print decorate the smoking section. Seating is on rust vinyl benches.

Atmosphere: ★★★ A popular place with a lot of local workers. Soft rock music plays in the background.

MONUMENT

Named for the rock formation west of town, Monument originally had two post offices in the county by the same name. One was changed to Edgerton, which no longer exists. The other was called Henry Station by the Denver & Rio Grande Railroad after Henry Limbach, who filed the plat for Monument in 1874.

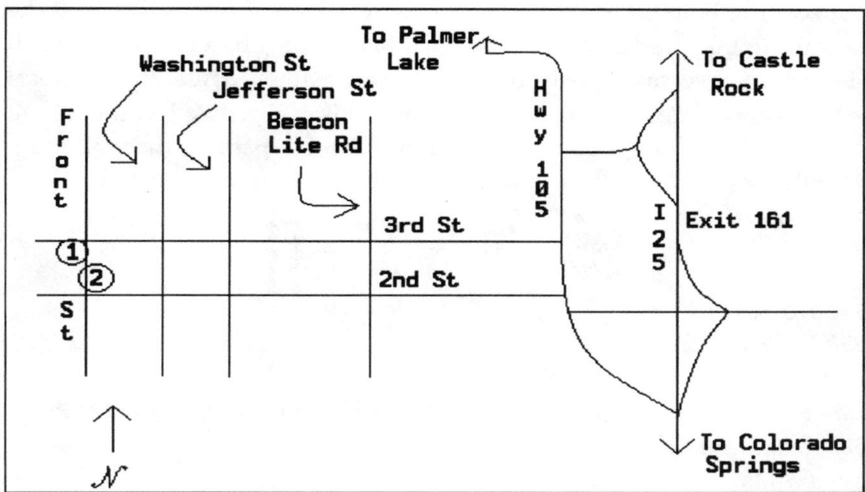

Restaurants and Ratings:	Food	Service	Decor	Atm	Overall
1. Coffee Cup Cafe	★★★	★★	★★½	★★	★★½
2. Ticino	★★★★	★★	★★★	★★★	★★★

Ticino serves spicy Italian food while the Coffee Cup Cafe prepares a good basic breakfast. Both restaurants have nonsmoking sections, but only Ticino accepts major credit cards and serves alcohol.

COFFEE CUP CAFE ★★½
251 FRONT STREET (719)488-0663

Breakfast/lunch$. TUE-SAT 6:30AM-2PM. SUN 7:30AM-1PM. Closed MON Type: Cafe.

***Food:* ★★★ *Service:* ★★ *Decor:* ★★½ *Atmosphere:* ★★**

I had a basic, but good, breakfast here consisting of two eggs over easy, bacon, country fries and rye toast. The country fries were plentiful and had pieces of fresh onion. While I was busy taking notes on the restaurant's decor, the waitress served my breakfast to another customer at the counter who came in several minutes after I had ordered. That did not seem to bother him. He ate it anyway. The waitress recognized the mistake to the other customer, but acted like nothing had happened when she returned to me. Rusty farm tools and leather artworks by a local artist decorate this two-room restaurant. This is strictly a local hangout. The place was full on Saturday morning. People passing through town usually stop at the Village Inn which is visible from the Interstate.

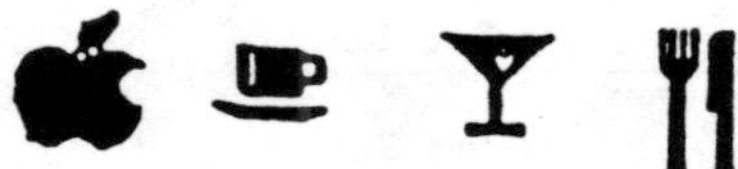

TICINO ★★★
230 FRONT STREET (719)488-9880

Lunch $, dinner $$-$$$. TUE-FRI: 11AM-2PM and 5PM-9PM. SAT 5PM-10PM. Closed SUN & MON.
Type: Italian (and Swiss).

Food: ★★★★ Cold, sliced Italian bread is served before your meal begins. The soup was homemade minestrone. The salad (lettuce, tomato, cucumber, red onion and pepperoncini) was served with "zesty" Italian dressing on the side. It was full of garlic and I strongly recommend it. My ravioli entree came with a spicy marinara sauce full of tomatoes. The three large al dente noodles were filled with meat. A delicious meatball spiced with oregano, basil and spinach, and an Italian sausage, were served on the side. The chef rolls out the ravioli noodles by hand after the order comes in. The meal was not overly filling, but I did not go away hungry either. The lunch appetizer menu features an antipasto of Italian meats & cheeses for two, carpaccio (thinly sliced raw beef), country-style veal pâté, and soup. Pasta, ravioli, baked mostaccioli, linguini in red clam sauce, fettuccine, and lasagna are the Italian entree choices. A cassoulet with duck, sausage, pork and Navy beans; Bratwurst; Hungarian noodles; sandwiches and subs are the non-Italian selections. You can finish lunch with homemade cheesecake or spumoni.

Dinner offers more veal dishes, such as scallopine, Parmigiana, alla Rusticana (sage, rosemary and white wine), saltimbocca (prosciutto & cheese), and Wiener schnitzel; seafood, like pasta marinara with scallops and clams; several chicken choices (chicken breast in Dijon or Hungarian paprika sauce); and rouladen (stuffed German beef).

Service: ★★ I somehow got lost in the shuffle after they seated me. I took notes on the decor and copied the entire dinner menu while I waited 20 to 25 minutes for someone to return to take my order. Finally, I asked the waiter, who had just served the table next to me, to send over my server. (I was also here when he took this table's order). He asked who that was. I said I did not know since I only had contact with the hostess and bus/water boy up to that point. He acted surprised that I had not ordered yet, "generously" offered to take my order and apologized. The bus/water boy, on the other hand, was very attentive to my needs: replacing the kerosene lamp that was out of oil, returning to relight it after it had gone out, and asking if there was anything he could get for me when he removed my salad plate.

Decor: ★★★ The restaurant is accessible by crossing over a small foot bridge. There are two dining rooms with a bar/lounge and outdoor patio. The nonsmoking section in the rear has 10 tables for 40. Its orange plaster walls with brown wood-framed windows and doors are sparsely decorated with eight small prints of English country cottages; a wreath over the entrance; a horn; an oval-shaped, brass-plated mirror; and a picture of a fortress by the sea. Lighting is provided by in-set ceiling lights and kerosene table lamps. The smoking dining room in front also has 10 tables for 40 diners. It is also sparsely decorated with a few prints and small horns. There are several tall-standing plants near the entrance to the nonsmoking dining room. Between the smoking room and the lounge is a two-sided cobblestone fireplace. The lounge has four high tables with 14 stools, four tables for 16, six barstools and is decorated with Italian advertisements and beer signs.

Atmosphere: ★★★ The Italian opera plays delightfully in the background. This is a family place with children (noisy at times) and middle-aged and older couples.

MORRISON

The town was named for pioneer George Morrison who founded the town in 1859. Located at the base of the foothills just west of Denver, Morrison is best known for adjacent Red Rocks Park Amphitheater.

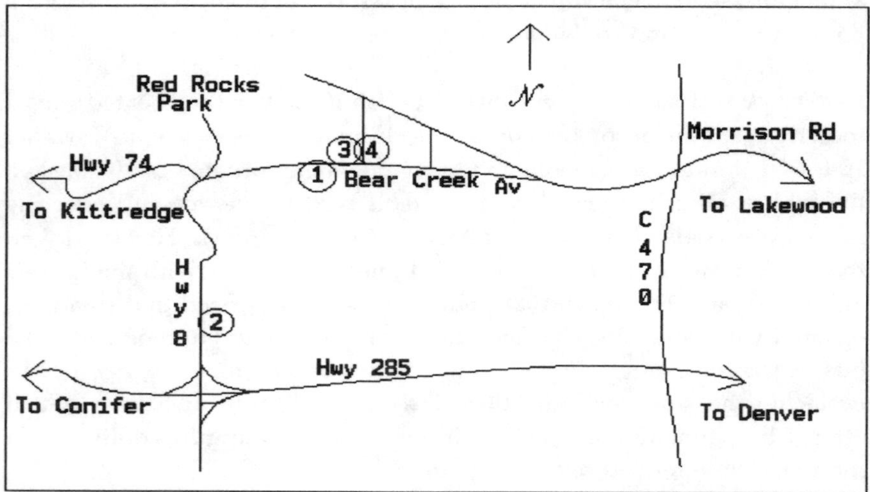

Restaurants and Ratings:	Food	Service	Decor	Atm	Overall
1. DARI TREAT	★★★	★	★	★½	★½
2. THE FORT	★★★★★	★★★★½	★★★★★	★★★★★	★★★★★
3. MORRISON INN	★★★★	★★★½	★★★½	★★★★½	★★★★
4. TONY RIGATONI'S	★★★½	★★★	★★★	★★★★	★★★½

The Fort lives up to its name and offers some excellent buffalo, wild game and seafood in a Southwest setting with an extremely amiable atmosphere. The Morrison Inn has some superb Mexican dishes and an interesting decor all in a party atmosphere. For very good Italian food in a quieter atmosphere, visit Tony Rigatoni's. Except for Dari Treat, each restaurant accepts major credit cards, has a nonsmoking section, and serves alcohol.

DARI TREAT ★½
316 HWY 74 (303)697-5721

Breakfast/lunch $. MON-FRI 6AM-5:30PM. SAT 7AM-5:30PM. SUN 8AM-5:30PM.
Type: Cafe.

Food: ★★★ *Service:* ★ *Decor:* ★ *Atmosphere:* ★½

My breakfast burrito was spicy and included potatoes, chicken, ground beef and egg. It was quite good and I would recommend it. The bacon was crispy. The coffee, however, was only fair. Service was quietly inefficient. My friend, who ordered scrambled eggs, bacon and wheat toast, was served pancakes. He gave it back to the waitress reminding her of his original order. She returned later with one egg over easy with bacon. My friend did not press the issue. This is a small, one-room restaurant with 10 formica tables for 36 and a counter with six short red stools. There are no curtains and no items of decor. A quiet, local clientele dines here.

THE FORT ★★★★★
19192 HWY 8 AT US HWY 285 (303)697-4771

Dinner $$$-$$$$ (a few $$$$+). MON-FRI 6PM-10PM. SAT 5PM-10PM. SUN 5PM-9PM.
Type: Steak. 17% service charge for tables of 8 or more. No separate checks. No pipes or cigars. Menus available in Japanese, French, German, Spanish and Braille. Minimum $6.50 service per person in dining area.

Food: ★★★★★ I had the opportunity to dine here twice, both times with friends. My first visit was to celebrate my 40th birthday. I finally tried Rocky Mountain oysters (as an appetizer): small, tender and quite tasty small calf fries with tomato relish and onion cocktail sauce on the side. We sampled a few of their spirituous specialties: Injun whiskey made with tobacco juice, red pepper, and gunpowder(!); a hailstorm, similar to a mint julip; and St. Vrain's Mule (a concoction of ginger brandy and ginger beer). I found the Injun whiskey to be a mild shot. The gunpowder is made from sulphur, charcoal and saltpeter ("to preserve your bacon," owner Sam Arnold says). The first sip of the St. Vrain's Mule tasted like ginger ale, but it got better. The salads were excellent and I recommend the bayou dressing: a green garden dressing with a hint of anchovy. Our entrees were quite good also. My Gonzales steak — top sirloin stuffed with real New Mexican pure green chili, then topped with a whole green chili pod and briefly broiled — was prepared to perfection. It came with pan potatoes, sprinkled with toasted canola seeds and slightly undercooked (I like them slightly undercooked) and peas. The meal was served with Indian blue corn and wild-blueberry muffins and pumpkin & walnut muffins (The Fort has baked more than five million pumpkin & walnut muffins!). The quail was moist, very flavorful, with a delectable seasoning and just slightly crispy. It was briefly marinated in teriyaki sauce, sherry and fresh ginger, then mesquite broiled. We finished out meals with glasses of port and sherry: a fine conclusion to an excellent meal.

On my second visit here, a month later to celebrate a graduation, three of us ordered the game plate: a combination of quail, buffalo, and elk, with fried potatoes and peas. The pheasant was deliciously tangy and sweet, prepared with teriyaki and orange slices and glazed with honey. The deep pink New Zealand elk was very tender and the buffalo broke apart easily with a fork. We ordered huckleberry sauce on the side: exquisite, but very sweet. It is something you would want to try on a few bites of meat, but don't pour it over your whole meal. The quail seemed to be the favorite of the three. One member of our group ordered the oysters Rockefeller (mixed with spinach, mushroom, butter and garlic) for an appetizer. He found them tender and tasty, .

The Fort offers many wonderful and unique items that you will not find in many other places. Starting with the appetizers, they have traditional Mexican guacamole made with avocadoes, tomatoes, onions, serrano chilies, cilantro, a little salt and a lot of lime; buffalo tongue served with Sam Arnold's famous capered horseradish; buffalo marrow bones, called "prairie butter", that you extract with a knife and spread onto toast; great American buffalo eggs (actually they're quail eggs. Even Sam Arnold can't make a buffalo lay eggs!): hard boiled and covered with buffalo sausage; pickled jalapeños stuffed with peanut butter; and Texas rattle snake braised, flaked and chilled with the texture of crab and the taste of chicken. The entrees feature buffalo, wild game, seafood and chicken. The prime rib roasts are rubbed with herbs, then slow-roasted with a little onion peel smoke. The mountain trout is broiled, basted in a mint sauce and topped with bacon bits. The yellow-fin tuna is charbroiled and served with "Uchucuta", a Peruvian peanut salsa. The piñon catfish is mesquite-broiled and topped with toasted pine nuts. "The bowl of the wife of Kit Carson", named after Kit Carson's granddaughter, who used to work at The Fort, is a spicy, peppered hot broth with chicken, rice, garbanzos, jack cheese, smoky chipotle chilies and avocado. The chicken adobe is a chicken breast, rolled with ham and cheese, breaded, and served with sour cream and mild green chili. The Santa Fe chops are charbroiled and served with New Mexico red chili sauce on the side. If you are a vegetarian, don't lose interest yet. They have a vegetarian plate, made to order, with in season vegetables like Arkansas Valley onions, white kernel shoe-peg corn, Anasazi beans, Cha-cha Murphys (mashed potatoes mixed with a little green chile and cheese), and quinoa (keen-wah), "the super grain of the future". You can compliment or finish your meal with Yuban coffee (THE coffee of the old west that Kit Carson enjoyed). The dessert selections vary, but you may see cheesecake (made with an amaretto crumb crust, rich dark Ghirardelli chocolate and Meyer's Jamaican rum), wild Montana huckleberry sundaes, Kir Royale mousse, The Fort ice cream pie (made with Dutch chocolate ice cream, coffee, crème de menthe, slivered almonds and Hershey's syrup in a chocolate cookie crust), or an amaretto flan.

Service: ★★★★½ On my first visit here the service was very pleasant and efficient. We wanted for nothing. Our waitress was quick and did not leave us waiting. My second visit was equally enjoyable. Only this time we had a jocular, "psychic", and flexible waiter who was prepared for anything, even the numerous interruptions of one member of our party who loves to give waiters (and most everyone else) a hard time (all in fun, though).

Decor: ★★★★★ Built in 1962, The Fort is patterned after an early Colorado fur-trade center called Bent's Fort located 160 miles to the southeast near

La Junta. It took 10 months for 22 New Mexican workmen from Taos to complete the project using 1800 tons of earth to make 80,000 mud and straw adobe bricks, each weighing 45 pounds and measuring 14" x 10" x 4". The restaurant, with its two-foot-thick walls, was opened on February 1, 1963. This is a very unique setting with an open-air courtyard in the middle complete with bonfire in the summer and fantastic views of Denver and Pikes Peak. 350 guests in nine dining areas can be served in this 12,000 square-foot structure. Talk about authentic! A few of the more notable items of decor are a 350 pound church bell built in 1840 located in the cupola under the flagpole; a 27 star flag: the one used in 1845 just before Texas was annexed; two 18′ x 18′ bastions or towers — one used for wine storage and tasting, the other as a special dining room with a fireplace; and cannons: a six-pound Napoleon, a 12-pounder on a naval carriage, and a "thunder mug".

The St Vrain bar, to the right of the front-gate portal, has a herringbone planked ceiling with vigas (log beams) and zapatas (footed supports). An adobe brick from the original Bent's Fort in 1834 can be found in a niche in the wall. As you pass through the dining areas of this restaurant you will notice an American Indian selling jewelry, Indian sketches and sand paintings; Padre Martinez chairs (an early New Mexican style wooden chair made of ponderosa pine and using peg construction), calico walls, decorated buffalo skulls, and oil paintings of the Bent brothers and San Miguel church in Sante Fe (the oldest church in the US) as it looked in 1845. It would be difficult to find a more elaborate restaurant in small town Colorado, or one requiring more work.

Atmosphere: ★★★★★ Most places this large and this crowded would leave the average person feeling a little uncomfortable, or at least self-conscious, especially visiting the first time. Not so with The Fort. The air is filled with laughter, joviality and high spirits. If you are looking for a good time come to The Fort. It is sure to delight your senses and enhance your mood. Several famous personalities have passed this way including James Michener, Dr. Arnold Toynbee, Ann Margaret, Louis Leakey, Sugar Ray Leonard, Michael Jackson, and Bryant Gumbel.

MORRISON INN ★★★★
301 BEAR CREEK AVE (303)697-6650

Brunch/lunch/dinner $$. Labor Day to Memorial Day: MON-THU 11:30AM-10PM. FRI 11:30AM-11PM. SAT 10AM-11PM. SUN 10AM-10PM. Same hours in the summer except opened one hour later each evening. Type: Mexican. 15% gratuity added to groups of seven or more. Absolutely NO checks.

Food: **★★★★** Their chips were light, very thin, warm and crispy. The salsa was spicy. My beef fajitas — three flour tortillas, mesquite-grilled beef, grilled green and red peppers, onions, guacamole, sour cream, pico de gallo, and cheddar — were scrumptious and filling. My friend for dinner ordered a fajita salad: an abundance of vegetables with grilled chicken in a giant tortilla bowl. He was also delighted, and full, after his meal. I also highly recommend Quan's gold house special margarita made with tequila, Grand Marnier, Cuervo gold and Cointreau. It is pleasing and potent. The list of appetizers includes petit chili rellenos, shrimp al carbon (mesquite marinated & grilled), and the poo poo (as opposed to pu pu) platter (a combination of their best appertivos). Chimichangas are their specialty. They are offered in two sizes ("macho" and "muy macho") and prepared with shrimp, pork, chicken, or beef. There are combination dinners, soft shell fajita and veggie tacos, a spinach enchilada, the original pork barbacoa (roasted pork with slightly sweet barbecue sauce rolled in a flour tortilla), and nonalcoholic specialty drinks. For Saturday or Sunday brunch (served from 10AM to 2PM) they offer eggs Benedict, Florentine, or Morrison (with guacamole), a steak & egg burrito, and Colorado huevos (three eggs with peppers and cheddar).

Service: **★★★½** Pleasing, helpful, attentive and delightful. The owner, Sal Siraguse (a good Italian name for a man from Buffalo), was a nice fellow and took me for a tour upstairs.

Decor: **★★★½** The bar/lounge is at the entrance with seven tables to the left for 28, seven tables to the right for 26, and a bar at the end with nine stools. A mural of a beach and boardwalk are painted on both side walls with their fictitious mascot, Quan, enjoying a tropical drink while stretching back in a dingy. A buffalo head hangs on the wall over the entrance to the rest rooms. Party photos adorn the walls as you pass through the lounge and again as you enter the dining areas to the right. Two life-sized human figures, known as "Gringo" and his friend "Gomez", along with a very tall wooden figure of a man they call "Woody", greet you as you enter the dining areas. Each of the two dining rooms, front and back, has 16 tables for 50 people. Old photos of Schneider's drug store and shoe shop, circa 1914 and 1920, the town band from 1902, and the Morrison school house in 1915 hang on the cement walls. Wagon wheels and fans hang from the brown-paneled ceiling that is cracking in places. Seating is on hardwood, rib-backed chairs set at varnished-wood tables. Ample lighting is provided by frosted ceiling lights. There is a green overhang outside. Upstairs, the original sandstone walls are still intact (they are cemented over downstairs). "Woody II" is on the patio that seats about 70 in a setting that features aspens, red-brick columns, an enclosed wooden fence, white plastic furniture and a bar. Inside, there is a large cactus in a square, wood-framed structure in the center section, pine log doorways and dividers, and full-length windows looking out onto the patio. This dining area seats about 60.

***Atmosphere:* ★★★★½** This is a happy, cheerful crowd. I have never visited here and not been exposed to people having a genuinely good time. For a bar-type restaurant, I really like the atmosphere in here.

TONY RIGATONI'S ★★★½
215 BEAR CREEK AVENUE (303)697-5508

Lunch $, dinner $$ ($$$ on some large portions). TUE-THU 11:30AM-9PM. FRI-SAT 11:30AM-10PM. SUN 12PM-9PM. Closed MON.
Type: Italian.

***Food:* ★★★½** My dinner salad consisted of lettuce, cucumber, one cherry tomato and several garbanzo beans in an Italian garlic Romano dressing. I tasted very little garlic and no Romano, which made it basically vinegar and oil. My ravioli Parmigiana, however, was delicious! Jumbo ricotta cheese ravioli with a lot of small pieces of Italian sausage, tomato cream sauce, topped (smothered is more like it) with melted provolone, a little parsley and grated cheese; served piping hot with white bread on the side. This was a cheese lovers delight, but I liked the tender pasta noodles, cooked to perfection, and light red sauce, the best. This was really a well-prepared meal. The lunch specials include home style spaghetti, calzones, and an individual pizza. You can also order a sandwich (marinated chicken, Italian sausage or meatball) with a side of spaghetti. Start your dinner off with the antipasto platter, nachos Italiano, caponata (sweet & sour relish made with eggplant, tomatoes, onions, celery and peppers), or polenta con gorgonzola (corn meal croutons topped with gorgonzola cheese and cream). Follow this with a chicken pesto salad or a bowl of deep-dish pizza soup. The special entrees include lasagna, eggplant Parmigiana, fettuccine Alfredo, tortellini, and chicken saltimbocca. The pasta dishes feature rigatoni, spaghetti, or ravioli with marinara sauce. They offer several specialty pizzas in medium and large, and let you create your own, as well, from your choice of three sauces, including tomato basil and pesto; five meats including prosciutto; three cheeses including ricotta and gorgonzola; 10 vegetables including spinach and artichoke hearts; and three specialty items like anchovies and fresh basil. For dessert, there's rigatoni roulade (white cake in raspberry cream swirl, rolled in chocolate and dipped in almonds), tirra ma su, bourbon pecan pie, and grannie apple pie with caramel topping. They usually offer two different cheesecakes, two pies, and a cake. Desserts change nightly. The dessert tray is brought to your table.

Service: ★★★ Prompt and courteous. The butter is served at room temperature, not straight from the freezer, and she returned quickly with a menu for me to take.

Decor: ★★★ There is a 108 year-old-bar with 12 stools at the entrance, but Tony Rigatoni's has only been around since December 22, 1990. Shelves at the entrance, open on both sides, hold canisters, bottles, chianti bottles and plants. The front dining area has portraits and photos of the Conte family hanging from the stucco walls. The room seats 28 at seven tables.

The middle dining area seats eight at two tables; the rear dining area seats 30 at nine tables. Seating is on hardwood chairs with armrests A high wall shelf is decorated with books, flasks, cans and clocks. The only items adorning the natural unfinished split log walls in the rear dining room are four wood-framed mirrors. An old-fashioned Martini & Rossi poster and a wreath hang in the middle dining area. Lights in the acoustic tile ceiling combined with table kerosene lamps, provide more lighting than one would think.

Atmosphere: ★★★★ This is a nice, quiet restaurant with several couples and families with small, well behaved, children. Very comfortable. Recorded accordion music plays through speakers set in the corner shelves near the ceiling.

The Fort - Morrison

NATURITA/NORWOOD/NUCLA

Naturita, meaning "close to nature" in Spanish, was named after a nearby creek by Rockford H. Blake, an early settler. Norwood was named by its founder, I.M. Coop, for a community in Missouri. Nucla got its name as a corruption of "nucleus," or "center," by C.E. Williams. The town was established in 1904 as a socialistic colony whose inhabitants believed that socialism would spread over the nation and their town would be the center of the movement (sounds like an ego problem to me).

I put these three towns together because they are located near each other geographically and, rather conveniently, they follow each other alphabetically in this book (with only Niwot interrupting). Located in the west central part of the state, south of Grand Junction and east of Montrose, these three small towns are located on, or just off of, U.S. Highway 141. I consider this highway from Grand Junction to be one of the most scenic in the state, especially if you can take it right before sunset. This is also deer country. Riding over the mesa and back roads near Naturita, we spotted about 700 or 800 deer, a few elk and a bald eagle, all in the same February evening. Recently, Nucla gained national attention for their annual prairie-dog shoot. The cute, but destructive, critters seem to be a pain in the leg for the ranchers' cattle. Animal-rights activists, more concerned with the burrowing rodents than with the larger mammals, have created a controversy over the annual event.

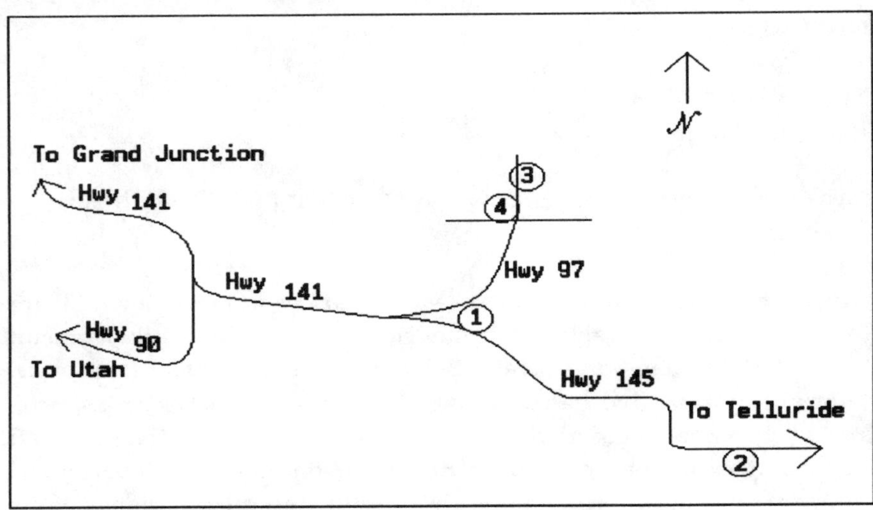

NATURITA/NORWOOD/NUCLA

Restaurants and Ratings:	Food	Service	Decor	Atm	Overall
NATURITA:					
1. Yellow Rock	★★★	★★½	★★★½	★★★	★★★
NORWOOD:					
2. Karen's	★★★★	★★★½	★★★★	★★★½	★★★½
NUCLA					
3. Chuckwagon	★★★½	★★	★★½	★★½	★★½
4. The Mustang	★★	★	½	½	★

I found the best overall restaurant and the best food to be at Karen's. They have a fabulous Mexican soup, called Fideo (fe-day-oh), and very good quiche. Wednesdays and Fridays are Mexican days at the Chuckwagon and it is worth the short four-mile trip off Hwy. 141 for some inexpensive and delicious Mexican food. The Yellow Rock Cafe is also good for any meal and has some attractive paintings for sale by a local artist. Only the Yellow Rock Cafe accepts credit cards and serves alcohol. None of the restaurants has a nonsmoking section.

NATURITA:

YELLOW ROCK CAFE ★★★
106 MAIN (303)865-2599

Breakfast/lunch $, dinner $-$$$. 7 days 6AM-10PM (9PM NOV-MAR). Type: Country.

Food: ★★★ I ate here on several occasions and I would recommend them for an inexpensive breakfast, lunch or steak dinner. The breakfast menu has pork chops, hamburger, crab omelets, cinnamon toast and sweet rolls. Lunch features sandwiches, such as a BLT bird (with chicken), roast beef, and a vegetarian; hot sandwiches (beef, steak, hamburger or ham) served with potatoes and gravy; several burger selections (including guacamole, chili, or mushrooms), chili, onion rings, soup, and salad. Dinner offers deep-fried breaded vegetables and shrimp cocktail for appetizers. Most of the entrees are steak selections, but you also have your choice of pork chops, roast beef, halibut, shrimp, or fried chicken. Homemade pies and ice cream complete the menu. Alcohol is available from the Incline Lounge behind the restaurant.

Service: ★★½ Service was always fairly standard: nothing special but no complaints either.

Decor: ★★★½ This is a two-room restaurant. The front room resembles a cafe and is used for breakfast and lunch. It seats 40 people in booths and at a counter. The back dining room seats about 60 people at tables. The dining room has a mantel with three reindeer heads. The walls are decorated with paintings by Betty Rutherford, a local artist. I purchased one painting of a cabin, waterwheel and lake with a lot of fall color.

Atmosphere: ★★★ Casual and homey.

NORWOOD:

KAREN'S ★★★½
1140 GRAND AVE. (303)327-4840

Breakfast/lunch $-$$. TUE-SAT 7AM-2PM. SUN 7AM-12PM. Shut MON. Type: Mexican.

Food: ★★★★ If you are in this area on any day but Monday, between the hours of 11am and 2pm, make sure you stop here and have some of their homemade Fideo (fe-day-oh)/a Mexican soup made with tomatoes and noodles/and some quiche (asparagus, seafood, or ham & cheese). Breakfast has some worthy selections like eggs Benedict, chorizo (sausage), cream cheese & eggs, new waveous (eggs, beans, cheese & salsa in a tortilla), blueberry pancakes and pigs in a blanket. The lunch menu offers homemade soup with homemade bread; salad; sandwiches featuring roast beef, chicken breast, and ham; burgers with mushrooms, avocado, green chili or cheese; and a patty melt. While this may seem like a limited menu, the quality of the food is the best you will find for miles around.

Service: ★★★½ The service is very good and the proprietor is interesting and humorous.

Decor: ★★★★ This is an attractive place with antique jars and canisters, a china cabinet, dinner plates from different states, and a pendulum clock. The walls are wood panel on the bottom with either striped or flower-patterned wallpaper on top. There is seating for 40 people at tables in two rooms.

Atmosphere: ★★★½ This restaurant offers the most pleasant setting of any in the area.

NUCLA:

CHUCKWAGON ★★½
475 MAIN ST. (303)864-2108

Breakfast/lunch $, dinner $$. MON-SAT 5AM-8PM (9PM in summer). SUN 5AM-4PM (5PM in summer).
Type: Country.

***Food:* ★★★½ *Service:* ★★ *Decor:* ★★½ *Atmosphere:* ★★½**

I recommend this place for their Mexican food on Wednesday and Friday. All of their Mexican entrees are inexpensive and very good. However, the sopapillas are thick and on the heavy side and the beans are not the refried variety. The rest of the lunch menu has burgers, halibut, chicken, roast beef, chili, soup, salad, and hot and cold sandwiches. The breakfast fare includes pork chops, crab omelets and cinnamon toast. Dinner offers a big selection of steaks, including "extra large steaks for hearty appetites," shrimp, roast beef, chicken, and pork chops. Soft ice cream is available for dessert. Service is inconsistent: a little slow on one visit, just fine the next. This is a single-room restaurant with six booths for 24, tables for 32, and a counter with six stools. A jukebox and a few paintings make up the decor. Good lighting is provided by windows along the front. A popular place with locals, especially on Mexican days.

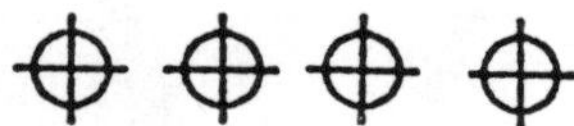

THE MUSTANG ★
490 MAIN (303)864-2111

Lunch/dinner $. MON-WED 10AM-9PM. THU-SAT 10AM-11PM. Closed SUN.
Type: Burgers.

Food: ★★ *Service:* ★ *Decor:* ½ *Atmosphere:* ½

Their burgers were fair, at best. Other food items include hot dogs; Mexican food; sandwiches, including a Reuben and corned beef; subs; and Cajun catfish. Ice cream cones, milk shakes, malts, floats and sundaes were also available. Service was slow and inefficient. There is one room for eating with five small booths, three tables and a bar for total seating of 34. A side room to the right has a pool table. A side room to the left is used for video games. This is the local teen hangout and, I suspect, the games are the main reason for the restaurant staying in business. There is no other decor. Atmosphere is "zip," none, "nada."

NIWOT

Originally called Modoc and founded by W. T. Wilson, the name was changed to Ni-Wot in 1879 for nearby Ni-Wot mine and mill. The name Ni-Wot derives from Arapahoe Chief Niwot, meaning "left hand". Chief Niwot greeted the early gold seekers to the area in 1858 and became known for his friendliness. The Arapahoe spelling of the name was Nawat, but through usage and time that spelling was changed to Niwot.

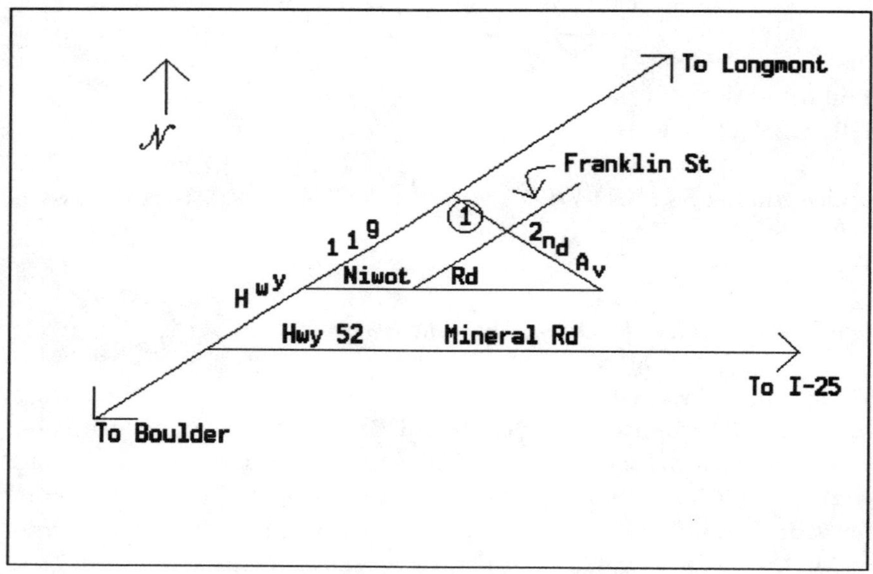

1. REV. TAYLOR'S ★★★½
121 SECOND AVENUE (303)652-2020

Breakfast $, lunch $-$$, dinner $$ (a few $$$). SUN-THU 8AM-8PM. FRI-SAT 8AM-9PM.

Type: Country. Located in an historic building where Rev. William E Taylor ("Old Niwot Bill" is what he liked to call himself) opened his meat market, grocery and general store in 1911, and later his popular soda fountain in 1926. Rev. Taylor's serves high quality, good-sized meals, in a comfortable and casual country atmosphere. They accept major credit cards, have a nonsmoking section, and serve beer and wine. A 15% gratuity is added for parties of six or more. Food items low in fat, cholesterol, calories and controlled for sodium are identified on the menu.

Food: ★★★½ Their dishes are homemade — prepared from scratch — and taken from prized family recipes. They use freshly made sauces, baked breads, muffins and desserts. The beer-cheddar soup was hot, creamy and delicious, made with thin slices of carrots and celery. The meatloaf was thick and filling, prepared with celery, onion and green pepper. A rich brown gravy covered the meat and real mashed potatoes, served with a homemade biscuit. This was a very good lunch in both quality and quantity. My lunch partner tried their ham & cheese omelet and was equally pleased and stuffed. The omelet was topped with melted cheddar and fresh ham and came with a hearty serving of hash browns. Breakfast, which is served until 2PM, includes a couple of country egg scrambles with ham, tomato & green onions, or with mushrooms & green onions; huevos rancheros; vegetarian or eggs Benedict; and Belgian waffles. The country lunches feature beef stew, country-fried steak, sandwiches (hot roast beef, vegetarian, chicken salad, Reuben, beef tip, and breast of chicken), burgers, soup, salads (chef or chicken), chili, a diet plate, and a fish of the day. Chicken wings & fingers, and fried cheese are offered as dinner appetizers. The list of entrees includes lemon & herb chicken breast, prime rib, NY steak, barbecue baby-back ribs and beef ribs, chicken burrito, and Mexicali chicken. On the dessert tray you will find pies (coconut cream, chocolate peanut butter, and French silk), carrot cake, chocolate eclairs, and a fruit kuchen. The soda fountain is still working and you can order an old-fashioned sundae, banana split, shake, malt, soda, float or ice cream cone.

Service: ★★★ Cheerful, helpful and attentive.

Decor: ★★★ This is a long, single-room restaurant in sections separated by short, four-foot plaster walls with wood frames and posts. The walls are literally cluttered with small and medium-sized wood-framed paintings; silhouettes; needle points; wreaths; dried flowers; and pans, saws and shovels with nature photos on the side or bottom. The tops of the plaster and wood dividing walls are covered with stuffed animals, ceramics, and dried flowers in tiny baskets. At the front of the restaurant is a small gift shop with more paraphernalia for sale. It's quite a concoction of varied artworks. Across from the gift shop is a small counter with eight stools, a soda fountain, a wood bench and a coffee table with a game of checkers set up. Rather quaint, I thought. Down the center of the restaurant are five booths for 16. The seating area to the left has six tables for 20; the area to the right, eight tables for 28. Hanging from the back wall are old photos of the Niwot Mercantile Military Band, the Post Office, a gazebo, and graduation day. Very ample lighting is provided by in-set ceiling lights accompanied by brass, frosted-glass wall fixtures.

Atmosphere: ★★★★ Classical guitar music plays through the sound system in the acoustic ceiling. This is a popular place with the white collar work force in town. Very pleasant. A lot of intelligent business conversations going on.

The Hot Springs in Pagosa Springs

PAGOSA SPRINGS

Pagosa comes from the Ute Indian word, Pagosah, meaning "healing water". The hot springs located here were a favorite camping place of the Utes who found them medicinal and beneficial. In the early 1870's, the Pagosa Hot Springs were a welcome rest and relaxation stop for travelers and miners. In 1878, the U.S. Army built Fort Lewis across from the Hot Springs, then moved to Durango in 1881. In the early twentieth century, sheep herding, cattle ranches and lumber were the main industries in this area. Today, you can still find cattle ranches, cowboys, and lumber mills, but tourism and sports, like skiing and biking, are the major industries.

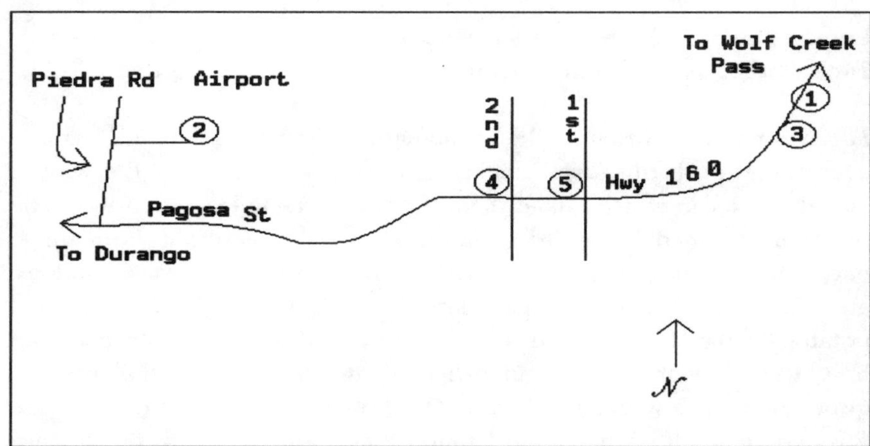

Restaurants and Ratings:	Food	Service	Decor	Atm	Overall
1. Branding Iron	★★★★	★★★	★★★½	★★★½	★★★½
2. Green House	★★★½	★★★½	★★★	★★★★	★★★½
3. Ole Miners	★★★★½	★★★★	★★★★★	★★★★½	★★★★½
4. Rolling Pin	★★★	★★½	★★½	★★★½	★★★
5. Spanish Inn	★★★½	★★	★★★	★★½	★★★

I found the best restaurants in Pagosa Springs to be three miles to the east or west of town. East of town, Ole Miner's Steakhouse serves delicious charbroiled steaks and seafood in a unique and very private setting resembling an old gold mine. A half mile farther east, The

Branding Iron has some lean meats with homemade barbecue sauce and a good lake-side view. The Green House, three miles to the west of town, serves good wholesome meals in a setting that features both an airport and a mountain range. All of the restaurants accept major credit cards, except the Rolling Pin and the Spanish Inn. They all have nonsmoking sections. Only the Green House serves alcohol.

BRANDING IRON ★★★½
HWY 160, SOUTH SIDE, 3½ MILES EAST OF PAGOSA SPRINGS (303)264-4268

Lunch/dinner $-$$. MON-SAT 11AM-8PM. Closed SUN. Closed JAN-MAR
Type: Barbecue. Take-out available.

Food: ★★★★ I ordered the combination platter so I could sample everything: pork ribs, beef, chicken and sausage, which, by the way, is also the order in which I liked them (from favorite to least favorite). The meat is trimmed, very lean, and served with warmed homemade barbecue sauce on the side. The meal comes with Texas toast, potatoes, and your choice of two vegetables. I found the long slices of fried potatoes somewhat dry and less than satisfactory. The pinto beans in brown gravy were hearty and delicious, and the corn on the cob was quite good. The whole meal was not as overpowering as it may sound. They serve small portions and I found that I still had room for dessert. The turtle pie is a mixture of vanilla ice cream, caramel, whipped cream, sliced pecan and a chocolate crust. It was a taste pleaser for sure. They also have excellent ice tea served in a huge glass mug. Children's plates, for those eight years and under, are available.

Service: ★★★ Very pleasant and helpful.

Decor: ★★★½ The decor for this restaurant really starts on the outside where there is a small patio with tables for about 20. Across the road is a pond with pine trees leading up to a ridge. It makes a great setting for summer sunsets. A boardwalk extends along the entire north side of the building with eight red-glass humming bird feeders hanging from a wagon wheel, and four more individual feeders on either side. There had to be, easily, 100 hummingbirds humming the evening that I was there. Inside there is a dining area to the right with seven tables for about 30 people and a main dining room to the left with four booths and eight tables for 42 more. The diagonal-cut pine walls display a variety of Western and Indian decor: branding irons; black-iron curios of howling wolves and big horn sheep; Indian rugs; and portraits. Beyond the dining room is a gift shop specializing in jewelry, rugs, dishes and cards.

Atmosphere: ★★★½ This is a family oriented restaurant. A red-haired, young fellow softly played folk songs on the guitar while a few boisterous children screamed, cried, yelled and ran. Still, the setting sun could not be spoiled by the little brats.

GREEN HOUSE ★★★½
3 MILES WEST OF PAGOSA SPRINGS ON PIEDRA RD, ½ MILE NORTH OF HWY 160. (303)731-2021

Sunday brunch/lunch $-$$, dinner $$-$$$$. JUN-OCT: MON-THU 11:30AM-10PM. FRI-SAT 11:30AM-11PM. SUN 11:30AM-9PM. NOV-MAY: SUN-THU 4PM-10PM. FRI-SAT 4PM-11PM.
Type: Steak/Seafood. Handicapped entrance. A 15% gratuity is added for parties of eight or more. No separate checks for large groups.

Food: ★★★½ I recommend their honey-mustard dressing for their salad. I ordered the turkey special for Sunday brunch: a wholesome meal with fresh tasting turkey, mashed potatoes, dressing with gravy, and peas. Other Sunday brunch items featured eggs Benedict, breakfast burrito, prime rib, Southern-fried chicken, and roast beef. The lunch menu offers sandwiches, burgers, grilled chicken breast, salads and French onion soup. The dinner menu starts off with fried cheese sticks, sautéed mushrooms, and shrimp cocktail. There are two soup choices: French onion and pepper cheese; and two salad choices: spinach and chef. The house specialties feature prime rib, filet mignon, steak Diane, lobster tail, Alaskan king crab legs, salmon, Rocky Mountain trout, roast beef, and pizza. There is a senior's menu for those 60 years and over and desserts (cheesecake with toppings, sundaes, sherbet, and ice cream pies).

Service: ★★★½ A very, pleasant young waitress. Service was very fast. They brought my salad in about three minutes and the dinner was served before I was half finished with the salad. Owner Paula Schoenenberger took me for a brief tour. They have been in business since April, 1990.

Decor: ★★★ This is a very clean, modern looking place with a consistent pattern of red tulips with green stems in the carpet and gold-framed glass prints. The main, nonsmoking, dining room has a one-way vaulted, pine ceiling with gold round studio lights which are also used on the pink walls. A large circular window, divided into fourths, is on the vaulted wall separating the bi-level nonsmoking section. Both levels have a clear mountain view featuring Pagosa Peak. The smoking section is adjacent to a small greenhouse at the front of the restaurant. The bar/lounge can seat 25 including nine at the bar and has a fireplace.

Atmosphere: ★★★★ Easy listening and new age music plays pleasantly in the background. The views, especially from the nonsmoking side of the jagged mountain peaks, are something special. This is a very nice setting for a restaurant. There is also the airport next door, so if you are lucky, you might catch a view of a plane taking off or landing.

OLE MINERS ★★★★½
HWY 160, SOUTH SIDE, 3 MILES EAST OF PAGOSA SPRINGS (303)264-5981

Dinner $$$-$$$$ (a few $$$$+). MON-SAT 5:30PM-9PM. Summer: SUN 5:30PM-9:30PM. Closed SUN the rest of the year.
Type: Steak/Seafood. Reservations are not accepted.

Food: ★★★★½ I ordered the sirloin/shrimp combination. It came with a loaf of fresh hot bread right out of the oven, and a 16-item salad bar featuring potato salad, cherry tomatoes, green peppers and pepperoncini. The main course had very lean, juicy, charbroiled sirloin with just a speck of fat; three large shrimp with melted butter, lemon and cocktail sauce; and authentic pinto beans with a lot of chopped bacon, onion and pickle. Try the beans for a very tasty alternative to rice, potatoes or vegetables.

A wide variety of charbroiled steaks are offered, everything from prime rib and filet mignon to ground sirloin and pepper steak. Alaskan king crab, Australian lobster tail, flounder, catfish, Rocky Mountain rainbow trout, and charbroiled shrimp are some of the seafood offerings. If barbecue is to your liking, you have sliced beef, a half-slab of pork, chicken breast, and baby-back ribs to choose from. The poultry selections include charbroiled chicken breast, pharaoh quail, and rock Cornish hen. Six kabob combinations featuring sirloin chunks, seafood, chicken teriyaki, and pork tenderloin, complete this rather extensive menu.

Service: ★★★★ Very pleasant, friendly and with a smile. Owner Paul Aldridge, who, with his wife Janet, opened this steakhouse on July 22, 1982, gave me a personal tour of the entire restaurant. He is a very down to earth, personal gentleman with a most interesting restaurant.

Decor: ★★★★★ This restaurant resembles an old, boarded-up mine. Outside you will find rusty old gears, a shovel, saw and anvil. Inside you will find one of the coziest restaurants anywhere. Raw natural wood with knot holes separate each dining section which has only one or two tables. It would be difficult to find a restaurant that caters more to privacy, so bring your significant other here. They have more private alcoves than any restaurant I have visited in Colorado. Owner Paul has put together a most unusual array of very old photos, paintings, stained-glass windows and doors from defunct churches, old pieces of totally unworked wood, a couple of Chardin prints, an old caldera — even a mirror-shaped saddle in the men's room and a salad bar upstairs made from a bath tub. Paul plans a stairway gallery of paintings for sale, a bookstore upstairs, and an outdoor barbecue. He has put together a remarkable restaurant and he continues to pursue new creative avenues. If you visit just one restaurant in Pagosa Springs, visit this one.

Atmosphere: ★★★★½ Quiet, easy listening music plays in the background. The atmosphere in here is just the opposite of the wide open scenery available at the Green House. At the Ole Miners, you sit in a cozy, enclosed area that is not much larger than a closet. Both restaurants are appealing for different reasons.

PAGOSA SPRINGS

ROLLING PIN BAKERY AND CAFE ★★★
214 PAGOSA (303)264-2255

Breakfast/lunch $. MON-SAT 7AM-5:15PM (6PM JUN-SEP). Closed SUN. Type: Cafe. Take-our available.

Food: ★★★ I had the broccoli and cheese quiche with fresh fruit cup for breakfast. The quiche was fair and the fruit cup fairly good consisting of a thick, juicy grapefruit slice, apples, orange, grapes and melon; but you must try their delicious, hot, fluffy and light buttermilk biscuits with homemade preserves (blueberry, strawberry, peach or plum). The blueberry was heavenly! The breakfast menu includes granola, huevos rancheros and an egg and cheese croissant. The lunch menu features quiche, salads, sandwiches, grilled chicken breast, burger, vegetable soup, and red or green chili. They also have a bakery counter that serves homemade pastries, cookies, breads, and cakes.

Service: ★★½ Service was provided by young waitress who was fast on her feet. In fact, a little too fast for this 40 year old. She would run off before I could complete my sentences.

Decor: ★★½ This restaurant is in a forties-style house with bay windows no window coverings, a stone wall along the sidewalk, and steps leading up to the stone front with green-shingled roof. The dining area is small: two rooms with six tables for only 28 people. The pale-orange wood walls have white trim along the doors, windows, base boards, and heat ducts. The rear room is sparsely decorated with pictures of an old ice chest (circa 1920) and an elderly, white haired, bearded man giving thanks before eating. The front dining room has a fireplace and wall-length mantel decorated with wicker baskets, pots and a can of "Clabber Girl Baking Powder". Below the mantel, on both sides of the fireplace are glass-door cabinets containing "Blue Diamond Almond Paste", plates, ceramic figures of houses, and an interesting black-iron replica of a pipe-stove and table, complete with pots, pans and other kitchen utensils. The bare-wood floors look appropriate here. One thing I particularly did not like was their use of plastic ware, plastic cups with lids for the homemade preserves and paper plates.

Atmosphere: ★★★½ A casual dining place, with families, children, and a radio in the kitchen playing rock and country music. A rather pleasant, well-lit place to be in the summer.

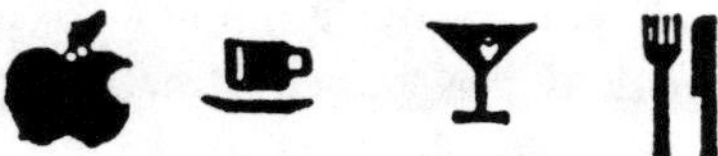

SPANISH INN ★★★
358 EAST PAGOSA (303)264-4676

Breakfast/lunch $, dinner $$. MON-SAT 7AM-8PM. Closed SUN. Breakfast served from 4AM during hunting season. (OCT to Mid-NOV). Type: Mexican

Food: ★★★½ I ordered the beef fajitas plate. The beef was charbroiled and the onions fried, just the way I like them. They were served with lettuce, mild green chilies, tomatoes, guacamole, sour cream and two flour tortillas. I thought the rice was only fair and the beans standard, not the authentic, refried kind. The breakfast menu offers eggs macho (eggs, cheese and salsa inside two corn tortillas). Lunch features burgers, sandwiches, chili, chili fries, salads and side orders of Mexican dishes. Soft tacos, tamales and steaks are on the dinner menu. A catfish fry is served on Friday nights. For dessert, there is homemade ice cream.

Service: ★★ A little slow initially getting to my table, but satisfactory after that.

Decor: ★★★ A main dining room and small adjacent dining room can seat 64 at a combination of booths and tables. An outdoor patio seats 16 at six tables in a covered section and 40 more at 10 tables in an uncovered section. The pine walls are decorated with wicker baskets, plate holders, a whisk broom, Mexican rugs and hats, cowboy hats, sheep and bull skulls, and paper mâché ornaments. Half the restaurant has a low ceiling and the other half has a high arch extending over the low ceiling.

Atmosphere: ★★½ I spent a quiet, rainy, late Saturday lunch here. The clientele was mostly families, but also a few local workers as well. Country music could be heard (barely) from the kitchen.

PALMER LAKE

The town and lake were named after General William J. Palmer of the Denver & Rio Grande Railroad. His railroad was extended to Palmer Lake in 1871. However, the first railroad station at this locale was named Divide and the lake itself was formerly called Divide Lake. The post office in this area was called Weissport, after C.A. Weiss, first station agent for the D & RG. A town plat was filed for Palmer Lake in 1883. The post office changed its name accordingly in 1887.

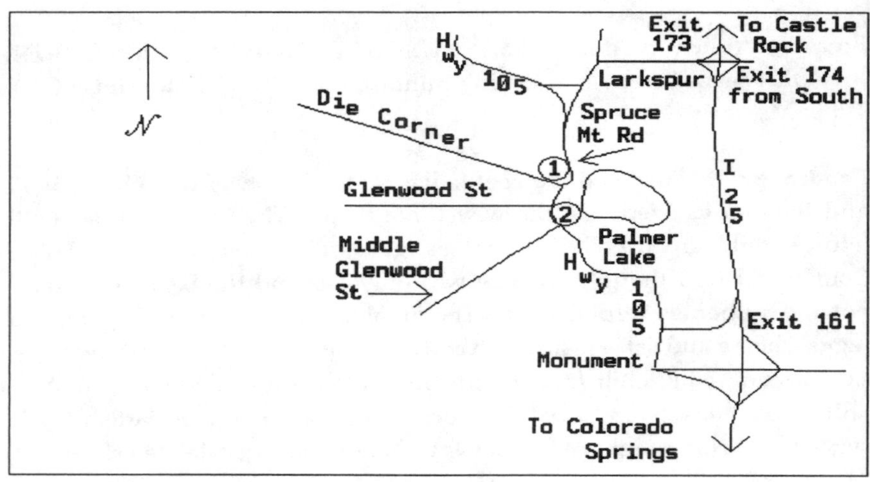

Restaurants and Ratings:	Food	Service	Decor	Atm	Overall
1. O'MALLEY'S PUB	★★½	★★★	★★	★½	★★½
2. ROMAN VILLA	★★★★	★★★★	★★★½	★★★★	★★★★

The Roman Villa offers superb quality Italian food in a Roman style setting featuring classical and operatic music. O'Malley's lets you prepare your own steak or burger on their grill, but the atmosphere is more bar than restaurant. Both restaurants serve alcohol, but only the Roman Villa accepts major credit cards and has a nonsmoking section.

O'MALLEY'S PUB ★★½
104 HIGHWAY 105 (719)488-0321

Lunch/dinner $-$$$. 7 days 11AM-2AM.
Type: Steak.

Food: ★★½ *Service:* ★★★ *Decor:* ★★ *Atmosphere:* ★½

You can grill a half-pound burger or steak to your own personal perfection. I found their thin rib eye with some fat to be quite good. However, their baked potatoes tasted microwaved with very little potato taste. They have a limited menu that includes a modest 10-item salad bar, sandwiches, nachos, hot wings, and chili. Service is very friendly and helpful and appears concerned for the customer's welfare. This pub is a bar/lounge with a small dining room. Beer signs, dart boards, sports trophies, beer bottles, games, and sporting events on television make up the decor. A few boisterous customers don't let you forget this is a bar.

ROMAN VILLA ★★★★
75 HIGHWAY 105 (719)481-2222

Dinner $$-$$$$. SUN-THU: 6PM-9PM. FRI-SAT: 5:30PM-10PM.
Type: Italian (Northern). 15% gratuity added to parties of five or more. This fine restaurant, featuring cuisine of Northern Italy, has been owned and operated by Linda Van Scoten Snyder since 1980. Constructed around the turn-of-the-century by John Lundquist, a Swedish carpenter, "the Villa" has served as a cafe and hotel, post office and ice cream parlor before the Romitti family opened the Roman Villa Restaurant in 1956.

Food: ★★★★ Their salad is a simple Romaine lettuce and cabbage, but the creamy Caesar's and fresh ground pepper add just the right flavor and spice. I ordered the cannelloni Florentine prepared with mushrooms and onions, stuffed with veal and spinach, and topped with a thick, rich marinara sauce. Garden fresh broccoli and green & yellow squash are served on the side. The portions are not large, but the quality is superb. Enjoy one of their desserts, like cheesecake topped with raspberries, spumoni, or a lemon cream puff, with the room you have left. The antipasto dishes include calamari for two, tortelli stuffed with spinach &

mozzarella, and deep-fried mozzarella wrapped in prosciutto. The pasta selections feature spaghetti in a Bolognese sauce (Italian sausage, red wine, tomatoes and herbs), linguini Alfredo, two lasagna dishes (Florentine and Florentine seafood), and cannelloni made with beef. Six veal entrees, including Parmesan, Marsala and saltimbocca; four chicken meals like cacciatori and orvietto (with artichoke hearts); and six fish dishes featuring scallops, mussels, and shrimp complete the dinner menu.

Service: ★★★★ Relaxed, yet efficient and very well-dressed. They exercised professional judgement in deciding when to approach a table.

Decor: ★★★½ This is a two-room restaurant separated by a small bar/lounge. The front dining room with 12 tables for 43 is decorated with pastel paintings and a large wall mural of an Italian village. The bar/lounge has five tables and a few barstools for about 20 people in total. Off the lounge is a very romantic little room with just three tables that seats eight. It is very reclusive and private. The rear dining room with 15 tables for 56 has a piano and a gas fireplace with a mantel atop two Roman columns. The walls around the fireplace are painted with scenes of villages and rural greenery. The back section of this room, which looks onto a patio, has a twisting vine plant hanging from a ceiling trellis with artificial grapes. The pink plaster walls with a combination of smooth and rough finishes are noticeably vacant of decor. Lighting is romantically provided by in-set ceiling lights, kerosene table lamps, woodsy wall lanterns and tiny white Christmas lights in the trellis.

Atmosphere: ★★★★ Classical and operatic music was playing throughout the restaurant when I arrived. The waiters and waitresses are dressed in cummerbunds and black ties. Music from a jazz flute replaced the classical/operatic music as more customers began to arrive. I thought the classical & operatic was more appropriate and in character for the building. This is one of the finest restaurants between Denver and Colorado Springs and well worth a short trip off the main highway.

PARKER

Formerly called Pine Grove, this town was a station on the old Happy Canon Road from Denver to Colorado Springs. The town was later named after James S. Parker, who served 33 years as postmaster. In the early 1860s he was a stage driver on the Smokey Hill South stage route.

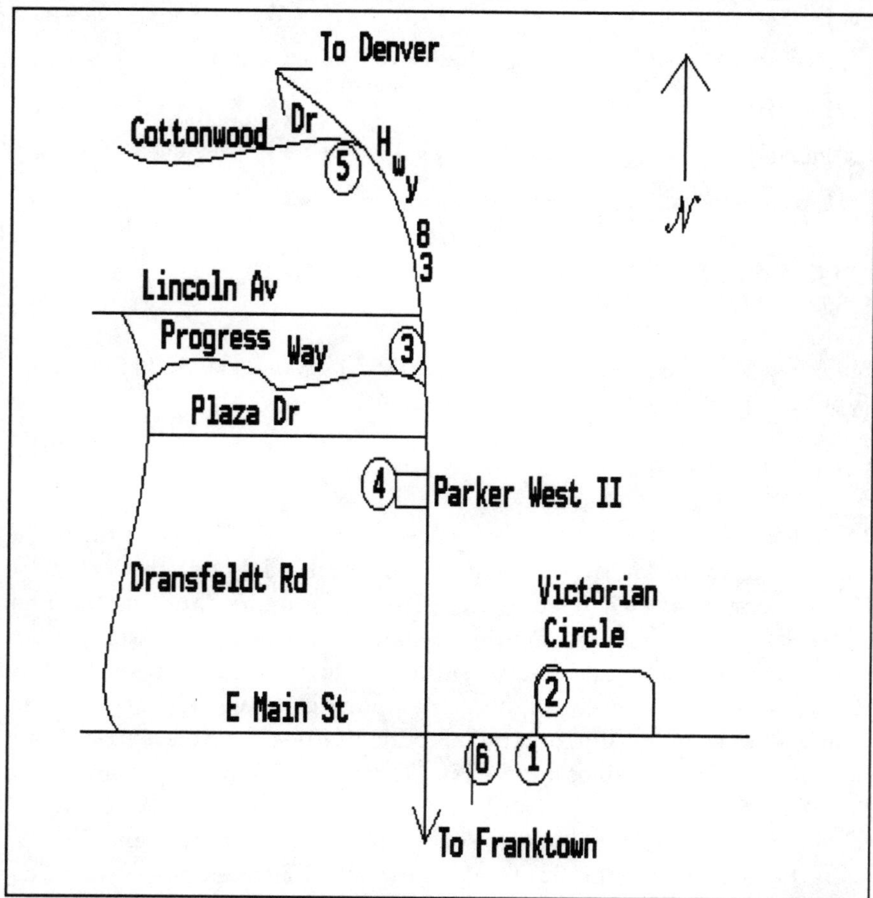

The finest restaurant is the Parker House, specializing in prime rib, steaks, and Mexican food. Betty's serves good sandwiches and curly fries. Prime Time serves a good bargain-lunch buffet and has some very interesting photographs of television and old movie stars: from Laurel and Hardy to Cheers. All of the restaurants accept major credit cards and have nonsmoking sections. Only Betty's does not serve alcohol.

Restaurants and Ratings:	Food	Service	Decor	Atm	Overall
1. Betty's	★★★	★½	★	★	★½
2. El Gallito	★★	★★½	★★½	★★	★★
3. Parker House	★★★★	★★★½	★★★★	★★★★	★★★★
4. Philomena's	★★½	★★★	★★½	★★★	★★½
5. Prime Time	★★★	★★★	★★★½	★★½	★★★
6. The Warhorse	★★½	★★★	★★	★★	★★½

Betty's Bar & Grill ★½
19552 E. Main St. (303)841-7179

Breakfast $, lunch $-$$, dinner $$. MON-SAT 7AM-10PM; SUN 7AM-2PM. Type: Country. They have a "smoke eater".

Food: ★★★ *Service:* ★½ *Decor:* ★ *Atmosphere:* ★

Their Monte Cristo sandwich on grilled Texas toast, served with curly fries and a dill pickle slice, was quite good. Other lunch items include a Philly hoagy sandwich, soup, salad, chili, burgers, and tacos. The breakfast menu includes O'Brien potatoes (potato skins with green peppers & onions). The dinner entrees feature steaks, pot roast, pork chops, spaghetti, seafood platters, and burrito plates. The server was young and friendly, but unfamiliar with the decor. This single-room restaurant with 10 tables for 34 people has part gray carpet and part linoleum for dancing. A band plays here on FRI and SAT. Gray tablecloths and ceilings match the carpet. A mandala, some Indian artifacts, and three cattle skulls adorn the wood-beamed blue walls. The rest of the decor is sparse: some pots and pitchers on a shelf in the rear. No curtains on the windows. A pesky fly bothered me throughout lunch. I sat by the window where there was a dead fly and an ant crawling about. Not surprisingly, there were not very many people.

El Gallito ★★
19553 E. Main St. (303)841-7411

Lunch/dinner $-$$. MON-THU 11AM-9PM. FRI-SAT 11AM-10PM. Closed SUN.
Type: Mexican.

***Food:* ★★ *Service:* ★★½ *Decor:* ★★½ *Atmosphere:* ★★**

My chili relleno was only fair and the rice was undercooked. The lunch/dinner menu includes a Mexican burger smothered with green chili, fajitas, pollo (chicken), carne guisada (tender beef with Mexican gravy), taco salad, huevos rancheros and tamales. The service is authentically Mexican and friendly. The front dining section has five booths and two tables for 24 people. The second larger section has booths along three sides and five tables for 53 people in total. The walls are decorated with colorful terry cloth artworks of Mexican peasants. The window coverings have a pretty fruit pattern on a white background with frills on top. Black metal-framed lamps with frosted glass hang two feet from the ceiling. Red carpet is used for the outer booth area while linoleum is used for the center area with tables. They were not very busy for lunch. Very few customers came in.

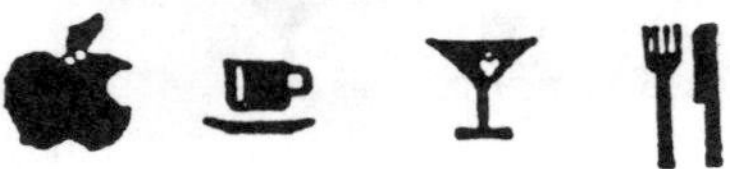

Parker House ★★★★
11473 N. State Hwy. 83 (303)841-0539

Lunch $$, dinner $$-$$$$. MON-FRI 11AM-3PM. MON-SAT 4PM-10PM. Closed SUN.
Type: Steak.

***Food:* ★★★★** They have excellent buffalo burgers and steaks. All of their food is high quality. Lunch items include sandwiches, such as cold prime rib, the Parker Philly, and pork tenderloin; soup; a limited Mexican fare that features chimichangas and fajitas; croissants, including one with shrimp; quiche Lorraine; taco or pasta salad; and a diet plate. They have homemade pies for dessert. The dinner menu features Rocky Mountain oysters, a soup and salad bar, steak or veal entrees, seafood selections (Alaskan king crab legs or lobster tail, shrimp and Rocky Mountain rainbow trout), surf and turf combinations, shrimp fettuccini, pork tenderloin schnitzel, a half-dozen Mexican dinners, a child's menu, and a few light selections.

Service: ★★★½ Service is most accommodating.

Decor: ★★★★ This restaurant has three dining rooms with smoking and nonsmoking sections. The first room has 12 tables for 38 people. The second room has 11 tables for 35 people and the last room has 10 booths, four tables and a bar for 66 people. This attractive restaurant is accentuated by red-brick interior walls, a stone fireplace, appealing light fixtures hanging from the wood-beamed ceiling, white curtains, and a walnut cabinet with mirrors. The walls are adorned with large brass plates and pictures of a red, lake-side cabin with an orange sky; a cattle drive; and an American Indian holding a baby.

Atmosphere: ★★★★ The clientele is mostly professionals. It is quiet and the most comfortable place in Parker.

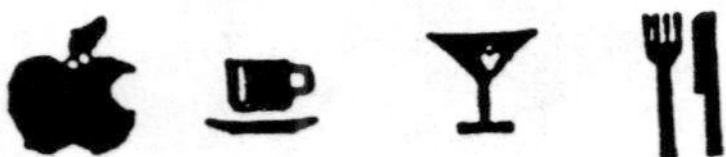

PHILOMENA'S ★★½
10471 PARKER RD. (303)841-4456

Lunch $-$$, dinner $$-$$$. MON-THU 11AM-9PM; FRI-SAT 11AM-10PM; SUN 10AM-8PM.
Type: Italian (with some Mexican, seafood and American).

***Food:* ★★½ *Service:* ★★★ *Decor:* ★★½ *Atmosphere:* ★★★**

I found the pasta to be on the bland side and the pizza to be a little too crusty. The lunch/dinner menu is quite extensive with jalapeño cheese bites and bite-size catfish for appetizers, soup and salads, calzones, pasta al pesto, spaghetti with clam sauce, manicotti, lasagna, three seafood selections, steaks, chicken or veal parmesan, Louisiana catfish, honey-dipped fried chicken, four Mexican dishes, pizza, sandwiches, burgers, a children's menu, and for dessert, spumoni, sundaes, and cheesecake. The service was friendly and jovial. This two-room restaurant has a bar and six tables in the first room for 32 people and seven booths and nine tables in the second room for 64 people. Maroon and black are the dominant colors. The country-kitchen-style wall decor includes an eggbeater, baskets, rolling pins, a spice grinder, a brass pail, crêpe pans, and a large 40-inch wreath. This restaurant is slow and quiet at lunch, but a popular place after work. Soft rock music was playing in the background.

PRIME TIME ★★★
17904 COTTONWOOD DR. (303)699-1010

Sunday breakfast buffet $, lunch $-$$, dinner $$-$$$. Daily 11AM-10PM. Type: Steak. The lunch and Sunday breakfast buffets are a bargain and the decor is entertaining enough to warrant a visit.

Food: ★★★ I had their all-you-can-eat lunch buffet which included soup, salad bar, fried chicken, mashed potatoes with gravy, and green beans. The chicken was a little underdone, but still good with the seasonings. The buffet menu changes daily. Their lunch/dinner menu has six appetizers, including shrimp cocktail and chicken wings; burgers; sandwiches, such as a patty melt, Italian sausage or meatball; a limited selection of Mexican entrees like chimichangas and fajitas; steaks; shrimp; snow crab; mahi mahi; barbecued beef ribs; and eggplant Parmesan. The choices for dessert include strawberry cheesecake, sundaes, chocolate mousse, and mud pie. The Sunday breakfast buffet includes eggs and meats, biscuits and gravy, waffles, and fruit, to mention a few items.

Service: ★★★ The service was friendly, helpful and informative.

Decor: ★★★½ This restaurant is one long, narrow room with five booths and 12 tables, plus a table for eight in the rear behind the buffet table and glass wall. Total seating for 64 people. To the left of the restaurant is a tavern with 12 barstools and seven tables. This is one of the most entertaining restaurants I visited in Colorado. The photos of television stars from the 50s through the 90s and the old movie comic greats includes such notables as the Star Trek Crew, Alfred Hitchcock, The Three Stooges, The Odd Couple (Jack Klugman and Tony Randall), I Love Lucy, Laurel and Hardy, the Golden Girls, Saturday Night Live, Cheers, David Letterman, plus many others. It is worth a stop here just to look at the walls.

Atmosphere: ★★½ There is a better crowd inside than what you might expect from the looks of the place outside. The clientele is a combination of business people and young people in cut-offs and t-shirts.

THE WARHORSE ★★½
19420 E. MAIN ST. (303)841-4018

Lunch/dinner $$. SUN-MON 11:30AM-9PM. TUE-THU 11:30AM-9:30PM. FRI-SAT 11:30AM-10PM.
Type: Steak. 50¢ charge for orders to go. 50¢ charge for substitutions. Personal checks with Colorado driver's license accepted.

Food: ★★½ ***Service:*** ★★★ ***Decor:*** ★★ ***Atmosphere:*** ★★

I liked the Mexican fare here. The menu offers mushrooms tempura, jalapeño Buffalo wings, soup, salads, fajitas, Mexican London broil, steaks, baby-back ribs, fried chicken, sandwiches, burgers, and, for dessert, pound cake with ice cream, or cheesecake with strawberries. The service was very friendly, courteous and helpful. Three sections seat a total of 114 people. Old-time photos of Parker, circa 1920, and American Indian paintings and rugs decorate the walls. A statue of a horse stands over the entrance on the inside. The ceilings are very high, about 16 feet, with exposed pipes and lamps on long chords hanging to within three feet of the booth tables. I found this very unattractive. Televisions and speakers made this place a little noisy.

PENROSE

The town was named after Spencer Penrose, Colorado Springs capitalist and largest stockholder of the Beaver Park Land & Water Company which established Penrose.

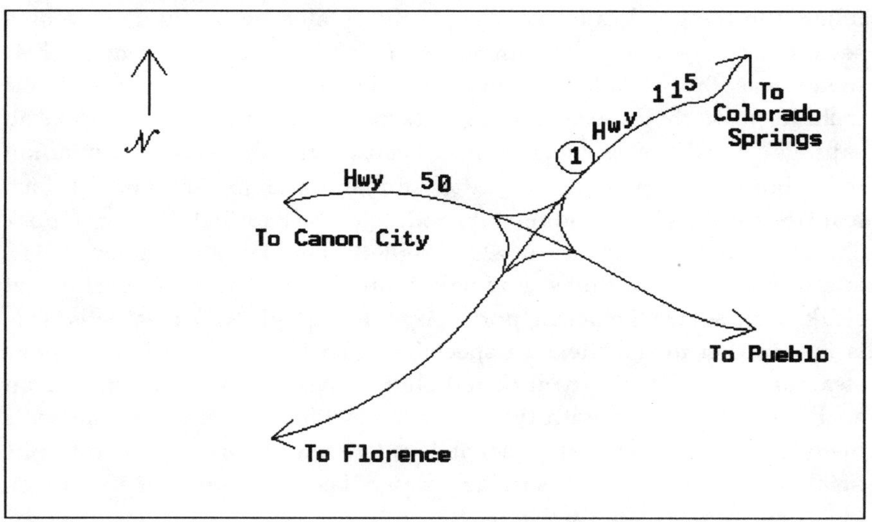

1. Mr. C's ★★★
895 Hwy 115 (719)372-6767

Breakfast $, lunch $-$$, dinner $-$$$ (a few $$$$ and $$$$+). Summer: SUN-THU 7AM-9PM (10PM FRI-SAT). Winter: SUN-THU 8AM-8PM (9PM FRI-SAT).
Type: Mexican (with steaks and seafood). Extra plate charge $1.50. They accept major credit cards, have a nonsmoking section, and serve alcohol.

Food: ★★★ I ordered the chili relleno plate: a full platter with two chili rellenos smothered with shredded cheese and green chili (red also available) with rice and beans. The stringy cheese is harder to eat than long spaghetti and the green chilies are buried somewhere underneath, but they are there. This is a challenge to finish. Personally, I did not care for the fluffy egg batter. I had eaten at this restaurant five years earlier and had forgotten how much egg they use in their batter. It is like a chili relleno wrapped in a fried egg. The refried beans were a pasty concoction and the rice with red and green peppers were dry. You do get two very large chilies, though, with quite a few pieces of pork in the green chili sauce. Either I have changed or Mr. C's has. Five years ago I would have rated their food excellent. More recently, I think it has fallen into the good category. People that I talked to in the Pueblo area seem to agree with my assessment. As I recall, my favorite item on their menu was the Matador (a smothered burrito). The breakfast items include pork chops, beef patties, huevos rancheros, chorizo (Mexican sausage), breakfast burritos, refried beans, Spanish rice, hot cinnamon rolls, buttermilk pancakes tortillas and avocado (in season). Lunch features sandwiches (sirloin, club, cod, and chicken filet), burgers, pork chops, shrimp & chicken baskets, spaghetti, tamales, stuffed sopapillas, and taco salads. For dinner you have your choice of several selections of steak, seafood, fried chicken, pork chops, and spaghetti & meatballs. This is in addition to the Mexican specialties like boneless chicken or pork steak smothered with green or red chili, a Mexican hamburger, and an enchilada torte made with two soft corn tortillas. There is a children's menu. A shrimp cocktail, guacamole salad or nachos can start off your meal. Ice cream, sherbet, sundaes, sopapillas with honey or ice cream, pies, or cheesecake can finish it off.

Service: ★★★ Straight forward and good.

Decor: ★★★½ There are two dining rooms. The front has six booths and eight tables with orange-vinyl chairs for a total of 62 people. Water colors (for sale) of ranches, corrals, yellow roses, ristras and landscapes decorate the white plaster walls above the wood paneling. There is a fireplace and hanging & potted philodendrons. Ample lighting is provided by octagon-shaped ceiling structures and brass, white, glass wall fixtures. The rear dining room has 14 tables for 70 on red-cushioned, black-framed chairs. The decor is actually more interesting in the less-used rear dining room with stone and stucco walls, fireplace, and country-style pictures. There is a lounge to the right of the front dining room with five tables, seven barstools and a television.

Atmosphere: ★★★ They played very pleasant, easy listening, music for an adult clientele.

PINECLIFFE

Originally called Gato, the Spanish word for "wildcat", Pinecliffe was named around the turn-of-the-century by Dr. Craig, a minister, for the beautiful pines on a nearby cliff.

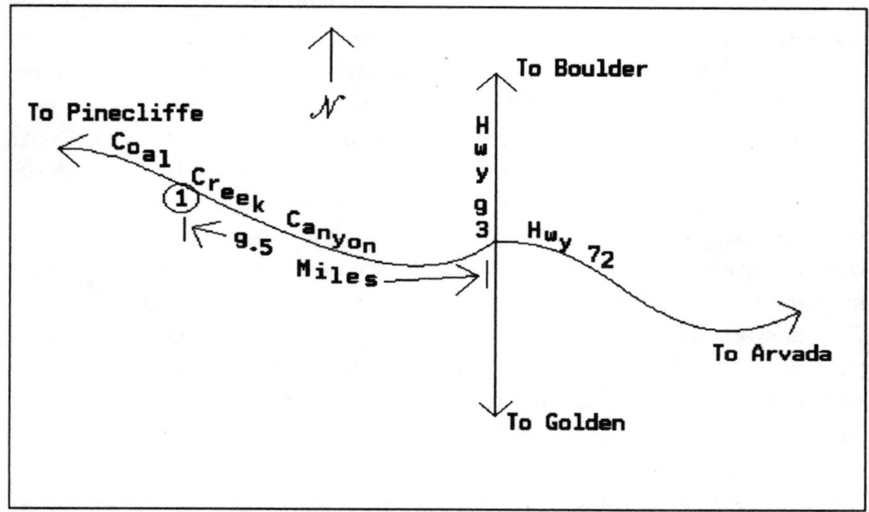

1. **Copperdale Inn ★★★★**
   32138 Hwy 72 (Five miles East of Pinecliffe in Coal Creek Canyon) (303)642-9994 or 642-3180

Dinner $$$-$$$$ ($$ for sandwiches & salads). TUE-SAT 5PM-9PM. SUN 12PM-8PM. Closed MON.
Type: German (Austrian and American). Major credit cards accepted, nonsmoking section provided, alcohol served. No separate checks. $2.50 charge on split dinners. 15% gratuity added on parties of five or more. Cholesterol free oils and fats used in cooking. All dinners cooked to order. Early dinner specials served TUE-FRI 5PM-6:30PM for $9.95.

Food: ★★★★ Their homemade soup was a delicious combination of all your favorite vegetables and slivered almonds. My pork and beef Bratwurst was very lean, tender and juicy, as was my smoked pork loin. The potato pancake was heavenly: nicely browned on the outside with a wonderful consistency. (I could have eaten a half-dozen). The red cabbage was sweet and delicious. All of this was served with apple sauce, candied apple, ground mustard and horseradish on the side. For a lighter meal you can order a sandwich (Bratwurst, Knackwurst, corned beef & Swiss, Reuben, and burgers), or chef salad. For an appetizer try marinated herring in sour cream, camembert or brie cheese, or smoked salmon. The German entrees feature smoked beef Knackwurst, veal Bratwurst, hot German potato salad, sauerkraut, cabbage rolls, Vienna rostbraten (braised NY steak, Viennese style), chicken Kiev, beef Stroganoff, Wiener schnitzel, schnitzel holstein (veal cutlet topped with fried egg), jaeger schnitzel, sauerbraten, veal Cordon Bleu, zigeuner schnitzel (veal cutlet with paprika & peppers sauce), and medallions of venison. If you are more of an American food eater, you can choose from a variety of seafood and steak entrees: filet of cod, Rocky Mountain rainbow trout, fantail shrimp, lobster tail, shrimp scampi, or filet mignon. The dessert list includes French vanilla ice cream, frozen raspberry yogurt, a daily pie, apple strudel, torts (chocolate raspberry, black forest, Viennese walnut, and German chocolate), mint parfaits, and chocolate sundaes. Espresso and cappuccino are also offered.

Service: ★★★ Friendly, courteous and adequate, but not overly attentive.

Decor: ★★★★ The restaurant overlooks a valley to the south with several hills beyond: a beautiful sight from the nonsmoking section. Posters of Innsbruck and Tirol, Austria, a sketch of the Trapp Family Lodge in Stowe, VT, and paintings of castles, snow-capped peaks and pine forests adorn the maroon and beige print wallpaper. This is a "woodsy" place with wood-framed windows, doors, dividers and ceiling. There is seating for about 80 at 24 tables set with kerosene lamps. Gold curtains and brass wall fixtures separate the row of southerly and easterly windows. The openings in the wall dividers have very attractive arrangements of wicker shades, green pompons and antlers. The front smoking section, with piano, organ and five-stool bar, features antlers hanging below the ceiling light fixtures.

Atmosphere: ★★★★½ They play tapes of Austrian tunes (accordion and organ instrumentals and female vocals) until 7PM when owner John Wallinger, who studied music in Salsburg, plays the piano and organ. This place has the setting and sounds of a true Austrian/German Inn.

PINE JUNCTION

Pine Junction is probably not on your map. It lies half-way between Conifer and Bailey on Hwy. 285 at the junction with the road that leads south to Pine and Buffalo Creek. It is six miles west of Conifer and six miles east of Bailey on the border between Jefferson and Park counties.

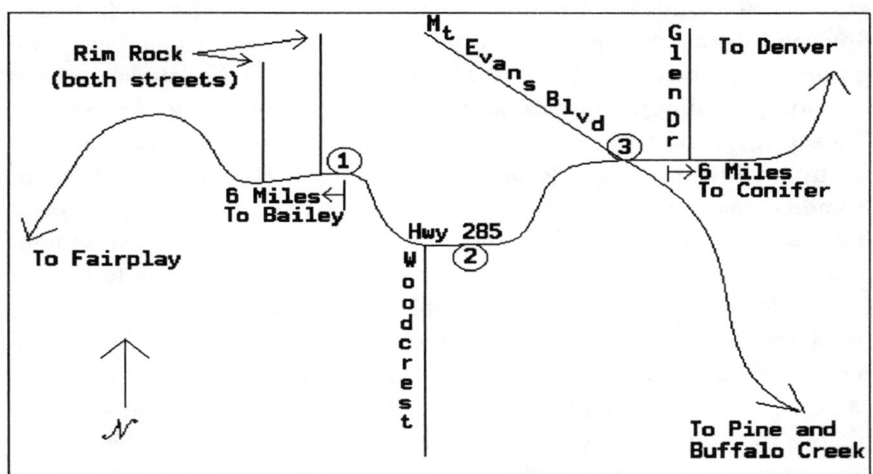

Restaurants and Ratings:	Food	Service	Decor	Atm	Overall
1. Red Rooster Inn	★★★½	★★½	★★★	★★★	★★★
2. Reggie's Will O' the Wisp	★★★★	★★★½	★★½	★★★½	★★★½
3. Woodside Inn	★★	★★	★★★½	★★½	★★½

Reggie's serves excellent lasagna while the Red Rooster offers a deliciously different omelet. Both are in a country setting offering outdoor seating. All three accept major credit cards. Only the Woodside Inn has nonsmoking. Only the Red Rooster does not serve alcohol.

Red Rooster Inn ★★★
16 Mt Evans Blvd (303)838-4537

Breakfast/lunch $-$$, dinner $$-$$$. 7 days 7AM-2AM.
Type: Country.

Food: ★★★½ For a uniquely different breakfast, try the chef's omelet: chock full of chicken livers, mushrooms, onions and cheese. It is quite good. Most of the members of our hiking group were well-pleased with their breakfasts. One member raved about the biscuits and sausage gravy. The biscuits were genuine homemade, the gravy did not taste like flour and the sausage was very good. However, another member of the group complained that the link sausage was fatty. We left her on the trail (only kidding). You can start your day here with eggs Benedict or Oscar, ham steak, or rainbow trout. The lunch menu has a wide selection starting with appetizers (sautéed brandied mushrooms, bull fries in brandied sauce, homemade onion rings, and peel & eat shrimp), French onion soup, red or green chili, and salads (house, chef, a stuffed tomato, and a vegetable or fruit plate). There are several sandwiches to choose from: Monte Cristo, club, hot or cold beef or turkey, tuna or chicken salad, Italian sausage or meatball, French dip, cold ham and burgers. The lunch entrees include chicken fried steak, spaghetti, chicken Marsala or Madeira, a luncheon steak, deep-fried rainbow trout, and a low-calorie plate. The dinner entrees feature fried chicken, sautéed or deep-fried chicken livers, shrimp scampi in garlic sauce or sweet mustard, filet of sole, deep-fried shrimp or rainbow trout, filet mignon, steak Oscar, and chicken Marsala, Madeira or piccata.

Service: ★★½ Satisfactory.

Decor: ★★★ Outside, the front has a very attractive black-iron fence on top of a stone wall. Beyond this is the Bier Garden with a black-iron gate entrance and three tables. Inside, to the left of the entrance, is a counter for 12, three tables and a booth. The dining room to the right has six tables and a booth for 25. There is a combination of wood walls and floors with red-velvet wallpaper and red carpet. The walls and mantel behind the wood-burning stove are decorated with copper pots, kettles, ladles and a caldron. There are three paintings: a scene of Venice; a portly, elderly gentleman with a smile looking over a vegetable stand; and an equally charming picture of a cobblestone alley with water barrels, potted flowers, and a wine bottle hanging from a balcony. Take a look up at the placard board ceiling. It is completely covered from end to end with graffiti. Seating is on red-cushioned chairs with white trim in varnished-wood frames. The tables have pink cloths covered with glass.

Atmosphere: ★★★ New age music, which I find appealing, plays in the background. This is a quiet place with mostly local people. The restaurant is difficult to see coming from Denver because it faces to the southwest, which may account for the lack of tourists.

REGGIE'S WILL O' THE WISP ★★★½
66803 HWY 285 (303)838-2092

SUN brunch $$, lunch $-$$, dinner $$-$$$ (a few $$$$). 7 days 11AM-10PM Type: Italian. 15% gratuity added to parties of six or more. All menu items available for take-out. $.30 box charge.

Food: ★★★★ I ordered the lasagna which comes with garlic bread and salad. I recommend the house Parmesan pepper dressing. The lasagna was excellent: layers of pasta noodles with ricotta, Parmesan and melted mozzarella, ground beef, Italian sausage, and a delicious tomato sauce properly spiced with oregano, basil and Italian seasonings. If you are hungry on your way back to Denver on a Sunday afternoon, this would be a good stop. The lasagna is also offered for Sunday brunch, which includes eggs Benedict or Oscar, NY steak, pork chops, and a vegetarian omelet. You can start off lunch with mushrooms in melted cheese, jalapeño peppers stuffed with cream or cheddar cheese, or an antipasto salad; continue with a burger, sandwich (French dip, NY steak, or chicken teriyaki), hot or cold Italian sandwich (meatball, sausage, salami & cheese, or vegetarian), a lunch entree (veggie lasagna, ravioli, spaghetti, fish & chips or Hawaiian chicken), a calzone, or a bowl of homemade soup. Pizza is available on homemade crust with 18 toppings to choose from in four different sizes. The dinner menu adds shrimp cocktail and onion rings to the list of lunch appetizers. Steaks, chicken, seafood and Italian are the featured dinner entrees: filet mignon, steak Oscar, chicken piccata or barbecue, trout almondine, salmon, shrimp scampi, crab legs, fettucini Alfredo, spaghetti & meatballs, and eggplant or veal Parmigiana to name a few. Pork chops, roast duck a l'orange and pizza are also on the menu. There is a senior citizens menu (55 and over) and most items on the dinner menu are available at half price for children.

Service: ★★★½ Friendly, courteous and pleasant.

Decor: ★★½ There is a deck enclosed in a yellow trellis perimeter that seats 30 to 35 at six varnished-wood tables with yellow umbrellas. The bar/lounge inside has eight barstools, four tables, a television and a video game. The bar is decorated with Michelob ceiling lampshades and several beer posters framed under glass. The dining room has 15 tables and six booths for a total of 84 people, a band stand, dance floor, and piano. The walls are decorated with paintings of mountains, lakes, country houses and barns, a collage of children & ducks playing in a pond, a wagon wheel, milk buckets, and other assorted items of country flavor. Posters of beer, vodka, wine coolers and John Wayne are also displayed. There are white-laced curtains in the windows and artificial flowers at every table.

Atmosphere: ★★★½ A combination of country cowboys and families. Despite the heavy local flavor, I did not get the impression that tourists were unwelcome. Owner Reggie reminded me of General George Armstrong Custer, or maybe it was Richard Mulligan, playing the part of General Custer in the movie "Little Big Man", that I was reminded of. On Fridays and Saturdays starting at 7PM and on Sundays starting at 5PM they have a big band, blues, jazz, ragtime, or Reggie's band playing.

WOODSIDE INN ★★½
67349 HWY 285 (303)838-9803

Breakfast/lunch $-$$, dinner $$-$$$. JUN-SEP: 7 days 7AM-10PM. OCT-MAY: 7 days 7AM-9PM.
Type: Country. 15% gratuity added to parties of 6 or more. No separate checks.

Food: ★★ *Service:* ★★ *Decor:* ★★★½ *Atmosphere:* ★★½

All of our breakfasts — six of them — were served lukewarm. Eggs ordered sunny-side up were served over hard. My hash browns were a combination of hard-stuck-together and underdone. Otherwise, most of the meals were good (biscuits & gravy, eggs Florentine, French toast, sausage & eggs and a Denver omelet) — just not warm enough. The portions were big. The Denver omelet had a spicy sauce and was very filling. The owner's daughter, Nancy, was a "hoot"! I asked for "cream, half & half, or milk" for my coffee and she responded with "the cow ran away!" When she returned later and I asked if the cow had come home, she said "our cow lays eggs!!" When I asked if that meant their chicken gives milk, she just gave me a strange look. Service was a little slow. This is a very rustic country restaurant with nailed-down wood chairs at tables with red & white checkered tablecloths, pine walls, and log beams on a slanted ceiling. The nonsmoking section to the right seats 24. The main dining room to the left seats 60. The bar can seat 20 and is adorned with posters of shapely young ladies selling beer and skis. Country music played softly from the bar. They have a live band on FRI & SAT.

Copperdale Inn — Pinecliffe

PLATTEVILLE

The town was named after the nearby South Platte River and founded by the Platte River Land Co., which purchased several thousand acres in the South Platte and St. Vrain River valleys.

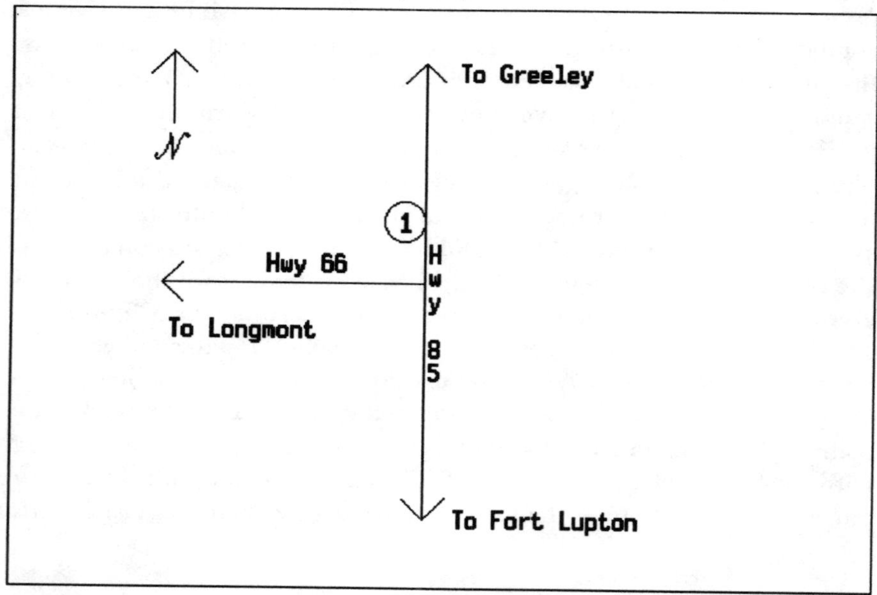

1. Double Tree ★★★½
701 Vasquez (West side of Hwy 85) (303)785-2238

Breakfast $, lunch $-$$, dinner $-$$$. MON-THU 6AM-10PM. FRI-SAT 6AM-11PM. SUN 6AM-8PM.
Type: Country. 15% gratuity added to parties of eight or more. Major credit cards are accepted and they serve alcohol, but do not offer a nonsmoking section.

Food: **★★★★½** When you think of Double Tree think of Thursday when their special is kraut burgers. I had one, without French fries, for only $2, then ordered three more to go. They were sensational! The meat is not the least bit greasy, the sauerkraut is chopped and it all comes in an enclosed white bread dough bun. Simply scrumptious. They also have terrific homemade pies. My fellow diners and I tried the coconut cream and banana cream. They were huge slices — almost a quarter of a pie —

with mounds of whipped cream and had a fresh, clean taste. Leave your calorie counter at home when you visit this restaurant and simply enjoy! The breakfast choices are Texas French toast, a breakfast burrito, huevos rancheros, Belgian waffles with fruit, and cinnamon rolls. The lunch menu features nachos; Rocky Mountain oysters; burgers; sandwiches, such as Italian sausage, rib eye, and a seafood salad croissant; light meals, such as quiche, or a fruit plate; homemade soup, chili or oyster stew; a salad bar; and dinner selections, including steaks, barbecued pork ribs, broiled or fried chicken, and jumbo butterfly shrimp. Several ice cream treats, pastries and pies are offered for dessert. The dinner menu is very similar to the lunch menu with additional items like orange roughy and broiled lobster tail. They have other specials during the week: chicken on SUN, T-bone on SUN-WED, and prime rib on FRI-SAT.

Service: ★★★ The service was a little slow during the very busy lunch hour, but it was friendly.

Decor: ★★★ This is a two-room restaurant with a cafe in front and a dining room in the rear. The cafe has five red-cushioned booths, five tables with red-cushioned chairs, and a counter for four. Total seating capacity in this room is 45. The dining room has seven booths and nine tables for a total of 72 people. The entrance to the rear dining room has a sign reading "Outhouse," which I thought was a peculiar name for a dining room. When I mentioned this, one of my fellow diners quipped, "limited dining." The sign was, of course, for the rest rooms which just happened to be where the cafe and dining room meet. Despite the white, concrete-block walls in the cafe, the decor does have some redeeming qualities, like the salmon curtains; the wall shelf with a toy train, oil cans, a miniature fire truck and bottles; pictures of nineteenth century gunslingers; a rack with purses for sale; pans and ladles; handsaws with panoramic pictures on the sides; and wagon wheel chandeliers. The dining room features a large mural on the rear wall showing mountains and lakes in autumn; mirrors; and a fireplace on the wall to the right.

Atmosphere: ★★★ There were a lot of local folks and ranchers here at lunch time. It got very busy with a lot of conversation, but it was not excessively noisy.

PONCHA SPRINGS

The town was named for Poncha Pass which lies just to the south. The word poncha may have derived from the Spanish word "pancho" meaning "paunch" or "belly", which describes the low bend in the mountain range found here. It may also have come from an Indian word meaning tobacco. A weed that grew on the pass was given this name and was an excellent substitute for tobacco. The springs, 99 of them, are located about three quarters of a mile north of town.

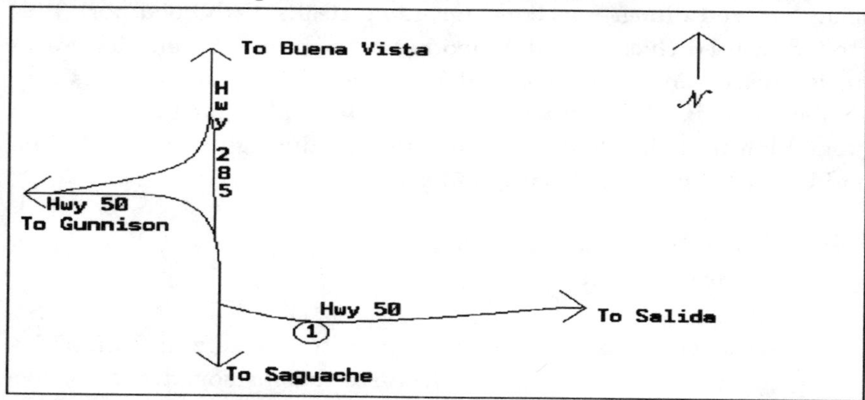

1. PONCHA TRUCK STOP CAFE ★★½
525 EAST HWY 50 (719)539-9907

Breakfast/lunch $, dinner $-$$. SUN-THU 6AM-9PM (10PM in summer). FRI-SAT 6AM-10PM.
Type: Cafe. Credit cards are accepted, there is no nonsmoking section, and they do not serve alcohol.

***Food:* ★★★ *Service:* ★ ½ *Decor:* ★★½ *Atmosphere:* ★★½**

They serve good burgers here. I ordered their Durango burger, with green chili and Swiss. Guacamole and French fries are served on the side. They have a 20 item soup/salad/fruit/dessert bar. Service was average. There is seating for 88 at 11 booths, nine tables and eight counter stools. Paintings of cowboys rustling cattle adorn the finished, but natural-looking wood walls. A row of windows extends along the front and right side. You can spend money at an adjacent gift shop or play the juke box. There were a lot of tourists combined with the locals.

PUEBLO WEST

Located just eight miles west of Pueblo on Hwy. 50, you might consider stopping here on your way to Cañon City.

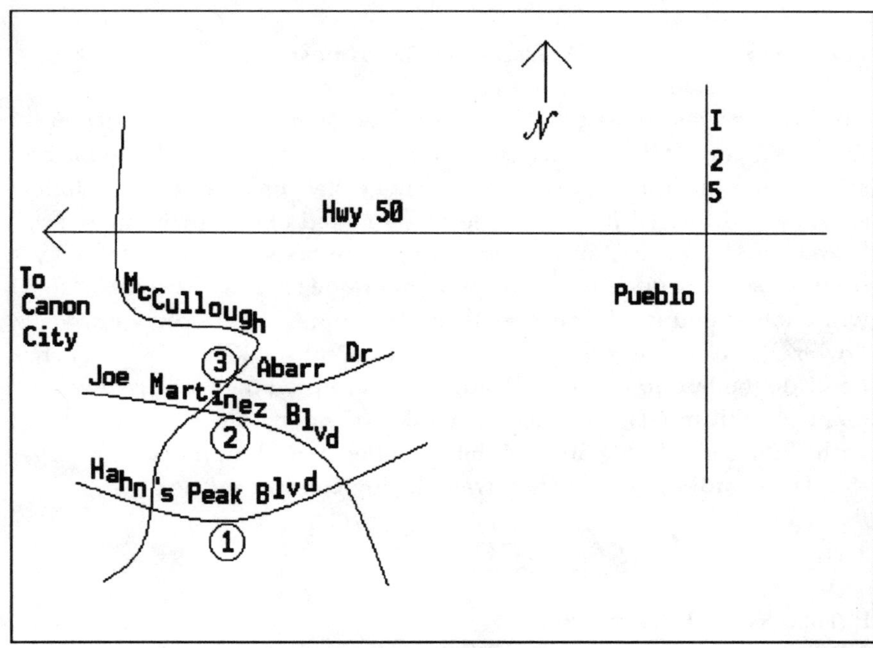

Restaurants and Ratings:	Food	Service	Decor	Atm	Overall
1. BRUCE'S	★½	★★½	★★½	★★	★★
2. PUEBLO WEST DELI	★★★	★★★	★★	★★	★★½
3. PUEBLO WEST INN	★★★½	★★	★★★★½	★★★	★★★½

The Pueblo West Inn serves very good steaks. The Pueblo West Deli has good chili and sandwiches. Only the Pueblo West Inn accepts major credit cards and serves alcohol. None of the restaurants offer nonsmoking sections.

BRUCE'S ★★
26 W. HAHN'S PEAK (719)547-0279

Lunch/dinner $ (Pizza $$). MON-THU 11AM-8PM. FRI-SAT 11AM-9PM. SUN 11:30AM-6:30PM.
Type: Diner.

Food: ★½ *Service:* ★★½ *Decor:* ★★½ *Atmosphere:* ★★

My burger was greasy. The French fries were fair. Bruce's offers a limited menu of thin crust pizza (anchovies available), burgers, and sandwiches such as a patty melt, chicken filet, breaded cod, or Italian sausage. Additional items include green or red chili, onion rings, fresh baked pie, ice cream, and cider. Orders are taken at the counter by a friendly server and cook. This is a small one-room restaurant with 11 white tables and red formica seats for 44 people. Nature photographs of flowers, wild mushrooms, and the Spanish Peaks, taken by a local artist, decorate the burlap fabric wallpaper. Higher up on the wall are three red mantels with mugs, candles, and bottles of cider. The room is well lit with fluorescent lights and exhibits a better look than most hamburger stands. A radio in the kitchen was playing country music.

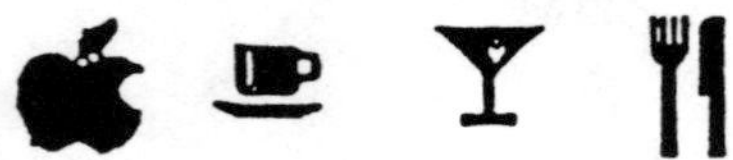

PUEBLO WEST DELI ★★½
279 JOE MARTINEZ BLVD. (719)547-3400

Lunch/dinner $-$$. MON-SAT 10:30AM-8PM. Summer: SUN 11AM-6PM. Winter: Closed SUN.
Type: Deli.

Food: ★★★ *Service:* ★★★ *Decor:* ★★ *Atmosphere:* ★★

The Savage, their version of the Philly steak sandwich, comes with three kinds of cheese and is very good. I would recommend it with a bowl of soup or chili. Other sandwich specials feature barbecue beef with jalapeño, a couple of vegetarian sandwiches, a French dip, a club, a grilled Reuben and a Monte Cristo made with Russian dressing. Eight-inch and 16-inch submarine sandwiches are also offered. The hot subs include cappicola, smoked turkey, and Danish ham. Cold salad subs and diet-salad platters are available in the following varieties: tuna, egg, chicken, turkey, and crab. Dogwood sandwiches are featured with various meats and Russian dressing on rye. Items from the grill include pepper or cheese steak, barbecue beef or ham, Italian or Polish sausage, burgers, pastrami and corned beef. No dessert items. Friendly and courteous counter service. This is a small one-room deli with only seven tables for 28 people. The decor is sparse. Pictures of sailing ships adorn the striped wallpaper which has a narrow strip of sailing ships bordering the wood panels below. The room is well lit with bright single lights under large metallic shades hanging on one-foot chains from the acoustic tile ceiling. There is a small ristra on one wall and a lifesaver on another. This is a busy place at meal times, but otherwise empty.

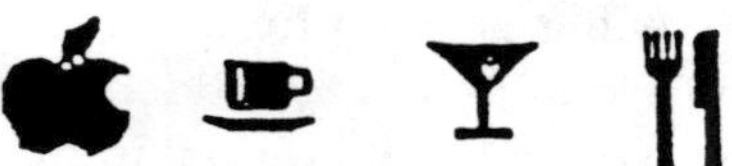

PUEBLO WEST INN ★★★½
201 S. MCCULLOCH (IN THE BEST WESTERN MOTEL) (719)547-2111

Breakfast/lunch $, dinner $$. MON-THUR 6AM-9PM. FRI-SAT 6AM-10PM. SUN 6AM-9PM.
Type: Family.

***Food:* ★★★½** Their cream of broccoli soup was very good. However, I felt they could improve the 20-item salad bar with more than three choices of dressing. It was only fair quality. The petite sirloin, medium-rare, was done just the way I like it. Breakfast features daily omelet specials, blueberry muffins, and — something I had not seen in a restaurant before — broiled grapefruit topped with brown sugar. The lunch menu offers stuffed mushrooms or potato skins as appetizers, a soup & salad bar, taco salads, western omelets, vegetarian stir fry, a light entree, and sandwiches. The dinner menu features six steak entrees, five chicken entrees, four fish entrees, and liver & onions. A few of the more notable entrees are boneless chicken with either wine & mushroom sauce or salsa & Cheddar, breaded shrimp, mahi mahi, Cajun snapper and trout amandine.

PUEBLO WEST

Service: ★★ I had a friendly, but inefficient waiter. He was quick to help light the kerosene lamp, answer my questions about the balcony, and run copies of the menu. However, I ordered the chopped steak with mushrooms and he brought me the petite sirloin ($2.70 more) instead. He also forgot to bring fresh rolls & butter.

Decor: ★★★★½ This restaurant has two dining rooms and an adjacent bar/lounge. The main dining room, divided by the soup & salad bar, has seven tables on the left side and 13 tables on the right for 84 people in total. The second dining room, used only when it gets busy, has 12 tables for 52. The lounge, with a big-screen television in the corner, has 12 barstools plus seating for 22 at nine tables. In the main dining room a vaulted, wood-beamed ceiling goes up from left to right, ending over a narrow balcony with no access except by ladder. The balcony is the best feature of the restaurant, with a black-iron rail in front and Spanish arch imprints in the wall behind. On the ground level, seating is on solid-colored, cushioned seats in a variety of colors: red, green, black, tan, blue, and orange. The table settings feature gray cloths, green paper table mats, kerosene lamps and turquoise napkins. There are two huge, eight-lamp, wagon-wheel chandeliers made from black-iron and yellow-tinted glass. The left wall is bare. The front and rear walls have four pictures of Indian pottery and four yellow-tinted wall lamps. The right wall, under the balcony, has two glass doors and two windows the size of doors leading to the courtyard. This dimly lit room has a romantic atmosphere. The second dining room has a single large mirror along the back wall, two ceiling fans, hanging plants, and no artworks. I gave an extra star for the balcony.

Atmosphere: ★★★ I was here in January, a dead month for Pueblo West and most other places north of the 38th parallel. Only one other table was occupied, by three young fellows who talked in whispers. The second dining room was set up for a banquet. According to the waiter, the balcony has only been used once in recent history: for a New Year's Eve celebration. The lounge's regular musician had his instruments hoisted up to the balcony for the occasion.

RIFLE

Rifle took its name from nearby Rifle Creek, which obtained its name from a small incident that occurred about 1880. Some soldiers were placing mile posts on the road between Meeker and the site of present-day Rifle. One of the men left his rifle at a night camp and when he returned for it, he found it on the bank of a stream which was immediately named Rifle Creek.

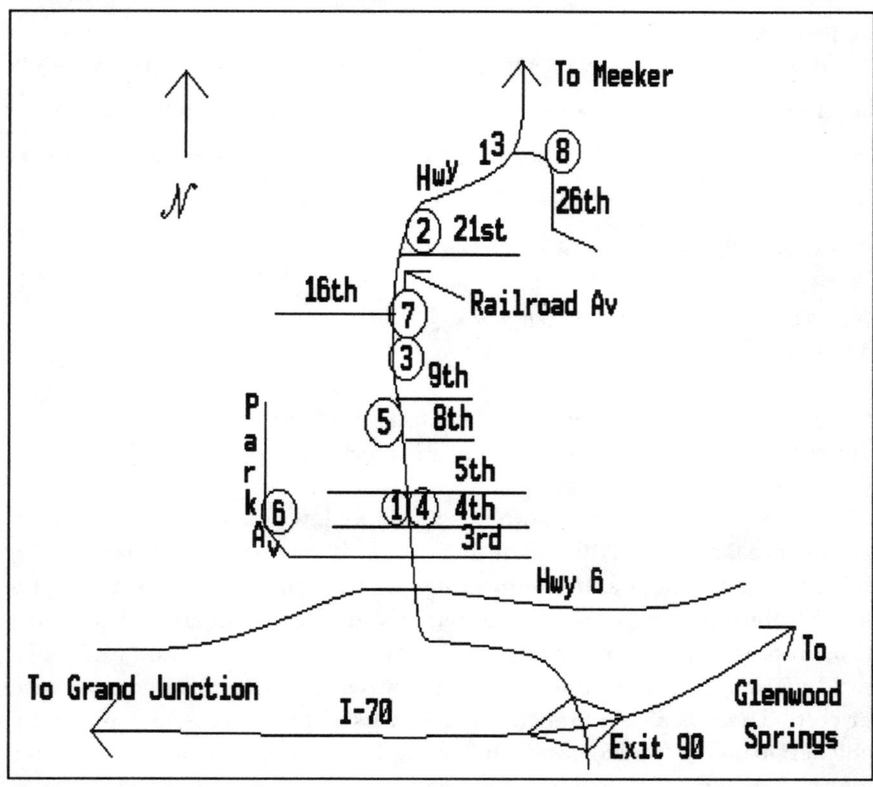

The best overall restaurant is the First National Fireside. It used to be the First National Bank of Rifle. For very good Mexican food, visit Que Paso. Martino's has a good all-you-can-eat pizza & salad lunch buffet. For fresh baked goods and breakfast anytime go to Audrey's. Four restaurants accept major credit cards: First National Fireside, Que Paso, Universal and Village Pizza. Only First National Fireside offers nonsmoking. Only Audrey's and Dairy Kreme do not serve alcohol.

RIFLE

Restaurants and Ratings:	Food	Service	Decor	Atm	Overall
1. AUDREY'S	★★★	★★½	★★★	★★★½	★★★
2. BURGER WORKS	★★½	★★½	★★½	★★	★★½
3. DAIRY KREME	★★½	★★½	★½	★½	★★
4. FIRST NATIONAL FIRESIDE	★★★★½	★★★★½	★★★★★	★★★★½	★★★★½
5. MARTINO'S	★★★½	★★★	★★½	★★½	★★★
6. QUE PASO	★★★★	★★★	★★★	★★★★	★★★½
7. UNIVERSAL	★★	★★	★★½	★★	★★
8. VILLAGE PIZZA	★★	★★½	★	★	★½

AUDREY'S BAKERY AND CAFE ★★★
401 RAILROAD AVE. (303)625-3163

Breakfast/lunch $, dinner $$. 7 days 6AM-9:30PM.
Type: Cafe. In business with the same specialty cook since 1975.

Food: ★★★ This restaurant offers good food, low prices, and fresh baked goods. Breakfast specialties include buttermilk biscuits with cream gravy, with Polish Sausage and cream gravy, or with ham, egg & gravy. The lunch offerings are primarily burgers, including a Russian burger with mushrooms and sour cream, and a chili burger; and hot and cold sandwiches. Beef, pork and ham come either hot with mashed potatoes, or cold. There is also a French dip and a fish sandwich. A shrimp plate, chicken basket, burrito, and chili complete the lunch menu. Dinner features steaks, roast beef, roast leg of pork, liver & onions, fried chicken, deep-fried perch or shrimp, soup, chef's salad, cottage cheese & pineapple, and a seniors menu. Ice cream, sherbet, and homemade pies can be ordered for dessert.

Service: ★★½ Satisfactory.

Decor: ★★★ This is a divided one-room restaurant with about 12 booths. There is also a bakery counter.

Atmosphere: ★★★½ A homey atmosphere is provided by this family-run business (mom, pop, and manager son). It appears to be well liked by the townsfolk.

BURGER WORKS ★★½
2178 RAILROAD AVE. (303)625-2620

Lunch/dinner $-$$. 7 days 10AM-9PM.
Type: Burgers.

Food: ★★½ *Service:* ★★½ *Decor:* ★★½ *Atmosphere:* ★★

This is not a bad place to pick up a burger. In addition, they offer Mexican specials, chili, chicken & beef fajitas, hot dogs, chicken, spuds, steaks, salads, and French dip sandwiches. The service is fast and friendly. You order at the counter and get served at your table. Inside there are enough booths for 44 people. Outside there are five benches for additional seating. This is a brick and wood-framed building. A high wall shelf is decorated with bottles and items from the old west. The atmosphere is, basically, that of a burger stand, but a little better.

DAIRY KREME ★★
1248 1/2 RAILROAD AVE. (303)625-3251

Lunch/dinner $. SUN-THU 10AM-8PM. FRI-SAT 10AM-9PM.
Type: Diner.

Food: ★★½ *Service:* ★★½ *Decor:* ★½ *Atmosphere:* ★½

You may want to stop here for an ice cream cone or sundae. They also serve burgers, hot dogs, chicken, fish, shrimp, Mexican dishes, sandwiches (including Polish sausage, pork tenderloin, beef barbecue, steak, and roast beef) onion rings, French fries, and milk shakes. Service is fast. This is a brown shack with four tables and eight booths for 48 people in total. This ice cream parlor attracts a young crowd.

FIRST NATIONAL FIRESIDE RESTAURANT ★★★★½
100 EAST 4TH (303)625-2233

Breakfast/lunch $, dinner $-$$. 7 days 6AM-10PM.
Type: Steak. I have a particular liking for churches and banks that have been converted into restaurants.

Food: ★★★★½ You can expect good-sized portions of quality food here. The breakfast menu offer eggs Benedict. The selections for lunch include salad, soup, burgers, chicken, Reuben sandwiches, pork, rib eye steaks, and Bratwurst. Dinner features German, Cajun, seafood, steaks, barbecue, and chicken. The entrees have appropriate names for this former bank, such as the Board Room Barbecue (smoked chicken, pork ribs or beef ribs), The Banker's Cut (a selection of steaks), From The Vault (seafood choices including red snapper, jumbo shrimp, Cajun catfish and swordfish), First Fund Specialties (chicken Marsala or chicken breast smothered with onions and mushrooms), and International Favorites (Wiener schnitzel and Bratwurst). They also offer a light menu.

Service: ★★★★½ The service here is very friendly, courteous and pleasant. You may find yourself wanting to tip extra.

Decor: ★★★★★ This former First National Bank of Rifle, which has found a better (and more profitable) home as First National Fireside Restaurant, seats 60 people in the main dining room and 22 in the loan office. Seating is mostly at tables. There are only two booths. The decor includes glass-covered red tablecloths, rectangular chandelier lamps made from brass and yellow-tinted glass, ceiling fans, and black & white pictures of the Colorado outdoors. I love the fact they made a restaurant out of a bank!

Atmosphere: ★★★★½ Sophisticated and elegant, yet comfortable and relaxed.

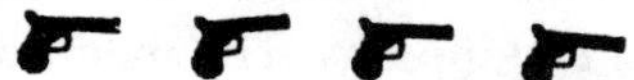

MARTINO'S PIZZERIA ★★★
851 RAILROAD AVE. (303)625-1666

Lunch/dinner $, pizza $-$$$. TUE-SAT 11AM-10PM. SUN-MON 5PM-9PM. Type: Italian.

Food: ★★★½ If you are looking for pizza, this is the place to come. TUE-FRI they have a pizza & salad buffet served from 11:30AM-2PM. Among the toppings offered are jalapeño peppers, anchovies, bacon bits, pineapple, shrimp, and hot or mild taco sauce. The rest of the menu includes lasagna; spaghetti; soup; sandwiches, such as Italian sausage and a ham, salami & Swiss sub; and garlic bread.

Service: ★★★ Good.

Decor: ★★½ This is a brown one-story building with 13 tables for about 50 people.

Atmosphere: ★★½ The atmosphere is a little on the dark side.

QUE PASO ★★★½
412 PARK AVE. (303)625-4699

Lunch/dinner $-$$. TUE-SAT 4PM-10PM. JUN-SEP: MON 4PM-10PM. Closed SUN. OCT-MAY: Closed SUN-MON.

RIFLE

Type: Mexican. 15% gratuity added to parties of six or more. $1 extra plate charge. Take-out available. One peculiarity about this Mexican restaurant is that it is owned by Germans.

Food: ★★★★ I must admit I did not care for their brown salsa. However, their chili relleno and smothered burrito were both very good and not heavily buried in sauce or toppings. The menu offers seven appetizers, including chili con queso, frijole dip (tortilla chips with spicy warm bean dip), and taquitas (deep-fried corn tortillas filled with beef, beans, and chili); the typical Mexican fare, either a la carte or as dinners, such as chimichangas, taco salad, and Mexican steak; a children's menu; a "Gringos" menu featuring sirloin, shrimp, and fried chicken; and a dessert menu with sundaes, sopapillas, and fruit-filled chimichangas with ice cream.

Service: ★★★ I had a humorless, yet quite efficient, waiter.

Decor: ★★★ This single-room restaurant has 13 tables for 50 people plus an outside patio. Pictures of a matador and bull on black cloth, flying geese, a Conestoga wagon, and a mountain house adorn the plaster walls. The brown, rust and tan carpet complements the brown, wood-finished tables. Potted plants in the window sills and kachina dolls also add to the decor.

Atmosphere: ★★★★ Music plays lightly in the background. A quiet, sophisticated presence was evident here. They do not offer a nonsmoking section, but the dining room is fairly large and spread out.

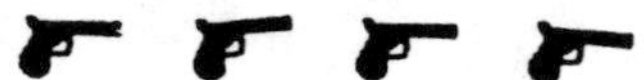

UNIVERSAL ★★
1600 RAILROAD AVE. (303)625-4736

Lunch/dinner $$-$$$. MON-THU 11AM-9:30PM. FRI-SAT 11AM-10PM. SUN 11AM-9PM.
Type: Oriental. Take-out available.

Food: ★★ *Service:* ★★ *Decor:* ★★½ *Atmosphere:* ★★

I found the food here to be only fair quality. Rather than specializing in one type of Chinese food, this restaurant offers Mandarin, Cantonese, Szechuan, Hunan, and Shanghai cooking. Like most Chinese restaurants, the menu is extensive featuring four combination dinners, ten family and ten regal dinners for two or more, eight house specialty dinners, and a total of 46 different meals from "The Four Basic Chinese Food Groups": pork, chicken, beef and seafood. Some of the more often seen items in these food groups are chop suey, chow mein, sweet & sour, curry, kung pao, and snow peas. The menu also offers ten appetizers, including pan-fried dumplings with ground beef and vegetables, and the poo poo platter. Six different soups are available, including crab meat or sea food. Egg foo yong, lo mein, and fried rice dishes complete the Chinese entree portion of the menu. Chilled Mandarin orange or lychee fruit, and sesame banana are offered for dessert. If you come to a Chinese restaurant to order American food, you have ten dinner selections, such as steaks, pork chops, fried fish, veal, chicken and shrimp; plus a few burger and sandwich selections. Service was acceptable. This restaurant has tables for 42 people. Silk screens and wall hangings add a Chinese flavor to the place. The walls have wallpaper on the upper half and wood panel below. The atmosphere is quiet.

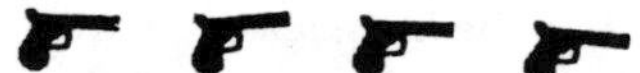

VILLAGE PIZZERIA ★½
160 EAST 26TH (303)635-0835

Lunch/dinner $-$$ ($$$ for medium and large pizzas). SUN-THU 11AM-9PM. FRI-SAT 11AM-10PM. Restaurant closes one hour earlier every night between NOV-MAR.
Type: Italian. Local checks accepts. Take-out and delivery available.

Food: ★★ *Service:* ★★½ *Decor:* ★ *Atmosphere:* ★

Try the breadsticks made with old-fashioned beer dough. They are light, fluffy, buttery and a pleasant change from hard Italian breadsticks. I liked the thin, fluffy dough used in making the pizza, as well as the ingredients. However, this pizza falls short on its sauce and greasy texture. Your choice of toppings includes pastrami, Canadian bacon, anchovies, pineapple, Ortega chili, and shrimp. The rest of the menu offers make-your-own submarine sandwiches; spaghetti with meat sauce, meatballs or sausage; salads (chef, stuffed avocado, shrimp, or dinner); ten sandwiches which include ingredients like puffy fried bread, baby shrimp, avocado, cream cheese, pepper steak, and roast beef; three croissant sandwiches, including shrimp or turkey; and three meatless sandwiches with avocado, tomato, or cream cheese. The waitress was young and friendly. Humorous, outrageous murals decorate this rectangular restaurant that can seat 60 people at a combination of booths and tables. The mural on the right wall shows a man, a monkey, a donkey and an ostrich working on a pizza assembly line. Another wall mural depicts skunks pointing the way to the rest rooms. A third mural has three pigs sitting at a table drinking. Depending on your sense of humor, or if you have children, you might consider stopping here just for a laugh. The tables are blue, the chairs are black-cushioned with wood rib-backs, and the benches are the color of poi. Poi is that edible (?) pasty substance served in Hawaii that some think is a cross between silly putty and Elmer's glue. It is sort of a dirty pink color. The windows have a frosted leaf pattern. You can see the mountains beyond the parking lot and convenience store next door. It was not too crowded the evening I was there. This seemed to be a place that attracted both families and giggly teenagers.

ROCKY FORD

Rocky Ford was originally located near a crossing of the Arkansas River about three miles northwest of the present site. When the Santa Fe Railroad was built through the area in 1875, Rocky Ford moved to be next to the railroad. The name is derived from the gravel-lined ford across the Arkansas River at the town's original site. If you are fortunate enough to be in Rocky Ford in late summer, be sure you stop at one of the roadside stands for some of their famous cantaloupes.

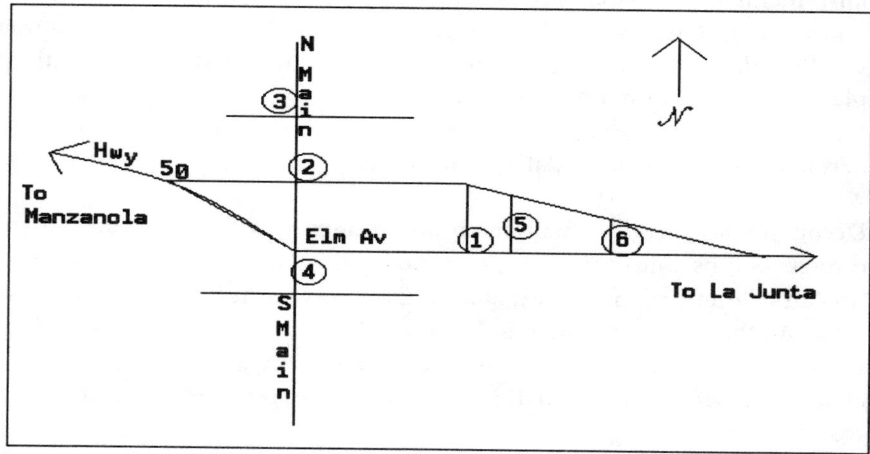

Restaurants and Ratings:	Food	Service	Decor	Atm	Overall
1. CASA LUZ	★★★	★★★	★★★	★★½	★★★
2. COUNTRY MORNING	★½	★★½	½	★½	★½
3. EL CAPITAN	★★★★	★★★½	★★★★½	★★★	★★★★
4. LA FIESTA	★★½	★★★	★★½	★½	★★½
5. MELON VALLEY	★★★½	★★★	★★★★	★★★½	★★★½
6. PEGGY'S CAFE	★★½	★★½	★½	★★	★★

For good Mexican food visit Casa Luz. For steaks and elegant decor, it is El Capitan. For a lunch buffet that provides a good spread go to Melon Valley. Only El Capitan and Melon Valley accept major credit cards and serve alcohol. Only El Capitan has a nonsmoking section.

CASA LUZ ★★★
1211 ELM AVE. (719)254-3557

Lunch/dinner $. MON-SAT 11:30AM-2PM and 5PM-8:50PM. Closed SUN. Type: Mexican.

Food: ★★★ This is good Mexican food at reasonable prices. The Mexican fare includes a flauta veracrusano (a rolled-up chicken taco with guacamole), tamales, chili rellenos, a potato & chorizo burrito or smothered burrito, and guacamole tostados and salads. Combination plates and ice cream are available.

Service: ★★★ Accommodating and friendly.

Decor: ★★★ This is a small one-room restaurant with only seven rusty orange booths and one lime-green table for a total of 34 people. An upstairs dining room is available if they become full. Black-iron bars decorate the outside of the windows; white curtains the inside. Wooden maracas and banjos adorn the window sills. An attractive black-iron chandelier with yellow-tinted, glass lamps and plants hang from the low, wood-beamed ceiling.

Atmosphere: ★★½ This is a nice, soft, quiet place.

COUNTRY MORNING COFFEE SHOP ★½
400 N. MAIN (719)254-6596

Breakfast/lunch $. MON-FRI 6AM-4PM. SAT 6AM-11PM. Closed SUN. Type: Country.

Food: ★½ *Service:* ★★½ *Decor:* ½ *Atmosphere:* ★½

The eggs breakfast special was fine, but they do have a limited menu. This is primarily a bakery offering donuts, long johns, and cinnamon or fruit rolls. Soup, sandwiches, burgers and pizza are available for lunch.

Service was talkative and friendly. This is a small restaurant with seating for 40 people. The tables are undersized for the size of the booths. They had some interesting, if not amusing, crooked hanging pictures: a watermelon with a clock, ladies dressed in full-length skirts, and sheep grazing with an abandoned farmhouse in the background. One side of the cafe had no curtains with a single hanging plant in the window. I was informed by my server that the restaurant had to raise the acoustic tile ceiling "to please the local health inspector." While I do not understand the exact nature of the problem, perhaps by the time you read this they will be presenting a better face. This was another hangout for "good ol' boys."

El Capitan ★★★★
501 N. Main (719)254-7471

Lunch/dinner $$. TUE-THU 12PM-2PM and 5PM-8:30PM. FRI-SAT 5:30PM-9PM. Closed SUN-MON.
Type: Steak.

Food: **★★★★** This is the place to go for steaks in Rocky Ford. There are several steak entrees, including porterhouse, filet mignon, and roast prime rib. They also offer a chef salad, hamburger, shrimp, and ham; a children's menu; and nightly specials, like cod fish filet. To start your meal, you can order marinated herring, garlic toast, or blue cheese chips.

Service: **★★★½** This has been a family-owned place since 1988. They are friendly and casual.

Decor: **★★★★½** Dinners are served in the Grand Imperial Dining Room which is to your right and to the rear as you enter the lobby. This room, with 13 tables for 56 people, has a high ceiling, wood-paneled walls, no windows, and a large, 12-lamp chandelier. It is regal and elegant, as well as dark. The principal objects of decor are five, large gold frames. Each frame borders a piece of red felt with a white, oval-shaped design and two lamps in the middle. This red felt also forms a four-foot wall border with the ceiling. A piano stands in one corner. In addition to the main dining room, there is also a banquet room to the right front which can seat 32 people, the Bonanza Room to the left of the entrance for 24 people, a small room behind this for 16, and a bar/lounge farther back with ten stools and four round tables.

Atmosphere: ★★★ Depending on the evening, you could be dining virtually alone or in a crowded dining room. I dined here twice and had both experiences. My main objection is the lack of natural light. It is quiet and dark, but not romantic.

La Fiesta Cafe ★★½
204 S. Main (719)254-9915

Lunch/dinner $. SUN-WED & FRI 11:30AM-8PM. SAT 11:30AM-9PM. Closed THU.
Type: Mexican.

***Food:* ★★½ *Service:* ★★★ *Decor:* ★★½ *Atmosphere:* ★½**

I had a chili relleno, smothered beef burrito, and beans. They were not bad, but nothing special either. There was nothing special about the chips and salsa either. Their menu offers several combinations featuring vermicelli, rellenos, stuffed sopapillas, red or green chili, Mexican steak, chicken flautas, menudo and avocado salad. A limited American menu offers burgers and a few sandwiches. Service was warm, friendly and with a smile. The room on the right has seven booths for 28 people. Three wood carvings, two conquistadors separated by a large banjo, and two black-iron decorations in the shape of a fan and candle holder, hang on the wood-paneled walls. Black-metal lanterns hang on the wall in four of the booths. The room also houses a jukebox and trophies. The plaster ceiling shows signs of wear. The room on the left, not in use the evening I was there, has six tables for 24 people with similar decor. The place was heavy with smoke.

MELON VALLEY ★★★½
1319 ELM AVE. (IN THE MELON VALLEY INN) (719)254-3306

Breakfast/lunch $, dinner $$-$$$. MON-THU 6AM-8PM. FRI-SAT 6AM-9PM. SUN 6AM-3PM.
Type: Family.

Food: ★★★½ Their all-you-can-eat lunch buffet for only $4.50 is a great deal. It includes a salad and dessert bar featuring pudding, lemon meringue, applesauce, peaches and cottage cheese; hot roast beef, mashed potatoes, creamed corn, fried chicken, spaghetti in meat sauce, and tostados. While some of these buffet lunch entrees may change from day to day, you can be assured of a complete menu and plenty of good food. If you are not in the mood for the buffet, you can order sandwiches (roast beef, open-faced prime rib, or French dip), chicken fried steak, or Mexican food from the menu. The dinner menu starts out with several appetizer choices including deed-fried vegetables, shrimp cocktail, bacon-wrapped chicken livers, and nachos. Following this are homemade soup, salads (dinner, macaroni, potato and a salad bar), and green chili. There are four Mexican entrees including fajitas, tacos, and burritos. The entrees feature seven steak selections, roast prime rib, calves liver & onions, ham, fried chicken, roast beef au jus, seafood (lobster, shrimp, trout, salmon, halibut, red snapper and catfish), and combinations from the land and sea. Ice cream desserts are featured from their own ice cream parlor.

Service: ★★★ The servers are very pleasant and will not forget to refill your beverage.

Decor: ★★★★ This is a very nice, even elegant looking, restaurant by comparison to most other places in this part of the state. Total seating is for 62 people at tables with high-back, red-patterned chairs in black brass frames. Wagon-wheel chandeliers hang from black brass chains. Each chandelier features a dozen rectangular black brass lamps with yellow-tinted glass. The white wallpaper with a little criss-cross blue pattern is fanciful. A local photographer advertises some of his subjects on the walls. Two sides of the room have large, ceiling-high windows with majestic red curtains.

Atmosphere: ★★★½ The dining room has an air of sophistication.

PEGGY'S CAFE ★★
1701 ELM AVE. (719)254-9956

Breakfast/lunch $, dinner $-$$. 7 days 24 hours.
Type: Cafe. They have a "smoke eater".

Food: ★★½ *Service:* ★★½ *Decor:* ★½ *Atmosphere:* ★★

They say their pancakes are average size, but each one is about eight inches in diameter and a good fluffy ¼ to ⅜ inches high. You be the judge. Breakfast items include pork chops and biscuits & gravy. The lunch menu has soup, salads, chili, burgers, and sandwiches (hot or cold roast beef, turkey, ham, fish, chicken, and a Philly). The dinner entrees include steak, chicken, halibut, shrimp, veal, pork chops, and those oysters from the high country. Service is very fast. This restaurant contains four booths, a counter for 12 and enough tables for 28. The decor consists of a hodgepodge of pictures showing a sailing ship, a mountain scene, a water pitcher, a loaf of bread with oranges, and a couple of sketches of wild flowers. This is a gathering place for local farmers and ranchers.

SEDALIA

The town originated in 1865 as the Round Corral, owned by John H. Craig who settled in nearby Happy Canyon. The corral was sold in 1870 and became known as Plum Station or the Town of Plum after East and West Plum Creeks. Later, one of the original settlers renamed the town after his hometown in Sedalia, MO.

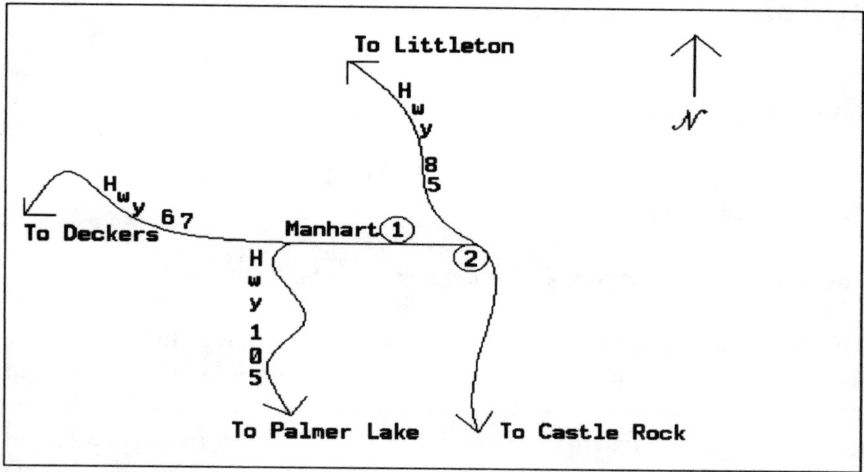

Restaurants and Ratings:	Food	Service	Decor	Atm	Overall
1. BUD'S BAR	★★★	★★½	★★	★★★	★★½
2. SEDALIA GRILL	★★★½	★★½	★★★½	★★★	★★★

The Sedalia Grill offers some good, down-home country cooking in a family-style atmosphere. If you are in the mood for a burger, and only a burger, in a friendly country atmosphere, visit Bud's Bar. Both restaurants serve alcohol, but only the Sedalia grill accepts credit cards and offers a nonsmoking section. Oh, there is another restaurant in Sedalia which some of you may wonder why I excluded. It is called Gabriel's. I attempted to dine here on a Friday evening, arriving at exactly 10:05PM after a long day. The host was on the telephone when I arrived so I mused over some brochures and newsletters on a counter. Being duly ignored after the host got off the phone, I moved in closer. He finally asked, "May I help you?" "Yes, one for dinner" I replied. "I'm sorry, we're closed" was his response. "Then I guess your sign out front that says you serve dinner from 5 o'clock until 11 o'clock on Fridays is incorrect," I stated in a rather matter of fact tone. "Oh those hours are for us (meaning the employees). We're out of here by 11 o'clock!" Funny, I always thought that the hours a restaurant posted were for the benefit of the paying customer, not the staff. Sorry, Gabriel, that kind of attitude and/or policy just does not make it in my book!

BUD'S BAR ★★½
5453 MANHART (303)688-9967

Lunch/dinner $. MON-SAT 10AM-9:30PM. Closed SUN.
Type: Country (Tavern).

***Food:* ★★★ *Service:* ★★½ *Decor:* ★★ *Atmosphere:* ★★★**

This is probably the most basic menu that you will find in this book. The entire menu is: "hamburgers, double hamburgers, cheeseburgers, and double cheeseburgers. Pickles, onion and chips included, but NO French fries." The price range is from $1.75 to $3.50. The folks from Sedalia and Castle Rock raved about the "Bud Bar burger". While the double (American) cheeseburger was a good burger, with a lot of lean, juicy medium cooked meat on a plain white bun, it was not, in my opinion, a great burger. Service was satisfactory. "Country Mom" brings you the food and "Country Pop", the bartender, brings the Bud. This is a single-room restaurant with four tables, five booths and 14 barstools on wood floors. The decor is rather interesting: a weight scale, a mural of a western town, a stuffed fish, a steer's skull, a couple of cardboard life-sized figures of saloon girls, paintings of "cow pokes", an upright piano, and an electric darts board. It is quiet and friendly during the week; noisy and jovial on weekends. The atmosphere is definitely country and very hospitable. They have a good selection of country-western tunes on the juke box.

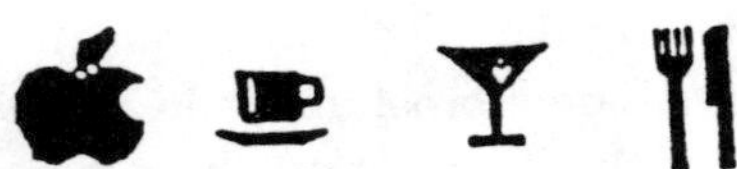

SEDALIA GRILL ★★★
5607 NORTH HWY 85 (303)688-1249

Lunch $, dinner $-$$. TUE-SUN 11AM-4PM and 5PM-9:30PM. Closed MON. Type: Family. All meals cooked to order.

Food: ★★★½ I ordered meatloaf — a dinner special and one of my favorites — with mashed potatoes and gravy and, my favorite vegetable, asparagus. It came with six-bean soup with vegetables in a brown broth and dinner rolls. The asparagus was lightly salted. The meatloaf, two large slices, was tender, flavorful and mildly spicy. The lunch menu features burgers, sandwiches (hot or cold roast beef, hot corned beef and Swiss, fish, club, smoked turkey, or Reuben), soup, salads red or green chili, and a few entrees (chicken fried steak, fish taco, fish and chips, and spaghetti). Milk shakes, malts or Columbian coffee can accompany your meal. Buffalo chicken wings and nachos can be ordered as appetizers for dinner. The entrees include beef or chicken fajitas, roasted chicken, red snapper, hot roast beef, and chicken burrito.

Service: ★★½ Partners Allison Prescott and Chef Jeff Rubach are friendly, talkative folks. The waitresses do an adequate job.

Decor: ★★★½ The main dining room to the right with 10 booths and six tables has four significant items of decor: a natural wood-framed wall structure about 20 inches high that extends around the entire room; in certain places, the wood wall structure widens into a diamond shape and features a picture in the center like an adobe building; a large square skylight; and a platform of potted plants in the center of the room below the skylight. This room is very well put together. A smaller dining room between the main dining room and lounge can seat 20 and has a large wall mural painting of a snowy mountain and lake with changing fall colors. The bar/lounge with five high tables and 10 barstools is decorated with football pennants, beer signs and darts.

Atmosphere: ★★★ This place surprised me. From the road it looked more like a country bar. However, inside was a family-style restaurant that played classic 50's rock n' roll. The combination of windows, skylight, plants and wall decor blended together well to provide a most comfortable surrounding. Don't judge this restaurant by the building.

SILVER PLUME

Established in 1870, there are two stories as to how the town got its name. One version is that the name was applied to a mine in the district that featured plume-shaped white streaks of silver in the rocks. The other version is that the town was named after a political figure, James G. Blaine, who was known as the "Plumed Knight".

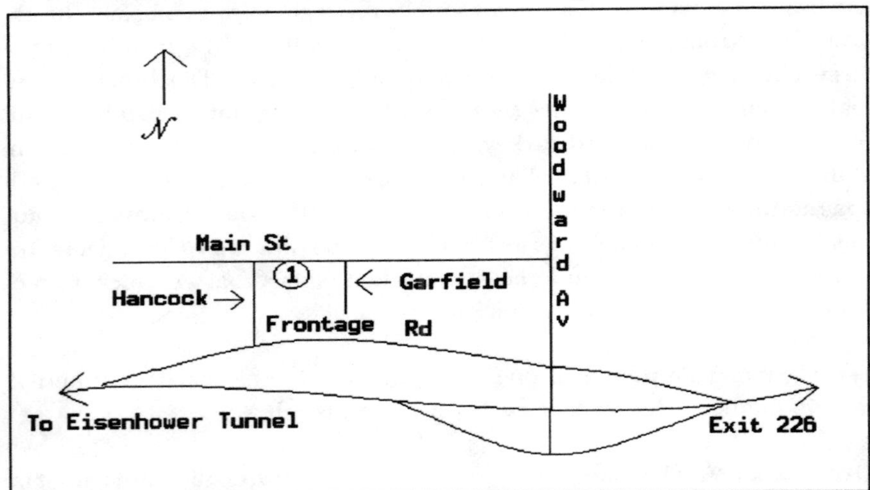

1. PLUME SALOON ★★★½
   246 MAIN ST (303)569-2277

Lunch/dinner $-$$. WED-MON 12PM-9PM. Closed TUE.
Type: Tavern. Major credit cards are accepted and they serve alcohol, but do not have a nonsmoking section. 15% gratuity added to parties of six or more.

Food: ★★★½ This has become a favorite stop after hiking or cross-country skiing, especially with one member of our group. In the past year we tried their "original Buffalo, NY style chicken wings", pizza, and the barbecued beef ribs dinner entree. All three were thumbs up! The first three Buffalo wings were moderately hot, then the next two were very hot! (kind of a delayed reaction). If you like the real thing, or are from Buffalo, try these. We had one of their pizzas with "the works", which in this case was six ingredients: sausage, pepperoni, green pepper, mushrooms, olives and onions. They use a crisp flour tortilla shell.

Personally, I prefer a crust with some dough. My friends thought the ultra thin crust hit their palates just right. All the toppings were fresh and nongreasy. The barbecued beef ribs are smoked locally with Rocky Mountain maple wood and grilled with their own special barbecue sauce. They were thick, meaty and great tasting! The dinner came with soup (split pea or tomato rice) or salad; and baked potato or rice. The other items on their short menu are baked French onion soup; beef stew; a fruit & cheese board; Cajun meatballs; burgers; hot dogs; Italian sausage; grilled chicken breast; chicken divan with broccoli & cheddar (casserole style); beef, chicken or vegetarian stir fry; and spaghetti & meatballs.

Service: ★★★½ The servers have always been friendly, jovial, and willing to join in the frivolity. One of the evening bartenders is from Buffalo: a testimonial to their Buffalo wings and good nature.

Decor: ★★★½ There is a bar at the entrance with ten swivel barstools. At the right end of the bar is a fireplace, a television, an Andeker of America draught supreme beer keg, a couple of rocking chairs, a French advertisement for Waverly Cycles, an old Coca-Cola advertisement, and a cozy booth with a small rust table. At the end of the bar to the left is a pot-belly stove and a small dining area for six. A second small dining area behind this seats seven at three tables. Decor consists primarily of portraits, including one of Francis Willard, the temperance woman of Colorado, the equivalent of Cary Nation from Kansas. (I wonder how she'd feel today about being featured in a saloon). Another major item of decor is pictures of Silver Plume from the 1920's and 1930's. White-laced curtains with figures of peacocks hang in the windows. The main dining room in the rear, which I have never seen being used, has 11 wood tables, 42 wood chairs, a black-iron stove, a piano, and a rectangular-shaped bar for nine. A few of the tables are rather interesting: semicircular-shaped along the wall. The room features stick figures of musicians, an aerial photo of the silver mines in Georgetown and Silver Plume, and several photos of silver mining.

Atmosphere: ★★★½ Very down to earth and peaceful. Not at all rowdy. Very jovial and relaxed. Rock music usually plays in the background. They have a regular group of locals.

SILVERTHORNE

Named for Judge Marshall Silverthorn who settled in Breckenridge in 1860. The Silverthorne Placer dates back to 1881 when there were visions of great mineral wealth in Summit County. Much later, Silverthorne become a construction camp for workers building the Eisenhower Tunnel and the Dillon Dam. The town was incorporated on September 5, 1967.

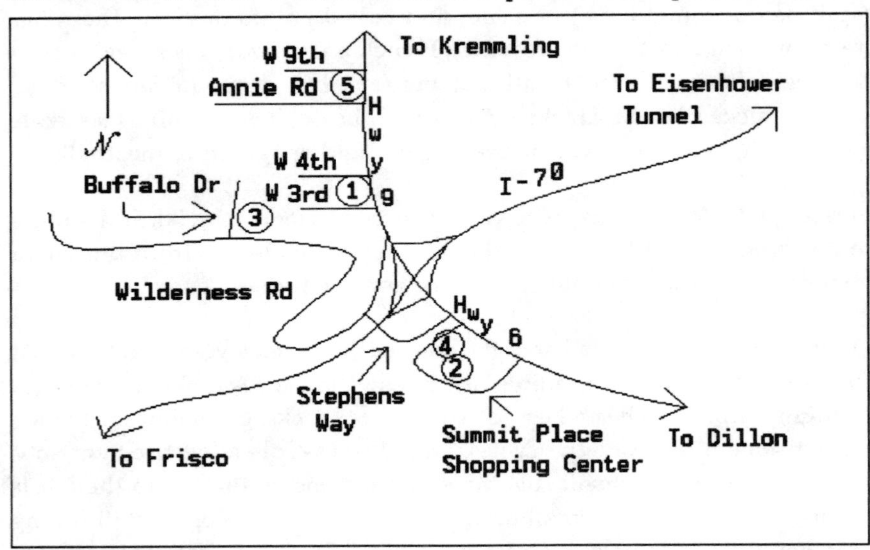

Restaurants and Ratings:	Food	Service	Decor	Atm	Overall
1. THE MINT	★★★★	★★★½	★★★★	★★½	★★★½
2. ROBERTO'S	★★★	★★½	★★	★★	★★½
3. SILVERHEELS	★★★★★	★★★★½	★★★★½	★★★★★	★★★★★
4. SUNSHINE CAFE	★★★½	★★★	★★★	★★★	★★★
5. WILLOW CREEK	★	½	★★★½	★½	★½

Silverheels is my selection for best restaurant in Summit Country. It is Southwest elegance at its best, offering some incredible stone-age cookery. The Mint will let you cook your own steak to its perfect conclusion. The Sunshine Cafe is your best bet for breakfast. All of the restaurants accept major credit cards, except Roberto's. Only Silverheels and the Sunshine Cafe offer nonsmoking sections. They all serve alcohol except Roberto's.

THE MINT ★★★½
347 BLUE RIVER PARKWAY (303) 468-5247

Dinner $$-$$$. 7 days 5PM-10PM.
Type: Steak.

Food: ★★★★ After the waitress shows you to your table, you walk up to the meat counter — just like in a butcher shop — and make your dinner selection from dry-aged or regular sirloin or NY strip, rib eye, filet mignon, shish kabob, chicken teriyaki or the daily seafood selection. The 20-item salad bar (included with the entree) features pasta and potato salads and Parmesan caper dressing. Sides of baked potato, corn on the cob, baked beans or rice are extra. They will also stir fry your own selection of vegetables from the salad bar for an extra charge. I chose the dry-aged NY strip, a hefty 14-oz to 16-oz piece of meat, and proceeded to the lava rock grill to flame broil my steak. The nice thing about cooking your own entree is you can not complain about it being overcooked. Being careful not to do just that, I returned to the grill three times before I got the perfect medium-rare steak. It was, for the most part, a lean and tender cut, but had a couple of areas of gristle. The dry-aged is a larger cut than the regular sirloin and costs more, so if you want the smaller cut, I would recommend you do that. I did not find that much difference in the taste of the dry-aged over sirloins that I have had in the past. They have a limited wine list of seven reds and five whites. Paul Masson is the house selection. They have a few noteworthy desserts: chocolate thunder made with a Chambord base and triple chocolate (chocolate cake, chocolate frosting, and chocolate chips), raspberry cream cheesecake topped with strawberries and whipped cream, Snickers pie, raspberry bush (a chocolate graham crust, dark chocolate, cream cheese and raspberry white chocolate), chocolate fudge brownie with walnuts, and carrot cake.

Service: ★★★½ My server was very courteous and helpful, especially when I first arrived. She described the entrees at the counter, explained the procedure for selecting and cooking my own entree, and handed me the entree. She even gave me recommended cooking times, which I nonetheless ignored for fear of over cooking. It turned out she was right after all.

Decor: ★★★★ There is a bar at the entrance which gives the whole restaurant the flavor of a bar. The barroom has 10 stools, two small round tables with four high stools, a long table with nine stools, a television and a dining section with six booths for 24. Seating is on hardwood bench seats with high turquoise wood backs. The unfinished natural-wood wall opposite the bar is decorated with antlers, a two handle wood saw, several stirrups, a sign of the Morton Salt girl ("When it rains, it pours"), an old pair of ice tongs, and framed and electric beer signs. Behind the barroom is the grill for cooking your own meat or fish and the salad bar. To the left is the second dining room which hosts 10 tables, a few in booths, for 46 people. A stone fireplace along the far left wall displays a pair of old wooden snow shoes and a couple of saddles. Old heat ducts painted brown run along the green vaulted ceiling which has two skylights. A third dining room around the corner and parallel to the barroom has seven tables for 37 and no decorations on the green and gold-patterned wallpaper on the inner wall or the red, flower-print wallpaper on the outer wall. However, the cross-beams overhead host an array of paraphernalia from skies and old Coke cases to milk jugs and old weight scales.

The barkeep took me for a tour of the upstairs that seats 25. He said this used to be an old bordello with some of the original barn wood from 1862. The back bar downstairs is also from 1862. It is very old looking, but a few beer signs spoil the natural aged look. Limited lighting is provided by lights in yellow shades hanging from ceiling chains. Three windows look out onto the street. Three old town photos at the top of the stairs show the horse and buggy days and 1930 style automobiles.

Atmosphere: ★★½ My server sat me in the barroom dining area, perhaps because she saw me stop for a moment in front of the television to watch the baseball playoffs. Depending on your mood and personality, this can either be a fun place to go with friends and drink beer around the grill while you watch your food cook, or it can be a smoky restaurant with a bar atmosphere that may not appeal to you. I liked the old pictures and decorations and the 130-year-old setting. I would have liked it better if the bar and dining areas were more separate.

ROBERTO'S ★★½
269 SUMMIT PLACE (303)468-5878

Breakfast $. Lunch/dinner $-$$. 7 days 8AM-9:30PM.
Type: Mexican

***Food:* ★★★ *Service:* ★★1/2 *Decor:* ★★ *Atmosphere:* ★★**

I ordered a smothered carnitas burrito with lettuce, cheese and tomato. The square-shaped flour tortilla had a good soft texture and was filled with beans and pico de gallo. Onions and green chilies gave it a moderate amount of spicy hot flavor. Service was fast and courteous. This small one room restaurant with five booths and two tables for 28 is decorated with Kachina dolls, Mexican hats and rugs, and other items of Mexico. The music started out at the hard rock level and progressed to light rock. This seems to be a place where people just drop in rather than plan to dine here.

SILVERHEELS ★★★★★
81 BUFFALO DRIVE (303)468-2926

Dinner $$$$. DEC-APR and JUN-SEP: 7 days 5PM-10PM. OCT-NOV: SUN-THU 5PM-9PM. FRI-SAT 5PM-10PM. Closed MAY.
Type: Steak/Southwestern. Gratuities of 15% are added to parties of six or more. No separate checks.

Legend has it that there once was a lovely dance hall girl called "Lady Silver Heels" who lived in Buckskin Joe, Colorado. She was much admired by the miners and known for the click of her silver plated high heel shoes. When a smallpox epidemic broke out in 1859, Lady Silver Heels visited the miners' sickbeds, giving aid and comfort, until she too fell to the disease. Devastated by the loss of her beauty, she disappeared into the mountains never to be heard from again. Mt. Silverheels in South Park near Fairplay was named in her honor.

Food: ★★★★★ Dinner starts with vegetables (carrot and celery sticks, radishes and cucumber slices) to munch on with red chili ranch dip. The dip had a sharp taste with just a little "zing". Incredible was the word that kept coming to mind as I delved into my entree, Gorditas, served with baked jalapeño-cheese onion rolls and corn-bread, jack-cheese muffins with red-chili and raspberry honey butter; New Mexico Rainbow Rice with green and red peppers, corn and peas; and mixed vegetables. The meal was a multitude of tastes that were a joy to the senses. This meal was a lot of food and I was not particularly hungry when I arrived (but, duty calls, as they say). Everything was so scrumptious, I had no problem finishing every morsel on my plate. The Gordita is a puff of brioche dough stuffed with marinated sirloin tips, sautéed onion, tomato, mild green chili, mild jack cheese, and topped with black bean salsa. You have to try it to believe it. If you only visit one restaurant in all of Summit County, visit this one.

The menu offers tapas (little dishes or appetizers): items such as taquitos (shredded smoked beef brisket, a warm mini flour tortilla and a tray of garnishes to make your own soft taco) and quesadilla camarones (spiced shrimp, cheese, onion, chilies and tomato folded in a flour tortilla). You can grill your own marinated sirloin steak, gulf shrimp or chicken breast right at your table on a fiery hot granite slab. They call this stone-age cookery. If you prefer to let someone else do the cooking, you can order one of their charbroiled entrees like NY striploin; lightly-marinated thick-cut pork chop loin; fillet of salmon; or beef tenderloin. The oven and sauté entrees feature Cornish hen on a bed of corn bread with chorizo sausage stuffing; a rolled spinach & cheese enchilada with three jumbo shrimp; and paella marlita (shrimp, scallops, crab legs, sweet hot sausage, and roasted game hen spiced with saffron and Achiote peppers). If you prefer your meats smoked, you can choose between four wild sage smokehouse selections: baby-back ribs; Mojave hen; a mixed grill with ribs, hen and sausage; or salmon.

Service: ★★★★½ Friendly and helpful. My waitress answered all my questions, or found the answers, and responded to all my requests.

Decor: ★★★★½ Four dining rooms and a bar/lounge can accommodate 120 people. The bar/lounge is to the right of the entrance and has a stone fireplace, cactus, wood ladder (Anasazi style), a Mexican hat, a picture of a silver slipper, a boot with a silver heel, and a picture of a buffalo head. Seating is on rust rawhide seats with wood frames and square, wood rawhide barstools. Three of the dining rooms are upstairs to the left of the entrance. The first two dining rooms feature wall to wall windows with views of blue spruces and fir trees that are illuminated with spot lights after dark. Double-framed glass posters by Edward R. Gonzales depict a solitary elderly Anasazi Indian on the desert and an Indian woman starting up a ladder. There are several hanging red chili ristras, baskets, and Indian corn cobs. Subdued lighting is provided by kerosene table lamps, brass and ceramic chandeliers, and green sconces featuring a star pattern of small holes emitting light. Aspen lattias, or beams, decorate the ceiling. The third dining room has some excellent photos of waterfalls and a fireplace. The fourth dining room is downstairs and features log walls adorned with brass, yellow-tinted, glass lanterns; two Great Chili posters; horse shoes; a branding iron; pot; and pan. There are three large, clear mirrors that will have you thinking there is another dining area; a cabinet at the entrance; a map of Colorado at the bottom of the stairs; and several red chili ristras.

Atmosphere: ★★★★★ Soft, relaxing music played quietly. A very romantic mood and setting with exterior lighting for the spruces and firs.

SUNSHINE CAFE ★★★
SUMMIT PLACE SHOPPING CENTER (303) 468-6663

SILVERTHORNE

Breakfast $, lunch $-$$, dinner $$-$$$. 7 days 7AM-3PM and 5PM-9:30PM (8PM APR-MAY and OCT-NOV).
Type: Cafe. A 15% gratuity is added to parties of five or more. No separate checks.

Food: ★★★½ Five of us stopped here for breakfast on our way to do some cross-country skiing. My crêpe, filled with green peppers, onions, tomatoes and American cheese, was very light, thin and quite good. We all raved about the potatoes and bacon. The wheat cakes are different from pancakes. They are thick and moist, like "a condensed bread with substance" is how one member of the group put it. There is quite a bit to choose from on the lunch menu: red chili, New England clam chowder, chef salad, gourmet burgers, and grilled sandwiches (like roast beef or ham, with turkey and Swiss on sourdough). A list of gourmet sandwiches features turkey, egg salad with avocado, and club. The hot entrees include chicken liver with bacon, onions & mushrooms on sourdough, vegetarian lasagna, spicy Italian sausage, and Philadelphia roast beef on a French roll. The dinner menu has even more to offer: chicken wings, fried calamari, or spinach & cheese quesadillas for appetizers; a house favorite soup made with potatoes, cheese and mushrooms; chef or Caesar's salad; and a choice of sesame soy, honey-mustard vinaigrette, or creamy herb dressings. The entrees feature charbroiled chicken breasts; pan-fried trout with tomato & fennel butter; grilled steak with salsa fresca; deep-fried breaded shrimp; blackened catfish; steamed vegetables; a green chili burrito plate; and pasta with goat cheese, tomato, basil & cream.

Service: ★★★ Fast, friendly and helpful, even when they were busy.

Decor: ★★★ There is a small counter with four stools around the corner from the host station. The adjacent dining area has nine tables and six booths for 56. Wood trellises with hanging plants separate the booths. There is ample natural light coming through the front windows, decorated by white curtains with beige trim on top. Additional lighting is provided by ceiling lights and frosted globe lights under wicker shades hanging on chains over the booths and tables. Beige, green, tan and red Indian rugs hang on the white plaster walls. Photos of mountain goats decorate the divider separating the dining area from the waiting area with two couches. Three slow moving ceiling fans spin overhead. A fish tank in the back hosts several racoon angelfish.

Atmosphere: ★★★ Rock music plays quietly through speakers in plant hangers. This is a popular place for young and old, locals and travelers: definitely one of the better places in the area to stop for breakfast.

WILLOW CREEK COOKERY ★½
102 ANNIE RD (303)468-8432

Breakfast $ (a few $$), lunch $-$$, dinner $$-$$$. 7 days 7AM-9PM.
Type: Country

***Food:* ★ *Service:* ½ *Decor:* ★★★½ *Atmosphere:* ★½**

Nine of us packed in here on a crowded Sunday morning, so admittedly, they were busy. Nonetheless, I found the service to be most IN attentive. Our waitress took our order after we were seated for ten minutes, then came back a half hour later to inform us that our breakfasts would be ready in ten minutes. "The chef is just starting to cook your orders now" is what she said! During the 40 minute wait for our meals, one of the less shy gals in our group got up and served everyone coffee...several times. Our waitress was noticeably absent the entire time. As for our food, the "south of the border" was heavy on onions; the biscuits and gravy had sweet, hard as a rock biscuits; the "kitchen sink" was good, but a little greasy; the sausage was a little dry; the eggs Sardoux with fresh, uncooked spinach and artichoke hearts was not bad; and the veggie skillet was probably the best of the meals. They do have good hash browns with chunks of seasoned potato, onion and green peppers. The decor was, by far, the best feature with old rusty farm tools and lanterns hanging from the walls, brass wall & ceiling lamps, and blue & white ceramic pots and plates. There were a lot of locals and cowboys.

SOMERSET

The town was established by the Denver & Rio Grande Railroad which brought coal out of the North Fork Valley. It was named after a coal mining community in Pennsylvania.

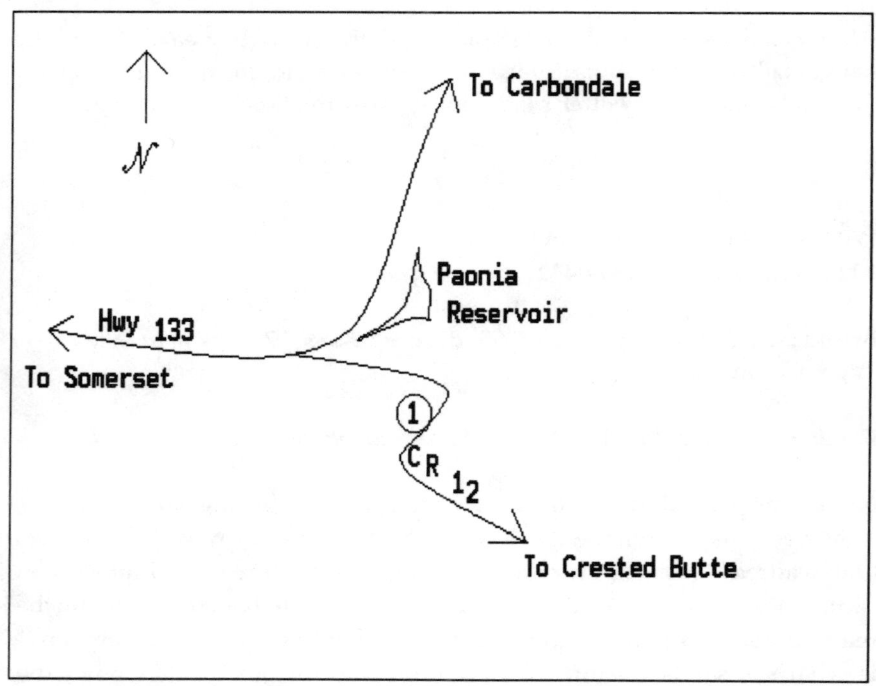

1. CRYSTAL MEADOWS RANCH ★★★★
   30682 COUNTY ROAD 12 (7 MILES EAST OF SOMERSET JUST OFF HWY 133 AT THE SOUTHERN TIP OF PAONIA RESERVOIR) (303)929-5656

Lunch $-$$, dinner $$. Late May to Mid-NOV: 7 days 11AM-9PM. Closed Mid-NOV to Late MAY.
Type: Country. Major credit cards are accepted, but they do not have a nonsmoking section and do not serve alcohol. Reservations are recommended. This was a delightful find for me: one of the real hidden treasures along the back roads of Colorado!

Food: ★★★★ I ordered the delta melta, medium rare: a thick, juicy half-pound burger on rye with Swiss and grilled onions. The burger was cooked closer to medium-well, but it was still an excellent burger, served with fresh fruit (cantaloupe and watermelon). It also comes with steak fries, potato chips, or potato salad. Besides burgers, for lunch you can order a sandwich (hot roast beef; barbecued beef; barbecued ham; broiled chicken breast; club; and cold turkey, ham, or beef), or something lighter like a quarter-pound burger, soup, chili, potato skins, chicken wings, a dinner or Caesar's salad, or a trip to the 14-item salad bar with four toppings (bacon bits, croutons, raisins and sunflower seeds) and four basic salad dressings. The dessert menu offers fresh pies and ice cream in addition to caramel crunch pie made with crushed Snickers, delicious dirt (a special pudding with crushed Oreo cookies served in a flower pot) and, occasionally, old-fashioned caramel baked custard. The dinner menu features a different steak selection every night; deep-pit, mesquite-wood, barbecued baby-back pork ribs, beef, or chicken breast with their own special barbecue sauce; rainbow trout almondine; chicken teriyaki; chicken pico with green chili sauce; and, Patsy's pasta: cheese filled tortellinni topped with a rich meat sauce that is simmered for hours.

Service: **★★★½** Young, friendly, delightful, enthusiastic, efficient and with a good sense of humor.

Decor: **★★★½** The front dining room, with its rock fireplace, chandeliers, and wall lights made from antlers, has six tables and 23 chairs with blue cushions and rib backs. The rear dining room is nicer and more comfortable with plastic table covers and mauve padded chairs. It has five tables for 26 and is decorated with prints (snow geese, Canadian geese, mallards, and elk) and stuffed animals (northern pike, striped Marlin and mallards). The ceiling is vaulted from four sides with a single fan with four lights in the center. The patio has five green-top tables with 18 plastic white chairs.

Atmosphere: **★★★★½** All indoor and outdoor seating areas have fantastic views of West Beckwith Mountain. Hummingbirds buzz, flutter, stop and go, around feeders hanging from the awning. This is a popular place with tourists in July, fall color seekers in September, and hunters in October. Hopefully, you too will add it on your list of dining pleasures.

SPRINGFIELD

Springfield was named after Springfield, Missouri, the hometown of Andrew Harrison, the original owner of the site.

I was in Springfield during the last days of Operation Desert Storm. The General Electric Catalogue Outlet Store, which takes up half a block, was decorated to the hilt with moving white lights along the railing and rain gutter, a huge American flag in red, white and blue lights, an outline of the 48 contiguous states in lights, a pair of hands at prayer with a sign reading "pray for our leaders and servicemen," and, to top it all off (literally), on the roof, a replica of the Statue of Liberty. What made it all the more interesting were the high winds we experienced. They knocked over the "Great Lady on the roof". Cut her off right at the knees, in fact.

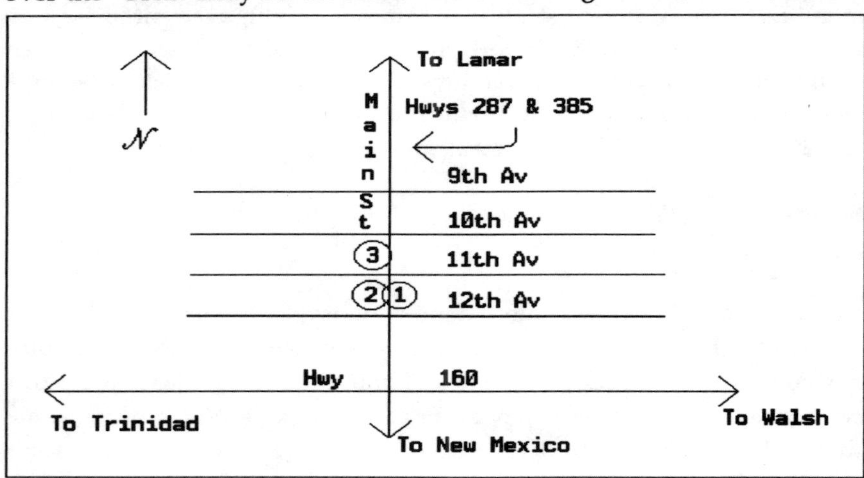

Restaurants and Ratings:	Food	Service	Decor	Atm	Overall
1. Bar Four Coral	★★★	★★½	★★½	★★	★★½
2. Main Cafe	★★½	★★	★★	★★½	★★
3. Princess Lanes	★½	★★	½	½	★

The Bar Four has a fairly decent salad and dessert bar for lunch and dinner, and a good burrito. For breakfast, you may want to stop at The Main Cafe. Only Princess Lanes does not accept major credit cards or serve alcohol. None of the restaurants offer a nonsmoking section.

BAR FOUR CORRAL ★★½
1124 MAIN ST. (719)523-4065

Lunch $-$$, dinner $$-$$$. SUN-THU 11AM-9PM. FRI-SAT 11AM-10PM.
Type: Country.

***Food:* ★★★ *Service:* ★★½ *Decor:* ★★½ *Atmosphere:* ★★**

I had the opportunity to eat here on three or four occasions. Their 20-item salad bar is probably the best of what they have to offer. It includes tuna, macaroni, potato, and green pea salads; cold spaghetti with meat sauce; and Jello, puddings, and a marshmallow treat for dessert. Their vegetable beef soup was homemade, but lukewarm. Their Mexican burrito was spiced right with good ingredients. My sirloin steak, medium rare, was prepared right, but only fair quality. Their pizza is the best in town, but don't expect Pizza Hut quality. It is too crusty and the ingredients are chopped too fine. Service is adequate. This is a two-room restaurant divided by a brown wood wall with window openings and an accordion-style sliding door. The front room has three tables and four booths for a total of 34 people. The room to the right has seven tables and three booths for 38 more people. Decor consists of pictures of cowboys, horses, and cattle; a wood-beamed, vaulted, stucco ceiling; and a free-standing pellet stove. They play "oldies" and current rock 'n' roll music. My first visit here was distracted by noisy children, but the other visits went just fine.

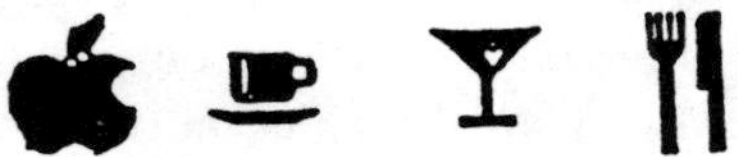

MAIN CAFE ★★
973 MAIN ST. (719)336-5736

Breakfast $, lunch/dinner $-$$. MON-SAT 6AM-9PM. SUN 6AM-2PM.
Type: Cafe.

***Food:* ★★½ *Service:* ★★ *Decor:* ★★ *Atmosphere:* ★★½**

I ate here on three occasions. Their beef broth soup with overcooked vegetables and no beef was only fair. Salad was basically lettuce with a few shavings of carrot and cabbage and was below average. The fried chicken was crispy on the outside but not very moist on the inside. Their liver was tender, however. Curly fries and baked potatoes were standard. Their grilled ham sandwich was average. Overall, the service was about fair. This restaurant is a single divided room with four tables to the right and six booths with three tables to the left. A Mexican hat and guitar made out of black wire and paintings of Indian pueblos decorate the fern green walls. Imitation red brick covers the lower half of the right wall. Potted plants are set on the four-foot, wood-framed divider. There are no curtains or shades on the front windows. This is a quiet place with no music.

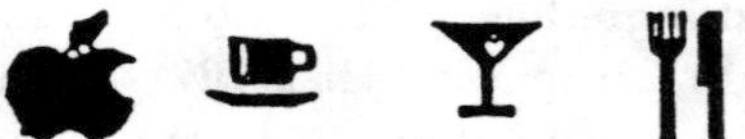

PRINCESS LANES ★
1165 MAIN ST. (719)523-6635

Lunch/dinner $. 7 days 10AM-10:30PM.
Type: Deli.

***Food:* ★½ *Service:* ★★ *Decor:* ½ *Atmosphere:* ½**

This restaurant is located in the bowling alley. My co-workers and I found their burgers to be fair, at best. The regular burger is an unimpressive grilled burger. Order the king burger or you will be asking "Where's the beef?" Also, give the spicy curly fries a try. Otherwise, bowl or shoot a game of pool. Orders are taken at the counter. There is also a drive-up, park-&-order car service, and a walk-up. Take your choice. There are eight red-cushioned stools at the red counter plus two separate seating areas with booths for 12 at each. The entertainment includes six bowling lanes, two pinball machines, two video games, and a pool table. That is also the decor. For atmosphere you have the sounds of pins falling. There is bowling every night, except SAT, starting at 7PM.

STEAMBOAT SPRINGS

Originally a summer playground for the Ute Indians, the town derived its name from a former mineral spring bubbling through a rock formation. To the trappers of the mid-1880's, it produced a sound similar to "a steamboat chugging". This spring, unfortunately, was destroyed during the construction of the Denver & Rio Grande Western Railroad in 1908. Steamboat is located in a big bend in the Yampa River with the springs on the south bank of that river.

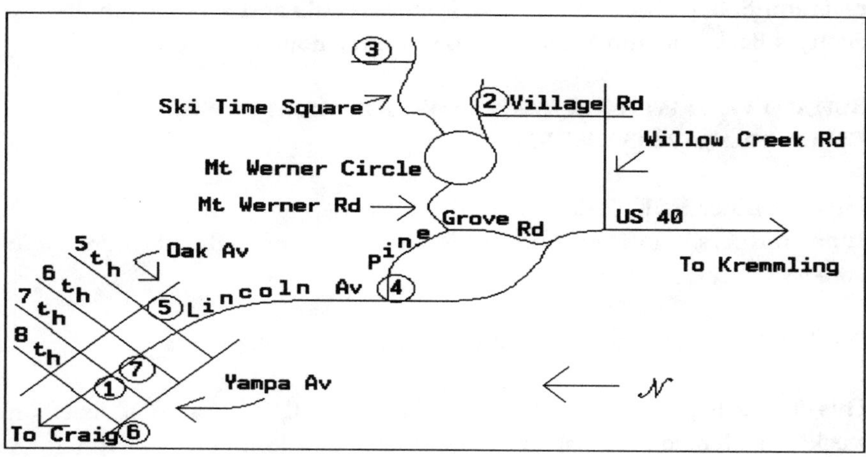

Restaurants and Ratings:	Food	Service	Decor	Atm	Overall
1. Buffalo Wild Wings & Weck	★★★½	★★	★★½	★	★★½
2. La Montana	★★★★½	★★★★	★★★★★	★★★★½	★★★★½
3. Mattie Silks	★★★½	★★★½	★★★★½	★★★½	★★★½
4. The Ore House	★★★★	★★★★½	★★★★	★★★★	★★★★
5. Scotty's Barbecue	★★	★★½	★★½	★★	★★
6. Steamboat Yacht Club	★½	★★½	★★★½	★★★	★★½
7. Winona's	★★★	★★½	★★★	★★★	★★★

STEAMBOAT SPRINGS

La Montana serves some award winning Southwestern, Texan and Mexican cuisine and has to be considered one of the best of its kind in the state. If you like wild game and old barns, you can find both at The Ore House. Mattie Silks offers some excellent continental cuisine in an elegantly "decked-out" restaurant. Buffalo Wild Wings & Weck is one of the few places outside of Buffalo, NY where you can get a genuine "roast beef on kimmelweck roll" (one of my personal favorites!). All of the restaurants listed here accept major credit cards and serve alcohol; only Scotty's Barbecue and Winona's do not offer nonsmoking sections.

BUFFALO WILD WINGS & WECK (BW-3 FOR SHORT) ★★½
729 LINCOLN AVE (303)879-2431

Lunch/dinner $-$$. 7 days 11AM-2AM.
Type: Burgers. 15% gratuity added to tables of eight or more. No personal checks.

***Food:* ★★★½ *Service:* ★★ *Decor:* ★★½ *Atmosphere:* ★**

This is the first place outside of Buffalo, NY that I found a "beef on weck": a delicious roast beef sandwich on kimmelweck roll. A kimmelweck roll is a hard roll with rock salt and caraway seeds. It was served au jus, which is not traditional, but acceptable (any of the beefs on weck that I had in Buffalo were never served with juice on the side), round French fries, cole slaw and a dill pickle slice. Outside of being in Buffalo, it doesn't get any better. The waiter was friendly, even tried to get me interested in starting a BW-3 franchise, but when I asked for horseradish (something you would not have to do in Buffalo), he spent five minutes looking for it, came back to tell me they were out of it, then returned a minute later with the bottle in hand. The restaurant is decorated with hanging plants, red-brick walls, green carpets, framed beer signs, posters of buffalos, buffalo T-shirts, and buffalo cigarettes. A big-screen television was showing "Andy of Mayberry", the television overhead had on the noon news, one of the televisions at the bar could be clearly heard blaring rock music from MTV, while the other bar television showed boxing with no sound. It was very disconcerting and incongruous.

LA MONTANA ★★★★½
2500 VILLAGE DRIVE (303)879-5800

Dinner $$-$$$$. JUN-MAR: 7 days 5:30PM-10PM. APR-MAY: WED-SUN 6PM-9PM. Closed MON-TUE.
Type: Mexican. 15% service charge added to parties of six or more. One check per party. $3.00 split plate charge. $.50 to go charge. Reservations recommended.

***Food:* ★★★★½** Their guacamole dip, made with tomatillas, avocado, sour cream, cilantro and fresh jalapeños, is superb. I ordered the chili relleno. The egg souffle batter was thick and spongy. The chili came filled with beef chunks and colby cheese, but could have been a little bigger given the size of the batter. Everything else was great, including the chili sauce. The rice was fine. The vegetables (zucchini, carrots, onions and red peppers) had just the right amount of cilantro seasoning and were cooked just enough. Authentic black beans from Mexico completed this superb dish. The cuisine is primarily Southwestern with a combination of Texan and Mexican (Tex-Mex). For appetizers they offer nachos; quesadillas; guacamole; mesquite-grilled elk, lamb and chorizo sausages (also available as an entree); half an avocado stuffed with mesquite-grilled chicken and topped with chili con queso; and red chili pasta made with red chilies and semolina flour (also available as an entree). Mesquite, by the way, is a hardwood native to Mexico and the Southwestern U.S. that imparts a unique flavor to grilled dishes. The Southwestern dishes are served with soup or Southwestern salad with piñon nut dressing and include blue corn tortillas rolled with goat and Montery Jack cheese; jumbo shrimp stuffed with crab meat; mesquite-grilled fish and chicken breast; and grilled elk tenderloin with pecans. The Tex-Mex specialties offer the usual Mexican fare, only they are much, much better. If fajitas are your thing, they have beef, chicken, pork, shrimp, elk, even a veggie. Also on the menu: a sweet pepper relleno (low in calories, cholesterol and fat), tempura shrimp, NY strip steak and grilled chicken breast.

Service: ★★★★ Joe was an excellent waiter. He gave me a table with a view, knew a few things about the food he was serving, even let me run back to the condo to get my credit card that I had forgotten. They have a laid back, "no problem", attitude.

Decor: ★★★★★ The dining room has some great superimposed photos taken from Escalante, Utah, the La Sal Mountains, and Fiery Furnace at sunset in Arches National Park. A small lounge to the left of the bar has more great prints taken from Zion National Park, California, Arizona, and Montana. These photographs, taken by the proprietor, Tom Garrett, show clear, crisp, clarity and make tremendous use of shadows. The bar/lounge area at the entrance has about a dozen stools, two small round tables for six with a view of the deck, and additional seating for 22 at seven tables. Between the bar and the main dining area to the right is a gazebo style, cozy setting with trellis walls and four small tables for 12. The dining area is in two sections: the first has an arched ceiling with wood beams, hanging plants over the booths, a maroon rug, and seating for 24 at cloth-cushioned bench seats and wicker seats in wood frames; the second presents a great view of the mountains to the west and north. With great views to the outside and terrific photography inside, you have a lot to gaze at while you dine.

Atmosphere: ★★★★½ This was the first place I dined at in Steamboat Springs that had some assemblage of patronage in the off-season. A variety of music played while I was here: jazz, Mexican, and rock. Someone kept changing the radio station. A warm, intelligent crowd comes here and I got some "good vibes" from this place!

MATTIE SILKS ★★★½
1890 MT WERNER RD (303)879-2441

Dinner $$$$, bar menu $-$$. 7 days 5:30PM-10PM. (In "mud" season, from Mid-APR to MAY, they only offer their bar menu).
Type: Continental. There is a five dollar split dinner charge and a 15% gratuity charge on parties over seven. The entire dining room is nonsmoking.

Mattie Silks first opened its doors in 1979. They have a quote in their menu that I like: "Virtue is its own reward, but vice is much more memorable." Mattie Silk is a legend when it comes to vice. Described as "a little Lily Langtry, with pouting lips and tightly curled blond hair," she claimed the title of Denver's "Queen of the Demimonde", becoming a madam at the early age of nineteen. The name "Silks" came from her love of silks and insistence that all her girls wear them. She died at the age of 83 in 1929 and is buried under the name Martha A. Ready.

***Food:* ★★★½** Being the "mud" season, they only had the bar menu available. I ordered the blackened snapper sandwich which comes with a spiced roll and chili mayonnaise on the side. The snapper was tender and flaky. It was served with a couple of new potatoes cooked just right, carrots in a delectable butter and caraway seed sauce, and green beans with crispy sliced almonds. A very tasty meal! All their sauces are made with homemade ingredients. The rest of the bar menu offers tossed or Caesar's salad, garden vegetable soup, sandwiches (steak Diane and broiled chicken teriyaki), filet mignon, Danish baby-back ribs, chicken fried chicken, and a nightly special like shrimp fettucini. They have different menus for winter and summer and they change every season. Their latest winter menu featured five appetizers that all sound delicious: seafood chowder, smoked salmon, warm smoked duck, shrimp & escargot fettucini, and crab & red pepper ravioli. This is followed by four salad selections: tossed, Greek, roquefort, and Caesar's. The menu gets even better with their choices of pasta: charbroiled chicken breast sliced over parsley and garlic fettucini with pine nuts and endive Alfredo sauce; shrimp, scallops and salmon in smoked tomato and garlic cream over saffron pasta; and spinach and riccota ravioli with sun dried tomatoes and calamari olive teppanade cream. Some of the special entrees include fresh grilled North Atlantic swordfish, pan-seared fresh salmon, blackened red snapper, Rocky Mountain trout in pecan crust with rock shrimp, lemon pepper veal with cognac sauce, and veal medallions with bay scallops and bernaise sauce. They offer 50 imported beers along with a full bar. A few of their desserts sound delicious: warm chocolate chunk bread pudding with heavy cream, carmel custard with fresh fruit, and apple and rhubarb Brown Betty with English cream.

Service: ★★★½ I had a very good waitress and a pleasant conversation with Bill Gander, one of the owners.

Decor: ★★★★½ The elegant decor of this restaurant reminded me of eighteen century Victorian Boston: high vaulted ceilings draped in rust-colored satin, red-felt drapes with white curtains, dark blue wallpaper with a leaf pattern, wax candles in silver and smoked-glass holders, red carpet to match the drapes, and white tablecloths to match the curtains. There are a couple of gold-framed mirrors, chandeliers, several potted and hanging plants, a trellis entrance from one dining room to the next, and a balcony dining area. There is one dining room downstairs and two upstairs with the bar/lounge. Total seating is about 115 in the dining rooms and 45 in the bar/lounge.

Atmosphere: ★★★½ Not much clientele here in the off-season; only a few patrons sitting at the bar and playing the video game. The dining rooms were vacant. It is difficult to rate atmosphere under these circumstances, but if appearances mean anything, the decor indicates a most pleasant dining experience during the regular seasons.

THE ORE HOUSE (AT THE PINE GROVE RANCH) ★★★★
1465 PINE GROVE ROAD (303)879-1190

Dinner $$$-$$$$. 7 nights 5PM-10PM.
Type: Steak. Located in a barn that is about 100 years old, The Ore House has been a restaurant since 1971.

Food: ★★★★ I had a hefty size meal here that had me taking some elk home for the next day's lunch. The 15-item salad bar included rainbow macaroni salad, gnocchi salad and seven dressings including poppyseed-mustard vinaigrette and tamari sesame. I liked the sweet tamari sesame dressing. My elk was a thick, eight-ounce serving, perfectly cooked medium rare, as I ordered it, and served with red current au jus on the side for dipping. The ranch potatoes were sautéed with onions. The mixed vegetables were properly cooked and included zucchini, yellow squash, carrots, onions, broccoli, and cauliflower. Dinner also came with wheat and cinnamon rolls. Their menu features buffalo and cherry smoked pheasant: all low in calories, fat and cholesterol. The list of appetizers includes coyote or popcorn shrimp, ribs, smoky steak bits, and, one you do not see too often: lemon pepper gator. Skewered venison with sweet onion, bell pepper and roasted corn; and duck à l'orange are the other game dinner offerings. Their charbroiled burgers are made with a combination of ground buffalo and top sirloin. The entree selections are prime rib; steaks (filet with cracked pepper & spices, marinated & grilled sirloin, and a center-cut filet wrapped in bacon and topped with crab & bernaise); seafood (shrimp scampi, salmon, crab legs, and lobster tail); baby-back pork ribs; and grilled, teriyaki, lime, barbecued, or mesquite-smoked chicken. King crab or Cajun chicken salads are available for the lighter eater and there is a children's menu. Kona coffee, my personal favorite, is on the list of beverages and, for dessert, you have your choice of mountain mud pie, cheesecake with berries, deep-dish cobbler à la mode, and ice cream.

Service: ★★★★½ The host and waitress were very friendly, pleasant, and full of smiles. They made you feel glad that you came.

Decor: ★★★★ Old photographs of Steamboat Springs and antique articles taken from the ranch provide a rich, historical ambiance for this rustic restaurant. Five dining rooms can seat about 250 in addition to the bar/lounge. Rough, natural wood walls with a lot of windows, and wood-beams on a flat ceiling, create a century-old mystic. Take time to look around at the big wagon-wheels, the huge skull with horns, and the sleigh at the top of the circular staircase. Upstairs you will find an enchanting night photo of snow-covered trees with long shadows under a full moon and pictures of Mt. Nefzger. Downstairs you can wander by attractive barrel-shaped light fixtures, kerosene lanterns, a cobblestone fireplace, white curtains with a flower pattern, potted jade plants in the window sills, saddles, spats, an iron wheel, a circular mirror, and a horseshoe. Outside you can view pine trees, mountains in the distance and the ski runs. This is a charming old place.

Atmosphere: ★★★★ Country music plays clearly over the speakers. A relaxed, jovial group dines here.

SCOTTY'S BARBECUE ★★
120 FIFTH ST (303)879-8177

Lunch/dinner $$-$$$. 7 days 11AM-8PM.
Type: Barbecue. $.50 per meal added for to go items

Food: ★★ *Service:* ★★½ *Decor:* ★★½ *Atmosphere:* ★★

This is a small, one-room, "hole in the wall" restaurant that has 10 tables covered with red-and-white-checkered tablecloths. There are a hodge-podge of pictures showing a skier, cowboys & rodeos, a railroad, Indians, a couple of stags butting horns, and two cute pictures of a cow girl carrying her ropes and stirrups with the captions "I don't do windows" under the first picture and "I don't make coffee, either" under the second. Coffee cans, canisters, milk buckets and similar paraphernalia can be found in an antique wood cabinet with glass doors setting along the left wall. As for the food, I found nothing special about the ribs. The waitress said they were baby-backs, but at five-to-six-inches in length, they were too big to be baby-backs. The meat was tender and the sauce served warm in a Glosch beer bottle, but it tasted like it came out of another store bottle. The beans with pork tasted like they came out of a can. The pickle was soft and the orange slice old. The best part of the meal was the fried corn. It was crispy and crunchy: an interesting alternative from the usual corn-on-the-cob. My server checked in on me between studying algebra. Rock music was playing quietly in the background while a World Football League game, with no sound, was on the television behind the bar. Only one other customer came in while I was there. This was typical "mud" season attendance.

STEAMBOAT YACHT CLUB ★★½
811 YAMPA AV (303)879-4774

Sunday brunch/lunch $$, dinner $$$$ (a few $$$). 7 days 11:30AM-2:30PM and 6PM-10PM (9PM Memorial Day to Labor Day). Afternoon menu 2:30PM-5:30PM.
Type: Seafood. Pipes and cigars discouraged in the dining room. A 15% gratuity added to parties of six or more.

***Food:* ★½ *Service:* ★★½ *Decor:* ★★★½ *Atmosphere:* ★★★**

Their food, overall, was very disappointing. The best part of the lunch was the clam chowder with fresh orange clams, onions and parsley in a thin broth. My broccoli, salmon and yellow squash quiche was very dry, as was my dinner salad. My co-worker's roast beef deli, made with cole slaw on the sandwich, was soggy and not very good. Service was satisfactory. The decor was very nice with an indoor and outdoor deck; pictures of the Yale and Columbia boat houses, clipper ships and crew teams; and a two-sided cobblestone fireplace. Soft rock music was playing a little too loud as a gentle breeze passed through the covered part of the deck. Outside, we could watch kayaks and a chocolate-colored labrador retriever make their way down the Yampa River.

WINONA'S ★★★
617 SOUTH LINCOLN AV (303)879-2483

Breakfast/lunch $. MON-SAT 7AM-3PM. Closed SUN.
Type: Deli. Travelers checks or local checks over #500 accepted.

Food: ★★★ I ordered the Philly cheesesteak: a nicely grilled steak that was not too greasy with Provolone, mild yellow peppers, onions and a few mushrooms on a hoagy roll. Other hot sandwiches include a mushroom cheesesteak, gyro, Reuben, and a veggie meltdown. The cold sandwich selections feature corned beef, pastrami, turkey, and hickory smoked ham on your choice of oat nut, rye or kaiser roll. Hoagies are served on an Italian roll with your choice of meat with the trimmings. You can also pick a burger or salad (chef, Greek, chicken or tuna) and finish your lunch with killer carrot cake, chocolate suicide cake (these people sound like they are into death!) key lime pie or Southern pecan pie. Everything at Winona's is homemade and cooked to order without any MSG or preservatives. For breakfast you can enjoy homemade granola and muffins; a strawberry yogurt smoothie; smoked pork chops; salami; buttermilk, blueberry, or sunflower-seed and raisin pancakes; and bagels with lox or cinnamon-raisin cream cheese.

Service: ★★½ You order at the counter and the waitress brings your food to your table. You also have to bus your own table. The orders are taken and the food served with a smile.

Decor: ★★★ This is a small one-room restaurant with 12 natural wood tables and 34 natural wood chairs. Six tables are along the right wall that is decorated with framed posters of Steamboat, the 75th winter carnival, summer and winter mountain scenes and American Indians. Five tables are in the front section looking out onto Lincoln Avenue and the red awning outside. A white, four-foot, wall separates this section from a single table for six. There is an eight-foot-long enclosed entrance way with tinted windows depicting tulips. Just inside the entrance way is a steer skull.

Atmosphere: ★★★ The clientele on the day I was here was a combination of housewives, businessmen, blue color workers, and a family. This is a popular place with a wide variety of locals and for good reason: it is a quiet place to enjoy an inexpensive meal and relax.

STERLING

The town derived its name from Sterling, Illinois, the home town of surveyor David Leavitt who started a ranch here in the 1870s. The South Platte River and the old Overland Trail pass through this area. Later developments included the arrival of the Burlington Railroad in 1887, Great Western Sugar Company in 1905, the Overland Trail Museum in 1936, and Northeastern Junior College in 1941. The Overland Trail Museum (open to the public) is a reproduction of Fort Sedgewick and records the migration of Americans into the West.

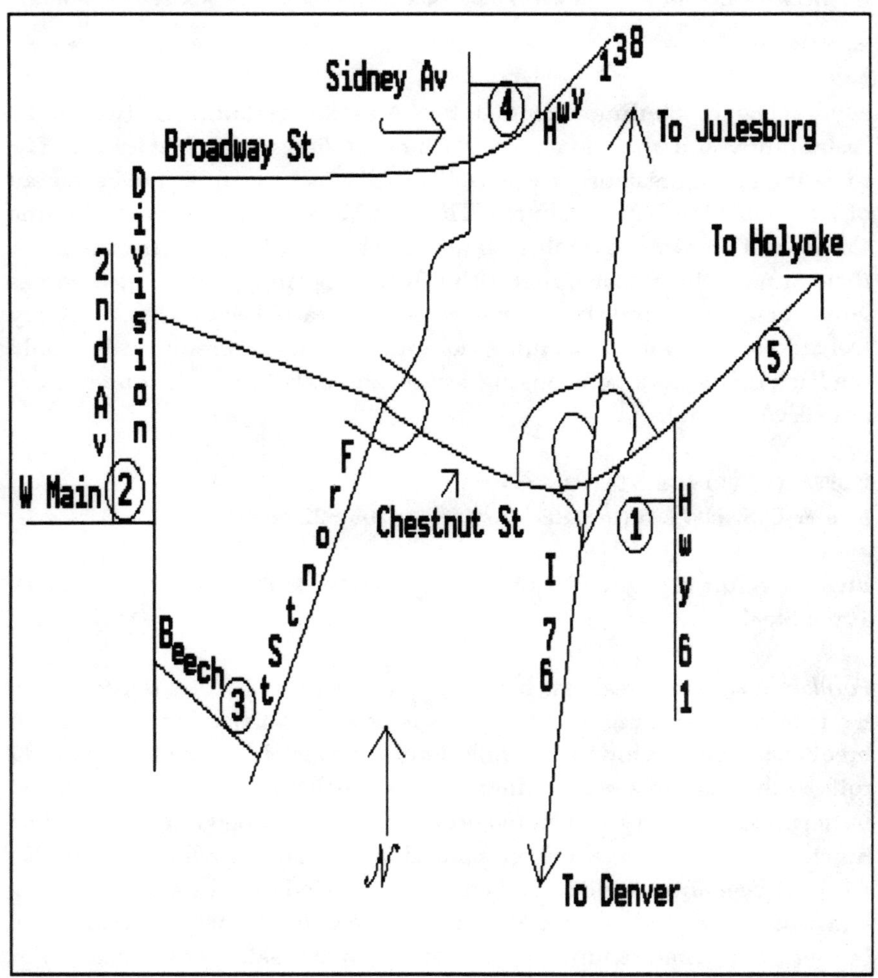

STERLING

Restaurants and Ratings:	Food	Service	Decor	Atm	Overall
1. BUFFALO SPRINGS STATION	★★★	★★★	★★★½	★★★	★★★
2. CHINA GARDEN	★★	★½	★★½	★★½	★★
3. DELGADO'S	★★½	★★½	★★★★	★★★½	★★★
4. MOMMA CONDE'S	★★★½	★★	★★	★★½	★★½
5. PARK INN	★★★	★★★½	★★★★	★★★★	★★★½

My review of Sterling included two Mexican restaurants, two motel restaurants, and the town's only Chinese/Vietnamese restaurant. The most interesting restaurant was Delgado's, which occupies the basement of a former First Baptist Church. The best Mexican food was at Momma Conde's. The nicest overall restaurant was the Park Inn. Try them for their Sunday Breakfast Buffet. The Buffalo Springs Station also serves good breakfasts and has some interesting articles of decor. Only Delgado's and Momma Conde's do not accept major credit cards. Only the Park Inn offers a nonsmoking section and only Momma Conde's does not serve alcohol.

BUFFALO SPRINGS STATION ★★★
I-76 & U.S. HWY. 6 (IN THE DAYS INN) (303)522-6660.

Breakfast/lunch $, dinner $-$$$. 7 days 6AM-9PM (10PM in the summer). Type: Steak.

Food: ★★★ I ate breakfast here: poached eggs with corned beef hash. Everything, including the coffee, was to my satisfaction. Additional breakfast items include low cholesterol sausage; homemade cinnamon rolls with cream cheese frosting; huevos rancheros; chicken fried steak; buttermilk, blueberry and strawberry pancakes; and Belgian waffles. The lunch menu features a dozen sandwich selections (including chicken Alfredo; beef and Cheddar; and crab with sautéed onions, green peppers, and mushrooms); five specials, such as deep-fried shrimp or linguini; burgers; homemade soup; salads, including a taco salad; and omelets. For dessert, there are pies, cakes, ice cream specialties, sherbet, cheesecakes, and strawberry shortcakes. Dinner specials feature a soup & salad bar, Alaskan snowcrab legs, Rocky Mountain trout, chicken teriyaki or ivory (with onions & mushrooms sautéed in Chablis), roast sirloin, and deep-fried fish. On FRI and SAT prime rib is available. THU is Mexican fiesta night. A SUN champagne brunch is served from 11AM-2PM for $7.95 ($5.95 for seniors). It includes a dozen entrees, such as roast baron of beef and sugar-cured ham; potatoes; vegetables; breads; homemade soup and salad bar; omelets; egg dishes; pastries; and desserts.

Service: ★★★ Accommodating. My waitress went out of her way to make a copy of the breakfast menu for me.

Decor: ★★★½ This single-room restaurant has six booths, three on each side, and eleven tables in-between, for a total seating capacity of 62. Rust-colored chairs and bench seats, pale green and white plaster walls, and pink table settings provide an attractive blend of colors. The plaster walls are uneven, as if someone had just slapped on the plaster. I found it both provocative and entertaining. Above the booths is an array of old farm aids: large milk buckets, a sewing machine, lanterns, a water pitcher and a gas tank, to mention a few. Accompanying these artifacts inside the booths are black-and-white sketches of farm and pasture scenes. White verticals separated by red-brick columns cover the windows along the rear wall. Ample lighting is provided by four copper-colored chandeliers with eight frosted-glass lanterns in a circle on each fixture. There is an additional dining room available for banquets, special parties, buffets, or SUN brunch. It has eight tables for 41 people, a piano in the corner, the same style chandeliers and jagged plaster, and no wall decorations.

Atmosphere: ★★★ This is a quiet family place with no music. Most of the clientele are motel guests.

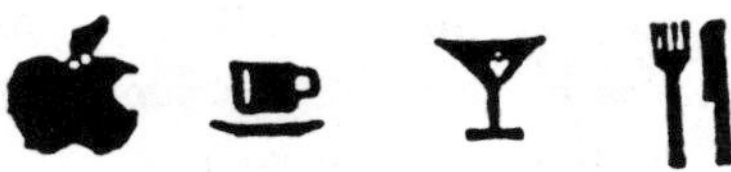

CHINA GARDEN ★★
126 W. MAIN ST. (303)522-1137

STERLING

Lunch/dinner $-$$. MON-SAT 11AM-2:30PM and 4:30PM-9:30PM. Closed SUN.
Type: Oriental (Chinese & Vietnamese). Take-out available.

***Food:* ★★ *Service:* ★½ *Decor:* ★★½ *Atmosphere:* ★★½**

I ordered the Vietnamese lemon-grass shrimp. It came with about a dozen small shrimp, an abundance of sliced onion, a few scallions, lemon-grass seasoning and sesame seed. It was advertised as "hot & spicy," but I only found that it had too much soy sauce and was not hot at all. This was only a fair meal. The tea was lukewarm. One of the more interesting Chinese choices is Tsing-Tao beer chicken. Some of the less-common Vietnamese selections are coconut chicken, honey crispy chicken, lemon-grass chicken or beef, and French steak (sautéed quickly on a high flame in French sauce). The table service was average. The waitress understood very little English. I tried to ask her what type of fish were in the fish tank and she responded with "Oscar." Either that is a type of fish my dictionary and I are unfamiliar with, or it is the fish's pet name, or she simply did not understand my question. She had one irritating trait: on certain occasions, when she entered the kitchen, she would practically shriek something in Chinese to the cook. The fish tank is at the entrance with three good-sized fish about a foot-long each. The tank needed cleaning badly. To the right of the entrance are two dining rooms divided by a cherry wood wall with bars. The first room has six booths and two small tables for a total of 28 people. The second room has nine tables for 40. The two rooms are decorated in red and gold with ornaments of Chinese letters and symbols and three large three-dimensional gold murals depicting Chinese life. The atmosphere was pleasant enough. There was a quiet clientele for lunch. Oriental music played softly in the background. As I was leaving, two women just entering the restaurant were having a discussion regarding the fish. One woman was trying to convince the other that the fish in the tank were piranha. The waitress came by and the women asked her what type of fish they were. She responded with "Oscar"!

DELGADO'S ★★★
116 BEECH (303)522-0175

Lunch/dinner $ TUE-SAT 11AM-2PM. TUE-SUN 5PM-9PM. Closed MON. Type: Mexican. Personal checks accepted.

Food: ★★½ Their salsa is a thick tomato sauce with red peppers; no green chili or jalapeño peppers. The chips are standard. Their regular Margaritas are very good. Apparently they have a reputation for good Margaritas and I would concur with that opinion. They also serve strawberry, peach and pineapple Margaritas. I ordered the chili relleno and bean burrito combination. They were both good. However, I thought the chili relleno could have used less breading and more onion and spices. I particularly liked the beans in the burrito. The meal came with lettuce, one tomato slice, sour cream on the side and was topped with cheese. Lunch is basic a la carte. A few noteworthy items are the guacamole tostado, softshell taco, and cinnamon ice cream. The dinner menu offers ten combinations. The entrees include beef and cheese sopapillas, and chili verde or pork meat with sauce. Nachos or quesadillas can be ordered as appetizers. Chimichangas, tamales and taco salad are available a la carte.

Service: ★★½ The service was a little slow, but I had a pleasant conversation with my server. They did seat me fifteen minutes before closing which is not something I can say about every restaurant that I have been to in Colorado. According to the waitress, they served 201 people in four hours that evening. That's about two and a half times their capacity.

Decor: ★★★★ Located in the basement of what used to be a First Baptist Church, this 13-year-old restaurant is in a white building with a red-brick front around the entrance. The stairway leading down takes you through a black-iron gate into a room with a low brown ceiling and red-brick walls that feature plaster cameos in the booths. There are five booths and 18 tables for total seating of 83. Corrugated-wood and dark-wood posts divide the booths, while light, unfinished-wood is used as dividers throughout the restaurant. I think converting a church into a restaurant is a great use for these classic and historic buildings. Delgado's also has a lounge upstairs for banquets.

Atmosphere: ★★★½ This is a very popular restaurant. It was about 75 percent full right before closing on a FRI night. Mexican accordion music is played in the background. My one main objection to this place was the lighting. They have very bright ceiling and booth lights that could use a shade. On the far side of the room is a nice, cozy alcove with a single table for six behind another black-iron gate. The alcove's walls are decorated with ornaments of knights, and the lighting fixtures, brass with yellow-tinted glass, provide much softer light.

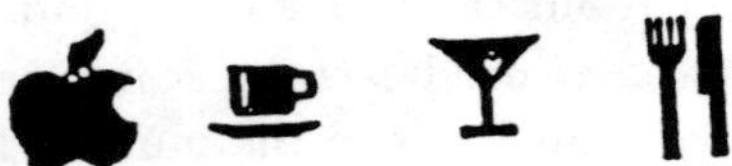

MOMMA CONDE'S ★★½
100 BROADWAY (BROADWAY PLAZA SHOPPING CENTER) (303)522-0802.

Lunch/dinner $. MON-THU 11AM-8PM. FRI-SAT 11AM-9PM. Closed SUN

Food: ★★★½ *Service:* ★★ *Decor:* ★★ *Atmosphere:* ★★½

This is a Mexican restaurant with burgers. I ordered a smothered chili relleno and a softshell taco. The relleno was excellent. The green chili practically falls over itself as you cut into it. This is one big chili! It comes with lettuce and tomato and is topped with pork sauce and melted cheese. The pork sauce was delectable. The softshell taco came in a large tortilla shell with a good portion of lean ground beef, plus lettuce and tomato. Despite the high quality of the ingredients, the taco was dry. I would still recommend it. Just order a side of picante sauce, sour cream or guacamole. Service was Fair. This is a long, single-room restaurant with eight booths and nine tables for a total of 67 people. Wood-framed free-standing dividers (that don't stand up straight) separate the small tables. Gold-framed colored-prints under glass depicting flowers, a gazebo, ducks, and a sailing ship (some of my favorite things), hang on the concrete block walls. Country music played from a small speaker that could be barely heard. This is a popular place for young families and young couples.

PARK INN ★★★½
I-76 & U.S. HWY. 6 (303)522-2625

Breakfast $-$$, dinner $$-$$$. MON-SAT 6AM-9AM and 4PM-10PM. SUN 7AM-2PM.
Type: Family. Reservations requested.

Food: ★★★ I ordered a light lunch. The vegetable soup had a lot of cabbage, celery and carrots, but primarily cabbage. The beef sandwich had a lot of lean fresh beef. (By the way, they no longer serve lunch). Breakfast specialties include eggs or crepes Benedict; breakfast, taco, or ham and cheese burritos; Belgian waffles; chicken fried steaks; and pork chops. Dinner offers a wide selection of appetizers, salads, Chinese, Mexican, Italian, poultry, seafood, steaks, sandwiches, light meals, and desserts. Some examples of these are nachos, Buffalo wings, shrimp or taco salad, chicken or shrimp stir fry, a sierra flauta, stuffed manicotti, chicken Cordon Bleu, prime rib, and German chocolate cake. The 20-item soup, salad and dessert bar is offered daily. On FRI there is a surf and farm buffet from 5:30PM-8:30PM.

Service: ★★★½ Friendly, very helpful, and with a smile.

Decor: ★★★★ This restaurant is one large, single room that wraps around the lounge. The front section of the dining room has five booths and 13 tables for a total of 72 people and is nonsmoking. The beige wallpaper is decorated with pictures of Civil War soldiers, cowboys, and horses. The section to the rear and right has six booths, the same number of tables, and is for smoking. This section has six large rectangular skylights and nature scene paintings of "Prewitt Reservoir," "Boulder Canyon," and "Elk in the Mountains." Kerosene candles and fresh green and white carnations add a nice touch to the tables. Seating is at rust-colored, cloth-cushioned, wood-framed chairs and brown cloth-cushioned benches. The buffet, soup & salad bars and an organ separate the two sections. The only negative aspect was the bright lights hanging above the booths.

Atmosphere: ★★★★ This is Sterling's premier restaurant and a little higher class than the others. Equally so are the clientele.

TRINIDAD

Named after the Holy Trinity, Trinidad was originally called Rio de Las Animas and first settled in 1859. Many famous western figures played a part in Trinidad's history: Bat Masterson, who was sheriff in the 1880s, Wyatt Earp, who drove the stage, Billy the Kid, and Kit Carson, whose statue graces the park that bears his name. While in Trinidad, I took an interesting side trip to Drop City, three miles northeast of I-25 and Exit 15, on Highway 239. Once a 1960s hippie settlement, there remains today a dome-shaped building made entirely of car parts, mostly fenders and doors. If you have an extra hour, take your camera and go see it.

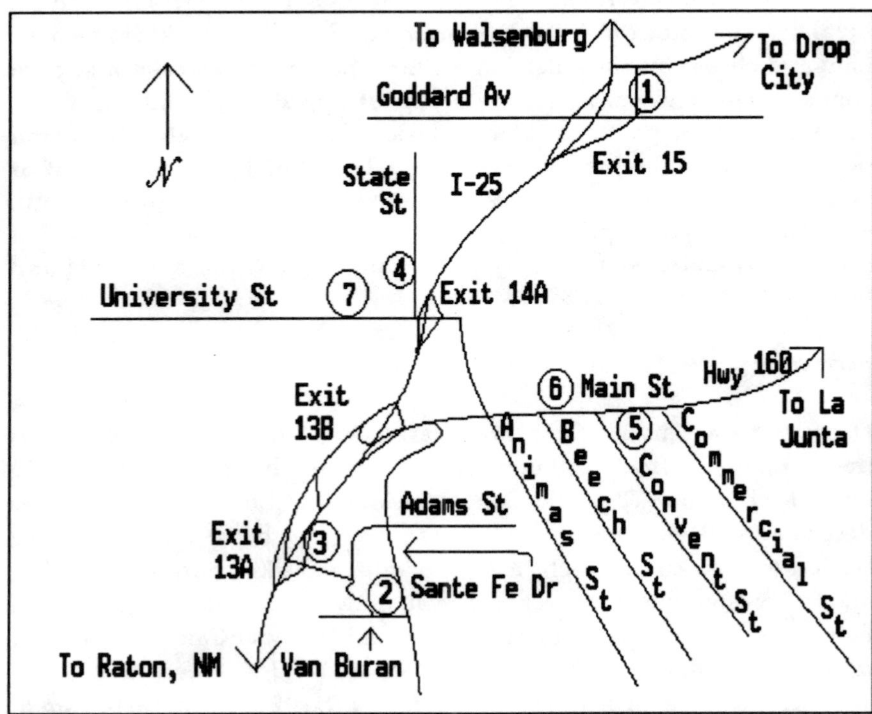

Nana & Nano's is a truly authentic Italian restaurant that you do not find very often in small town Colorado. La Fiesta serves excellent homemade Mexican food and Maria's has outstanding chili rellenos. Maria's is the only restaurant that does not accept major credit cards. All restaurants, except El Capitan, provide a nonsmoking section. Chef Liu's, El Capitan, and Herllee's are the only restaurants that serve alcohol.

Restaurants and Ratings:	Food	Service	Decor	Atm	Overall
1. BOB LEE'S	★★★	★★★	★★	★★	★★½
2. CHEF LIU'S	★★★½	★★★	★★★	★★★½	★★★½
3. EL CAPITAN	★★	★	★★★½	★★	★★
4. HERLLEE'S	★★★	★★½	★★★★	★★★	★★★
5. LA FIESTA	★★★★	★★★★½	★★★½	★★★½	★★★★
6. MARIA'S	★★★★	★★★½	★★½	★★½	★★★
7. NANA & NANO'S	★★★★½	★★★★★	★★★★½	★★★★	★★★★½

BOB LEE'S ★★½
2008 FREEDOM ROAD (719)846-4570

Breakfast/lunch $, dinner $$. MON-SAT 6AM-8PM. SUN 6AM-7PM. Type: Family. $5 minimum order. Free delivery in city limits.

Food: ★★★ *Service:* ★★★ *Decor:* ★★ *Atmosphere:* ★★

I ordered the Santa Fe Trail Burger: a half-pound of ground meat on a sesame seed bun with Cheddar cheese, mild green-chili strips, Swiss and bacon. Lettuce, tomato, onion and pickles are served on the side and it comes with French fries. I was literally cracking my jaw trying to open my mouth wide enough to eat this monster. It was a good charbroiled burger, even if it was a little overdone for my liking. The fries were average. There were many tables cluttered with dirty dishes when I arrived about 6:30PM on a Sunday evening. They were very apologetic about it. As I later learned from the busboy, he had been at work since they opened at 6AM. One of his replacements called in sick and the other did not show up at all, so he had the burden all day. I can sympathize with that. They were quick to take my order and my meal was served in about seven or eight minutes. They did try very hard to please and had the right attitude. This restaurant is located at the end of a strip shopping center with Walmart at the other end. There are two rooms. The first has ten tables for 40 people. The second room, to the left, has 14 tables for 64 people. It is in two sections divided by the soup and salad bar. The first dining room has several polished-wood picture clocks for sale. They include pictures of Elvis Presley, kittens, a husky, a unicorn, ducks, and a mountain cabin and waterwheel by a stream with full fall colors. The second dining room has framed displays of arrowheads for sale. Separating this display is an unusual artwork of skyscrapers made from a reflective silver material. This is a good family restaurant: quiet, no music, and, with its location on the far north side of Trinidad, somewhat detached from the main activity of the town.

CHEF LIU'S ★★★½
1423 SANTA FE TRAIL (719)846-3333

Lunch/dinner $-$$ (with some $$$). 7 days 11AM-9:30PM. (DEC-MAR: Closed TUE).
Type: Oriental (Chinese).

Food: **★★★½** I ordered the triple delight: beef, chicken and shrimp in a brown spicy sauce with black mushrooms, bamboo shoots, broccoli, green beans, baby corn and black beans. Hot tea, sweet and sour sauce made with pineapple, orange and lemon; and hot mustard sauce are served on the side. The meal came with hot and sour soup made with a rich eggflower broth. It was hot, spicy and quite good. For the entree, the beef and chicken were tender, but the shrimp were small and average. The meal was not filling. In fact, I would call it a light meal. They offer several lunch specials in all the major Chinese food groups: pork, chicken, shrimp, beef and noodles; as well as a half-dozen lunch combinations. They have 11 appetizers, such as shrimp Rangoon with cream cheese and onion, paper-wrapped chicken, and barbecued pork or spare ribs; eight different soups, including crabmeat with asparagus, and abalone with chicken; a dozen chicken entrees, like curry, almond, cashew or lemon; nine pork entrees, such as Mongolian, mu shu, and in plum sauce; ten beef entrees, including broccoli, Hunan, and pepper steak; 17 seafood entrees, mostly shrimp, but also scallops, lobster and crab legs; five vegetarian dishes; soft noodles; fried rice; seven family dinners; and a dozen specialties, including Peking shrimp or duck, beef and scallops, volcano shrimp, and sizzling lobster and beef.

Service: ★★★ Pleasant.

Decor: ★★★ This restaurant has dining room seating for about 90 people, plus additional seating around a dance floor. At the entrance are two small rooms: one to the left with three tables for 12 people and one to the right with a single table for six. Two white arches provide the entrance to the nonsmoking room which has 11 tables covered with white tablecloths for 48 people. The decor is typical Chinese with hanging lights in orange, pumpkin-style holders; red tassels with green bobs; gold fans; red and gold dragon ornaments; and, a large colorful mural with several characters in what resembles a royal palace scene. The smoking room in the back has six tables for 20 people plus a bar with four black stools. There is a jukebox, brown wood-beamed ceiling and brown carpet, painted red-brick wall and fireplace with beige fans, and brown-cushioned chairs in gold-metal frames. There is an additional room three steps down to the right with 11 tables for 46 people around a dance floor. At the end of the room is a stage. Mirrors cover the right wall; windows are on the left. Country-western music is played here every Thursday night starting at 9pm.

Atmosphere: ★★★½ Chinese music plays softly in the background. They have a quiet clientele.

EL CAPITAN ★★
321 STATE ST. (719)846-9903

Lunch/dinner $-$$. MON-THU 11AM-9PM. FRI 11AM-10PM. SAT 4PM-10PM. Closed SUN.
Type: Mexican.

Food: ★★ *Service:* ★ *Decor:* ★★★½ *Atmosphere:* ★★

The homemade vegetable beef soup with potatoes was good. The salad bar was minimal. I ordered the chicken fillet, which turned out to be five deep-fried chicken strips. They were not moist and tender and just a few drops above dry. The potato and peas were satisfactory. El Capitan has a full Mexican menu with stuffed sopapillas, tamales, green chilies, red or green chili, beef chimichangas, and eggs rancheros. The lunch/dinner menu also features burgers, sandwiches, steaks, Italian dishes, chicken, and shrimp. A busgirl seated me immediately upon entering, but at an uncleared table. I chalk that up to inexperience. Dinner took 25 minutes from ordering to being served. The salad bar "greets" you when you first walk through the entrance. The first dining room has eight tables for 30 people. The room is divided by a wall with very large - about four-inch-by-16-inch - gold-colored stones. In style with the Mexican/Italian menu, there is a painting of Venice and another of a fountain in front of an adobe building. The carpet looks more like a runner: brown and flat. The second dining room has 12 tables for 50 people, a picture of a courtyard with Spanish arches and an interesting picture which reminded me of Italy (a woman wearing a turban and walking up some alley steps). Both rooms are well lit and divided by a wall with a large mirror and two sliding doors. There is an adjacent bar/lounge to the right of the restaurant entrance with two tables, four booths and seven bar chairs for a total of 33 people. Upstairs there is a banquet room. Carly Simon music played in the background, but you could barely hear it. It was quite busy in here on Saturday night. One large party of 15 took up a third of the back room and another party of about eight took two tables at the other end. Some whining children entered the scene before I had a chance to leave to make matters worse. A varied clientele could be found here, however. Overall, I would have to say that El Capitan was more like Le Ensign, or perhaps even El Kid.

HERLLEE'S (FORMERLY THE COUNTRY CLUB) ★★★
I-25 & EXIT 13A (IN THE BEST WESTERN MOTOR INN) (719)846-6246

Breakfast/lunch $, dinner $$. 7 days 6AM-9PM.
Type: Family. $1 extra plate charge.

Food: ★★★ Their coffee is good. My mushroom and cheese omelet had fresh mushrooms that tasted like mushrooms and not tofu. The hash browns were average. Other breakfast items include pigs in a blanket, coconut or pecan pancakes, eggs Benedict, buttermilk biscuits, and giant blueberry or banana nut muffins. The lunch menu features seven burger choices, soup, salad, sandwiches (French dip, club, turkey or roast beef with Cheddar, and charbroiled chicken breast or sirloin), and the following specials: roast turkey or sirloin, fried chicken, baby beef or chicken liver, pork chops, and cod filets. A children's menu and desserts (pies, carrot cake, cheesecake, ice cream and sherbet) are also available. Dinner entrees specialize in seafood (trout, shrimp, cod, halibut, and red snapper) and steaks. Other items include charbroiled chicken teriyaki, chili rellenos, chili, and omelets.

Service: ★★½ Pleasant, but a little slow. They have a tendency to forget to bring the check.

Decor: ★★★★ A wall of windows to the left and rear provides a view of the hills to the west, over I-25, and to the north — which IS the decor in this restaurant. The nonsmoking section, along the left row of windows, has ten tables for 40 people. The smoking section has 12 tables for 48 people. Additional seating is provided by eight tables for 32 people in a room adjacent to the smoking section and separated by a folding wall divider. The room between the front lobby and the restaurant has nine tables without settings. The cloth chairs are an orange-rust color in a gold-metal frame. The matching rug is a combination of brown, beige, rust, and a touch of blue. The orange verticals complement the decor. Chandeliers in glass-umbrella structures with gold edges, and plants in wicker baskets, hang from the ceiling. The salad bar is set up along one smoking-section wall decorated with two mirrors, a wreath, and two pictures of flowers and butterflies. The smoking section is separated from the bar/lounge by a brick fireplace with a picture of wild horses.

Atmosphere: ★★★ Comfortable, quiet and relaxed. The live entertainment on weekends in the lounge next door does not begin until 9PM when the restaurant closes. The clientele was varied and obviously included tourists and people staying at the motel. This is a good, clean, wholesome restaurant. Also, it is a popular place for the local police, which should tell you something about their coffee. And then there is the view!

La Fiesta ★★★★
134 W. Main St., Suite #14 (719)846-8221

Breakfast/lunch/dinner $. MON-SAT 10AM-8PM. Closed SUN.
Type: Mexican. Take-out available. 20¢ charge per container. 20¢ charge for special orders.

Food: ★★★★ This is one of the few Mexican restaurant I have been to that serves its chips hot, straight from the oven. They are fresh and crisp. Make sure you order some with guacamole to munch on while you wait for your meal. The guacamole is fresh also and is made with onion, garlic, cottage cheese, tomato, and chili or jalapeño peppers. It is spicy, but not too hot. Everything here is homemade. I ordered the green chili burger, their FRI specialty. It is a ground burger, in a sopapilla, topped with lettuce, tomato and cheese. The gravy sauce was especially good. It will put just a little fire in the back of your throat. It is spicy, but not red-hot. Their menu for the first meal of the day includes huevos rancheros, menudo, and hot apple cider. The lunch/dinner menu is complete Mexican with red or green chili, chili fries, and tamales; with (a slight touch of American) burgers. The daily specials on the other days of the week are: MON-enchiladas, TUE-tacos, WED-chicken crispas, THU-Mexican, and SAT-chili rellenos.

Service: ★★★★½ Ask for Brenda. She is exceptionally pleasant.

Decor: ★★★½ This restaurant is located in the basement of the Bell Block. It consists of two rooms separated by the kitchen. The nonsmoking room to the right has three booths and four tables for a total of 30 people. Stone walls are to the right and left; the back wall is pink with baby blue doors and door frames. The ceiling is low with heat ducts visible overhead. There is very little decor: menu signs on the back and left walls and small Mexican weavings and hats. However, the rock walls speak for themselves. Each table has a ceramic artwork resembling either a Spanish house with cactus or some Mexican lads in big sombreros. These ceramic pieces contain the salt, pepper, sugar, cream and honey. Seating is on comfortable and attractive brown-cushioned benches and orange-cushioned chairs in wood frames. The smoking room, back and to the left, has two sections: three booths and a table in the lower section, and six booths in the upper section to the rear. Total seating in this room is 46. The stone wall extends around the three sides with a few red bricks filling in the right side. There is a fireplace on the left and just a few Mexican weavings, hats, and a mirror. The room is well lit with track studio lights. In the front of the restaurant, by the windows, are three stone columns and two booths. A point of historical interest: this building burned in an arson fire in 1975, but was restored by community leaders. It now consists of red brick, mortar, and stone from the old days, combined with new wood and plaster from the restoration.

Atmosphere: ★★★½ This restaurant attracts both locals and tourists. It provides a nice atmosphere for people of all ages. The owner, Lou Ann, has been in the restaurant business since she was 16.

MARIA'S ★★★
219 W. MAIN ST (719)846-4962

Breakfast $, lunch/dinner $-$$. TUE-SAT 7AM-8PM. SUN 8AM-4PM. (NOV-FEB: Closed MON).
Type: Mexican.

Food: ★★★★ Their salsa carries a little "kick." I highly recommend their chili rellenos. They are outstanding: golden brown, fluffy, perfectly fried with just enough cheese oozing out so you can eat them with a fork or with your hand. I ordered them with green chili, but they are just as grand alone. They are served with beans, rice, lettuce, tomato and two sopapillas. Honey is provided at every table. This is a close second to La Fiesta for best Mexican food in Trinidad. The lunch menu offers tamales, stuffed sopapillas, chili caribe, flautas, chicken or steak fajitas, carne adovada rancheros, posole, menudo, chili, burgers, green chiliburgers, hot dogs, sandwiches, fish & chips, and salads. Fruit and cream pies, ice cream, and homemade Danish can be ordered for dessert.

Service: ★★★½ A very pleasant and cheerful young waitress.

Decor: ★★½ This is a long, divided, single-room restaurant. The front nonsmoking section has six tables and three booths for a total of 32 people. The back smoking section has seven booths and 10 tables for 58. A wood-paneled structure with Mexican rugs, hanging plants, ristras, and candles separates the two sections. Wall decor includes mantels with ceramic pots and potted plants, Mexican hats and rugs, a picture of a señorita playing maracas, and a picture of a señor taking a siesta under a palm tree. The restaurant runs into the coffee station on the left and the server station and kitchen in the rear.

Atmosphere: ★★½ There was a lot of noise coming from the kitchen which you can see into through the server window. No music. A quiet, mixed clientele of differing ages and ethnic backgrounds.

NANA & NANO'S ★★★★½
415 UNIVERSITY (719)846-2696

Lunch $, dinner $-$$. Memorial Day to Labor Day: MON-FRI 11:30AM-1:30PM and 4:30PM-8PM. Labor Day to Memorial Day: WED-FRI 11:30AM-1:30PM. TUE-FRI 4:30PM-8:00PM. Closed MON. Year-round: SAT 4:30PM-8:30PM. Closed SUN.
Type: Italian. 15% gratuity for parties of seven or more. Bibs available-5¢.

Food: ★★★★½ The salad dressings (Italian and creamy Italian) are part of the table setting. I tried both. I preferred the regular Italian which has a sweet taste. The salad comes with a homemade breadstick. I ordered the FRI special: Mostoccioli with meatballs. I had the small portion, which, with the salad and bread, I found very filling. The sauce was moderately spicy. I personally prefer my tomato sauce with a little more oregano and basil, but this was very good. The pasta noodles were tender, al dente, cooked just right. It was almost as good as my mother used to make (her maiden name is Middione. I am half Italian).

The lunch menu features these sandwiches: turkey, ham or pastrami with your choice of cheese (Provolone, American, Swiss, or mozzarella); Italian sausage; meatball; gyro; or Italian beef. Salad, chef salad, pizza, and a soup or pasta of the day are also available. For dessert, the choices are cheesecake, turtle or grasshopper pie, and spumoni or vanilla ice cream. Dinner entrees include spaghetti, ravioli, gnocchi, fettuccine Alfredo or con sugo (with Italian tomato sauce), alla olio (spaghetti with olive oil, garlic & parsley), polenta (corn meal with tomato sauce), and rib eye steak. All pasta dishes come with meatball or Italian sausage, in large or small portions, and take 20 minutes to prepare. It is well worth the wait!

Service: ★★★★★ Fran Monteleone, her daughter Kim, and their friends run a very friendly and successful Italian restaurant. They are very personable and eager to tell their story. Give them an ear while you enjoy some great pasta.

Decor: ★★★★½ The nonsmoking room has 13 tables with red-and-white-checkered tablecloths and red-cushioned chairs in black-metal frames for 50 people. There are red window coverings with white-rope ties, potted plants in the window sills, smooth natural-wood walls, and green napkins and carpet. The wall decorations include two paintings by Fran's aunt, wedding photos of Fran's parents and grandparents, a picture of the Trevi fountain in Rome, a colored map of Italy, Alitalia posters, wreaths from Mexico, and a poster of the different pasta noodles. The room is well-lit by light fixtures with red, cone-shaped shades that hang on three-foot chords. Waitress/daughter Kim informed me that the branding-iron marks on the wood border at the top of the walls was left over from Dairy Queen. These marks look out of place with the Italian decor, but they provide an interesting remnant of the history of the building. Nana & Nano's first opened on July 4, 1988. The rear, smoking section, has seven tables for 30 people in a room with small wicker baskets and artificial flowers hanging from the wood-paneled wall.

Atmosphere: ★★★★ Perry Como, sings "Hot Diggity, Dog Diggity, Boom, What You Do To Me." To some Italians, it just does not get any better than this. This is a good place for families and couples.

Walden was home for the 1990 National Capitol Christmas Tree. In December, 1990, a 65-foot spruce from nearby Routt National Forest was cut and transported to Washington, D.C. to stand in front of the Capitol building. The tree shown here was decorated and stood in this spot for all of 1990 in tribute to this event. This picture was taken in January, 1991, when they were taking the tree down.

TWIN LAKES

This town was named after two natural lakes, each about two miles wide and five miles long. In the 1880s and early 1890s Twin Lakes became a staging center on the wagon route between the silver camps of Aspen and Leadville. Later, the Denver Rio Grande Railroad put a stop in Twin Lakes which further developed the town's growth. Today, The Village of Twin Lakes is a National Historic District.

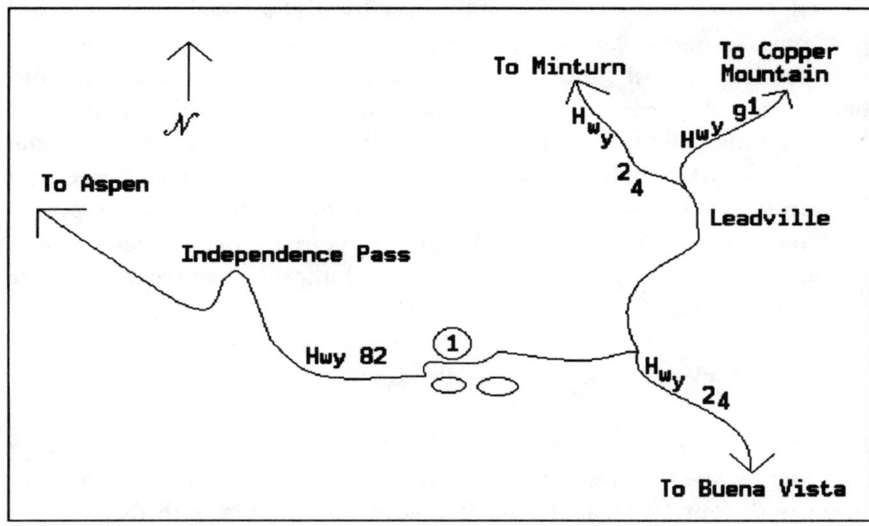

NORDIC INN ★★★★
6435 HWY 82 (719)486-1830

Breakfast/lunch $, dinner $$-$$$. JUN-OCT: 7 days 7AM-10PM. NOV-MAY: SAT 8PM-11PM. SUN 5PM-9PM. (Open on holidays and by reservation in the winter).
Type: German. Credit cards are accepted, they have a nonsmoking section, and they serve alcohol.

Constructed in 1879 as a stagecoach stop, the original name of the inn was The Twin Peaks Hotel, named after Mt. Twin Peaks due south of the inn. During the silver boom of the 1880s and early 1890s, a toll booth was constructed directly in front of the inn. To accommodate the miners, the inn served as a brothel and continued in this capacity until the 1920s. Today, the inn is used as a mountain getaway resort for vacationers.

TWIN LAKES

Food: ★★★★ The inn offers several excellent German dishes as well as some American. I recommend the sauerbraten: spicy marinated beef with potato dumplings, red cabbage, and applesauce. It is a delectable dish. The other German dinner entrees feature pork: schnitzel and jaeggerschnitzel; smoked pork: kassler rippchen; steak: rinderrouladen; sausage: Bratwurst; and chicken Bavaria. Homemade soup and bread are served with all entrees. Side dishes served with the meal include boiled potatoes, German potato salad, sauerkraut, and vegetables. The American entrees include rib eye, rainbow trout, vegetarian lasagna, and hamburger. A garden salad, children's menu, nightly dinner specials, baked goods, a wine list, and dinner cordials are also available. Special breakfast items include a homemade sweet roll with fruit and cheese, and buttermilk pancakes. Lunch offers German meals: Bratwurst or potato pancakes; American meals: a burger, tuna melt or Reuben; and a vegetarian or fruit plate. Imported and domestic beers may also be ordered.

Service: ★★★½ The barkeep handles it all.

Decor: ★★★★ This restaurant consists of two small rooms: a long, narrow room along the perimeter with seven tables for 14 people and an inner room with four larger tables for 21 people; a bar area with three tables for 10; and a patio with five tables. The wall separating the two dining rooms is constructed of wood logs and cement, which adds a natural flavor to the place. Several 3½ inch plates hang over the window in this dividing wall. On the sill of this window are some colored bottles and wooden dolls. The windows to the outside have a short, one-foot, white-knit curtain at the top and books in the sill. Chandeliers hang on gold chains from the log beam ceiling. The inner dining room is decorated with an Ansel Adams poster, beer mugs on the fireplace mantel, a picture of a cute seal, a very old pair of wooden skis, and a chest with Teddy bears on top. This is a small place, but the decor has a distinctive quality that combines Germany and the Colorado Mountains.

Atmosphere: ★★★★½ The mountain setting is perfect for this small, but exquisite, restaurant.

VAIL

The valley of Gore Creek, where Vail resort now stands, was first settled in the 1880's by silver prospectors. Unsuccessful at silver mining, they developed homesteads instead and raised cattle and grew crops. Vail and nearby Vail Pass (10,603') were named after Charles D. Vail, Colorado State Department engineer and director in the 1930s and 40s. The town of Vail is relatively new having been established in 1959 and incorporated in 1966. Vail ski area opened in 1962 and was chosen as the site of the 1989 World Alpine Ski Championships.

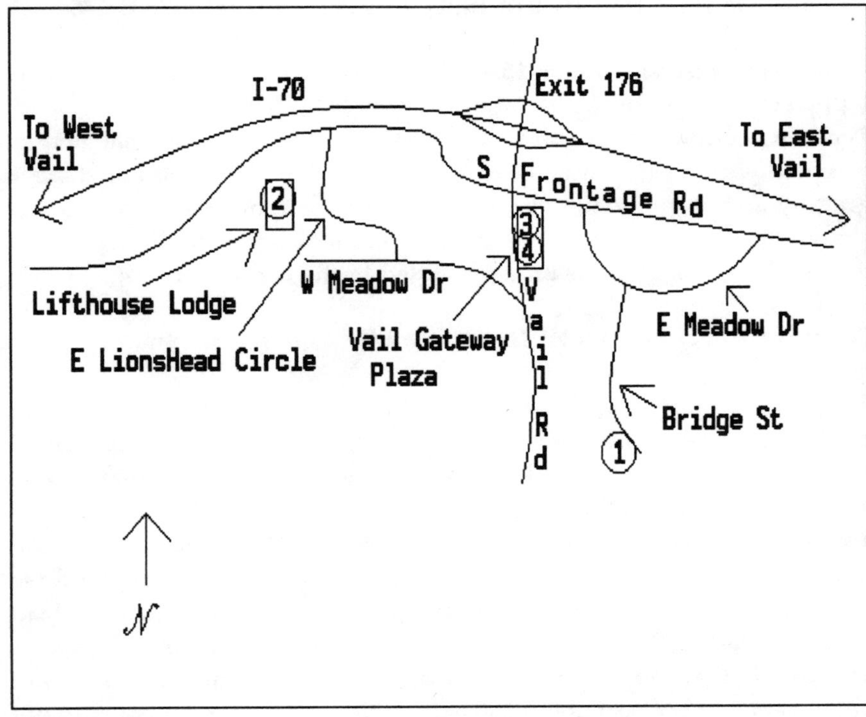

Restaurants and Ratings:	Food	Service	Decor	Atm	Overall
1. CYRANO'S	★★★	★★½	★★★½	★★	★★½
2. MONTAUK	★★★½	★★½	★★½	★★★	★★★
3. PIZZA & PA'NE	★★★★	★★★½	★★★	★★★½	★★★½
4. SIAMESE ORCHID	★★★	★★★	★★★½	★★★	★★★

Pizza & Pa'Ne offers sizable Italian dishes, delicious marinara sauce, and a good second-story view of the ski slopes. Montauk serves lightly seasoned grilled fish for the naturalist and offers Vail's only raw oyster bar. If you like your Chinese on the hot side, try some of the selections at the Siamese Orchid. All four restaurants accept major credit cards, have nonsmoking sections and serve alcohol.

CYRANO'S ★★½
298 HANSON RANCH RD(TOP OF BRIDGE ST, VAIL VILLAGE) (303)476-5551

Breakfast/lunch $$, dinner $$$-$$$$. 7 days 8AM-3PM and 5PM-10PM (appetizers served in the bar/lounge from 2:30PM-6PM).
Type: American/Continental. No separate checks. Personal checks accepted with check guarantee card. U.S. travelers checks accepted. 15% gratuity added for parties of nine or more. There may be an additional charge for substitutions, extras or split plates. The entire dining area is nonsmoking. Smoking is only permitted in the downstairs bar.

***Food:* ★★★ *Service:* ★★½ *Decor:* ★★★½ *Atmosphere:* ★★**

Their spicy Cajun gumbo made with scallops, turkey, sausage, onion, and black & red pepper in a beef broth was very good. I ordered the grilled marlin with a Caesar's salad and mango pickle relish. The marlin was a thin slice with a very nice grilled taste. The mango relish was a good accompaniment. This was not an overpowering meal, but flavorful and high on quality. The service was pleasantly adequate. There are three dining areas upstairs with 17 tables for about 70 people. Glass doors lead to a patio facing the ski slopes. There is limited knotty-pine wallspace. The bar/lounge downstairs serves only hot dogs, chips & salsa and appetizers, but can seat about 150 at 25 tables and 50 barstools. I did not care for the heavy rock music they played. There were a lot of skiers and tourists at lunch time and it did appear to be a popular place.

MONTAUK ★★★
549 WEST LIONSHEAD MALL (303)476-2601

Dinner $$$-$$$$. NOV to Mid-APR: 7 days 5PM-10PM. Memorial Day-OCT: 7 days 5:30PM-9:30PM. Closed Mid-APR to Memorial Day.
Type: Seafood. No separate checks. 25% off early bird specials 5PM-5:45PM, every day.

Food: ★★★½ I ordered one of the blackboard grilled-fish entrees: Louisiana pink salmon with pineapple chutney sauce. Each evening they offer a different selection of grilled fish. There is no mesquite flavoring or special seasoning, only a little salt and white pepper. The idea here is to preserve the natural flavor of the fish. You also have your choice of four sauces each evening. The other three were tomato salsa with cilantro, white-bean, garlic-cream, and tequila lime-butter. My salmon was flavorful and I could definitely taste the fish, but I think I still prefer the mesquite flavor or special seasoning. I did enjoy the pineapple chutney and recommend it. The French fries, lightly seasoned with garlic salt, were thin and average. As much as I love vegetables, they managed to select what are probably my least favorite: Brussels sprouts and turnips. The also served carrots. The other grilled-fish selections were Florida mahi mahi, yellow-fin tuna, Florida grouper, jumbo sea scallops, Florida swordfish, and Rocky Mountain rainbow trout. Other blackboard specials included Alaskan king crab, live Maine lobster, and baked orange roughy with sun-dried, cherry-butter sauce, wild rice and basil. If you are into raw oysters and clams before dinner, and I definitely am, I strongly recommend you arrive early and visit their raw bar to try their little neck clams, oysters (blue points, appalachicolas, and malpeques), stone crab claws, rock shrimp, and Northwest smoked salmon with a mini bagel and cream cheese. It will set the mood for a fine evening of seafood dining. For an appetizer you can choose from fried calamari, peel & eat shrimp, steamed mussels, Manhattan-style clam chowder, and roast duck salad. The regular menu entrees, for those of you — and me — who prefer spices, include blackened Pacific snapper, pecan coated rainbow trout, pan-roasted breast of chicken, steamed salmon wrapped in napa cabbage, grilled T-bone, seared sea scallops, roasted sea scallops, roast swordfish, and grilled prawns. A children's menu is also available. The dessert selections, which change nightly, may feature a rum crème en glaze (a flan), pecan brownie, mascarpone cheese with fresh fruit, an apple crêpe crème en glaze served hot, Grand Marnier cheesecake, or ice cream cake made with chocolate chip ice cream, roasted almond sauce and graham cracker crust.

Service: ★★½ Satisfactory, nothing more or less.

Decor: ★★½ To the right of the entrance is a single divided main dining room with glass doors facing the ski slopes. The outer section has 15 tables for 56 diners, the inner section has six tables for 24. White paper place mats and crayons are set at each white-clothed table. The kids seem to enjoy using the crayons on the white placemats and it serves its purpose in keeping them quiet and not fidgety. The outer section has the evening's grilled-fish menu on three different blackboards, one of which is positioned on a three-dimensional figure of a fish about to devour a much smaller fish. The only other items of decor are a skylight and two large brass lanterns. The inner section has a large mirror at one end. Lighting is provided by in-set ceiling lights and brass wall lamps with tan ribbed shades. To the left of the entrance is a small smoking section with six tables for 20. Behind it is the bar/lounge and raw bar. It features 10 basil-colored, wood barstools, 11 tables for 36, and photos of sailing ships in high waters. The two patios on either side of the entrance can seat a total of 50 in the summer.

Atmosphere: ★★★ They seem to like their rock music here. At dinner time, though, it has more of a family-type atmosphere.

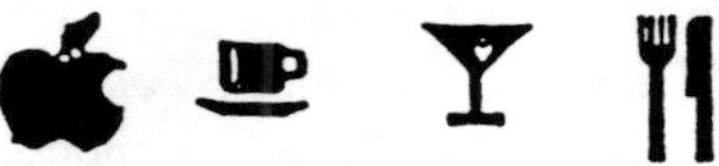

PIZZA & PA'NE ★★★½
12 SOUTH FRONTAGE AND VAIL RD (VAIL GATEWAY PLAZA) (303)476-7550

Lunch $$, dinner $$-$$$, (pizza $$$-$$$$). Thanksgiving to Mid-APR and Memorial Day to Mid-SEP: 7 days 11:30AM-2:30PM and 5PM-11PM. Mid-SEP to Thanksgiving and Mid-APR to Memorial Day: 7 days 11:30AM-2:30PM and 5PM-10PM. Happy hour from 2:30PM-5PM: pizza & pasta. Type: Italian. 10% senior's discount. Smoking only permitted at the bar.

Food: ★★★★ I tried their stromboli for lunch: a pastry shell filled with sausage, green peppers, pepperoni & onions, with marinara sauce on the side. This was a huge serving. The stromboli and small dish of marinara completely filled a 10" plate. I especially liked the thin-cut pepperoni, the Italian parsley, and the marinara. This should please anyone with an appetite for Italian food. (I know it pleased this half-Italian). Other lunch sandwiches and entrees include meatball, sausage, eggplant Parmigiana, chicken breast, calzone, and stuffed pizza. Salads, which are also available for dinner, feature Greek, Italiano chicken, and Caesar's. They serve both white pizza prepared with chopped fresh garlic and olive oil sauce, as well as Roma (tomato sauce) pizza in 10" and 14" sizes. Some of the more flavorful toppings include shrimp, goat cheese, fresh basil, feta cheese, artichoke hearts, eggplant, chicken, and meatballs. You can start dinner with an antipasto of mussels marinara, cockles, or clams. The dinner entrees feature an assortment of different pastas: spaghetti, ravioli, lasagna, baked ziti, linguini & clams, chicken or eggplant Parmigiana, and shrimp Florentine. They have a short children's menu.

Service: ★★★½ A very friendly young lady, well spoken with a cheerful smile. They have a sign at one end of the bar which says "please be patient with us. Your order is carefully prepared with love." My stromboli, ordered when the restaurant was empty, took about 20 minutes. It was worth the wait.

Decor: ★★★ This is a small, one-room restaurant with a long narrow section opposite a bar and an open section with views of Vail Village and the ski slopes. There are 16 tile-topped tables for 46, plus 10 short, round, brown barstools. Table seating is on hardwood, rib-backed chairs. Decor consists primarily of photographs taken in Italy showing an American girl in 1951, a couple dancing, and another couple having a rendezvous under a row of columns. Other photos feature "Spanky and his dog" and a boy and girl sitting on a beach. A poster of the Brooklyn Bridge greets you at the entrance. At the end of the bar is an old photo of owner David Gambetta's father's store in New York City: "Gambetta Snuff".

Atmosphere: ★★★½ Jazz plays in the background. The restaurant has been around since 1978. There are good southerly views of the ski slopes.

SIAMESE ORCHID ★★★
12 SOUTH FRONTAGE AND VAIL RD (VAIL GATEWAY PLAZA) (303)476-9417

Lunch $$, dinner $$$-$$$$. Mid-NOV to Mid APR: MON-SAT 11:30AM-2PM. SUN-THU 5PM-10PM. FRI-SAT 5PM-10:30PM. JUN-SEP: MON-SAT 11:30AM-2PM. 7 days 5:30PM-10PM. Closed Mid-APR to MAY and OCT to Mid-NOV.
Type: Oriental (Thai). The entire restaurant is nonsmoking.

Food: ★★★ I ordered a bowl of lemon-flavored soup with shrimp - hot, very hot!. It was prepared with full-tail shrimp, mushrooms, leaks and lots of fresh chili pepper. If you love hot dishes you have to try this one. Have the ice water and napkins ready. For my entree, I had stir-fry graprou mint with pork — spicy hot again. It was prepared with green and red peppers, scallions, onions and, more fresh chili. Give your taste buds a challenge and try some of their extra hot offerings. The same dishes with milder sauces are also available.

Service: ★★★ Friendly, smiling and efficient.

Decor: ★★★½ This is an L-shaped restaurant. A small dining area to the left has four tables for 10 diners. White tablecloths and napkins are used. The middle of the dining room has a low wall with bench seating on both sides at six tables for 24. Green and orange cushions are used on the hardwood benches. Around the perimeter are seven tables for 24 additional diners. There is a back dining area with five tables for 26 and a large gold and black oriental rug with portraits of oriental people. The two distinctive items of decor are the solid-color red, blue and yellow umbrellas, sort of super-large versions of the ones used in exotic drinks, and a two-column pagoda style overhang. The artworks hanging on the solid green walls feature Chinese warriors and peacock feathers in gold frames with black mats. Windows occupy two sides of this corner restaurant. Subdued studio lights are used with no wall or table lighting.

Atmosphere: ★★★ Chinese instrumental music plays in the background. This is a nice, comfortable, low-keyed place with skiers and travelers — somewhat sporty and sophisticated — and intellectuals in sweaters.

WALDEN

Formerly called Sagebrush, the town's present name is for Mark A. Walden, who was a postmaster at Sage Hen Springs, now a ghost town, about four miles to the southwest. Walden is situated in a wide valley with the Park range section of the Colorado Mountains visible in the distant west. I was here during the cold, dark, desolate days of January (as opposed to the "lazy, hazy, crazy days of summer"). I was so moved by the remoteness of this place in the dead of winter, that I got up about 2AM on my first night in town and wrote the following poem:

To Walden

Somewhere in the cold, dark, silent, void
        recesses of space;
Somewhere over remote, barren, desolate
        stretches of frozen wasteland
        looking outward toward icy sunsets;
Somewhere under chilly, clear, windy
        full moonlit skies, lies...

Walden, Walden.
The name burns bitter on the lips
        of those who speak it.
Say it softly and not very often,
        lest you be next to walk this path.

O.K., so scholars will not confuse this with Thoreau's "Walden." But, how many other restaurant guides offer poetry?

Restaurants and Ratings:	Food	Service	Decor	Atm	Overall
1. Elk Horn Cafe	★★★½	★★½	★★½	★★	★★½
2. Teedo's	★★	★	★★	★	★½

For good homecooking, go to the Elk Horn. For a great cinnamon roll, visit Teedo's. Both restaurants accept major credit cards, neither has a nonsmoking section, and only the Elk Horn serves alcohol.

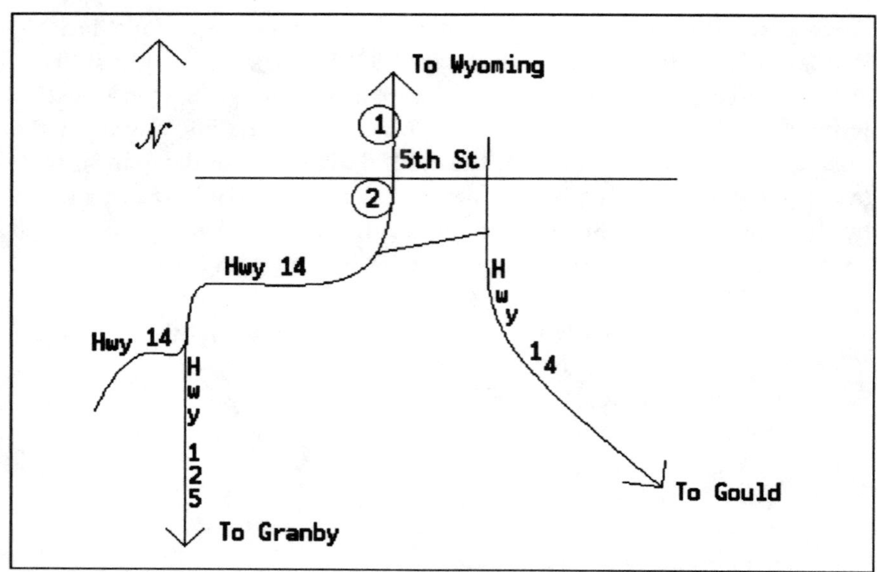

ELK HORN CAFE ★★½
486 MAIN (303)723-9996

Breakfast $, lunch/dinner $-$$. 7 days 5:30AM-8:30PM.
Type: Cafe.

Food: ★★★½ *Service:* ★★½ *Decor:* ★★½ *Atmosphere:* ★★

I had a couple of opportunities to eat dinner here with my co-worker. The meatloaf special, made with bacon, mushrooms, green peppers, and carrots, is very good. It comes with real mashed potatoes, creamed peas, roll, and soup (cabbage and Swiss) or salad. The salad bar had a limited, but well-chosen, selection: potato and macaroni salad, green and black olives, pepperoncini, rice pudding with marshmallows, pears and cottage cheese. Their chicken fried steak and breaded veal are fairly good. The stir-fried chicken on white rice had moist, flavorful slices of chicken, but it came with "mushy" vegetables. They also serve a good, decent burger with spicy curly-Q fries. Service was satisfactory. This restaurant has a casual cafe in front with ten tables for 40 plus a counter for nine more. The blue and white plaster walls are decorated with horseshoes, ropes, belts, wooden planks with branding-iron marks, and pictures of cowboys, deer, and rodeos. Behind the cafe is a dining room with 11 tables for 36. There is a big mural along the back wall titled "Trees in Autumn," a large mirror to the left, and dividers on the right separating the bar/lounge. The clientele includes locals and passers-through on their way to ski vacations in Steamboat.

TEEDO'S ★½
508 MAIN (303)723-8272

Breakfast/lunch/dinner $ (pizza $-$$$). 7 days 6AM-10PM.
Type: Diner.

***Food:* ★★ *Service:* ★ *Decor:* ★★ *Atmosphere:* ★**

The locals claimed their pizza is the best item on the menu, so I tried it. The waitress said it would be a 20-30 minute wait. It took 25 minutes. The cheese was soupy and tasted like plain whole milk cheese, although the cook claimed it was mozzarella. I did not think it was worth the wait. They do, however, have excellent cinnamon rolls, so you might want to stop by in the morning. Make sure you inform the waitress to "go easy on the ice" if you order a beverage. She served me a cup literally overflowing with ice and a few swallows of lemonade. I hate that! This is a single-room restaurant with 12 booths and a single table for a total of 54 people. The room has a divider with potted plants and plant hangers. The hangers are a creative design made with several small pieces of wood in an egg shape. They come in three sizes and are for sale. Seating is on nailed-down, wood-rail benches at white formica tables. Prints of flowers and butterflies in glass-covered gold frames hang on the wood-paneled walls. A service counter, kitchen and gift shop are to the right. The walls to the right are used as a community bulletin board. They have a jukebox and a video machine. Each table has a cute and creative miniature picnic table that houses the salt, pepper, catsup, and mustard. I found it different and unique. Known locally as a teen hangout, two teens and a heavyset gentleman were the other diners.

WALSH

Walsh was named after a retired general baggage agent for the Atchison, Topeka, & Santa Fe Railroad. One item of moderate interest in Walsh: on the northwest corner of Oak and Nevada, across from the Walsh United Methodist Church, there is a miniature Statute of Liberty. Swing by and see it on your way through town.

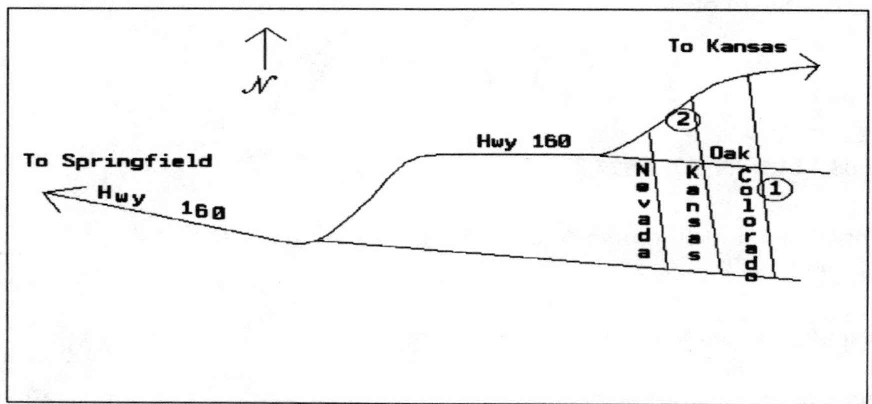

Restaurants and Ratings:	Food	Service	Decor	Atm	Overall
1. BEN'S CAFE	★★	★★½	★★½	★★	★★
2. GET AND GO	★½	★★	★	★	★½

Your best bets in Walsh are a salad or baked potato at Ben's Cafe or tater tots at the Get and Go. Only the Get and Go will accept major credit cards. Neither restaurant has a nonsmoking section nor serves alcohol.

BEN'S CAFE ★★
438 N. COLORADO (719)324-9900

Breakfast/lunch/dinner $ (a few $$). MON-SAT 7AM-7PM. Closed SUN. Type: Cafe.

Food: ★★ *Service:* ★★½ *Decor:* ★★½ *Atmosphere:* ★★

This restaurant is popular at lunch time. The chef salad comes with a lot of American cheese, ham, carrots and tomatoes. Their baked potato is good also. The chili is like hamburger soup with no kidney beans or spices. Their Mexican food and burgers are average. No complaints on the service. This is a single-room restaurant with 11 booths along the right and left walls and seven tables in the middle for a total of 76 people. A half-dozen, wood-framed oil paintings of horses, mountain cabins, an Indian weaver, and an Indian tepee decorate the walls that are white plaster on top and wood panel below. The plaster is chipping and peeling in several places. The clientele is mostly older and wearing cowboy hats.

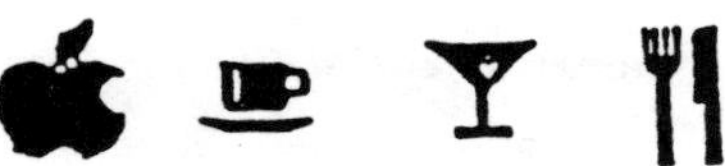

GET AND GO ★½
CORNER OF HWY. 160 & KANSAS AT THE GAS STATION (719)324-5501.

Breakfast/lunch/dinner $, (pizza $$-$$$). 7 days 5AM-9PM (10PM APR to Mid-NOV).
Type: Deli.

Food: ★½ *Service:* ★★ *Decor:* ★ *Atmosphere:* ★

Their tater tots are probably the best item on the menu. They are crispy and nongreasy. The chef salad, which comes with turkey, beef, ham, or cheese, is fair. The fries are average. Their grilled burgers are thin and unpredictable. They can be anything from cold and underdone to average. As for the pizza, I did not care for the cheese. The other toppings - pepperoni, mushrooms, and green peppers - were average quality at best. Place your order at the counter and they will bring your food to the table. There are nine brown formica booths for 36 people; particle board walls, posts, and ceiling; and a community bulletin board. A washboard and what appears to be a giant plunger hang on the wall behind the counter. Store shelves are in the same room as the small seating area. The floors are dirty. A lot of local outdoor workers visit here. Along with the high winds, they track a lot of dirt inside.

WINTER PARK

Winter Park began as a construction camp for the Moffat Tunnel and was originally called West Portal, after the west portal of the tunnel. A ski area started up in 1927 with a 25¢ rope tow. Several years and two fires later, the world's first double chair lift was completed in 1947. Today, Winter Park is one of the finest winter sports centers in the country, home to a handicap ski clinic, and host of the special olympics.

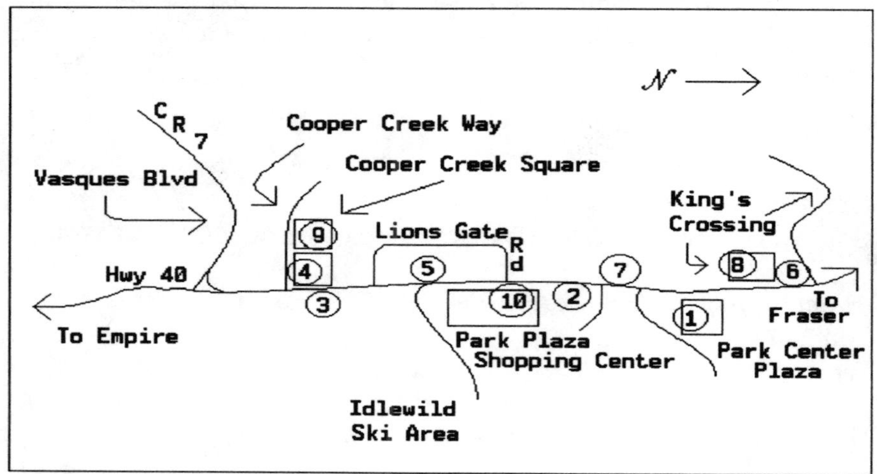

Restaurants and Ratings:	Food	Service	Decor	Atm	Overall
1. Bev's Bunnery	★★½	★★	★★	★★	★★
2. Chalet Lucerne	★★★★	★★★★	★★★½	★★★★	★★★★
3. Deno's Swiss House	★★★½	★★½	★★★	★★½	★★★
4. Divide Grill	★★★	★★★	★★½	★★★	★★★
5. Gasthaus Eichler	★★★★★	★★★★½	★★★★½	★★★★★	★★★★★
6. Hernando's	★★★★½	★★★½	★★★	★★★	★★★½
7. The Kitchen	★★★★	★½	★★½	★★★	★★★
8. The Last Waltz	★★★	★★½	★★★	★★★½	★★★
9. New Hong Kong	★★½	★★½	★★	★★★	★★½
10. Rudy's Deli	★★★½	★★	★½	★½	★★

Gasthaus Eichler is, in my opinion, by far the best restaurant in the Winter Park/Fraser area, with superb German cuisine made with exquisite sauces, special treatment from the servers, and all in a restaurant that emphasizes Colorado and Germany. Chalet Lucerne is another excellent continental restaurant specializing in Swiss cuisine. Hernando's serves a great Roma style pizza in a friendly and popular place with some unusual decor. All of the restaurants accept major credit cards except Bev's Bunnery, The Kitchen and Rudy's Deli. Surprisingly, only the Divide Grill, The Last Waltz and the New Hong Kong have nonsmoking sections. All of the restaurants serve alcohol except Bev's Bunnery and Rudy's Deli.

BEV'S BUNNERY ★★
PARK PLACE CENTER (303)726-5774

Breakfast/lunch $. 7 days 7AM-2PM (8PM NOV-APR). Closed for two weeks in MAY.
Type: Cafe. They offer a variety of breads and pastries baked fresh daily.

***Food:* ★★½ *Service:* ★★ *Decor:* ★★ *Atmosphere:* ★★**

My breakfast waffle was over an inch high and filled the plate, but was heavy rather than fluffy. Service was just fine until after I was served, then I became invisible. This is a small, one-room restaurant for 30 people with a pastry counter in the back; a wood cabinet; and stoneware mugs, aprons, and t-shirts for sale. A quiet clientele listens to the sounds of avant garde music emanating from the kitchen.

CHALET LUCERNE ★★★★
78521 US HWY 40 (303)726-5402

Breakfast $ lunch $$, dinner $$-$$$. Mid-NOV to MAR: 7 days 11:30AM-2:30PM and 5:30PM-9:30PM. FRI-SUN 8:30AM-11:30AM (Closed MON Mid-NOV and Mid-DEC). Memorial Day to Mid-OCT: TUE-SUN 11:30AM-

2:30PM and 5:30PM-9:30PM. SAT-SUN 8:30AM-11:30AM. Closed MON. Closed APR-MAY and Mid-OCT to Mid-NOV.
Type: Continental (Swiss).

Food: ★★★★ Dinner started with a rich, full-bodied beef consomme: light, but deep in beef broth flavor. The veal Zurich-style entree was a sizeable portion of tender, delicious veal chunks and mushroom slices in a creamy white wine sauce. The spatzle, chopped into little tid-bits, was a bit "doughy" and a little dry. Swiss cuisine, according to their menu, is light and sprightly by comparison to German food with no heavy gravy to weigh you down. The breakfast menu offers Mussli, vanilla yogurt and rib eye steak. Your favorite sandwiches are on the lunch menu: corned beef, club, grilled Knockwurst on sauerkraut, pastrami with Swiss, grilled marinated chicken breast, burger, and a their own version of a Reuben. There are also several salads to choose from: pasta, chef, chicken, a wurstsalad (a variety of salads), and buendnerfleisch (same as a wurstsalad only with air-dried beef cured with spices). A few of the lunch specialties include seafood fettuccine, crêpe Florentine, cannelloni (their version is a crêpe with chopped sirloin and melted Swiss), veal Bratwurst, breaded pork schnitzel, kassler rippchen (smoked pork loin with sauerkraut and boiled potatoes), and beef or cheese fondue.

Start your dinner off with an appetizer of escargot, the buendner plate, sliced smoked salmon, artichoke hearts, Swiss raclette (cheese melted over new potatoes), or just a house salad. A half-dozen light, less expensive dinners, are available: beef stew, vegetarian crêpe, fried chicken, veal Bratwurst, tortellini, and roast pork loin. If you are in the mood for charbroiled meats, you can order filet mignon with artichoke hearts, lamb chops with mint jelly, NY sirloin, rib eye, or buffalo. The seafood selections include rainbow trout, grilled salmon, breaded butterfly shrimp, Alaskan king crab legs, and rock lobster tail. There are four veal specialties: veal Marsala, Wiener schnitzel, and veal medallions sautéed with lemon butter or mushrooms in a creamy white wine sauce. The house specialties feature roast duckling à l'orange, sauerbraten, pork or beef tenderloin, lamb sautéed in a mild curry sauce, marinated venison in piquant red wine sauce, and beef or Swiss fondue for two or more people. It might be worth your while just to come here for one of their off-the-menu desserts. In fact, a group of four or five came here just for that purpose. They chose from a variety of cheesecakes (white chocolate, raspberry, and fudge brownie), homemade apple strudel, black forest cake, Swiss honey nut torte, coupe maison (French vanilla ice cream, Grand Marnier, and whipped cream), and coupe Denmark (French vanilla ice cream, hot chocolate sauce and whipped cream).

Service: ★★★★ This is a family-run business headed by chef/owner Hillary Henz — a true, old, Swiss-style gentleman all the way. His son waited on my table. He was friendly, talkative, informative and intelligent.

Decor: ★★★½ This is a two-dining-room restaurant with seating for 80 people. An outside patio is used from Memorial Day through September. Cantons, or miniature flags, representing most of the 25 states of Switzerland hang from the ceiling of the larger dining room. Posters of Lucerne and Interlaken, a pair of antlers, a wooden clock, and a couple of water colors depicting town scenes adorn the walls. Picture plates decorate the wallspace above the windows. Potted plants and stained-glass brighten the front of the wood-framed windows. A maroon and grey, padded bench seat extends around two sides of the larger dining room which matches the curtain over the top of the windows, the grey tablecloths and maroon napkins.

Atmosphere: ★★★★ This is a dimly-lit restaurant with yellow-tinted, brass lanterns hanging from the ceiling, and kerosene lamps at each table. Not withstanding that, and the fact that they do not offer a nonsmoking section with two dining rooms, these are still very pleasant surroundings. Classical music played quietly in the background at just the right volume. A quiet, sophisticated clientele was here.

DENO'S SWISS HOUSE ★★★
78911 US HWY 40 (303)726-5332

Lunch $-$$ (Pizza $$$-$$$$), dinner $$$. 7 days 11AM-9:30PM.

WINTER PARK

Type: American (burgers, steaks, pasta, pizza, seafood). 15% service charge for parties of six or more. No separate checks.

Food: ★★★½ Their cream of celery soup was thick and contained celery salt. The linguini marinara was cooked al dente with a mild marinara sauce and Parmesan cheese. My personal preference would have been a spicier sauce with the sharper tasting Pecorino Romano. The meal was served with Italian bread. I also had a chance to sample their pizza and found it quite good. The crust is thick and doughy and the ingredients fresh. I had a slice with tomatoes, green peppers, mushrooms, pepperoni and sausage. I would recommend the pizza over the pasta if you are undecided between the two. The lunch menu offers appetizers (artichokes Parmesan, chicken wings, onion rings, nachos, and garlic cheese bread), salads (house, Greek, Caesar's, and grilled chicken), soup, chili, a roasted pork loin burrito, burgers, sandwiches, pizza, and baby-back ribs. The dinner menu features more appetizers (French onion soup, chili con carne, Cajun-barbecued shrimp, and smoked trout), pasta (angel hair al fresca or with wild mushrooms, fettucine Alfredo or primavera, and linguini with shrimp & tomatoes), steaks, chicken or veal (picatta, Marsala, or scallopini), seafood (shrimp scampi, snow or king crab legs, and Australian rock lobster), and combination dinners.

Service: ★★½ A little slow, but otherwise satisfactory. I had a new waiter who spent considerable time chatting with customers.

Decor: ★★★ There is a bar to the far right with lounge areas to the left, near right and straight back. The main dining area is in the back with a big-screen television in front of a red-brick fireplace. The booths are decorated with metal-framed glass posters of skiers, ski slopes, eagles and wine. Seating is on wood, rib-backed chairs with brown-vinyl cushions. Kerosene lamps and green-clothed napkins are set on beige tablecloths. There is ample lighting provided by bright lights under metal shades hanging close to the ceiling so as not to be annoying. In-set ceiling lights shine down on the booths. The bar/lounge area seats 80. The dining area seats an additional 70.

Atmosphere: ★★½ This is a sports bar and restaurant with 10 televisions simultaneously showing Monday night football, or whatever the sporting event of the day or evening happens to be. The atmosphere is casual and relaxed: a good place to socialize.

DIVIDE GRILL ★★★
78930 US HWY 40 (TOP FLOOR OF COOPER CREEK SQUARE) (303)726-4900

Dinner $$-$$$. Mid-NOV to APR: 7 days 5PM-10PM. JUN to Mid-OCT: THU-TUE 6PM-9PM. Closed WED. Closed MAY & Mid-OCT to Mid-NOV. Type: Italian (with Continental). A 15% gratuity is added to parties of six or more. $2.50 service charge for extra plate. Take-out available. Owners Wolfgang Wendt, born and raised in Germany, and his wife, Robyn, a native of New Zealand, (a unique combination) have combined their culinary and managerial talents to bring you this fine restaurant.

Food: ★★★ They have a twenty-five-item salad bar that includes tortellini, and two Italian vegetable salads. Fresh, thick Italian bread is served with meals. My linguini with clams in Alfredo sauce was made with very tender al dente noodles and mild, creamy white Alfredo sauce. However, the clams were canned and the grated Parmesan cheese, served in a jar, could have been fresher. The dinner menu features appetizers (marinated artichoke hearts, mushroom caps stuffed with Italian bread crumbs and sausage, and calimari fritti), the soup and salad bar, pasta (spaghetti, lasagna, fettuccini Alfredo, pasta primavera, shrimp scampi, and manicotti), and continental specialties (veal picatta or Marsala, egg plant Parmesan, chicken topped with artichoke hearts, trout almandine, swordfish, and a steak sandwich). You can choose a dessert from their pastry case to go along with a cup of their freshly ground espresso.

Service: ★★★ Friendly and efficient. Where else will you find a restaurant where one German chef plus one New Zealand office manager equals one Italian/Continental restaurant? I had a pleasant chat with Robin Wendt who brought back fond memories of my trip to lovely New Zealand in 1986.

Decor: ★★½ The entrance is on the walkway level. Then, it is one flight up to the dining room. A solid row of windows on the south and east sides provide good views of the surrounding pines, aspen, and mountain scapes. This is a single, divided dining room with 16 tables for 56 along or near the windows for good viewing, and three tables inside a brass railing for 16. The bar/lounge area to the left, the only area where smoking is permitted, has seven barstools and five tables for 10. The long row of windows, trimmed with white lights, leaves little room for decor. Artificial plants and green-shaded lamps hang from the walls.

Atmosphere: ★★★ They played light jazz throughout the restaurant. The effects of the off-season were being felt here as I was the only customer. With the view, though, who needs a crowd?

GASTHAUS EICHLER ★★★★★
HIGHWAY 40 (303)726-5133

Breakfast/lunch $-$$, dinner $$$-$$$$ (a few $$$$+). Mid-NOV to Mid-APR: 7 days 7:30AM-10AM. MON-FRI 5PM-9PM. SAT-SUN 5PM-9:30PM. JUN-AUG: WED-MON 11:30AM-2PM and 5PM-9PM. Closed TUE. SEP to Mid-NOV: WED-MON 5PM-9PM. Closed TUE. Closed Mid-APR to MAY. Type: Continental (German). 15% gratuity for parties of six or more. $10 per person minimum for those 12 years and up. No cigars or pipes. Some entrees available in children's and Senior portions. They do not take reservations. Winner of the Award of Excellence from the International Association of Food Critics for quality of food and service.

Food: ★★★★★ Dinner entrees come with soup and salad. The soup was a chicken consomme with flat egg noodles, chunks of chicken, parsley and onion. The salad consisted of lettuce, tomato, cucumber and cabbage, topped with poppy, wheat and sunflower seeds. The blue cheese dressing was flavorful, but without any blue cheese chunks. My entree was rahmschnitzel: sautéed veal topped with fresh mushroom and brandy cream sauce. Whoever gave credit to the French for the expression "the secret is in the sauce", did not dine here first. The creamy, brandy mushroom sauce was exquisite and very rich. The veal was a whole piece, not as tender as medallions, but still excellent. All of the vegetables on the plate (cauliflower, broccoli and carrots), tasted garden fresh, although they were not. The spatzle was moist and tender. Breakfast, only served in the winter months, offers smoked loin of pork, veal or smoked pork Bratwurst, blueberry or peaches & cream pancakes, eggs Benedict, smoked trout or salmon with bagels, Bloody Marys and hot toddies. Lunch is only served in summer and features light entrees like smoked trout served cold, smoked salmon served with caviar, salads (shrimp, almond & avocado, chef, or chicken in a melon half), soup, sandwiches, and burgers. A children's menu is also available. Early bird dinner specials are served year round and include jagerschnitzel, Wiener schnitzel, rainbow trout, petite filet mignon, Bratwurst, huhner ragout, kassler rippchen and paprika goulasch. A half-dozen appetizers are available before dinner: potato pancakes, shrimp cocktail, escargots, smoked Colorado trout or Alaskan salmon, and baked camembert. Other veal entrees are veal Cordon Bleu, Oscar, Cordon-Oscar, and supreme (topped with lobster, crab, shrimp, asparagus and Bernaise). Other delectable entrees include rindsrolladen (rolled beef stuffed with onion, bacon & spices), steak or grilled chicken breast Diane, Australian lobster tail, fillet of sole stuffed with crab meat, rainbow trout, Alaskan king crab legs, and shrimp scampi. For dessert, you can choose from a variety of cheesecakes, homemade hot apple strudel, or chocolate mousse.

Service: ★★★★½ Pleasant, cheerful, lovable, efficient and friendly, to mention just a few characteristics. I think you will like the way you are treated here.

Decor: ★★★★½ An interesting display of Colorado and German decor is presented here. There is a bar/lounge at the entrance with a stuffed hawk, mallard duck and boar's head hung on the wall. The main dining room in the rear is divided into two sections. The first, to the right, has seven tables for 26. The second section, behind the first, has 19 tables and two booths for 84. A four-foot wall-divider, separating the two dining areas, is decorated with a ski trophy, a shiny brass pitcher and plant holder, a lantern, a wagon-wheel, a Hal's pal doll with one short arm (given to Hans, the owner, by the handicap ski clinic in Winter

Park), and a ceramic bottle. Frosted-glass wood and brass lanterns hang on the stucco walls. Brass kerosene lamps are set on the tables. Dining is on high-back, wood chairs set at tables with green-clothed napkins. Green tablecloths are set over white tablecloths. Two interesting items of decor are the picture puzzles hanging on the wall in wood frames. They were put together by Hannelore Eichler "years ago" according to my waitress. The puzzles are of Miltenburg in Germany and Schloss Neuschwanstein Castle in the Bei Garmisch section of Bavaria. The larger dining section is decorated with glass-framed posters of German beer, two stained-glass hangings of hummingbirds, flowers, grapes, and plates, and a small German deer skin. The hallway outside the first dining section has a wine rack on one side and a signed poster of world famous skiers Phil, Steve, and Paul Mahre. Betty White was another celebrity to have dined here. The best always attracts the best!

Atmosphere: ★★★★★ Beautiful classical, instrumental and easy listening music is played in the restaurant. The clientele are quiet and sophisticated, yet witty and fun-loving. This is the most pleasant dining experience you will find in Winter Park. Despite the fact they do not offer a nonsmoking section, they do try to accommodate both smokers and nonsmokers.

HERNANDO'S ★★★½
78260 US HWY 40 (KING'S CROSSING INTERSECTION) (303)726-5409

Lunch/dinner $$-$$$. Winter: 7 days 4PM-11PM. Summer: 7 days 11:30AM-10PM. Fall & Spring: WED-MON 5PM-9:30PM. Closed TUE. Type: Italian. 15% gratuity for parties of eight or more. No separate checks. No cigars. All items available for take-out. Free local delivery in the winter only.

Food: ★★★★½ I ordered one of Jerry's pizza's - Roma style. I found that I <u>really</u> liked the Roma style. They start with homemade dough, brush it with a fresh marinated mixture of virgin olive oil, fresh basil and minced garlic, add sliced Italian Roma tomatoes, mozzarella cheese, pepperoni, sausage and mushrooms. This pizza is nongreasy, despite all the meat. The marinated virgin olive oil mixture adds a flavor to the pizza that I had not experienced before. It was, in many respects, the **BEST** pizza I ever had. Hernando's offers a traditional pizza in addition to their Roma style, but I would strongly recommend you go with the Roma style. There are 17 toppings to choose from including anchovy, jalapeño, almonds, and artichokes; white or whole wheat crust; and 10- and 14-inch sizes. One of their specialty pies uses fresh basil (Intoxicating!) and garlic. If you are looking for something extra before the meal, you can order minestroni soup, garlic bread, or a tossed or antipasto salad. Not in the mood for a pizza? Select a sandwich: meatball, sausage, vegetable Parmigiana, or a cold Italian submarine. There is a full list of pasta dishes to choose from as well: spaghetti, ravioli, meat or vegetable lasagna, rigatoni, and tortellini. Cheesecake, spumoni, Italian ice and a dessert of the day can end your meal.

Service: ★★★½ The folks here will treat you right.

Decor: ★★★ This is a single-room restaurant with 14 polished walnut tables with benches for 56, plus a small bar with six hardwood stools. A wood-burning, red-brick fireplace sets in the middle of the room. Chianti bottles in wicker baskets hang from the wood-beamed ceiling. Over 300 one dollar bills, left behind by customers leaving their mark, trim the inside entrance and wood post in front of the bar. Old-styled server trays with high rims and beer labels hang on the wall over the bar. The rest of the decor is a paraphernalia of beer signs, banjos, and brass wall lamps with green shades.

Atmosphere: ★★★ A very friendly and popular place. Rock music played in the background. Folks come in here expecting a good time and don't leave disappointed. Smoke may be a problem.

THE KITCHEN ★★★
78542 US HWY 40 (303)726-9940

Breakfast $ ($$ for large orders), lunch $. Winter and Summer: 7 days 7:30AM-12:30PM. Fall and Spring: MON-FRI 8AM-12PM SAT-SUN 7:30AM-12:30PM.
Type: Cafe. 15% gratuity added to parties of six or more. No separate checks. 50¢ added to total price of to go orders. $1.00 extra plate charge. Checks accepted with I.D.

Food: ★★★★ They do serve excellent breakfasts here. The eggs, over easy, were perfect and the hash brown potatoes, onions and shredded corn beef was a scrumptious combination. Texas toast with raspberry jam on the side and cinnamon flavored coffee compliment the meal. The breakfast menu includes corn torts, beans, salsa, egg sandwiches, a children's selection, egg or veggie burritos, huevos rancheros, and potato huevos (home fries substituted for beans). Tomatoes may be substituted for home fries. For lunch, or if you don't like eggs, you can order a sweet roll, enchilada, quesadilla, BLT, grilled cheese, or burger.

Service: ★½ Arguably "the slowest restaurant in the west"! However, they do warn you with signs and advertisements like "If you are in a hurry, eat somewhere else", "We serve no egg before its time" and "If you are the last group in after a 'rush' that fills the house, it may take about 1 hour to be served". If you have the time, this is the place to come for breakfast, or even an early lunch. The slow service did not keep people away in the slow season. Everything is cooked to order. My meal took about a half-hour, so I guess the wait could have been longer. As for the servers, they are friendly and hospitable and will keep your tea or coffee filled while you wait.

Decor: ★★½ This is a small, one-room restaurant with eight tables for 32. The main item of decor is the literally hundreds of polaroid photos of former customers — with their names, home towns, and year they visited — taped to the beige wallpaper above the windows. An S-shaped wood log hangs from the ceiling behind the entrance door and serves as a coat rack. Other items adorning the walls include a color cartoon sketch of the front of the kitchen, a wreath, three-dimensional wood carvings of a Friar monk and flowers, and a string of red Christmas lights along the rear wall. Mostly, though, there are a lot of windows on the three sides with white, transparent, banded curtains. A single, five-lamp brass and frosted-glass light fixture provides the only other source of light.

Atmosphere: ★★★ Very popular and usually crowded, but in a quiet and jovial atmosphere. Don't let the crowds keep you away. You can feel comfortable in here.

THE LAST WALTZ ★★★
78336 US HWY 40 (KINGS CROSSING SHOPPING CENTER) (303)726-4877

Breakfast $, Sunday brunch/lunch $$, late afternoon fare $-$$, dinner $$-$$$. 7 days 7AM-9:30PM.
Type: Mexican (mixed with Country).

Food: ★★★ I ordered the chicken chimichanga. I enjoyed the crisp flour tortilla, but would have favored whole chicken pieces to shredded chicken. Lettuce, tomatoes, black olives and onions are served cold on the side along with salsa. It came with mushy pinto beans and crispy black or brown chips. For dessert, I had their flan with whipped topping and orange sauce with bits of orange. It is light, nonfilling, delicious and I highly recommend it. Breakfast features some interesting delights: blueberry or apple pancakes, omelets with cream cheese and strawberry jam, lox and bagels, chorizo (sausage), corned beef hash, migas (eggs, salsa, and corn tortilla chips), and machacas (scrambled eggs and special spicy beef). Lunch offers soup, salads (chicken Caesar's, Mexican beef, shrimp, and lemon-ginger chicken), tamales, egg roles, green chili, and sandwiches (blackened ham, fish, grilled chicken breast, Rocky Mountain Reuben, club and burgers). Between lunch and dinner from 2PM to 5PM they serve appetizers (buffalo rings, broiled artichoke hearts and calientitas) and a few sandwiches. The dinner menu features fajitas, blackened ham steak, honey-pecan fried chicken, pork chop, Rocky Mountain pan-fried trout, scampi, steaks and pasta. Children's portions are available on some meals. Their list of homemade desserts includes NY cheesecake, pies (fudge, grasshopper or mud), ice cream, and apple dumplings.

Service: ★★½ Friendly and helpful, but a little slow returning.

Decor: ★★★ The nonsmoking section takes the center and rear of the dining room with six tables, four booths and four half-booths that can seat 56. There are several glass-framed old photos of miners at work and play. One such photo depicts the miners making music with a guitar, accordion and scrub board. There are also several oil landscapes of "Mountain Lake", "Devil's Thumb" and other select places in the surrounding area. A white piano and small red-brick fireplace are in the rear. Brass wall lamps, brass ceiling lights with frosted-glass, and in-set ceiling lights provide a moderate amount of light in the nonsmoking section which only has two small windows on the back side. The smoking section is in the front of the building where there is a solid row of windows providing an ample amount of light. It seats 30 at eight tables and has a small bar with six stools. Seating is on hardwood rib-backed chairs with comfortable armrests and blue woven seat mats. The table setting is modest with blue paper placemats and kerosene lamps.

ATMOSPHERE: ★★★½ This is a popular place, even in the off-season. Many local business people dine here for lunch.

NEW HONG KONG ★★½
331 COOPER CREEK SQUARE (303)726-9888

Lunch $, dinner $$-$$$. TUE-FRI 11AM-9PM. SAT-SUN 12PM-9PM. Closed MON.
Type: Oriental (Chinese). Take-out available. Delivery available during winter months.

Food: ★★½ *Service:* ★★½ *Decor:* ★★ *Atmosphere:* ★★★

I ordered the sesame seed lunch special, supposedly one of their "hot & spicy" dishes. It came with hot-and-sour soup. Both were good, but not as spicy as my favorite local Chinese restaurant. The menu advertised "bone in chicken", but mine came without any bones. It was crispy, but a little heavy on the dough. Service was quiet, even shy; a complete opposite from the experience I had the night before at Deno's. This is a two-dining-area restaurant separated by a row of potted plants in a wood-framed structure. There is a bar/lounge and waiting area at the entrance. The walls are, for the most part, void of decor. Full length pale-green curtains add a touch of formality to the otherwise casual surroundings. Windows that look down on the pedestrian walkway allow in a lot of sunlight. Pleasant, relaxing, new age music is piped in.

RUDY'S DELI ★★
US HWY 40, PARK PLAZA CENTER (303)726-8955

Lunch/dinner $. Mid-NOV to Mid APR: 7 days 10AM-9PM. JUN-AUG: 7 days 10AM-5PM. SEP to Mid-NOV: THU-TUE 10AM-3PM. Closed WED. Closed: Mid-APR to MAY.
Type: Deli.

***Food:* ★★★½ *Service:* ★★ *Decor:* ★½ *Atmosphere:* ★½**

I had their Reuben with a cup of chili topped with cheese. The light rye on the Reuben became a little soggy, but it had plenty of lean corned beef, Swiss, sauerkraut, and Dijon mustard in place of the traditional Thousand Island dressing. It was quite good. The chili I definitely recommend. It is prepared with whole chunks of beef rather than ground beef. It is spicy, but not too spicy hot. You place your order and pick up your food at the counter. Service is friendly and efficient, with one small problem. They insist on keeping the door open because it gets too hot behind the counter. Unfortunately, in the fall and winter, that results in some "chilly chili" for the customer in front of the counter. In bad weather, take-out may be your best bet. Seating is at small round tables and seats. The chairs, in black-iron flexible frames, are uncomfortable. Old photos of basketball, baseball and rugby teams and individual players hang on the white plaster walls. Rock music attracts a few long-haired individuals. This is probably the best "fast food" you will find in Winter Park.

WRAY

The town was named after John Wray, a foreman for the Print-Olive Cattle Company. Wray is the county seat of Yuma County, which ranks second in Colorado in total agricultural production and first in corn production. Three interesting sites in and around Wray are the Beecher Island Battle Ground, site of many prehistorical artifacts; the Wray Museum, which contains many Beecher Island relics; and the Wray Amphitheatre located in a canyon with overhanging cliffs east of Wray.

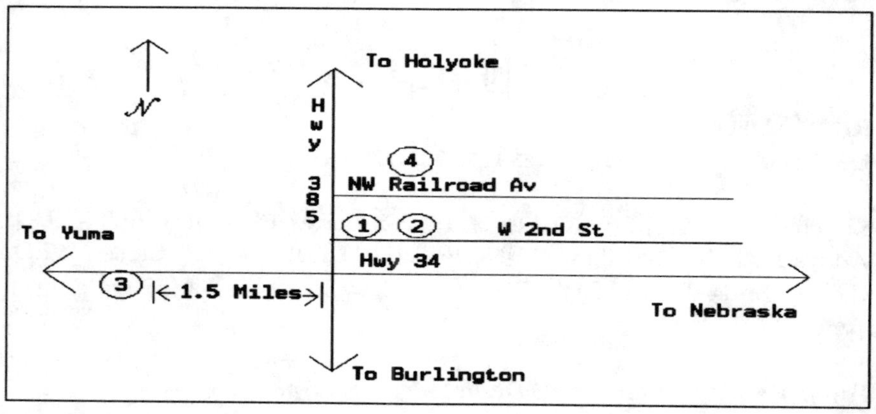

Restaurants and Ratings:	Food	Service	Decor	Atm	Overall
1. BIG RED CAFE	★★½	★★★	★	★★	★★
2. LA FAMILIA	½	★	★	★	★
3. PIZZA FACTORY	★★★	★★½	★★	★★½	★★½
4. SANDHILLER	★★★½	★★½	★★	★★★½	★★★

The Sandhiller is the best all around restaurant. They have a very good lunch buffet, soup and salads. Pizza Factory makes good pizza. For breakfast, I would recommend the Big Red Cafe. None of the restaurants has a nonsmoking section; only the Sandhiller will accept major credit cards; and only Pizza Factory serves alcohol. The people in Wray must think that walls were only made to keep the outside from the inside. Apparently none of them have given much thought to decorating walls with pictures, plants, or artwork. This is a town with (almost) no decor.

Big Red Cafe ★★
369 West Second St. (303)332-5864

Breakfast/lunch/dinner $. MON-FRI 6:30AM-8PM. SAT 6:30AM-3PM. Closed SUN.
Type: Cafe.

***Food:* ★★½ *Service:* ★★★ *Decor:* ★ *Atmosphere:* ★★**

I recommend either the biscuits and gravy, which comes with a lot of sausage gravy, or oatmeal for breakfast. Their coffee was weak on one visit, but just fine on two other occasions. Lunch features homemade chili, chef salad, a diet plate, burgers, sandwiches, hot dogs, and burritos. Dinner entrees include steak, fish, chicken, Rocky Mountain oysters, and shrimp. A children's menu and desserts (apple dumpling, pecan pie, hot fudge cake, homemade chocolate chip cookie, and ice cream treats) are also available. Service was good, friendly and helpful. Sixteen booths with rust-colored benches and blond formica tables can seat 70. A single decoration - a small, half-moon-shaped, wood-framed mirror with an emblem - decorates the wood-paneled walls separated by tan window curtains. This is a hangout for soft-spoken "good ol' boys."

La Familia ★
Wray Shopping Center (Hwy. 34 & Hwy. 385) (303)332-5157

Lunch/dinner $-$$. MON-SAT 11AM-8PM. SUN 11AM-2PM.
Type: Mexican.

***Food:* ½ *Service:* ★ *Decor:* ★ *Atmosphere:* ★**

Large quantities of low-quality food that is extra, extra dry. I took some take-out back to my motel room. After several attempts at swallowing, I had to return to the restaurant for lubricants. It was 7:45PM, but they had already locked their door (see hours above). They did let me in and made another sale, charging extra for the salsa and sour cream. The meals come with lemonade or iced tea, unless you order to go, then it's extra. The restaurant is run by teenagers. The front room has ten tables for 40 people and the back room has ten tables for 60 people. Decor, like the moisture in their food, is virtually nonexistent. The front room has wood-paneled walls on one side with a single oval mirror and concrete blocks on the opposite side. The back room has some needlepoint hangings of matadors and bulls and large wagon-wheel chandeliers with plain white bulbs. What "Plan Nine from Outer Space" was to the movie industry, La Familia is to the Mexican restaurant business in Colorado.

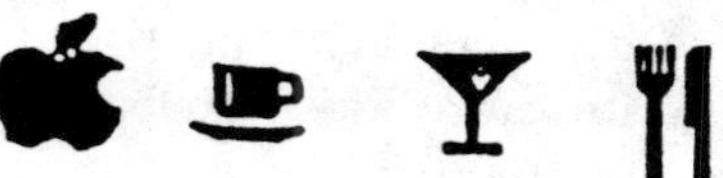

PIZZA FACTORY ★★½
29544 HWY. 34 (303)332-4041

Dinner $, (pizza $-$$$). WED-SUN 5PM-10PM. Closed MON-TUE.
Type: Italian (pizza).

Food: ★★★ *Service:* ★★½ *Decor:* ★★ *Atmosphere:* ★★½

Their pizza is very good: made with fresh ingredients, not overcooked, and in 10-, 13-, and 15-inch sizes with the usual offering of toppings. Other items on the menu are fish, chicken, Rocky Mountain oysters, curly Q's, chef salad, and sandwiches on warm Italian rolls. This has the appearance of a family-owned business. Twenty tables with brown chairs can accommodate 80 people in a single room with a low acoustic tile ceiling and pictures of carousal horses. This is a family place.

SANDHILLER RESTAURANT ★★★
411 NORTHWEST RAILWAY (303)332-4134

Lunch/dinner $-$$$$ (mostly $). MON-THU 11AM-9PM. FRI-SAT 11AM-9:30PM. Closed SUN.
Type: Steak (and seafood).

Food: ★★★½ Their soup is very good and their steaks are respectable. They offer T-bone, prime rib and chicken fried. The seafood selections include lobster, crab legs, cod, halibut, shrimp, scallops, and oysters. The other choices are chicken, charbroiled pork, ham, sandwiches, burgers, salads, soup, and chili. They also provide a salad bar and serve appetizers and desserts (homemade pies, ice cream and bread pudding).

Service: ★★½ Average.

Decor: ★★ Twenty-eight brown formica tables with brown, low-back, hard, but comfortable, chairs provide seating for 110 people. The decor is sparse: a single sketching of a tractor and a local emblem adorn the gold-striped wallpaper above the wood paneling. Plants hang from the low, flat ceiling in the long, narrow window wells.

Atmosphere: ★★★½ I found this place to be comfortable.

Gasthaus Eichler - Winter Park

YUMA

The town was named after the Yuma Indians. The word "Yuma" means "sons of the river." The townsite was established in 1886 when Fred Weld and Ida P. Alrich married and joined together their two quarter sections of land on opposite sides of the railroad. A year later the town was destroyed by a fire and had to start over. Yuma was the county seat for a short time, between 1889 and 1902, before Wray took away that honor.

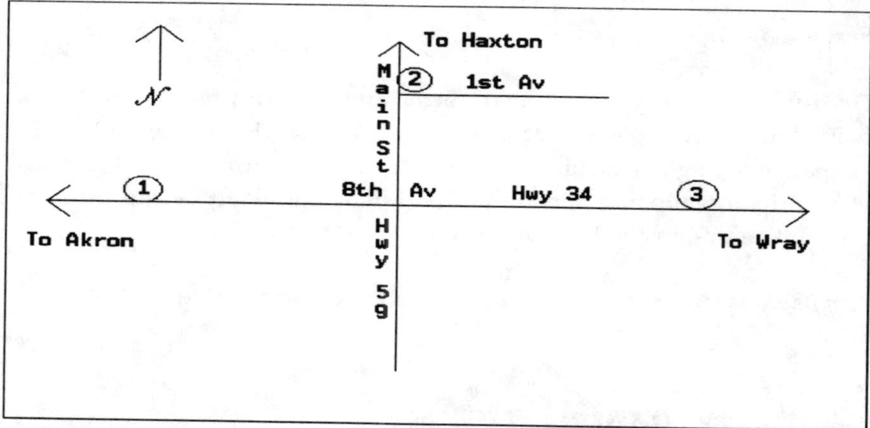

Restaurants and Ratings:	Food	Service	Decor	Atm	Overall
1. Beacon Inn	★★	★★	★	★	★½
2. Fernando's	★★★½	★★★	★★★	★★½	★★★
3. Popcorn Shack	★★★	★★½	★★	★★½	★★½

I would recommend Fernando's for good Mexican food and the Popcorn Shack if you are looking for a good family restaurant. None of the restaurants in Yuma accept major credit cards; none have nonsmoking sections; and only Fernando's serves alcohol.

Beacon Inn ★½
900 West 8th Ave. (303)848-3356

Breakfast/lunch/dinner $. 7 days 4:30AM-7:30PM.
Type: Diner.

Food: ★★ *Service:* ★★ *Decor:* ★ *Atmosphere:* ★

I had a fair Belgian Waffle here. Their menu is limited and includes burgers; tacos; taco salad; sandwiches, including barbecue Polish sausage; chicken nuggets; fruit pies and ice cream. Service is fair for a drive-up place. There are 11 tables for 44 people in this austere diner with no decorations, only video games. The walls are wood-paneled. Spherical light fixtures hang from the acoustic ceiling. Very little atmosphere.

FERNANDO'S ★★★
123 SOUTH MAIN (303)848-5313

Lunch/dinner $. MON-SAT 11AM-9PM. Closed SUN.
Type: Mexican (and American).

Food: ★★★½ I highly recommend their stuffed sopapilla, either the all-beef, chicken, beef and beans, or chicken and rice. It is about eight inches long, three inches wide, and two inches high. They also serve chimichangas, hamburgers, chicken, and cod.

Service: ★★★ Good.

Decor: ★★★ There are ten booths for 40 people and tables for another 32. The walls are decorated with pictures of Mayan ruins, including some from Chichen Itza; the head of a Toltec warrior; and Navy emblems with anchors and sabres. The decor has no particular theme, but I liked the pictures of Mayan relics.

Atmosphere: ★★½ This is a popular place for lunch, as well it should be.

POPCORN SHAKE & DELI ★★½
720 EAST 8TH AVE. (303)848-2993

YUMA

Lunch $, dinner $$. MON-SAT 7:30AM-8PM. SUN 11AM-2PM.
Type: Family.

Food: ★★★ *Service:* ★★½ *Decor:* ★★ *Atmosphere:* ★★½

I ordered their sirloin, medium-rare. Although it came out medium-well, it was still a good steak. Some small towns have a difficult time not overcooking. Their lunch menu offers burgers, sandwiches, chicken, pizza, and hot dogs. Dinner features steaks, soup and salad. True to their name, assorted flavors of popcorn are available. The service is about what you would expect for a family-style restaurant. This is a large, single, L-shaped room with 12 booths and enough tables to bring total seating capacity up to about 130. The decor is simple. They have pictures of farming, a windmill, and a barn in winter. This is a family dining place that is popular with the local folks. It is relaxed and casual.

The Author - Turning 40 at The Fort Restaurant in Morrison

Index by Overall Rating

(The number of restaurants per rating is in parenthesis.)

★★★★★ (12)

★★★★½ (19)

★★★★ (37)

★★★½ (57)

INDEX BY OVERALL RATING

City	Restaurant
Gunnison	Cattleman Inn
Gunnison	Dos Rios
Hot Slphr Spgs	Riverside
Idaho Springs	Buffalo Bar
Keystone	Bighorn Steakhouse
Kittredge	Dick's Hickory Dock
La Junta	Kit Carson
Lamar	Abitia's
Limon	Fireside Junction
Mancos	Millwood Junction
Manitou Spgs	Adam's Mt Cafe
Montrose	Red Barn
Morrison	Tony Rigatoni's
Niwot	Rev. Taylor's
Norwood	Karen's
Pagosa Springs	Branding Iron
Pagosa Springs	Green House
Pine Junction	Reggie's
Platteville	Double Tree
Pueblo West	Pueblo West Inn
Rifle	Que Paso
Rocky Ford	Melon Valley
Silver Plume	Plume Saloon
Silverthorne	Mint
Steamboat Spgs	Mattie Silks
Sterling	Park Inn
Trinidad	Chef Liu's
Vail	Pizza & Pa'Ne
Winter Park	Hernando's

★★★ (86)

City	Restaurant
Aspen	Aspen Mine
Aspen	Little Annie's
Bayfield	Choice Burgers
Breckenridge	Fatty's
Breckenridge	Prospector
Brighton	Brighton Depot
Brush	Drover's
Buena Vista	Delaney's Depot
Burlington	Western Motor Inn
Castle Rock	Khaki's
Castle Rock	Pegasus
Conifer	La Cantina II
Conifer	New China Dragon
Cortez	Nero's
Crested Butte	Idle Spur
Crested Butte	Wooden Nickel
Dacono	Lawana's
Del Norte	Tin Cup Cafe
Delta	Fireside
Dillon	Antonia's
Elizabeth	Botana Junction
Empire	Jenny's
Estes Park	Molly B
Estes Park	Roth's
Evans	Portofino's
Evergreen	Jonathan Wolf's
Fort Lupton	Branding Iron
Fort Morgan	Park Terrace
Fraser	Amazenburgers
Frisco	Log Cabin Cafe
Fruita	Dinosaur Pizza
Georgetown	Place
Georgetown	Swiss Inn
Glenwood Spgs	Buffalo Valley Inn
Glenwood Spgs	Florindo's
Golden	Kenrow's
Granby	El Monte
Grand Lake	Mountain Inn
Gunnison	Sundae Shoppe
Hot Slphr Spgs	Stagecoach Stop
Idaho Springs	Marion's
Keenesburg	Charlie D's
Keystone	Commodore
Keystone	Edgewater Cafe
Kremmling	Wagon
La Junta	Capri
La Junta	Copper Kitchen
La Junta	El Camino
La Junta	El Azteca
Lamar	Main
Las Animas	Bent's Fort Inn
Leadville	High Country
Leadville	La Cantina
Limon	Flying J
Limon	Southside
Louisville	Blue Parrot
Lyons	Don David
Manitou Spgs	Craftwood Inn
Monte Villa	Movie Manor
Montrose	Jim's Texas Barbecue
Montrose	Starvin Arvin's
Monument	Ticino
Naturita	Yellow Rock Cafe
Pagosa Springs	Rolling Pin
Pagosa Springs	Spanish Inn
Parker	Prime Time
Penrose	Mr. C's
Pine Junction	Red Rooster Inn
Rifle	Audrey's

INDEX BY OVERALL RATING

Index by Type

Several restaurants offer a variety of food. Each restaurant in this index is listed only once by the most predominant type of food offered. Some restaurants may offer other types of food as well. The number of restaurants per type is in parenthesis.

INDEX BY TYPE

DELI (11)

DINER (9)

FAMILY (26)

GERMAN (6)

ITALIAN (38)

MEXICAN (55)

Index by Restaurant

INDEX BY RESTAURANT

INDEX BY RESTAURANT

INDEX BY RESTAURANT

INDEX BY RESTAURANT